KT-567-857

Work and Organizational Psychology

An introduction with attitude

In this unique text, Christine Doyle provides the student with a cutting-edge introduction to the field of work and organizational psychology. The main focus is on recent changes that have occurred in the world of work, incorporating their causes, consequences, proposed solutions to the associated problems, and above all, the challenges they pose for work and organizational psychology.

Among the topics covered are motivation at work, the concept of stress, and the causes of individual accidents and organizational disasters. The proposed solutions to these problems include lifelong learning and training, performance management, career development, and employee assistance programmes.

This lively, provocative, and highly readable book will be an essential resource for advanced undergraduate and postgraduate students of work and organizational psychology, as well as business management students and anyone with an interest in human resources management.

Christine Doyle is a chartered occupational psychologist and is currently Director of the Professional Doctorate in Occupational Psychology at the University of East London.

Psychology at Work
Edited by P. Robinson

The *Psychology at Work* series, edited by Peter Robinson, provides comprehensive coverage of the central issues and debates in work and occupational psychology today. Its aim is to take specific areas or problems within the world of commerce, industry, and public service, and establish a dialogue between their practical concerns and the academic theory and research of work and organizational psychologists. It is hoped that the series will provide a resource that generates debate and facilitates the process by which policy and practice become informed by (and inform) critically evidence-based research.

The comprehensive text by Christine Doyle, *Work and Organizational Psychology: An introduction with attitude*, covers the central areas of the subject. Further texts cover options found on advanced courses in work and organizational psychology or examine contemporary and controversial topics within the field. The series will be of use to undergraduate and postgraduate students of work and organizational psychology, and will be particularly suitable for the British Psychological Society specification syllabus of accredited MSc courses in occupational psychology. It will also be of interest to those professionals in business and management eager to find out more about how work and organizational psychology can inform and improve the working environment.

Also available in this series:

Designing for Humans
Jan Noyes

Work and Organizational Psychology

An introduction with attitude

Christine E. Doyle

Psychology Press
Taylor & Francis Group

HOVE AND NEW YORK

First published 2003 by Psychology Press
27 Church Road, Hove, East Sussex BN3 2FA

Simultaneously published in the USA and Canada
by Taylor & Francis Inc,
29 West 35th Street, New York, NY 10001

Psychology Press is part of the Taylor & Francis Group

© 2003 Christine Doyle

Typeset in 10/12pt Times NR by Graphicraft Limited, Hong Kong
Printed and bound in Great Britain by
TJ International Ltd, Padstow, Cornwall
Cover design by Jim Wilkie

All rights reserved. No part of this book may be reprinted or
reproduced or utilised in any form or by any electronic,
mechanical, or other means, now known or hereafter
invented, including photocopying and recording, or in any
information storage or retrieval system, without permission in
writing from the publishers.

British Library Cataloguing in Publication Data
A catalogue record for this book is available
from the British Library

Library of Congress Cataloging in Publication Data
Doyle, Christine E., 1950–
    Work and organizational psychology : an introduction with
attitude / Christine E. Doyle.
        p. cm. — (Psychology at work)
    Includes bibliographical references and index.
    ISBN 0-415-20871-8 — ISBN 0-415-20872-6 (pb.)
        1. Psychology, Industrial.   2. Work—Psychological aspects.
    3. Organizational behavior.   4. Organizational change.
    I. Title.   II. Series.
HF5548.8 .D674 2002
158.7—dc21   2002073967

ISBN 0-415-20871-8 (hbk)
ISBN 0-415-20872-6 (pbk)

To Thomas, Barbara and Chris, Keiron and Mike

Contents

Figures

Acknowledgements

A large number of people helped me to write this book. Special thanks must go to my editor Peter Robinson who patiently read every word more than once, invariably gave good advice, and never failed in his good humour and encouragement. Other people also read draft chapters and boosted my confidence as well as pointing out my failings: John Skelton, Ruth Sage, Sarah Lewis, Mark Holloway, Steve Fisher, two anonymous reviewers, and the entire classes of 1999/2000 MSc students endured at least some of my earlier efforts. (Of course any deficiencies are still my own.)

My students were also a source of inspiration as well as guinea-pigs—virtually everything in this book has been presented to or tried out on them—which probably explains why one reviewer wrote, "You can imagine the author delivering this material in a lecture theatre." I also thank my doctoral students, in particular, Andrew Day, Guy Lubitsh, Georgina Slaven, and Mike Rugg-Gunn for the many insights their "real world" practitioner research provoked. Caroline Osborne, Lucy Farr, Susan Rudkin, Kathryn Russel, and the staff of Psychology Press, were very supportive.

Lastly I must thank my son Thomas for his patience in putting up with the book writing in addition to my full-time job and long-distance commuting. It's a wonder he got any attention from me for the past 2–3 years!

0 Read me ... (It's all in the subtitle, or I'd like to disagree with Aristotle's principle of moderation in all things)

My approach

You will have noticed that this book is "An Introduction with Attitude"—a subtitle that has been chosen with care. This book is pervaded with the expression of attitudes—*my* attitudes. "With Attitude" also has connotations of assertiveness and of a forcefully held position, and this book most definitely "comes from a certain direction". Since both characteristics are rather unusual in academic textbooks this calls for some explanation. Certainly, if you do not bother to read this chapter you may find it difficult to understand what I am about and what this book is about.

Serious academic textbooks are usually cool, balanced, and impartial, giving the arguments and evidence for and against, drawing cautious conclusions and with some trenchant criticism of virtually every theoretical position and piece of research evidence. Serious introductory academic textbooks also tend to be comprehensive in their coverage, starting with the early work in the field and laying out the history of the development of ideas in any topic area in meticulous detail. There is nothing wrong with this sort of approach and there are many excellent "Introduction to Occupational/Work and Organizational Psychology" texts already on the market—indeed, I recommend a good many of them in my suggestions for further reading.

This book is different. It is chatty, opinionated, personal, biased, and selective in its coverage, and is specifically designed to provoke the reader. Academic purists may be mystified, even outraged by my approach. So why have I done it this way? There are several reasons. First, I see no merit in producing yet another conventional academic textbook when so many others have already done it so well. Yes, my book might be more up to date because it has been written more recently, but most of the solid body of knowledge built up over the years in work and organizational psychology remains the same, so what is the point of trotting it all out again? My aim is to present a fresh "take" on traditional issues and to emphasize what I see as the challenges and growth points of the discipline and profession of work and organizational psychology. Second, I am a person with a mission—or rather, with several missions!

Mission number 1 is that I want my text to engage my readers fully. I am passionate about the content of this book and it would be nice if I could inspire you to be too. This means that I don't want you to be just interested, I want you to be fascinated, excited, enthusiastic, argumentative, irritated, annoyed, angry even. I want you to argue with me, rush off to read more, put pen to paper, try out ideas in the workplace, and generally behave (in terms of activity *not* aggression!), like a nest of hornets that has just been stirred with a stick! Conventional academic textbooks do not usually make particularly good "sticks". Why do I want to inspire such activity? This approach is informed by what I know about the process of learning—active learning, arguing with concepts and ideas, and searching for better arguments and evidence—leads to better learning and the creation of new ideas.

Mission number 2 is to provide a good read. Some (by no means all) academic textbooks can be a trifle dull. Some other academic work seems to pride itself on being wholly incomprehensible to most readers, as if the density of the text contributes in direct proportion to the intellect and prestige of the author compared to the rest of us mortals. Some publishers seem to be taken in by this but, as one who has spent her life struggling to make truly profound ideas understandable, this sort of thing infuriates me. To steal a famous phrase, "Life is too short to stuff an ego." I hope my book is entertaining as well as informative and provoking. I do not pretend to be an expert in every aspect of work and organizational psychology—no-one could be; but this book is based on scholarship, only I try to wear it lightly. To steal another famous phrase, "Why should the devil have all the best books?" Throughout the sciences, there is great effort to communicate knowledge in a form accessible to the "lay person" without distortion or oversimplification. Since I hope that this book is aimed at trainee work and organizational psychologists and may even be of interest to people without a background in psychology, I have aspired to join this admirable trend. Whether I have succeeded is for you to judge.

There is ample reference to easily obtainable sources, but there are also a lot of references to conference presentations that are harder to track down. This is because attendance at conferences is one of my main ways of keeping not just up to date but ahead of the game. Conferences allow one to detect emerging trends and learn about research in progress, and I am very fortunate to be able to go to one or two a year. Conference "Books of Proceedings" will usually be available from national collections such as the British Library or occasionally for sale from sponsoring bodies such as the British Psychological Society. Authors may also provide copies of manuscripts, reprints, or eventual publication details. If you cannot locate the original papers do not despair—much of this work can already be seen or will shortly emerge in databases such as PsychInfo or on scholarly websites on the internet. However, my main aim in including such references is to share this emerging knowledge with you and to back up points made in the text, not to send you on frustrating detective hunts. If all else fails, at least you heard it from me!

Mission number 3 is probably most important and tells you (in the current jargon) "where I am coming from". To read much of the introductory work and organizational psychology literature you might sometimes be forgiven for thinking that the world of work has remained fairly static for much of the 20th century and that the issues that confronted our professional fore-bears 20, 30, 40, and even 50 years ago are as relevant today as they were then. In some cases this is a reasonable stance, in many more this leads to serious difficulty. Other commentators (and I also) caution that we should not over-estimate and over-react to changes in the workplace in the past decade or so, but it seems to be generally agreed that there has been some-thing of a revolution in the nature of working life, if only in the fact that work has been "intensified". We are all expected to work harder and longer than our parents were expected to do, and this applies to everyone from the cleaner of the corporate bathroom or hospital ward, to the smiling hotel receptionist, from the "client-centred" professional, to the City banker. This book is an exploration of these changes: their nature, causes, consequences, proposed solutions to the problems thereby created, and, above all, the challenges they pose for work and organizational psychology.

It is a book in two halves. The first half presents the problems as I see them; the second half evaluates the proposed solutions. At the beginning, Chapter 1 provides the essential background—what work and organiza-tional psychology is all about. This account is not exhaustive. The discus-sion starts with a question that is never far from the mind of a reflective practitioner but is articulated less often: "What is work and organizational psychology for . . . ?" The answer to this question is important since it deter-mines the nature of the profession, the activities of practitioners, and even the nature of the research evidence that gets published to inform practice. I have a clear position on this but it isn't always shared by my professional colleagues. As I argue in Chapter 1, one cannot ignore wider historical, soci-etal, economic, and political contexts when considering the world of work. I also agree with Malnick's (2001) view that work and organizational psycholo-gists ought to be willing to be controversial and challenging in "promoting healthy, sane work environments and practices" (p. 26). This means that the discussion can become more "political" than is usual in an academic text but, in accordance with my mission to provoke, you are allowed to disagree!

I then use the labels for the eight areas of knowledge currently deemed by the British Psychological Society as essential background for a would-be practitioner to proceed with training, to introduce my subject matter. For each area of enquiry and intervention, I state the main aims as I see them, and describe a little history and what I perceive as interesting growth points. Having split the discipline and profession of work and organizational psy-chology into arbitrary "chunks", I then attempt to put it back into a unified whole, using the issue of teamwork to show how it can be the basis of analysis and intervention at many levels from the "global" to the individual. This chapter is your passport to the rest of the book. In the final chapter I do a similar job, but this time taking a selection of topics that I think represent the growth areas of the future—their threats, opportunities, and solutions. This is a possible passport to your contribution to the future of our discipline and profession. What you do next is up to you . . .

In between we explore the problems. Chapter 2 sets out the main difficulties facing workplaces now and in the future, their causes, and consequences. For many people's working lives "change is the only constant"; job insecurity and risk the main parameters of their lives; "work" the only "life" there is time for. How widespread is this change, and are human beings adaptive enough to cope with this? Is this all a storm in a teacup? Chapter 3 looks at theories of motivation—what makes people work hard (and well) for their living? Do these frameworks need to be revised if everyone is now out for her/himself and cares nothing for the employing organization, clients, customers, products, or whatever, except where they serve personal gain/aims? Chapter 4 looks at stress or rather the stressors in the work environment that engender negative reactions or strain in the workers. Has the workplace become so stressful that it is unbearable for most people or have we all talked ourselves into exhaustion and depression? Chapter 5 considers human error and creating a safety culture. If people are "stressed out" and exhausted, and productivity takes precedence over safety, what hope of eliminating individual accidents and organizational disasters?

Then there are the solutions. Chapter 6 deals with lifelong learning and training; if we become more skilful in our work, can we cope better with the challenges the new conditions present? Chapter 7 deals with selecting the right people to do the job; would all organizational problems disappear if only we could select people who are made of the "right stuff"? Chapter 8 discusses performance management and career development so that employees can grow to meet the challenges they are expected to deal with and organizations can achieve their business goals. Chapter 9 deals with counselling in organizations—employee assistance programmes—primarily designed to treat the "walking wounded". But could this function have a more important role to "re-humanize" the workplace? Each of the approches to solving the challenges that face us is described and evaluated, but none of these chapters is exhaustive.

In fact readers must exercise caution. On its own, the content of this book is probably not enough to pass exams, though I hope it will fire you with passion to make sure that you *do*! You should note that I make no reference to many key areas in the BPS "benchmark" syllabus for the Postgraduate Certificate of Occupational Psychology. What has been included or excluded has been very carefully considered. What has been included has been selected according to my main themes already described. A note on some of the main areas I have excluded, or given scant attention to, follows so that you know what information to seek in other texts. You may, for instance, wish to consult other books in this series, which deal with specific areas in depth and detail. Otherwise, every chapter ends with suggestions for further reading.

Some areas that have received little or no attention in this book

Organizational development and change

Theories of the management of change, employee resistance; organizational culture and climate; processes of change; power and politics in organizations.

Reason

I think the conditions of work have changed so much for a large number of people that many frameworks are no longer relevant; e.g., how should one try to overcome resistance to change when "change fatigue" is driving people out of the occupation or into clinical depression or anxiety? The need is to inform change agents, including top management and Government, of the likely human consequences of their actions and policies.

Employee relations

Trades Union negotiations; ingroup/outgroup conflict; theories and methods for conflict resolution.

Reason

In the UK at least, Trades Unions have been weakened to the point of irrelevance and relationships between individuals are more important. There is a huge amount in this chapter on the potential for conflict in the workplace (also covered in Chapter 2) but it is explicit to the main arguments only and implicit to the BPS syllabus. I do not trot out all the usual theories.

Design of environments and of work

Very little on traditional areas such as the effects of heat, noise, etc., in the workplace.

Reason

There are good treatments elsewhere (e.g., Chmiel, 1998, 2000; Oborne, 1995); I have concentrated on topical issues, e.g., the increase in night shift work, the increase in mental workload. I have also focused on contemporary concerns such as workplace bullying and control over work. Earlier work has served us well in informing practice. The topics I have selected are what I think we ought to be addressing now.

Human–machine interaction

Nothing on "knobs and dials" and little on human–computer interaction. Sad . . . both aspects are absolutely fascinating! Our whole lives are surrounded by machines with knobs and dials, even given the dominance of computers. What's more, good old print and "hard copy" will *not* go away so the design of these materials is also important. I have vast fun teaching Ergonomics to MSc students and they all go on to hunt their houses and workspaces for failures of design and safety with great enthusiasm, but I have no space in this book to include all this. I have also said very little about the introduction of new technology.

Reason

I have chosen to focus on macro-ergonomics and issues surrounding automation and the control of hazardous systems such as nuclear power plants. Replacing workers with "smart" machines has many important implications for remaining employees, especially in safety-critical systems. Bad design in the home or office usually creates nothing worse than frustration and inefficiency. In a hazardous industry it can lead to catastrophe; so may an emphasis on production at the expense of safety. See J. M. Noyes (2001). *Designing for humans.* Hove, UK: Psychology Press—a companion volume in this series.

Training

Very little on theory and research that should inform the design of training programmes or on the evaluation of training.

Reason

Again, given specialist texts in this area, it is a question of selecting topics that are interesting and fit in with the overall themes of the book. The notion of a learning organization has been posited as a cure for many organizational ills and fits well with themes such as lifelong learning and a flexible workforce that can cope with rapid organizational and technological change. However, there are many obstacles to achieving such a vision, not least that training often occupies a very lowly status in the organizational scheme of things.

Selection and assessment

This is perhaps the most traditional chapter in that it covers most of the BPS syllabus.

Appraisal and career development

Nothing on traditional forms of appraisal, design of rating instruments, and sources of bias in supervisor ratings. Not much on career development theory or on how people make career decisions.

Reason

There is a large number of career development theories: to try to cover too many of them would be confusing and comprehensive coverage appears in Patton and McMahon (1999). One of the consequences of the changing nature of work is that appraisal systems that have a strong developmental strand are becoming most popular, so this is the main focus of the chapter.

Counselling and personal development

There is very little on different approaches to counselling or on the development of counselling skills.

Reason

Comprehensive coverage of these aspects would be impractical in a short chapter. I have concentrated on the role that the counselling function can play in re-humanizing the workplace. See J. Irving and D. Williams (in press). *Counselling and personal development*. Hove, UK: Psychology Press— another companion volume in this series to be published soon.

(Note: Several other volumes in this series are nearing completion as I write and may appear at the same time or shortly after publication of this book.)

Be assured that this is an idiosyncratic selection and you need to read more. However, what you do find here is a large amount of discussion of topical and emerging issues that you may not find in other introductory texts.

A final note: Why didn't I entitle this chapter a Preface or a Foreword? The reason is that almost no-one reads Prefaces or Forewords—unless they really loved the book and can't bear to stop reading it. In that case the information given here would be far too late. The number zero is also important. Some mathematicians think it is the most important number of all. So in a sense, I regard this chapter as perhaps the most important in the book. I hope you did read it and I hope you enjoy the rest!

Christine Doyle
December, 2001

1 What's it all about . . . ? (Introduction to work and organizational psychology)

May you live in interesting times.

Chinese curse

Defining work

Benjamin Franklin once wrote memorably that there are only two certainties in life—death and taxes. It is arguable whether he ought to have added work to this duo. The fact that he didn't probably has something to do with the difficulty of characterizing what work is. One thing is clear; our attitudes to work have always been ambivalent. The Christian Bible gave work as one of the punishments visited on humanity following expulsion from Paradise. For centuries the less pleasant forms of work were delegated to slaves and peasants. Part of the attraction of being rich and powerful has been that you don't necessarily have to work and that you can get others to do it for you. Perhaps because work was such an unpleasant necessity, it was elevated to a virtue. Medieval monks made work part of their discipline, either as a form of "mortifying the flesh" or for the "glory of God". This may be the source of the "Protestant Work Ethic" (Furnham, 1990; Weber, 1958), which perhaps reached its peak when prosperity through hard work was regarded as evidence that the person was predestined to be "saved" from damnation. And there lies the paradox. Work may be a necessary evil, but for most of us, work is a powerful source of our personal and social identities irrespective of whether we enjoy it, whether we are paid for it, or whether those identities are thereby enhanced or undermined.

Have a look at Exercise 1.1 opposite. If you spent any time at all thinking about the questions in Exercise 1.1, you will have realized that work and our attitudes towards it are not as straightforward as you might have first thought. According to Porteous (1997, pp. 4–5), "work is normally conceived as involving some element of giving away control of the way one can distribute one's time and effort to someone else in exchange for money or its equivalent". However, he acknowledges that this definition is too narrow. I once did a study in which 100 people were asked what were the most

EXERCISE 1.1
Reflecting on the nature of work

Before reading on, take a little time to think about this. What is one of the first questions that you typically ask a stranger after you've said hello? Why, until quite recently, did many a woman describe herself as "only a housewife"? How many forms can work take (e.g., from a school child to a homemaker to a political or business leader)? If you love your work is it still work? When do leisure pursuits such as sport and hobbies become work? (For instance, is the amateur squash player who competes in national competitions working?) Why does losing one's job often have devastating effects over and above the loss of income? If you won millions, what would you do after the initial euphoria wore off and how many of your activities would be classed as work? What kinds of work do you do and what do they mean to you? What do you think are the defining features of work?

important features of work as opposed to play or leisure. The top features on which there was over 90% agreement were as follows:

1   Work activities are necessary for survival and usually involve some form of compulsion. True, one can choose whether or not to work but leaving the tasks undone or stopping when you get bored has costs. A filthy home is a health hazard, a lazy worker risks being sacked and losing income, the would-be writer who never gets down to it loses the satisfaction of having written, the uncommitted student risks failure, the "idle rich" may feel bored and that life lacks direction. Work also imposes structure. You can play in any way you choose but work has to be done methodically, and there is often a best way to do it.
2   Work activities are almost always undertaken in the service of some higher aim. The voluntary worker wants to make life better for someone, the "breadwinner" wants to provide for his or her family, the business executive wants the success of the company, the teacher wants students to fulfil their potential, entertainers want to give pleasure, artists want to create something of lasting value. It is for this reason that work is such a powerful source of identity and why it can be a source of satisfaction. It is also why being deprived of work can be so painful.

Both these features may explain why many people enjoy having worked even if they did not enjoy the work itself. A job well done promotes a sense of mastery and achievement—it enhances one's self-esteem.

Having come to these conclusions, I then discovered reversal theory (Apter, 1982, 1989, 2001), which develops the distinction between work and nonwork activities within a general theoretical framework. One of the core ideas in reversal theory is that how people feel and what people want are determined by distinct psychological states that are essentially *transient*. These psychological states have also been referred to as "ways of being" or "selves within the person", which capture the idea that at any given moment we can experience the world in very different ways. Apter calls these psychological states meta-motivational states because they determine what people want at any given time. Frey (1997, p. 3) gives a succinct summary: "Reversal theory is a general psychological theory that posits the existence of eight meta-motivational states that combine in various ways to determine one's motives and experiences at a given moment in time . . . Switches between opposite states are called reversals . . .". Two particular meta-motivational states seem germain to the work/play divide. When we are in the telic state we are primarily goal oriented. The goal involves something that is significant to us and the means to achieve that goal is largely immaterial. If, for instance, we could magically push a button to get the house clean, the pile of marking done, the business deal signed, etc. then most of us would. In a paratelic state, it is the doing of the activity itself which is important, not the goal. Thus, a person may play tennis for pleasure and just enjoy . . . playing tennis. The idea that one might get someone (or something) else to play the tennis or listen to the music, or drink the glass of wine and so on to achieve the enjoyment is nonsensical. This seems to get at the kernel of work and play. When we work, we are primarily in a telic state, when we play we are primarily in a paratelic state. Once the goal of winning becomes more important than playing the game, it becomes work, or at least something very like it. Conversely, we can expend a great deal of "worklike" effort on some activity and still regard it as leisure or play. Thus, the true gardener enjoys the gardening; the person who cuts the lawn to avoid the neighbours' censure is working.

The great strength of reversal theory is that it proposes that people can suddenly switch between these states with consequent profound changes in emotional experience. Thus meeting a liked colleague at work and exchanging pleasantries can switch us into the paratelic state and leaven an unpleasant or boring task. The extreme anxiety one can feel before having to give a presentation can turn to enjoyment or elation if the audience responds enthusiastically. Thus, many people would say that the social rewards of paid employment are among the most important to them. One of the consequences of the drive for ever-increasing efficiency and productivity is that people are often too pressured to switch into paratelic states and so the work is frequently perceived as stressful. Conversely, people who love their work and would do it for enjoyment of the activity alone, will spend much of their time in a paratelic state, whatever the pressures. So here we have the germ of an explanation as to why some people thrive on long hours and constant pressure while others suffer stress-related illness. We will return to reversal theory again in this book because it seems to be a very promising framework which is attracting increased research attention (see, e.g., Apter, 2001; Svebak & Apter, 1997).

Defining work and organizational psychology

Useful though this wider definition of work is for understanding the meaning of work for individuals, work and organizational psychology is primarily concerned with paid employment and often with people who work for large or medium organizations. It attempts to understand and explain the behaviour and experience of people at work by applying theory and research methods from psychology.

However, this simple description hides a great deal of complexity. Even the name of the discipline cannot be agreed on. In the UK it is called occupational psychology, in the USA it is called industrial/organizational psychology, and in Europe it is work and organizational psychology. There has been much recent debate within the British Psychological Society's (BPS) Division of Occupational Psychology as to whether the name should be changed to come into line with the rest of Europe but as I write no consensus has yet been reached. So what is an author to do? If I use "occupational psychology" in the title, the term may be obsolete before the book is published and in any case, I want the title to reflect the mainly European focus. On the other hand, the name of the Division has not yet changed and, in the UK, practitioners are still known as chartered occupational psychologists. In the end there has to be an unhappy compromise. The title reflects the European focus but some parts of the text conform to current UK practice. From now on readers should regard the terms "work and organizational psychology" and "occupational psychology" as synonymous.

To make matters worse, work and organizational psychology is by no means the only discipline to concern itself with people at work. To name but a few, there are management science, human resource management, personnel management, and a hybrid discipline known as organizational behaviour which, according to Cherrington (1989), developed from psychology, sociology, and anthropology with minor influences from economics, political science, and history. There is not space here for an extended discussion of the similarities, differences, and definitions of all these disciplines, which in any case have been explored elsewhere (see, e.g., Brotherton, 1999; Furnham, 1997). Suffice it to say that theory and research in work and organizational psychology contribute to all these related disciplines though not always at a very sophisticated level. For instance, Porteous (1997) describes the role of a personnel manager as being largely concerned with administrative duties such as benefits, pensions, holiday rosters, and so on. He continues, "Many companies are totally unaware of the value of good occupational psychologists. Being qualified in occupational psychology is not the same as being qualified in personnel" (p. 17). Not everyone agrees with this view. Some have argued that human resource professionals can have at least as much, if not more competence in their specialist areas than occupational psychologists (Ridgeway, 2000; Shaw, 1992). St Ather (1999) makes the point that management consultants, trainers, personnel specialists, recruitment consultants, etc. are practitioners' main competitors, not other occupational psychologists. The debate continues (Crawshaw, 2000b; Duncan, 2001).

Work and organizational psychology tends to focus on individuals and groups and to explore what goes on in organizations in terms of underlying psychological processes. So for instance, leadership is coming to be understood in terms of the social constructions of followers. In other words, followers interpret what is going on around them and come to a consensus about what that "reality" is. Leaders are the people who influence these socially constructed interpretations through their exceptional social and communication skills. (Alimo-Metcalfe, 1998a; Smith & Peterson, 1988). Having said that, occupational psychologists are not afraid to borrow from other disciplines, if that helps understanding. For instance, analysing the causes of disasters such as Chernobyl and the Piper Alpha North Sea oil platform requires understanding of the social, historical, and political contexts as well as engineering design—both of which issues go far beyond the psychology of the human operators (see, e.g., Reason, 1987, 1990, 1997).

Work and organizational psychology also brings a degree of scientific rigour to the study of people in the workplace. For instance, procedures for selecting new employees are carefully designed to be as fair and accurate as possible and the effectiveness of the methods are evaluated later by measuring the work performance of successful candidates. The one great strength of work and organizational psychology is that its practice is based on systematic research evidence and, in theory at least, all its interventions should be properly evaluated. Thus, a programme to help employees to manage stress would be followed up with research to establish whether or not stress levels actually were reduced. This emphasis on systematic methods and research does not always endear itself to top management, who want instant solutions to pressing problems and do not want to hear about costly failures. However, it does make it less likely that 6 months after the consultant has left, the "miracle cure" is discovered to be worse than the original disease!

But what is work and organizational psychology FOR . . . ?

The question of the basic purposes and aims of work and organizational psychology is something which needs to be tackled at the start even if the reader cannot make up his or her own mind on the matter until the book has been read and digested. There is a very real problem here. We might start by asking what is psychology in general for? An informed answer will probably involve something to do with understanding the human condition in order to improve it. As psychology graduates will be aware, this debate is hedged around with horror stories of past mistakes, post-modernist critiques, and so on, but I believe that a concern for human welfare has always been close to the purposes of both psychology and psychologists. This is seen clearly in the work of professional colleagues in, e.g., clinical, educational, and health psychology. Work and organizational psychology is different. Work can be a mixed blessing for individuals and most organizations have priorities and agendas which leave little space for human weakness and well-being.

The private (commercial) sector is first and foremost concerned with making a healthy profit for shareholders and directors. This means producing the best quality goods and services at the lowest possible cost. Pursuing this efficiency could mean paying subsistence wages and demanding up to 16 hours of work on 6 days a week. These practices are not confined to the 19th century—they exist today in the developed West and in many other parts of the world and companies are not averse to relocating production to take advantage of them. However, another option is to increase automation, drastically reduce the size of the workforce, and leave every two survivors doing the work previously done by three or more people (Herriot & Pemberton, 1995). In the public sector too, successive UK Governments have demanded ever higher quality services whilst simultaneously driving down funding. Thus, public sector workers tend to be low paid and overworked. Expecting all organizations in either sector to behave automatically like charitable institutions with human well-being at their core is not only naive but stupid. It isn't going to happen.

So the question is: Who are the clients of occupational psychologists— the organization, which pays their fees and wants greater productivity, or the employees and their well-being? Given the realities of the current system, it is inevitable that work and organizational psychology is in the service of business priorities. Luckily for those of us who feel that there should be some ethical dimension to our work—a need to make a positive difference to the quality of people's lives and not simply via the creation of wealth— the choice is not so stark.

In the UK in the 19th century, reformers of the worst abuses of the Industrial Revolution were not simply naive idealists. The various Factory Acts became law partly because employers realized that it was in their own best interests to have a healthy, well-fed workforce. The Government of the day was itself appalled at the poor physical state of men from the slums and factories who presented themselves as recruits for the armies of World War I. (A terrible irony yes, but the defence of the realm was a serious matter.) So despite many false starts and halting progress, things did gradually improve, not least because the social evils of a vast underclass were unacceptable in a Liberal Democracy. The process continues today in the current UK Labour Government's campaign against "social exclusion". Thus just because a system appears all-powerful and all-pervasive does not mean that there should be no attempt to change it or that such attempts are doomed to failure. A key way to achieve change for the better is still to demonstrate that the goals of productivity, profit, and excellence of service are best served by ensuring the well-being of the workforce.

EXERCISE 1.2
Evidence-based practice

To illustrate the caution needed, let us take one example from the *Times* newspaper on Saturday 13 May 2000. "Ailing teachers take 2.5m days off" shouted the headline and the story went on to report that more than half the teachers in UK state schools took an average of 9 days sick leave in 1999. Representatives of the teachers' Trades Unions immediately attributed this to stress created by high workloads and relatively low pay and status relative to other professions, compounded by rigorous (and some would say punitive) Government inspections. If this were true, then the consequences for children's education and the nation's health-care bill would be serious indeed and the causes of teacher stress would need urgent attention.

What questions would you want to ask and have answered before accepting the Trades Union interpretation of these statistics? (Remember that it often appears to be in the best interests of employers to be sceptical too, so "forewarned is forearmed".)

However, in contrast to the stark realities of the 19th century, the issues are not quite so clear-cut as the link, say, between unguarded machinery and a mangled arm. For a start, there has been an awful lot of history—not least the general failure of Communist economies. It also has to be admitted that work systems that made people part of the machinery have been very successful in creating affluent societies. One should pause, therefore, before taking to the soapbox. Perhaps you would like to pause here to consider Exercise 1.2.

Thinking about Exercise 1.2, here are a few of the questions that occur to me:

- How accurate are these figures anyway?
- How does this sick leave rate compare with other workers in the public and private sectors?
- What proportion of days actually worked by UK teachers does 2.5 million lost represent?
- Is this rate of sick leave worse than in the past?
- What is the evidence that teachers are under more stress than other workers?
- Could other factors be implicated? For example, children tend to suffer a lot of infectious diseases so perhaps teachers are more exposed to infection. What were the most common illnesses anyway?
- Could poor training and low expectations of the professionalism required by teaching in the past mean that there are more people in post who are "not up to the job" than in other professions?

- Could teachers' low morale, born of resistance to necessary reforms and change, mean that more teachers stay away in protest?

There are many more questions that could be asked but even if they were all answered to our satisfaction we'd still have to prove that teachers' jobs are making them ill. We would need objective measures of workload and other stressors and a clear link between these and, e.g., deficiencies in the body's immune system. From this it can be seen that the enterprise is far from easy.

Psychologists in general, and occupational psychologists in particular, have the training and the tools to conduct the necessary research to help answer such questions. Beech (2000, p. 23) suggests, "our first priority is not to advance the interests of the employer and in the process advance the interests of employees; it is to advance objective truth and advance human well-being". That may be the first priority but recommendations based on often complex and abstract research will not be implemented if they are impractical, are too long in coming, or threaten the financial viability of the organization. Occupational psychologists need to take account of the political and social context of organizations and "talk the language of business" as well as adhering to the ethical principles of their profession (Arnold, Cooper, & Robertson, 1998). Making a difference for the better is not easy but then it never has been in any aspect of life. Sir Peter Medawar once defined science as "the art of the possible". The same could be said of the theory and practice of work and organizational psychology. So what is it for? Well, for me, it's for taking a critical look at the world of work, gathering good evidence, and suggesting solutions which serve *both* human wellbeing *and* the bottom line. The tensions between the two are just part of the fascination. The fact that work and organizational psychology might not always succeed is no reason to give up trying. Malnick (2001), arguing for "well founded interventions that foster and develop humanity at work" (p. 26), calls for "A more proactive, campaign-based Occupational Psychology . . . by being more outspoken, challenging and focusing first and foremost on human wellbeing in the world of work." So if some of my arguments seem overly political for a sober academic text, that is because the issues *are* political. Of course, as in all political discussion, you, dear reader, are allowed to disagree!

A brief (and selective) history of occupational/work and organizational psychology

Work and organizational psychology developed in the early 20th century in response to the increasing complexity of organizations. For a discipline that has the well-being of people at work as a major focus, it is ironic that its growth was stimulated by social disasters such as the Great Depression and World Wars I and II. Occupational psychology is generally agreed to have begun in the UK during World War I when the health and work performance of munitions workers became a national priority. The activities of early occupational psychologists led to the setting up of the National Institute of Industrial Psychology in 1921. C. S. Myers, who had been professor of Psychology at Cambridge University, was its first director and he did much to establish psychology in Britain (see Bunn, 2001 for more details). Myers was succeeded by Frederick Bartlett. Bartlett, more commonly known for his book *Remembering* (1932), also did some pioneering work on the effects of extreme fatigue on work performance (Bartlett, 1943).

Between 1924 and 1932, one of the most renowned early studies in industrial / organizational / occupational psychology / work and organizational psychology (!) was conducted at the Western Electric Company in the USA (Roethlisberger & Dickson, 1939). The Hawthorne studies, as they became known, showed the importance of social factors at work. Originally conceived as an investigation of the effects of lighting conditions on productivity, it soon became clear that the increased attention paid to the workers in the course of the study was possibly the main factor in raising performance levels. Moreover, group processes and unofficial norms of work output were more influential than the exhortations of management. The Hawthorne studies have been severely criticized since (e.g., Rice, 1982; Yorks & Whitsett, 1985; & see Furnham, 1997 for a general discussion). Apart from methodological flaws and meagre effect sizes, the most common criticism is that the researchers were evangelists who wished to promote better working conditions and so over-emphasized social relationships. Despite all this, these studies were hugely influential and culminated in the foundation of the Human Relations Movement (Bellows, 1954; Maier, 1952) and the Quality of Working Life Movement (Davis, 1972; Moldaschl & Weber, 1998), both of which emerged between the 1950s and late 1970s. Also during this interwar period, Jahoda, Lazarsfeld, and Zeisel performed a seminal study of the effects of unemployment, which also focused attention on the importance of paid employment for psychological health (published in English in 1971).

Mass conscription in World War II stimulated a growth in selection techniques to identify those with officer potential. The increasing complexity of military hardware also promoted an interest in how to design machines which fitted human capabilities. (It has been estimated that one plane in every thousand missions crashed because pilots misread badly designed altimeters! See Fitts & Jones, 1947/1961). As a result, ergonomics was established as a subdiscipline in the 1950s by people such as Fitts (1962), who among other things attempted to define criteria to inform decisions as to what aspects of work were best done by humans and which by machines.

More recently there has been a huge increase of interest in work and organizational psychology because great changes in the nature of work and workplaces have created major "people management" problems and a need for lifelong learning and career management. But of that, more will be said throughout this book. (For more on the history of occupational psychology see Shimmin & Wallis, 1994.)

The scope of work and organizational psychology

Arnold, Robertson, and Cooper (1991) suggested that there are 12 distinct areas of work and organizational psychology, but in Britain and Ireland the British Psychological Society currently stipulates that occupational psychologists should be familiar with the theory and practice of eight. At the time of writing there is still a debate about which areas should concern occupational/work and organizational psychology. The eight areas are collapsed into four generic categories of practice—namely work and the work environment (including health and safety); the individual (including assessment, selection, guidance, and counselling); organizational development and change; and training. Despite this state of flux, I still think that an examination of what each of the current eight areas entails is a good way of introducing what occupational psychologists do.

Human–machine interaction/human–computer interaction

The basic aim is to design machines or complex human–machine systems such as power plants or aeroplanes so that human physical and psychological needs are met—to promote maximum efficiency, productivity, safety, and well-being. Traditionally, research concentrated on making machines "user friendly" in order to maximize human strengths and capabilities, and to minimize human limitations, not least because badly designed systems lead to errors, accidents, and disasters. In 1987 the Three Mile Island nuclear reactor came within a whisker of meltdown partly because 1800 alarms and error messages in the first 2 minutes made diagnosing the original fault near to impossible (Reason, 1990).

The Human Relations School based at the Tavistock Institute in London in the 1950s/1960s (see e.g., Trist, 1982; Trist & Bamforth, 1951) emphasized the need to harmonize the social system (people and their relationships with each other) with the technical system (the machines they use in their work). This is exemplified in the famous Volvo experiments (Jonssen & Lank, 1985). Instead of the traditional assembly line, groups of workers collaborated to make entire cars. Not only was the job itself drastically redesigned to give workers more varied, interesting, and autonomous work, but the machines and their layout had to be changed too.

Recent rapid changes in information technology and advanced manufacturing technology mean that the nature of much work is changing in fundamental ways. Skilled operators frequently become "machine minders", aircraft exist which do not need pilots, the "workplace" can be your bedroom or your car, and people dispersed across continents can work as "virtual teams". This means that most specialists in this area now deal with human–computer interaction and how to keep the operator "in touch" with the state of the system. Further, as most accidents and disasters involve some element of human error, issues concerned with risk perception and the promotion of a safety culture have come to the fore (Cooper, 1998; Reason, 1997).

Design of environments and of work

The basic concern of this area is to investigate how to design jobs and workspaces to maximize comfort, well-being, safety, and efficiency with particular reference to the physical and psychological needs of people. Earlier research concentrated on how poor physical conditions (e.g., excessive noise, heat, etc.) contribute to inefficiency, accidents, and stress-related illness (see, e.g., Galer, 1987; Oborne, 1995 for reviews and examples). In the 1940s Bartlett and colleagues such as Kenneth Craik conducted classic research in this vein known as the Cambridge cockpit studies (Bartlett, 1943; Craik, 1940). (For interesting historical accounts see Rolfe, 1996 and Vince, 1996). With wartime concerns about excessive fatigue in pilots, volunteers spent up to 50 hours working in one of the world's first flight simulators. They were periodically tested on their performance on a reaction-time task and towards the end they were exhausted. Notwithstanding this, their performance on the reaction-time task was remarkably little impaired. With characteristic flair, Bartlett noticed other more sinister signs of degraded performance. Attention narrowed so that pilots focused on the altimeter but not on the fuel gauge, skilled movements became disrupted and were performed out of sequence, and moods altered so that participants became increasingly irritable and their language more violent as they blamed the instruments and the machine. At the same time participants were convinced that their performance had not suffered in any way.

It would be reassuring to know that after 50 or more years Bartlett's lesson that overtired people are potentially dangerous would have been learned. Not so. Contemporary employment involves increasing amounts of night shift work, long hours, work overload, jet lag, and mental fatigue. As recently as 1983, Holding found that fatigued workers are likely to adopt less effortful but riskier strategies, such as driving faster to complete a journey more quickly. Hockey, Payne and Rick (1995) found that junior hospital doctors at the end of a long weekend shift made mistakes in a simulated dispensing task as well as showing signs of quite severe physiological stress. Carpenter (2001) reports on research by Stickgold and colleagues at the Harvard Medical School demonstrating that deep sleep soon after learning a new task seems to be essential for effective recall of it in subsequent weeks. These findings are somewhat alarming because Connor (2000) reports that as many as one in five workers claim that that they are so short of sleep that it affects their daily lives, and Rice (2000) quotes UK managers remarking that "sleep is the new luxury".

Together with human–machine/computer interaction and in collaboration with specialists in physiology, experimental psychology, and engineering, this area has developed into the hybrid discipline of ergonomics. Once largely concerned with physical design issues and stressors, this discipline is now equally involved in investigating social factors such as the effects of the way new technology is introduced into the workplace and the influence of social stressors on well-being and health.

Personnel selection and assessment

If ergonomics is concerned with "fitting the work to the person", selection is "fitting the person to the work". Its aim is to choose the best person for the job by means which are as reliable, valid, and fair as possible, in order to maximize worker well-being and productivity. There are probably more occupational psychologists practising in this field than in any other. Selection begins with job analysis—a detailed specification of what the work entails and the attributes, skills, abilities, and aptitudes the person needs to perform it well. Then a procedure must be devised to assess candidates' characteristics reliably and validly in these respects. Finally, the success and fairness of the selection methods needs to be evaluated in terms of the selected candidates' later job performance.

Recently there has been a great increase in the use of cognitive tests and personality inventories in selection, but still the most popular methods by far are the familiar trio of application form, references, and interview. The persistent popularity of the interview as a tool for selection has prompted an interest in what goes on in interviews and how fair and effective they are. Springbett (1958) found that interviewers tend to make up their minds about the suitability of a candidate in the first 4 minutes and then spend the remaining time looking for confirming evidence. However, from the mid-1980s, a consensus has emerged from the research evidence that properly conducted, carefully planned, and structured interviews done by trained interviewers can be very effective (Boyle, 1997). Silvester (1997) used attribution theory to analyse what candidates said in interviews. She found that interviewers were more impressed with people who admitted personal responsibility for past failures and showed that they had learned from the experience than with people who blamed anyone or anything but themselves.

Work and organizational psychology is facing a number of challenges in this area. Equal opportunities legislation and the globalization of economies mean that there is far more diversity in the workforce than hitherto. This gives rise to issues such as how to assess fairly candidates with disabilities or to take account of cultural differences when selecting for a multinational corporation. The environment in which businesses have to operate has also become much less predictable and stable so it is increasingly difficult for employers to be able to specify the workforce they will need in the future. How does one analyse a job that does not yet exist or assess skills and attributes when one does not know what these will be (Landis, Fogli, & Goldberg, 1998)?

The rise of information technology and the internet has also stimulated an interest in computerized testing. Not only does this raise difficult practical and ethical problems (Bartram, 1997, 1999, 2000) but the dynamic nature of the VDU screen allows assessment of abilities that could not be measured using traditional paper and pencil instruments. Bartram's (1995) MICROPAT test battery used in trainee pilot selection, for instance, assesses the ability to attend to and act on multiple sources of rapidly changing and unpredictable information—something that would be very useful in a fighter pilot!

Performance appraisal and career development

Traditionally the "Achilles' heel" of work and organizational psychology, performance appraisal concerns the measurement of how well people are doing their jobs. Appraisal can be related to rewards (pay, promotion, the sack) or development—helping people to improve their performance in the future. Reliable and valid measurement of job performance is vital for many other processes such as evaluating the effectiveness of selection procedures, identifying training needs, designing development/training programmes, and succession planning. Needless to say, if workers perceive the process to be unfair, this can cause great resentment especially when pay and promotion are involved. It is unfortunate, therefore, that methods of measuring work performance are generally flawed. Even objective indicators such as the number of widgets made, sales figures, or absenteeism can be inaccurate or affected by factors beyond the worker's control such as machine breakdown. A common method is to have the person's supervisor rate his or her performance, but this is open to all manner of biases. The problem is compounded by the increasing complexity of work. There has been a great decline in manual and semi-skilled jobs and many people are now "knowledge workers", most of whose activities are covert and difficult to observe. Perhaps for these reasons, performance-related pay initiatives have not been conspicuously effective (Herriot & Pemberton, 1995). In today's turbulent business environment, promoting lifelong learning is a major concern for individuals who must increase their "employability" to be sure of the next job and for organizations that require a flexible and innovative workforce.

For all these reasons there have been moves to greater use of developmental forms of appraisal. Here the person is helped to identify strengths and weaknesses, to set goals and devise personal development and career management plans. One form of this which is gaining in popularity in management development is multirater (or 360-degree) feedback (Alimo-Metcalfe, 1998a). Here, a manager rates himself or herself on an instrument designed to assess important skills or competencies. At the same time, the manager's boss, subordinates, and peers use the same instrument to rate the manager's performance. The idea is that the combined views of all these people will give a more accurate and rounded picture of the manager's performance. Any discrepancies between self-ratings and others' ratings will indicate possible strengths and weaknesses. For instance, if managers rate themselves highly on their ability to communicate but their staff do not, then this is obviously an area requiring attention in terms of further enquiry, and possible training and development.

Developmental forms of appraisal must be seen as nonthreatening if they are to be effective and to motivate people to improve their performance. (How many people would be honest about weaknesses if they thought that pay rises might be withheld or their careers damaged by such admissions?) Handled badly, multirater feedback has the potential to be devastating rather than motivating. Alimo-Metcalfe (1998a) has published a set of best practice guidelines and argues that if these are adhered to, multirater feedback is a very powerful management development tool. However, Fletcher, Baldry, and Cunningham-Snell (1998) warn that multirater feedback instruments are as prone to bias and inaccuracy as any other rating method. They also report a worrying trend for some organizations to tie this method to formal appraisals and even performance-related pay awards. No wonder Handy (1996) entitles his report, *360 degree feedback: Powerful tool or unguided missile?*

Counselling and personal development

If the distinction between personal and career development has become blurred in recent years, the role of counselling in work and organizational psychology has undergone a huge expansion such that many consultancy firms now employ chartered counselling or even clinical psychologists. Originally, counselling was used in two main arenas: in careers guidance for young people and to help people to cope with and resolve personal problems that might interfere with their work performance. These functions are still important but others have been added. So for instance, the death of a "job for life" means that most people can expect to change jobs and even occupations in the course of their careers. There is thus an increasing need for careers guidance and advice on career management for people of all ages and not just the traditional groups of school leavers and young graduates (see, e.g., Arnold, 1997a). Helping people to make career transitions also extends to "outplacement" where firms implementing redundancy programmes provide a service to help their employees cope with job loss and find alternative employment. Herriot and Pemberton (1995) argue that this practice makes good business sense too, because shabbily treated ex-employees may next work for a competitor; if good times return, there is less potential to recruit them back.

The changing nature of work also means that counselling services are required by increasing numbers of people for work-related and not just personal problems. Many organizations are undergoing major changes in terms of mergers, acquisitions, or business re-engineering to improve efficiency and effectiveness. It is generally agreed that employees perceive major organizational change as stressful and disruptive (Carnall, 1995; Connor & Lake, 1994), and perceived job insecurity is rife even though in Britain average job tenure actually rose during the 1990s (Smith, 1997). The concept of occupational stress has been challenged (Briner, 1997), but there is no doubt that stress-related illness has huge financial costs for organizations. Osborn (2000) estimates that the annual cost of lost productivity in the UK is £5.3 billion, in addition to the toll of human misery. For these sorts of reasons many organizations provide confidential counselling services either "in-house" or via an external Employee Assistance Programme provider.

In addition to the specialist role of counsellor as therapist, there is a need for counselling skills such as active listening and empathy in many management tasks. For instance, a major concern of enlightened management is how to reconcile the goals and aspirations of employees with the business needs of the organization. Developmental forms of appraisal are often seen as the key to achieving this but they require the sensitive handling characteristic of a trained counsellor to be effective (Alimo-Metcalfe, 1998a; Payne, 1998; Randell, 1989). Counsellors may therefore find their roles expanding to include training and facilitating organizational change (Carroll, 1996).

Training

The aims of this area of work and organizational psychology are to identify training and development needs, design and deliver training programmes, and evaluate their effectiveness to increase people's work performance and well-being. Traditionally, the concerns have been how to promote effective learning taking into account differences between people and their preferred learning styles, and how to evaluate the effectiveness of training, particularly whether it translates into enhanced performance in the workplace. Best practice suggests that training should lie at the heart of human resource management. Training needs should be identified and considered in the design stage of creating human machine systems, in the selection of candidates, and in career, personal development, and succession planning. Training and development issues should also inform top management's strategic thinking to create a "learning organization" which will provide an innovative, flexible, and multiskilled workforce (see chapter 6).

Many forces operate to undermine this vision, and typically the training budget is the first to be cut in hard times. For much of this century, in manufacturing industry at least, the emphasis has been on de-skilling work and replacing expensive people with machine automation, with the assumption that there was a lesser need to invest in training programmes. There was also the fear that having invested large sums in training, people would take their costly new skills to competitors. Far better, therefore, to "head hunt" appropriately qualified people or to "buy in" specialist contractors as and when needed. These trends were exacerbated in the last recession when many organizations "outsourced" noncore functions to firms of contractors and many employees became disposable "assets" to be hired and fired as circumstances demanded. In these conditions it became employees' responsibility to invest in their own futures by paying to acquire new skills and competencies.

The essential folly of this short-term perspective is beginning to be realized. Highly qualified "key players" could only be retained, if at all, by very high salaries (Korabik & Rosin, 1997). When employees took charge of their own development, this was not always in the best interests of organizational goals (Arnold, 1998). Skills shortages hampered company expansion after recession (Herriot & Pemberton, 1995). The UK Government itself became seriously concerned by high levels of unemployment, which had poorly developed or obsolete skills as their root cause, while competitor nations, such as Germany, had a much better trained and effective workforce (Hamlin, 1995). In addition to this, Senge's (1990) concept of the "Learning Organization", which gained competitive advantage via the ability of its workforce to learn, adapt, and share knowledge, became increasingly influential.

The result is that training, or to be more accurate, learning, is back on the agenda. More organizations are taking responsibility for developing their workforces (Arnold, 1998), and many now have "Staff Development" units where the emphasis is on multimedia computerized learning resources and the internet, which employees can use when they have a spare half hour. The nature of training is changing too. In the past the emphasis was on the acquisition of technical skills needed to do the job and promotion often followed from this. Now the emphasis may be upon changing workers' attitudes and values, improving their social, leadership, and teamwork skills, and promoting an organizational culture that values development and change (Alimo-Metcalfe, 1998a; Pearn, 1995; Steel, 1997).

Experiments are also being conducted in the delivery of training. "Just-in-time learning", "job-based challenge" learning, and many forms of distance learning, including the use of multimedia packages and the internet, are increasingly important (McConnell, 1997; Stewart & Winter, 1995).

Employee relations and motivation

This aspect of work and organizational psychology is most closely allied to "people management". It aims to harness our knowledge of social processes at work to increase worker motivation, well-being, and effectiveness. This area also includes industrial relations and conflicts between groups such as managers and shop-floor workers. However, given the decline in trades union power in many workplaces, there has been a shift of interest from collective, intergroup processes to a focus on relationships between individuals such as managers and direct reports or within members of a team. Issues include the factors which influence the amount of effort expended at work, the influence of job satisfaction on levels of performance and organizational commitment, the processes that underly group behaviour and decision making, and the exercise of power and influence in organizations. Also of interest is the nature of leadership and followership, and the management of organizational change.

Much research and theorizing has been expended on exploring the characteristics of jobs that make the work meaningful and worthwhile, so that the work itself becomes the main reward for effort (e.g., Hackman & Oldham, 1980; Herzberg, 1966; Maslow, 1954). Although such theories provide interesting insights, they generally fail to account for individual differences in what people want from work. Early theories tended to assume that everyone needed challenge, achievement, and recognition in their work, and the hunt was on to try to offer these within the constraints of assembly lines and such like. Although it is true that monotonous work appears to be extremely stressful (Davies, Shackleton, & Parasuraman, 1983), Schein (1988) is probably closer to the truth of many people's working lives when he argues that the greatest satisfaction from work is the social relationships between workers. Well and good—a lot of people want to work mainly for the company and comradeship; but social relationships can also be very stressful. For instance, West and Slater (1995) argue that working in a team can be a potent source of strain.

Warr's (1987) vitamin model is more general and more promising. He argues that the person's environment (which can include the workplace) can provide nine principal features, which act on psychological well-being rather like vitamins act on the physical body. Just as deficiencies in vitamins lead to physical ill-health, too little of any one feature such as pay, social status, opportunities to use your skills, etc. leads to poor mental health. However, beyond a certain level these features provide no further benefit, and high levels can be "toxic" and cause actual harm. Thus, beyond a certain level, pay rises are no longer motivating, and overwhelmingly complex and fast-paced jobs can lead to serious health problems. The beauty of Warr's theory is that the workplace is only one environment in which the person is involved and so it can explain why many millions of people who do not have or want paid employment can lead perfectly fulfilled and happy lives. However, paid work is probably the richest source of these "vitamins"—it has the potential to provide all of them, including what is essential to most people: access to money. It is therefore also extremely useful for explaining bad (and indeed good) reactions to unemployment.

Nevertheless, at a practical level, it does not predict how any one person will react to a particular job or how much of any one "vitamin" any individual needs for good psychological health. Some progress has been made in recent years (Warr, 1996a, 1998) in that job satisfaction and well-being are recognized as multi-faceted concepts. (Few people like every aspect of their jobs, and although job challenge may increase anxiety, it may also increase enthusiasm and reduce the chances of depression.) There is also increasing evidence that personality characteristics such as "negative affectivity" (e.g., emotional volatility) strongly influence job satisfaction—in other words, people who are habitual "worriers" are likely to dislike their work whatever its characteristics.

This area of work and organizational psychology faces many challenges, as old certainties in work are swept away (for instance, the expectation that one will progress steadily up the promotion ladder in the course of one's career). Most of the theories need to be re-evaluated in the light of the changing nature of work, but the importance and fascination of this area is thereby enhanced. For many organizations the main question is how to create a "totally committed and totally expendable workforce". For most occupational psychologists, the question is how to do this without also doing harm to individuals.

Organizational development and change

The aims of this area are to assist organizations and the individuals within them to adapt to change to cope with an increasingly turbulent business environment and so survive and flourish. Organizations of all types have undergone unprecedented change. There are many reasons for this. Some forces are economic (increasing competition, the global economy, "boom and bust" financial markets); others are driven by rapidly advancing technology (e.g., the rise in telephone banking and insurance, advanced manufacturing technology, virtual teams). Political forces (e.g., privatization of utilities, Government intervention in public services) and social trends (e.g., increasing diversity in the workforce) have also had an influence. These trends were apparent in the UK throughout the 1980s but during the last recession (circa 1990–1993) companies were forced to take drastic action. Business re-engineering led many organizations to "outsource" all but their core functions, to cut out whole tiers of management to push responsibility lower down the hierarchy (delayering), and to make large numbers of people redundant (downsizing). These changes were particularly traumatic because they also affected people who thought they were in secure jobs and expected to remain with their organizations until retirement. It is generally agreed that after the recession the old jobs did not return and that there are now more different ways of working. When I started this book, commentators were remarking on a growing realization that full employment may never again be possible. (In 1998 around 10% of the European labour force was out of work.) According to Herriot and Pemberton (1995) the revolution in the nature of work is still underway and the concern felt by many European work and organizational psychologists is reflected in the titles of recent conferences. "Health Hazards and Challenges in the New Working Life" was held in Sweden in January 1999, and "Innovations for Work, Organization and Well-being" was in Helsinki in May of the same year. The concern is ongoing; the 10th European Congress on Work and Organizational Psychology held in Prague in May 2001 had "Globalization: Opportunities and Threats" as its main theme.

Occupational psychologists working in this area have always been concerned with issues such as the design of organizations to promote maximum efficiency and effectiveness and the factors that underly the creation and expression of an organization's culture and climate, as well as with the management of change. Now a number of new issues are emerging such as the psychological contract (Guest, Conway, Briner, & Dickman, 1996), which concerns the unwritten and often implicit "agreement" between employers and employees about what each expects of the other. Unilateral violations of this contract by employers have very serious consequences for the workforce. Other issues concern the promotion of commitment and innovation, a customer service orientation, and quality control. To try to achieve this, workers are increasingly organized into teams, product-centred groups, and temporary project groups. Understanding what leads to effective team performance is thus a major focus (see e.g., Costa, Roe, & Taillieu, 2001; Curral, Forrestier, Dawson, & West, 2001; Hackman, 1994; Slater & West, 1995; Van Mierlo, Rutte, Seinen, & Kompier, 2001; Van Offenbeek, 2001; Van Vianen & De Dreu, 2001; West & Slater, 1995). Organizations have become more complex and effectively "boundaryless" with partnerships, consortia, mergers and acquisitions, and a focus on "stakeholders" such as suppliers and customers. There is also more interest in international management and promoting organizational culture across national boundaries. Many of the theories that have served in the past appear too static to explain the process of constant change (e.g., Lewin's 1951 theory of unfreezing, change, refreezing—see Chapter 2). Others are too internally oriented for the "boundaryless" organization.

These are certainly "interesting times" for everyone at work, but very exciting and challenging for occupational psychologists.

Levels of analysis and teamwork

In practice, there are no clear-cut boundaries between areas in work and organizational psychology since each impacts on all the others. So job analysis may influence the design of technological systems, the design of jobs, selection procedures, performance appraisal, training courses and employee development programmes, reward systems, social interaction between workers, and ultimately the culture and climate of the organization. So another way of characterizing the discipline is to consider the different levels of analysis that can be applied to any problem. This is summarized in Box 1.1 and is illustrated by the specific example of teamwork.

The "global" environment

At the most general level there is the "global" environment in which the organization operates. This includes societies, cultures, history, political systems, markets, and other organizations such as partners and competitors.

BOX 1.1
Levels of analysis in occupational psychology: The example of teamwork

Level of analysis	Aspect of process	Professional area	Relevant theory in "mainstream" psychology
"Global" environment Society, culture, history, politics, economics, markets, other organizations, global competition	Reasons for emphasis on teamwork, e.g., to enhance competitiveness	Organizational development and change plus other disciplines	Mainly the domain of other disciplines; economic and consumer psychology
Organizational environment	Climate/culture, mission/goals, nature of tasks, resources, diversity management process: All impact on team effectiveness	Organizational development and design	Open systems theory, management theory, communications theory
Physical environment Workspaces, human–machine systems, etc.	Influences effectiveness of interactions between team members, e.g., in virtual teams	Human–machine/human–computer interaction, design of environments and of work, training	Social psychology, cognitive psychology, environmental psychology, individual differences plus other disciplines, e.g., human physiology
Social environment	Selection of team members, teambuilding, operation of team, appraisal of team performance	Personal selection, training, employee relations, counselling, performance appraisal	Individual differences, psychometrics, personality and learning, social psychology, including social cognition, clinical psychology
Internal environment	Team members' behaviour, feelings, etc.	Personnel selection, training, personal development	Almost all psychology!

For many organizations this environment is truly global, for others it may be national, and yet others may operate within local communities. For many it will involve all three. Take an organization such as a university, an institution not conspicuously associated with global enterprise in the public mind. Here at the University of East London an important aspect of our mission is to serve the local community, which, this being London, is among the most culturally diverse in the world and contains many small to medium enterprises. East London is not an affluent area but a new campus has just opened in nearby Docklands to serve the local and business communities there. These encompass individuals with little formal education on the one hand and multinational corporations on the other. Individuals, groups, and departments have forged partnerships with many different local organizations in the London area. Nationally, we compete with other UK universities for students and income-generating contracts, whilst being subject to the imposition of Government policies and levels of funding. Corporate plans, business plans, course viability, and income generation are all high on the agenda. Also nationally, there is a network of individuals, groups, and professional bodies collaborating in research, the maintenance of academic standards, and entry to various professions. Internationally, there are links with Europe and a worldwide community of scholars as well as a large number of collaborative projects such as accreditation of overseas courses and involvement with other projects. The recent downturn in Far Eastern economies affected our recruitment of overseas students and hence our income, and competition from distance learning courses via the internet is likely to prove the next major challenge. All this in an organization more popularly associated with ivory towers! The point is, however, that the behaviour and experience of those working within this organization cannot be understood without reference to this "global" environment.

So it is with other organizations. The current importance afforded to teamwork cannot be understood without reference to the global forces that have created major changes in the nature and organization of work. Optimists might say that effective teams encourage innovation and get products faster to market ahead of the competition. Cynics might argue that having destroyed the basis for employee commitment and high performance, organizations are clutching at straws, hoping that commitment to one's team-mates will replace organizational commitment.

The organizational environment

The next level of analysis is the organization itself. As Chapter 2 will show, top management philosophies of human nature exert a profound effect on culture and climate and thus on managerial practices and the way work is organized. In the case of teamwork, Hackman (1994) emphasized that many aspects of an organization will determine the effectiveness of teams. Calling a group a team but managing them as individuals; calling a team an autonomous work group but retaining traditional forms of control; specifying challenging team objectives but skimping on organizational supports both in terms of resources and appropriate structures and systems, all undermine team performance. West, Lawthom, and Patterson (1995) noted that the several chains of command in primary health-care teams made them some of the most dysfunctional teams the researchers had ever encountered. Hackman reported that even administrative matters like duty rosters can prevent effective teamwork. Flight crews on passenger aircraft work best when they know each other well, but the complexities of allocating the same people to the same flights may mean that they rarely work together.

The physical environment

At another level of analysis we have the physical layout and technology of the workspace. It has long been known that people interact best and form friendships and good professional relationships when they are geographically close—a maximum radius of 50 yards from a person's desk has been quoted (Festinger, Schachter, & Back, 1950). Open-plan offices were introduced to counteract the "isolationist" tendency of the closed doors of individual offices but there is evidence that this creates a noisy and distracting environment which reduces work performance (Sundstrom, Town, Rice, Osborne, & Brill, 1994). Meanwhile, the practice of "hot desking", where people use whatever desk happens to be available when they are in the office, means that there is no stable base for developing relationships. Others who are permanently "chained" to their computers have no opportunity to interact face-to-face with their colleagues (Briner & Hockey, 1988).

Finally we have people dispersed across buildings, cities, countries, and continents who are expected to function as "virtual teams" via technological links such as e-mail and video conferencing. To date there is almost no evidence of the effectiveness of such teams beyond case studies of facilitated product launches and general hype about the technology's potential (Lipnack & Stamps, 1997). Meanwhile David Oborne in *The Psychologist* (1996) warns about deficiencies in the technology, and there are complaints about virtual team members wasting time "chatting" on e-mail. The personal experience of many suggests that e-mail can be both a boon for effective communication and a pain. I once spent 2 months trying to arrange a meeting with someone only to discover by chance that we actually lived within 15 minutes' drive of each other—something that would probably have emerged within a few minutes of a "real" conversation. Most organizations accept that virtual teams need regular face-to-face meetings to be truly effective (Pape, 1997). Given the problems that arise in the operation of "real" teams, it is fascinating to speculate on the obstacles and barriers confronting virtual teams. At the same time, the very distance, both geographically and psychologically, may facilitate the workings of virtual teams. There may be less likelihood that people will come into serious conflict when they must write their communications—a process traditionally involving more reflection on what one says. It is also possibly more difficult to detect hidden agendas and power plays in electronic communications, which could result in more harmonious relationships, at least superficially. Whatever the truth of the matter, one thing is clear—more research is needed!

The social environment

If physical conditions and technology deeply influence the workings of a team, the relationships between team members are also vital. Part of the rationale for team-based work is "synergy"—the belief that teamwork produces results over and above what would be achieved by the individuals working alone. West (1994) considers a number of barriers to effective teamwork, one of which is termed "social loafing" and concerns the tendency of people to work less hard when they are working in a group. Sometimes this is exacerbated by hierarchies in the team. In a classic study, Maier and Solem (1952) planted people who knew the answers to mathematical questions in groups, yet many of the groups failed to come up with the right answers. The "experts'" views had not been heeded because they lacked status. Similarly, in West's health-care teams, doctors had greater influence than health visitors and receptionists. Consequently, the latter felt that their work was not valued. An extreme example of how hierarchy can lead to bad decisions occurred when a co-pilot wondered aloud whether the captain was landing rather fast. The co-pilot was ridiculed and ignored and the plane crashed (Brown, 1988).

Janis (1982) proposed the notion of "groupthink", which he used to explain the disastrous decisions made by President Kennedy and his group of advisors in the Bay of Pigs fiasco in Cuba in 1962. Groupthink is a danger in very cohesive teams where there may be overwhelming pressure on dissenters from the majority view to change their views or remain silent. (See Nemeth & Owens, 1996 for a recent review of research on minority opinion in group decision making.)

There are many questions concerning the right mix of personalities and skills necessary for optimum team performance. De Jong, Bouhuys, and Barnhoorn (1999) found that extroverts and people with a high sense of self-efficacy were more likely to contribute in management teams. However, people with dominant personalities can often prevent others contributing and so reduce the effectiveness of teams.

Thus teamwork has to be understood from the point of view of the processes involved in the composition of the team, the way teams develop their modes of operating, and the group dynamics. Anderson and West (1995) have developed an instrument to try to measure some of these aspects of team functioning. The Team Climate Inventory attempts to assess the extent to which team members share information, listen to one another, give each other feedback, and strive for high performance.

The internal environment

At the level of the person there are individuals—with all their knowledge, abilities, skills, competences, personalities, agendas, and roles. For instance, Sonnentag and Schmidt-Braße (1998) review the literature on differences between high and moderate performers. High performers pursue more specific goals and put more emphasis on analysing the task than moderate performers do. In a team context they make use of highly developed communication and cooperation skills (Curtis, Krasner, & Iscoe, 1988). West (1994) cites a study of military teams, which showed that people of high ability performed best when in teams where the other members also had high ability.

Individuals may be assigned to a team on the basis of their function in the organization, their position in the hierarchy, or their particular skills. However, people are also said to have preferred team roles. Belbin's (1981) typology of team roles has been particularly popular in management circles. He describes nine different roles that people could occupy when working within a team, each of which has particular strengths and weaknesses (see Box 1.2). Each of us is said to have a natural tendency to occupy one or more of these roles. For instance, a Teamworker is cooperative and diplomatic and tries to avert friction or defuse conflict, but can be indecisive. A Shaper is challenging, dynamic, and thrives on pressure. Such a person has the drive and courage to overcome obstacles, but is easily provoked and can offend people's feelings. If people really do have a tendency to behave consistently in these ways, then it would be useful to be able to identify them when deciding on the composition of a team. A team composed mainly of Shapers, for instance, is likely to be a hotbed of conflict. Unfortunately, the reliability and validity of the instrument used to assess people's preferred team role—the Belbin Team Role Self-Perception Inventory—has recently been questioned. Senior and Swailes (1998) found that observers of team members' behaviour did not agree at all well on which role individuals were playing and individuals' own assessment of their roles did not agree well with that of observers. Senior and Swailes comment that there is very little evidence that people actually do occupy stable team roles. This conclusion is supported by a study that employed measures of personality and video observation and analysis of people taking part in business simulation exercises (Fisher, Hunter, & Masrossen, 2001). Analysis of the data showed that the Belbin team role model lacked validity but that personality characteristics could well influence people's behaviour in teams.

Teambuilding with the Myers–Briggs Type Indicator

Another popular approach in teambuilding is to assess individuals' personality using the Myers–Briggs Type Indicator (MBTI)[1] The MBTI is an

---

1 MBTI and Myers–Briggs Type Indicator are trademarks of Consulting Psychologists Press Inc. Distributed in the UK by OPP Ltd.

BOX 1.2
Description of Belbin's team roles

Roles	Team-role contribution	Allowable weaknesses
Plant	Creative, imaginative, unorthodox. Solves difficult problems.	Ignores incidentals. Too preoccupied to communicate effectively.
Resource investigator	Extravert, enthusiastic, communicative. Explores opportunities, develops contacts.	Over-optimistic. Loses interest once initial enthusiasm has passed.
Coordinator	Mature, confident, a good chairperson. Clarifies goals, promotes decision making, delegates well.	Can be seen as manipulative. Offloads personal work.
Shaper	Challenging, dynamic, thrives on pressure. The drive and courage to overcome obstacles.	Prone to provocation. Offends people's feelings.
Monitor evaluator	Sober, strategic, and discerning. Sees all options. Judges accurately.	Lacks drive and ability to inspire others.
Teamworker	Cooperative, mild, perceptive, and diplomatic. Listens, builds, averts friction.	Indecisive in crunch situations.
Implementer	Disciplined, reliable, conservative, and efficient. Turns ideas into practical actions.	Somewhat inflexible. Slow to respond to new possibilities. Inclined to worry unduly. Reluctant to delegate.
Completer-finisher	Painstaking, conscientious, anxious. Searches out errors and omissions. Delivers on time.	Inclined to worry unduly. Reluctant to delegate.
Specialist	Single-minded, self-starting, dedicated. Provides knowledge and skills in rare supply.	Contributes on only a narrow front. Dwells on technicalities.

Source: Adapted from B. Senior & S. Swailes (1998). A comparison on the Belbin Self-Perception Inventory and Observer's Assessment Sheet as measures of an individual's team roles. *International Journal of Selection and Assessment, 6*, 1–8. Copyright © 1998 Blackwell Publishers Ltd.

BOX 1.3
Characteristics of each of the four MBTI scales

Extraversion (E)
Prefer bustle, activity, variety, and frequent interaction with others

Introversion (I)
Prefer quiet, private settings which allow reflection and concentration on tasks; dislike interruptions

Sensing (S)
Prefer to pay attention to detail and like tasks that are concrete, practical, and useful; prefer to use tried and trusted methods and well-developed skills but good at following through; dislike major changes and prefer to fine-tune

Intuition (N)
Prefer to focus on the general and the "big picture"; like to try new things—innovative solutions to problems, new ways of working, learning new skills; trust their inspirations and like "big ideas"; prefer to change things radically

Thinking (T)
Prefer to focus on logic and analysis and getting the job done; base decisions on principles and truths and sometimes hurt others' feelings without being aware of it; readily offer criticisms and suggestions for improvements

Feeling (F)
Prefer to focus on people and relationships; like harmony and pleasing people; sensitive to people's needs and feelings; allow others' likes and dislikes to influence their decisions; dislike criticizing others

Judgement (J)
Prefer structure, order, planning, and organization; like to make plans and stick to them

Perception (P)
Prefer to be spontaneous, flexible, and to leave things open so that last-minute changes can be made

---

interesting personality instrument which is based on Jung's theory. Although it has been criticized as distorting Jung's theory (McCrae & Costa, 1988) and the evidence for its validity is somewhat patchy (see, e.g., Furnham, 1992), the general consensus seems to be that, on the whole, it is useful and worthwhile as a basis for exploring personality issues.

It is an unusual instrument in that instead of measuring personality traits such as extraversion or conscientiousness, it purports to classify people according to personality type. According to the theory people have certain natural preferences which influence the ways they typically react to their environments. There are eight personality preferences organized into four scales with two opposite preferences on each scale (see Box 1.3).

To perform well at work, people may have to use all eight preferences at different times but usually feel more comfortable using the preferences that come most naturally to them. People can be classified into one of the 16 different personality types according to their dominant preference on each of the four scales.

For instance, people classified as ENTJ might be energetic managers, frequently seeking people out and taking charge of situations. They are likely to be highly innovative and are likely to create a lot of change and "uproar" as they may "leap" before they "look", that is, acting before checking out all the details of any plans. While they are logical, analytical, and well organized, their task orientation may lead them to be insensitive to others' feelings, and they may be too forthright in criticizing people's ideas or work performance. They may also be rather rigid in sticking to plans and projects long after a change in course of action would have been desirable.

The MBTI is often used in teambuilding and management development because it gives people insights into how they may come across to others, who may see things differently. Knowledge of their own and others' preferences not only aids understanding and communication but also helps them to appreciate that their own limitations might be compensated by others' strengths.

Since we have been talking about teamwork, you might like to start applying the skills of an occupational psychologist to a case study of a dysfunctional team in Exercise 1.3. This exercise is best done with one or two friends and then you can act as a problem-solving team and simultaneously observe the way you work together. Some suggested answers to this exercise are included.

Summary

In this chapter I have discussed the nature of work and work and organizational/occupational psychology and some of the political and ethical issues surrounding the study of people in the workplace. Using the eight areas stipulated by the British Psychological Society I have briefly introduced the content of the next eight chapters of this book. (See Chapter 0 for more on the rationale for the organization of this book and what has been selected for inclusion.) In a sense, Chapters 2–5 present the problem, and Chapters 6–9 explore the solutions. The final chapter examines growth points in the discipline.

However, this chapter has also emphasized how the different areas of work and organizational/occupational psychology are inter-related. Using teamwork as an example, it has shown how effective teamwork can be analysed at different levels from the "global" environment to the individual worker. It has ended with an opportunity for readers to think like an occupational psychologist by applying theory to suggest solutions to a case study of a workplace problem.

EXERCISE 1.3
Using the MBTI to resolve conflicts in a work team

You have been asked to investigate why a marketing team of two people are just not getting on well together and are holding up the launch of a new product. If some solution cannot be found, the company will have to consider "releasing" one or both of the parties, which will be expensive both in terms of redundancy payments and recruiting replacements.

After extensive interviews with the two people and other staff and managers you manage to piece together the following sequence of events.

Fred and Jean work for a company that manufactures biscuits and are expected to work as a team. They have the task of choosing which of two new chocolate biscuits should go into production and designing a marketing strategy. "Yummy Chocs" has run-of-the-mill milk chocolate, known to be popular with the punters but is not much different from the competitions' biscuits. "Moonlight Dreams" has high quality continental-type chocolate, which has less mass appeal and is more expensive but is a sophisticated and distinctive product.

Jean prefers to play it safe and go for "Yummy Chocs" with its mass appeal but Fred sees "Moonlight Dreams" as a great opportunity to take the company upmarket and establish a distinctive brand image. Jean points out that the company already has a brand image which is very much middle of the road. Moreover, market research has not yet been completed and shouldn't they wait before making a decision? Fred argues forcibly for his choice and seems impatient with Jean's objections.

When it comes to thinking about a marketing campaign, there is little agreement either. Jean wants to target "Yummy Chocs" at children and put relatively cheap and cheerful adverts in amongst kids' TV. Fred wants exotic adverts with shots of swans flying by moonlight, 1920s Rolls Royce Silver Ghosts drawing up outside country houses, and a launch including a hot air balloon complete with "beautiful people". Jean points out that this would certainly exceed their marketing budget. Fred begins another heated monologue. Jean goes very quiet and looks strained.

Over the next few days Jean tries to process the market research results but Fred interrupts her whenever he thinks of another argument to support his position. Eventually she goes along with his ideas. Fred sets about the detailed planning of the project.

You realize that there is a personality clash here and get Jean and Fred to take the MBTI. Unknown to them, Fred has an ENTJ personality type while Jean has an ISFP personality type. By looking at their respective MBTI personality profiles it is easy to see that these two people would make a dreadful team with constant conflicts and breakdowns of communication because they have diametrically opposed preferences. To gain a deeper understanding of the dynamics of their relationship:

1   Using the characteristics list and the sample of their interactions given previously, write descriptions of what each is likely to think privately about the other.
2   Jean, particularly, is likely to be suffering from severe work strain—why?

However, to keep their jobs they have to continue working as a team. So having explained the strengths and weaknesses of their respective personality profiles, what advice would you give regarding:

3   What Fred can do to modify his behaviour to make life less stressful for Jean?
4   What Jean can do to modify her behaviour to improve their working relationship?
5   How they could each use the other's strengths to compensate for their weaknesses to achieve better work outcomes?

Note: you may find it amusing and instructive to role play Fred and Jean's discussions before and after the MBTI revelations.
    Feel free to reverse the personality types so that Fred becomes Jean and vice versa—does this make any difference to your answers and interpretation of the situation?

Suggested answers
1   *Fred (ENTJ) on Jean (ISFP)*. Jean is a real nit-picking bean counter who wouldn't recognize a good idea if it got up and bit her. Half the time she's barricaded in her office and I can't get anything out of her and next thing she's sucking up to me and agreeing with everything I say. Hasn't she got any independent thoughts? And what a stick-in-the-mud! She always has to do the same old thing and no wonder—she couldn't plan her way out of a paper bag!
    Jean (ISFP) on Fred (ENTJ). Fred is a loud brash bully with the social sensitivity of a hippo! He never stops pestering me so I can't get on with my work and he's always ready to criticize—there's no pleasing the man! Half the time he's off on his wild ideas with never a thought about whether they're practical or not and then he plans everything like a military campaign and I get frogmarched into it. Never mind whether the plan is a good one! Nothing is ever good enough for him—he wants to change everything. I don't think I can stand this much longer.
2   Jean's feeling preference will make her especially vulnerable in this personality clash because she likes harmony in working relationships and to please people. She will also be acutely aware of Fred's feelings of frustration when they come into conflict. Her unwillingness to criticize also means she is likely to suffer in silence. Her sensing preference means that she will find constant change very stressful and Fred's

frequent interruptions mean that she can't work in her preferred way and is likely to suffer performance anxiety.

3   Note that Fred and Jean would undoubtedly need counselling to help them to develop a better working relationship if things had really deteriorated as badly as the descriptions imply.

However, Fred could use his thinking and judgement preferences to make Jean's life more tolerable. He should analyse what causes her most distress and then plan to minimize it. For instance, he could plan set times during the day for meetings and avoid interrupting her between those times. He should recognize that Jean's strengths in attention to detail and social sensitivity can complement his own weaknesses in this regard. By understanding and thus respecting where she is coming from, he should be less abrasive in meetings. Indeed, knowing his own limitations he should listen to her views all the more carefully because she can see his blind spots. This would please Jean because she enjoys meeting people's needs. He could also try to develop his nonpreferred side, e.g., by social skills training. By harnessing his planning and organizing skills he too could give more thought to the detailed implementation of his schemes.

4   Jean should also recognize Fred's strengths, particularly his capacity for innovation and organizing, and realize that she too has much to contribute to their team. She might develop the thinking side of her personality by taking an assertiveness training course so that she feels more comfortable standing her ground and offering constructive criticism. She can use her social skills to negotiate changes with Fred and tone down some of his more extravagant schemes instead of agreeing to them and suffering in silence. Now that she understands Fred's personality better she is less likely to misinterpret his behaviour and take things personally.

5   Fred is the ideas man and his capacity for innovation is one of his main assets. Jean, on the other hand, is the practical one and she can act as a valuable "reality checker". He should run his ideas past her, listen to what she has to say, and then find innovative solutions to the practical problems she raises. It would be sensible for Jean to take over any aspects of the work that require attention to detail such as gathering information, conducting market research, and implementing the minutiae of the marketing campaign. Her social sensitivity might make her more suitable for dealings with service providers such as advertising agencies. In addition to having ideas, Fred is the organizer, which makes him a good project manager, but here again Jean can act as a valuable check on his tendency to rigidity. He can review his plans with her periodically so that her flexibility can promote necessary changes in emphasis and direction. They could both compromise more. Fred could go along with Jean's level-headed choice of "Yummy Chocs" but then market it with such brilliance and originality that it becomes a huge success. In these ways Fred and Jean could become a very effective team.

Learnings and further reflections

- This is a simplified version of the theory behind the MBTI and of course, in real life, teams tend to be much larger with a more complex mix of personalities. This has also been an extreme example—in real life Fred and Jean wouldn't have been able to work together for more than a week, if anyone had been stupid enough to force them to do so in the first place! Even with the MBTI and counselling there might still not have been a happy ending. Even so, I hope this has demonstrated how the MBTI could be used in teambuilding before members get down to the real work. The processes described here have also been used to improve the functioning of ineffective and strife-ridden teams. Try experimenting with other combinations of MBTI types and with three or more protagonists. What further clashes of personality might occur and how might harmonization of their different perspectives and preferred ways of working be achieved?
- Have you felt uncomfortable with the gender relations portrayed in this account or did you accept them without much thought? (Having a male and female protagonist was merely for the sake of clarity of exposition—they could just as easily have been two men or two women.) Try reversing the the personality types so that Fred becomes Jean and vice versa. Do you feel that this makes the case study less "realistic" in some way? Does this tell you anything about your own attitudes to the roles and behaviours of men and women at work?
- Note that although this is a hypothetical case study it illustrates the twin goals of occupational psychology—achieving business objectives and making working life better for individuals.

Suggested further reading

Apter, M. J. (2001). *Motivational styles in everyday life: A guide to reversal theory.* Washington, DC: American Psychological Association.

Arnold, J., Cooper, C. L., & Robertson, I. T. (Eds.). (1998). *Work psychology: Understanding human behaviour in the workplace* (3rd ed.). Harlow, UK: Financial Times/Prentice Hall.

Chmiel, N. (Ed.) (2000). *Introduction to work and organizational psychology: A European perspective.* Oxford, UK: Blackwell.

Furnham, A. (1992). *Personality at work.* London: Routledge.

Furnham, A. (1997). *The psychology of behaviour at work: The individual in the organization.* Hove, UK: Psychology Press.

Porteous, M. (1997). *Occupational psychology.* Hemel Hempstead, UK: Prentice Hall Europe.

Svebak, S., & Apter, M. J. (Eds.) (1997). *Stress and health: A reversal theory perspective.* Washington, DC: Taylor & Francis.

2 All change . . . the past and future of work: Organizational change and development

A historian is a prophet in reverse.

Schlegal, 1772–1829

As we begin the 21st century, it is arguable whether there has ever been so much disagreement about the nature of work and how it should be organized, to say nothing of debate about a future when large sections of the population may have no paid work at all (e.g., Wilpert, 1997). The optimists, mainly in the USA but including Charles Handy (1995) in the UK, see work undergoing a revolution to which people will adapt, becoming multiskilled, resilient, and self-sufficient as they manage portfolio careers. The pessimists, mainly centred in Europe (e.g., Frese, 1997), but including Herriot and Pemberton (1995) in the UK, are not so sanguine. They perceive a workforce under increasing strain where two people in employment now do the work previously done by three, where the UK is generally agreed to have the longest working hours in Europe, feelings of job insecurity are rife, and organizational commitment is severely threatened. Meanwhile millions are in enforced idleness and poverty, and some commentators (e.g., Wilpert, 1997) predict increasing social unrest and societal breakdown.

Work smarter, not harder . . .

What is really happening in the workplace and what are its consequences for individuals? The truth is that at this time no-one really knows. As Thompson and Warhurst (1998, p. 8) say, "The banal but simple truth is that there is no universal direction." For many millions in many sectors of the economy work goes on much as it has always done. Many people working in the retail industry, in maintenance, repair, and construction firms, and in the hotel and leisure industry, for instance, might scoff at the notion that a revolution in the nature of work is underway. But for millions of others, their working lives have been transformed in recent years. There is undoubtedly a growing consensus about trends in working life, but the complexities of what is actually happening on the ground are well illustrated in two recent collections of papers (Mabey, Skinner, & Clark, 1998; Thompson & Warhurst, 1998). Both demonstrate that reality often falls short of the rhetoric (e.g., performance-related pay fails to motivate because of its lack of objectivity) and that there are many contradictions between the rhetoric and management practice (e.g., greater employee autonomy is actually accompanied by increased coercive control). There is a plethora of anecdote, case studies, general "feelings", and opinion, but little hard evidence.

All this seems to be neatly reflected in an article published in the *Financial Times*. Richard Tomkins (1999) begins with the comment that the 1990s seem to have been a time when "everyone" is "stressed out" with ever more to do and fewer hours to do it in and blames, among other things, the advance of technology which makes work portable and brings it into our cars and homes and even onto the beach. Technology does not save us time, it enables us to do more things in the time we have and meanwhile the information explosion makes it impossible for today's "knowledge workers" to know more than a tiny fraction of what they need to know. He then moves on to quote an interview with Paul Edwards of the London-based Henley Centre forecasting group, who suggests that feeling time pressured can be exaggerated or self-imposed—if you are not stressed by too much to do in too little time, you are not a success, so people actually want to claim time pressure. Moreover, Geoffrey Godbey, professor of Leisure Studies at Penn State University in the US, points to research showing that since the 1960s the average American has gained 5 hours' free time per week. He believes that as people's horizons have expanded, so they now have a surfeit of choices of what to cram into their time. That then, is the real problem—if only we lowered our expectations about the number of good things we feel we need to cram into our lifetimes the problems would be eased. We are thus the authors of our own misfortune.

What is one to make of such a mix of arguments? Even-handedly, Tomkins mentions that time pressure may apply to only half the population, with increasing numbers taking early retirement and others unemployed. He also mentions gross inequalities between men and women. "According to the Henley Centre, working fathers in the UK average 48 hours of free time per week. Working mothers get 14." What does that do to Godbey's argument that the *average* amount of free time enjoyed by US workers has increased but not fast enough to keep pace with everything they want to do with it? Herriot and Pemberton (1995) quote evidence that, in 1993, 89% of managers reported an increase in workload, 82% increased responsibility, 58% worked more than 50 hours per week, and 85% were concerned about leading a more balanced life than they had been 5 years ago. In a very different context, Hind and Doyle (1996; Doyle & Hind, 1998), found that 77% of their sample of lecturers in UK higher education reported an increase in workload over the past 5 years and 67% said they worked most evenings and weekends. Arnold (1997a, p. 21) notes that "there is no doubt" that British workers perceive themselves to be working longer and harder than in the past and it is often claimed that they work the longest hours in Europe (Rubery, Smith, & Fagan, 1995). Average numbers of hours of overtime have also increased with a significant rise in evening, night shift, and Sunday working. Also, there are now about 1.25 million people with two or more jobs, mostly, says Arnold, because of financial necessity. Clearly some people are more "time starved" than others.

But is there anything particularly new in all this? Social historians of the 19th century quote horrendous working hours; servants who rose to begin work at 5 am and went off duty to bed close to midnight; factory workers doing 14- and 16-hour shifts with appalling rates of industrial injury as exhausted workers made mistakes and got entangled with unguarded machinery; and so on. Industrial reformers of the time were in no doubt that such long hours were injurious to health and fought long and hard to reduce them against determined opposition from the owners of business who forecast bankruptcy in the face of such reforms in rather the same way that our own times have produced a great deal of protest against the European Directives on the maximum working week and the minimum wage. At the beginning of the 21st century, very long working hours are more likely to be suffered by managers, professionals, people juggling two or three part-time jobs, and mothers in full-time employment who start another "day's work" when they get home.

Interestingly, commentators at the dawn of the new millennium (at least, in management circles), appear to be far less convinced that current working practices could damage health and well-being than our predecessors 150 years ago. According to much of the rhetoric people working 60, 70, 80, and more hours per week are likely to be told that they are inefficient (could organize their time better), are lacking in ability or skills (could work faster and smarter), are personally inadequate (unable to manage stress), are rigid and inflexible (cannot handle necessary change), or, as already mentioned, simply have too much choice of leisure activities for a comfortable personal life. In contrast, the voices raised against intolerable work demands are less often heard (see, e.g., Hockey et al, 1995). Warhurst and Thompson (1998) believe that "most managers would be too embarrassed by the evidence of their own eyes and ears to repeat the 'working smarter not harder' mantra" (p. 10). The long-term consequences of an apparent return to 19th-century working hours for both organizations and the people who work within them are simply unknown. However, in Japan, *karoshi*, or death by overwork, is a matter of public debate (Kyotani, 1996, unpublished paper cited in Thompson & Warhurst, 1998). In 1996, the journal *People Management* reported that Japan's biggest advertising agency had been forced to pay £780,000 to the family of an employee who committed suicide after working 17 months without a day off and frequently with only 2 or 3 hours sleep per night. The Japanese Ministry of Labour reported 63 such deaths in 1995, but this was the first case where the employer was held responsible for suicide through overwork.

Such considerations can easily be dismissed as a political polemic. True, but this is the landscape confronting occupational psychologists who are generally employed to maximize an organization's financial success but who also, for the most part, believe that ultimately this is best achieved through the well-being and commitment of the workforce. Occupational psychologists have no monopoly of the truth, whatever that might be, and have many "rival" professionals who will dispute interpretation of the available evidence. Nevertheless, if work and organizational psychology is to offer anything more than the latest "management guru" creed, it must be based on sound, empirical research evidence and the onus is on the discipline to produce rigorous evidence. However, employers are very unwilling to allow, let alone fund, such research, even to the extent of refusing to try to find out whether their investments in interventions have been worthwhile. It is ironic, therefore, that throughout the 20th century, management's philosophy of human nature has been deeply influenced by theory and research in psychology, and this in turn has deeply influenced management practice and the organization of work for good and ill. It is to these that we next turn, before examining the "revolution" in the workplace in more detail.

Management philosophies: Two extremes?

It seems to me that the majority of the 20th century was dominated by two major management philosophies that have deeply influenced the organization of work. These two main philosophies were encapsulated around the middle of the century by McGregor (1960) in his contrast between theories X and Y.

Managers who espoused theory X were said to believe that the mass of ordinary people are inherently:

- Lazy.
- Self-centred.
- Lacking in ambition/willingness to take responsibility.
- Resistant to change.
- Gullible and not very bright.
- Motivated by "sticks and carrots"—fear of the sack and wages.

Managers must therefore organize, direct, persuade, punish, reward, and, above all, control workers to meet the needs of the organization. It was this view of human nature which seems to underly the metaphor of the organization as "machine".

The dominant philosophy of human nature encapsulated in theory Y is that people are not by nature passive and lazy but may become so because of their experience of organizational life. On the contrary, people are thought to want challenge, development, achievement, and recognition and will work hard to get these in the right conditions. People can also learn to want responsibility and self-direction and to become committed to organizational goals. People are:

- Naturally motivated to work for goals which they value and this includes organizational goals.
- Intelligent and capable of imagination and innovation in solving organizational problems.

Management must therefore create the conditions for people to develop their full potential and so that people can achieve their own goals best by directing their efforts towards organizational objectives. This philosophy underlies the metaphor of the organization as living organism and more recent ideas of the "learning organization" (see Chapter 6).

Metaphors of organization as intellectual tools

Morgan (1997) gives a lucid and impartial account of each metaphor (in amongst many other ways of conceptualizing the nature of organizations, all of which contribute to our understanding in different ways). Morgan stresses that these are merely metaphors. Powerful tools for understanding, yes, but they share the limitations of all metaphors in that they seek to help us to understand the unfamiliar in terms of what we do understand about the familiar. In this sense, we explain something in terms of what it is *not* in order to understand and communicate what it *is*. The danger of metaphors is that just because they are so useful they may be over-exploited, and this can result in misleading comparisons and over-simplification. We must remember that at some stage the metaphor must break down when we discover aspects of what we are trying to understand that are fundamentally different from the model we are using to explain them (Boden, 1981).

One trouble is that what starts off as a "hook" to hang our imperfect understandings on, all too often becomes an ideology about what ought or should be. Part of our current muddle is that we cannot decide whether organizations are, or should be, machines, living creatures interacting with their environment, or "brains", when in certain respects they may be like these things or all of them at once.

The machine metaphor

Morgan (1997) reminds us that an effective and efficient organization is often seen in machine terms—running like clockwork and equally routinized, reliable, and consistent in its standards and outputs. The goal of the organization is to achieve this consistency, and the messy and unreliable human participant must either be eliminated (through automation) or forced to conform to "machine" standards (through rules, regulations, quality control, close supervision of work, etc.).

This philosophy is most often associated with organizations based on Taylor's (1911) Scientific Management, usually manufacturing industry with traditional assembly lines. However, it could also be said to characterize bureaucracies with their rigid hierarchies, tightly specified roles and responsibilities, and sets of rules and procedures. Thus, its influence pervades not only factory floors but also public institutions such as the Civil Service, the UK's National Health Service (NHS), and increasingly, all levels of the education system (see Pollitt, 1993).

Many of these ideas are not new. The ancient Classical world gives many examples of the use of machines to make labour easier, of factories, and of mass production. The Roman Empire, with its Civil Administration, and the medieval Christian Church were superb bureaucracies. Frederick the Great revived many of these ideas in his organization of the Prussian Army in the 18th century. However, before the Industrial Revolution most manufacturing activity was domestic in scale, often home-based, highly skilled, often involved self-employment, and was frequently intermittent or part-time. Examples include the 17th-century cloth-making and lead-mining and smelting industries in Yorkshire. Farming families supplemented their income by these means and took to say, mining, for only a few months of the year. All this changed with the introduction of steam power, when expensive machinery and plant sited close to water supplies required the concentration of workforces close to large factories. To gain an adequate return on their investment, owners required workers to work for very long hours, and the different machines dictated a division of labour and a gradual de-skilling of jobs. Not surprisingly, people were reluctant to give up their independence to become "machine slaves", so employers became focused on how labour was to be organized and controlled.

Early in the 20th century, Frederick Taylor published his book *Principles of Scientific Management* (1911), which described techniques to standardize work activities to achieve maximum efficiency of effort and time. By means of a "time and motion" study, the unfortunate Schmidt (a pig iron handler) was induced to increase his production by 280% from shifting 12.5 to 47.5 tons a day. Time and motion studies involved observing and analysing tasks into their simplest components and working out the most efficient way to perform them. As a result, workers were obliged to behave like mechanical machines, in very precise and regular ways. When Henry Ford invented the moving assembly line, the system of mass production was complete. In the process, work was split into its simplest components and became coordinated, routinized, monotonous, and de-skilled.

Interestingly, the original idea behind bureaucracies was essentially philanthropic. By vesting authority in the fixed role in the hierarchy rather than in the person occupying that role, the arbitrary exercise of power over the workforce was curtailed. An owner might indulge in nepotism or sack workers on a whim. In theory at least, a bureaucratic role was obtained on merit and was hedged around with rules and procedures to ensure that everyone was treated equitably. Bureaucracies were meant to be rational and quasi-legal systems.

Both forms of organization have had a bad press. Henry Ford is reputed to have had to increase wages to unprecedented levels to prevent the equivalent of his entire workforce leaving every 3 months. A few years ago BBC television broadcast an excellent series called the "People's Century" which included interviews with people who had lived through the events depicted in archive film. One programme was entitled "On the Line" and it contains extraordinary footage of Ford's giant River Rouge plant in full swing. What a scary place! The hectic pace of work, the chunks of ironmongery constantly moving overhead, the noise, are all apparent. No wonder former workers said that many could not abide the conditions for more than a few weeks. (The whole series was released on video in 1997 and was available from BBC Worldwide Ltd; striking "still" images can also be found in Hodgson, 1995.) Fletcher and Payne (1980) found that rates of ill-health and mortality were highest not in business executives but in shop-floor workers—although it is difficult to disentangle the additional effects of unhealthy lifestyles. Weber (1949) was a famous critic of bureaucracy which he believed had the potential to routinize and mechanize every aspect of human life, eroding the human spirit, capacity for creativity, flexibility, and human action. Even today, the greatest problem with both types of organization is their inflexibility in the face of major external change and their capacity to stifle individual initiative and innovation.

Somewhat surprisingly, both forms have been remarkably resistant to extinction and remain alive and flourishing into the 21st century (Taylor, 1998; Wall & Martin, 1994; Wright & Lund, 1996). The strengths of these systems remain—they provide reliable and consistent products and services remarkably efficiently (and profitably!)—as is manifest in a very well-known fast food outlet, branches of which can be found in the most unlikely quarters of the globe, all selling the same familiar product to the same standard, all held together by time and motion techniques and rules and procedures specified down to the required smile as one greets a customer. However much the human cost, we cannot deny that such systems have been largely responsible for the steady rise in affluence in Western countries throughout the 20th century—an argument made persuasively in the "On the Line" programme. Though much of manufacturing industry has moved on towards greater and smarter automation, forays into autonomous work groups, and greater worker empowerment and so on, the principles remain firmly in place (Danford, 1998) and are likely to do so for the forseeable future. This is not to say that Taylorism has not developed into more sophisticated forms. For instance, Wright and Lund (1996) use the term, "computerised Taylorism" in connection with the introduction of new engineering standards systems, and Adler (1993; Adler & Cole, 1995) dub activities such as worker participation in job analysis in order to develop new systems of work measurement, "democratic Taylorism". Control is often more subtle.

If workers internalize management's strictures as regards acceptable behaviour then less supervision is necessary (Warhurst & Thompson, 1998). However, control can also be very explicit. We see its influence in data entry operators whose every pause and mistake is recorded electronically (see Briner & Hockey, 1988) and in what have been deemed, fairly or unfairly, as the "new sweatshops"—24-hour call centres, where dialogues with telephone customers are randomly sampled for deviations from company regulations. More startling is the suggestion that microchips, placed under the skin of staff, might be used to monitor their every movement and keep track of efficiency, time-keeping, and productivity (*Metro London* newspaper, 1999). Kevin Warwick of Reading University has reportedly been approached by several firms to explain how the microchip technology he has been developing might be used for these purposes. He is also reported as saying, "It is pushing the limits of what society will accept but it is not such a big deal." Some would beg to differ! De-skilling also continues apace. Warhurst and Thompson point out that the much vaunted "knowledge workers" are often engaged in extremely routine, repetitive tasks.

The recent history of bureaucracy is even more interesting. Bureaucracies such as the UK National Health Service (NHS) and nationalized industries were deemed to be wasteful and inefficient at the end of the 1970s so the then Conservative Government set about much-needed reform. National utilities were privatized, and it is a matter of debate whether their services are now more efficient and effective. They certainly appear to be more profitable. However, public services proved much more intractable. The introduction of "internal economies" of customers and providers, of local control of budgets (e.g., of GP practices, schools, and university departments), of the imposition of external controls in the form of, for instance, the National Curriculum and OFSTED inspections, seem to have improved standards but, paradoxically, at the cost of a huge increase in . . . bureaucracy! Control is now enforced by appraisal systems linked to performance targets and "quality audits". Many of the long hours put in by teachers, academics, and medics can now be laid at the door of the need for extensive documentation and "paper chases", often in parallel with a raft of new administrators and managers. For instance, Milhill (1996) documents that the NHS lost 50,000 nurses and midwives between 1989 and 1994 but gained over 18,000 managers. *Management Today* (Tester, 1998) recently profiled the head of a secondary school, likening her role to that of a chief executive of a medium-sized company. Unfortunately, her pay bore little resemblance to her colleagues in industry and this is perhaps a contributory factor in the current shortage of school heads (Lyons, 1997).

In fact, there is growing evidence that these changes in the public services, coupled with low pay in comparison with related professionals in the private sector, are having an adverse impact on recruitment and retention. In the UK in the winters of 1998/99 and again in 1999/2000, in order to meet a crisis in demand, the Government was forced to raise the pay of nurses to tempt back those who had left the profession. One of the last acts of the 1992/97 Conservative Government was to stem the flood of early retirements of teachers by changing the rules to make it almost impossible, which itself precipitated a flood of early retirements in experienced teachers who may have been intending to continue working for longer. As I write, the present Labour Government is running advertising campaigns to recruit more nurses, doctors, teachers, and police officers. There are regular news reports of short-ages of such personnel and of the need to recruit abroad to fill vacant posts. Also in the UK there are complaints that universities are not providing IT graduates with the skills the industry needs (Merridenand & Bird, 1999). However, starting salaries are so low that few of the brightest IT graduates and established professionals are tempted into university teaching. Similar problems occur in the recruitment of staff with professional expertise in many areas. The position of university research staff is also cause for con-cern. Research carried out for the Brett enquiry on academic pay in 1999 found that 93% of all researchers were on short-term contracts, some lasting only a few months, and some earned as little as £10,000 per annum. Also, early in 1999, junior hospital doctors were threatening industrial action in protest against their long hours (up to 100 or more hours per week) and "derisory" rates of (supplementary) pay (£4 per hour) when they were "on call". The same is true of hourly paid staff in higher education, where low pay may be threatening the quality of professional training. Most professionals are minded to help to foster the next generation by part-time teaching to pass on their skills, but universities can rarely afford to match commercial rates of pay so practitioners often find themselves making a net loss when they spend their time contributing to postgraduate training courses.

Lest this foray into public sector pay be regarded as an irrelevant diver-sion, it is well to remember Henry Ford's difficulties in retaining his workforce. The "machine" philosophy regards workers as being primarily motivated by the pay packet and fear of the sack. Herriot and Pemberton (1995) remark that long hours and total commitment to the organization can be bought with high pay, at least temporarily. However, they also note that in times of high unemployment, the privilege of having a job at all is as much reward as many can expect. They also warn that in economic upturns, companies can expect to suffer severe skill shortages.

The organic metaphor

Von Bertalanffy (1950), a biologist, defined living organisms as a collection of parts interacting and functioning as a harmonious whole in a continuous process of exchange and interaction with the environment. This idea was applied to organizations, which came to be seen as complex open systems (Katz & Kahn, 1978). Like living bodies, organizations are composed of many interacting parts and processes, which take inputs from the environment, transform them in some way, and produce outputs back into the environment.

Since the parts are interdependent, changes in one part can have profound and unpredictable effects on the other parts in the network. The system must adapt to the demands of its external environment but at the same time it must preserve its internal stability whilst engaging in constant change. Complex systems can be analysed at many levels, from the total organism within its environment to the workings of an individual cell. Similarly, understanding a work organization and people's behaviour within it can range from analysis of the historical, political, economic, and cultural environment in which it operates through the social interactions within work groups to the goals, aspirations, and abilities of individual workers.

This way of thinking about organizations arose from a general dissatisfaction with mechanistic approaches, which could not explain the complexities and unpredictability of what goes on in an organization. Homans (1950), for instance, identified the existence of informal systems which ran alongside of, and were often more important than the official formal system. Cyert and March (1963) described organizations as being composed of coalitions, and organizational life as a process of negotiation, bargaining, and power play between shifting coalitions in accordance with environmental demands. Scott (1987) also stressed that organizations functioned as coalitions of shifting interest groups which negotiate to develop goals, whilst Kahn, Wolfe, Quinn, Snoek, and Rosenthal (1964) talked of overlapping role sets and introduced the useful notions of role ambiguity and role conflict. Bureaucracy, with its rigid hierarchies, clearly defined roles, rules, and procedures was not a good model to describe such messy complexity.

Similarly, researchers at the Tavistock Institute (Rice, 1963; Trist, 1982) pointed out that organizations were composed of a social system (the people and their interactions) and a technical system (the machines and processes). Both these systems needed to be in harmony if the organization is to be effective and this would imply also meeting the social and psychological needs of people who complemented the technology. Sociotechnical systems were therefore somewhat separable from the notion of treating people as if they were part of the machinery.

This way of thinking led to an appreciation of the true complexity of organizations. Sources of this complexity have been summarized by Schein (1988). The first issue concerns boundaries—where does a large company end and its community begin and what is its relevant environment? The devastation wreaked on entire regions when major industries fail is all too familiar and demonstrates the interconnectedness of local economies. The organization's stakeholders can include suppliers, outsourced services companies, partners, customers, shareholders, even competitors, and not just the workforce. A good example of this blurring of organizational boundaries concerns recent urban renewal programmes in the UK when private corporations, local government, and voluntary sector agencies may all work together in a complex set of inter-organizational relations. Of course the global restructuring of production magnifies this complexity.

Organizations also have multiple purposes and functions. The primary function may be the provision of a product or service for profit but an organization may also provide focus and meaning for the whole community. The manifest functions of higher education are teaching, research, and scholarship but there are also numerous latent functions such as sorting talent for society, training a multiskilled flexible workforce for economic prosperity, encouraging social cohesion by providing opportunity for disadvantaged groups, and so on. Not surprisingly, many of these agendas conflict with each other.

Another source of complexity is that the workforce is only partially involved in the organization. Employees are representatives of the external environment and occupy multiple roles. They are members of society, of a local community, of ethnic, cultural, and religious groups, of a network of family and friendship ties, and also of other groups such as professional bodies, trades unions, consumer groups, etc. They bring with them a diversity of demands, expectations, values, cultural norms, and so on which may conflict with organizational norms and values. However much top management may wish that employees would display total commitment and behave as if they had no lives outside work, this is simply not the case.

The open systems approach has gained in influence as the pace of environmental change has accelerated in recent decades. Increasing global competition and rapid technological change mean that organizations now face a "turbulent" environment that demands a different kind of capacity to respond. Instead of slow evolution or reacting to change, organizations must anticipate change and be proactive. Very often, the most important input from the environment is knowledge, which is then transformed into output products. The static, unresponsive, mechanistic forms of organization will no longer serve and employers need "brains", not "hands". Hence the lazy, dull-witted, tightly controlled workforce of theory X has been replaced by the smart, multiskilled, innovative, autonomous, and internally motivated knowledge workers of today. It has led to the development of the metaphor of organizations as brains and to notions such as the learning organization (Senge, 1990—see Chapter 6). It is also the reason why the Labour Government in 1999 is reported as wanting 50% of the UK's young people to undergo higher education and why "lifelong learning" is high on the political agenda.

A new quality of working life?

This shift in management's philosophy of human nature would doubtless delight the founders of the quality of working life movement (Davis, 1972; Moldaschl & Weber, 1988) who were protesting the mindless drudgery of much work in the wake of scientific management. However, as we have seen, scientific management is also alive and well. Paradoxically also, this enlightened view of human capabilities has taken place within the context of human resource management (HRM). Brotherton (1999) gives a useful summary of the development of this thinking. He traces its emergence to Beer, Spector, Lawrence, Quinn-Mills, and Walton (1984), who suggested that people's skills and abilities were frequently underused and undervalued. People should be regarded as an organization's greatest asset, and managed and developed as stringently as capital and financial assets. Whereas in the past, top managers tended to achieve their positions by avoiding the personnel function, the management of human resources has now assumed a strategic importance. Legge (1989) made a distinction between "hard HRM", which emphasizes the rational, strategic, calculative business of managing and deploying the workforce as efficiently as one might the plant and machinery, and "soft HRM", which takes on board the ethos that employees deserve respect and consideration and are valuable assets requiring care and development.

Herriot and Pemberton (1995) are particularly scathing about "hard" HRM, which seems to regard people as business costs to be used and discarded as needed and often appears as exploitative as any "dark, satanic mill" scenario. Martin, Beaumont, and Staines (1998, p. 73) characterized the nature of many organizational change processes as "programmes of culture reconstruction designed to constitute new identities for all levels of employees which were consistent with the overarching 'vision and values' of the organization". In other words, there is an attempt to change people's personalities and not simply their behaviour. This level of control has almost Orwellian overtones. Taylor (1998) shows that employees often react very negatively to being told to "act naturally" while being subject to a plethora of coercive management strictures coupled with surveillance techniques to enforce compliance. There is also some evidence that customers, too, clearly perceive the falsity of the "Have a nice day culture" (Mann, 1998).

Even when reality matches the rhetoric, the impact of such a change in emphasis on a workforce that has always been told what, how, and when to do often simple and routine tasks, can also pose considerable problems (e.g., Pearn, Roderick, & Mulrooney, 1995). Job satisfaction has not necessarily increased either. Summers (1993) reported that the Royal Mail staff attitude survey revealed that 70% of employees were unhappy at work. As long ago as 1980, Hackman and Oldham warned against increasing the complexity of jobs without regard for the readiness of the workforce to embrace training, personal development, and greater responsibility. Warhurst and Thompson (1998, p. 11) conclude, "it seems clear that in terms of what management set out to do, employees often *dis*engage and treat expanded demands as a form of additional calculative performance" (emphasis in original). That is, employees are well aware that all the rhetoric of empowerment and greater job satisfaction often really means more work, more responsibility, and more stress for no more or even less reward than before. Hirsh and Jackson (1996, p. 17) express this memorably: "For all the talk of empowerment, never have so many been disempowered by so few." Frese (1997) also asks tellingly, "What about the not so smart people?"

In short, for many commentators, the ideals of the quality of working life movement have been cynically subverted and distorted in a possibly doomed attempt to serve the "bottom line".

Forces for change in the nature of work

Thus we seem to have a fusion of the two dominant managerial philosophies of human nature and this is accompanied by a growing consensus that a revolution in the nature of work is taking place. As we have seen, how widespread this actually is "on the ground" is not easy to assess given the available evidence. It is all too easy for discussion of these issues to sound like an extreme left-wing polemic so let us start with an analysis of the forces that have produced these changes. Hartley (1997) produced a useful summary of these (see Figure 2.1), which, incidentally, is also a nice illustration of a systems approach.

The technological context

Hartley does not give differential weightings to these forces for change, but for some commentators (Brotherton, 1999; Castells, 1997a, 1997b, 1998) the most profound and far-reaching of them is the advance in technology, which has proceeded rapidly in the last decade or so. According to these writers, this can justifiably be called a revolution, for it is already influencing the very fabric of our lives. Advances in "smart" automation in advanced manufacturing industry is only the tip of the iceberg, though it means, for instance, that changes to a computer program can greatly increase the flexibility of an assembly line. Computer-aided design means that the lead times for getting innovative products from idea to market are measured in weeks or months rather than years and once there, a host of cheaper imitations can soon appear. Expert systems can perform complex operations that once required the presence of highly trained and experienced human beings. Technology has swept away whole occupations and fundamentally changed others. High street banking is being replaced with 24-hour call centres and automatic cash machines. In fact, one aspect of the technological revolution that has as yet received little attention, is the vast increase in night shift work. The "global village" never sleeps! Paradoxically, the ethos of customer service is accompanied by customers doing the work of former employees. Thus, UK visitors to the US can be startled by an irate petrol pump attendant as they attempt to serve themselves. One UK supermarket chain has recently experimented with bar code gadgets to get us to add up our own shopping bills.

Underlying all this, says Castells, is the fact that we are on the verge of a network world. "What characterises the current technological revolution

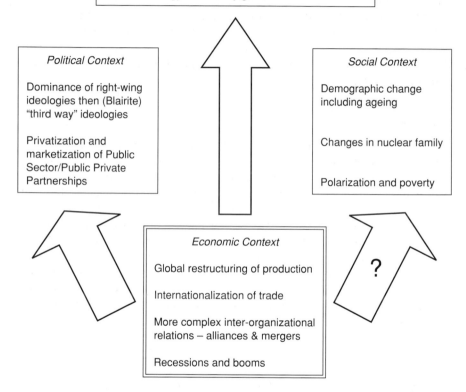

Figure 2.1 Forces for change in the nature of work (adapted from Hartley, 1997). Reproduced with permission of the author.

is not the centrality of knowledge and information, but the application of such knowledge and information to knowledge generation and information processing/communication devices, in a cumulative feedback loop between innovations and the uses of innovation" (Castells, 1997a, p. 147). It is this revolution in the technology of information processing and communication that has allowed the creation of a global economy, of virtual teams that can communicate and work together across continents, which gets products to market ever more rapidly and, as users apply innovations to new areas, creates yet more innovation. Intranets within organizations give employees wide access to information and remove the need for whole tiers of middle managers, while anyone with a computer, modem, and telephone line can access the internet and a supply of information on a scale almost inconceivable only a few years ago. Moreover, much of this information is dynamic, interactive, mutually generated, and globally shared in a way that was impossible with any previous technology. However, the absence of any "vetting" means that the quality of this information can also be very poor and untrustworthy.

This revolution is having profound effects on all aspects of our lives and especially on our working lives, if only to vastly increase the social exclusion of those who lack access to this network. However, the efficiency gains from the introduction of technology cannot be ignored by any organization that wants to survive.

The economic context

Within the economic context we have many of the forces that have already been described and which reflect technological change. The world economy is increasingly interdependent such that financial crises far away can threaten domestic economies, but more than that, production can be shifted to any part of the world where costs are cheaper and workers more productive. This trend is not confined to manufacturing industry; for instance, a UK organization's payroll can be administered from a centre in Eire or India. Meanwhile, distance learning degree courses via the internet are already available meaning that, potentially, any student could study at any university in the world. As the costs of study fall increasingly on students and their families, this could prove a very attractive option and could fundamentally change the provision of higher education.

The political context

Within the political context, in Western countries the 1980s were dominated by monetarist, free market ideologies and as we enter the 21st century there seems little evidence of any fundamental change in this respect despite the "Blairite Third Way". Though there are some warning voices (e.g., Giddens, 1999; Klein, 2000; Monbiot, 2000), and several disturbing or downright horrific signs that all is not well with the world of globalized capitalism, many would argue that there should not be a decrease in free market influence. All sectors should be accountable and give value for money. State-run enterprises were seen as inefficient organizations that needed fundamental reform or to be swept away. The need for a flexible workforce led to attacks on organized labour and, where the interests of professionals were perceived to dominate at the expense of those of clients and customers, this was also tackled by a barrage of reforms and controls.

The social context

In the social context there are also many forces for fundamental change. Globalization means a far more diverse workforce than hitherto. Further, women and members of minority groups are succeeding in occupations previously the sole domain of white middle-class men, though their lives are far from easy (see, e.g., Davidson, 1997; Davidson & Cooper, 1992). In developed Western countries, the workforce is ageing with far fewer young people available to enter it in 2020 than elderly people who will need to be supported in retirement. Meanwhile in developing nations the reverse may be true, with many more young people wanting jobs than there are job opportunities (Johnson, 1991). Simultaneously, in some countries large proportions of the adult population are being affected by the AIDS epidemic.

Turbulence in people's personal lives can also impinge on productivity and well-being at work and influence the supply of well-adjusted and suitably qualified employees. In the UK, there is now a one in three chance of marriages ending in divorce. This has led to a huge rise in single-parent families and children being brought up in poverty. Remarriage leads to complex family relationships of step-siblings and parents, varying amounts of contact with family members, and children often having more than one home. All this leads to stressful life changes and adjustments as well as increasing social exclusion for large sections of the population and polarization between the haves and have nots. The rise of the "knowledge workers" and the decline in traditional manual jobs are exacerbating such polarization for those without educational opportunity or who lack the means or intellectual capacity to pursue lifelong learning.

The result of all this, says Hartley (1997), is increasing complexity, uncertainty, turbulence, and upheaval both in people's personal and their work lives. The consequences of this for individuals and the implications for organizations and organizational psychology will be explored in the rest of this book. Here we will briefly explore four issues.

1   What changes in the workplace have these social changes unleashed?
2   What have been the reactions of working people to them?
3   What are the implications of these reactions for organizations?
4   Given all this fundamental and continuous change, what contribution has occupational psychology made to understanding this process?

What changes in the workplace have these forces unleashed?

It is worth starting this discussion with a consideration of the received wisdom of the nature of work in the past—the "old deal" as reported by Herriot and Pemberton (1995). First of all, it seems to revolve around the notion of "career". This could be said to have had the following characteristics:

- Permanent, full time.
- Something you train for when young.
- Then learn mainly from experience.
- Your employer provides any necessary further training.
- Remains pretty much the same for life except for more responsibility, etc.
- Involves fairly predictable moves up the hierarchy to some level.
- And often within the same organization from leaving education to retirement.

It is debatable whether this "golden age" ever really existed except for a relative few; it is heavily biased to a traditional white, middle-class, male career path. Millions of workers, including most women and shop-floor/ manual workers had very different experiences. Whatever the truth of this, it is generally agreed that all these career characteristics have been threatened or swept away.

There is no doubt that for many people the old certainties of their working lives disappeared. During the last recession in the late 1980s and early 1990s, many organizations were forced into major restructuring or re-engineering, which also took place against the background of the introduction of "hard" HRM practices. Downsizing, reducing the workforce to cut costs, led to large-scale redundancies, whereas delayering, reorganizing the organization to cut out whole tiers of management, resulted in redundancies too but also greater responsibility and workload for the survivors. Very often, say Herriot and Pemberton, redundancy programmes were carried out with "the inter- personal sensitivity of a rhinoceros" (1995, p. 71). However, it also has to be said that some organizations, e.g., BT in the UK, provided such enlightened and generous programmes that they suffered contrary problems—key workers who were not allowed to take redundancy felt aggrieved.

The landscape of organizations also changed. Organizations focused on their "core" activities and "outsourced" many service functions. So for in- stance, local authorities issued tenders for refuse collection and the supply of school dinners to private firms and allowed their IT departments to set up as commercial companies. They then paid these outside companies for services which they had formerly provided in-house. (In hindsight, many organizations have come to realize that outsourcing was a costly mistake [Steel, 1997] and the conditions governing the wisdom, or not, of outsourcing have been debated in the *Harvard Business Review* [Chesbrough & Teece, 1996; Pisano, 1996] and elsewhere [Hurley & Schaumann, 1997]). Simul- taneously, there was a tendency to employ only the minimum number of full-time, permanent staff and to hire part-time or temporary staff to meet peaks in demand. All this led to what Handy (1984, 1995) has described as a "shamrock" organization with a small number of core staff who are full time and permanent. They are expected to show total commitment to the organization, work very long hours, and are sometimes highly paid. The other two "leaves" of the shamrock are composed of contract workers who are self-employed or are outside specialist firms, and an army of part-time hourly paid workers, some of whom are treated very badly. The notorious "zero hour" contract demands that workers are available for work at any time but does not guarantee any work at all. Since many part-time workers are women with young children who cannot be available for paid work at all times, this often destroys the possibility of doing part-time work. Similarly, although some contractors were former employees who became self-employed and then earned enhanced incomes on long-term contracts for doing what they had always done, other contract workers might only be employed for as long as it took to avoid employment protection legislation, such as rights to maternity leave and redundancy pay. Whatever . . . it is generally agreed that when the recession lifted, many of the old, full-time permanent jobs were not replaced. Many of the new jobs were temporary or part-time (Gregg & Wadsworth, 1995; Naylor, 1994). (Hakim, 1999, gives an admirable analysis of these trends in employment and draws comparisons with research for the USA, France, Germany, and other developed nations. However, her data were drawn from the 1991 British census. Though this is the first such detailed analysis of the data, released only in the mid-1990s, there is no reason to believe that the trends identified have not increased in the meantime, particularly the growth in "marginal" employment.)

Even for full-time, permanent staff, the landscape has changed. Work is often organized around project-led, flexible work teams and the old hierarchies have gone, so that steady promotion has become increasingly difficult, however well the person is performing. Most of all, continued employment is not assured, again, notwithstanding how well one is performing. Much is said about "employability" as the only hedge against job insecurity—the extent to which one has marketable skills and can get another job easily. Paradoxically, at a time when technological change was destroying whole occupations (for instance, traditional newspaper printing), and continuous updating of skills was imperative, employers put the onus for personal development on employees. Given the imbalance of power between employers and employees at the time, the consequences of this policy were temporarily masked but as jobs became more plentiful again, Arnold (1998) reported that organizations were returning to working in partnership with staff to achieve the skill mix they needed.

Technology also meant that more people were spending at least part of their time working from their homes or in cars, trains, and planes. As already mentioned, "hot desking" became fashionable so that one did not have a personal workspace but took any available desk or workstation, thus disrupting much of what social psychology has said about social identities and relationships at work. Mobile phones, faxes, and modems meant, as Lucy Keloway once remarked in the *Financial Times*, that one could not escape work even on a mountain top. Yet all this dislocation of traditional ties of loyalty to one's organization also came with the expectation of total commitment. As it has been memorably remarked, organizations wanted a "totally committed but totally expendable workforce". As is the way with such powerful statements of the *Zeitgeist*, no-one can remember who said it first, and no-one can quote it accurately. No matter, the phrase has entered into history as a description of "how it is".

Despite all this gloom, it is actually quite difficult to ascertain exactly how accurate or widespread this general picture is (Thompson & Warhurst, 1998). Even those who have been most influential in spreading the message of these fundamental changes present some statistics that indicate some grounds for hope. Herriot and Pemberton (1995) note that 68% of companies in South East England declared redundancies during the depths of the recession in 1991/92, mostly in the banking, insurance, retail, and leisure sectors. As the recession began to lift in 1994, only 3% of professionals and 5% of managerial, administrative, and technical staff were unemployed, as compared with the much higher rates of 13% for craft and operative staff. Although 52% of companies in a survey had downsized and/or delayered, 35% employed *more* managers than they had 5 years previously. However, it is significant that large organizations (utilities, retail, and government sectors) had been most likely to downsize and delayer. Herriot and Pemberton also quote figures showing that although in 1982, managers had been more likely to move jobs for career development reasons (49%), this percentage had dropped in 1992 (34%). Instead, managers in 1992 were more likely to have suffered enforced job changes than they had 10 years previously (41% vs. 21%), which is likely to reflect more sideways or downwards moves as a result of structural changes such as delayering, mergers, and so on.

It is interesting to note that the outcry against current employment practices arose from job losses in a traditionally prosperous part of the UK and it hit employment sectors hitherto considered particularly secure, e.g., branch bank managers. There is no reason to doubt that those in mid-career, who saw themselves progressing steadily up the career ladder, were particularly traumatized, and this is supported by research showing that lack of promotion prospects is a major source of job dissatisfaction (Goffee & Scase, 1992). Mallon (1998), documenting the transition of public sector workers into "portfolio" work, describes these people as "refugees", feeling embittered, betrayed, and bewildered. Nevertheless, it is intriguing that large sections of the working population may have scarcely noticed these momentous changes—job insecurity, frequent changes of job and even occupation, short-term contracts, and the like were probably seen as business as usual, whereas tiny companies and one-man-bands remained, as ever, obsessed by filling this week's order books. Guest, Williams, and Dewe (1980) also provide a fascinating insight when they report that 25% of employees who had made the transition to working in autonomous workgroups perceived no significant change in the nature of their work. Day (2001) conducted an equally fascinating longitudinal study of manufacturing workers, before and after the introduction of semi-autonomous work groups. Initially, there was a marked split between the attitudes of production and maintenance workers. The highly skilled maintenance men were apprehensive about the change and concerned about their loss of status, while many production workers were either excited by the prospect of greater responsibility or anticipated little change in their jobs. After a short period of enthusiasm and cooperation, disillusionment set in. Old pay differentials survived despite the fact that both groups were now doing similar work; team leaders were almost invariably chosen from the ranks of the maintenance men; team meetings petered out because the overtime in which to hold them was no longer on offer and teams' suggestions were largely ignored by management; more conflicts about overtime pay led to the end of cooperation—production workers no longer did minor maintenance and maintenance workers refused to do production tasks. In short, despite much initial goodwill and large sums spent on training and reorganization, working lives had returned to the previous *status quo* within a year. This is a nice illustration of the gap that can exist between rhetoric and reality and the processes that can contribute to that gap. Even so, the writing is on the wall. Few working people in the 21st century will be able totally to ignore gathering global forces for change.

What have been the reactions of employees to these changes?

In the literature on this topic, the notion of the psychological contract is central. Argyris (1960), Kotter (1973), and Schein (1980) have all stressed that, in addition to the formal, legal, written contract of employment, there was another unwritten and implicit set of expectations existing in the minds of employers and employees, equally if not more powerful. Herriot and Pemberton (1995, p. 17) expressed this succinctly (see Box 2.1).

Hayes (1999) notes that the hallmarks of the old "psychological contract" notion were that it was:

• Implicit and unwritten.
• Concerned with expectations and obligations.
• Mutual—involving both parties.

BOX 2.1
The psychological contract

You offered	*Organization offered*
Loyalty—not leaving	Security of employment
Conformity—doing what you were asked	Promotion prospects
Commitment—going the "extra mile"	Training and development
Trust—they'll keep their promises	Care in trouble

However, she believes that the writings of Rousseau (1995) subtly changed this concept. Rousseau blurred the distinction between the economic and psychological contract such that some aspects were explicit and written. Thus "psychological" shifted from a focus on the expression of an interpersonal but unstated relationship into an area of managerial concern—employee rights and reciprocal obligations. As a result, says Hayes, violations of the psychological contract came to be seen as employer and employee not sharing the same understanding of the written contract. The psychological contract was thus transformed into a set of beliefs about the written contract and was no longer one of mutual, shared beliefs. As a result, employee protest against unilateral employer violations of the psychological contract could be interpreted as the irrational misperceptions of employees, e.g., that their jobs were secure.

Guest et al. (1996) proposed a more comprehensive model of the psychological contract, which is shown in Figure 2.2. The implications of this model are that the psychological contract is broader than the written contract; is continually renegotiated, particularly during the progress of an individual's career; defines the employment relationship; manages the mutual expectations of the employer and employee; includes some economic aspects such as fair pay, but is mainly "psychological" in that it involves such things as the expectation of being treated with fairness; includes the expectation that

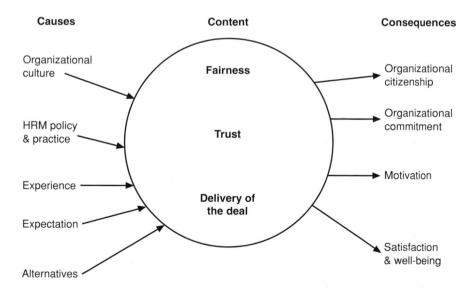

Figure 2.2 A model of the psychological contract (Guest et al., 1996). This material is taken from *The State of the Psychological Contract in Employment* by Guest, Conway, Briner, & Dickman, 1996, with the permission of the publisher, the Chartered Institute of Personnel and Development, CIPD House, Camp Road, London SW19 4UX.

employees will be loyal, do their best, keep trade secrets, and so on (organizational commitment and good citizenship). On this model, unilateral violations have very serious consequences, yet Hayes found that few managers in her study had any awareness of the psychological contract concept. Whether they were unfamiliar with the term rather than the concept itself is not clear, but Herriot and Pemberton (1995) argued that the last recession, coupled with "hard" HRM and consequent wholesale violations on the part of employers, have resulted in the destruction of the old "relational (Psychological) contract". It has been replaced by a "transactional contract" whereby employers and employees continually renegotiate explict, written contracts which, instead of being based on mutual trust and good citizenship, are on strictly "you give me this, I'll give you that" agreements where the parties don't go beyond the contract and continually check that the terms are being fulfilled.

In their case studies of the traumatized victims and survivors of often poorly managed downsizing and delayering exercises, Herriot and Pemberton (1995) document what they term as the "Get safe, Get out, Get even" set of reactions. "Get safe" involves outward compliance with company strictures while often doing the minimum and currying favour with those in power. "Presenteeism", whereby people are keen to be seen to be working long hours but may not be doing anything especially productive, may be a reflection of this. This, they say, encourages a "yes person" climate and a stifling of innovation. The "Get out" strategy means that anyone with the ability or opportunity to do so will exit the organization, often at short notice. Thus, key employees go to competitors or set up as competitors themselves. When the good times return, employers may find themselves critically short of skilled staff. The "Get even" option is even more damaging to organizations since it involves sabotage and anti-role behaviour. Examples are given of customer complaints personnel conceding to every request for replacement or reimbursement without even checking proof of purchase, and of aggrieved individuals leaving their jobs having installed unknown passwords on their computers so that valuable company databases are inaccessible. All this is accompanied by evidence of a sense of powerlesness, a betrayal of trust, and a loss of social identity amongst both survivors and those made redundant.

How widespread these reactions are and whether they will persist as a new generation, which never expected the old psychological contract, enters the workforce, are moot questions. Certainly, employees do not appear to be the passive, compliant individuals that top management often seem to believe they are. Mabey et al. (1998) and Thompson and Warhurst (1998) provide many examples of workforces exerting a considerable influence on their own working conditions. Mabey et al. (1998), summarizing the evidence from the point of view of those on the receiving end of HRM, conclude that at best the claimed benefits for organizations remain unproven, and at worst they are unfulfilled. (They also point out that many of the goals of HRM are unrealistically high and therefore doomed to "failure".) Hall (1999) reports an interesting cross-sectional study of two age cohorts of blue-collar postal workers. He found that there were no age differences in the considerable degree of distrust and hostility towards management despite the introduction of HRM practices. However, the under-35 age group who grew up when Trades Union power was waning in the UK showed far less personal identification with the Union than older workers. Conversely, the younger group were more "self-oriented", seeing the company as a resource which they could exploit to their own ends—for the benefit of family or their own careers. Thus, the "us and them" attitude prevails but the concept of "us" has shifted from worker collectivity to a more individualist stance. This study indicates that while industrial relations have improved in the UK since the 1970s, in terms of stoppages and strikes, the basic cynicism and hostility of the workforce towards employers has not changed, and work is still a means to an end and not an end in itself. Workers may be less inclined to take industrial action, but they are dissatisfied and may resort to more devious means to get what they want.

There are also indications that managers are adapting to the new circumstances. A recent survey of nearly 2000 UK managers was reported in *Management Today* (Rice, 2000). The results were that two thirds of the younger managers (under 35) said that a "job-for-life" was lowest on their list of career priorities, and nearly three quarters said that they intended to move on from their current employers within the next 2 years; 91% believed that career development was the responsibility of the individual. One particpant is quoted as saying, "It's people staying with people as long as they get the deal they want." Luckily (perhaps) for organizations, the majority of job changes were for greater responsibility and challenge, but over half the sample wanted to retire at 55 or younger. The similarity with the attitudes of shop-floor workers is striking.

In an interesting analysis of the effects of workplace changes in the US, Feldman (2000) talks of people's desire not to "work their way up" an organization but to "work their way out". Increasing numbers of younger and older workers do not want organizational careers. Rather, young people use large organizations for a few years to gain experience, contacts, credibility, and so on. They then leave to set up enterpreneurial enterprises themselves. Similarly, established workers are often keen to take early retirement to become self-employed. Feldman also argues that when job insecurity is rife it makes no sense to remain loyal to one company. He quotes the example of two managers who are both made redundant after 20 years of employment. One person has worked for 5 years in each of four different companies in four different industries. The other has worked for just one company. The first person is likely to be perceived by new employers as having wide experience and flexibility, the second is likely to be seen as lacking in both. Thus, one permanent effect of the changes is likely to be that people are committed to their own careers rather than to their organization. (See also Loughlin & Barling, 2001 for more on the work values, attitudes, and behaviour of young workers.)

The literature on stress-related ill-health paints a sombre picture of billions of pounds lost each year in absenteeism and health costs, quite apart from the human suffering (see Chapter 4). Cooper (1998) reports on decreasing job satisfaction and rising sickness rates. One source of evidence is an IRS survey in 1995 which covered 400 companies employing some 8 million workers in 17 European countries. This showed that the percentage reporting feeling satisfied with their jobs in the UK fell from 64% in 1985 to 53% in 1995. Over the same period, the percentage of workers who felt that their jobs were secure fell from 70% to 48%. Smith et al. (1998a, 1998b) also report that over half their pilot sample of 254 UK workers felt that their jobs were moderately to excessively stressful (17,000 people are to be included in the main study).

Recent TV programmes in the UK have also debated the effect on women and presented case studies of highly qualified and talented women finding it impossible to balance the demands of a family with long working hours and the intensification of work. A female Chair of the Confederation of British Industry (CBI) remarked that mothers cannot hope to succeed in the workplace if they cannot "compete" with men and women without children, in terms of time and commitment. Further case studies showed women determined not to have a family. In the US, Feldman (2000) claims that the number of hours American employees are working has increased by 15% over the past 20 years and that women have been especially badly affected by this change (Hochschild, 1989, 1997). In the West we have spent much of the past 30 years raising a generation of highly educated young women with high expectations for their careers, most of whom think that they ought to be able to combine this with having children. What may have now happened is that the "goalposts have been moved"; employers are making it increasingly difficult to combine a career and motherhood. The consequences of this for women's rights and future demographic trends remain to be seen.

Moreover, workplace bullying, which can often be confused with "firm management", may also be exerting a price. Leymann (1996) estimated that 10–20% of suicides in Sweden had workplace bullying in the background, and a report published by the Industrial Society in 1999 suggests that workplace bullying may cost firms up to £200,000 per employee in sick leave, redundancy pay, and pensions. One problem is that no-one has adequately compared the undoubted efficiency gains in recent years with these hidden costs.

Despite the weight of this evidence, there are some dissenting voices. Guest and Conway (1997, 1998, 1999), who have conducted three annual surveys, plus a separate study of those working long hours, show that most UK workers "report a positive psychological contract, with high levels of commitment, and low levels of job insecurity" (Department of Organizational Psychology Birkbeck College Annual Report: 1998–99, p. 6). They report that meta-analyses of reliable surveys tend to support these some-what surprising findings. They also provide evidence that short-term contract workers profess to have a better psychological contract than those on per-manent contracts and that they are equally motivated. This paradox may be partly resolved by even more recent research (Stevens, Faragher, & Sparks, 2000). Excess working hours in managers predicted poorer physical health even after unhealthy lifestyle factors (which were also associated with work-ing long hours) were statistically controlled, and even though those who worked longer had higher job satisfaction. Thus, high job involvement, and thus a willingness to work long hours, did not protect people from the negative effects on health. Moreover, working excess hours had no relation-ship with organizational commitment. This finding would follow from the research which showed that younger managers, especially, tend to use com-panies to further their own career objectives and then to move on to better things (Rice, 2000). Together, these sets of research findings illustrate the complexities of the true picture, but we are getting there!

One consistent theme in the literature is that there is an increase in the *intensity* of work for those who are employed, and an emphasis on con-trolling one's natural reactions and personality to comply with company standards, of which employees are well aware (McKinley & Taylor, 1997). Although Mabey et al. (1998) conclude that the benefits of HRM to the majority seem to outweigh the costs to the minority, it is a sobering thought that we may only be able to judge the effects of what is happening in retrospect—in terms of the long-term morbidity and mortality of today's workforce.

What are the implications of these reactions for organizations?

If you believe Herriot and Pemberton and their ilk, the consequences are dire. According to them, organizations lose their best people and are left with self-serving, traumatized survivors, who remain only because they have no alternative (continuance commitment). But the real picture may not be this bleak. For those at the bottom, things may not have changed that much, and employers may simply be faced with the age-old problem of how to control and direct the productivity of the workforce for maximum effect-iveness in terms of profit or quality of service. In the future, with a decreased working life due to extended education, and (possibly?) early retirement plus a more self-reliant and self-efficacious workforce (Bandura, 1997), people may be more able to withstand and even thrive in the intensification of work climate. In recent years we have seen the "Tiger economies" of the Pacific Rim falter despite their supposed HRM virtues, which the West has striven to emulate with varying degrees of success (Danford, 1998). This may indicate that we have less understanding of the forces for economic success than governments, multinational corporations, and management gurus (and occupational psychologists!) would like to believe. So far as one can tell, the wholesale abandonment of whole swathes of society to their own devices after years of faithful service, and of increasing numbers of people who can no longer cope with the pace and intensity of contemporary work, has not led to the collapse of societies and economies, except on the "margins". Commentators note such social ills as the rise in youth crime in the UK, nationalist violence even in "developed nations", the horrific actions of psychopaths, "anti-capitalist" riots, and social exclusion in general, etc. Whether such social problems are related to changes in the nature of work is far from established. However, the appalling events in New York and Washington on 11 September 2001 may have changed things. Several analysts (e.g., Barber, 2001; Prowse, 2001) have been prompted to question US-led globalization. As Barber writes, "Too often for those in the second and third worlds south of the US, Europe and Japan, globalisation looks like the imperious reach of predominantly US economic power; too often what we understand as opportunities for liberty and prosperity seem to them a rationalisation for exploitation and oppression" (p. I).

Be that as it may, disentangling the effects of the policies of major organizations from wider historic, social, and political forces is never going to be easy. However, we do know from history that communities were once welded together by the work they did, whether this was in agriculture, mines, factories, or whatever. In my opinion, we ignore possible signs that this basic fabric is unravelling, or even that recent fragile stability is being undermined, at our peril. Occupational psychologists, with the only claim against competitor professionals that they are researcher practitioners basing their recommendations on "hard" evidence and reliable theory, have to investigate what is going on, regardless of commercial exigencies and the pressures for a "quick fix". Academics, supposedly removed from the hurly-burly of the real world, can be accused of irrelevance. But someone has to reflect on the *total* cost.

The contribution of occupational psychology to organizational change management

Hartley (1996) makes distinctions between the nature and scope of change. Change can be developmental, in that it takes place in many small incremental steps, or tranformational—more like revolution than evolution. Transformational change involves completely new structures, processes, and ways of working. Change can also be piecemeal, involving only a small function or a single department, or it could be organization-wide—a merger or major restructuring or an attempt to completely change the culture of the organization—as happened in the NHS, from a professionally oriented bureaucracy to a client-focused, internal market. Large organizations are likely to have experienced organization-wide transformational change in recent years, whereas for a small family business change may have been confined to the introduction of a computer for book-keeping and adjustments in practices to meet Government directives. However, whatever its nature and scale, continuous change is now the norm rather than the exception.

Therefore, it is dispiriting to see how little impact occupational psychology has made on theory and research concerning the processes underlying the initiation, management, and impact of organizational change. Partly this is because there is a paucity of research evaluating the effects of change. Porras and Robertson (1992) found only 71 evaluation studies conducted between 1975 and 1988. This may be because top management is unwilling to risk unwelcome news or suppresses the publication of findings which may reveal sensitive company information. Or it may simply be that by the time change agents are called in, the change process is already well underway so before and after comparisons are impossible.

However, an equally plausible explanation lies in the theoretical underpinnings of the field and the general orientation of many psychologists working in this area. Open systems theory was a major influence, but some claim that it was too complex and too imprecise in its predictions to provide an adequate guide to practitioners. Organizational development (OD) was another approach which, according to French and Bell (1999, p. 1) is "a systematic process for applying behavioural science principles and practices in organizations to increase individual and organizational effectiveness". OD programmes concern "long-term, planned, sustained efforts" focused on organizational culture, processes, and structure. It is an iterative process of diagnosing, taking action, diagnosing and taking action; in other words there is a strong orientation to "action research" which involves information gathering, setting goals, performing actions, information gathering to evaluate the outcomes of those actions, re-defining goals, performing new actions, and so on. Action research also aims to empower the particicipants and/or recipients of interventions so that they fully engage in the change process and learn continuous improvement of their own functioning. Each OD programme will be unique because every organization and its problems will be unique but they are all "identifiable flows of inter-related events moving over time towards the goals of organizational improvement and individual development" (p. 3). However, Hartley (1996) believes that, especially in its heyday in the 1960s and 1970s, OD had more of the flavour of a missionary crusade than rigorous scientific endeavour. The emphasis was and is on practice rather than theory, social processes within groups, and experiential learning from feelings and experiences. Hartley notes that its techniques are still used but are more suited to the impact of change processes on individuals and small groups than to the wholesale, radical changes we have been talking about. There has also been a tendency to neglect the development of theory. In all fairness it has also to be said that many commentators have argued that organizational change is so complex that attempts at rigorous scientific investigation of process or evaluation of outcomes are inappropriate (see, e.g., French & Bell, 1999). Many believe that more progress may be made by taking other approaches to investigation such as action research and the careful analysis of discourse, both of which are favoured by OD. Day (2001), for instance, expressed regret that he had not employed an action research approach in evaluating the introduction of autonomous work groups because this might have helped to prevent some of the mistakes leading to its failure or might have contributed to more "ownership" of the research findings and consequent commitment to putting things right. Certainly a good case can be made for using both qualitative and quantitative methods in our search for understanding.

One of the most influential approaches was also the earliest. Lewin's field theory (1951) conceptualized the change process as involving three phases. First, "unfreezing" involves showing the organization that it needs to change and overcoming resistance to change. Second there is the change process itself. Finally, there is "refreezing", when the changes are sustained and become a normal and accepted part of organizational life. It is interesting that both Hartley (1996) and Brotherton (1999) comment on the continued influence of Lewin's approach (in for instance the stress on worker participation in the unfreezing process and the need to sustain change) and attribute this to the general failure of theoretical advance. As to the central change process itself, little or nothing is said, and Brotherton quotes an example from the change management literature typical in that its advice is so abstract and general as to be almost useless for practitioners and managers faced with pressing realities. In any case, Lewin's process assumes some stability before and after the change process, which clearly does not often obtain in today's turbulent business climate. As a small example, Hind, Rowley, and Frost (1997, p. 297) found that team membership rarely remains stable for more than 4 months "with change being the only constant". These sorts of figures also question the relevance of the famous "forming, norming, storming, and performing" model (Tuckman, 1965) of the social processes which lead to effective teamwork. Many work teams are just too unstable in their membership for the processes of getting to know one another's agendas, learning each other's "language", establishing "ground rules", overcoming conflicts, and eventually performing effectively, to be feasible. And what, may one ask, of *virtual* teams who rarely meet face-to-face?

That said, there is an interesting research literature which explores the initiation of the change process. Many authors stress the influence of external forces that compel change, but Hartley (1996) points out that this is to overlook the influence of human agency (as has this chapter!). She quotes a case study of a US transport authority (Dutton & Dukerich, 1991) where large numbers of homeless people began living in their premises. Though the homeless people constituted an external threat, forces internal to the organization also determined how this problem was dealt with. For instance management perceived that the organization's identity and image as a high quality transport company was being threatened by the presence of these people. Management's perceptions that customers and the media were changing their attitudes to the company in a negative direction was an important trigger to take action. A burgeoning literature on management decision making could add much to our understanding of the processes that lead to change and why a particular course is chosen (see, e.g., Miller, Hickson, & Wilson, 1999 for a review). Herriot and Pemberton (1995) are less persuaded that change is a rational, internally driven process. They claim that the introduction of HRM policies were often reactions to external events (the 1989/93 recession) and were only later given the dignity of being called a coherent business strategy.

However, Kirton (1961, in press) suggests that there is a discernable structure to the way organizational change processes typically occur. Based on an extensive series of case studies of organizations in the process of change and stripped down to the essentials, the management initiative process can be represented as six steps. (Although Kirton says that, in the real world, organizational change can seem more like a plate of spaghetti than this neat linear sequence.)

1   PERCEPTION OF THE PROBLEM

For any change to take place someone has to notice that a problem exists and that change is necessary. Then that person has to persuade top management that the problem exists and needs to be addressed. Some problem perceivers are "voices crying in the wilderness"; others find a ready ear; but nothing happens until the senior decision makers are won over to the problem perceiver's position.

2   ANALYSIS OF THE PROBLEM

Kirton says that this is frequently the weakest and least considered stage of the change process. Once the problem is accepted, the least possible effort and time is expended on investigating its nature and seriousness or gathering information which might inform the choice of solutions.

3   ANALYSIS OF THE SOLUTION

Unlike the previous stage, this one is often very protracted and involves a great deal of effort. Kirton suggests that people are now anxious not to "back losers" so analysing the solution and deciding to go with it takes much time and effort. This stage is often conducted in extreme secrecy but there are nearly always leaks to those lower in the hierarchy, and some of the resulting rumours can be gross distortions of the truth. Despite all this effort, Kirton says that new problems generated by the solution to the old problem are frequently overlooked or accorded minimal importance. In other words, the new problem that the solution has just made for them is given as little attention as the original problem.

4   AGREEMENT FOR CHANGE

Getting senior management to agree to the change process could take a very long time too (years rather than months or weeks) but on other occasions, changes just as large and expensive "slid through" without problems. This was a puzzle in need of explanation.

5   ACCEPTANCE FOR CHANGE

Once the senior decision makers have slowly and painfully agreed upon a solution, they then launch it upon those who are likely to be most affected by it and who may already be extremely anxious as a result of mis-information. Forgetting their own difficulties in reaching this point, the senior decision makers expect *immediate* acceptance and label any hesitation and questioning as "resistance to change". It is very often forgotten that change which is good for the organization can be bad for the individual and that in every change, even if it is change for the good, something valuable is almost always also lost. Kirton says that people are not "resistant to change" in general, but they may be resistant to this particular change.

6   IMPLEMENTATION

Several things puzzled Kirton about this stage. First, the originators of some successful interventions are sometimes "damned with faint praise" while the perpetrators of costly failures may be forgiven and promoted. He also noted that both unexpected success and failure were rarely dissected for the lessons to be learned.

Kirton (in press) developed his theory of adaption–innovation from the study of the process of change in many different organizations. Many residual puzzles can be explained by the fact that there are two main preferences for/styles of problem solving. Adapters tend to favour change within the existing structure—adapting what is already in place. Innovators go for more radical solutions—they tend to propose changes that go outside the generally agreed boundaries of "the way we do things around here". Kirton suggests that the status of the "problem perceiver" and the proposed solution determines the speed and smoothness with which stages 1–6 occur. Adaptors are likely to occupy the "establishment" of any organization since they maintain the culture and *status quo* (even if the latter are actually quite radical and progressive). Thus, an adaptor "problem perceiver" and a problem solution that fits the dominant paradigm are likely to be accepted and adopted even if the eventual outcome is failure. An innovative "problem perceiver" is much less likely to belong to the "establishment" and will find it hard to get a hearing. His or her "mould-breaking" solution will also have a rough ride to acceptance and even if successful may not be properly valued.

Kirton makes the point that the adapter–innovation distinction is a continuum, as is the degree to which solutions can be "paradigm consistent/inconsistent" but the most important point is the potential for conflict. Adaptors are likely to regard innovators as irresponsible and "off-the-wall" risk takers. Innovators are likely to perceive adaptors as "stick-in-the-mud", unimaginative, "no-hopers". He believes that it is vitally important to dispel these mutual incomprehensions. Complex, diverse problems demand complex, diverse solutions devised by a complex diversity of people.

This analysis has shed some light on my general incomprehension of the actions of some top management teams in recent years. For instance, expecting "instant acceptance" of organizational change may stem from a "macho" management culture guarded by an adaptor inner-clique. The failure to anticipate the negative effects of traumatized survivors after downsizing is also explained in the relative lack of attention given to both the original problems and solution-generated problems. The paradox of my own "resistance to (imposed) organizational change" (of which I have frequently been guilty of in the past decade) while pursuing vigorous and radical change within my own sphere of influence is also explained. (Imposed change, "dropped from on high", is very different from a committed team working out their own solutions together.) How many other insights into the current world of work does this framework generate for you?

So far we have largely been talking about top management. The focus on top management has also led to a renewed interest in the processes of leadership both within senior teams and at every level within the organization (see, e.g., Schruijer, 1992; Sparrow, 1994). Shell, for instance, encapsulates its vision as "Leaders leading Leaders" (Steel, 1997). Much is made of the ability to formulate and communicate vision. From ideas such as this, Bass and his colleagues proposed the concept of transformational leadership, in which the leader's ability to inspire and empower followers and to create a belief in the attainability of the vision are stressed (Bass, 1999; Bass & Avolio, 1990). (See Chapter 6, pp. 13–16 for more on transformational leadership.) Many culture change programmes begin with leadership development of senior managers, which then spreads more widely throughout the organization. Schruijer and Vansina (1999a, 1999b) edit and provide a commentary on a fascinating collection of papers that consider the role of leadership in organizational change. They raise a number of important and difficult questions concerning top-level leadership in organizations, including the extent to which one should focus on the individual qualities of the leader or on the incredibly complex set of relationships between leaders and followers. For instance, followers may exhibit dependence on, trust in, loyalty, and commitment to the leader but nevertheless aspire to and compete strongly for his or her job (Berg, 1998)! Schruijer and Vansina conclude that one thing characterizing successful leaders in today's turbulent business environment is their capacity to collaborate with diverse groups and stakeholders to achieve strategic objectives. The dynamics of this kind of shared leadership are illuminated by the work of De Vries, Roe, and Taillieu (1999) and Rijsman (1999), who both emphasize a "follower-centred" approach. Alimo-Metcalfe and Alban-Metcalfe (2000) are also considering the influence of "nearby" leaders rather than top management and conceptualizing the former as "servants" to their followers. However, as Bass (1999) and others have stressed, transformational leadership is needed as well as more mundane management that organizes and coordinates work and provides the structure for implementing the fine detail of change.

Much is made of the importance of worker participation in the process of change and sometimes this can be successful. For instance, Hellgren and Isaksson (1997) and Isaksson (1995) found that survivors of downsizing programmes had better morale and a greater sense of procedural justice (perceptions of how fair the process/procedures are) when they had been consulted and kept informed. Pearn et al. (1995) describes three case studies of apparently successful culture change when workers participated via focus groups. However, as Hartley (1996) points out, much change is highly coercive and there is some evidence that this approach is effective. For instance, the Government's imposition of a National Curriculum may well have raised the standards in UK schools. The privatized public utilities in the UK appear (mainly) to be profitable, likewise many commercial organizations that engaged in widespread downsizing and delayering exercises. However, it is likely that such changes can only be forced through in conjunction with costly systems of control. In UK schools, OFSTED inspections, the publication of league tables, and "public shaming" of failing schools probably did as much to push through change as the National Curriculum. The Quality Assurance Agency is performing a similar role in UK higher education. There may be hidden costs in this process. There is much anecdotal evidence of hugely increased workloads and distress in educators on the receiving end of inspections, but little systematic study. The NHS is often claimed to be one of the most efficient health services in the world (at least in terms of bed occupancy), but the imposition of commercial values on its staff, who see this as conflicting with their commitment to patient service and care, has been linked to increased levels of burnout (Traynor, 1994). (Moreover, the lack of "slack" in the system seems to provoke a crisis with every winter's 'flu outbreak, despite their predictability.) Several studies have shown similar effects across a range of occupations where employees report feeling that the needs of service users are no longer a central consideration in their organizations' core values and goals (Forgacs, 1995; Hunter, 1995; Jones, 1992; Miller, 1995). Then there is the "Get safe, Get out, Get even" triumvirate documented by Herriot and Pemberton (1995). Meanwhile, British workers have the longest working hours in Europe (Rubery et al., 1995). The implication is that coercive change has led to greater efficiency and effectiveness at the expense of individuals' well-being. If so, we do not know what the long-term consequences will be.

Complexity theory

Most recently, there have been some stirrings of renewed theoretical debate prompted by mathematical chaos theory, which is based on the premiss that tiny changes at any one point in time set in train further changes that have powerful and unpredictable consequences on future outcomes. A prime example is the minute but cumulative changes that can turn an ocean squall into a major hurricane which devastates the mainland. Neither the conditions governing the growth of the storm nor its eventual appearance on land can be reliably predicted in advance. This theoretical turn, now labelled complexity theory (Battram, 1998), seems well suited to develop the old and very vague notion of equifinality in open systems theory—the fact that we can never predict the final consequences of organizational change. Amongst other things, complexity theory proposes that organizations are composed of people who are self-organizing within clear boundaries. This means that a relatively few rules could explain apparently complex behaviour. The example is given of the flocking behaviour of birds in flight. A computer simulation shows that remarkably complex behaviour can be explained by the application of only three simple rules: keep a suitable distance from other birds, match velocity with other birds in the vicinity, and move towards the perceived centre of the flock. The resulting computer program simulates the behaviour of a flock of birds in flight so accurately that ornithologists have suspected that the computer graphics were derived from film footage, not the three simple rules. Actors in initial conditions have great room for manoeuvre and choice but as more enter the scenario, the conditions created by the first-comers provide little or no choice. Thus, the first bird to be released in a large space has to obey only one rule—to avoid obstacles —whereas later-comers are constrained by all three rules. Organizations can be viewed in a similar way to the flock of birds. The initial conditions provide the rules (or more correctly, tendencies) of self-organization and these mean that people's behaviour eventually "shakes down" into relatively stable patterns according to these rules. "It is often the case that a few underlying rules are 'powering' all the complex behaviour observed on the surface" (Battram, 1998, p. 125). According to complexity theory, organizations in constant flux cannot develop a stable system because it is always changing and adapting—applying new rules if you like. It is on the boundary between order and chaos but because of the self-organizing properties of the system, it does not descend into total chaos.

This sort of thinking is not new. Chomsky (1965) was able to describe the vast complexity, endless variety, and creativity of the grammar of language production in similar terms. Given a finite number of grammatical rules and a finite vocabulary, the number of different grammatical utterances one can make is infinite. Similarly, once a language community has become established, especially when one also adds social and cultural rules, there are considerable constraints on what one says when, which prevent the system from descending into chaos. Many of us choose what we say with care but we generally do not feel a great burden of constraint as we speak and write. So it may be with organizational behaviour. Because we have learnt the rules, and given that the "behavioural vocabulary" is very large, there is scope for almost infinite variety even though there is a clear underlying structure. Perhaps for these reasons, people tend not to feel that they are subject to "mind control" at work except when coercive constraints are very explicit and rigorously enforced. The complexity of language use is also a useful analogy in that living languages are in a constant process of development and change, yet the system always maintains its internal consistency and coherence, otherwise people would not be able to communicate. Chomsky argued that this tendency for rule-based self-organization is an inborn human characteristic as far as language is concerned. Later writers suggested that rule-based self-organization is a general property of human cognition and functioning (see, e.g., Donaldson, 1978). If so, it is good news for organizations. It could be argued that it is this general property of human cognition that prevents organizations from descending into chaos in the face of continuous change. However, we must not stretch the analogy too far. Living languages undergo evolutionary, rather than revolutionary, change and humans seem to be "pre-wired" to cope with the former. It is much less certain whether they are equipped for constant re-writing of the rules and "behavioural vocabulary". It's also wise to remember that Chomsky's rules only explain how we produce utterances that are grammatical. Nothing in this scheme guarentees that anything meaningful will be said. Chomsky illustrated this truth with a sentence obeying all the rules of English grammar, that became famous in developmental psychology circles: "The little pie with mud eyes was making a blue girl." By analogy, in the case of organizations, there is no guarantee that anything sensible will be done.

Complexity theory has the potential to explain current transformational and continuous change, thus replacing Lewin's theory. However, its utility for hard-pressed managers and occupational practitioners remains to be seen. It is much safer to believe in a simple, unfreeze–change–refreeze process than to subscribe to the fact that your next memo could precipitate a catastrophe!

Two interesting points can be raised in conclusion. One concerns the prevalence of self-employment in many countries—1 in 8 workers in the UK in 1993 and around 29% in Italy in 1990 (Castells, 1998; Jones, Hodgson, Clegg, & Elliott, 1998). Further, by far the greatest proportion of employers in the UK are small to medium-sized enterprises with 20 or fewer employees (Bartram, Lindley, & Foster, 1992). In part, this must reflect the changing nature of organizations with their greater reliance on outsourcing and contract and part-time workers. But at least one delegate to a symposium on the changing nature of work held in Dublin in 1997 was of the opinion that young people were less accepting of the tyranny of organizational life. As already discussed, Feldman (2000) believes the "flight from organizations" is already well underway in the USA.

Second, Flynn (1998) argued that the changes in the nature of work merely reflect a return to the conditions of working life before the industrial revolution. The notion of total commitment to one organization that guaranteed "a job for life" was, she said, a short-lived aberration in the history of work and, in any case, only ever applied to a privileged few, mainly male and middle class.

It is interesting to reflect that the dominance of large organizations in working life may be largely illusory or, at least, waning (and this could well flow from complexity theory). Further, we should never underestimate the effects of the media on public perceptions of the nature of working life and this industry has itself been hard hit by the demise of the "old deals". For instance, Wells, in an e-mail introduction to a seminar series held at UEL in 1999, commented that, "for every fashionable success, there are literally thousands of [media] practitioners who barely manage on social-benefit levels of income or who have to find less creative work". Maybe the importance of life in large organizations has been grossly exaggerated—it is not the experience of most of the world's workforce. Meanwhile, work and organizational psychology is showing early signs of a shift in emphasis from multinational corporations to small to medium enterprises (SMEs; Bartram et al., 1992; Bartram, Lindley, Marshall, & Foster, 1993; Chapman, 1999; White & Doyle, 1998).

Certainly, Hartley (1996, p. 426) is right when she says "Psychological theory needs to catch up with reality in researching the processes and outcomes of these types of [coercive] change." Practitioners, too, need to publish more of what they find in organizations of all sizes.

Summary

In this chapter I have argued that global forces for change have transformed the nature of work in ways which many commentors consider is for the worse. Two dominant management philosophies—the machine and organic metaphors—have influenced the organization of work throughout the 20th century and are still pervasive. However, it seems that there is a trend for work to become increasingly constrained and coercive while it can be argued that the principles of the quality of working life movement have been subverted by "hard" HRM. The adverse impact these changes have had on individuals and their organizations have been considered. Although it is possible that the extent to which work has changed can be overestimated, the potential damage to individuals, organizations, and societies should not be ignored. This chapter has "set the scene". Much of the rest of this book examines these issues in more detail. But first you might find it useful to work through Exercises 2.1–2.3.

EXERCISE 2.1
The mechanistic approach

1   To what extent, in your view, are mechanistic practices still pervasive in employment? Do they still succeed? Why?

2   Keep a brief (and discreet!) diary for a week and note examples of mechanistic practices as they occur in your worklife. What was your own/work colleagues' reactions to these instances? Were there any consequences for the quality of work, for employee well-being, etc., good or bad? Now that you are observing closely, would you change your answers to question 1?

3   Read something on reinforcement theories of motivation—did you notice any instances of inappropriate rewards/punishments and what were the consequences of this? (Note that the most frequent type of reinforcement in the workplace is punishment for errors and failures, whereas high quality work is often taken for granted.)

EXERCISE 2.2
The organic organization

1   Think of any organization you have worked for and answer the following questions:

   •   Who seemed to be most influential in your workgroup—was this the supervisor/line manager or someone else?

   •   If you needed something doing or wanted something to help you get your job done better or to enhance your career, how did you do it? Write a memo/talk to your line manager/supervisor/ Trades Union rep; make a formal presentation to a committee; "collar" someone influential on the corridor; negotiate with other individuals or groups; network with people outside the organization; any or all of these things or by other means too? Which were most effective and did they correspond to the official hierarchies, rules, and procedures of your organization? If not, why do you think they were effective?

   •   Have you ever been involved in a organizational change programme—either towards greater bureaucracy and control or greater autonomy and responsibility? How did you and your colleagues react? What did you do about it?

   •   Have you ever had a manager who was really inspiring and made you feel good about your work? Have you ever had a dreadful manager who made your life a misery? Can you put your finger on the crucial differences between the behaviour of the two?

How well does open systems theory help you to explain these things?

2 Keep a diary for a week and note down any evidence/incidents that indicate your organization is working as an open system. Compare it with your answers to the exercises on the mechanistic organization. Which model seems to offer a better explanation of what is going on? Why? If your experiences seem to support both camps equally, is open systems theory still a better explanation of the processes occurring? (Hint: The formal structure etc. may be mechanistic but "real life" may be organic.)

EXERCISE 2.3
The future of work

1 Although the changes in the nature of work discussed in this chapter are generally agreed to be widespread, Herriot and Pemberton report that the implementation of "hard HRM" practices is "patchy". It is likely that for very large sections of the workforce, things haven't changed very much. Indeed, it could be argued that the changes have only affected traditional middle-class (predominantly male) careers. Shop-floor workers and women may have always had to cope with job insecurity, flexible working patterns, etc. It is therefore well worth examining your own work experience for instances of the changed working conditions. Do they "ring true" for you? Have you ever had experience of working for a company that has undergone downsizing and delayering? How were these processes managed? What were the effects on yourself and your colleagues? Have you any direct experience of the "Get safe, Get out, Get even" reactions described by Herriot and Pemberton? If you have no direct experience, talk to friends and relatives about their experience of work. What do they report?

2 Views of the changes seem to fall into two camps—the optimists and the pessimists. The optimists (concentrated in the USA) argue that people adapt, and that it is only the people in mid-career who had expected a job for life who are hit hard. Young people entering the workforce will accept and even relish the career challenge so the problems will fade with time. It is also argued that there

will be a "withering away" of work as careers become curtailed by longer periods of education and early retirement. People will find their identity and life satisfaction outside work.

The pessimists (concentrated in Europe) view the future of work with alarm. Advances in technology will create mass unemployment and social unrest. Long hours, work overload, and job insecurity will create mass stress-related ill-health. The increasing complexity of work will mean that large sections of the population will effectively become unemployable. A demographic timebomb plus ageism at work means that fewer younger workers will have to support an increasing population of old people. Young people will refuse the tyranny of organizational life and become self-employed, leaving organizations with a shortage of skilled labour. Poverty and the gap between the "haves" and the "have nots" will increase.

Which camp do you belong to and why?

Further study and reading

Arnold, J. (1996). The psychological contract: A concept in need of closer scrutiny? *European Journal of Work and Organizational Psychology*, 5(4), 511–520.

French, W. L., & Bell, C. H. Jr. (1999). *Organisational development* (6th ed.). Upper Saddle River, NJ: Prentice Hall.

Guest, D., Comway, N., Briner, R., & Dickman, M. (1996). *The state of the psychological contract in employment*. London: IPD.

Herriot, P., & Pemberton, C. (1995). *New deals*. Chichester, UK: Wiley.

Morgan, G. (1997). *Images of organization* (2nd ed.). London: Sage.

Rousseau, D. M. (1995). *Psychological contracts in organizations: Understanding written and unwritten agreements*. London: Sage.

3 Why work? (Or life, the universe, and everything!): Employee relations and motivation

Why should I let the toad *work*
Squat on my life?

Philip Larkin

It is interesting to speculate whether Philip Larkin would ever have risen to the dizzy heights of being asked to take the post of Poet Laureate, if he hadn't written this, possibly his most famous poem. In it, he combines a passionate outcry against "the sickening poison" that work spreads through lives, with despair about his moral cowardice in not shouting "*Stuff your pension!*" This poem has some personal resonance for me because when I was an undergraduate at Hull University, Larkin was employed as its chief librarian. His lanky and rather gloomy figure was a familiar sight and I often wondered whether his celebrated denunciation of work and our mean-spirited acceptance of its deadening hand extended to his role as custodian of our most important learning resource. I, who had come through adolescence via the nascent revival of feminism, saw work, or rather a career, as liberation. Being confined to the home and financial dependence was the slavery! Be that as it may, this is a nice illustration of the vast differences which can exist in the meaning of work for individuals and the fact that our attitudes to it are complex indeed. It also hints at another issue—work can mean different things to us at different points in our lives. Perhaps the differences between my views and those of Larkin are not as diametrically opposed as they once were!

Measuring our attitudes to work is a bit like trying to capture woodsmoke but that doesn't stop people trying. You may wish to begin this chapter with some evaluation of what work means to you, using the questionnaire in Exercise 3.1. It is based on expectancy theory (Vroom, 1964). This theory proposes that we will expend most effort to gain rewards that are important to us, but only when the expectation that we will actually get what we want is high.

Thus, $B = V \times E$ where B is motivated behaviour, V is valence (how much we value the rewards on offer), and E is expectancy (how confident we are that we will actually get these valued rewards). It follows, therefore, that if

EXERCISE 3.1
What motivates you at work? The expectancy questionnaire

(Adapted from D. A. Nadler & E. E. Lawler (1977). Motivation: A diagnostic approach. In J. R. Hackman, E. E. Lawler, & L. W. Porter (Eds.), *Perspectives on behaviour in organizations*. New York: McGraw-Hill. Reprinted with permission of the authors.)

If you wish to answer this questionnaire in relation to your paid employment, rather than your work as a student, you will need to adapt the questions mentally. This is quite easy to do. For instance, a prize might be a wage increase; instead of exam success substitute promotion; instead of respect from fellow students and praise from tutors substitute the respect of colleagues and praise from your boss; and so on.

Answer questions 1, 2, and 3 by circling the answer that best describes your feelings.

Question 1
Here are some things that could happen to people who do their work especially well. How likely is it that each of these things would happen to you if you performed your work as a student especially well?

		Not at all likely						Extremely likely
a	You will get a tangible reward, e.g., prize or award	1	2	3	4	5	6	7
b	You will feel better about yourself as a person	1	2	3	4	5	6	7
c	You will have an opportunity to develop your skills and abilities	1	2	3	4	5	6	7
d	You will have better job security in the future	1	2	3	4	5	6	7
e	You will be given chances to learn new things	1	2	3	4	5	6	7
f	You will get a better job in the future	1	2	3	4	5	6	7
g	You will get a feeling that you've accomplished something worthwhile	1	2	3	4	5	6	7
h	You will be given more freedom to pursue your own interests	1	2	3	4	5	6	7
i	You will be respected by the other students	1	2	3	4	5	6	7
j	Your tutors will praise you	1	2	3	4	5	6	7
k	Other students will be friendly with you	1	2	3	4	5	6	7

Question 2
Different people want different things from their work. Here is a list of things a person could have as part of his or her work. How inportant is each of the following to you with respect to your work as a student?

		Moderately important or less				Extremely important		
a	Tangible rewards you may get	1	2	3	4	5	6	7
b	The chance you have to do something that makes you feel good about yourself	1	2	3	4	5	6	7
c	The opportunity to develop your skills and abilities	1	2	3	4	5	6	7
d	The amount of future job security you will have	1	2	3	4	5	6	7
e	The chances you have to learn new things	1	2	3	4	5	6	7
f	Your future chances for getting a better job	1	2	3	4	5	6	7
g	The chances you have to accomplish something worthwhile	1	2	3	4	5	6	7
h	The amount of freedom you have for doing your work	1	2	3	4	5	6	7
i	The respect you receive from the other students	1	2	3	4	5	6	7
j	The praise you get from your tutors	1	2	3	4	5	6	7
k	The friendliness of the other students	1	2	3	4	5	6	7

Question 3
Below you will see a number of pairs of factors which look like this:

warm weather sweating never 1 2 3 4 5 6 7 almost always

Indicate by circling the appropriate number, how often it is true for you personally that the first factor leads to the second with respect to your work as a student.

working hard high productivity never 1 2 3 4 5 6 7 almost always

working hard doing my work well never 1 2 3 4 5 6 7 almost always

working hard good exam performance never 1 2 3 4 5 6 7 almost always

we don't value the rewards, or think it is unlikely we will get them anyway, we won't be motivated to try very hard to get them. The questionnaire has been revised to look at student motivation so if your main life activity at present is studying for a degree, you can complete it as it stands. It would also be instructive to adjust the wording of the questions in your mind to cover your current paid employment or, if you don't currently have a job, what you hope for in your future career. Box 3.1 provides guidelines for interpreting your responses.

BOX 3.1
Interpreting your responses to the expectancy questionnaire

Although there is a way to calculate your total motivation score, it is much better to use the results qualitatively to diagnose what motivates and demotivates you.

Look first at your responses to question 1, which assesses the extent to which you believe that rewards will follow from high work performance. Note that a score of 4 is in the middle of the scale so if you scored higher than this it means that you expect that it is more likely than not that the rewards will come to you as a result of high performance. A score of less than 4 means that you think is more unlikely than likely that you will get these rewards. If you have a lot of low scores, this means you are rather disillusioned about getting any rewards for good work.

However, it is probable that you will have a mix of responses. Look at the rewards you do expect to get and those you least expect to get, even if you do well. What are the reasons for your responses? Is there anything you could do to increase the chances of getting the rewards you think are unlikely to occur?

Then look at question 2, which assesses how much you value these rewards, and ask similar questions. What do you least value and why? What do you most value and why? Again, if you have a lot of low scores this indicates that you don't much want any of the rewards on offer. If you have answered the questionnaire on the basis of your student work, you might question why you are bothering to do a degree.

Now look carefully at any discrepancies between your responses to questions 1 and 2. Is there anything that you value very highly but which you have very little expectation of getting even if you perform well? For instance, if the reward you value most is also the one you least expect to get, this could do much to explain lack of motivation and dissatisfaction. Is there anything that you could do to increase the chances of getting this valued reward?

Question 3 could be said to indicate your confidence in your own abilities or feelings of self-efficacy and is possibly the most important factor. After all, who is motivated to do anything when success seems impossible however much effort is put in? If you think that working hard will not lead to high performance, consider whether you are being too self-critical, whether changing your work strategies might increase your chances of success, and what else you might be able to do to improve your self-confidence.

Now consider how this instrument could be used in a work setting. If employees feel that however well they work, valued rewards such as job security or promotion are highly unlikely, then their morale is likely to be low and there is little incentive for good work and high effort. If employees think that they can't achieve good results however hard they work, then perhaps they are so overloaded they feel they can't do anything well, or perhaps they need training. In such circumstances, a good employer would try to do something to improve matters.

Motivation: Some issues

Conceptualizing motivation at work

Essentially, motivation is concerned with effort at work. The motivated employee is assumed to work harder, longer, and to a higher standard than the less motivated. There are four basic issues: (1) arousal of motivation—how to induce effort in the first place; (2) direction—how to get the effort directed at organizational goals; (3) magnitude—how to get the maximum effort; (4) maintenance—how to maintain a high level of effort. In a humorous (but very politically incorrect) article, Herzberg (1968) described the various methods used to try to achieve all this, albeit in his view, with little success. The simplest method of getting someone to move, he says is to "kick him in the pants—give him (sic) what might be called KITA". Negative physical KITA is illegal but has proved reasonably effective in the past—one thinks of Roman galley slaves and the like. Negative psychological KITA reads like a classic account of workplace bullying, long before its recent emergence in the work psychology literature. As we will see in Chapter 4, these tactics are far more widespread than hitherto imagined, although, like child abuse, we do not know if it is increasing or whether it has always been around but people are now more prepared to talk about it. Whatever the case, it is pretty much counterproductive as a motivational technique and is more likely to lead to worker absenteeism, exit, and in severe cases, post-traumatic stress disorder (Leymann, 1996; Randall, 1997). Various forms of positive KITA such as increasing pay and fringe benefits are also discussed and found wanting.

Herzberg's (1968) basic point is this. If you kick your dog, it moves, but was it motivated to move? Well, I would certainly be motivated to run away if someone kicked me, but presumably that is not what employers want. True motivation comes from within the person who *wants* to move. Thus, says Herzberg, "hygiene" factors such as pay and work conditions only prevent job dissatisfaction. The true motivators come from "that unique human characteristic, the ability to achieve and, through achievement, to experience psychological growth" (Steers & Porter, 1991, p. 230). Thus, such job characteristics as challenge, autonomy, advancement, and recognition are what lead to job satisfaction and, hence, motivated workers.

Herzberg's two factor theory (1968) has been severely criticized (see, e.g., Steers, Porter, & Bigley, 1996) but, here, two interesting points can be made. First, Herzberg was making a distinction between factors external to the person and those internal to the person, which is still used today. For instance, Katzell and Thompson (1990) speak of exogenous causes of motivation—independent variables that can be changed by external agents, such as pay. In contrast, endogenous reasons involve processes or mediating variables (expectancies and attitudes, etc.) that are modifiable by indirect means. Though Herzberg was right to draw attention to the importance of internal factors, the distinction is actually very muddled. In fact Katzell and Thompson's exogenous/endogenous distinction does not map well onto the extrinsic (external to the person)/intrinsic (internal to the person) distinction. For instance, making jobs interesting and satisfying and work goals clear, challenging, and attainable are included in the exogenous category because external agents (employers) can change them. However, all are directly related to potentially increasing the intrinsic rewards of the job—the extent to which performing one's work is rewarding in itself. At the same time, theories such as Hackman and Oldham's (1980), which are explicitly concerned with the job characteristics that make work intrinsically rewarding, include extrinsic rewards such as pay and conditions (context satisfaction) as important moderator variables. Meanwhile, satisfaction (internal) with pay (external) is heavily influenced by one's expectancies and values (internal). Confused? I'm not surprised! I think that perhaps it is time to abandon this distinction between external and internal motivators and to concentrate instead on the complex inter-relationships that exist.

Second, Herzberg explicitly links job satisfaction with motivation and implicitly with worker well-being and productivity. His theory assumes happy workers are motivated workers are productive workers. Despite the intuive plausibility of this line of reasoning, there is very little evidence to support it. In general, job satisfaction has not been found to have much relationship to productivity (Iaffaldano & Muchinsky, 1985). In fact, it could well be that many people enjoy their work because it does not require too much effort. Meanwhile, the increasing intensity of work (i.e., more effort) appears to be leading to more job dissatisfaction and psychological distress (see Chapters 2 and 4). If expending increased effort at work equals motivation, then it could be argued that the UK's workforce has never been so motivated! Moreover, effort does not necessarily lead to high performance. A host of factors can intervene to thwart us. We may not have the necessary skills or ability; we may be so overloaded we cannot do anything well however hard we work; we may be so constrained that we cannot employ the most efficient and effective work methods; external forces may render our best efforts null and void; we may even expend most of our effort into "beating the system" and avoiding work . . . In other words there may be little or no direct relationship between motivation, job satisfaction, psychological well-being, or productivity.

Katzell and Thompson (1990) list seven imperatives for a motivated workforce:

- Ensure workers' motives and values are appropriate for the jobs they are doing.
- Make jobs attractive to workers and consistent with their motives and values.
- Define work goals that are clear, challenging, attractive, and attainable.
- Provide workers with the personal and material resources to do the job.

- Create a supportive social environment.
- Reward good performance.
- Harmonize all these elements into a consistent sociotechnical system.

There is the feeling here that this is doing little more than stating the obvious. However, the fact is that each one of these imperatives is almost impossible to achieve in practice, which is why pleas of "How can we motivate the workers?" are as loud today as they were in 1968, and doubtless have been ever since people started to give their labour to others to secure personal survival rather than just working for themselves.

Money as a motivator

At the most basic level, most living creatures try to avoid death. For plants and invertebrates this may be more a matter of propagating their genes than securing personal survival but even a humble house fly will go into a frenzy of avoidant manoeuvres when I start trying to swat it. (Try it!) Human beings are more complex in their motivations in that as self-reflective beings, they can decide that life is no longer worth living or that some greater cause demands its sacrifice. Even so, if work is the price of physical survival, then most people will pay it, whatever else it may cost them in pain and humiliation. (Why else did slaves continue to work despite frequently terrible conditions and little hope of any improvement?) Thus there seems little reason to doubt that one of the main reasons people work is to earn money to buy the necessities for sustaining life. Yankelovich (1979) suggested that material rewards for work have become less potent as motivators as a result of various forces including the availability of unemployment benefits and high standards of living which made pay rises less of an incentive. In a similar vein, Porteous (1997) writes, "The social and financial support emanating from social security legislation in advanced countries has also led people to recast their view of their relationship to work. People are not prepared to be exploited and most do not have to put up with bad treatment by employers such as their parents and grandparents may have experienced" (p. 6). Whether social welfare benefits really do lead to people being less concerned about their pay or keeping a job is open to doubt. However, factors such as these led to an emphasis on internal rewards that has tended to obscure the role of monetary rewards. In fact one is tempted to return to something akin to Herzberg's much-criticised position. Money is important so long as it meets people's expectations and needs and is seen as fair. Even when it fails to meet these conditions, it is still important and will keep people working even when it is a source of serious dissatisfaction and grievance. As an anecdotal example, I once saw a TV interview with a homeworker who earned just 50p an hour. As a single mother with chidren she felt that anything was better than nothing. Felstead and Jewson (1999) in their study of homeworkers also found many examples of people who earned less than

£1 per hour. On the other hand, as Warr (1998) points out in his "vitamin model", there may well be a curvilinear relationship between pay and the motivation to work. Beyond a certain level, pay rises may cease to be significant motivators. We should not forget, however, that individuals also have their "bottom line" and if their particular work no longer serves this, then they will seek alternatives. We see this in the growth of the "black economy" (sic) where people eschew organizational life to set up as unofficial contractors, touting their skills to individuals, obtaining work as and when they please, and insisting on cash payment. Even so, pay is the reason why millions of people get out of bed and go to work. What they do having arrived can be entirely another matter, and this is where the difficulty starts. Once we have satisfied our needs, can material rewards really motivate us to greater effort at work, and if so how?

We might start with a comparison of traditional reward systems and conditions which tend to obtain under the "new deal". This is shown in Box 3.2. As always, the true state of affairs was and is more complex than the broad analysis in Box 3.2 suggests. Even so, it is immediately apparent that there are serious flaws in both systems. In terms of pay the traditional system tended not to reward individual effort and performance. Thus, good and poor workers on the same grade would be paid the same and, in many higher status occupations, provided one stayed in the job, annual increments would be awarded regardless of performance (at least until one reached the top of the pay scale). Visible signs of status could be divisive. The "works canteen" would be very different from "the executive dining room" and the contrast would be stark indeed if, as sometimes happened, the two were contained in the same room divided only by a screen. However, under this system, effort and high performance were more likely to be rewarded with promotion. The "new deal" cannot deliver promotion in the same way since hierarchies have been flattened and, in any case, rigid hierachies do not meet the new priorities. It therefore tries to increase what Katz and Kahn (1978) called the "connectedness factor" in other ways, so that people can see that effort and performance is linked to reward. Thus exceptional work performance might lead to a large pay rise or bonus but not to promotion. A "cafeteria" system of rewards (Brown, 1997) allows individuals to choose the "perks" they value most. However, the emphasis on individual appraisal and reward conflicts starkly with the espoused values of teamwork. Furthermore, managers who lose their former trappings of status are likely to react negatively to any new system of "perks" (Steel, 1997). Moreover, the success of any reward system oriented to appraisal of individual performance is very heavily dependent on the fairness and accuracy of measures of job performance. As Chapter 8 will show, all too often appraisal systems are deeply flawed with the result that performance-related pay systems are rarely successful (see, e.g., Herriot & Pemberton, 1995). Goffee and Scase (1992) showed also that lack of promotion prospects was one of the most important sources of job dissatisfaction in managers.

BOX 3.2
Comparison of traditional pay and reward systems and conditions under the "new deal"

Traditional	*New conditions*
Emphasis on conformity, following rules, etc.	Emphasis on innovation and initiative
Emphasis on collective bargaining, group pay awards, and perks	Emphasis on individual, localized bargaining, appraisal of performance, performance-related pay (PRP)
Emphasis on individual performance	Emphasis on teamwork and group work performance
Clear hierarchy: 20 or more tiers	Fewer tiers or project-led work makes hierarchy meaningless; hierarchy incompatible with learning organization
Strict pay range applied to each tier: Each job is assigned a number of points based on its level in hierarchy and paid accordingly	"Broadbanding"—large number of grades, tiers collapsed into a few bands, often with very wide salary ranges. Level of pay is determined by appraisal of individual's performance
"Perks" also closely tied to level in hierarchy; often little personal choice	Visible signs of status often abolished; "cafeteria" system of "perks"—workers choose which to receive
(Sometimes) annual increments for service and experience	Pay rises depend on individual's performance
Good workers expect steady promotion up the hierarchy	Much less opportunity for promotion; if good work is rewarded at all it is through individual pay rises, company prizes, etc.

The "connectedness" factor

It is worth pausing here to consider this notion in relation to one of the oldest but still very useful theories of motivation—reinforcement theory. At the risk of considerable over-simplification, reinforcement theory predicts that behaviours that are rewarded will increase, whereas behaviours that are not rewarded or punished will decrease or become extinct. Over-simplified though this is, and with all its mechanistic connotations, it can still act as a powerful explanation of behaviour at work. For instance, Komaki, Coombs, and Schepman (1996) document an example of reinforcement principles in practice in engineering manufacture. Workers doing good quality work received the same pay as people doing poorer quality work. They received little management recognition and promotions were rare. At the same time they were given extra work to check on quality (which did not endear them to their peers), and were held responsible for the return of substandard work. Meanwhile, workers doing poorer quality work were rarely reprimanded, still got the same pay, didn't lose their friends, and didn't have to do the extra quality control work. All these things could be expected to lead to the extinction of good quality work because workers were not being rewarded for it. Indeed, in many respects they were being punished for it.

In a classic article, Kerr (1975/1996) documents "The folly of rewarding A while hoping for B", which showed that in a wide variety of work contexts, employers reward the wrong things. This "folly" is still widespread today and it is not difficult to find examples from industry and commercial life. Day's (2001) research (detailed on pp. 57–58) charts the failure of an expensive scheme to introduce semi-autonomous work groups in a manufacturing plant. Most of this failure can be attributed to the fact that cooperative teamwork was not rewarded. In 1992 the Sears Group, in the US, was forced to pay circa $15 million in out-of-court settlements because customers sued the company for unnecessary repairs to their cars. In a bid to raise productivity, Sears had decided to pay their garage mechanics on the basis of volume of repairs completed, instead of paying a fixed salary. The number (and thus speed) of repairs logged was being rewarded; good workmanship, customer care, and employee honesty were thereby punished— at least (presumably) until Sears discovered its mistake.

Another major problem in the world of work is that punishment, or at best lack of reward, is more common than reward itself. For the ordinary employee, good work is often taken for granted and little noticed, whereas mistakes are often conspicuously obvious and so attract punishment. Although organizations want innovation, this necessarily involves risk taking and a greater possibility of mistakes and failures. This has led many commentators to commend an organizational tolerance for failure and an emphasis on learning from mistakes (see Chapter 6), but the extent to which this is followed in practice is debatable.

There are also many irrationalities and inconsistencies in reward systems, which prevent people being rewarded for doing the right things (Brown, 1979). Before reading on you may like to think about Exercise 3.2. The answers to the questions in Exercise 3.2 are not always completely obvious. Women often "select themselves in" to low or lower paid occupations (Baron, Davis-Blake, & Bielby, 1986; Hunt, 2001; Maitland, 2001; Sachs, Chrisler, & Sloane-Devlin, 1992; Stromberg & Harkness, 1978). Many jobs are obtained via personal recommendation from existing employees (Bartram et al., 1992, 1993) so the

EXERCISE 3.2
Factors affecting unfairness in pay levels

On the basis of your knowledge and experience, list as many factors affecting unfairness in levels of pay as you can think of.
   To get you started:

*   Why do men and women, majority and minority groups, etc. typically get paid differently despite equal opportunities legislation?
*   Why do some kinds of work attract much higher rates of pay even though they are equally valued by society (e.g., city traders vs. nurses)?
*   Which undesirable aspects of jobs deserve greater compensation?
*   What factors influence the person's ability to achieve bonuses for high output/performance?

status of your job may depend on what your friends and family happen to do. In the army, "danger and foreign service" translated as "adventure and travel abroad" may be the main reason for joining! Professionals who have to do a task where they get dirty are often compensated for it, but those who do the dirtiest jobs are often paid the lowest wages. A multitude of factors from machine breakdown to a depressed "sales patch" thwart the productivity efforts of individuals. Doubtless you have thought of many other examples of, and reasons for, pay differentials and inequities.

The importance of perceived fairness in reward systems

According to a number of process theories of motivation which stress social comparisons (e.g., Adams, 1965; Homans, 1961) the perceived fairness of reward systems is crucial in determining the motivating potential of pay and other material rewards. People are assumed to take a rational, calculative stance when judging the fairness of their treatment in terms of their effort and rewards in comparison with significant others.

Equity theory (Adams, 1965) is one of the most well known and influential of these. According to this, people consider their outcomes over their inputs in relation to the outcomes of another reference group over their inputs. A simplified equation representing these relationships is as follows:

$$\frac{\text{Outcomes (P)}}{\text{Inputs (P)}} \neq \frac{\text{Outcomes (O)}}{\text{Inputs (O)}}$$

where P = the person, O = comparison group, and ≠ means "not equal to".

If the ratio of personal inputs to outcomes is perceived as being unequal in some way to the input/outcomes ratio of the out-group/comparison group, then an uncomfortable sense of "cognitive dissonance" (Festinger, 1957) is said to exist and the person takes steps to resolve this. People are hypothesized to have several means at their disposal to resolve inequity:

1   *Change one's own inputs/outcomes.*   Get safe, do the minimum? (In practice, this can be difficult because it may threaten the person's work identity to do a less than optimum job, especially if the work is seen as important for the well-being of others, e.g., that of a nurse or junior hospital doctor.)

2   *Change others' inputs/outcomes.*   Get even, out-of role behaviour/ sabotage? (Again, this might threaten identity if the consequences for others are particularly severe, e.g., the controller of a safety-critical system is unlikey to withhold information that may prevent an accident just because a colleague is unfairly paid more.)

3   *Cognitive distortion.*   Focus on O's costs. (One may, for instance, reason that the other group has less congenial co-workers, less job security, less pleasant working conditions, less interesting work than oneself, etc., which reduces the perceived imbalance.)

4   *Change reference group* (usually "downwards").   Accept a "lower standard" for comparison. (This has considerable implications for feelings of self-worth and self-esteem since it implies that the value of one's work and expertise is less than one had imagined. The result is likely to be a loss of morale.)

5   *Exit.*   Get out? (One goes to where one hopes the "grass is greener" and one is more appreciated and rewarded.)

The implicit idea behind this theory is that perceived inequity is uncomfortable and the person is motivated to resolve it. There is some support for this theory. Adams and Jacobsen (1964) predicted that perceived over-payment would increase effort because of positive inequity. They conducted a laboratory study which involved students being hired to proofread. One group was told they were unqualified but would be paid the same as qualified persons (positive inequity). A second group was told that they were unqualified so would be paid less (reciprocal group), and a third was told that no qualifications were needed so everyone would be paid at the same rate (equity group). As predicted, the positive inequity group worked harder and detected more errors than the other groups. In their zeal, they even reported more "false positives"—"errors" that were in fact correct. There were many criticisms of Adams and Jacobsen's interpretations of these results. It was not a feeling of inequity but the challenge to the self-esteem in the positive inequity group that had produced the extra effort—they needed to prove themselves. Another explanation could be that the people who believed they were overpaid felt uncomfortable working alongside others who were perceived as more qualified but paid less for the same job. As a result, they needed to work harder to demonstrate they were earning their money to avoid resentment and possible retaliation from their fellow workers. However, both alternative explanations could be seen as different reactions to perceived inequity. Greenberg (1988) tested the theory in the field using "overpayment and underpayment" in terms of status symbols, in this case, the quality of the work office. This was an ingenious, opportunistic study that occurred when offices were being redecorated. On the hypothesis that a nice office also enters into the equity equation, people were moved temporarily into higher, equal, or lower status offices. Over 2 weeks, the people moved into higher status offices improved their performance whereas those moved into lower status offices showed a decrease, and the magnitude of the change was directly related to the degree of status change.

Equity is a powerful explanatory concept, especially (in the context of organizational change detailed in Chapter 2) if we allow that the "comparison group" may be the job people and their peers had before organizational change transformed it out of recognition. The inequity comparison is not with others but with the perceived inputs and outcomes which one had with what one has now. Most of the "balancing" options to reduce inequity have costs for the person. The fact that the "get safe, get out, get even" options (Herriot & Pemberton, 1995) have not caused more disruption to organizations than they have, may be because the perceived costs are too great —one might lose one's job, and there are few alternative employment opportunities. People are forced back onto cognitive distortion (others are even worse off than I am) or to accept that their knowledge, skills, and competences are of less value than they had come to assume (my work isn't very important in the general scheme of things but just having a job is important to me). Neither option bodes particularly well for psychological health in that identity is likely to be threatened and morale lowered. These options imply that workers comfort themselves with self-deceptive resignation or "realistic" resignation. And who wants a nurse motivated by continuance commitment (there is no better alternative) or a teacher who thinks that educating the next generation can't really be that important? Combined with the general intensification of work it may explain why people are working harder for less personal reward while stress-related ill-health appears to be increasing. Of course, young employed people with more energy and raw enthusiasm coupled with a work identity yet to be fully established, have different comparisons for judgements of inequity. Maybe it is no coincidence that negative attitudes to older workers appear to have increased in recent years, despite little evidence that their performance is inferior to that of younger people (Warr, 1996b, 2000). It is also a sobering thought that anecdotal evidence often categorizes "older workers" as anyone over the age of 35! For a Western economy heading towards a demographic shift in the numbers of young people entering the workforce beginning circa 2010, this seems extraordinarily short-sighted, even if currently expedient.

Are these theories still useful?

Goffee and Scase (1992) conducted a study of managers in six major UK organizations all undergoing major structural change. They found that reduced promotion prospects were the greatest source of job dissatisfaction among the managers who valued development, autonomy, security, pay, and status but felt disappointed in their expectations of all these things. Goffee and Scase noted that the main reactions to this situation were anger and exit (get out), anger and minimal effort (get safe), and anger and anti-role behaviour (get even). The main effect of the changes was a great increase of continuance commitment—a negative attachment to the organization due to a lack of employment alternatives accompanied by low morale and little effort (Meyer & Allen, 1984). Can expectancy value theory and equity theory explain these effects? From Box 3.3 it does appear so.

BOX 3.3
Can expectancy value theory and equity theory explain Goffe and Scase's results?

Expectancy value theory

$$B = E \times V$$

where E = expectancy of success (increased pay and promotion) is low, and V = value of reward is low (job is only important because there are no alternatives). Value of other rewards (security, autonomy, status etc.) is high but these are unavailable. Therefore, B (motivated behaviour) is low.

Equity theory

$$\frac{\text{My outcomes (pay, promotion, etc.)}}{\text{My inputs (effort)}} \neq \frac{\text{Top managers' outcomes}}{\text{Top managers' inputs}}$$

OR

$$\frac{\text{My outcomes (pay, promotion, etc.)}}{\text{My inputs (effort)}} \neq \frac{\text{My previous outcomes}}{\text{My previous inputs}}$$

Therefore:

- Change own inputs/outcomes reduce effort (get safe).
- Change other's inputs/outcomes: anti-role behaviour, sabotage (get even).
- Exit (get out).

The fact that both theories could account for these reactions is not very helpful for understanding the processes involved but the analysis indicates that they are still relevant in today's circumstances. It is also worth mentioning that equity theory has recently led to the interesting distinction between "distributive" and "procedural" justice (Cropanzano & Folger, 1992). Distributive justice lies at the heart of equity theory and concerns the perceived fair distribution of rewards to people in the workforce—essentially who gets what. Procedural justice concerns the means by which this distribution is achieved. It concerns perceptions of the fairness and impartiality with which jobs are graded, of appraisal systems, of promotion procedures, and so forth. In redundancy programmes the perceived fairness of the process has a markedly positive effect on the morale of both survivors and those made redundant (Brockner, Grover, & Blonder, 1988; Brockner, Tyler, & Cooper-Schneider, 1992; Hellgren & Isaksson, 1997; Herriot & Pemberton, 1995). As Steers et al. (1996) point out, the concept of procedural justice is not, strictly speaking, part of equity theory but a logical extension of it, but again this indicates its continued value.

What these theories have more difficulty in explaining, are findings such as those of Guest et al. (1998, 1999) who found that the majority of UK workers who they surveyed did not exhibit the "get safe, get out, get even" reaction. On the contrary, most of their respondents appeared well motivated and did not object to long working hours. It is probably a common feature of many people's work experience that they and their colleagues continue to do the best possible job even in the most difficult and demotivating circumstances and even when expressing the intention to leave. This is particulary true of public sector workers (e.g., Alban-Metcalfe & West, 1991; Doyle, 1998) who are more likely to value the interest of the job and "making a difference to society" rather than pay, "perks", and status. So, despite everything that has been said about the muddled and generally unhelpful distinction between intrinsic/extrinsic rewards, it is to these sorts of motives that we must now turn.

Work as its own reward: Sources of internal/intrinsic motivation

Intrinsic rewards are said to flow from merely doing the job. In reversal theory terms, we are primarily in a pleasant paratelic state where it is "the doing" rather than the "having done" which provides the satisfaction. Unfortunately, there is little that is particularly playful about internal motivators. Katz and Kahn (1966) propose that these internal rewards have three main sources. Value expression involves the extent to which we self-identify with the job. In an important sense, I *am* a teacher, an artist, a skilled tradesperson, and so on. In this sense we have internalized the values of our chosen occupation so that they have become an expression of our own identity. A great deal of the investment of ourselves in our work comes from the skills we use. Teachers who can inspire students to understanding, hard work, and success have their sense of identity, self-esteem, and self-efficacy enhanced because their skills have been instrumental in this outcome. Plausible though these ideas are, there are some complications. There is a strong sense that self-identification stems primarily from the feeling that the work is "socially responsible" or is benefiting others in some way. Katz and Kahn thought a strong work identity was likely only in professional and other high status jobs. But how true is all this? The most mercenary city trader can be influenced by the same processes if making a personal fortune is internalized as a legitimate goal and his or her skills have achieved it. And I once knew an "intellectually challenged" village street sweeper who plied his trade for years with dedication and enjoyment but died within weeks of being made redundant in a council efficiency/cost-cutting drive. Indeed, the main query about work-identification comes from consideration of boring, monotonous jobs. For many, such work does not contribute specifically to a *work* identity but nevertheless lies at the core of other aspects of their identities—as "breadwinners" for their families for instance, and their ability to provide promotes self-affirmation. Thus we can have strong self-identification with a job which may be experienced as very unpleasant. This seems to be another example of our futile attempt to impose the extrinsic/ intrinsic distinction onto our motives for working.

A second source of intrinsic reward is self-determination—the extent to which we have autonomy and discretion in our work and thus feel in control of our lives. As we saw in Chapter 2, there is a paradox in that workers are expected to be more autonomous and responsible at the same time as being subject to ever more coercive forms of control. Lucky the people who freely choose to internalize the "hearts and minds" aims of "hard" HRM! While they adopt the dress, attitudes, and behaviour codes of the organization they can feel completely in control of their work and lives. This concerns a tired old debate going back to freedom vs. determinism. Here we may merely note that autonomy and job discretion is a topic that will receive extended treatment in Chapter 4. We may also note in passing that if self-determination is a powerful source of internal motivation then a perceived gap between rhetoric and reality may also act as a powerful *demotivator*.

Finally Katz and Kahn (1966) cite affiliative expression—the extent to which our work fulfils our social needs—as an important source of internal rewards. Schein (1980) emphasized social motivators and the importance of social relationships at work, which he said were the principal means of shaping personal identity. Among the reasons cited for this emphasis were that the de-skilling of much work removed its intrinsic meaning so this had to be sought in social relationships. Further, it has been known since the Hawthorne studies that employees are more responsive to peer pressure when establishing unofficial norms of work performance than they are to management's exhortations and incentive schemes (Whyte, 1955). Though this "solidarity" has often been seen as lowering productivity, the opposite can occur. Loggers in the southern states of the USA, when they were allowed to set their own goals, actually exceeded the performance targets that management would have demanded (Locke, Shaw, Saari, & Latham, 1981). Barker (1993) found evidence that autonomous work groups develop internal systems of norms and values which exert a powerful influence in controlling members' behaviour. Because the pressure to conform comes from colleagues with whom one is in close proximity, the influence is more potent (and more subtle) than old bureaucratic forms of control. It follows that if the team's norms concern long hours, commitment, and high achievement, then the individual has little choice but to "go along" with this. Tales of the entire staff of Japanese offices afraid to go home until the boss has left attests to the potential power of these processes. The perceived importance of social relationships at work seems to have prompted the current popularity of autonomous work groups and teamwork. Finally there is the evidence that superior–subordinate relationships are important in the workplace. For instance, the single most important influence on people's work attitudes, commitment, job satisfaction, and well-being is the relationship with their immediate boss. (See Chapters 4 and 8.)

Content theories of work motivation

Content theories propose that within individuals, there exist certain psychological characteristics, usually termed needs, which predispose the person to initiate, direct, and maintain effort. Earlier theorists assumed that these were universal, inborn, human characteristics but later models introduced the notion of "learned needs" (McClelland, 1961, 1962, 1965a, 1965b, 1971). Other content theories include Herzberg's two factor theory, already mentioned, and Alderfer's (1972) existence-relatedness-growth theory. There is a great deal of overlap between these conceptual frameworks and here we will consider just one theory. (See Steers et al., 1996 for more extended discussion.)

Maslow's hierarchy of needs

One of the earliest and still very influential theories was Maslow's needs hierarchy (Maslow, 1954, 1968). This was a general theory of what energizes people to action but it was quickly applied to the work situation. According to Maslow, the most basic needs are physiological—those that sustain physical life, such as the need for food. Next in the hierarchy are security needs—the need for physiological safety and shelter. Also in this group of what Maslow terms social deprivation needs is the need for affiliation—to feel that you belong, are loved, and so forth. If this latter need is not met the person cannot achieve a healthy personality. Next are the growth needs, which are forward looking, driven, incentive motivators. The first of these is the need for self-esteem—to achieve self-respect, to feel that one is a worthwhile and successful person. Finally, there is the need for self-actualization—for self-fulfilment and to achieve all that one is potentially capable of. These two growth needs will drive the person to want recognition from others, development, challenge, and the freedom to be creative and innovative.

According to Maslow, these needs are activated in a dynamic cycle of deprivation. If a lower level need is not met, the person is energized to remedy the deficiency and does not attend to higher level needs until it has been satisfied. Self-actualization is the exception to this in that satisfying this need motivates more attempts to self-actualize. In other words, providing our lower order needs are met, we never tire of trying to achieve our potential.

Despite the theory's intuitive plausibility, there is actually very little research evidence to support it (Wahba & Bridwell, 1976). However, it is easy to understand its popularity with managers: It is a simple and sensible framework. For instance it is possible to apply it to the development of work practices, particularly those related to the activities of trades unions, and to assess the extent to which work has changed to meet these needs, as shown in Box 3.4.

However, as Chapter 2 showed, the reality may be very different from the rhetoric and if Maslow is right, then HRM has a major difficulty in that it fails to meet workers' lower order needs while expecting them to pursue self-actualization. For instance, job insecurity violates security and affiliation needs. It also undermines the need for belongingness—for organizational commitment. The increasing isolation of many workers, e.g., on night shifts, working from home, tied to one's terminal or one's telephone, also fails to meet the social needs of workers. Finally, the fear that one may be made redundant however well one performs violates the need for recognition and self-esteem.

Maslow's theory actually explains the reactions of some workers to the changing nature of work quite well. Herriot and Pemberton's (1995) "get safe" reaction whereby workers keep their heads down, play by the rules, and do the minimum can be understood as a preoccupation with fulfilling

---

BOX 3.4
Maglow's hierarchy applied to work practices

Need	*Practice*	*Timing*
Physiological	Health and safety legislation	Late 19th/early 20th century
Security	Pensions, sick pay, unemployment benefits, etc.	Mid 20th century
Affiliation Self-esteem	Human relations movement	1950s and 1960s
Self-actualization	HRM	1980s and 1990s

security needs. The trauma suffered by Mallon's "refugees" (see p. 57) can also be seen as a reaction to the destruction of the basis for fulfilling security needs. However, Maslow's theory cannot be the whole story because the failure of many organizations to meet fundamental needs would lead to the prediction that they would become untenably dysfunctional—indeed this is Herriot and Pemberton's essential argument. Despite the pessimist's view, however, this is clearly not the case. Some people continue to expend a great deal of effort and deliver high standards of performance regardless of whether their needs are met. School teachers in the UK, for instance, have endured a barrage of public criticism, major organizational change, and increasing classroom violence which could be argued to have undermined their sense of safety and self-esteem, while they are not conspicuously well paid. Nevertheless, the vast majority of the profession remain dedicated to doing the best job they possibly can. This point is not negated by the fact that given alternatives, many choose to escape (exit) or indeed avoid entering the profession. Most of those who do stay, do not take the "get safe" and "get even"options.

Perhaps one possibility is that the application of Maslow's theory to the world of paid work has obscured the fact that it is a general theory and was never built on the premise that *only* work could fulfil these needs. People can pursue their social needs outside work, for instance. Indeed, Robertson (1985) charts the development of the concept of a "proper job" and concludes that dependency on an employer for work, money, identity, social role, and so on is relatively recent. Both Robertson (1985) and Handy (1984) argue that too much weight is placed on paid employment with the result that large sections of the population who do not have a "job" but who certainly regard themselves as working, are demeaned. However, the high divorce rate in the UK could be in part a symptom of the need to work such long hours that close personal relationships are neglected—a possible indication that conventional employment is now reducing the opportunity to fulfil important needs.

However, the theory really starts to unravel when we come to consider which factors could fulfil which need. For instance, a preoccupation with development and "employability" could reflect an attempt to satisfy safety needs and have nothing to do with the pursuit of self-esteem or self-actualization, though there are obvious spin-offs which are connected with higher order needs. The role of money as a motivator is even more ambiguous. Potentially, money can fulfil all the needs simultaneously. Money not only supplies a comfortable lifestyle, security, and social status but it could buy friendship. For instance, it could be argued that more affluent people can afford to socialize more and so are likely to have a wider circle of friends. Finally, if it is part of your potential to successfully pursue wealth, activities related to the accumulation of yet more money, and the skills you employ to achieve this become self-actualizing. Thus, in a sense we do not need empirical evidence to reject the notion of a hierarchy of needs—the concept itself is untenable, even though the general idea that we do have inborn needs which must be fulfilled has merit.

More recent theories of intrinsic motivation

Hackman and Oldham (1980) proposed a theory whereby the characteristics of jobs were said to engender critical psychological states within the person which led to positive work outcomes. An overview of the theory is presented in Figure 3.1 along with details of how core job characteristics are said to influence critical psychological states and outcomes. Context factors were a later addition to the model and include such factors as pay and conditions, ability and skill, social relationships, and organizational climate, which act as moderators of the relationship between job dimensions, critical psychological states, and outcomes. One of the most important of these factors is the extent to which the person wants development through job challenge, autonomy, and so on. Hackman and Oldham call this characteristic growth need strength.

Skill variety concerns the extent to which one's job allows the full use of one's skills and abilities and the greater the number of different tasks there are to perform the greater this is likely to be. Task identity concerns the extent to which a person has to complete a "whole job". Task significance involves the extent to which the work is important for others or society as a

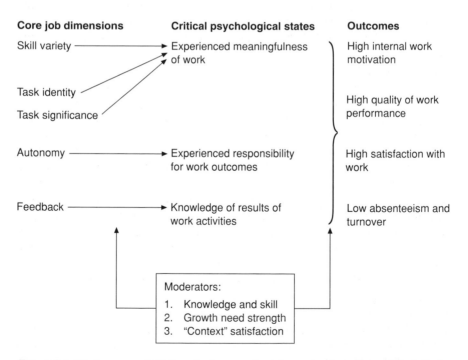

Figure 3.1 Hackman and Oldham's theory of work motivation. From *Work Redesign* by Hackman/Oldman, © 1980. Reprinted by permission of Pearson Education, Inc., Upper Saddle River, NJ.

whole. So for instance, the person who is responsible for checking the wheel nuts on a passenger jet has a job with a great deal of task significance. Together these characteristics contribute to a feeling that the job has meaning and is worthwhile. Work that is high on these characteristics will lead to the person being intrinsically motivated to perform well. Autonomy refers to the extent that people can decide on how they will perform their work and the extent to which they are closely supervised. People who are subject to explicit and coercive control are likely to feel little sense of responsibility if they have followed the rules but things then go wrong. Conversely someone who has been personally responsible for decisions can take satisfaction from success and a job well done. Finally, feedback from the job and from others tells people how well they are doing and how they can improve their performance. Knowing that you are doing a good job and that others value your performance makes it less likely that you will add to the organization's absenteeism and turnover statistics.

Hackman and Oldham (1980) developed the job diagnostic survey (JDS), which is an instrument designed to operationalize the concepts in the theory. Every job can vary on each core dimension and the JDS yields a motivating potential score (MPS), which indicates the extent to which job incumbents perceive that their work is high on the five core dimensions. This instrument has received some support and although there has been little research on the critical psychological states, core job dimensions do appear to be associated with the predicted outcomes, especially in professional and managerial jobs (Abrahams, 2001; Harvey, Billings, & Nilan, 1985; James & Tetrick, 1986; Loher, Noe, Moeller, & Fitzgerald, 1985).

However, Hackman and Oldham (1980) stressed that their model should not be applied indiscriminately. If the workforce has low growth need strength, then job redesign to increase MPS could prove a costly failure. HRM practices that have forced people to take on more responsibility and a wider range of work frequently ignore this caveat. The feeling among employees that they are being asked to take on roles that should properly belong to management, without any increase in pay, often causes resentment and hostility (Herriot & Pemberton, 1995). Ability and skill also moderate the effects of improving jobs in terms of the core dimensions—if people feel inadequately equipped to meet increased task demands then they are likely to experience anxiety and strain. Thus, this model too could explain negative reactions to the "new deals".

But can it explain why some people continue to work to the best of their ability even when feeling very demoralized? Perhaps it can. Take the job I know best—lecturing in a university—though by all means substitute your own job as you read this, noting parallels and possible differences. There can be few areas of work that call for so much skill variety—one has to be daily a presenter, a teacher, a scholar, a researcher, an author, an assessor, a counsellor, an administrator, and (sometimes) a manager, as well as a filing clerk and general dogsbody. The great thing is that no 2 days are ever the same, and every day calls for the exercise of a variety of different skills. Task identity also tends to be high—although you need to consult and work with colleagues, you are generally responsible for the courses you teach, which also adds to autonomy. Task significance is also high—students come to higher education with all manner of motives but most of them hope that it is going to make a difference to their lives and for the better. Feeling that you personally can and should contribute to these aspirations is a powerful motivator. Traditionally, job autonomy is high. Lecturers can generally decide what and how they will teach and to a certain extent when and how they will work. Finally, the feedback is good—it ranges from enthusiastic student participation in classes to excellent exam results. All these things can be expected to increase the MPS of the job and they do. Thus, one can become and remain very work involved. The "get safe, get even" reactions, for instance, are hard to indulge when you feel that this behaviour may damage someone's future life chances. My own research showed that senior women academics often felt that the enjoyment they felt in advancing knowledge and communicating it to a new generation meant that they often had difficulty in distinguishing between work and pleasure (their words) (Doyle, 1998). And yet, an increasing volume of research shows that, worldwide, academics are suffering low morale and high work strain (Doyle & Hind, 1998; Gmelch, Wilke, & Lovrich, 1986; Winefield, 1997). All in all, Hackman and Oldham's (1980) theory can explain why very large numbers of people in very many occupations continue to expend considerable effort long after other theories would predict low work performance.

Nevertheless, Hackman and Oldham (1980) always stressed that job re-design to raise the level of the core job characteristics was a double-edged sword. It seems that their major concerns were with jobs that had been simplified into routine and monotonous tasks and thus they were interested in the means to improve motivating potential. The theoretical model does not lend itself to improving the motivating potential of already complex jobs to make them even more complex. Indeed within the model, there are the seeds of *demotivation* and even the potential for serious psychological and even physical damage. What if the person does not have the competence to cope with the necessary skill variety, if task identity leads to work overload, if task significance and personal responsibility (autonomy) are experienced as terrifying, and if the feedback is mostly negative? What if people "soldier on" regardless, either because they feel that the work is too important to neglect or they have no viable alternatives for financial survival? Xie and Johns (1995) found a curvilinear relationship between job scope and mental health; too little or too much had negative effects on well-being. Hockey, Payne, and Rick (1995) found that junior doctors who exhibited a "passive coping" style were more anxious but less tired at the end of a normal "heavy" work day than "active copers", who were more tired but less anxious. This fits in with Bandura's (1997) contention that people's beliefs about their own competencies (self-efficacy) will be powerful determinants of their own internal goals and perceptions of how their performance measures up to these. At the end of the long weekend shift, however, the differences between active and passive copers had disappeared and both groups were showing signs of quite severe physiological stress (see Chapter 4). In other words, intolerable work demands are beyond anyone's capacity to cope. All this seems to be summed up in the comment of a junior doctor interviewed for a TV programme. "Every night", she said, "I go home thinking 'Thank God, my decisions didn't kill anyone today' ".

It is quite possible that many jobs today have too much motivating potential and, together with a hectic pace, may have become too complex and overloading for most of us. At least part of the apparent rise in work-related ill-health may be the result of highly internally motivated people working themselves literally into the ground.

Warr's vitamin model

Warr (1987) proposed a general model of mental health in which he said the environment affords us characteristics or opportunities that act on our sense of well-being rather as vitamins act on the body. We all need a certain amount of each vitamin for good physical health and too little leads to ill-health. However, beyond a certain level, too much of any one vitamin offers no further benefit or can actually be toxic. The nine characteristics of the environment which provide us with "psychological vitamins" are as follows:

- Opportunity for control.
- Opportunity for skill use.
- Externally generated goals.
- Variety.
- Environmental clarity.
- Availability of money.
- Physical security.
- Opportunity for interpersonal contact.
- Valued social position.

Though not really a theory of work motivation, it is easy to see how this framework could be applied to the world of work, and Warr himself uses it to explain the negative effects of unemployment. Work can provide all these characteristics and being made redundant with little prospect of finding another job can suddenly remove many of these characteristics from a person's environment. Hence, mental health suffers. In addition, all the characteristics have been linked to job motivation in one theory or another, so the extent to which people's jobs provide these characteristics, the greater their well-being is likely to be . . . up to a point. Jobs that are too high on these characteristics could be experienced as stressful, and mental health may deteriorate. Thus, Warr's model could be used to explain people's reactions to both monotonous, routine work and work that is too complex and demanding. However, note that in this model the "vitamins" relate to well-being, not to motivation per se. It could, however, prove useful as an explanation for greatly increased levels of stress-related ill-health in today's workforce.

Goal-setting theory

Recent theories have stressed the role of cognitive and motivational factors in determining people's behaviour at work. Goal setting as a powerful motivational force was first proposed by Locke in the 1960s but has been developed since (Locke & Latham, 1990). This theory and its variants are generally believed to be the most adequate models of work motivation now available. The goals that we formulate are said to drive and provide direction for all human action and the goals to which we commit ourselves determine our performance. People who set themselves hard, specific goals perform better than those who set themselves easy or vague goals. There is evidence that having work goals which are clear, challenging, attainable, and attractive does lead to higher effort and performance in a wide range of occupations (e.g., Frayne & Gerlinger, 1990).

However, a number of factors limit the usefulness of goal setting as a motivational force. One concerns a person's sense of self-efficacy (Bandura, 1989, 1997). Self-efficacy refers to the extent to which one has confidence in one's ability to succeed, to perform well and achieve valued goals. Self-efficacy develops in part from previous experiences. The most self-efficacious people are those who have had to strive hard and persevere, overcoming setbacks and obstacles on the way to success. They become resilient and persevere in the face of difficulties and are not too much affected by occasional failures because they have had enough experience of mastery and success to believe in their capabilities. Such people are likely to set difficult goals for themselves and to expend a great deal of effort to achieve them. People who have found that success comes very easily, perhaps because of exceptional intelligence, social skills, or even just luck, are likely to become quickly discouraged when they meet setbacks and they may abandon their goals. Other people who have experienced a great deal of failure are likely to suffer self-doubt and to set very easy goals for themselves or give up trying when they hit problems. Thus, the value of goal setting in producing high effort and performance depends very much on the person's level of self-efficacy. Other important processes influencing self-efficacy are modelling and social comparisons. A good role model at work will provide a great deal of information about strategies for success which the person can then adopt to increase their own success and, hence, belief-in-self. If people see others achieving success through sustained effort this raises their own belief in their capabilities—if I work hard, I could do that too. On the other hand, if others fail despite high effort this lowers self-efficacy—look at what X did and she failed, so how can I hope to succeed?

Applying this to the sorts of reactions detailed by Herriot and Pemberton (1995), the model can be seen to be very useful. Let us take the person whose goals are to have a secure job and achieve a balanced life with plenty of time for family, friends, and other interests. Such a person is likely to want to work for only the number of hours specified in his or her formal contract. If this person then sees that people who behave in this way are more likely to be made redundant, a change of goals is needed if he or she is to avoid downsizing. The goal is then revised and becomes to work longer hours for no extra pay, thereby giving managers the illusion that *this* worker is loyal and committed and so encourages them to keep him or her in the job. This is the "get safe" reaction but manifests itself in apparently greater effort. Human resource commentators often term this sort of behaviour presenteeism—when people put in the hours at their desks but are not necessarily productive. Consider also the traumatized survivors of downsizing who saw people sacked who had put in sustained effort and had achieved excellent results. In addition, the circumstances surrounding such sackings were often perceived to lack procedural or distributive justice. In these circumstances, the lack of justice in the system undermines the person's belief that they can achieve their goals by persistent effort. Perhaps it is not surprising that Herriot and Pemberton also chart the development of the "reluctant manager"—people who actively avoid and do not want promotion. One way of interpreting this reaction is that such people have had their self-efficacy so undermined by downsizing experiences and failures to achieve imposed goals because of lack of resources, that their work goals for success and promotion have been abandoned.

Consider these two comments from managers, cited in Herriot and Pemberton's (1995) book:

> There is no scope for personal input; everything is centrally planned. I personally am prepared to stand (or fall) by what I can deliver, provided I have some input to targeting, admin levels, budget and resource management. Until that unlikely day arrives, the only planning I am doing is for my retirement. I believe I have a lot to offer, but "they" know best.
>
> (p. 75)

> My organization wants to employ flexible and agile (young) heads at the cheapest rate ... You are considered to be slow, inflexible and expensive in your late 30s/early 40s.
>
> (p. 78)

The sense of injustice is palpable in these comments but there is also a strong feeling of helplessness—however talented, experienced, and hard working the manager, the prospects are bleak.

However, these sorts of reactions are not inevitable. According to Bandura (1989, 1997), someone who has been set a very challenging work goal and succeeds despite all the difficulties is likely to have his or her self-efficacy enhanced; thus we can also explain the people who continue to work hard and perform well even against great odds. This doesn't mean, however, that people have to feel happy about the situation.

Another problem with implementing goal-setting theory to increase motivation is that it is far from easy to set goals at the right level of difficulty and specificity. There is personal reward in achieving goals but if the target is too high then effort will be punished with failure. I have known many students who regarded an upper second degree as relative "failure"—they had put in years of intense effort pursuing the goal of a first class degree. Others who had more modest goals were ecstatic simply to have passed. Further, goals perceived as unattainable discourage the person from putting in any effort to achieve them. Second, if the goals are too vague or too long term, then people have very little idea of what to do to achieve them or, reviewing their progress, they become discouraged as the current results of their efforts appear so meagre in comparison with what the ultimate aim is. If my goal is to become rich and famous, then I am not likely to see publishing an academic textbook or appearing in the local amateur panto as significant progress towards celebrity. If my goal is to see my name in print or on the billboard advertising a show, then I have succeeded. Notice that these latter goals are not simply more modest but more specific. How will I know when I'm rich and famous—when I can't leave my hotel room for fear of being mobbed by adoring crowds; when I have exceeded the personal fortune of Microsoft's Bill Gates . . . ? The motivating potential of vague and long-term goals is severely limited by the fact that one simply does not know when one has achieved them and so their reward potential is poor.

Recognizing this, goal-setting theories have emphasized the role of cognitive factors in self-regulation (e.g., Heckhausen, Schmalt, & Schneider, 1985). They make a distinction between goal setting—deciding on a course of action—and goal striving—actually trying to achieve the goal. Both processes involve information processing and decision-making theory. The more specific the goal or subgoal, the easier it is to decide how it may be achieved. Thus, "getting a good degree" or "getting promoted to area manager" are not helpful as guides to action. "Getting a first class mark for the next essay" or "successfully negotiating the next business deal" or "achieving a 2% increase in productivity" are more useful. They are more likely to lead to strategies and behaviours that lead to success on the road to the long-term goal. Factors influencing both goal setting and goal striving include self-efficacy as already described, but are also social constructions of reality (Bandura, 1986). If the general perception is that high work performance does not avoid redundancy but currying favour with the boss does, then the goal-striving strategy will be very different from what the organization is aiming for. If the goal is to achieve employability and earn more money in a better job, the organization may be severely disappointed in a person who strives constantly for self-development and challenge in the job and then leaves at a moment's notice. (Remember the folly of rewarding A whilst hoping for B?)

These latter theories also emphasize individual differences in cognitive abilities that underlie skills in self-regulation. This concerns the extent to which people can identify successful strategies and can discipline themselves to pursue them. This points again to the importance of setting specific work goals but also to the tenuous links between effort and performance. If the person lacks the skills and abilities to "do the right things" or is prevented from using optimal strategies by coercive controls, then effort will not be rewarded by success. Since information processing is so important in the goal-striving phase, feedback on how well one is doing is also important to success. However, feedback can have costs for the individual and often depends on social relationships. If you suspect a subordinate is competing for your job, will you ask that person for feedback on how well you are performing? Even if feedback is valid, if it tells you that you are *not* achieving your goal, it can be dispiriting and demotivating. As already mentioned, in most occupations, good performance is taken for granted whereas any lapse or failure is punished, sometimes severely. So feedback—so important for monitoring progress towards goals—which is claimed to be motivating, often has the opposite effect. Of course, the worst feedback of all is being met without warning by a security guard toting a plastic bin liner and being marched to your desk to retrieve personal belongings before being escorted off the premises.

Taking stock

So far so bad. We have a plethora of theories of motivation (only some of which have been considered here), and all of them can provide perfectly plausible explanations of almost any work behaviour even if supporting evidence is often somewhat weak and their predictions sometimes contradict each other (Locke & Henne, 1986). To make matters worse, many of the theories can explain all outcomes and completely opposite patterns of behaviour in response to the same "objective" work conditions. We are in danger of falling back on the lame conclusion that different people are motivated by different things. This has led some commentators to suggest that we now have quite enough theories and evidence about work motivation to call a halt and integrate what we do know into something which has more coherence and usefulness (Landy & Becker, 1987). Not so, says Shamir (1991/1996). The problem with all these theories is that they implicitly claim to have universal applicability when they are only really useful in "strong situations" where for instance, "goals can be clarified, where there is an abundance of rewards, and where rewards can be closely linked to performance" (p. 150). Typically, organizations do not enjoy such conditions— indeed the "new deals" suggest the opposite—and what is needed are theories which can account for individual differences and the fact that motivated work behaviour can occur in adverse circumstances. Drawing on research literature from sociology, Shamir argues that what is missing from most work motivation theories is any consideration of the role played by people's self-concepts in determining work behaviours and the amount of effort the person expends. If my earlier analysis is correct, this is not entirely true, but Shamir's ideas are new in that he explicitly considers the influence of such things as work identity and feelings of self-worth, whereas these concepts tend to be implicit or are ignored in most other formulations. As such, his ideas deserve attention.

Shamir's self-concept based theory of work motivation

Shamir (1991/1996) argues that theories of motivation are too individual-istic and hedonistic in their orientation and ignore the person's values and sense of moral obligation which, he says, operate on a molar level. That is, they influence a person's whole approach to work and not just specific tasks or situations. They will determine such things as how much of our personal time we devote to work, levels of attendance, the care with which we carry out tasks, the extent to which we strive to improve our performance, and so on. His theory rests on five assumptions.

1   Humans are not only goal oriented but also self-expressive.   "Behaviour is not always goal-oriented, instrumental and calculative but is also expressive of feelings, attitudes and self-concepts." (p. 154) In other words our behaviour is often a manifestation of our self-concept. Thus, if we see ourselves as morally responsible we may not behave in our own self-interest but in the light of what we believe to be right.
2   People are motivated to maintain and enhance their self-esteem and self-worth.   "Self-esteem is based on a sense of competence, power or achievement. Self-worth is based on a sense of virtue and moral worth and is grounded in norms and values concerning conduct." (pp. 154–155) Thus, much of our behaviour is guided by internal standards, and we evaluate our actions in terms of these standards.
3   People are also motivated to retain and increase their sense of self-consistency.   "People derive a sense of 'meaning' from a sense of unity of their self-concept, from continuity between the past, the present and the projected future (McHugh, 1968) and from the correspondence between their behaviour and self-concept." (p. 155) Self-consistency leads not just to "corrective" behaviour when there is a perceived dis-crepancy but is also a positive motivation. The self-concept acts as an ideology which people attempt to validate in their behaviour.
4   Self-concepts are composed, in part, of identities.   People can hold a number of identities which, according to Stryker (1980), are organized into hierarchies according to their salience—"the importance of an identity for defining one's self, relative to other identities held by the

individual" (p. 156). Identities are expressed in behaviour and the more salient the more likely the person will perceive a situation as an opportunity to act out that identity and the more the person will actively seek such opportunities.

5   Self-concept based behaviour is not always related to clear expectations or to immediate and specific goals.   Shamir invokes Levinson's (1978) concept of the "Dream"—"a personal construction that contains the imagined self associated with a variety of aspirations, goals and values" (p. 156). In other words, ideas of what we might become or would like to become. These possibilities only have to have probabilities greater than zero to exert a powerful influence on our behaviour. Thus, the eradication of poverty and suffering from the world is not a likely outcome but millions of people work hard towards achieving this.

Shamir argues that when applied to work these motivational forces can explain motivated behaviour in less than optimal work conditions; when, for instance, goals are not clear or external rewards are not clearly related to performance. It explains, for instance, why nurses will continue to strive for high standards of performance when they are poorly paid, squeezed of resources, and plagued by staffing shortages. However, when the job starts to undermine the person's self-esteem and self-worth, then work motivation is reduced. Though Shamir does not say so, the implication is that such a person is more likely to exit the job than to lower their standards of performance and so damage their self-concepts still further. Thus for nurses who feel that financial considerations rather than quality of patient care are driving the system, continuing to serve that system will be detrimental to their self-concepts. It is, therefore, not surprising that following such changes to the NHS, large numbers of nurses have left the profession.

Shamir does not claim that the self-concept theory of work motivation will apply to everyone. People will differ in the extent to which their work identitity is salient within their self-concepts, the extent to which they are "pragmatic" rather than "moral" in their social relationships, and the extent to which they have firmly established or "crystallized" self-concepts. He gives some evidence to support his five assumptions and goes on to suggest a number of research strategies that could operationalize these difficult concepts and establish support for the theory, but as yet there does not appear to be much directly relevant research evidence.

This theory deserves further study because it has a number of important implications. First, maintaining high levels of effort and performance to protect the self-concept in adverse circumstances has costs for the person, especially if there are no perceived alternatives but to continue in the job (see Hockey, 1997). Just because people continue to work harder and perform well does not mean that organizations can be as complacent in the fact that they are "fitter and leaner". They may be living on borrowed time, as recent difficulties in staffing the UK public services, especially in expensive areas such as London and the South East, may be beginning to show. Increased levels of burnout and stress-related illness within the workforce may be real effects with real structural causes within organizations. This issue will be explored further in Chapter 4.

Second, the theory prompts a reconsideration of what we mean by work motivation. At the beginning of this chapter we defined it in terms of effort at work—its arousal, magnitude, direction, and maintenance. But it is clear from a number of the theories reviewed that it is not as simple as this. If effort can be caused by everything from fear of the sack to the actualization of a person's central identity and if effort can be accompanied by severe job dissatisfaction and threatened identity, to say nothing of the tenuous link between effort and performance, are we really talking about a single concept? We have operationalized motivation in terms of one dimension of behaviour but it seems to me that this will not do. Even effort itself can take so many different forms that the term covers a range of distinguishable meanings. Take, for instance, a hotel receptionist who is genuinely pleasant and helpful versus someone who is following a rigid set of rules laid down and enforced by management. Both may work equally hard, both may do the job competently and efficiently, but the experience of the guest is likely to be very different in the two cases. It seems to me that Herzberg (1968) was right when he said that true motivation comes from within the person, some mysterious quality that makes the person *want* to do a good job. Being forced or bribed to do a good job isn't at all the same. Shamir's theory may tell us something of the processes which lead to this mysterious inner quality. However, I think that his notion of the role of the self-concept is too narrow and moralistic in tone. We come back to a point made earlier—if you hold being a maker of a great deal of money as a salient identity, then your work behaviour will be just as much an enactment of your self-concept as that of the dedicated nurse or teacher. Maybe that is what true work motivation is—not effort at work, not the instrumental getting of what you want, but the expression of your self-concept.

Towards an integrated model of work motivation

Perhaps we have been asking the wrong question all these years. Instead of asking what motivates us to work, we should have been asking what are we motivated to do? The person whose job is so unpleasant that it cannot form the basis of a salient work identity is not motivated to work; he or she is motivated to earn money, which might support a more salient identity— perhaps to be a good provider for the family. Alternatively, people may be motivated to seek social rewards from the job—being a good work-mate and making friends. People are not motivated to work for fear of the sack, they are motivated to avoid getting the sack, which might threaten other salient identities such as being a successful and well-respected person. Does such a distinction matter? Well, yes it does, because you will put effort into what you want to achieve but no more than is necessary. If doing "a good enough job" gets you the pay packet or avoids the sack then that is what you will do and no more. If the organization demands more for the pay packet then you will deliver more, but never more than you need to and never as much as the person who is truly motivated to work. Meanwhile the organization may mistakenly believe it has increased motivation to work and thus productivity, while in reality the workforce is looking for ways to support their non-work identities in less effortful ways—getting safe, for instance.

If the job even fails to support salient nonwork identities by, for instance, becoming so insecure that being a good family provider is untenable, or workloads threaten other salient personal identities by, for instance, leaving little time for family and friends, then you get even or get out. Notice too that even in people who have a strong *work* identity and enact their self-concepts through their jobs, if job changes start to threaten that identity, getting out is the likely reaction if there are any employment alternatives. If not, stress related ill-health is the other outcome. Another very negative reaction is to revise the salience of the work identity downwards—the job ceases to be an important expression of the person's self-concept. This has great potential for damage to the person's feelings of self-esteem and self-worth, and burnout, get safe, and get even reactions can then ensue. However, painful as the revision of self-concepts may be, successful adaptation is possible—the City trader "downsizes" his or her job and becomes the "family person" or the local charity worker. It can work the other way too—the teacher becomes a successful business entrepreneur. It is the individuals who cannot escape their current jobs who suffer the most damage to themselves and potentially create most damage to their organizations.

These ideas have the potential to integrate the best points from all the theories considered here—equity/expectancy theories, job characteristics, goal-setting, and self-concept theories. A possible model is shown in Figure 3.2. In this model, a fundamental distinction is made between those whose self-concept is primarily sustained by a highly salient work identity and those for whom work is only a means to an end in that it supports other salient aspects of the person's self-concept. Many factors may affect the salience of the person's work identity, but probably Hackman and Oldham's (1980) core job characteristics will have a bearing. The more "impoverished" the work, the less likely that the person's self-concept will be centred around a work identity. Growth need strength plays a more problematical role in this scheme. Highly work-involved people are all likely to have high growth need strength, especially in an age of greater educational opportunity. So younger workers and those who embark on educational and professional qualifications later in life, and who are also high on work involvement, are likely to have high growth needs. This lack of variance may mean that high growth need strength appears to have no relationship with a salient work identity in this group. Within the "work-as-a-means-to-an-end" group, growth

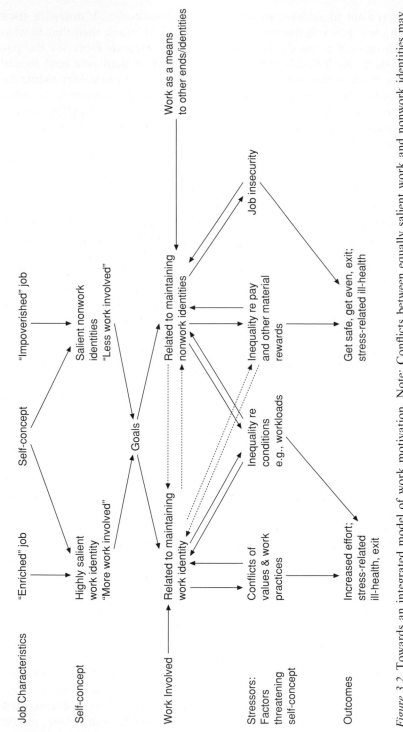

Figure 3.2 Towards an integrated model of work motivation. Note: Conflicts between equally salient work and nonwork identities may provoke shifts in degree of work involvement.

need strength may predict the extent to which people seek to sustain their nonwork identities, e.g., as homeworkers or in the pursuit of hobbies.

In any case, the fundamental goals of each group are likely to be different. For those whose central identity revolves around work, the goals will be strongly work related, perhaps at the expense of other nonwork identities. For the less work-involved group, the goal will be to ensure economic survival with the minimum of effort and nonwork goals will predominate. The two groups are likely to respond to work stressors in rather different ways. Anything that threatens the central work identity of the "involved" group (e.g., conflicts between core values and required work practices) will have most impact on this group. The short-term response may be increased effort and a neglect of other valued but less salient aspects of identity. In the longer term, stress-related ill-health and exit from the job or occupation may result. In the "less involved" group, anything which appears to threaten the role of the job in supporting valued nonwork identities such as job insecurity, reductions in overtime pay, or increased responsibility and workload without corresponding material reward, will be experienced as particularly aversive. "Get safe, get even, and exit" reactions are more likely but so is stress-related ill-health—assaults on one's sense of self when there is no obvious means of escape have serious consequences, whether or not a work identity is most salient.

Interestingly, the response to inequity may be different in each group. The "work involved" group may be more sensitive to violations of the conditions underlying the ability to do a good job such as an excessive workload. Those without a strong work identity may be more sensitive to perceived injustice in pay and other material rewards.

All this is a matter of degree, of course. People do not *either* live to work *or* work to live—for many of us it is a struggle to maintain a balance between the two extremes. And even the most work-involved person needs to sustain other aspects of self—maintaining good family and social relationships too prevents us from becoming workaholic nerds! Thus, most of the concepts in the model represent continuums rather than "type" categories. What is perhaps most interesting in this model is the career of women, especially those who enter professional, managerial, and technical occupations. We have raised a generation of bright, ambitious, and talented young women who expect to succeed in the world of work and "have it all" in terms of family life. Successful career women may experience a serious crisis of identity when thay have their first child. Suddenly another identity—that of mother—competes strongly for priority. Subsequent children may exacerbate the conflict since society exerts strong pressure to be a "perfect mother" and organizations demand the perfect professional person. Thus, there has to be a major reorganization of salient identities and work identity can be downgraded. (Men too can experience this conflict when they encounter fatherhood, but society is far less censorious of men who put their careers before the welfare of their children.) We see the effects of this in the UK by the number of women MPs elected in 1997 who are deserting their Parliamentary careers. There is also a lot of research showing that women report higher work-related strain than men (e.g., Doyle & Hind, 1998; Karasek & Theorell, 1990) even though paid employment can also be good for women's well-being (Baruch, Biener, & Barnett, 1987; LaCroix & Haynes, 1987). However, researching women making the transition from FT career person to working mother may be a fruitful way of testing this model. And at least it gives us some framework to avoid "one man's meat is another man's poison" explanations of work motivation, which we all knew in the first place!

So can we answer Phillip Larkin's question? Why do we let the toad work squat on our lives? Well, the first reason is obviously economic survival, but some of us are rather fond of toads and I wonder if Larkin ever had the good fortune to meet one.

Summary

In this chapter I have reviewed a number of theoretical frameworks for explaining what motivates people to work. All these perspectives have value in that they can explain different people's work behaviour but none offers a complete explanation. Pay explains why many people go to work in the first place but isn't a particularly good explanation for what they do once there. Theories of what makes work intrinsically motivating usually neglect the fact that one can have "too much of a good thing", and don't explain why people continue to strive for excellent performance even in very adverse conditions. I suggested that consideration of the person's self-concept may hold the key to understanding what motivates different people. I suggested that we have been asking the wrong question—it is not What motivates people to work? that is important but What are people motivated to do? A highly work-involved individual is driven by very different goals from those who use work to sustain salient nonwork identities. I used this idea to attempt an integration of all the theories considered and to suggest ways in which this model could be tested.

Suggested further reading

Brotherton, C. (1999). *Social psychology and management: Issues for a changing society*. Buckingham, UK: Open University Press (especially Chapter 3).

Mabey, C., Skinner, D., & Clark, T. (Eds.) (1998). *Experiencing human resource management*. London: Sage.

Steers, R. M., Porter, L. W., & Bigley, G. A. (Eds.) (1996). *Motivation and leadership at work* (6th ed.). New York: McGraw-Hill.

4 A study of stress: Design of environments and of work

The mass of men lead lives of quiet desperation
Henry David Thoreau, 1817–1862

A few years ago I was minded to teach a course on the Design of Environments and of Work, which is all about how to make jobs and workplaces fit for human beings so as to maximize health, well-being, efficiency, effectiveness, and safety. Fascinating stuff, I thought but the students did not agree. I had forgotten that they are now "customers" and all consumers like goods to come attractively packaged. "Design of Environments and of Work" sounded so dull that eyes swiftly moved on to other options in the handbook. Then I considered the crux of the issue. So many workplaces are manifestly unsuited to human beings that what we are really talking about is how environmental and psychosocial stressors create strain, ill-health, accidents, and disasters. I changed the title of the course to "Work and Stress" and I had many more "takers" even though the content of the course remained exactly the same.

It is not surprising that the word "stress" provoked interest. Judging from Thoreau's famous comment, it has been around for a very long time. However, in recent years the amount of stress-related ill-health appears to be increasing to levels that have attracted the concern of governments and bodies such as the World Health Organization (WHO). For instance, the Labour Force Survey (Hodgson, Jones, Elliott, & Osman, 1993) found that after musculoskeletal disorders, stress and depression were most frequently cited as causes of work-related health problems. Moreover, Griffiths and Cox (1993) found evidence to suggest that stress may be a significant factor in the development and reporting of musculoskeletal disorders. Fredriksson et al. (1999), reporting a longitudinal study of 500 Swedish workers, found that overtime and high mental workload were among the predictors of disorders of the neck, shoulders, hands, and wrists 24 years later. The Labour Force Survey: Fifth Wave (Jones, Hodgson, et al., 1998) investigated the prevalence of work-related ill-health in the UK in 1995; 40,000 workers were asked if they had suffered any work-related illness in the past 12 months and 70% of those answering "yes" to this question were later interviewed and had their reports confirmed by their GPs. Unusually in a study of this nature, a control sample of those answering "no" were also interviewed and asked about their working conditions. On the basis of this research, the estimated prevalence of self-reported work-related illness in the UK population was 2.0 million; 0.7 million of those affected were no longer in work and half a million people lost 19.5 million working days because of their illness. Again the main problems were musculoskeletal problems (1.2 million), and stress (anxiety and depression) (0.5 million). The main reported risk factors were workload and pace, work schedules, and lack of support at work either socially or in terms of resources. The groups most at risk of work-related illness were teachers and other professionals and older workers. Smith et al. (1998a, 1998b) conducted a pilot study of 254 respondents and found that over half reported themselves moderately to extremely stressed at work and that the problems associated with high work stress "are of the same magnitude as those seen in unemployment" (17,000 are to be included in the main study).

In my own modest research involving 600 academic staff in UK Psychology departments, reported levels of burnout on the Maslach Burnout Inventory (Maslach & Jackson, 1986) equalled the norms for the medical profession, itself regarded as a particularly stressful occupation (Doyle & Hind, 1998; Hind & Doyle, 1996). (Burnout is often seen as the final stage of adverse reactions to prolongued exposure to stressors. It is characterized by a feeling that one no longer has the resources to cope [emotional exhaustion], emotional distancing of oneself from the recipients of goods and services [depersonalization], and feeling that one has achieved little of value [lack of personal accomplishment]; see also pp. 135 and 141) What is especially striking about our findings is that the "groves of academe" were commonly assumed to be removed from the "real world" and uniquely stress-free (Argyle, 1989). Rose (2000), analysing large sociological data sets and comparing 100 occupations for the ESRC Future of Work project, confirms that teachers at all levels are high on his "misery index". He concludes, "On this evidence, then, there seems little question that the education 'family' of occupations has been that experiencing the highest stress in recent years . . . Arguably, they lie at the core of national stress problems" (p. 9). But teaching is not the only stressful occupation. Rice (2000) reports on a survey of nearly 2000 UK managers where nearly half reported being too mentally and physically exhausted to do more than work and sleep and nearly a third said their lives and work were out of control.

These and hundreds of similar research findings worldwide (see, e.g., Box 4.1) indicate that whatever the processes underlying work stress-related illness, it is not merely a figment of employees' imaginations and it constitutes a growing social problem.

However, as Hartley pointed out (Chapter 2), all aspects of our lives appear to be increasingly stressful so to what extent can pressures at work

---

BOX 4.1
The results of the UN International Labour Organization Survey:
Work-related ill-health in five countries

The *Guardian* newspaper (Osborn, 2000) carried a report of a survey of stress in five countries carried out by the United Nations International Labour Organization (ILO). According to the ILO report, "Workers worldwide confront, as never before, an array of new organizational structures and processes which can affect their mental health." Some statistics follow:

- In the UK, as many as 3 in 10 employees experience mental health problems and 1 in 20 suffers from major depression. Stress accounts for 14% of sickness leave and £80 million lost working days each year. The annual cost of lost productivity is £5.3 billion.
- In the US, 1 in 10 workers suffer from clinical depression with 200 million lost working days per year and costs in terms of lost earnings and treatment amount to £30 billion annually.
- In Finland more than half the workforce have stress-related symptoms, 7% are "severely burnt out", and there is a high suicide rate.
- In Germany almost 7% of early retirements are caused by depression. Stress-related absenteeism is estimated to cost £1.5 billion.
- In Poland anxiety caused by "soaring" unemployment increased by 50% last year.

---

be blamed for rising levels of stress-related ill-health? There is little reason to doubt that much worker stress-related problems stem from personal difficulties rather than anything to do with the workplace itself. However, we must also remember that personal and work-related causes are unlikely to be independent. Problems at home can impact on work and vice versa (Cooper, Cooper, & Eaker, 1988). Work stress seems to be associated with a more stressful personal life. Smith et al.'s pilot study (1998b) found that those who reported low levels of stress at work were unlikely to perceive life as being generally stressful, whereas a third of those reporting high work stress also perceived life to be generally stressful. Even if we grant that less than half of stress-related ill-health stems from people's work then it still represents huge costs in terms of human misery, lost productivity, and health-care bills.

Related to this, another controversy concerns the extent to which the individual or the organization can be held responsible for stress-related ill-health. There is one school of thought that could be termed "If-you-can't-stand-the-heat-get-out-of-the-kitchen" approach. If only companies could recruit workers made of the "right stuff" (abilities, competencies, personality, values, attitudes, energy, etc.) then the problem would go away. The opposing camp holds that organizations, through their management, work practices, and job design, create environments which will be experienced as stressful by most, if not all, their workforce.

In practice many organizations attempt to occupy the middle ground by placing great emphasis on selection whilst also redesigning jobs, promoting a safety culture, and, sometimes, providing stress management programmes and counselling services (see Chapter 9). This makes researching and understanding the processes underlying work-related ill-health in the field somewhat difficult because there are too many things going on at the same time to be able to disentangle their effects. However, there is some evidence that despite much talk of "worker empowerment", there are general trends towards reduced job discretion and increased job strain (Karasek, 1990; West et al., 1995). Some job redesign interventions may therefore be more a matter of rhetoric than reality. Day (2001), investigating the introduction of autonomous work groups in a manufacturing plant, found exactly this. The change increased stress by producing conflict between the skilled maintenance men and the less skilled production workers, and threatening the work identity of many, but didn't actually deliver the benefit of increased worker autonomy. All this was accompanied by a decrease in machine uptime and thus lower productivity—exactly the opposite of what management had intended.

Day's was a longitudinal study (2001) and he was able to chart the changes in productivity and worker attitudes over 2 years. Much stress research is cross-sectional but such studies have limited value since one thing that everyone agrees about is that psychosocial and other stressors exert their effects over time. For instance, Cooper (1997) investigated the effects of major reorganization on worker morale. He found a large decrease in morale immediately after the change but, as workers began to adjust, morale began to recover (although not fully up to its original level). Numerous studies of the effects of sleep loss in night shift workers show increasing effects as the number of nights on shift increase (Akerstedt, 1985). Thus there is a need for many more longitudinal studies if we are to understand workplace stress fully.

Considerations such as these mean that although stress is possibly the most widely researched area of work and organizational psychology, it is still not well understood. The huge literature and many controversies also create problems about what to include in a short chapter on this topic. I am going to concentrate on four main areas:

1   Major concepts of and theories about stress.
2   The physical stressor of fatigue and the related concepts of mental effort and fatigue.
3   The psychosocial stressor of workplace bullying.
4   The concept of control over work as a mechanism for ameliorating stress reactions.

I have no better or worse justification for this choice than that these are the areas attracting contemporary research interest.

Major theories and concepts concerning stress

Terminology

In the introduction to this chapter I have tended to use the term "stress" to mean both the things that make us feel bad and the experience of feeling bad because this is how the word is used in common parlance. But readers may also have noticed the term "stressor" and in fact theorists in this area make an important distinction between sources of pressure and people's reactions to them. A stressor is some feature of the person's environment that has the potential to be interpreted as threatening, dangerous, damaging, etc. Stressors can be mainly physical in origin, e.g., excessive heat, noise, vibration, or mainly psychosocial in origin, e.g., poor management, hostile or inimical colleagues. Other stressors do not fit neatly into these categories. Long working hours, night shift work, high work demands, high workloads, inadequate resources and support, and job insecurity can be said to originate in the external environment but their effects are heavily influenced by the person's perceptions. In fact it could be argued that perceptions influence the experience of even extreme physical stressors. Noise loud enough to damage hearing is enjoyed in nightclubs and heat intense enough to cause quite severe burns can be enjoyed on a beach.

Strain is the person's negative reaction to stressors, which may or may not be consciously experienced. Negative effects can manifest themselves in physical symptoms such as insomnia, excessive fatigue, gastrointestinal disorders, headaches, and serious disease, e.g., cardiovascular complaints. Or the effects may be psychological, such as depression and anxiety. In some instances, the person may suffer the effects of stressors without being aware of it, as when someone goes gradually deaf as a result of excessive noise or the first sign of strain is sudden cardiac arrest. Very often physical and psychological symptoms are related so that anxiety may produce insomnia and fatigue. Sometimes strain leads to secondary behaviours that exacerbate the effects of the stressors, for instance, smoking, alcohol and drug abuse, failure to take exercise, and so on. The negative reactions to stressors are generally called distress.

However, as already mentioned, even extreme stressors can also be experienced as enjoyable and a challenge. Sky diving and bungee jumping come to mind as behaviours that would be inexplicable if we didn't sometimes seek out and enjoy stressors. In fact, boredom is itself a significant stressor, and all of us need some stress in our lives. This has led to the concept of Eustress —the good effects of stressors.

However, the link between workplace stressors and ill-health is actually quite controversial, not least because of individual differences.

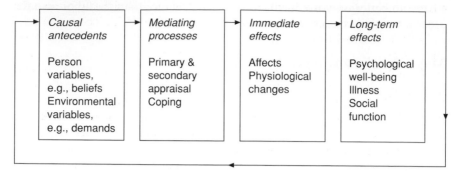

Figure 4.1 Lazarus and Folkman's (1984) model of the stressor–strain relationship. From R. Lazarus & S. Folkman (1984). *Stress, appraisal and coping.* Springer Publishing Company Inc., New York 10012. Copyright (1984). Used by permission.

Major questions

What we all want to know is, do certain job or organizational characteristics cause reduced well-being or ill-health and if so, how? We know that noxious substances and physically hazardous environments can cause biological damage, but can psychological distress cause biological damage too, and if so, how? Distress is usually conceived as involving objective or subjective environmental demands exceeding the person's objective or subjective resources to cope. One of the most influential theoretical frameworks was proposed by Lazarus and Folkman (1984) and is presented in Figure 4.1.

According to this model, causal ancecedents of stress reactions include both environmental factors, such as work demands, and person variables, such as beliefs and expectations, e.g., about what work demands are reasonable or achievable. Perceptions of these factors prompt an appraisal of the situation, which may then be construed as threatening or stressful in the short term and, in the longer term, provoke attempts to cope. These mediating processes create immediate changes in affect—such as feelings of anxiety —and physiological changes—such as fatigue as a result of increased effort. Long term, the person may experience reductions in psychological well-being, increased ill-health, and deterioration in social functioning. This process can be iterative. For instance, strain may lead to poor work and family relationships, and this itself feeds back to exacerbate the original causal antecedents. Thus, difficulties in personal relationships at home may further reduce the person's emotional resources for coping at work; deteriorating social relationships at work make a bad situation worse and further reduce the person's feelings of being able to cope. And so the process continues.

Since the person's appraisal or interpretation of the stressor is so important in the stress response, this immediately raises the question of whether stressors are "real". That is, whether they are objectively present and measurable in the environment or whether they are individually or socially constructed. Most researchers are agreed that we need objective measures of workplace stressors but this can be surprisingly difficult to achieve. A good illustration of this concerns job insecurity. There is much objective evidence that some jobs have become more insecure than they once were and that organizations no longer promise a "job for life" but, at the same time, average job tenure in the UK has increased and so feelings of job insecurity can be dismissed as "paranoia" (Smith, 1997). Although the first "objective fact"—that jobs are less secure than they were—seems relatively clear-cut and is generally accepted, the second—that tenure is increasing—is open to various interpretations. One may be that, in a general climate of job insecurity, people are more likely to stay put in the job they have rather than moving on in search of something better. Another is that crude averages conceal wide variations in people's personal experiences. Thus, a sample of people whose average job tenure is 10 years could include someone who has stayed with the same firm for 20 years and another who has been made redundant several times in quick succession. So average length of tenure is not a good measure of objective job insecurity.

Better objective measures include looking at the financial situation in specific companies. The prevalence of downsizing, reorganizations, and mergers in recent years has allowed researchers to conduct longitudinal studies of the reactions of workers whose jobs are under real threat (see, e.g., Hellgren, Sverke, & Isaksson, 1999; Kinnunen, Mauno, Natti, & Happonen, 1999). These studies show that real job insecurity does have a negative impact and is related to job exhaustion and sickness absence at a later point in time. In an earlier series of studies, Van Vuuren and colleagues (Van Vuuren, 1990; Van Vuuren, Klandermans, Jacobson, & Hartley, 1991) found a direct relationship between the financial health of companies and subjective feelings of job insecurity amongst employees. When the outlook appeared bleak, subjective job insecurity increased; as the outlook improved so did feelings of job security. Klandermans and Van Vuuren (1999) comment that such relationships indicate that job insecurity is not simply a matter of social construction. However, they also point out that "not all the variance in job insecurity can be explained by the company's situation. Workers who are facing identical situations differ in their feelings of job insecurity" (p. 145).

Complexities such as this allow organizations to claim that they are not creating objectively stressful environments. The exhortation to "work smarter, not harder" is in part a denial that the intensification of work is an objective stressor. However, Klandermans and Van Vuuren (1999) argue that the objective/subjective debate related to job insecurity is rather missing the point. Even in the best of circumstances, some people will experience feelings of job insecurity, perhaps because they suffer from low self-esteem or are basically pessimists. However, when jobs are *really* under threat, such personality influences on worker reactions "become irrelevant". Then factors such as employability and the availability of other jobs become important in determining how well people are able to cope. The very interesting set of research papers these authors edit demonstrate:

1   The power of good research in clarifying the factors that influence negative reactions to workplace stressors.
2   That negative reactions are not simply a consequence of personal "defects" or faulty perceptions in workers.

We need far more good research like this.

However, the notion of "the person's resources to cope" still invokes individual differences, the implication being that some people have more resources than others and are thus less likely to experience strain when faced with the same objective stressors. Common sense tells us that this is undoubtedly true. For instance, more intellectually able or more skilled people can cope with complex and demanding tasks better than the less able and less skilled (see, e.g., Westman & Eden, 1996). But here again we meet the objective versus subjective distinction. Self-efficacy theory leads to the prediction that some people will underestimate their resources for coping, whereas others may overestimate them. Those who underestimate will experience strain even though, objectively, they are capable of coping with the stressor. Examples may include the very able student who suffers unnecessary exam anxiety or the capable health worker with severe performance anxiety. Overestimation of resources to cope is interesting but little researched. The person who believes that increased effort will resolve an insoluble situation is likely to suffer severe long-term effects. An example might include a dedicated but less than charismatic school teacher who perseveres in the face of a hostile, disruptive class of youngsters from socially dysfunctional families. Even when the person accurately assesses that the objective situation exceeds their resources, it is important to demonstrate that it is the job and not the person's shortcomings which causes the distress.

Psychological health and well-being

Physical health/ill-health is the result of complex processes—genetic predispositions, lifestyles, psychological well-being, and a host of other factors seem to be implicated as well as physical pathogens. The relationship between psychological health and well-being could be even more complex and involves at least three different levels of functioning.

1   At the most serious level there is severe mental disturbance such as clinical depression and post-traumatic stress disorder (see Chapter 9 for more information on this).
2   At the next level there is general psychological well-being which concerns feelings about oneself in relation to one's world and can be context specific (e.g., job related) or context free (satisfaction with life in general).

3   At another level we have people's moods or affective states which can be relatively permanent orientations (feeling generally miserable at work) or relatively transient (reacting badly to the latest hassle).

Warr (1996a, 1998) contends that psychological well-being is not a unitary concept but has three principal dimensions. These are displeasure to pleasure, anxiety to comfort, and depression to enthusiasm. Thus, people may experience their work as difficult and effortful (high displeasure) and may suffer performance anxiety (high anxiety) but still feel enthusiastic about their work, perhaps because it is seen as meaningful, worthwhile, and bound up with the expression of their self-concepts. In fact, Warr cites evidence that higher level jobs are indeed associated with more job-related anxiety but less job-related depression. However, such jobs could be experienced as impossibly demanding and exhausting. Job characteristics also impact more on some dimensions of well-being than others. Thus, jobs with high work demands affect the anxiety–comfort dimension more than the depression–enthusiasm dimension, and jobs that allow little personal control over the way work is performed impact on the depression–enthusiasm dimension more than on the anxiety–comfort dimension. It follows from this that experienced strain is not a unitary concept either. However, I think that suffering from job-related anxiety is as bad for mental health as suffering from job-related depression. Nevertheless, Warr's framework tells us that the concepts of job satisfaction, stress, and so on are meaningless unless these dimensions are considered. For instance the low correlations typically found between job satisfaction and work performance could be partly explained by the fact that jobs promoting pleasure and comfort could create well-being at the expense of high performance.

A further complication is that personality factors are also implicated in how people react to job stressors. Warr (1998) reviews evidence that negative affectivity (a facet of personality including a tendency to think negative thoughts and worry about things) is a good predictor of low job satisfaction. For instance, Staw and Ross (1985) showed that being a "worrier" predicted job dissatisfaction even when people moved jobs and occupations. Some researchers (Arvey, Bouchard, Segal, & Abraham, 1989; Arvey, McCall, Bouchard, Taubman, & Cavanaugh, 1994) have even claimed that up to a third of the variance in people's reactions to work could be genetically based via ability and personality. If this is the case, then employers may well dispute the argument that they are making their workers ill.

Is workplace stress a useful concept?

Briner (1997, 1999c) argues that the concept of stress has now become so muddled and unhelpful that it should be abandoned in favour of focusing on people's feelings and emotions at work (Briner, 1999a, 1999b). He argues that stress is a trivial concept because there is confusion about whether stress is a stimulus or a response. We talk about being in a "stressful environment" and being "stressed out" when what we mean is anything bad we feel or experience at work. He also criticizes the research tradition in workplace stress. This comes from at least four theoretical bases:

- "Stress" as a biological/physiological phenomenon based on engineering concepts.
- "Stress" as a disruptor of performance.
- "Stress" as a factor in the development of illness.
- "Stress" as an antecedent of psychological adaptation.

He says that "none of these is clearly conceptually or empirically related" but they are now all conflated to mean the same thing. Thus, when we ask "what is stress?" we have no answer because there is no one thing that is "stress". He also attacks most stress research as being very poor methodologically. The better the research, the weaker the relationships between stressors and adverse reactions that are found. Stress, he says, is a "modern myth".

I have much sympathy with Briner's critique but until his alternative framework and methods to investigate it are better developed I am opposed to abandoning the concept. Consider the supposed lack of evidence. Much early stress research was conducted in the controlled conditions of laboratory experiments. There was a remarkable failure to demonstrate any adverse effects of stressors on performance. Broadbent (1958) had to devise "sensitive tasks" to detect any deterioration of performance even in the presence of objective stressors such as very loud noise. As an example of just how resilient people can be, Chiles (1955) had volunteers working continuously in an aircraft simulator for up to 56 hours without rest. During this time, participants were regularly tested on their performance on a tracking task which involved keeping a stylus on a small moving target. Some were so exhausted that they had to be carried to the test apparatus!!! Despite this there was no decrement in performance on the tracking task throughout the study. If this happens in artificial controlled lab conditions with objective stressors and precise measures of performance, how much harder must it be to demonstrate adverse effects in the "real world", when measures of objective stressors and performance may be much less accurate and people are even more motivated to protect their performance? All these studies may be telling us the well-known ergonomic principle that people are capable of "graceful degradation"; they will put up with an awful lot, when they have to, before they start to become dysfunctional. Therefore, I am less impressed by the lack of evidence than Briner. Rather we need better research. The example of job insecurity, given earlier, is a good illustration of how we can demonstrate the adverse effects of objective stressors.

However, my main objection to Briner's critique is unashamedly political. With the injunction to ensure a psychologically "healthy" workplace in the

1992 amendments to the Health and Safety legislation and various landmark cases which have penalized employers for placing unreasonable demands on workers, companies are beginning to take their responsibilities for worker well-being to heart. In my view, this is not the time for theoretical disputes within the profession to give organizations the impression that work-related ill-health does not exist when patently it does. Even Briner admits the damage perpetrated by workplace stressors, while stoutly defending the principle that outmoded and muddled concepts are not helpful for advancing "objective truth" and should be replaced. Quite so! But . . . what we need is better research, not the abandonment of a potentially useful concept which has a great deal of public acceptance and understanding. Hockey, Payne, and Rick (1995) found distinct differences between junior doctors in terms of their active versus passive coping styles following a heavy normal work shift. "Active copers" had higher adrenaline levels in their blood and were more fatigued, but less anxious. This pattern seemed to indicate that these people were actively striving to meet challenges. "Passive copers" had higher cortisol levels in their blood and felt less fatigue, but more anxiety. This pattern was more indicative of passive endurance. Thus, the effects of similar objective stressors appear to be moderated by cognitive appraisals, which in turn may be moderated by personality differences. After the long weekend shift, however, these differences disappeared. Excessive fatigue caused by severe sleep deprivation and prolonged mental effort meant that passive coping predominated and cortisol levels were high in both groups. The conclusion is that *no-one* could cope with the demands of the long weekend shift—the organizational demands were just too great. (See p. 123 onwards for more on the physiological mechanisms underlying adverse reactions to stressors.) In a similar vein, Decker and Borgen (1993) found that the negative effects of stressors such as role ambiguity were still significant even when negative affectivity was controlled statistically. Rydstedt, Johansson, and Evans (1998) obtained similar results in a longitudinal study of bus drivers. Increases in workload over an 18-month period were strongly associated with exhaustion, fatigue spillover from work to personal life, and psychosomatic symptoms. Controlling for negative affectivity made no difference to the pattern or significance of the results. The implications of these studies are that, at some point, most people become dysfunctional, that no-one can cope any more, or that different aspects of the person come into play (as in the job insecurity literature).

In addition, recent studies suggest that the relationship between negative affectivity and outcome variables such as job satisfaction and strain are not straightforward. For instance, Hochwarter, Perrewe, Zellars, and Harrison (1999) found that managers with high negative affectivity who also perceived their jobs as being higher in job scope reported more job satisfaction than individuals low in negative affectivity. Thus, the relationship between personal disposition and job satisfaction was mediated by job complexity. Judge, Bono, and Locke (2000) looked at the relationship between several "core self-evaluations"—self-esteem, generalized self-efficacy, locus of control (feelings of being in control or of being controlled), and negative affectivity—and found evidence supporting their hypothesized model that perceived job characteristics and job complexity mediate between self-evaluations and job satisfaction. Warr (1998) also concludes that both personality and the nature of the work influence how people feel about their jobs. In fact, Judge et al. (2000) consider that their main contribution to our knowledge in this area is that both their cross-sectional and longitudinal studies provide evidence that people with low negative affectivity seek out and gain jobs which have higher complexity and are therefore more satisfying. However, greater job complexity is not always an advantage. Xie and Johns (1995) looked at the relationship between job demands, ability, and stress. Job complexity was measured by objective measures, namely the dictionary of occupational titles (DOT; Roos & Treiman, 1980), which is based on job analysis, and the occupational prestige index (OP; Treiman, 1977), which is based on levels of formal education and salary levels achievable by incumbents. They found a curvilinear relationship between job complexity and emotional exhaustion as measured by the Maslach burnout inventory (Maslach & Jackson, 1986). Specifically, both low levels of job complexity and very high levels were associated with high emotional exhaustion. These findings fit very well with Warr's vitamin model (see Chapter 3), which proposes that both too little and too much of a good thing is bad for health. Having a more interesting job does seem to reduce the negative effects of a generally gloomy disposition but impossibly demanding jobs could well be objective stressors that reduce the chances of anyone being able to cope adequately.

Moreover, several authors warn against drawing causal inferences in cross-sectional research. For instance, Cropanzano, James, and Konovsky (1993) point to the evidence that personal dispositions do seem to be relatively stable over time so it seems reasonable to assume that dispositional affectivity determines work attitudes. However, they go on to say that other causal paths are possible and quote Davis-Blake and Pfeffer (1989), who review evidence that working conditions can change personality. Judge et al. (2000) note that perceived job characteristics might determine job satisfaction or vice versa, since enjoying your work could lead to more positive evaluations of its characteristics. More longitudinal studies are needed to sort out the directions of causality.

Further insights may be gleaned from research concerning people with disabilities. First, in a review of the literature, Reid (2000) notes that there are significant differences between the scores of people with visual impairments on various measures of personality and the instrument norms, based on sighted individuals. She suggests that for visually impaired individuals, the difficulties of achieving independent functioning in a modern society may impact on their adult personalities. She also presents evidence that people with visual impairments tend to select occupations on the basis of how they interpreted the occupational titles in relation to the perceived limitations their disability imposed. In other words, their experience of visual impairment influenced what they thought they could achieve in the world of work. It is quite plausible that self-efficacy is heavily implicated in this process.

Finally, there is some evidence from people who suffer disabilities such as visual impairment later in life. Hershenson (1981, 1996) has proposed a model of how people adjust to work when disability follows illness or accident. Three developmental domains are involved: one concerns work personality, self-concept, and motivation; another concerns work competencies, skills, and habits; the final area concerns work goals. According to this framework the onset of a disability may have a devastating impact on people's work competencies and this in turn will have a negative impact on people's work personality and self-concept and their work goals. The person may decide that a return to work is impossible. If the onset of disability can have a profound impact on people's self-concepts, work identity, and sense of self-efficacy, may not other adverse experiences also impact negatively on personality? People may be courageous, resilient, hardy, stubborn, determined, what you will . . . But to what extent do these qualities just delay the inevitable? Even someone who demonstates all these admirable qualities may succumb to clinical depression eventually.

These considerations of the direction(s) of causality bring me to my third fundamental objection to Briner's arguments. This is that we now have a much greater understanding of the physical effects of stressors and this research indicates that "mind" can most definitely exert a negative influence over "matter". If true, the debate about whether "real stressors" or people's interpretations are more important in creating negative reactions is largely irrelevant, because it is the subjective appraisal which triggers the physiological response. Lack of enough clear evidence that workplace stressors have negative effects on productivity and well-being also becomes less important as an objection to the claim that the way work is organised can make people ill. If research can demonstrate that workplace stressors have the potential to impact on worker health, what we then should become concerned about is what is "reasonable" in legal terms in the demands employers place on employees and what "reasonable care" they should take to ensure that the health and well-being of employees are not put at risk.

Physiological mechanisms underlying stress-related illness

Frankenhaeuser (1986) investigated the relationships between the neuroendocrine system, work performance, and physical/psychological health (see Figure 4.2). She proposed that there were two main mechanisms. In the first, environmental demands trigger perceptions of threat in higher brain centres, which in turn provoke signals to stimulate another brain structure known as the adrenal medulla, via the hypothalamus. This provokes release of catecholamines (adrenaline and noradrenaline) into the person's blood

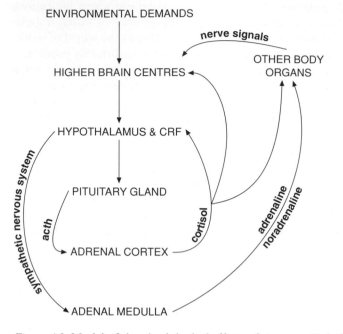

Figure 4.2 Model of the physiological effects of stressors: Relationships between the neuroendocrine system, performance, and psychological/physical health. From M. Frankenhauser, *Dynamics of Stress*, 1986. Reprinted with the permission of Kluwer Academic/Plenum Publishers.

stream. Adrenaline is associated with the traditional "fight or flight" reaction to environmental stressors. In our evolutionary past this could have been the appearance of a hungry sabre-tooth tiger. Nowadays it is more likely to be associated with high work demands. In any case the catecholamines have a "fuelling" effect on the body and are strongly associated with psychological and physical effort, active coping, and a feeling of challenge and control.

A second system also has its origins in environmental demands, higher brain centres, and the hypothalamus, but this time the brain signals go via the pituitary gland and the neurotransmitter ACTH to stimulate the adrenal cortex. As a result of this, cortisol is released into the person's bloodstream. Cortisol is found in injured animals and is thought to produce the immobilization that may aid healing. A high level of cortisol indicates that the body is reacting as if physically damaged and is linked to subsequent organ damage, in particular, heart disease. Cortisol is associated with passive coping—a helpless, hopeless endurance.

This model offers an explanation of how psychological factors such as appraisals of environmental threats can exert a direct effect on bodily processes. Something in the higher conscious brain centres determines which system is activated. Further insights are provided by research investigating stress and the immune system (Evans, Clow, & Hucklebridge, 1997). The central question here is whether stressors lower the body's natural defences so that people become more susceptible to disease. Caution is needed when interpreting research findings because there are methodological problems. First, people differ in their reactions to stressful events so it is difficult to measure experienced strain. Generally we are forced to rely on self-reports, which may not be reliable. Second, the state of people's immune systems vary considerably even when people are not experiencing strain. Thus, the preferred terms to describe it are "up-regulation", which implies enhanced immunity, versus "down-regulation", which implies suppressed immunity, relative to the average state of the immune system. Measuring levels of immunity at any time is not easy. The presence of lymphocytes, various "natural killer cells", and antibodies in the blood are all used, but different indices can give different results.

Despite this, some tentative conclusions can be drawn. Longitudinal studies of people suffering long-term severe stressors such as caring for a close relative with Alzheimer's disease, or enduring separation and divorce, do seem to link with overall down-regulation of the immune system (Kiecolt-Glaser, Dura, Speicher, Trask, & Glaser, 1991; Kiecolt-Glaser et al., 1993; Zisook et al., 1994). However, acute stressors are often temporarily associated with up-regulation of the immune system. For instance, Evans, Bristow, Hucklebridge, Clow, and Walters (1993) conducted a longitudinal study of differences in stress-related measures (e.g., mood and everyday events) with secretion of a particular antibody (sIgA). Over a week, sIgA levels were associated with quality of life experiences, i.e., the lower the quality of life the lower the sIgA levels. However, daily measures showed raised sIgA levels on the *worst* days. In other words, temporary up-regulation of the immune system occurred in response to days with a lot of hassles even though the general trend was towards down-regulation in response to prolonged stress. Similar results occurred in studies of student stress. Having to give a presentation resulted in temporary up-regulation, whereas exam periods are associated with a general trend towards down-regulation (Evans, Bristow, Hucklebridge, Clow, & Pang, 1994). Similarly, laboratory experiments involving demanding tasks such as computer games and mental arithmetic were associated with temporary up-regulation (Carroll et al., 1996).

Evans et al. (1997) invoke Frankenhauser's two systems to explain these effects. Acute stressors activate the catecholamine system, which energizes us to active coping with environmental challenges. Thus do we exert ourselves to cope with daily hassles. Long-term stressors, which do not admit any real solution whatever our efforts, promote passive endurance and are associated with activation of the damaging cortisol system. In reversal theory terms, the emotional experience of challenge, excitement, and mastery activates the adrenaline system; the emotional experience of anxiety, helplessness, and hopelessness activates the cortisol system, which can lead to lasting physical damage.

I am not going to get embroiled in the argument about whether emotions cause bodily changes or bodily changes cause emotions. Suffice it to say that cognitive acts must result from physical processes within the brain. Thus, the appraisal of stressors that occur in the higher brain centres could well lead to activation of either the active or passive physiological mechanisms and mind can indeed influence matter. Personality and prior experience are also implicated because these determine, at least in part, the nature of the cognitive appraisals of threat. However, organizations cannot assume that, just because some employees can appear to "thrive on chaos", others are not being seriously harmed. Moreover, even the "stars" may not thrive for long. We may be able to rely on active coping and the adrenaline system in the short term. However, chronic stressors over which the person has little control, such as long-term intolerable work demands, are likely to activate the cortisol system, which leads to suppression of the immune system. Thus, psychosocial workplace stressors could cause physical ill-health.

Notice that in this discussion I have moved seamlessly between worker strain and well-being at work, and researchers do appear to be changing their focus to well-being (Briner & Daniels, 1999). Though these two concepts "ought" to be different sides of the same coin, this is by no means clear. For instance, the factors which promote well-being could be different from those engendering strain. Even though the *same* stressor is involved. Challenging work, for instance, could be experienced as negatively stressful but still contribute to a general feeling of well-being if the person copes successfully. In this case the difficulty of the work creates strain but the feeling of mastery promotes well-being. Reversal theory (Apter, 2001; Svebak & Apter, 1997) may come to our aid here. Apter and Batler (1997, p. 119) hypothesized that the pursuit of potentially self-damaging behaviour can be explained as deliberate self-exposure to risk with the aim of achieving excitement. Anxiety is an unpleasant emotion, but excitement is pleasurable. "The theory posits that . . . danger increases arousal levels in the telic state, producing anxiety, and then mastery of the danger triggers a reversal to the paratelic state in which the high arousal is enjoyed instead as excitement." (See also pp. 9–10 in Chapter 1.) To test this, they conducted a questionnaire study of people who indulged in the sport of parachuting and found that reported anxiety was highest just before the moment of maximum danger, as people prepared to jump, and excitement was most prevalent after this, when people were out of the aircraft. Most people hate the waiting for anxiety-provoking action more than the action itself. However, few other theories can explain such "paradoxical" behaviour at all—unless one invokes Freud's concept of thanatos—an inborn death wish—which itself is not really adequate since the excitement stems from having successfully avoided death. At a less spectacular level, emotions and particularly reversals of emotion at work could explain some aspects of organizational behaviour and experience. One person's challenge is another person's nightmare; one person's excitement is another person's intolerable anxiety and strain. Perhaps the most important point is that it is also possible for the *same person* to switch rapidly between these states, maybe several times during the course of a single day.

The conclusion seems to be that situations can be stressful but provided that we can overcome them to achieve a sense of mastery, our health and well-being can be enhanced—at least in the short term. Once we begin to feel that our best efforts are no longer effective or that the outlook is bleak whatever we do, then the consequences can be serious. We will return to the role of mastery and the associated concept of self-efficacy throughout this chapter and particularly in the final section on control over work.

Meanwhile, perhaps organizations should take note that their past failures to acknowledge the effects of physical stressors, which caused, e.g., lung diseases in asbestos workers and miners, came back to haunt them in successful court settlements many years later. As more governments enact legislation to require organizations to provide a healthy psychological environment for their employees, claims for psychological damage may also become the reality that many thought unthinkable. Indeed, this is already happening (e.g., *Walker v Northumberland County Council*, 1995), while the "hidden" costs of "stressed-out" employees and the army of unemployed people in Western countries has barely begun to be calculated. A cynic might even be forgiven for thinking that this is all a global plot to ensure the premature removal of the burden of too many retired people on the scant workforce that will be needed (or available) in the 21st century! I never impute malice where incompetence will do, but I don't rule it out entirely either.

The effects of physical stressors

This was the focus for most of the history of the design of environments and of work as an area of work and organizational psychology. It stretches back to the worries of the UK Government during World War I about the effects of fatigue in munitions workers. I wonder whether this concern was caused by care for the well-being of workers or the loss of efficiency and productivity, particularly when exhausted workers may have made mistakes and blown up themselves and their factories.

Whatever the source of governmental concern, the next 60-odd years saw a vast amount of research investigating the effects of physical stressors on work performance. Space precludes discussion of this work but for a good review see, e.g., Hockey (1986) or Oborne (1995). Suffice it to say that laboratory studies found an astonishing absence of any effects at all. Broadbent (1958) conducted one of the best thought out and controlled series of studies but, as already mentioned, found it necessary to use "sensitive" tasks to detect any decrements in work performance. "Sensitive tasks" were mind-bogglingly boring reaction-time tasks where people were required to either respond as quickly as possible to a light stimulus by simply pressing a lever or, in a more difficult version, to press the button corresponding to the position of a light stimulus in a particular display. Thus, if the third light arranged in a circle came on, you had to press the third button in a circle of buttons. Reaction times (performance) in such tasks was shown to be remarkably resilient to adverse conditions but stressors such as extreme noise or sleep deprivation could have an effect. Very often these decrements in performance could be attributed not to a general slowing down of reaction times but to a few serious "lapses" when the person failed to respond at all for some time. When the person was seriously fatigued by sleep deprivation this could be attributed to "micro-sleeps"—when the person failed to see the signal because he or she was momentarily unconscious! Broadbent also found that stressors tended to interact with each other so that, for instance, loud noise tended to keep the seriously fatigued person awake and so prevented "lapses" in reaction times. However, these simple reaction-time tasks are far removed from the complexity of much of today's knowledge work. Generalizing from these results to conclude that stressors such as serious fatigue would not cause decrements in performance in the workplace would be dangerous.

With the luxury of hindsight, I am rather more impressed with Bartlett's "Cambridge cockpit" work (1943), which showed that whereas performance on a reaction-time task was relatively unaffected after up to 50 hours or so of continuous work in one of the world's first flight simulators, many other indicators of performance in the primary task of flying an aircraft were seriously affected. Bartlett's mainly "qualitative" findings were largely ignored by a psychology dominated by behaviourism, but how many airline passengers today would be content to entrust their lives to a fatigued pilot who was concentrating on the altimeter at the expense of the fuel gauge and was swearing at the controls for their failure to respond to uncoordinated commands, yet still had complete faith in his or her ability to fly the plane? And yet this is exactly what Bartlett found. In fact, airline companies take pilot fatigue very seriously because they also have to contend with jet-lagged pilots. Their safety record is examplary amongst all forms of transport and even after the terrorist attacks of September 2001, it is still probably safer to fly the Atlantic than to drive your car to work. Other industries seem less concerned about the effects of fatigue. Long working hours are commonplace in the UK despite the European Directive on the maximum working week and there has also been a great increase in night shift work.

Fatigue comes in three main forms. The first can be termed sleepiness and occurs naturally after people have been awake for about 16 hours. Being forced to stay awake much longer than that is termed sleep deprivation, and sleepiness increases dramatically after about 30 hours (see, e.g., Empson [1989] and Horne [2001] for reviews of relevant research). It also builds up when there is sleep "debt"; when people have had less than their usual amounts of sleep over a number of days. The second type of fatigue state occurs after physical activity. Finally, there is mental fatigue, which follows prolonged effort on a demanding cognitive task. The physiological mechanisms underlying physical fatigue are quite well understood and include such processes as the build-up of waste products in the muscles and the efficiency with which oxygen can be supplied to all parts of the body. It is less clear why prolonged mental activity can make us feel physically tired, except that the brain is a physical organ and, like any other, requires energy to function. As anyone who has engaged in intense and prolonged mental effort can tell you, the feelings afterwards can be experienced as being as draining as having run a marathon. Few employers either need or expect people to expend that amount of physical effort at work but there often appears to be the expectation that people can sustain hard mental effort for 10 hours or more.

Sleep debt and sleep deprivation

No-one really knows why we need to spend about a third of our lives largely oblivious of the world around us, but it is so essential to life that our bodies have a built-in mechanism for making us sleep. Dieters can ignore the pangs of hunger, and very busy people may even forget to eat for a time, but sleepiness cannot be ignored. If we do try to ignore it, we are apt to lapse into involuntary "micro-sleeps" where we may be effectively unconscious for a few seconds at a time (Williams, Lubin, & Goodnow, 1959). The early studies of severe sleep deprivation (Patrick & Gilbert, 1896) had volunteers staying awake for 3–4 days. The researchers reported that it was almost impossible to keep them awake in the last 50 hours, and it was not safe to let them sit down on their own. In the 1960s at UCLA, four volunteers went for 8 days without sleep (Pasnau, Naitoh, Stier, & Kollar, 1968). After 4 days it appeared that only their shared determination to stay awake sustained them—they kept each other awake. Other studies have also shown that social stimulation and a shared sense of purpose is the most effective means to overcome the effects of sleep deprivation (Dinges, Orne, & Orne, 1984). This may help the staff of a busy hospital accident and emergency department, but doesn't bode well for the lone night security guard or radar operator. Sleep deprivation is so stressful that it is frequently used as a means of torture. Sleep deprivation combined with social isolation is associated with hallucinations and paranoid symptoms. The UCLA volunteers didn't suffer hallucinations, but, as happened with the Cambridge cockpit participants, there was a breakdown of conventional social behaviour.

There is only one cure for sleep deprivation and that is to go to sleep. Rats totally deprived of sleep die after about 14 days, but animals allowed to sleep towards the end of that time make a full recovery (Rechtschaffen, 1998). It is not clear why the rats die but Horne (2001) suggests that sleep serves more than one function and may change its emphasis with evolution. Small mammals have a need for constant activity to find the food to satisfy their high energy needs so sleep may be the only opportunity for physical rest. In humans bodily repair and recuperation can occur just as well if not better during relaxed wakefulness as during sleep. However, apart from when we are sleeping the cortex is constantly active, which means that sleep may be essential for the recovery of cerebral function. Recent brain-imaging studies show that the prefrontal cortex undergoes paricularly profound changes with sleep deprivation (Drummond et al., 2000; Thomas et al., 2000). Significantly, as Horne (2001) points out, the prefrontal cortex is one of the hardest working areas of the cortex during wakefulness. It is responsible for the performance of tasks involving verbal fluency and nonverbal planning (Horne, 1988) and "for directing and sustaining attention, inhibiting distraction, aspects of working memory, and flexible thinking" (p. 305). All these functions are impaired in sleep-deprived people (Harrison & Horne, 2000).

Sleep debt is far more common than total sleep deprivation and occurs when people have less sleep than they need. A night shift worker, for instance, may get only a few hours' disturbed sleep during the day, and sleepiness will build up over a week of shifts until the person is showing symptoms of sleep deprivation (Tilley & Wilkinson, 1982). It is true that people vary quite a lot in the amount of sleep they need and some individuals seem to be able to stay fit and healthy on very much less than what most of us consider to be essential. (See Empson, 1989 and Horne, 2001 for discussions that attempt to disentangle the folklore and wishful thinking from the facts.) Even so, most people need at least 6½ hours of sleep per night to remain alert during the day.

The study of sleep was revolutionized in the 1960s by the electro-encephalograph (EEG), which allowed the recording of electrical activity in the brain (see, e.g., Empson, 1989). EEG recordings show that sleep is a complex process and, according to the pattern of brain waves, consists of five distinct stages. Stage 1 sleep is light sleep and often alternates with brief periods of wakefulness and stage 4 is the deepest sleep, which is punctuated by periods of REM sleep, so called because it is associated with rapid eye movements. Throughout the night we shift up and down the stages, but there are usually four or five episodes of the deepest sleep per night. Horne (2001) cites evidence that deep sleep is associated with cerebral recovery, particularly in the prefrontal area. Night shift workers sleeping in the morning often report "less restful" sleep. Tilley and Wikinson (1982) recorded the sleep of such workers in their own homes. They found that the normal pattern of sleep was disrupted with more REM sleep, less deep sleep, and more awakenings. Hence, both the amount and quality of sleep was degraded.

Circadian rhythms

We are naturally diurnal creatures—active during the day and asleep at night. Very many bodily processes are linked to this wakefulness cycle. So for instance there is a 24-hour fluctuation in body temperature, which is lowest during the night. The body clocks or circadian rhythms are normally synchronized with the sleep/wake cycle. When they become desynchronized, as for instance when we fly across time zones, our bodies take between a week and a fortnight to adjust. Even when we get adequate sleep, the effects of jet lag can be severe. Night shifts also desynchronize circadian rhythms, and even if the person is on permanent night shifts, the body rarely adjusts completely because most people revert to normal daytime activities on their rest days. The most popular type of shift rotation system in the UK and the US also appears to be the most disruptive. "Slowly rotating" shift patterns, where workers spend a week, fortnight, or month on the night shift followed by similar periods on the early morning and afternoon/evening shifts, result in circadian rhythms always being "out of sync" with the sleep/wake cycles and an inability of such workers to adjust lifestyles to fit the pattern of any one shift. Wilkinson, Allison, Feeney, and Kaminska (1989) found that student nurses on a rotating shift showed the same pattern of decrements in performance from the first to the seventh night on the night shift throughout their course. Student nurses on a permanent night shift adjusted so that their performance levels were back to normal by the 90th night. However, this study also showed great individual variation in adjustment. Those who adjusted best were flexible in their sleep patterns (could easily sleep during the day) and showed a commitment to the changed lifestyle associated with the night shift (i.e., didn't try to fit the night shift round normal daytime activities). In fact, one of the factors that makes people least able to tolerate night shift work is if their circadian rhythms *do* adjust readily (Reinberg et al., 1984). When this happens it leads to the circadian rhythms being permanently desynchronized or they adjust rapidly back and forth so body processes are permanently destabilized.

Even being on call shortens and disrupts normal sleep patterns. Torsvall and Akerstedt (1988) studied the sleep patterns of ships' engineers who were briefly disturbed from sleep approximately twice a night and found the same pattern of more REM, less deep sleep, and more wakefulness, as had been found in shift workers sleeping in the morning. These effects occurred before any alarms and might be attributed to uneasiness and the anticipation of being disturbed during the night. Thus, even if junior hostital doctors can snatch a few hour's sleep on their 72-hour "long weekend" shift, the quality of that sleep is likely to be poor.

Although still being debated, there is increasing evidence that night shift work entails greater risk of heart disease than day work (Kawachi et al., 1995; Waterhouse, Folkard, & Minors, 1992). Gastrointestinal disorders are also common, possibly because people have to eat at hours that do not fit in with their body clocks (Bohle & Tilley, 1989; Rutenfrantz, Haider, & Koller, 1985). Personal problems and the disruption of family and social life are also more likely (Colligan & Rosa, 1990; Tepas et al., 1985).

Night shift work

Given all these negative effects, it might be thought that employers would avoid having night shifts unless it was absolutely necessary, as in the emergency services or in "continuous process" industries such as the power and chemical plants, which cannot be shut down every evening. Not so! Night shifts are being introduced to thousands, maybe millions more workers for reasons as trivial as allowing you and me to check our bank statements in the middle of the night. So if 24-hour work patterns are being introduced for purely economic reasons, what effects do sleep debt and deprivation and disruption to circadian rhythms have on work performance?

As already mentioned, it would be a mistake to put much faith in early lab studies, which showed quite spectacular failures to find any effects at all. Later EEG studies of the performance of sleep-deprived people show that brain activity is not normal except for the occasional micro-sleeps. Rested people sometimes exhibited slow waves indicative of stage 1 sleep but sleep-deprived participants showed this pattern at best. Physiologically, they were continuously on the edge of deep sleep even though their performance on various tasks seemed unaffected except for lapses (Kjellberg, 1977). These findings have been supported by more recent studies showing that the prefrontal cortex is particularly affected (Drummond et al., 2000; Thomas et al., 2000).

Out in the workplace the news is not good. Akerstedt (1988) attached portable EEGs to workers and found that sleepiness increased during the night shift and a quarter of all workers showed EEG patterns of sleep, sometimes as much as five times in the second half of the shift. When sleepiness cannot be indulged, periods of involuntary sleep are always preceded by a struggle to stay awake, which diverts attention from the task onto bodily sensations of discomfort. In fact, one of the effects common to most stressors is a narrowing of attention (Hockey, 1970), so, for instance, Bartlett's pilots attended to their altimeters but not their fuel gauges. Thus, performance is degraded even if the person stays awake. Vigilance tasks, which are very boring but depend on constant attention to detect infrequent signals, are particularly affected by fatigue (Horne & Pettitt, 1985; Horne & Wilkinson, 1985; Johnson & Naitoh, 1974). As already mentioned, Harrison and Horne (2000) found decrements in performance on many cognitive tasks after short-term sleep deprivation. Folkard and Monk (1979) concluded that the most carefully controlled studies do show that job performance is low over most of the night shift, and Folkard reiterated this point in a review of the evidence in 1996. Most sobering of all is research concerning safety and accidents on the night shift, which is summarized in Box 4.2.

Before leaving this topic, it has to be said that not all shift workers dislike their work patterns. Harrington (1978) estimated that 10% of workers liked their shift work pattern and a further 60% were able to tolerate it reasonably well. Some 10% even enjoyed night shift work. Given that increasing

---

BOX 4.2
Summary of research concerning safety and accidents on the night shift

Findings include the following:

- Train drivers go through red lights more often (Hildebrandt, Rohmert, & Rutenfranz, 1974).
- Rotating shift workers showed a 23% increase in risk of injury on the night shift as compared with the morning shift. This increased to 82% greater risk when only the more serious injuries were considered (Smith, Folkard, & Poole, 1994).
- "Unexplained" road traffic accidents peak between 4 and 6 am even though roads are quiet at that time (Horne & Rayner, 1999).
- Some studies have indicated that if commuting to work is added to commercial driving, road traffic accidents may be the single most important cause of fatalities at work (Harrison, Mandryk, & Fromer, 1993).

and . . .

- 28% of a sample of lorry drivers reported driving whilst tired (Adams-Guppy & Guppy, 2000).
- Stress-related sleep disturbances, loss of energy, and tiredness in airline pilots have been linked to air traffic incidents (Loewenthal et al., 2000).
- After one night in an A&E department, junior hospital doctors showed significant memory deficits when trying to relate patient's previous histories to current evidence (Dreary & Tait, 1987). After the long weekend shift junior hospital doctors switched to a "high risk" strategy and made twice as many prescribing errors on a simulated task (Hockey, Payne, & Rick, 1995).

Some people have argued that many serious disasters have occurred during the night or early in the morning when people have been working all night, e.g., Chernobyl, Three Mile Island, the US Challenger disasters (Mitler et al., 1988). However, this evidence of the detrimental effects of sleep loss are indirect and controversial—accidents and disasters occur during the day too.

---

numbers of people have no choice but to work shifts, it would be interesting to see if this level of acceptance still obtains. However, it is the night shift and others that disrupt sleep patterns, which cause most problems (Kogi, 1985).

Long working hours

Little considered in the research literature are the increasing numbers of commuters who are expected to be at their desks at 8 am or earlier and who cannot leave to travel home again until early to mid-evening. Especially in London and the South East of England, where house prices are high, such people may be forced to live at some distance from their place of work in order to secure more affordable accommodation. Given an inadequate and unreliable public transport system and a great deal of congestion on the roads, this long working day is often exacerbated by a long time spent commuting. Such people are likely to be suffering considerable sleep debt by the end of each week simply because they have to rise so early and get home so late. Rice (2000) reports that some respondents wrote of "sleep as the new luxury". Granted the problem may be partly self-imposed as the person could choose to live closer to work, but it is perhaps the 10- to 12-hour working day in between that could be the real stressor.

Guest et al. (1996) conducted a survey of UK workers and provided evidence that long working hours were not resented. Stevens et al. (2000) surveyed over 5000 managers worldwide and also found positive results. The number of hours worked voluntarily in excess of formal contracts was positively correlated with mental well-being and negatively correlated with sickness absence. However, it would be wrong to conclude from this that long hours were not having any adverse effect. The greater the number of excess hours worked the poorer the person's reported physical health became, and the strongest relationship was between excess hours and an unhealthy lifestyle. However, even taking account of factors such as little exercise, smoking, alcohol consumption, etc., excess hours still predicted reduced health levels. When the overtime was forced rather than voluntary, excess hours also correlated with poorer mental health and low organizational commitment. How are we to explain these somewhat contradictory findings? How can poorer physical health go hand in hand with fewer sickness absences? Why should long hours be associated with greater mental well-being? The answer may lie in the fact that if these people tended to be very work involved they would enjoy their jobs and would keep working even when they were physically ill. There were some indications that the excess hours were not always truly voluntary in that some were worked as a means of coping with the stress of an excessive workload. Other factors that may have contributed to excess hours include pressure from the organizational culture and a desire to further careers, but commitment to the organization does not seem to be a significant factor. Rice (2000) reports that of nearly 2000 UK managers, 78% say they want to spend more time with their families and partners and nearly 43% say that their loyalty is now to themselves and their careers rather than to their employers; 68% believe that "presenteeism" (being seen to be present at work but not being very productive) dominates the culture of work. Beyond about 40 hours a week, time spent working appears to become increasingly unproductive (Sparks, Faragher, & Cooper, 2001).

The Stevens et al. (2000) and Rice (2000) studies are both cross-sectional and rely solely on self-reports. It would have been good to have had some more objective measures of physical health over a period of time but the results are still quite striking. In Stevens et al.'s sample, the vast majority do not appear to be "disgruntled workers" since excess hours correlated positively with mental well-being. Further, a link between long working hours and heart disease has been known since the 1960s. Breslow and Buell (1960) found that workers in light industry who worked more than 48 hours a week had twice the risk of death from a heart attack than people who worked a maximum of 40 hours a week.

In an interesting study involving over 2000 US Army soldiers, Jex and Bliese (1999) looked at how self-efficacy might moderate the effects of long working hours and work overload. They found clear interaction effects between work hours and self-efficacy in predicting psychological strain and physical symptoms. Respondents with strong self-efficacy beliefs reacted less negatively to long hours and work overload than people with low self-efficacy. The authors suggest that self-efficacy may impact on stress reactions through the success of coping efforts. This echoes the discussion of mastery in the context of reversal theory. However, they note that we can't rule out the possibility that very high work demands could have a negative impact on people's beliefs about their competence and ability to cope. Indeed, the literature on burnout (see Schaufeli & Buunk, 1996 for a review) indicates that this is a very real possibility. Apart from emotional exhaustion, which is a feeling that one simply hasn't the resources to cope, one major symptom of burnout is a loss of feelings of personal accomplishment.

Whether or not people report that they have no objection to long working hours, it is clear from these studies that they are damaging to both individuals and organizations.

Workload, mental effort, and mental fatigue

In today's network society, many workers are "knowledge workers" and their jobs involve mental effort—monitoring and supervising complex systems, information processing, decision making, problem solving, and so on. Sustained complex cognitive effort can lead to physical fatigue but mental fatigue can also occur when people can no longer "think straight" or are overcome with reluctance to complete the task. Fatigue is a very slippery concept because it is a subjective feeling and may not reflect the amount of work done. Even with physical fatigue the main barriers to continued effort appear to be cognitive/psychological. People seem to decide that muscular work is no longer possible long before they reach their physical limits (Caldwell & Lyddan, 1971; Schwab, 1953). Anecdotal evidence also comes from marathon runners who will tell you about having to "go through the

pain barrier" in order to stay the course. Mental fatigue is even more difficult. Some authors report spending a whole day getting a single paragraph
or page "just right"—some people would find it difficult to describe such
activity as "hard work"!

Holding (1983) defines fatigue as "a subjective residue of feelings of bodily discomfort and *aversion to effort*" and provides evidence that the main
effect of fatigue is to prompt the person to use less effortful but more risky
strategies (in terms of likelihood of success), to perform the task. This leads
us to the concept of mental effort. This notion has been investigated in three
main areas of enquiry:

1   Individual differences in performance on cognitive tasks: Why do some
     people find tasks easy (low effort), whereas others find them difficult
     (high effort)?
2   Explaining mental workload: Why are complex cognitive tasks that are
     not physically demanding often experienced as exhausting?
3   Explaining the effects of stressors such as noise, sleep deprivation, etc. on
     performance: It is assumed that these stressors produce a state that is
     detrimental for optimum performance so the person has to exert com-
     pensatory, active, effortful responses to maintain levels of performance.

Individual differences

The nub of this issue is quite simple—people who are intellectually more able
than the rest of us tend to find complex cognitive tasks easier and so do more,
in less time, and to a higher standard. My favourite definition of intelligence
is "learning facility", i.e., the amount of time and effort we have to expend
to learn something new and the ease with which we can apply this learning
to new situations. The implications of this view are far more optimistic than
the old fixed, mainly inherited IQ argument (or rather arguments, since this
is one of the most bitterly contested areas in psychology). It implies that
with sufficient time, effort, and application most of us have the capacity to
achieve far more than we think we can. This does not mean that we all have
the potential to become brilliant mathematicians, rocket scientists, and brain
surgeons, etc. However, it may mean that we have underestimated the learning capacities of most of the population and also underestimated the extent to
which lack of learning opportunities is responsible for underperformance.
These points are demonstrated by the achievements of people with quite
severe intellectual handicaps (Howes, 1991) and the fact that once they have
learned to do a task, people with learning disabilities are as capable of
remembering it and performing it well as anyone with "normal intelligence".
Older workers, supposedly inflexible and less able to learn, can learn well
given sensitive and appropriate training courses (see Chapter 6).

But there is a snag—we don't have unlimited time to learn to perform tasks,
and especially when our work is constantly pitching us into new situations,

a limited ability to learn and apply our knowledge is a serious handicap. Even when we come to consider learned skills, which undoubtedly make the performance of complex tasks easier for the experts, the more able have an advantage since they can acquire the skills more quickly, leaving them more time to acquire yet more skills. When jobs and technology are changing so fast this too confers a considerable advantage. Small wonder, then, that one of the best general predictors of future job success, in almost any occupation, is performance on cognitive tests (Cook, 1998; Schmidt & Hunter, 1984).

Even the bare crux of the issue isn't as simple as this, of course. People's self-efficacy will deeply influence what they will attempt to learn and how much they will persevere before giving it all up as hopeless. Self-efficacy (Bandura, 1986, 1997) seems to have a great deal of potential explanatory power. However, it does not appear to be a general aspect of personality. Rather, belief in our ability to perform well and cope with stressors is specific to certain aspects of our functioning and limited to particular contexts. Thus, a manager may feel comfortable dealing with financial management but lack confidence in his or her interpersonal dealings with staff. He or she may be confident when leading staff meetings but consumed with anxiety when giving a presentation to the Board of Directors. Bandura (1986) defined self-efficacy as "people's judgements of their capabilities to organize and execute courses of action required to attain designated types of performances" (p. 395). Vrugt (1996) argues that the key to self-efficacy lies not so much in the possession of necessary skills for the job but in an attitude of mind, which leads the person to believe that mastery and success are possible. Bandura developed this theory of how attitudes to achievement influence performance in 1989. He proposed that a "mastery orientation" stems from believing that personal inadequacies can be remedied by means of training, practice, and personal effort, not because the person is necessarily supremely confident of success in any situation. Such people set themselves goals just beyond their current level of competence and strive to achieve them. If they fail or encounter setbacks, this is interpreted as stemming from a need for more self-development and effort, rather than from some fundamental and unchangeable personal deficiency. However, in general, such an outlook engenders success, which then breeds more success and increases the capacity to take on new challenges. An "outcome orientation" involves a more rigid and helpless view of one's capacities. Intelligence is often seen as fixed and incapable of change or development and yet is also perceived as the key to good performance. Such people can then conclude that since their own perceived abilities are modest, that they can do little to influence their own growth or better their performance. Such people avoid setting challenging goals and so do not experience the success that might increase their self-efficacy. Faced with a constant stream of change and therefore new challenges, people with an "outcome orientation" are likely to experience severe anxiety and work stress, which will further reduce their performance and experience of success.

In my previous incarnation as a developmental psychologist, I always found it heartbreaking to see so many lovely little kids effectively defeated before they even completed primary school. Many adults lack confidence as learners (see Chapter 6), but one of the great joys of teaching in higher education in recent years has been seeing so many mature students, who may have been "school failures", succeeding in degree courses and going on to great careers. Vrugt (1996) gives an account of how such things can be achieved both in education and in work and is optimistic about the extent to which people's fundamental self-evaluations can be changed for the better.

However, most organizations are not charitable-cum-educational bodies. They want people who can "hit the ground running" and make a difference to the "bottom line" immediately. They want people who are confident and competent already and usually have little interest in or understanding of, the need to nurture a "mastery orientation". For this reason, cognitive ability tests are being used increasingly in job selection and selection techniques are seen as vitally important parts of the solution to the strain generated by the pace and complexities of contemporary work. (This will be explored further in Chapter 7.) Here we need only note that since ability plays such an important role in the experience of mental effort and mental fatigue, it makes calculating the workloads of "knowledge workers" difficult. As we shall see, the person's level of experience and skill, and, by inference, self-efficacy, also influence how workloads are perceived.

Mental workload

Mental overload can occur for four main reasons:

1   Time pressures: Too much to do in the time available.
2   Task competition and switching: Having to do two or more things at once or very frequent switching between tasks.
3   Task complexity: When the task itself is highly complex, e.g., integrating and acting on information from many different sources.
4   Presence of other stressors: e.g., heat, noise, drugs, sleep deprivation etc.; attention gets focused on bodily discomfort so there is less "capacity" for the task.

In the 1950s and 1960s these effects were explained in terms of Broadbent's (1958) notion of limited channel capacity. People's ability to process information was said to be limited by the number of symbols that could be retained and manipulated in short-term memory. Since Miller's (1956) research seemed to indicate that the capacity of short-term memory was no more than about seven "chunks" of information, our information processing capacity appeared limited indeed. Too limited, in fact, to explain much of what we do in everyday life. My husband, for instance, can write complex computer programs while listening to the news on the radio. Skilled drivers can perform equally complex feats of intellect, judgement, decision making, and action. We can

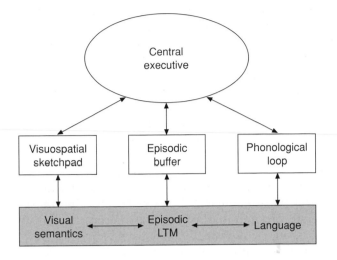

Figure 4.3 Baddeley and Hitch's model of a working memory: A further development
of the model. Reprinted from A. Baddeley (2000). The episodic buffer: A
new component of working memory. *Trends in Cognitive Sciences, 11*(4),
417–423. Reproduced with permission from Elsevier Science.

all listen to and comprehend what someone else says while processing a host
of nonverbal signals, making judgements about what we should say, and
actually composing our reply.

For these sorts of reasons, the concepts of short-term memory and limited
channel capacity have been replaced by that of working memory (Baddeley,
2000; Baddeley & Hitch, 1974), which is represented in Figure 4.3. This
model of memory suggests that there are two separate but related systems: a
memory system and the central executive that runs it. The memory system
includes multiple stores with different functions. The phonological loop can
hold speech-based information and could be termed the "inner voice". The
visuospatial sketchpad performs a similar function for visual information
and might be termed the "inner eye". The most recent addition to the model
is the episodic buffer, which is capable of integrating information from
visual, auditory, and long-term memory sources into coherent episodes or
episodic representations. The central executive appears to be an almost pure
attention system—it involves what we are consciously aware of at any one
time. Initial evidence for this theory comes from people's performance on
"double tasks". Baddeley and Hitch (1974) asked people to hold seven or
eight numbers in mind while performing another task such as sentence
comprehension and verbal reasoning. According to limited channel capacity
theory, remembering seven–eight numbers should fill short-term memory
and make the verbal reasoning task impossible to do. In fact, a few people
could remember the numbers without any loss of speed and accuracy in the
verbal reasoning task and most could perform well, provided they didn't
have to remember more than about three numbers.

The implications of this research are as follows:

1   If the task is within the limits of the memory system it will place few demands on the central executive, which can use its capacity for performing the verbal reasoning task.
2   Once the memory system becomes overloaded, the central executive has to bring in more resources to avoid losing the stored numbers.
3   If the memory component requires more attention from the central executive, fewer resources are available for the reasoning task; therefore there are more errors.

Over the years, a great deal more evidence has emerged to support the model (see Baddeley, 2000 for a summary). For our purposes, the main point is that the central executive has a limited capacity (in general we can only think one thought at once) but has the flexibility to direct its resources (we can move on to another thought or switch our attention to another task). However, tasks which exceed the capacity of the central executive will lead to poor performance and anxiety. Anyone who has learned to drive a car will have experienced this kind of information overload—there is simply too much to attend to and do all at once—and all but the most foolhardy experience considerable anxiety when they first get behind the wheel and attempt to negotiate the traffic.

So how come skilled drivers can control the car at speed, successfully negotiate all manner of hazards, *and* argue politics with a passenger? The answer lies in automization. Conscious control of attention and information processing is expensive in terms of mental effort and remember that the conscious mind—the central executive—has limited resources. However, the human brain has enormous resources at its disposal outside of consciousness. Take perception, for instance. The brain processes vast amounts of information in parallel but we are not consciously aware of this. All we experience are the results of all this activity; we see the scene before us, we hear the music, and so on. Therefore, the brain tries to relegate as much as possible to unconscious processing so that it becomes automatic and does not require expensive and effortful conscious processing.

This process of automization can be seen very clearly in the example of learning to drive. The early stages of learning are very effortful because all aspects of the task have to be consciously attended to, frequent switches of attention are needed, and the central executive is almost always grossly overloaded. Skilled driving is largely under automatic control and, unless a hazard arises, the driver can direct attention to daydreaming, listening to the radio, talking to passengers, etc. This is why most experienced drivers will have had the alarming experience of having been on "automatic pilot". When this happens you may have absolutely no recollection of how you traversed the last few miles of road. However, at some level you were aware of what you were doing because if a hazard had arisen you would have snapped your attention back to take avoiding action. The brain also has the capacity for pre-conscious processing of information (Dixon, 1981), which is available to the "searchlight" of the central executive if an environmental event or a thought triggers a switch of attention.

Coming back to the notion of mental effort and mental workload, then, we can see that it is conscious or strategic processing, using the central executive component of working memory, which has to be done serially (one thing at a time), which gives rise to the subjective feeling of effortfulness, strain, and fatigue. These subjective feelings are also accompanied by physiological changes, e.g., in heart rate, muscle tension, secretion of adrenalin, cortisol, etc. So mental effort also involves physical effort. Mulder (1986) reviews evidence of two types of mental effort. One is related to the difficulty of the task and the other is related to controlling the state of the person—mobilizing mental resources, speeded thinking, etc. He terms this latter type of effort compensatory control and suggests that "mental fatigue may best be characterised by the inability to continue to exert 'executive resource control' (compensatory control) in the face of task difficulty". (See Tattersall, 2000 for a recent review of workload research.)

We can now apply all these ideas to cognitively complex work. Take the work of a middle manager involving frequent switching of attention not just within one main task but within several different task domains, all of which require equal levels of skill, e.g., analysing accounts and financial planning, project management and problem solving, leadership, and interpersonal skill use, etc. Though with increasing experience and skill these disparate tasks will become easier (because, for instance, there may be overlearned routines for dealing with common problems), these sorts of tasks can never come fully under automatic control. Add to this constant interruptions from the telephone and colleagues, urgent e-mails, sudden crises, etc., and it is easy to see why 8–10 hours of constant executive resource control can lead to feelings of mental exhaustion. Interestingly, "emotional exhaustion" is a major component of the process known as burnout. In a recent review of theory and research on burnout, Schaufeli and Buunk (1996, p. 311) actually write, "Burnout is a metaphor that is commonly used to describe a state or process of mental exhaustion, similar to the smothering of a fire or the extinguishing of a candle." Burnout is often considered as the "final stage in a breakdown in adaptation that occurs from the long-term imbalance of demands and resources" and is particularly prevalent in those who begin their careers with high ideals and levels of enthusiasm. Chronic mental exhaustion is therefore something to be taken very seriously.

The psychosocial stressor of workplace bullying

Until quite recently bullying seems to have been considered as something that took place in school playgrounds rather than in adult workplaces. Brodsky appears to have done the first study of workplace bullying in 1976, and although much work was conducted in Northern European countries (Sweden, Norway, Finland, Germany) very little of this was published in English until Zapf and Leymann edited an issue of *The European Journal of Work and Organizational Psychology* devoted to this topic in 1996. Since then, workplace bullying has become a major issue in societies as a whole and not just in academic and professional research (see, e.g., Farquarson, 1999). In the UK there is a raft of employment legislation designed to protect workers from bullying and harrassment. Under the Health and Safety at Work Act 1974, employers have a duty to provide a healthy environment and the Sex Discrimination Act 1975, the Race Relations Act 1976, and the Disability Discrimination Act 1995 make harassment on the grounds of gender, race, and disability illegal. The Public Order Act 1994 and the Protection from Harassment Act 1997 make abuse or harassment criminal offences, whereas the Employment Rights Act 1996 covers victimization, injuries to health, and unfair and wrongful or constructive dismissal. Despite all this the Institute of Personnel Development estimates that one in eight workers is bullied. In March 1999 Industrial Relations Services (IRS) published a survey of 157 employers in the manufacturing, services, and public sectors with more than 650,000 staff between them. They found that only 40% of these organizations were dealing with reported bullying in that specific policies were rare, even though 11% had faced industrial tribunals because of harassment. The IRS claims that in most cases "Workers have little confidence their complaints will be taken seriously."

Part of the problem may be that compared with, say, racial harassment, defining what counts as bullying is difficult. Randall (1997) subsumes a huge range of activities under the term bullying—racial and sexual harassment, discrimination, sabotaging the victim's career, physical assault, and even murder. This makes the whole concept very muddled. Leymann (1996) and most of the European researchers prefer the term "mobbing" because "bullying" has too many connotations of physical attack, whereas workplace bullying is often very subtle and is characterized by destructive communication and socially isolating the victim. In the workplace, the emphasis is on the deliberate attempt to cause psychological harm to individuals. An Institute of Personnel Study (see Ishmael, 1999 for details) found that only 8% of respondents reported any physical contact. There is also some debate about whether sexual or racial harassment should also be considered as a form of bullying. Bullying may be motivated by racism, and sexual harassment may develop into bullying if the victim rejects advances or reacts "badly". Randall (1997) reports a case of bullying because a group of lesbians objected to working with a "straight woman". So the boundaries are blurred but bullying does seem to be a process somewhat distinct from racial and sexual harassment. Leymann (1996, p. 168) defines bullying/mobbing as "Psychological terror . . . [which] involves hostile and unethical communication which is directed in a systematic way by one or a few individuals towards one individual, who due to mobbing is pushed into a helpless and defensive position." As opposed to the inevitable conflicts which occur between people in the workplace, the major characteristics of bullying are its frequency (hostile acts occur at least once a week and often daily) and its prolonged duration (at least 6 months). I will confine this discussion to the phenomena of Leymann's research—psychological terror and destructive communication—rather than physical threat or racial and sexual harassment. I will also use the term bullying rather than mobbing because it has gained currency in the UK and is more likely to be understood by managers.

Bullying is hard to investigate for a number of reasons. Ishmael (1999) found that bullied staff are very reluctant to report incidents or make formal complaints. Leymann also shows that one of the worst aspects of bullying is managements' tendency to blame the victim rather than the bully. Bullies are often in positions of power over victims and present themselves in the role of "good manager" to higher management. There is often a general failure in higher management to distinguish between "strong/firm" management and bullying, which also favours the bully.

The subtlety and deviousness of much bullying behaviour also make it difficult to recognize. Many tactics deliberately put the victim in a bad light. A boss might give the victim an impossible workload or withhold vital information so that it is easy to criticize the person's quality of work. Further, bullying activities are often a normal part of social interaction. For instance, workmates often make insulting remarks to each other or play practical jokes that can be accepted with good humour if there is no malicious intent behind them. Similarly, people often get left off the list of invitations to a staff outing and most people gossip about work colleagues. However, when such incidents occur in a bullying context, they take on a sinister meaning—they become deliberate attempts to humiliate, ridicule, and socially isolate the person. Moreover, individually, each bullying incident may be quite trivial, but it is the sheer cumulative volume of incidents that causes the psychological damage. As a result, victims may be afraid to complain or seek help. "They deliberately left me out of the Christmas party" may sound like a childish complaint. Finally, the victim's psychological distress might lead him or her to break down and behave in inappropriate ways. Consequently, victims are often branded as people with personality disorders.

Much of the evidence for the processes involved in bullying comes from case studies and court cases and is necessarily retrospective and often biased to the victim's version of events. It is virtually impossible, if only for ethical reasons, to observe or investigate the process as it occurs. However, the accumulated evidence from case studies is now allowing us to piece together the typical course of events and understand more of the processes involved.

One such case study is provided by Leymann (1996) and is summarized in Case study 4.1. This case illustrates the course of bullying over time. Most cases of bullying begin with some incident or triggering situation that creates conflict. In Eve's case, it was the cooks' misinterpretation of management's change of policy. In other cases the appointment of a new

Case study 4.1:   Eve: A case study in workplace bullying

Eve was appointed as a canteen supervisor in a large prison and had a staff of six long-standing female cooks. Management instructed Eve to institute a new regime of economy and healthier food, but did not tell the six cooks of the change in policy, and did not propose to arrange or fund any training for them. The cooks' style of cooking was completely at odds with the new policy and they believed it was all Eve's idea. They interpreted her attempts to get them to change their cooking methods as a personal criticism of their skills. They began to gossip about her, to criticize her personality and home life, and to ignore her instructions. Soon conflict and hostility and negative communication was the norm. In response to the cooks' behaviour Eve made repeated requests to management for a job description, but this was interpreted by management as insubordination. The cooks believed that this meant that management was 'on their side' and that it legitimized their harrassment. Frequent heated arguments ensued and one particularly virulent incident was overheard by a manager. Eve was summoned to an interview, severely criticized, and ordered to see a psychiatrist, who diagnosed a personality disorder. Eve was ordered to take sick leave and after 2 years was dismissed from her job. Several years later she had still been unable to find another.

manager or colleague can create conflict with existing workers; if, for instance, a preferred person is not appointed or the new manager has very different values and styles from the previous one. It is not clear how simple conflict becomes full-scale bullying but in Eve's case it was exacerbated by management failures and possibly because she was just one person against an established group of six who all shared the same grievance.

Leymann calls the next stage "mobbing and stigmatization". Behaviours that are not necessarily aggressive on their own, if repeated frequently enough over a long period, become changed in meaning. The underlying intent is to "get at" a person and cause him or her psychological harm. The conflict escalates and leads to verbal abuse, public criticisms, and furious arguments. At this point, says Leymann, senior management and personnel may become involved and frequently add to the victim's distress. As in Eve's case, management may misjudge the situation and accept the prejudices that led to the bullying and blame the victim's personality rather than the bully or environmental factors (e.g., the unannounced change of policy). As a result, management and bullies confirm each other's behaviour and there is a desire to "get rid of the problem", i.e., the victim. This often leads to serious violations of employment law and employees' rights. The final stage is expulsion. The victim becomes physically ill or psychologically disturbed and leaves or is forced to leave. Management often disbelieve the victim's story and don't investigate the triggering social events. Victims are branded as substandard workers or managers. Unjust suspension or dismissal or incorrect medical diagnoses are common. Victims are categorized as suffering from paranoia, manic depression, or personality disorders. Leymann takes the view that prolonged misery at work causes personality disturbance rather than vice versa. Evidence for this view comes from many case studies where the victims had very successful careers before the incident that triggered the bullying. Many victims suffer from post-traumatic stress disorder as a result of their suffering and, as has been mentioned in Chapter 1, Leymann (1996) estimates that as much as 20% of the annual suicide rate in Sweden has workplace bullying in the background.

Leymann (1996) believes that there is no evidence that there is a "victim personality" which predisposes some people to be bullied. He analysed 800 case studies and found that two main factors led to bullying in the workplace. The first was poorly organized production and/or working methods and the second was inadequate or uninterested management. Bullying is often more common in the public than the private sector—nurses, teachers, and social workers are particularly prone to being bullied. Nursing can be used as an example of Leymann's two factors at work. Hospitals have two separate hierarchies—one relating to doctors and the other to nurses. Nurses may thus have two "bosses", which creates the potential for conflict. Staffing shortages and poor organization of work may lead to work overload and unclear lines of authority. Whether the potential conflicts are resolved or escalate to full-scale bullying may depend more on the group dynamics (e.g., a supportive and cohesive team) rather than management's training in conflict prevention and solution. Impoverished management may join in or exacerbate bullying as in Eve's case or may even initiate the bullying so as to drive people out of their jobs and avoid having to make redundancy payments. Management denial that a conflict exists allows it to escalate by its inaction.

The causes of bullying: A continuum?

Randall (1997) argues that childhood bullies become adult bullies and that vicious personalities are almost always involved. However, what emerges from Leymann's analysis is that bullying is not necessarily the result of people with malicious or pathological personalities. The cooks in Eve's case felt that they had a legitimate grievance against her. Their initial reactions were probably more understandable "mutterings of discontent". Only as the situation deteriorated and Eve also reacted badly, did behaviours on both sides become more extreme until full-scale bullying was in progress.

I personally believe that the initiation of bullying can stem from a number of causes forming a continuum from deliberate maliciousness to behaviour that looks like and is interpreted as bullying, but where there is no actual intent to create harm.

Maliciousness

Here the bully sets out on a deliberate and systematic campaign to make the person's life a misery or to seriously damage the person's career. These sorts of instances may well involve people with pathological personality traits and the aim is often to "get rid" of an unwanted colleague by whatever unscrupulous means present themselves. As already mentioned, bosses may impose impossible workloads and targets and then publicly criticize and humiliate victims when these are not met. Alternatively, the victim may be given no work at all or forced to complete only mundane, low status tasks. Sometimes the tactics can be quite ingenious. Randall quotes a case of "Jodie", an assistant administrative officer who, unbeknown to her, had a line manager who had wanted someone else appointed in her place. The line manager seemed very sympathetic and friendly, encouraged Jodie to take time off for family responsibilities and to take up training opportunities. Then at her first appraisal, the line manager reported that she had too much time off, required excessive instruction, was not fully work committed, and was overly familiar. As a result, Jodie felt she had to leave her job. This case is a good example of the difficulty of defining bullying. There was no overtly hostile behaviour involved until the end—no long months of misery for Jodie—but the eventual betrayal must have been traumatic and the end result was the same—the line manager "got rid" of her. Such "behind the scenes" machinations must be all too common in working life, especially when people in authority feel threatened by bright, "up-coming" staff, but is this really bullying as we have defined it? I don't think it is.

"Abnormal" cultures

Sometimes the official or unofficial culture of an organization leads otherwise quite decent people into totally unacceptable behaviour. The most obvious example of this is when "macho" management practices prevail. Leadership that is excessively task oriented with no consideration for the person can lead to authoritarian and aggressive ways of dealing with people, which is then experienced as bullying. Though some such managers may consciously enjoy the exercise of their coercive power, others may simply believe this is "the way it should be done around here". Neither is such behaviour confined to management. In many shop-floor contexts there may develop a culture of putting new recruits through "initiation rites", which may involve considerable torment in the form of practical jokes, derogatory language, and general indignities. If people can endure this with humour then they are accepted into the group. If not, they are rejected and bullying ensues.

Vansina (1998) believes that there is increasing pressure on managers to transform human beings into a sheer economic resource and this dehumanizing stance has negative effects on both individuals and organizations. The human resources perspective implies a failure to attempt to understand employees as human beings. For instance, in one Danish company there was an attempt to introduce autonomous work teams but only Trades Union representatives were consulted. In this case "participation" was no more than a vehicle to overcome resistance to the change and the project soon ran into great difficulties. Vansina argues that people need time and space to "worry through" the implications of change, express their fears for the future, and "grieve" for the loss of valued aspects of their jobs and old certainties.

When management treats employees as an amorphous mass to be coerced into conformity to company policies, then the whole process starts to look like bullying. Such cultures can get out of hand, especially when exacerbated by incipient racism and other forms of discrimination. The most notoriously enduring example of an abnormal culture leading ordinary people to appalling extremes of behaviour is the Nazi Holocaust, but there have been many other horrific examples in recent years. "Abnormal" cultures exist in organizations too, and though they may be less extreme they are equally difficult to resist. An abnormal culture usually originates at the top. If top management passes down impossible demands and requires the next level of management to achieve them or suffer themselves, bullying cascades down the hierarchy. It may be that the currently common ethos of treating the general workforce as expendable, and expecting "core" workers to give themselves "body and soul", encourages bullying behaviour.

Escalation of conflict

As in the Eve case study, if conflict is allowed to escalate unchecked and unresolved, then full-scale bullying is the likely result. The "eventual bullies" may not have deliberately set out to destroy another human being but as feelings of bitterness and hatred grow this becomes increasingly likely. In the maelstrom of negative emotion almost anything short of physical harm may seem justified to the bullies. Less commonly, it doesn't stop there and physical assault also occurs.

"Unintentional" bullying

I am not sure whether this type of behaviour is distinguishable from that manifest in "abnormal" cultures as already discussed. However, it is possible that people who have no malicious intent to do harm, and do wish to treat their staff with consideration and respect, can behave like bullies because of pressures beyond their control. Possible examples may include managers who hit unpredictable peaks in workload and have to interrupt their staff's normal work and make unreasonable demands to get the job done. Similar effects may be found when cost cutting means there are insufficient staff for the workload so the climate encourages things like people being forced to do overtime and being refused permission to take holidays when they want. Requests to attend to pressing personal matters such as a sick child or family bereavement may be greeted with irritation. Constantly pressured management and staff can lead to a dangerous situation when tempers get frayed and angry outbursts become more likely. People may regret their actions and apologize later but the "bullying stamp down" has already occured. Working mothers may be particularly at risk of this kind of bullying since they may be reluctant to attend evening meetings and childless staff may become resentful about the extra demands placed upon them by "family-friendly" policies.

The experience of being bullied in such circumstances can be exacerbated if people impute such behaviour as steming from deliberate malicious intent, rather than intolerable work pressures and factors beyond the person's control. I come from a sector that relies on goodwill and many hours of unofficial overtime to function effectively. Staff brought in from outside this culture are often shocked and appalled by the amount of work that is demanded in addition to the official contract hours. In this situation, conflict becomes likely.

It is an interesting question whether "unintentional bullies" have any place in the workplace if they are insensitive to the effect they are having on the people around them but I wonder whether the increase of concern with and reported bullying at work has anything to do with the general intensification of work and the changes employees are expected to embrace, often without adequate consultation, preparation, or training. A recent article in *The Lecturer* (October, 2000) reports on a survey of 249 lecturers in further and higher education by Christina Savva, which gives some evidence for this view. In a 3-year follow-up study, she found that 6 out of 10 of her respondents reported being bullied. "As pressure on the system grows, so does the experience of bullying. Financial pressures, funding cuts and organizational change were cited time and again as reasons for the bullying they encountered" (p. 3). Although poor management skills and lack of training were given as reasons by nearly half and over a third of respondents respectively, insecurity (77%), work pressure (35%), and inability to handle the work (48%) were also viewed as most likely causes of bullying.

Whatever the causes of bullying, the outcome is always the same—a great deal of trauma and suffering for those on the receiving end. Luckily, the problem of bullying is now being accepted and there are a number of Trades Union hotlines and internet websites offering help and advice for sufferers. Those who feel they are being bullied are advised to keep a diary of incidents since any one instance alone may appear trivial—it is the cumulative, daily expectation of misery and humiliation that saps the spirit and does so much damage to individuals and their organizations.

As it happens, this brings us nicely to the issue of control over work. Often, one of the hallmarks of bullying is that the victim is reduced to a state of helplessness and the only control the person can take is to exit the organization.

The concept of control over work as a mechanism for ameliorating stress

Control over one's work is generally seen as a good thing and the most promising means to reduce stress reactions. It is also widely believed to lead to greater commitment, personal responsibility, and job satisfaction. Worker "empowerment" is reflected in many work practices such as quality circles and autonomous work groups as well as being an important component of the concept of transformational leadership (see Chapter 6). The notion of control is included in several theories of work motivation. In Hackman and Oldham's (1980) model, autonomy is one of the core job dimensions. Another very influential theory is Karasek's demand-control theory. In its original form (Karasek, 1979), this argues that the primary sources of work stress lie within two job dimensions: psychological job demands and job decision latitude, or the amount of control the person has over work. When demands are high and decision latitude is low this is likely to lead to job strain. Such jobs might include a schoolteacher who must comply with the demands of the National Curriculum and a host of regulations and policies. When demands are high but decision latitude is also high then this is likely to lead to job involvement and low job strain. Such jobs were said to include university teachers and other professionals but these examples may be much less appropriate today. The least stressful jobs are those which are low on demands and high on decision latitude. The work of forest rangers was given as an example of these types of jobs. Karasek provided evidence from demographic studies that serious illness such as heart disease was more prevalent in his high strain occupations.

In 1990 Karasek and Theorell presented an expanded model, which proposed an interaction between stress and learning, as in the diagram in Figure 4.4. In active jobs (high demands, high decision lattitude) there is a positive spiral because learning inhibits strain. The person is empowered to find new ways of performing their work and more effective forms of coping. This in turn creates a sense of mastery and confidence, which helps people to cope with strain and frees them up to take on new challenges, to learn more, and cope yet more effectively, which promotes mastery and so on. In passive jobs (high demands but low decision latitude) a negative spiral occurs. The accumulation of strain in such jobs means that people are less able to take on new challenges and so they learn fewer coping strategies. This results in a loss of a sense of mastery, which inhibits the person's ability to cope with strain, which leads to more strain and so on.

Johnson and Hall (1988) introduced a further elaboration of the model by introducing a third dimension—work support. This is the extent to which workers enjoy social and emotional support from colleagues, the amount of help and trust between workers and supervisors and colleagues, etc. The most unfavourable jobs are those imposing high demands with little decision latitude and the person is "isolated" with little work support. The

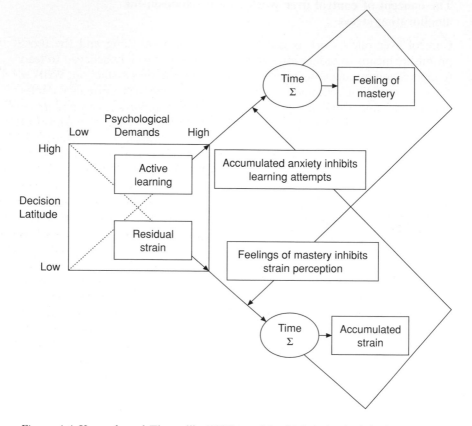

Figure 4.4 Karasek and Theorell's (1990) model of job latitude, job demands, and learning. Copyright © 1990 by Robert Karasek. Reprinted with permission of Basic Books, a member of Perseus Books, LLC.

schoolteacher alone in front of a class all day, or dealing individually with parents, governors, and local industry, might come into this category. As we have seen, teaching is one of the highest risk occupations for job strain in the UK. On the other hand, effective teams of professionals where demands are high but autonomy is also high would be expected to show least strain.

In evaluating this model commentators tend to praise its apparent simplicity (Jones, Bright, Searle, & Cooper, 1998; Le Blanc, de Jonge, & Schaufeli, 2000), which in theory should commend it to managers as a basis for redesigning jobs to promote health. However, it has been criticized on conceptual grounds and on the operationalization and measurement of its basic concepts. For instance, Ganster (1989) said that Karasek's measure of decision latitude related to the length of training needed to do a job and did not measure job control directly at all. Le Blanc et al. (2000, p. 164) conclude that although the epidemiological data gives most support to the model, "the assumption that the combination of psychological demands, decision latitude and social support involves stronger responses (such as more physical symptoms or more work motivation) is often not supported". More often, the three components are found to have separate impacts on outcomes rather than operating in combination. A review by Terry and Jimmieson (1999) also finds little support for the theory. Jones, Bright, et al. (1998) believe that the popularity of the model has led to the neglect of a range of other psychosocial factors that might affect health. Furthermore, there has been a disappointing lack of impact on the design of jobs. If anything, the evidence is that, despite the empowerment rhetoric, jobs are becoming more constrained.

Refining the concept of control

Ganster (1989) argued that control is a multi-dimensional concept with at least seven different components. These are:

- Amount of discretion over work tasks (how the work is done).
- Pacing (to what extent can the worker control the level of effort, take breaks at will, etc.).
- Scheduling (can the worker control what is done, when, and in what order?).
- Control of the physical environment (heat, light, ventilation, organization of the workspace, etc.).
- Decision making (to what extent can people participate in decisions which govern their work?).
- Social interaction (to what extent is the person free to interact with colleagues?).
- Job mobility (can the person get another job easily?).

Ganster argues that variations in any one aspect could interact with or compensate for any of the others. For instance, if things become really unbearable, knowing that one can always go to where "the grass is greener" might be a significant moderator of stress reactions. Feeling completely trapped in a job one hates may be particularly aversive. Ganster also argues that person variables such as locus of control (feeling that you are personally in control of your own life vs. feeling controlled by external forces) may also be important in determining the relationships between control and positive outcomes.

This conceptual analysis of control and the processes that may underlie its moderating effects on perceived stress and ill-health are taken further by Frese (1989; Frese & Zapf, 1994) using the framework of action theory. Action theory has a long history (Hacker, Skell, & Straub, 1968) but not much has been published in English, and outside Europe it has had little impact on managerial thinking. It is essentially a goal-oriented approach to explaining motivation. Work behaviour is goal driven and actions are carried out in the service of goals. Control therefore equals the freedom to flexibly pursue goals.

Frese (1989) elaborates on the dimensions that make up the concept of control. As well as those proposed by Ganster, there are also levels of control. There is objective control—the extent to which the person really can control work tasks—and subjective control—the extent to which the person perceives they can control work tasks. Mismatches between the two have already been discussed in the context of self-efficacy (see p. 118). In addition, person variables such as knowledge, skills, and experience determine the extent to which people can realize the potential for control. There is also the distinction between "actual" and "hoped for" control. Outcomes can be particularly poor when the person perceives little control and doesn't expect this to improve. Individual versus collective control is another dimension. Is the person directly involved with decision making or is this done via intermediaries such as Trades Union representatives? Social support from co-workers can wrest control where none was previously available. So for instance, a threatened "walk-out" of all workers can reduce the speed of an assembly line, or a more experienced worker can assist a less experienced one and make an otherwise daunting task possible. In September 2000 there was a most striking example of collective control in the "blockade" of oil refineries and the disruption to travel by convoys of slow lorries and tractors across Europe. These protestors against high fuel prices brought sophisticated Western societies to a standstill. This may also be an example of the distinction between objective and subjective control. For several years hauliers and farmers in the UK have been making their views known to the UK Government about the damage being done to their industries by high fuel prices. The impression one gains from the media reports of the time is that they previously felt powerless to effect significant change, but were somewhat overwhelmed by their ability to bring transport across the country to a halt.

Frese also postulates the mechanisms possibly underlying the effects of control upon adverse reactions to stressors. To explain these I will take an example from my own work, presented in Case study 4.2. While you are reading this, it would be a good idea to substitute any problematical aspect of your own work in order to consolidate your understanding.

According to Frese, these control mechanisms can act as moderators of stress reactions at every point in Lazarus and Folkman's (1984) model of the stress process. The objective stressor can be reduced, the appraisal process can be modified, short-term stress reactions can be controlled, and long-term ill-health can be prevented. Effective control can also enable the use of strategies so that objective stressors are not even perceived as threatening. For instance, in my case study, the appointment of an additional administrative assistant at the start could have prevented the escalation of workload.

Frese's rich framework allows us to make conceptual hypotheses that other models have difficulty in handling. A small selection follows:

Case study 4.2:   Frese's mechanisms in academic life

Let us take the bane of most academics' lives: too much administration. Given that in my own study (Doyle, 1998; Doyle & Hind, 1998), 77% of university teachers cited this as having increased significantly over the previous 5 years, most did not regard it as the most important part of their jobs as teachers, scholars, and researchers, and many reported having to spend evenings and weekends "doing the real work" that administration had squeezed out of their normal work time, we can be reasonably sure that this is an objective stressor.

The direct effects of control include direct stressor reduction. These include delegating or sharing administrative tasks, employing more administrative staff, and so on. However, this strategy can only succeed if one has the means to control resources: colleagues who can be called upon to assist, money to employ extra people, etc. People can also use persistence in coping. I may reorganize my filing system, streamline procedures, devise systems, prioritize, use time management, and so on. However, these strategies can only work if I can control the way work is done and the scheduling of tasks.

The indirect effects of control include fitting the environment to the person. Thus I can make representations to superiors to improve systems or provide more resources. However, this strategy can only be used if I have control over access to those with the power to effect changes. And of course exit is the ultimate exercise of control but only if there are job alternatives.

- If task complexity/work overload is too high then the potential for control cannot be realized.
- Inappropriate coping strategies (e.g., misperceiving control) make a stressful situation particularly aversive.
- Perceiving a stressor as aversive stimulates the need for control.
- Control can facilitate an adjustment reaction to stressors (e.g., I don't mind spending the best part of 3 days a week on administration so long as I can work at home on the aspects of the job that I love, even if this includes working in the evenings and at weekends; similar sentiments were expressed by the senior women academics in my 1998 study).

Strengths of this model include the fact that responsibility for adverse stress reactions can be placed firmly at the door of objective stressors. Thus, people alone cannot be blamed for their inadequacies and employers have a duty to provide a work environment more conducive to health. In fact, Briner's (1996) critique of the general failure of stress management interventions is largely predicted by this model. The new, nonautomatic coping strategies promulgated on stress management courses are not those people favour in crisis situations. Under high stress conditions people favour highly automated actions instead of intellectual strategy formulations. Non-automatic "problematic" coping strategies are the ones most likely to be tapped in questionnaire studies and could be an additional source of strain when people feel guilty about finding themselves unable to implement them in the "real world" following stress management courses! In a particularly well-designed study of three different stress management training interventions in a UK Government agency, Whatmore, Cartwright, and Cooper (1999) found that a structured, physical exercise programme followed for 45 minutes twice a week, gave the most beneficial outcomes after 3 months, but most of these had dissipated after 6 months. (The other stress management programmes involved personal stress awareness—information about sources of stress for the individual and action plans to combat these; and cognitive restructuring—identifying and combating irrational beliefs, which contribute to the negative appraisal of stressors.) Resource limitations meant that there was little contact with participants after the initial training workshops that launched the three types of stress management programmes, so it was not clear how many participants were persevering with their programmes. However, there was a very high drop-out rate from the excercise programme—42% had given up after 3 months. Similar effects were found by Harma, Ilmarinen, Knauth, Rutenfranz, and Hanninen (1988), who evaluated the effects of a physical exercise programme on nurses working variable shifts. The exercise group improved on a number of dimensions of physical health and reported less fatigue over the whole shift cycle than a control group. However, there was a high drop-out rate, an increase in fatigue on the evening shift after exercise, and there was no decrease in reported psychological distress. In fact, the difficulty of trying to fit the exercise programme into a busy professional and personal schedule may have increased stress for some participants.

In fact, Frese's (1989) model predicts what coping strategies are likely to be successful in what situations and suggests different types of intervention for particular circumstances. For instance, in the administration example (in Case study 4.2), better systems, prioritization, and time management can be effective first lines of defence to stem escalating workloads. However, if these are not sufficient, other measures are needed such as a general reduction in the amount of imposed paperwork or the appointment of more support staff. Some stress management interventions are less appropriate. Spending time on meditation, relaxation, or physical exercise may help my blood pressure but doesn't solve the underlying problem or clear the backlog.

However, one concept this model has the potential to highlight is that of self-efficacy. Schaubroeck and Merritt (1997) believe that self-efficacy plays a key role in mediating the effectiveness of control in ameliorating stress reactions. They found that in two samples of participants (health professionals and an occupationally diverse group) there were interactions between demands, control, and self-efficacy in predicting blood pressure. For people who experience a high level of mastery in their jobs, increasing their control over work could well reduce the negative effects of stress. However, for people with low self-efficacy, increasing their control could well lead to higher levels of strain than before. These authors conclude that, "If self-efficacy had not been included as a moderator in these analyses, this would be yet another study that failed to support the demands–control [Karasek] interaction" (p. 750). Schaubroeck and Merritt suggest that it is as important for organizations to increase people's sense of self-efficacy and mastery as it is for them to redesign jobs for greater control. Jex and Bliese (1999) also stress the importance of fostering self-efficacy. Vrugt (1996) provides an interesting discussion of the factors that influence perceived self-efficacy and effective training programmes to promote it. However, we might note here that downsizing and delayering programmes often forced greater responsibility on people without regard to their feelings and certainly without self-efficacy training. In those circumstances, it is hardly surprising that stress levels rose and "empowerment" has often been more a matter of rhetoric than reality. On the other hand, "delusions of self-efficacy" where people overestimate their ability to solve possibly insoluble problems could also be dangerous, as has been mentioned on p. 118.

Hockey (1993, 1997, 2000) integrates many of the ideas covered in this chapter into a model of mental effort and stress reactions. He takes the idea that mental effort involves the intervention of a "supervisory conscious controller" when work outputs do not match quality control standards. This process involves increased effort to maintain standards and is expensive in terms of energy and cognitive resources. Those who can control their work have a choice of strategies. They can increase their effort to maintain goals and performance; they can adjust and reduce their goals to maintain adequate performance; they can change their task strategy so that there is less effort but more risk of unsuccessful outcomes; or they can maximize personal comfort at the expense of work goals (though fear of the sack may make this strategy rare at work). If the person has no control over work, then the strategies may be limited to grim determination to "hang on", taking sick leave, or exiting. Hockey stresses that coping has costs for the individual. Increased effort, for instance, is only effective if the situation is capable of change, increased effort will resolve the problems, and the person has the necessary resources to produce high effort. If intolerable demands continue indefinitely and increased effort does not solve problems, then the outcomes can be the worst of all worlds. The person becomes exhausted and suffers various psychological and physical symptoms, personal life and relationships suffer, and work performance deteriorates.

What is worrying about today's work climate is that people are often expected to maintain high levels of conscious effort all the time, in terms of the amount and complexity of work, their relationships with colleagues, their adjustments to major changes, and their capacity for innovation. (In some companies workers are discouraged from chatting to their colleagues because this is "wasting time"!) Demands for continuous improvement, frequent change, the endless challenging of old methods and the search for new ways of doing things, and lifelong learning imply that *very little* ever comes under full "automatic" control. What's more, we expect this sort of activity to be sustained for up to 10 or more hours per day on maybe 6 or 7 days per week. Demanding this level of *physical* labour from workers today, in a Western society, would probably be greeted with criminal prosecution. However, because many (most?) employers do not appear to understand what they are asking, equivalent levels of mental labour are being routinely expected. (And we have not even covered "emotional labour"—an additional cost incurred by people who must deal with the public either by presenting an unruffled, corporate stance whatever their feelings or by maintaining emotional stability during continuous exposure to human inadequacy and suffering (see, e.g., Briner, 1999a). Small wonder, then, that professional workers tend to be at the top of Rose's (2000) "misery index", and burnout is particularly prevalent in "human care" professions (Shaufeli & Buunk, 1996).

There are already some signs that this situation cannot be sustained indefinitely. Nixon (2000) reports on City of London workers who have "downsized" their careers after "relentless routines of 14 hour days and working weekends". He suggests that many such workers see their careers as a 5-year "tour of duty", to accumulate enough money to move on to a more balanced lifestyle before they "burn out". This may be all right for high earners who will then have other options at 35, but it offers little hope for those with more modest salaries and fewer options. Are today's employers any more ethical than the Victorian mine-masters and factory owners? Or have those of us on the receiving end just become "soft"?

Summary

In this chapter I have argued that workplace "stress" is a complex matter since so many factors mediate between objective stressors and adverse reactions to them. These include appraisal of threatening events and situations, the person's ability, skills, and personality, the person's feelings of self-efficacy, and job factors such as control over work. This may lead to some employers refusing to accept that the work conditions they create can have an adverse impact on people's health and well-being even though the financial costs of work-related ill-health are high and appear to be rising. I believe that the theories and evidence reviewed in this chapter support the following conclusions:

1   The physiological mechanisms linking reactions to stressors with ill-health are well understood. Just as there is now no argument about asbestos or coal dust causing lung disease, so it is clear that adverse working conditions such as shift work, long working hours, excessive workloads, and workplace bullying can lead to ill-health.

2   Although person characteristics such as neuroticism and self-efficacy may be implicated in people's reactions to stressors, there is also evidence that prolonged exposure to adverse working conditions can negatively

impact on and change person characteristics. So intolerable work demands may lower people's self-efficacy and in some cases may lead to post-traumatic stress disorder and clinical depression. Such factors as person-ality characteristics also become less important in mediating reactions when "objective" stressors such as prolonged sleep deprivation, excessive mental workload, job insecurity in financial downturns, and bullying are severe. Even those who "thrive on chaos" may not be able to main-tain their performance and well-being indefinitely, and some workplace stressors are impossible for any human being to cope with adequately.

3   Control over one's work can ameliorate the effects of stressors but only up to a point. Control also has costs for the person and active coping strategies over long periods of time may not protect the person from ill-health. Stress management interventions in the face of intolerable pressures may actually make things worse.

4   Working conditions nowadays can seem as inhumane as any 19th-century factory or mine because many jobs involve so much coercion and surveillance or excessive mental workload demands that they are unmanageable for most people. These conditions assault psychological health, which can lead to physical illness.

5   The long-term consequences of all this for the health of nations already seem to be revealing themselves.

Perhaps the questions in Exercise 4.1 will assist you to make up your own minds.

EXERCISE 4.1
Work and stress

1   Taking any aspect of your work that causes you problems and makes you feel bad, analyse the causes, consequences, and pos-sible solutions using any of the theoretical frameworks covered in this chapter.

2   Speak to friends about their experiences of job stress. What stressors have they encountered, what coping strategies have they used, were these successful and if not why not; how have these work pressures impacted on their personal lives and vice versa? Conduct an analysis as in the previous exercise and write a "dummy" report that might be presented to management in a real consultancy situation.

3   Take your own job and redesign it to promote greater well-being and effectiveness, using the theory and research covered in this chapter.

4   Design a stress audit process for your organization. How would you gather initial information, what methods would you use to assess the health and well-being of the workforce, and how would you seek to identify major stressors?

Suggested further reading

Chmiel, N. (1998). *Jobs, technology and people*. London: Routledge.

Hockey, G. R. J. (Ed.). (1983). *Stress, fatigue and human performance*. Chichester, UK: Wiley.

Klandermans, B., & van Vuuren, T. (Eds.). (1999). Job insecurity. *European Journal of Work and Organizational Psychology, 8* (whole No. 2).

Kroemer, K. H. E., & Grandjean, E. (2000). *Fitting the task to the human* (5th ed.) London: Taylor & Francis.

Monk, T. H., & Folkard, S. (1992). *Making shiftwork tolerable*. London: Taylor & Francis.

Moore-Ede, M. (1993). *The 24 hour society: The risks, costs and challenges of a world that never stops*. London: Piatkus.

Parker, S., & Wall, T. (1998) *Job and work design: Organizing work to promote well-being and effectiveness*. London: Sage.

Schabracq, M. J., Winnubst, J. A. M., & Cooper, C. L. (Eds.). (1996). *Handbook of work and health psychology*. Chichester, UK: Wiley.

Sparks, K., Faragher, B., & Cooper, C.L. (2001). Well-being and occupational health in the 21st century workplace. *Journal of Occupational and Organizational Psychology, 74,* 489–509.

5 The ironies of automation and other disasters: Human–machine interaction

> Whoever uses machines does all his work like a machine. He who does his work like a machine grows a heart like a machine, and he who carries the heart of a machine in his breast loses his simplicity. He who has lost his simplicity becomes unsure in the strivings of his soul.
>
> Chuang-tzu, 4th century BC, quoted in Morgan, 1986

> To err is human but to really foul things up you need a computer
>
> "Techie" joke

My students often groan when I tell them that this semester's timetable is to include human–machine interaction (HMI). I find this reaction puzzling because for every second of every day we are surrounded by machines of one sort or another. We live and work in buildings that are effectively machines in their own right. (If you doubt this, just wait until the plumbing decides to cease cooperating!) We use machines constantly, and frequently find the experience frustrating. The burnt dinner, the wrong programme recorded on the video, the car's lights left on and the battery flattened, the computer crash and work lost—the list of what can go wrong in our inter-actions with machines is endless. So wouldn't you think that the study of the design of machines to make them better fitted to our human capacities and limitations would be an interesting prospect?

Maybe many of us secretly harbour similar attitudes to machines as the Chinese sage quoted at the beginning of this chapter. Most of us tend to take it for granted when machines work properly and how they work is their affair—we neither know nor care. When they break down (which they always do eventually), we are filled with rage at our impotence in the face of this inanimate lump resolutely refusing to do our bidding. Somehow it is an affront to our human dignity—"Why won't this wretched computer do what I say!" It is also true that many people's working lives make them feel as if they are just parts of the machinery. A data entry clerk whose every keystroke, pause, and mistake is recorded by the computer, or the machine operator spending 8 hours loading and unloading a metal press, could be forgiven for thinking that the natural order of things had been overturned.

Machines are supposed to serve us, aren't they? Of course, it isn't quite as simple as this but it may help to explain my students' reactions. Maybe only an engineer can truly love the innards of a machine.

However, there is a much darker side to human–machine interaction compelling us to achieve greater understanding. When things go wrong in hazardous technologies such as chemicals manufacture, nuclear power generation, or complex transport systems such as airlines, the results can be catastrophic. At 8.11 am on 5 October 1999, two commuter trains collided almost head-on, at an estimated impact speed of over 100 mph, just outside Paddington station in London. A devastating fire, which exceeded temperatures in a crematorium, then engulfed the two trains and added to the horror and loss of life. Soon after the crash, newspapers were predicting a death toll of a 100 or more but in the event it was "only" 33 killed, but with hundreds injured, some very seriously. As human-made disasters go, this is far from the worst. In 1972 a dam gave way at Buffalo Creek in West Virginia, USA and the resulting flood left 125 people dead and 5000 homeless. Symptoms of anxiety and depression were still evident in the survivors 14 years later (Green et al., 1990a; Green, Lindy, Grace, Gleser, & Leonard, 1990b). In Bhopal, India in 1984 an escape of toxic gas from a chemical plant killed at least 2500 people and injured over 200,000 more. But perhaps the worst technological disaster so far was the Chernobyl nuclear power plant explosion in 1986. Although this was a conventional, and not a nuclear, explosion a large amount of radioactive material was released into the atmosphere and scattered over much of the former Soviet Union and Northern Europe. Three hundred power plant and fire fighting personnel were admitted to hospital and 31 had died by the end of 1986. However, the human and environmental consequences are still in progress. An estimated 150,000 people's thyroid glands were seriously affected by radiation (*Los Angeles Times*, 27 March 1989), and a report issued soon after the disaster (Collier & Davies, 1986) estimated that as many as 40,000 people might eventually die as a direct consequence of exposure to radiation.

Unfortunately, there is no consensus on the numbers of people killed or made seriously ill by the accident. Sources close to the nuclear energy industry accuse anti-nuclear organizations of gross exaggeration of the effects on people's health and they also blame this mis-information campaign for increasing the negative psychological effects on people then living in the area by raising their fears. For instance, Adams Atomic Engines Inc. (1996) claim that up to 200,000 women decided on abortion because of fears that their foetuses may have been damaged by radiation yet, the article says, there is no evidence of birth defects caused by radiation after the accident. Anti-nuclear groups (e.g., Chernobyl No More, 2002) report that in 1994, the official death toll directly related to Chernobyl was estimated at 125,000 in the Ukraine alone but this included many older people who might have died anyway in the decade following the accident. The same source reports that among the clean-up workers, the rate of the incidence of tumours has increased 2 times and 5.7 times in those most exposed to radiation and only 18% of this group are now considered to be in good health. The Ukraine's Health Ministry (BBC News, 2000) estimates that 3.5 million people became ill as a result of the contamination and that the incidence of some cancers has increased as much as 10 times the national average. First Deputy Health Minister Olga Bobylyova claimed that death rates in the clean-up workers were rising because they were ageing faster than normal. Even Adams Atomic Engines Inc. admits that on the "best available data" there have been 500–600 excess cases of thyroid cancer, mostly in children, in the areas most affected and that some of the surviving emergency workers still need periodic treatment for radiation-related diseases. The UK's BBC, usually regarded as a trustworthy source of information, reported that according to a group representing the emergency workers involved, 15,000 were killed and 50,000 disabled in the clean-up.

If the death toll is disputed, the social and economic costs seem clear. By 1994, 200,000 people had been evacuated and resettled, some without belongings or other resources. Chernobyl No More (2002) estimates that 1.7 million people were directly affected and 2.4 million live on contaminated land. They also say that about 7% of the Ukraine's GDP goes on continuing clean-up operations but that 20% would be needed for a thorough job.

Whatever the disputes, this was some considerable disaster. Obviously it is important to investigate the causes of such accidents, especially the human contribution to them, in order to try to prevent them happening again. What prompts me to single out the Paddington rail crash here is the way the accident was reported in the media. The immediate cause appears to have been that one of the train drivers passed through a red stop signal and so moved onto the line occupied by the express speeding from the opposite direction. Only a decade or so ago this might have been considered sufficient explanation—inattentive, negligent, incompetent train driver ignores red signal and causes crash; end of story. In fact, after only 30 hours, the media, in consultation with various experts, had supplied a catalogue of other possible contributory causes of the disaster including: Government failure to privatize the rail network sensibly; senior management's failures to emphasize safety and spend money redesigning confusing track and signal layouts; inadequate technical safety systems; and unsafe carriage design. The role of the train driver in passing two danger signals and one red stop signal was immediately acknowledged as only the end point in a long chain of inadequacy. In the eyes of the media, Paddington was a disaster waiting to happen.

As I write, all these contributory causes are matters of informed speculation, yet to be confirmed by a formal enquiry. However, the important point is that there is an appreciation of a "systems approach" to explanation— accidents and disasters in complex human–machine systems (such as rail transport) do not have a single cause and many of their causes have their origins as "accidents waiting to happen", buried, and therefore not fully appreciated or noticed, in the system. Even if only a few of these factors were really implicated in causing the Paddington crash, it still illustrates the complexity of accidents and disasters and the fact that operator errors may be only the last link in a very long chain. Certainly, other disaster enquiries, e.g., the Piper Alpha oil platform fire, the Chernobyl nuclear disaster, the *Herald of Free Enterprise* ferry sinking, all display this pattern of multiple causes. Moreover, this essential message is getting through to the public consciousness so we do not automatically look to blame "human error" or faulty technology.

One person who has done a great deal both to construct and disseminate this message is James Reason, and I have drawn heavily on his work in writing this chapter. His recent book, *Managing the Risks of Organizational Accidents*, published in 1997, is important, fascinating, and scholarly but lucid. (Read it; buy it; it's worth it!)

In this chapter I am going to focus on macro-ergonomics, that is, the general issues that arise in human–machine interaction, rather than micro-ergonomics—the principles that should inform design for the safe and easy use of machines. I will be exploring the multi-causality of technological accidents with a view to understanding and preventing them. Surely that is worth more than a groan?

And now for something completely different . . .

At the end of an extended news bulletin largely devoted to the tragedy at Paddington, the BBC announced the broadcast of a comedy programme immediately following on, as "some light relief". I feel the need to do likewise.

What do you think of the following copy, which originally appeared in the computing press?

BOX 5.1
The ultimate notebook unveiled in Birmingham

By Ken Bresman

The Luddite 2000, unveiled in Birmingham yesterday, has been proclaimed a quantum leap in mobile data capture and retrieval.

The compact A5-sized PDA is a pen-based system that boasts a user-friendly Handwriting Recognition algorithm. It allows Random Access data storage, as well as accepting graphics input.

The full-size "display" is modelled on the familiar "ring-bound" format found on other PDAs, but is far more sophisticated. The surface has an opaque, paper-like texture that allows for very natural "feel" when using the pen.

The pen itself is a step up from the usual stylus. For a start, it actually transfers a microscopic film of graphite onto the display area, allowing immediate visual feedback of the pen movements. Deleting can be accomplished in two ways; either by moving the pen up and down over the offending words until they are obliterated, or by reversing the pen and passing the "eraser" end over the words.

Information and images produced on the device can be easily transferred to other people by "tearing out" the relevant "pages" and posting them on a convenient mail system.

The notebook (£0.60) and pen (£0.12) are available separately from most good newsagents.

Have you smelled a rat yet? Read the last line again. This amazing machine is just an everyday paper notebook and pencil. Sorry! But this example illustrates two very important points:

1 Our notions of a "machine" are very stereotyped—especially today. We think of hi-tech gizmos and banks of incomprehensible displays and controls, when in reality, we are surrounded with very effective "low-tech" machines—and some of these are not as simple as we assume. Forests are demolished to produce writing paper (which we know), and huge technology is devoted to creating a pen or pencil (which we may not know so well). A flush toilet, for instance, is actually a very sophisticated machine that depends on an extensive public infrastructure and is thus quite unsuited to many developing countries. Similarly, pen and paper is a sophisticated technology—civilizations were built on variations of them and the wisdom and knowledge of societies were thus passed on to contemporaries and later generations in a far more reliable form than had been possible via oral transmission. The invention of the printing press speeded the process up and made the transmission of knowledge more affordable. Information and communications technology is similarly transforming our lives—just as the printing press did.

2 Even the simplest "machine" forms part of a system—you, the user, and the technology. But the system does not end there. Paper and pencil are useless unless there is a written language system and people trained to use it. This implies a society committed to educating the young, and people with ideas and information that seem worth writing about. From this perspective the human–pen–paper system is complex indeed. A driver and a car, a pilot and an aircraft, or an operator and a nuclear power plant are even more complex examples but the same principles apply. History, politics, economics, culture, and a host of other macro factors are involved. However, as we shall see, with technologies such as power and chemical plants, the human–machine system is itself highly complex too. Not much can go wrong when you commit pen to paper except for crossings-out and inkblots. Similar technological mistakes in a nuclear power plant invite catastrophe because a seemingly trivial error has unforseen consequences as it "ripples" through the system creating more

and bigger effects as it goes. (A similar effect can occur when you submit written material to an audience and thus to the wider system, and then almost anything can happen—Karl Marx's *The Communist Manifesto* is one example, Gregor Mendel's paper on inheritance in peas is another, Darwin's *Origin of Species* yet another, and this list could be extended indefinitely.)

The allocation of function

Traditionally, machines enhanced people's capacities, thus helping to reduce human limitations. Digging a field with your bare hands is not effective; using a spade is somewhat better; but a tractor and plough transforms the farmer into a superhuman. Within this simple example we also find an issue very close to the heart of HMI—what jobs should we give to humans and which to machines? It is an issue that arises whenever human machine systems are being designed, and the technical term for referring to it is the "allocation of function". With some systems the decision appears straightforward. Ploughs are manifestly better at digging up earth than human hands; humans are manifestly better at driving tractors than ploughs; and so we have a happy solution ensuring that they each do what they do best and the system is maximally efficient. However, with the advent of "smart" machines and the increasing costs of human labour (especially in developed countries), allocation decisions are usually far more difficult.

Very crudely speaking, there are two schools of thought on the matter.

According to the "Machine School", humans are expensive, unreliable, prone to error, puny, unpredictable, intractable, truculent, and limited in many other ways. Thus, they should be replaced by machines whenever possible.

According to the "Human School", humans are flexible, creative problem solvers capable of high level planning, fault diagnosis, and correction, and who can make good evaluations of the evidence. They are the designers of the systems and unique controllers of them. Thus, humans have skills no existing machine can match and should be retained whenever possible.

Of course, there is truth in both "camps", so many commentators believe that the best combination is a system where human limitations are compensated for by machines so that full human potential can be realized. That represents my opinion. The trick is to achieve the right balance and to avoid a blinkered mentality. I once read a fascinating anecdote about engineering students, the source of which I cannot now locate. No matter, it is too good a story to leave out. The engineering students were asked to allocate functions in an exercise involving a human–robot manufacturing system. One group was doing wonderfully well and suddenly went downhill. Asked why they had suddenly decided to give a difficult task to the robot and a mundane task to the human instead of vice versa as originally planned, they said that to do otherwise was a "waste of the robot's capabilities". No wonder many people hate machines!

There seems little reason to doubt that the "machine school" is currently in the ascendant and has been for several years. We see it in fly-by-wire aircraft, pilotless jets, and attempts to automate driving. Meanwhile human experts' knowledge and experience is being incorporated into computer programs known as expert systems, which can then replace the humans; experienced operators are being replaced with automatic computer systems or being reduced to "machine minders", and there appears to be a hope that teachers and trainers can be similarly dispensed with via the internet, etc. The justifications vary (and very often have merit), but the main motive is economic—cost cutting to save on wage bills. Not all these "economies" are conspicuously successful. In 1999, the British public were treated to scenes of chaos as hundreds of people hoping to go on holiday abroad queued in the rain to get passports from a system overwhelmed by (predictable?) demand. Changes to the law requiring children to have their own passports undoubtedly exacerbated the uproar because it prompted a great increase in passport applications, but the root problem seems to have been not enough employees and a new computer system that was not properly up and running. This is not an isolated example. As the lead story in *Computing* (2000), "Labour delivers its plan to end IT disasters", points out, the UK Government has been associated with a string of such "fiascos". The article claims that the private sector has as many problems, but is better able to suppress news of adverse consequences. Maybe it is not such a good idea to sack the people before you're sure that the computer system can deliver.

But let's not be negative. Good automated or semiautomated systems greatly improve efficiency and effectiveness and, especially in hazardous industries, undoubtedly prevent accidents and save lives. In the latter case, we have an imbalance of evidence since we know a great deal about the incidents the technology has contributed to, but much less about those it has prevented. One exception to this general rule occurred on Sunday, 20 August 2000. Two airliners carrying 700 passengers and crew were heading on a collision course as they flew over London on their approach to Heathrow airport. Air traffic controllers did not notice until a computer-activated "conflict alarm" sounded. By that time the aircraft were just hundreds of feet apart, but an ATC ordered one to take emergency action to avoid a crash. But for the computerized alarm, there would have been devastation in central London (*Metro London* newspaper, 2000). Like the machines in our homes, good technology is taken for granted until it goes wrong. In addition, we should not underestimate the difficulty of making the right decisions regarding the allocation of function.

Fitts lists

In the 1950s Fitts (1951) produced a list to specify the relative strengths and weaknesses of humans versus machines, which could then be used to guide allocation of function decisions. Over the years, several ergonomists

EXERCISE 5.1
Allocation of function

Think of the capabilities of machines and write brief descriptions (e.g., greater accuracy and precision). Then do likewise for humans (e.g., ability to sort/categorize information). Then think of any task with which you are familiar that you currently do manually. Try to split the task into its component parts. Using your list as a guide, decide which aspects you could automate and which you would still have to do yourself.

(e.g., Chapanis, 1965; Kamali, Moodie, & Salvendy, 1982; Nof, Knight, & Salvendy, 1980; Singleton, 1969) have elaborated on the original list and the term Fitts lists has come to be used to refer to them all. Before reading further you may like to conduct your own allocation of function exercise as described in Exercise 5.1.

A case study in the allocation of function

As an example, one of the tasks I would love to automate is filing (oh, for a paperless office!). I could use machines to scan in documents and store the information in directories. My job would be to feed the scanning machine, decide on a suitable title and directory, and perform periodic deletions and reorganization of the stored information. Notice, though, that such a system would probably not save me much time as regards the actual filing. All this categorization and feeding the scanning machine would probably take me half the morning every day given the average amount of paper arriving in my in tray. But provided my directories were accurate and well organized, I could retrieve information much more efficiently and it would clear my office of filing cabinets and mounds of paper. I might be able to do what the management gurus used to recommend—never handle the same piece of paper twice. (Such electronic filing systems are already being considered (and used) by solicitors, many of whom currently have expensive temperature- and humidity-controlled warehouses full of legal documents, which must be kept for many years.)

It is true that if all documents were sent electronically, the scanning process would be unnecessary, but as yet, people still use paper and even if they don't, there are umpteen software incompatibility problems to contend with. To make matters worse, if some authorities are to be believed, the transience of many electronic storage systems is quite frightening. Messages recorded on papyrus have lasted 2000 years. Magnetic discs degrade after about 5 to 10 years and that's taking no account of whether the hardware and software to read them is still available (Tyler, 2000). Changes in paper and ink technology since the 1860s means that paper-based material decays after about

100 years but that will do for me and my filing system. This example illustrates some of the problems of automation. I still have the major task—deciding where to put what and actually getting it into the right place so I can find it again—and it may even take me longer initially than the manual system. Five years may seem a long time in the commercial world but how much company history and expertise can be lost if your "electronic memory" lasts only for that time? Maybe there is something to be said for the old-fashioned filing clerk and paper-based systems.

Early Fitts lists tended to be quite positive about people's capacities. Fitts (1951), for instance, stressed the cognitive superiority of humans over machines. Humans can perceive patterns, improvise and use flexible procedures, store large amounts of information, exercise judgement, and so on. Machines excel at routine repetitive tasks, fast and accurate computation, and doing several things at once. Whereas machines are subject to sudden breakdown, humans are capable of "graceful degradation" (!). Chapanis (1965) also emphasized human flexibility, particularly as regards handling unexpected events, and finding alternative ways of doing things when the primary means fail. However, as machines became "smarter", the Fitts lists began to sound more like woeful catalogues of human inadequacy. For instance, Nof et al. (1980), comparing humans and robots, list people as inferior on the ability to access information stored in memory, to store and integrate large amounts of information, and to communicate quickly, precisely, and accurately. Even the much-vaunted human ability to learn and adapt is challenged—it is easier to re-program a robot!

Although in engineering terms this negative view of human ability is undoubtedly true, one wonders where, within this scheme, people like Nof categorize their own abilities to design systems and to write programs! Fitts lists have always suffered from vagueness and imprecision, particularly where they relate to cognitive functions. It is rather ironic, therefore, that intelligent systems are increasingly being driven by advances in our understanding of human cognition. For instance, known principles of human memory organization are being used to inform the design of expert systems, and programs mimicking neural networks are being used to "teach" robots quality control. In 1965, Chapanis was calling for ergonomists to be included in more design teams. Twenty years later, Price (1985) was making exactly the same plea. Perhaps, as Price argues, one reason for this lack of progress is that the human side of the allocation equation can never be as precise as the engineering solutions and therefore Fitts lists, and their ilk, are not particularly useful in the design process.

In the field of human–computer interaction (HCI) things were rather different. Booth (1989) puts human needs at the centre of HCI research.

Areas of study in HCI are:

- Matching models: How to match the system's model of the task to that of the user's model. Concentrates on *how* users perform the task.

- At task level: How to fulfil users' information needs and allow users the freedom to perform the task in the way they wish. Concentrates on the overall nature of the task and the user's information needs.
- Interactional hardware and software: How does the user communicate with the system and how does the system communicate with the user? How does the nature of the system affect the quality of this interaction?
- Design and development: Making the design process *user* centred rather than *system* centred—fitting the system to user needs, not just a system that can do the job.
- Organizational impact: The impact new systems have on individuals, groups, and the organization. Concentrates on design and implementation techniques to prevent problems such as job de-skilling and conflict between groups.

HMI versus HCI

At this point the reader may be somewhat confused about the distinction between HMI and HCI. As more and more machines come under computerized control and computers are machines, surely there can't be much difference between the two? A good question! I think the difference lies in the history. HMI grew out of a concern during World War II that machines should be more fitted to human use. At that time most machines were mechanical and much work involved perceptual-motor skills, so HMI focused on human physical capacities. So for instance, you get the famous example of "Cranfield Man" (1969) where the design of a lathe required the human operator to be four feet tall with an arm span of eight feet in order to use it comfortably. Also, as control rooms in power and chemical plants became more complex, the problem of how to arrange all the displays and controls such that the controllers could use them easily and safely became acute. As late as 1987, Woods catalogued a series of inadequacies in control rooms where ergonomics had been ignored in the design. Displays that could not be read and controls that could not be reached were common. The Three Mile Island incident in 1979, when a nuclear reactor came close to meltdown, also highlighted the problems. In the first 2 minutes of the emergency, 1800 different error messages and alarms were activated, making it almost impossible to diagnose the original fault.

HCI originated later and didn't really take off until the personal computer revolution in the 1980s, when computers were first used widely by non-specialists. The nature of the machine also forced an emphasis on cognitive processes from the start and this was aided by the development of cognitive science (see, e.g., Aitkenhead & Slack, 1985), which occurred around the same time. (Cognitive science is concerned with modelling human cognition in computer programs and with developing artificial intelligence systems.) HCI is also much concerned with the individual computer user rather than with the operation of large industrial systems that may include many different kinds of machines. Thus, the emphases of HMI and HCI were different. Although HCI has to be a subclass of HMI, albeit a major one, they are still relatively distinct. This can be seen very clearly simply by a quick look at commonly used textbooks. Oborne's (1995) book, *Ergonomics at Work*, shares little content with Preece et al.'s (1994) and Dix, Finley, Abourd, and Beale's (1998) textbooks on HCI. Even so, it is making less and less sense to distinguish between HMI and HCI, since most ergonomists nowadays have to concern themselves with HCI. Ships and power plants are now more likely to be controlled by a computer interface than banks of dials and controls, but that doesn't mean that all the problems have been solved. Now questions include how to help the operator integrate information over time, as it may be presented on different screens, or how to avoid deluging the person with unwanted information as he or she gets lost in the system trying to find the information that *is* wanted. Neither is the question of the allocation of function solved. So . . .

Back to the allocation of function

Two possible models are given in Figure 5.1. In the first model the expert system gathers the information from the environment (e.g., the industrial process), generates solutions such as how to maintain maximum efficiency, and monitors the success of its "decisions". In this model the process is largely automatic and the computer controls it via its expert system. The human contribution is very little more than monitoring the process—"machine minding". His or her job is to check that all is going well and to look out for any developing faults. The only reason the human is there at all is to diagnose and correct such faults. In the "smartest" systems the human is dispensed with altogether.

The second model is quite different, and the computer provides the human with the information to support his or her decision making. The human decides on the goal, e.g., to increase production with maximum efficiency, and the expert system provides necessary information, perhaps presented in a display integrating information from several sources. The program might also suggest alternative courses of action and run predicted sequences of events so that the human can select which is likely to be most successful. The system can also aid in fault diagnosis by running primary fault sequences so the human can understand what has gone wrong. The system might also generate hypotheses about the cause of the fault and possible corrective actions. In this system, the machine's capacity to integrate information from many sources rapidly and accurately complements the human's ability to evaluate, test hypotheses, and exercise judgement.

Which system is better depends on circumstances and the purposes of the system but all too often the first is chosen to cut the human operator out of the control loop, either in an attempt to prevent human error or as a cost-cutting exercise. As we shall see, selection of the first model when designing

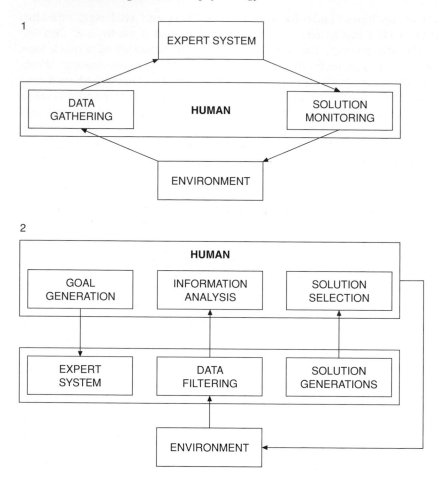

Figure 5.1 Two models of human–machine systems. Source: Woods (1986).

a system is not always a wise choice, not least because the valuable skills of the human are lost. As a recent example, Schwartz (1992, cited in Oborne, 1995) reported the case of an astronaut who retrieved a "lost" satellite by grabbing an antenna when all the automatic mechanical options had failed. Be that as it may, ergonomists such as Oborne (1995) are calling for person-centred ergonomics. Human beings should not be regarded as a part of the machinery and subordinate to the system, but as unique controllers of the system. Oborne, Branton, Leal, Shipley, and Stewart (1993) list four important features of the situation that can influence the process of HMI and which need to be taken into account in the design process: The human operator should be seen as purposive, information seeking, uncertainty reducing, and responsible. Operators are " 'doers' who are continually active, computing . . . the implications of the incoming information and the nature of their responses to it" (Oborne, 1995, p. 12). Thus, the designer needs to understand their purposes and their need for anticipation and prediction. Operators need to be able to "see" the results of their actions before they are carried out. The task also needs to be interesting since boredom leads to inattention and errors. The human need for control and autonomy helps to reduce the uncertainties of outcomes. An operator who is "out of the control loop" may not understand the current state of the system, which makes fault diagnosis and correction an almost superhuman task (Reason, 1990). As regards responsibility and trust, the human operator must be able to trust the incoming information. Too many false alarms lead to the "cry wolf" scenario in which real emergencies are ignored. Too much trust can also lead to disaster. In 1958 the human pilots in the Everglades air crash attended to a false alarm "fault", while the automatic pilot flew the plane into the ground.

Chmiel (1998) makes similar points and adds that the "static" allocation of function in advance takes no account of variations in workload, changes in environment, and the state of the individual. For instance, air traffic controllers may prefer to guide the landings of aircraft individually when workload is light but when the traffic is heavy they may switch to more "automated" modes of stacking and orderly descent, since this reduces the load on working memory (Sperandio, 1978). Similarly, pilots may prefer to use automatic landing systems at difficult airports or in poor visibility. Hancock and Scallen (1996) advocate "dynamic" allocation when decisions can be made during the execution of tasks. For instance, the technology may detect when the operator is getting overloaded or bored and switch allocation to automatic control. Interesting that the technology gets to decide!

In poorly designed systems this sharing of control can be disastrous. Reason (1997) reports the case of Airbus Industrie, who wanted to increase their market share of commercial jet aircraft by producing more automated cockpits—known as the "glass cockpit". Automation proved highly successful when the aircraft was flying horizontally; aids such as an electronic map showing the aircraft's position relative to the ground topography, and displays of weather en route were extremely useful. The problems arose in vertical flight—take-off, landing, and other changes in altitude. These involve complex processes of elevator control and engine thrust inputs, which make these manoeuvres the most vulnerable stages of the flight. The Airbus Flight Management System (FMS) offered at least five ways (modes) for changing altitude, each with different levels of automation. Some modes were selected by the pilot, and some were triggered automatically. "Hard protection" was also built into the system so that if certain design tolerances were exceeded (e.g., flying too fast or too slow) the system would automatically over-ride the pilot's actions. These features had at least two unfortunate consequences. First, pilots often became confused about which mode was active at any time, and, second, they found it difficult to predict what would happen next. To keep ahead, pilots would have to know:

- Which mode they were currently in.
- How FMS selects new modes.
- Which mode it would select next.

And all this had to be done just when the pilot's mental workload was greatest and the flight was at its most dangerous stages—take-off and landing! Further, if the aircraft's speed dropped below a critical value when coming into land the program would automatically switch to "go around" mode and abort the landing. All this resulted in unexpected flight deviations and pilots fighting (sometimes unsuccessfully) to regain control of the aircraft. Weiner (1989) coined the phrase "clumsy automation" to describe such confusing and potentially dangerous systems. They are not confined to the unfortunate Airbus Industrie, which at the time was pioneering highly innovative systems. Hansman (1995, reported in Hughes, 1995) analysed 184 cases of mode confusion incidents that occurred between 1990 and 1994, some of which involved fatal accidents. By far the most common causes of these incidents (45%) were pilots entering data incorrectly into the FMS or entering it into the wrong mode. In 20% of the incidents the FMS executed an unexpected mode change or failed to perform an expected one. In 12% of the incidents the FMS itself failed. All this prompted Reason (1997, p. 46) to propose another irony of automation to add to Bainbridge's original (1987) list: "in their efforts to compensate for the unreliability of human performance, the designers of automated control systems have unwittingly created opportunities for new error types that can be even more serious than those they were seeking to avoid".

Even the well-known "switching to manual" can also have its problems. Studies of car automatic cruise control systems, designed to ease the driver's workload, have shown that they tend to fail badly in emergencies. Drivers were unable to regain manual control in time to avoid collisions (Stanton, Young, & McCaulder, 1998). Thankfully these studies took place in driving simulators, but the authors recommend a "back to the drawing board" approach before such systems are let loose on our roads.

It seems that the allocation of function issue is set to run and run.

A "diversion" to modern manufacturing technology and practices

Lest it be thought that this book is overly concerned with the work of managers, technical experts, and professionals, let us go to the factory floor because here, too, there is scope for a revolution in the nature of work. Chmiel (1998) makes the point that even in industrial processes, there has been a big shift from mainly manual work to jobs involving mental effort:

monitoring, supervisory control, information processing, problem solving, and so on. Parker and Wall (1996, 1998) detail the trends in modern manufacturing that have set the fuse for this potential revolution. Most are driven by the need for economic survival. Global competition means that there is a need for cost cutting (i.e., wages) and high quality goods that are responsive to market demands and get there ahead of the competition. The ability to meet these demands is facilitated by new technologies and production methods.

Advanced manufacturing technology

The first trend is in advanced manufacturing technology (AMT). Though the machines vary greatly according to their function, these systems have in common that they are computer based/controlled and are linked to materials handling devices and robots. Their advantages over earlier machine automation are that it is easier to reset the machines, since changing the software takes less time than physically resetting the machine. This in turn allows small "batch" production so that goods can be customized for individual purchasers without loss of the economies of scale associated with traditional assembly lines. Parallel developments include computer-aided design systems, sometimes linked across continents by information and communications technology and "groupware", which can allow design teams to work collaboratively together across time zones and get new products to market within months instead of years. Computer-aided production management—stock control, etc.—also allowed the development of the next trend.

Just-in-time inventory control

In traditional production, a manufacturer bought in raw materials, produced the goods, and stockpiled finished products ready to sell to customers. There also tended to be lots of "work in progress" to occupy the workforce in slack times or when the lines were down. All this was expensive in terms of the capital tied up in raw materials, components, and finished goods, as well as the space needed to store them. Just-in-time (JIT) systems are driven by customer demand and every aspect of the production process is delivered "just in time" for the next aspect. Thus, raw materials would not be bought in until a specific order had been received, there would be little "work in progress", and no stockpile of finished goods. Suppliers of raw materials and components would also be forced into JIT if they wanted to survive, since they could not rely on a steady flow of orders. Thus, the interdependence of different firms was reinforced and the growth of "stakeholder thinking" involving suppliers and customers encouraged.

　　JIT is all very well in theory but it requires very close cooperation between the different stages of production, from supply of raw materials to finished product, and very fast production at that—the customer is waiting!

This in turn means that the machines and transport systems must be very reliable since a breakdown in any one part of the process causes disruption and loss of production at every other stage. It is also essential that the quality of the products emerging from one stage of the process is "right first time"; poor quality goods provoke an immediate negative reaction from workers next in line whose bonuses can be threatened by their co-workers' poor performance. (One can easily imagine fist fights!) Thus, we get the third trend.

Total quality management

In traditional manufacturing, separate quality inspection staff were employed to check that work was up to standard. Production and quality control were separated by time, space, and personnel so that substandard work had few personal consequences for the perpetrator. Total quality management (TQM) makes quality control an inherent part of the production job and checking is achieved either through automatic monitoring systems or by training the operator in quality monitoring. Either way, the onus for ensuring quality now rests with the individual worker and deviations from accepted standards not only become very visible but very personal.

Cellular manufacturing

Traditionally, stages in the production process are separate, and the raw materials flow through the system towards finished product with each worker only concerned with a small part of the process. In cellular manufacturing all the machines and people needed for a larger part of, or even the whole, process are grouped together (a cell) and specialization of the workers is by product rather than by task. Autonomous or semiautonomous work groups are often introduced at the same time as cellular manufacturing, since it makes sense for workers to pool their skills, rotate jobs, cover for absences, remedy quality issues, set targets, and conduct preventative maintenance to minimize machine downtime. Wall (1996) has shown that giving "lowly" operators a role in machine maintenance, as opposed always to calling in the specialist maintenance workers when things go wrong, can result in significant gains in productivity.

Integrated manufacturing systems

Since all these developments complement each other, they are often introduced simultaneously as integrated manufacturing systems. None of these developments is inherently a bad idea in itself. Indeed, according to many of the theories of motivation reviewed in Chapter 3, they could be expected to improve worker motivation and satisfaction via enrichment of the job. The question is, do they actually work, and if they work, what are the costs to

those on the shop floor? Pease (1994/2000) offered a trenchant criticism of
the practicalities of JIT from a purely business perspective. What if prospective customers want to see examples of the finished product but they are not
in stock, or the customized item won't be available for inspection for several
weeks? What if *your* JIT isn't JIT enough for *them*? What if the JIT of your
suppliers is not JIT enough for you? Pease's (1994) article was republished
in April 2000 and he was asked to update his arguments if he felt it necessary. His reply was, "No additional comments. I said it all the first time.
Many readers agreed." (As an interesting aside, Pease extolled the virtues of
practices based on the theory of constraints [Goldratt, 1989; Goldratt &
Cox, 1986] as a more viable and realistic alternative to JIT. Lubitsh [2002]
is evaluating the use of this technique to cut down NHS waiting lists. I will
return to this topic in Chapter 8.)

Meanwhile, back in the Ivory Towers . . . Martin and Wall (1987) documented the profound changes that these practices had effected in production workers' jobs. AMT was said often to reduce the operator to a "machine
minder", but also to increase responsibility for fault detection, correction,
and maintenance to reduce downtime. TQM increases attentional demands
and makes failures highly visible and quantifiable—a single error made by
one person could mean thousands of pounds in lost production. JIT leads
to increased planning and problem-solving demands to keep production
running smoothly. There is a need for tight coordination and a high reliance on the work of others for any individual's performance. Teamwork
and "distributed cognition" (i.e., many people pooling their knowledge and
experience to get the job done rather than relying on one person's resources)
become the order of the day. This new manufacturing system creates a
highly uncertain environment, which needs flexible practices and decentralized decision making (see later). Operators need to be "given the necessary
skills, information, and freedom to respond to unforseen circumstances
affecting the production system and its task environment" (Cummings &
Blumberg, 1987, p. 48).
   Can anything more different be imagined from the job of traditional
assembly line workers riveting their rivets all day every day? Parker and
Wall (1998) argue that many new systems fail to achieve their potential.
Martin and Wall (1987) found that workers could deal with the high
attentional demands of TQM *or* the high production responsibility implied
by the increased personal visibility of contribution to production, but
together they caused severe work strain. Day (2001), in a review of the literature regarding the effectiveness of the introduction of autonomous work
groups (AWGs) in industrial contexts, could find little reliable evidence of
their success. In his own study, the introduction of AWGs appeared to fail
because of threats to work identity (skilled maintenance workers felt demeaned by having to do production jobs) coupled with incompatible reward
systems. And all this happened despite much initial goodwill on the part of

the workforce (albeit mixed with a great deal of apprehension), and vast sums poured into training.

The integrated manufacturing systems vision is exciting but it faces a number of challenges, not least that, to be successful, there has to be a high quality workforce. It is ironic that when educational opportunities were relatively few, millions of very intelligent people must have been forced into mundane jobs and treated as if they had no talents or aspirations. Now that we have need of those same talents and aspirations, the numbers available to provide them may be much fewer as the expansion of higher education leads such people to seek professional and managerial jobs. The Dublin Motorola plant, which was attempting to enact a learning organization (McConnell, 1997—see Chapter 6), reported a shortage of high quality applicants. Day's (2001) research shows that there may be no inherent hostility to more complex industrial work—many of his production workers relished the prospect—but expecting the entire workforce to cope with such a sudden change in the complexity of the job may not be realistic. Interestingly, in another study, Day found that a line where the workers had volunteered and been selected for work in autonomous groups functioned far more effectively than a similar line where the men had not been selected and had felt forced into it, even though both groups had been drawn from a similar original workforce.

Complex process control and organizational accidents

If production work has sometimes become more complicated, changes to the nature of complex process control are more ambiguous—in some ways automation has made the job easier, in others it has made it more difficult. But what is complex process control? Typically, it involves hazardous industries such as chemicals manufacture, power generation, and oil and gas extraction. Production is continuous because the process cannot easily be halted. However, complex transport systems such as airlines are also included in this category and, in fact, much of the best research in recent years concerns aviation. Reason (1997) makes a distinction between individual accidents and organizational accidents. All jobs (and indeed life in general) carry some risk of personal injury. Hazards in the workplace, combined with mistakes and unsafe behaviours, can lead to accidents but these mainly affect one person or a very few individuals—the effects are localized. In hazardous industries, however, organizational accidents, which can involve catastrophic loss of life and severe environmental damage, are likely. Indeed, in a seminal work entitled *Normal Accidents: Living with High Risk Technologies*, Perrow (1984) argued that organizational accidents are inevitable (normal) in such highly complex systems. Since the cost of errors are potentially so high, these industries try to achieve error-free performance. However, as we saw in the Paddington rail crash, simply preventing errors in front-line operators is an inadequate strategy. Understanding the multiple causes of organizational accidents is therefore vital.

Characteristics of complex process control

Because industries that require complex process control involve toxic, hazardous environments, operators are distanced from the processes and cannot physically see what is going on. The machinery cannot be handled manually, and much of the process will be under automatic control. Machines relay information back to a distant control room and the operator has to interpret and integrate this information in order to understand the state of the system and decide what actions to take. Such systems are "tightly coupled", which means that all the parts are so interdependent that a fault can have a series of unpredictable effects on many other parts—a "ripple effect". The initial cause of the Three Mile Island near-meltdown was a single maintenance error, which allowed a cupful of water into a sensitive part of the system. This tripped the turbine and shut down the feedwater pumps that cooled the reactor. Emergency feedwater pumps came on automatically, but the flow was blocked by two closed valves, and so heat and pressure began to build up in the core. This in turn tripped the reactor. An emergency relief valve came on automatically, but then got stuck in the open position, setting the scene for a catastrophic loss of coolant. All this happened in *13 seconds*. Note that up to this point the front-line operators had not made a single error, though they did make errors later because they did not understand what had happened (Reason, 1990). Other features of these systems are illustrated in this example. First, their complexity can make them very opaque to the operator, and the more components there are, the greater the likelihood that at least one will fail. Indeed, several components may go wrong in unexpected combinations. Second, since sophisticated automatic systems mediate between the process and the operator, it is not always clear who, or what, is in control.

The main characteristics of the job of a complex process operator can be summarized:

- No direct access to the state of the system.
- Constantly changing information.
- Adjustments needed to keep the plant running at maximum efficiency and safety—involves prediction.
- Time-lags between adjustments and effects.
- Prediction also needed when faults are developing.
- Diagnosis of faults require reversal of thought processes from when the plant is working normally—thinking *backwards* from effect to cause.
- Correcting faults requires more prediction and hypothesis testing.
- "Ripple effects" can make diagnosis very difficult.
- Control can be ambiguous.

Defences in depth and latent conditions

Not surprisingly, the designers of such potentially dangerous beasts put in successive layers of protection, each one guarding against the possible breakdown of the one before. The philosophy underlying defence in depth is that there should be redundancy in the safety system; if one layer fails then the next takes over and the whole process resembles a "rearguard action" of successive damage limitation exercises. When the plant develops a fault, as in Three Mile Island, various automatic safety systems will be triggered, which in theory should render the plant safe enough for the operators to correct the fault and regain normal control. If, nevertheless, control is lost, then various other automatic systems kick in—perhaps leading to shutdown. If that too fails, then the aim is to contain the damage, by for instance limiting the release of toxic substances into the atmosphere. The final defence is evacuation and denial of access to the affected area.

What may be rather surprising, is that such elaborate defences should ever be breached at all. Reason (1997) gives the analogy of the defences being like successive, unbroken steel doors but this, he says, is misleading: The reality is that these "doors" are full of holes. When these "holes" line up what he calls "the accident trajectory", hurtles through all the defences to create loss of life and property. The set of circumstances that combine to create the alignment of all the "holes" in the defences can be extremely unlikely. This is why Wagenaar (1986; Wagenaar & Groeneweg, 1987) use the term "impossible accident". Most organizational accidents cannot be predicted in advance. These "holes" really are what Reason terms latent conditions, which lie dormant and unnoticed in the system for a long time. (This is in contrast to active errors on the "front-line", which have immediate effects and so can be perceived and corrected.) Latent conditions are rather like pathogens that lurk within the human body. Individually, they do us no harm and can be tolerated and may go unnoticed. However, if enough pathogens accumulate and there is some additional factor, e.g., long-term stress, the combination can cause illness. In a similar way, latent conditions can cause the collapse of complex sociotechnical systems. Thus, at Three Mile Island, *if* maintenance had done their job properly, *if* the valves had not blocked the flow of the emergency feedwater, *if* the emergency relief valve had not stuck at open, and *if* the operators had been able to understand quickly what had gone wrong, then the accident would not have happened, but they all lined up and it did.

Latent conditions can exist at any level of the system and beyond it. The Piper Alpha North Sea oil and gas platform fire tragedy, in which 167 men died, illustrates this. One of the latent conditions that contributed greatly to the loss of life was the enormous pressure from top management to maintain production. Hence, local managers were reluctant to shut down nearby platforms, which kept pumping and so fed the fire. No doubt economic and political pressures influenced top management. Other latent conditions were that the platform had been modified to pump gas, and, to cut down costs, inadequate blast walls had been fitted. This in turn allowed the fire to engulf the living quarters where the men had been instructed to go to await rescue. Those who obeyed the instructions all perished. Only those who decided to jump 175 feet into the sea survived, despite having been told that this would mean certain death. None of these latent conditions would have led to disaster had there not been sloppy safety procedures surrounding the maintenance operations that led to the initial explosion.

Cognitive ergonomics and the ironies of automation

Reason (1997) maintains that the defences themselves can become latent conditions and perhaps the greatest danger may involve attempts to replace unreliable humans with machines. Before we start on this discussion, it cannot be over-stressed that good automated systems with defences in depth undoubtedly prevent unknown numbers of accidents and disasters. However, by their very nature, they also contain the seeds of disaster. Bainbridge, in 1987, gave a masterly description of the ironies of automated systems designed to compensate for the unreliable and error-prone human. First, she says that automation, by taking away the easy parts of the operator's job, makes the difficult parts more difficult. Human operators spend most of their time as "machine minders", merely monitoring the process, but are also left with the tasks that the designers and programmers do not know how to automate, i.e., diagnosing and correcting faults. People tend not to perform well on vigilance tasks, which watching out for rare faults developing entails, and they may become de-skilled in the abilities needed in an emergency. Worse, if they are "out of the control loop", they may lose the capacity to understand and diagnose correctly what the state of the system is. It is a matter of months/years of boredom punctuated by terrifying quarter hours. Thus, a further irony is that the most successful automated systems, with a rare need for the human operator to do anything, also require the greatest investment in operator training. This is why the pilots of "fly-by-wire" airliners still need to spend many hours a year in flight simulators practising for incidents that may never occur in the course of their careers. Plant operators similarly have to undergo hours of training dealing with computerized simulated fault scenarios.

The problem is that no-one can anticipate every emergency that could occur, since most organizational accidents are "impossible". Reason (1997) cites a hair-raising example of an incident where an airliner's engine blew up and a piece of debris cut through the entire hydraulic system making the aircraft uncontrollable (Haynes, 1992). Who could have foreseen that an aircraft's entire control system and all its fail-safe mechanisms would be destroyed at a stroke? However, as the aircraft began to roll onto its back, from which it would have fallen out of the sky, its brilliant captain experimented with opposite side thrusts of the remaining engines. In this manner

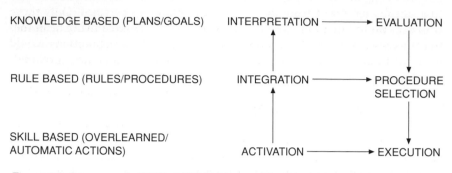

TYPE OF BEHAVIOUR   DECISION-MAKING ELEMENTS

KNOWLEDGE BASED (PLANS/GOALS)   INTERPRETATION ————→ EVALUATION

RULE BASED (RULES/PROCEDURES)   INTEGRATION ————→ PROCEDURE
                                                   SELECTION

SKILL BASED (OVERLEARNED/
AUTOMATIC ACTIONS)   ACTIVATION ————→ EXECUTION

Figure 5.2 Rasmussen's (1981, 1986) ladder model of decision making.

he and two other pilots were able to maintain reasonably level flight and even to crash-land. Of the 285 passengers and 11 crew on board, 174 passengers and 10 crew were saved from what would have been certain death. It is quite possible that only years of experience of manual flying and an intimate knowledge of the handling characteristics of the aircraft could have enabled the captain to use his strategy successfully.

Rasmussen's ladder model of decision making

Rasmussen (1981, 1986) provides an extremely useful and influential model, which helps us to explain how people control complex systems. This is presented in Figure 5.2. At the skill-based level, experts perform actions automatically in response to environmental stimuli. Thus, when a plant is running normally, operators make minor adjustments without much thought. It is rather like a skilled driver whose foot automatically hits the brake pedal at the sight of a hazard ahead. However, errors can still occur. They are likely to involve slips where we accidentally select the wrong action as when we may inadvertently turn on the windscreen wipers instead of the indicator in a car because we've overlearned responses in a previous car where the controls were on opposite sides. Slips can also occur because of lapses of attention, e.g., hitting the fog-light button instead of the rear windscreen heater. Such errors are more likely when the displays and controls are badly designed. Lapses are where we forget to perform some action at the right time. Norman (1981) gives the everyday example of putting boiling water into a teapot having forgotten to put the tea in first. An interesting variant of lapses is "capture errors", where we continue with well-rehearsed routines instead of doing what we intended to do. In effect we are "captured" by our automatic routine. The most familiar example for many people is driving home from work and forgetting to divert to a shop to buy a loaf of bread or whatever. Good systems give immediate warning of slips so that they can be quickly corrected—when the windscreen washers come on you know you have made an error. Lapses are more problematic—you may only remember that you forgot to buy milk when you come to make a drink at home. Both types of error can be serious when you are controlling a power plant. For instance, a serious lapse occurred at Chernobyl. The emergency core cooling system was disconnected early in the sequence of events leading up to the disaster and was not reconnected later. However, on their own, skill-based errors are not usually fatal.

Rule-based behaviour tends to occur when the situation demands more than an automatic reaction, perhaps because it is unfamiliar in some way. However, the situation will have been anticipated so that it is covered by appropriate rules and procedures. So for instance, either by luck or judgement, only a few weeks before the Paddington rail crash, London's emergency services had staged a "simulated disaster" using just such a crash as a scenario. As a result, rescue efforts were very prompt and well coordinated. It was reported that fire crews were training the first water on the blaze within 3 minutes, despite problems gaining access because of a high security perimeter fence. The first doctor on the scene resisted his instincts to help everyone crying for assistance but established priorities and assessed what resources would be needed. He directed all the doctors and ambulance crews as they treated people in the wreckage and arranged for victims to be ferried to many hospitals so that no one hospital was overwhelmed by the number of casualties arriving all at once (*Evening Standard* report, 6 October 1999). Without all this disaster planning and training, the death toll would undoubtedly have been much higher. Similarly, Reason (1990) reports a nuclear power plant emergency when the supervisor arrived and systematically went through the rule book, reading instructions aloud, which the operators then followed, until the situation was brought under control. As Reason comments, they were a very good team!

The main error that can occur with rule-based behaviour is misinterpreting the situation and selecting the wrong rules and procedures. In the Piper Alpha disaster, when a pump failed, the operators followed the "correct" procedure of switching to a second pump line. However, unfortunately, a misunderstanding caused by two separate job sheets led them to believe that the second pump line was safe to use, whereas it was in the middle of undergoing maintenance and only a temporary cover was preventing the escape of gas. When they switched to the second pump line, the cover blew off and caused the first explosion. In fact, the correct procedure in these circumstances would have been to shut down production. Piper Alpha also provides a tragic example of following rules which did not fit the circumstances. The men who sought rescue in the accommodation block died. Those who broke the rules and jumped into the sea, survived.

Knowledge-based behaviour

The final and most difficult level involves knowledge-based behaviour. This is where the situation is so novel that neither skill-based actions nor rules and procedures will suffice. People are forced back onto their own knowledge resources to laboriously construct a model of what is happening and how to resolve the situation. Skriver and Flin (1997) provide a model of what may occur in these situations. They start by invoking the familiar distinction between long-term and working memory. Long-term memory (LTM) contains episodic memories for specific prior experiences, procedural memory about how to behave in particular circumstances, and a general semantic memory about how the world works. Information in LTM is organized into schemata—"a vehicle of memory allowing organisation of an individual's analogous experiences, that include identification, elaboration, planning and execution knowledge" (1997, p. 48). LTM is a very strong system within human beings; messier and more fallible to be sure, but far more powerful than any existing computer's memory. LTM allows the successful execution of skill-based and rule-based behaviour. Working memory (WM) can loosely be described as consciousness—what is currently the focus of the person's attention. It is the conscious processing of information, thinking, problem solving, reasoning, imagery, and so forth. It is far more limited than LTM; in general we can only think about one thing at a time, or more accurately, we can only turn the "searchlight" of our attention on one thing at once although frequent switching of attention to direct resources flexibly is also a fundamental feature of WM. WM can also draw on the vast resources of knowledge within LTM, although this can be an effortful and slow process. Faced with a totally unfamiliar situation, the person is thrown back on the WM system and the decision making, according to Skriver and Flin, then becomes a three-stage process:

1 Interpret the situation using WM and pattern matching (WM searches LTM for previous experiences similar to current situation).
2 Retrieve relevant schemata from LTM to build a mental model of the current situation.
3 Decide on an appropriate procedure.

To this one might add, inventing a wholy new procedure, since nothing known fits the exact current circumstances. This would be difficult enough if emergency situations were static, but typically they involve fragmentary, unreliable, and rapidly changing information, severe time pressures, and extreme hazard. Reading the accounts of process operators, air traffic controllers, and firefighters in such circumstances, one can scarcely suppress gasps of awe at their ability to think at all!

Thankfully, experts have more complex and detailed schemata to draw on and are good at focusing on important cues to make better predictions.

In other words, they are able to perceive and recognize large meaningful patterns within their domains of expertise. A striking example of this comes from an anecdote told by Burke at the British Psychological Society's Occupational Psychology conference in January 2000. A fire chief pulled all his men out of a burning building minutes before it collapsed into an inferno. When questioned later about how he came to make this decision, he said that he had a heard a subtle change in the noise the fire was making, which reminded him of a previous incident when a building had also collapsed.

However, the heavy reliance on WM necessarily involves a narrowing of attention. Reason (1990) talks of "keyhole vision" where people can consider only part of the problem space. Thus, they may get locked into one hypothesis and seek confirming evidence instead of considering many alternatives and seeking disconfirming evidence. Indeed, professors of maths and logic have been shown to fall into the trap of seeking confirmatory evidence when confronted with abstract problems in the calm of a laboratory task (Wason & Johnson-Laird, 1972). It is very interesting that in several nuclear power plant incidents, including Three Mile Island, it needed the "fresh eye" of someone not involved in the formation of the original faulty hypothesis to deflect operators into a more accurate line of reasoning (Reason, 1990; Woods, 1984). Skriver and Flin's research, in which senior managers of North Sea oil and gas platforms participated, also demonstrated exactly this effect. Their research involved semistructured interviews where the managers thought aloud about how they would manage three emergency scenarios. These scenarios were based on "routine emergencies", in which they were well trained, so rule-based behaviour predominated. However, when routines failed (e.g., emergency escape routes became dangerous), they lost the big picture and switched to local problem solving—how to circumvent the immediate hazard. Such a reaction is to be expected when the person is forced to rely mainly on WM.

The US Nuclear Regulatory Commission (1994) sponsored the study of 21 reports of incidents at nuclear power plants. All of these incidents were safely resolved, but there were big differences between the most and least successful recoveries. The most successful recoveries involved incidents when the reactors were running at full power. This is the normal condition for a nuclear reactor and the procedures and training worked well. The least successful recoveries occured when the reactors were running at low power or were in shut-down mode. Such circumstances are not unusual since reactors have to be shut down regularly for repair, maintenance, and refuelling, but they are less familiar to the operators. In these situations the operators often appeared confused or uncertain about the state of the system and made mistakes that exacerbated the fault and delayed recovery. Even skilled operators appeared to be working at their limits. This study provides a classic example of the problems created by being forced into knowledge-based behaviour.

The greatest danger of knowledge-based behaviour (apart from the fact that it is slow and laborious when speed is of the essence) is that the wrong goal can be selected. This appears to have happened at Chernobyl. The operators seem to have been "locked in" to the goal of maintaining the dangerous low power conditions needed (ironically) for a safety test, when in fact, the goal most certainly should have been to abandon the test. In the process, they systematically dismantled every one of the system's defences during an "heroic" struggle to maintain test conditions in the face of the increasingly unstable condition of the reactor. They were undoubtedly operating in knowledge-based mode since the test conditions were highly unfamiliar and, if such a word is appropriate in these circumstances, they were successful. At one point they managed to stabilize the reactor at 7% full power, when the recognized safe minimal power level was 20%. Thus, says Reason, a prize-winning team violated every safety rule, forgot to be afraid, and caused possibly the worst organizational accident to date.

We can now see why attempting to cut the fallible human operator out of the control loop via automation could be the most dangerous defence of all. By all means, we can agree that it is vital to avoid the need for knowledge-based behaviour whenever possible, and if automated systems achieve this, well and good. If, however, they cannot achieve this, then the results can be disastrous, since anything that undermines knowledge reduces the probability of any success. And we should not forget that system designers and programmers are fallible humans too.

More, dangerous defences

Reason (1997) describes other safety systems that can pose greater dangers than those they are designed to prevent. Even quality control can cause problems. TQM means that everyone is responsible for quality, but does that mean that no-one owns it? In aircraft maintenance, for instance, maintenance engineers sometimes sign off their own work, so the valuable "fresh eye" of a quality inspector is lost. Maintenance is implicated in so many organizational accidents that it is a potent latent condition. Reason gives a marvellous illustration of why this should be so. Take a simple bolt with eight nuts screwed onto it. Taking the nuts off is easy—there is only one right way to do it and the knowledge is in the world rather than in the head of the operator. However, there are 40,000 ways the nuts can be screwed back on in the wrong order! Multiply the nut and bolt example by the complexities involved in, say, reassembling a passenger jet, and it is small wonder, Reason argues, that in modern reliable systems, a *reduction* in the amount of maintenance would significantly enhance safety.

Written safety procedures can also create greater risks. Near misses and minor accidents get reported, and another rule gets written. Sometimes the rules become so restrictive that the only way to get the job done is to break them. Train wagon couplers, for instance, were not allowed to begin work until the wagons were stationary. However, the coupling mechanism only worked when the buffers of each wagon were pressed together at the point of impact so the couplers had to get between the wagons while the train was still moving. Many times this dangerous behaviour did not lead to an accident, but given another factor—a trip, a momentary loss of concentration—and disaster struck. The most insidious thing about unsafe behaviours that become part of the culture is that they make workers liable to forget to be afraid of hazardous systems because they do not usually lead to bad consequences.

Finally, the new rules that get written to prevent the next accident may not be appropriate for the next emergency. For instance, after Three Mile Island the US Nuclear Regulators prohibited the cut-off of high pressure water injection, but 3 years later at Ginna, the nature of the emergency actually required operators to perform this action.

Rasmussen (1993) speaks of the "fallacy of defences in depth". The main problem is that they tend to make the system more opaque and can conceal the occurrence of errors that may have long-term consequences. And they require yet more components that can go wrong. They can also create a false sense of security. Perhaps the most notorious example of this kind of thing was the fate of the "unsinkable" *Titanic*, which continued full steam ahead across the North Atlantic in the teeth of iceberg warnings, and with only a fraction of the lifeboats needed to save all the passengers and crew.

Reason's latest refinements on the causes of organizational accidents

In his latest book Reason (1997) concludes that the causes of organizational accidents are so complex and far-reaching it is difficult to know how far back we should go in tracing their origins. To give just one, very sad, example, Legasov, the chief Soviet investigator of the Chernobyl disaster said, in a message left after his suicide, that Chernobyl represented "the summit of all the incorrect running of the economy which had been going on in our country for many years". In this judgement he was almost certainly correct (see e.g., Reason, 1990, p. 193), but does this really help to prevent such occurrences? Reason suggests that we start with the organization and its safety culture. In the worst scenario, there is a "pathological" culture, which ignores, punishes, or conceals all safety warnings, responsibility for safety is shirked, and any new ideas are actively discouraged. At the other end of the spectrum, a "generative" culture actively seeks, rewards, and promotes safety information. New ideas are welcomed, and safety failures lead to far-reaching reforms. Perhaps surprisingly, given all the examples taken from hazardous industries, the most telling quote comes from the Group Treasurer of Baring's Bank shortly after its collapse at the hands of "rogue trader", Nick Leason. Speaking of the bank's failure to act on alarms about fraud and to review risk controls in time to avert the disaster, he said, "Perhaps there was always something else more pressing." Reason adds, "That is an appropriate epitaph for most organizational accidents" (p. 39). We shall discuss this issue in more detail later.

BOX 5.2
Reason's (1997) six categories of behaviour and error types

	Good rules	*Bad rules*	*No rules*
Correct performance	Correct compliance	Correct violation	Correct improvization
Incorrect performance	Misvention	Mispliance	Mistake

© Reason, J. (1997) *Managing the Risks of Organizational Accidents.* Reproduced with permission from Ashgate Publishing Ltd.

Meanwhile, Reason (1997) went on to make a distinction between "correct" and "incorrect" actions, which expands his previous analysis of error types. Correct actions are taken on the basis of accurate risk appraisal, but this is often unknowable in advance and unknown at the time. (Hindsight is a wonderful advantage when deciding on the best course of action in an emergency.) This distinction gives us six kinds of behaviour, as in Box 5.2.

This new scheme allows us to fine-tune the categorization of the errors that typically lead up to organizational accidents. Correct compliance is when you follow the rules and the outcome is good. Correct violation is where you break the rules but the outcome is good. Nelson ignoring orders by putting his telescope to his blind eye before the Battle of Copenhagen is a good example. A mispliance is where you conform to a bad rule and the outcome is also bad. Reason notes that only history can judge between generals' correct violations and mispliances. Very often the "great" war leader is one who ignored the rules but achieved victory. The mediocre general is often the one who sticks to the rules and is defeated. Certainly, the unfortunates who took refuge in the living quarters of Piper Alpha were victims of mispliance, whereas those who jumped performed correct violations. A misvention is a deviation from a good rule with an unsafe outcome. The operator errors at Chernobyl were almost entirely composed of misventions—the violation of good rules. But who knows? If their actions had led to a successful test, they may have become heroes of the Soviet Union and their actions would be judged as correct violations. When there are no rules, as when knowledge-based behaviour is called for, you can either engage in successful improvisation or fail miserably. Either way, you are "flying by the seat of your pants", and success may owe more to luck than judgement. Not included in this scheme, but still considered vitally important, are incorrect but successful violations of good rules. This behaviour includes that of the train wagon couplers, and everyone else who engages in unsafe actions because the informal culture dictates that this is the only way to get the job done.

In my view, the value of this taxonomy of errors lies not so much in the greater precision with which we can analyse and categorize them, but in that it prompts the realization that what counts as an error at all can be quite arbitrary. In large measure, this is judged on the basis of outcome—at least in any ambiguous and risky situation, which, incidentally, includes a lot of work nowadays. Take JIT, for instance. The difference between financial success and disaster can depend on whether the assembly line runs smoothly or breaks down. Similarly, the success of any innovative scheme can hang by a thread—on being in the right place at the right time. There is little new in this. "Captains of industry" always pride (and pay) themselves on the basis of their ability to take calculated risks that lead to successful outcomes. However, it is a little sobering to think that this ability is also needed in the "front-line troops", especially in safety-critical industries.

It has to be said that top management are frequently forced into the position of knowledge-based problem solving because the conditions they face are both highly complex and largely uncharted. Sometimes, however, like the "out of loop" operators, they lack the basic knowledge to make "correct" decisions in this mode and, like the "gung-ho" Chernobyl operators, forget to be afraid. This is illustrated in the *Herald of Free Enterprise* ferry disaster. The top management of the ferry company sent the ship into a port for which it was not designed, and which entailed much trimming of ballast whilst at sea. They insisted on a turnround of 15 minutes, which did not allow for correction of the ballast whilst in port. Further, they refused to install a cheap bow-door safety signal on the bridge because they were employing a seaman to report that the bow doors were closed when she sailed. Presumably they did not intend to sink the ship and kill a large number of passengers, so their actions were misventions—based on experience of many voyages involving successful violations of good rules. They were also guilty of a major mistake; the goal of maximizing profitability led to "key-hole vision"; the possibility that the ship *would* sail with bow doors open and capsize in seconds didn't enter into their calculations. In the wake of the Paddington and Hatfield rail crashes, corporate ignorance of the true risks may come to carry heavier penalties than a lot of bad publicity and a failed corporate manslaughter lawsuit. Accurate risk assessment thus becomes of central importance to both individuals and organizations when attempting to create a safety culture to avoid individual and organizational accidents.

Creating a safety culture

It may be useful to start this section with a definition of organizational culture. The one provided by Uttal (1983) seems as good as any: "Shared values (what is important) and beliefs (how things work) that interact with an organization's structures and control systems to produce behavioural norms (the way we do things round here)." Translated into a safety culture this means that everyone will put safety at the top of their priorities (shared values). They will believe that safety is achievable and that management shares this belief such that there is top-level support for safety and that pre-ventative procedures and practices are both designed with safety uppermost and will be effective (shared beliefs). Finally, everyone will behave in accordance with these values and beliefs so that unsafe acts will not be tolerated (behavioural norms).

I must admit that I find this a rather unrealistic Utopian vision. However, Reason (1997, p. 220) comforts me with the following observation. "It is worth pointing out that if you are convinced that your organization has a good safety culture, you are almost certainly mistaken. Like a state of grace, a safety culture is something that is striven for but rarely attained. As in religion, the process is more important than the product. The virtue—and the reward—lies in the struggle rather than the outcome." It is in this spirit that I proceed.

The Health and Safety at Work Act (1974)

Safety at work has long been on the agenda. From the early 1800s a plethora of Acts of Parliament in the UK, supported by much case law, attempted to protect people from death and injury at work. Even so, in 1972, the Robens report found that, in the UK alone, in any one year, about 1000 people were killed and 500,000 suffered injury at work. This caused an average of 23 million workdays lost every year. This prompted the judgement that contemporary measures were not effective enough, and something had to be done. The result was the 1974 Health and Safety at Work Act, which was specifically designed to be updated. From 1992 onwards, it has been the main vehicle for the enforcement of the European Union Health and Safety at Work Directives. (See Barrett & Howells, 1997 for a lucid account of the Act and its workings.) The 1974 Act placed wide-ranging duties on employers to provide a safe working environment for employees and anyone else who might visit their premises, including contractors and the general public. Suppliers were enjoined to provide safe materials or to control and safely store hazardous substances. Employees were charged with care for their own safety and those of others. Any interference with health and safety measures was declared unlawful, and employers were not allowed to charge employees for anything done or provided in the interests of safety. To enforce the Act, the Health and Safety Commission (HSC) was set up. This was a Government department exclusively concerned with advising on health and safety policy. The Health and Safety Executive (HSE) was set up to "police" the Act by conducting inspections and bringing prosecutions under the Act. Both bodies issue codes of practice and practical guidance, which while not legally binding, can be used in evidence in cases brought against statutory breaches.

So far so good. Unfortunately, the 1974 Act was hedged about with phrases such as "so far as is reasonably practicable", which made interpretation of the law in particular cases quite difficult. From 1992, however, more "teeth" were introduced in phrases such as "employers should provide . . .", and so on. As a result, more employers appear to be eager to comply with the "letter", if not always the "spirit", of the Act. (One ploy is to have a mammoth Health and Safety manual with which no-one could be wholly familiar, and then to fight every claim against violation of the law with the counterclaim that the plaintives didn't comply with company safety procedures.) But even with the best will in the world, creating a safety culture is no easy business. Case study 5.1 illustrates the pitfalls.

Case study 5.1: The pitfalls that can occur when trying to create a safety culture

Cooper (1998) provides a wonderful case study of what can go wrong. A national company brought in external consultants to design and implement their safety culture procedures and spent a six-figure sum in the process. All the right ingredients were put in place including management safety systems, training all managers in safety management auditing, setting up a series of safety committees, and instituting a variety of communication and publicity measures including an "in-house" safety newsletter. All this was to no avail. In the third year, a steep rise in accidents began again and after 30 months the company had still not recouped the consultants' fees in savings on sick leave, compensation claims, etc. To their great credit, the mystified senior management asked people on the shop floor what had gone wrong. They were told . . . forcibly.

- The consultants had been perceived as being used to impose safety.
- The safety procedures had not always been appropriate to local conditions.
- The workforce had not been properly consulted or involved.
- The whole thing had been predicated on discipline and a climate of fear of reprisals.
- The scale of the consultants' fees had been resented, especially when contrasted with a concurrent redundancy exercise to reduce labour costs.
- Reported safety problems were met with inaction on the grounds that solutions were too costly.
- But ever-increasing targets for production were always met.

Meanwhile . . .

- Accident investigations were superficial.
- There was a tendency for management to blame the "carelessness" of the victims.
- Employees thus became reluctant to report near-misses and minor accidents.
- Junior and middle managers stopped attending safety meetings and conducting audits because they said they were too pressured by production targets.

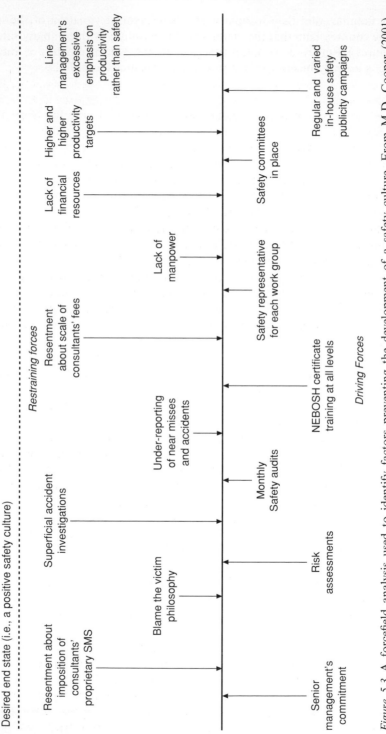

Desired end state (i.e., a positive safety culture)

Restraining forces

Resentment about imposition of consultants' proprietary SMS

Superficial accident investigations

Under-reporting of near misses and accidents

Resentment about scale of consultants' fees

Lack of financial resources

Higher and higher productivity targets

Line management's excessive emphasis on productivity rather than safety

Senior management's commitment

Blame the victim philosophy

Risk assessments

Monthly Safety audits

NEBOSH certificate training at all levels

Lack of manpower

Safety representative for each work group

Safety committees in place

Regular and varied in-house safety publicity campaigns

Driving Forces

Figure 5.3 A forcefield analysis used to identify factors preventing the development of a safety culture. From M.D. Cooper (2001). *Improving safety culture: A practical guide.* Hull, UK: Applied Behavioural Sciences. Reproduced by permission of the author.

A forcefield analysis (see Figure 5.3) helped senior management to refocus their efforts and change their approach. But what a catalogue of mistakes! Both management and consultants appear to have been "flying by the seat of their pants", and they failed. Three things strike me about this case study. First, there was commitment from senior management, which Cooper (1998) and others regard as vital for the success of any safety management system, yet this, on its own, was not enough. Second, the people actually doing the job, who could be expected to know most about its potential hazards, were barely consulted. Worse, they felt forced, through a climate of fear, into inappropriate behaviours. Third, production targets took precedence over safety concerns. And therein lies the grave of many a would-be safety culture.

The cost of organizational accidents are so enormous that most hazardous industries are rightly obsessive about safety. They are also closely regulated. For instance, after Piper Alpha, the HSE took over the monitoring of safety in the North Sea and all companies have to carry out periodic risk assessments on all their rigs. The US Federal Aviation Authority now requires that pilot workload analyses be carried out for all types of aircraft. Promoting safety in less hazardous work can be more of a problem because management may perceive few risks in, say, office work. In fact, management typically perceives fewer risks in any type of work than do those most exposed to the risks (Ostberg, 1980).

Cooper (1998) makes the point that management often equates productivity with a fast pace of work and safety with a slow pace of work, so the two are seen as being in conflict, and in the contest productivity usually wins. We have already seen that systems can be quite forgiving of unsafe acts for long periods, so there is a real danger that any behaviour that gets the job done will become part of the informal culture (the way we do things round here), regardless of the rule book. However, the costs of individual accidents in the workplace are very high. Cooper cites an HSE (1993) report that put the ratio of insured versus uninsured accident costs at 1:11, and a Confederation of British Industry report (1990), which estimated that the minimum nonrecoverable cost per accident was £1500, whether or not it was investigated. He also reports evidence that, in the US, projects driven by safety were more likely to be delivered on time and on budget, with reduced absenteeism, more positive attitudes to quality, and improved product quality. Research in the construction industry (notorious for its individual accidents) showed that every 2.5% spent on safety provided a return of 6.5% overall— a net increase in profit of 4% (Cooper, Phillips, Robertson, & Duff, 1993). Stewart and Townsend (2001) cite several studies which show that improving safety is associated with improved productivity. In one meat-producing company, reduced costs of accidents gave a cost benefit of +7% and productivity increased by 11%. The authors concluded that this was because the actions taken to improve safety, e.g., better ergonomics and housekeeping, are the same as those needed for increased productivity. For instance, the discipline provided by risk assessment and the process of working out what could go wrong and measures to reduce the risks, also applied to increasing productivity. (Visit www.behavioural-safety.com for a wealth of information, further compelling evidence, and a list of peer-reviewed journal articles.)

Stages in the development of a safety culture

A safety culture results from the successful integration of policies and practices of three components of the system: people (psychological), jobs (behavioural), and organizations (situational). Cooper (1998) suggests three levels of intervention.

1   Immediate level of effort: Establish a strategic direction. This phase would involve information gathering, e.g., a communication analysis, job analyses, risk assessments, audits of control measures, etc.
2   Intermediate level of effort: Establish systems and procedures. This phase would involve integrating management information systems to facilitate organizational learning, establishing safety strategies, and disseminating best practice for reviewing the adequacy of safety controls, etc.
3   Ultimate level of effort: Winning hearts and minds. This is the implementation phase and involves publicity of safety information, safety training, risk perception analyses, and constant updating of policies and procedures.

The aim of all this is to eliminate unsafe behaviours. Sensible and laudable as this is, there is a potential snag. If this process seems like a lot of extra work and bureaucracy, that is probably because it is. There is the risk that safety will be perceived by already overloaded staff as the intolerable imposition of extra bureaucratic burdens. One answer to this is to recognize safety as a legitimate business cost and to provide the necessary extra people and resources. The general tone of some safety procedures may be more difficult to solve. For instance, one safety audit checklist for an office environment includes sensible precautions such as checking that electrical leads are not posing a trip hazard and that high shelves are not overloaded or difficult to access, but the overall tone is "nannying". Some people might find it offensive that they were being checked to see if they were putting their chairs underneath the desk every time they left it for a few moments or were holding the handrail when they walked down the stairs. Yes, people can bump into chairs and running down the stairs two at a time is not a good idea, but such "nit-picking" might bring the whole safety system into disrepute and divert attention from its really important aspects.

Reason's safety culture philosophy

Writing mainly for hazardous industries, Reason (1997) adopts a less bureaucratic approach. Rather than being a matter of imposing a large number of rules and procedures, he believes a safety culture is more concerned with creating a frame of mind. He says that a safety culture is an engine that propels the system to the goal of maximum safety regardless of individual leaders' personality and current commercial concerns. Its power is derived from not forgetting to be afraid. The most important component of a safety culture is that it is an informed culture, and that the best way to sustain a "state of intelligent and respectful wariness" is to collect, analyse, and disseminate the right kinds of data. These should include accident and near-miss reporting, but also the use of regular proactive checks, i.e., risk assessments.

An informed culture

For this one needs a reporting culture, and this in turn requires a just culture. There is some controversy about how to get people to report accidents, near-misses, and other essential safety information, especially if they fear reprisals for "carelessness" or breaking the rules. Cooper (1998) believes there should be a "no blame" culture and that people should have immunity from punishment for any personal contributions to the incidents they report. Certainly, a "shoot the messenger" mentality will suppress vital safety information, but in hazardous industries, "no blame" will not do. Deliberately reckless behaviour, gross incompetence, or serious violations of the standard operating procedures cannot be tolerated.

Reason (1997) suggests that the answer is to be very clear about the limits and to have fair and just procedures for dealing with all reported incidents. He presents British Airways (O'Leary & Chappell, 1996; O'Leary & Fisher, 1993; O'Leary & Pidgeon, 1995) as a case study of an informed culture. First, BA issued the following statement to encourage reporting:

> It is not normally the policy of British Airways to institute disciplinary proceedings in response to the reporting of any incident affecting air safety. Only in rare circumstances where an employee has taken action or risks, which, in the Company's opinion, no reasonably prudent employee with his/her training and experience would have taken, will British Airways consider initiating such disciplinary action.

This seems to have done the trick. Between 1990 and 1995, the number of reported incidents trebled. Simultaneously, BA introduced a Confidential Factors Reporting Programme, which asks about the circumstances surrounding each incident, such as whether all the relevant flight, FMS, and system information was clearly available. The replies are then analysed by ergonomists to determine the types of error made and whether deficiencies in the displays or controls might have contributed to them. Finally, there is regular expert analysis of flight recorders. All this information is fed back to management and to pilots by a newsletter and other means.

Reason (1997) believes that this kind of information is important but, since most accidents cannot be foreseen, more proactive risk assessments should be carried out. According to an HSE leaflet a risk assessment involves five steps.

1　Look for the hazards. They recommend concentrating only on significant hazards "which could cause serious harm or affect several people". The people who actually work in the environment should be asked for their opinions.
2　Decide who might be harmed and how. Hazards should also be considered in relation to others who might use the space—cleaners, visitors, contractors, etc.
3　Evaluate the risks arising from the hazards and whether the existing precautions are adequate. Some risk usually remains even after all precautions have been taken, so the next step is to decide for every significant hazard whether the remaining risk is low, medium, or high. For high risks, questions must be asked whether legal requirements and general industry standards are met. Creative thinking about what more could be done is also needed, e.g., putting some nonslip material on slippery steps is a cheap and effective way of reducing the risks.
4　Record your findings (and inform employees). All companies employing more than five people have to put their risk assessments in writing.
5　Monitor and carry out periodic reassessments. Details of incidents and "near-misses" should also be recorded and appropriate action taken.

All this sounds like sensible advice that does not impose too many additional burdens. In hazardous industries, however, something more is needed. Reason (1997) discusses several methods, and a particularly interesting technique—Tripod Delta—was developed by teams from the universities of Leiden and Manchester for Shell oil exploration and production operations (Hudson et al., 1994). The elements of the system are given in Figure 5.4.

One of the main safety measures is LTI (lost time injuries per million working hours). Tripod Delta tries to reduce LTIs indirectly by addressing general failure types (GFTs). GFTs are effectively latent conditions that provoke or encourage unsafe acts and active errors. After observing operations and a study of accident levels the designers of Tripod Delta identified 11 categories of GFTs most likely to contribute to LTIs. A summary is given in Figure 5.5a. For instance, incompatible goals might include instances where the informal norms of a work group are incompatible with safety goals or where there is incompatibility between safety and production goals. Information is then collected about the symptoms of the presence and degree of GFTs from the people doing the job. This leads to checklists that

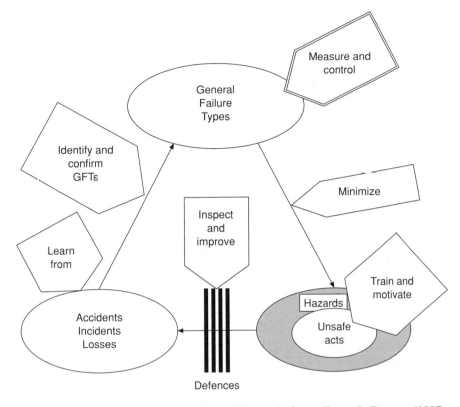

Figure 5.4 The elements of the Tripod Delta technique. From J. Reason (1997). *Managing risks of organizational accidents*. Aldershot, UK: Ashgate. Reproduced by permission of the publishers.

can be used to assess specific work spaces. Eventually this leads to a failure state profile (see Figure 5.5b), which identifies the most pressing issues for attention. Also identified are the safety management actions necessary at each stage. The most important of these is to measure and control the GFTs.

The strengths of Tripod Delta are that it identifies the causes of unsafe acts rather than just treating the symptoms; it describes things as they are rather than how they ought to be, and it involves the people doing the job. Although it is deliberately noncomprehensive, it does address the most important accident-causing dimensions, i.e., the latent conditions.

A flexible culture

Reason (1997) also believes that there needs to be a flexible culture. By this, he means that in emergencies or critical situations the normal chain of

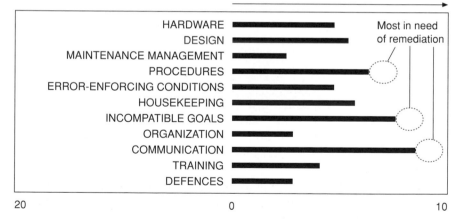

(a)

PROCESSES	GFT's
STATEMENT OF GOALS	INCOMPATIBLE GOALS
ORGANIZATION	ORGANIZATIONAL DEFICIENCIES
MANAGEMENT	POOR COMMUNICATIONS
DESIGN	DESIGN FAILURES POOR DEFENCES
BUILD	HARDWARE FAILURES POOR DEFENCES
OPERATE	POOR TRAINING POOR PROCEDURES POOR HOUSEKEEPING
MAINTAIN	POOR TRAINING POOR PROCEDURES POOR MAINTENANCE MANAGEMENT

ERROR-ENFORCING CONDITIONS

(b)

GENERAL FAILURE TYPES

CAUSE FOR CONCERN AS REVEALED BY CHECKLIST SCORES

HARDWARE
DESIGN
MAINTENANCE MANAGEMENT
PROCEDURES
ERROR-ENFORCING CONDITIONS
HOUSEKEEPING
INCOMPATIBLE GOALS
ORGANIZATION
COMMUNICATION
TRAINING
DEFENCES

Most in need of remediation

20 0 10

Figure 5.5 Tripod Delta: Summary of the 11 categories of GFTs and a failure state profile: (a) The relationship between the basic systemic processes and the general failure types, and the combined impact of the GFT's on the error-enforcing conditions; (b) A Tripod-Delta failure state profile identifying the three GFTs most in need of improvement in the near future (in this case, procedures, incompatible goals, and communication). From J. Reason (1997). *Managing risks of organizational accidents.* Aldershot, UK: Ashgate. Reproduced by permission of the publishers.

command disappears so that local experts take over control, whatever their rank. LaPorte and Consolini (1991) give some interesting case studies illustrating this in action. One concerned an aircraft carrier when 70 out of its 90 planes were simultaneously flying on missions. In this situation, the normal hierarchy disappeared and everyone from commanders to junior officers deferred to the technical expertise of noncommissioned officers who effectively directed operations. In another example, a sudden change in wind direction created a crisis in a busy air traffic control centre when very many aircraft had to have their flight paths reoriented in double quick time. Again it was the "experienced controller virtuosos" who took charge, rather than the supervisors who had the formal authority. As soon as the emergencies were over, the normal hierarchy returned.

Interestingly, both these organizations are normally bureaucratic and hierarchical, but Weick (1987) argues that this is what is needed for decentralized decision making because a very strong, centralized culture creates a homogenous set of assumptions and decision premises. Reason adds that first-line supervisors need to be high quality employees and highly trained. It is interesting to note that the local manager on the Claymore rig kept pumping towards Piper Alpha while he spent time trying to contact his superior in Aberdeen for authorization to shut down. If ever there was a need for decentralized decision making, this must have been it.

A learning culture

Finally, Reason (1997) argues that a safety culture must be embedded in a learning culture, the elements of which must include:

- Observing: noticing, attending, heeding, tracking.
- Reflecting: analysing, interpreting, diagnosing.
- Creating: imagining, designing, planning.
- Acting: implementing, doing, testing.

From this it can be seen that promoting safety is as integral to the job as actually getting the "real" work done. For all this to happen, people need a certain amount of free time. If they are already overloaded with the primary tasks, then there will be no time to pursue safety in this way. Perhaps the real key to creating a safety culture is resources. But very often economic considerations take precedence over safety. As recently as September 1999, David Woods, President of the Human Factors and Ergonomics Society of the US, felt compelled to place a strongly worded article on the Society's web site. Speaking about public controversy regarding proposed regulations on workplace ergonomics, he writes, "The debate seems to have focused on economics alone, as if safety is a meaningful goal only when it also produces short-term economic benefits. Isn't safety a meaningful goal, regardless of costs involved?" These sorts of points are made by most commentators and do not only apply to the industries themselves but also the regulatory bodies for those industries. Reason (1997) tells a sorry tale of cost cutting in the HSE, which has reduced the available resources to oversee health and safety. Numerous case studies of regulatory bodies in many countries tell the same story of workload increasing while resources have been cut. In addition to this, there is often more concern about colluding with companies to maintain "commercial viability" than with enforcing regulations. In the UK, three serious rail crashes in 3 years have undermined public confidence in this form of transport. After Paddington, many people were outraged to learn that fitting an advanced warning device, which may have prevented the accident, had been rejected on the grounds that it was "uneconomic" in terms of the number of lives that would thereby have been saved. In the autumn of 2000 the Hatfield rail crash was blamed on a broken rail on poorly maintained track, which derailed a high speed passenger train and resulted in the death of four people and injuries to many more. In turn, Railtrack, the company that owned and maintained the UK rail network, blamed the rail regulator for forcing an emphasis on train punctuality at the expense of safety. But for this, they argued, the train would not have been travelling at such speed on this particular stretch of track. From these sorts of examples it is clear that there are many potentially conflicting goals involved. Despite what has already been said, productivity, profitability, quality of service, and health and safety are not always compatible. At some point, "difficult decisions" have to be made and sometimes safety wins. The Chairman of Railtrack promised the UK months of disruption and delays as the cost of putting things right and the travelling public were not "disappointed" in the ensuing chaos! However, this example also illustrates the difficulty of putting safety above everything else. Within a couple of weeks, Railtrack was being accused of "over-reaction" in the media and travellers abandoned the trains for their cars or stayed at home. Railtrack was soon in a very serious financial position as a result of all the engineering works, compensation payments, and lost revenue. It has since been shut down by the UK Government and replaced by a new organization. As I write, late-running trains are still more common than those on time. However, some people may direct their outrage not at inconvenience and bankruptcy, but to the fact that the track infrastructure had been allowed to deteriorate to such an extent and that people had to die before serious remedies were implemented. Woods (1999) is unequivocal in his assessment of which goal—safety or profit—should take precedence. At the end of his web article he says, "in the final analysis, I represent those who work at the 'sharp end' of systems".

Maybe, also, a "stressed" culture is incompatible with a safety culture, a point that should perhaps be borne in mind when psychosocial stressors are being unfavourably compared with the more tangible physical risks. After all, a frantically busy person is more likely to run down the stairs two at a time.

Summary

In this chapter I have argued that machines should be kept in their place and that place is to augment human abilities by compensating for human limitations; to do the things we hate doing, the things we are particularly bad at doing, or the things that would be too dangerous for us to do. The Industrial Revolution made huge numbers slaves to the machinery and now the Information Revolution may not be dissimilar in its dehumanizing potential. Paradoxically, although new technology and associated work practices have increased the complexity of many manufacturing jobs, perhaps beyond the capacity of much of the current workforce, it has reduced many other workers to the status of "machine minders". When safety-critical systems are involved, automating the fallible human out of the control loop is a dangerous defence. Far from cutting out human error, it merely moves it further from the front line to the designers of the system, management, and maintenance. Meanwhile the human operator is left with the tasks the designers don't know how to automate—diagnosing and correcting faults. This combination can be disastrous. Health and safety issues are too often sacrificed to production and profit. They can also become bureaucratic nightmares that are unworkable in an already overloaded workforce. The best "safety culture" is more of a philosophy or a "state of mind" characterized by good proactive information, good communication, trust, fairness, and a willingness to learn. For this to happen there must be adequate resources. A safety culture is not something you can add on at little extra expense. However, we all pay the price of poor safety cultures in one way or another —death, injury, post-traumatic stress disorder, grief, loss of income, environmental damage, and higher taxes to sort out the havoc. I'm pleased to see that the current Labour Government in the UK seems to agree with me that the companies responsible should be made to pay more of the price ("Safety at work", 2000).

Exercise 5.2 is designed to consolidate your understanding of the content of this chapter and may be suitable for writing up in a Log Book for chartership applications.

EXERCISE 5.2
Analysis of Piper Alpha disaster

The following is an outline of the events that occured before and during the Piper Alpha tragedy.

First go through each event and categorize it according to the type of error it represents, paying particular attention to latent conditions versus active errors. Next, imagine you are an HSE representative, arriving on another rig in the wake of the disaster. Outline how you would go about carrying out a risk assessment and what priorities you would set for immediate safety improvements and longer-term changes.

Background

The UK Department of Energy was responsible for checking on North Sea oil workers, but it was also responsible for getting as much oil and gas out as possible—the Government needed the revenue (£12 billion extra in the 1980s). Shutting down for safety checks or repairs cost about £30,000 per hour so there was enormous pressure on managers to keep up production. Workers who complained about safety standards were sacked. Maintenance was always being reduced or postponed. There was a preponderance of (cheaper) contract workers, and Trades Union membership was strongly discouraged.

The original rig had been designed for oil extraction only, but it had been modified to take gas, which brought the production area much closer to the accommodation block. The accommodation block was heatproof, and the men had been instructed to go there in the event of a fire to await rescue from the helipad on its roof. The area containing No. 2 pump did not have blast-proof doors because requests for these had been rejected on the grounds of unnecessary cost.

On the day

Two maintenance jobs were being performed on No. 2 pump: one was expected to be completed during the day; another had it booked out for a major service within the next fortnight.

The shorter first job took longer than expected and a temporary cover was fitted until work could be completed the next day. The temporary cover was situated high up on the wall and obscured by other pipework. The maintenance crew went off duty, leaving two separate job sheets which do not appear to have been filed together.

Meanwhile, since a diving crew were at work, the automatic sprinkling system was shut off. This was to avoid the danger of divers being sucked into its intake pipe but on other rigs this shutting down procedure was only implemented when the divers were working close to the intake. In fact, the divers were working a long way from the intake.

In the evening

A new shift was on duty when No. 1 pump failed. The supervisor found the long-term, major service job sheet for pump No. 2 and assumed that work had not begun on it. He does not appear to have known about the temporary cover. Pump No. 2 was started up and after a few minutes under intense pressure, the temporary cover blew off. The escaping gas caused the first explosion which blew down the walls of the area, and the fire quickly spread to the location where the automatic sprinkling system would have to be turned back on manually. At this stage only two or three men had been killed.

Piper Alpha sent out distress signals, but the communications room then had to be abandoned. Piper Alpha had ceased production but two neighbouring rigs continued production, sending a "backwash" of oil up the pipes, which then fed the fire. Men took refuge in the accommodation block as instructed. A wind was blowing the smoke towards the block and making it impossible for rescue helicopters to land. The block gradually filled with smoke.

Meanwhile on an adjacent rig, the manager was trying to contact his supervisor on the mainland to get permission to shut down production. He continued production despite the exhortations of a subordinate, radio messages of Piper Alpha workers being picked up from the sea, and the blaze being clearly visible on the horizon. Such fires had occurred before and not knowing the circumstances, especially that the sprinkler system was turned off, he assumed that it would be brought under control. This belief was encouraged by the presence of the firefighting vessel *Tharos*, which was moored near to Piper Alpha. It proved totally inadequate, e.g., an extendable ladder moved so slowly that it could not be positioned to effect rescue until it was too late. Meanwhile the intense heat ruptured the gas pipes, causing a massive explosion. When rescue helicopters arrived they could not get near the platform because of heat, flames, and smoke.

The adjacent rig manager finally got through to his supervisor and shut down production. But by then it was too late. Only those men who left the "safety" of the acommodation block and jumped into the sea survived: 167 were killed; 30 bodies were not recovered. Most of the platform collapsed into the sea, and the rest was later demolished by Occidental. Occidental's insurers paid out £116 million in compensation, and the company later withdrew from North Sea operations.

Risk assessment
Using the following guidance notes and the material in the chapter, supplemented by further reading, conduct a risk assessment of your workspace or an area in your home. Things to consider include whether you have sufficient space for the tasks you have to perform there, whether you can see and reach everything you need comfortably, whether lighting, heating, equipment, and furniture are adequate. You also need to look out for more serious risks such as the safety of electrical items, the dangers of falling, tripping over, or slipping, and of things falling on you. (Interestingly, when people were asked about the risks of working on an oil platform, they rated the risk of explosion higher than that of falling or being struck by objects and yet the latter hazards have been the biggest causes of injury [Rundmo, 1992;

Flin, Mearns, Gordon, & Fleming, 1996].) If you choose a space in your home, e.g., the kitchen, it may be particularly useful to do this also from the point of view of children as the users of this space. Not only will this encourage a "fresh eye", to pinpoint hazards that you may have got used to, but it could help to reduce home accident statistics, which are at least as bad as, if not worse than, those for the workplace.

Notes for guidance

Some definitions: A hazard is a source or agency of possible harm; a risk is a function of that harm being caused and the severity of its consequences; a risk assessment is an evaluation of the chance that a hazard will cause harm.

One method used to measure the risk severity of a hazard is the following simple equation:

Hazard factor × Person factor = Risk severity factor

The hazard factor is assessed on a sliding scale which can be interpolated. For instance, a minor hazard could be more serious in certain circumstances, e.g., if a mildly toxic substance was ingested in sufficient quantity—if in doubt, err on the high side.

Hazard factor 10	minimal risk	causing strain or stress, etc.
Hazard factor 20	low risk	causing minor injuries, e.g., cuts, bruises, sickness, etc.
Hazard factor 50	moderate risk	causing injuries such as broken bones, burns, scalds, etc.
Hazard factor 80	high risk	causing disease, serious injury, maiming, etc.
Hazard factor 100	serious risk	causing death

To obtain a risk severity factor, the appropriate hazard factor is then multiplied by a person factor, which is proportional to the number of people affected. (Of course, you would be right to feel that the serious injury or death of one person is unacceptable, especially if it happened to be you or your child. However, in the workplace, it is necessary to set priorities for immediate remedial action and one important factor in this decision is the number of people at risk.)

Person factor 1   for 1 to 5 people affected
Person factor 2   for 6 to 10 people affected

Person factor 3   for 11 to 20 people affected
Person factor 4   for 21 to 49 people affected
Person factor 5   for 50 and above people affected

By inserting the appropriate factors into the equation, a risk severity factor can be calculated. For instance, if a hazard is rated as moderate risk (factor 50) and it may affect up to 10 people (factor 2) then the risk severity factor is $50 \times 2 = 100$.

The next step is to decide on the action needed to eliminate or reduce the risk.

Severity factor 1 to 19   3 months to remedy
Severity factor 20 to 49   1 month to remedy
Severity factor 50 to 79   7 to 10 days to remedy
Severity factor 80 to 99   1 to 2 days to remedy
Severity factor 100 and over   immediate action

It is always sensible to take remedial action as soon as possible.

Another way to prioritize action is to construct a risk severity/probability grid.

Probability/likelihood	*Description*
Likely/frequent	Occurs repeatedly; event only to be expected
Probable	Not surprising; will occur several times
Possible	Could occur sometime
Remote	Unlikely, though conceivable
Improbable	So unlikely that probability is close to zero

	Likely	*Probable*	*Possible*	*Remote*	*Improbable*
Fatal	1st	2nd	2nd	3rd	
Major injury/ permanent disability	2nd	2nd	3rd		
Minor injury	3rd	3rd			
No injury					

1st rank actions = immediately; 2nd rank actions = within a few days; 3rd rank actions = within a month; remote or improbable + minor or no injury may be acceptable risks (no action).

Suggested further reading

Chmiel, N. (1998). *Jobs, technology and people*. London: Routledge.
Faulkner, C. (1998). *The essence of human computer interaction*. London and New York Prentice Hall.
Kroemer, K. H. E., & Grandjean, E. (2000). *Fitting the task to the human* (5th ed.). London: Taylor & Francis.
Noyes, J. M. (2001). *Designing for humans*. Hove: Psychology Press.
Oborne, D. J. (1995). *Ergonomics at work* (3rd ed.). Chichester, UK: Wiley.
Reason, J. (1990). *Human error*. Cambridge, UK: Cambridge University Press.
Reason, J. (1997). *Managing the risks of organizational accidents*. Aldershot, UK: Ashgate.

Internet sites:

www.behavioural-safety.com
www.ergo.human.cornell.edu   Cornell University's website with link to HFES, USA
www.ergonomics.org.uk   Ergonomics Society (UK) with links to related sites worldwide
www.open.gov.uk/hse/public.htm   HSE website

6 Lifelong learning:
Training and development

Education makes a people easy to lead but difficult to drive; easy to govern but impossible to enslave.

Lord Brougham

The only thing worse for an organization than training its people and having them leave is not training them and having them stay.

Microstation Institute Training advert

The history of training in Britain during the 20th century makes remarkably depressing reading (Hamlin, 1995). In general, it is one of a failure to provide the right skill mix in sufficient numbers for the economy. Latterly, large-scale unemployment has been created because the pool of potential employees have few or obsolete "marketable skills". Hamlin believes that repeated failed attempts to improve the nation's training systems have resulted from two entrenched traditions: controlled apprenticeships and voluntarism.

Traditionally, boys leaving school learned their work skills by undertaking apprenticeships. These lasted between 5 and 7 years, during which time the apprentice was paid low wages and learned on the job, usually under the supervision of a master of the relevant craft. There were no national standards or accreditation systems apart from "time served", and the training given was of very variable quality. At the same time powerful trades union interests ensured that only those who had served their apprenticeships were able to take jobs in that particular trade. By these means the unions effectively controlled the supply of skilled workers and simultaneously operated a "closed shop" policy.

The second factor of voluntarism was based on the belief that the state should not interfere in labour relations, including training, and that such matters were not the concern of government but of industry alone. This contrasts strongly with policies in other European countries such as Germany, where there has been a strong tradition of partnership between government and industry to provide a framework of nationally agreed training procedures and standards.

In the 1970s this deeply flawed UK system began to break down. Trades unions had used their collective bargaining power to raise the wages of all, including apprentices, so that the costs of training them had escalated and made industry uncompetitive in comparison with other countries. Combined with general short-termism in industry, this led companies to reduce drastically the number of apprenticeships they offered and sometimes not to provide any training at all, instead, relying on poaching to get their trained labour.

The position was untenable even before the revolution in work practices began to require a flexible and multi-skilled workforce. There was virtually no provision for adult workers to update their skills or retrain, and girls were largely excluded from the apprenticeship system. Mass unemployment was rising. During the 1980s the incumbent Conservative Government took concerted action. They instituted the National Council for Vocational Qualifications (NCVQ), which was tasked with creating a coherent framework of vocational qualifications and national standards based on job competencies. This proved to be a more difficult task than anticipated, and it took until 1993 for some 509 NVQs to be put in place, covering occupations representing 80% of the working population. The take-up of these NVQ qualifications was slow and patchy. According to Hamlin, the main reason for this has been controversy about how generic the skills taught in NVQs should be. Some employers would only support workers to take those modules most relevant to their current jobs, which meant that they did not complete the full qualification.

The government also instituted a national network of Training and Enterprise Councils (TECs) in England and Wales and Local Enterprise Councils (LECs) in Scotland. These bodies involved partnerships between business and training providers at the local level. They required great commitment from employers to plan and deliver training and to develop small businesses locally. Most importantly, the TECs and LECs were supposed to deliver training for adult unemployed people, but there was a time lag between the start of the Employment Training scheme (ET) and when the TECs and LECs could take operational responsibility. As a result the TECs and LECs were starved of government funds and drastically reduced their provision just at the time when the ET scheme was getting established.

Various youth training schemes have not been conspicuously successful for a variety of reasons. In the early 1980s the YTS scheme had the misfortune to be launched during a deep recession and was criticized because employers used it as a source of cheap labour whilst giving little training. Political opponents accused it of being a cynical ploy to "massage" the unemployment statistics. A later attempt to provide "training credits" so that all school leavers could "purchase" training was hampered by the fact that there was a disturbingly low enthusiasm for self-improvement amongst school leavers, as the Department of Employment eventually conceded. In the pilot schemes only 45% of the credits given to school leavers were actually taken up. Part of the problem appeared to be that young people could earn more in unskilled jobs than they could in training. Later initiatives at last began to address the needs of adult workers, but by 1997/1998 it was all change again. As new provisions begin to emerge from this state of flux it is probably still too soon to judge their effectiveness.

Certainly, one success story that has received little official recognition is the expansion of higher education throughout the 1980s and 1990s. The university population rose from 10% of young people to 30% in a decade, and many of the new students were mature people who had not succeeded at school or who wanted a change of occupation. Many others were from groups whose families traditionally left school at the earliest legal age. So successful was this initiative, that the government of the day was forced to "consolidate" and introduce controls so that numbers did not escalate out of control, and the imposition of student fees and the abolition of maintenance grants appear to have deterred mature and economically disadvantaged students most (Midgley, 2000). Even so, the Open University still provides a highway to higher education for students who follow largely distance learning courses in their own time.

Readers may be surprised that I have brought higher education into this discussion of training, which has traditionally been concerned with the acquisition of physical skills. This is quite deliberate. Today, the need for training and indeed, lifelong learning, has never been greater. Neither is it confined to men engaged in the "skilled trades" learning largely "manual" skills. Downs (1995) notes that the need to develop cognitive skills—developing concepts and so on—is fast overtaking the reliance on rote learning and using physical skills. Learners need to "learn how to learn" and many argue that graduates are most likely to have achieved this. In addition, much knowledge work requires graduate-level understanding. Whatever the differences between education and training may have been in the past, these are becoming increasingly blurred given the demands of the new workplaces.

In a climate where workers need to be flexible, multi-skilled, and innovative, and where there is a need for constant updating of skills in the wake of rapid technological change, training and lifelong learning are seen as essential. There is also a belief that skilled workers will be able to cope better with the pace and complexity of contemporary jobs and therefore to be less likely to succumb to stress-related illnesses. Finally, in a world where "employability" is often the only insurance policy people have for continued employment and economic survival, the opportunity for self-development is often the characteristic of jobs most valued by employees (Doyle, 1992; Sunman, 2000). For all these reasons, the whole concept of training has expanded from an emphasis on formal courses to the inclusion of almost any aspect of job-related learning, however achieved. Similarly, lifelong learning (and by implication, training) is seen as a major solution to the ills created by the revolution in the workplace and is central to the human resource enterprise (Keep, 1989).

In this chapter we will first look at the "ideal"—what the "best" organizations are striving to achieve. Then, despite the absence of much "hard" evidence, we will examine what is known about the barriers that currently exist (at least in the UK) and which must be overcome if the "ideal" is to be achieved. I discuss a general model of what is involved in planning, implementing, and evaluating a training course using theory and a case study from Patrick (2000). Finally, I invite you to undertake an exercise in concept learning based on Downs' (1995) technique and then to devise your own based on your organization's mission statement.

The "ideal"—the learning organization

Transforming a traditional, bureaucratic organization into a learning organization is a cause often pursued with missionary zeal as the answer to all ills. But what exactly *is* a learning organization?

Pearn et al. (1995) identify four themes that characterize a learning organization. It is one that involves:

1   Creating a shared vision for the future to guide and even inspire.
2   Acquiring an organizational capacity for renewal and self-transformation.
3   Encouraging and sustaining the learning of all members of the organization.
4   Creating organizations that provide increasing satisfaction and fulfilment to all the stakeholders.

Learning organizations aim to "bridge the gap between the world of work and the rest of people's lives" (1995, p. 2). Intelligent, creative, resourceful people too often become passive, dependent, and "brainless" when they encounter the command and control ethos at work. Learning organizations aim to create a climate of continuous learning and improvement at individual, group, and organizational levels. Though by no means all learning takes place in formal training courses, training is obviously high on the business agenda. According to many commentators the learning organization is *the* solution to the "crisis in organizations" (p. 2), so it is worth examining the concept in some detail.

Origins of learning organization thinking

The learning organization is based on the metaphor of organization as a brain (Morgan, 1986) and the idea was influenced by cybernetics—the study of information, communication, and control. Engineers attempting to design "intelligent" machine systems capable of flexible and adaptive behaviour attempted to emulate the functioning of the human brain.

The ability to self-regulate behaviour depends on processes of information exchange, particularly those involving negative feedback, i.e., the detection and correction of errors. These processes depend on the system's ability to scan the environment and detect discrepancies between actual and desired states of affairs, so that corrective action can be taken. The detection of

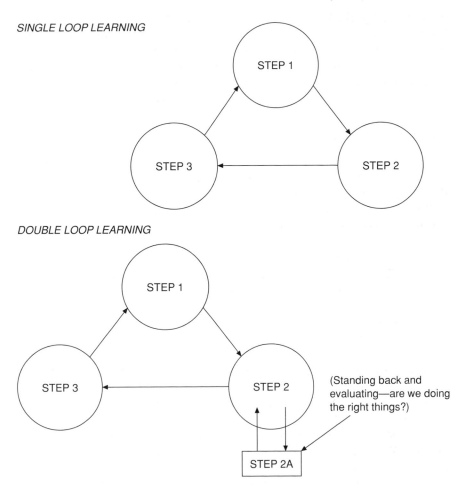

SINGLE LOOP LEARNING

DOUBLE LOOP LEARNING

(Standing back and evaluating—are we doing the right things?)

Figure 6.1 Single and double loop learning. Page 88 from G. Morgan, *Images of Organization*, 1986. Copyright © 1986 Sage Publications. Reprinted by permission of Sage Publications Inc.

discrepancies involves some comparison with a set of standards. If the standards are appropriate, well and good. However, if the standards are or become inappropriate, then the "intelligence" of the system breaks down.

Argyris and Schon (1978) applied these ideas to single and double loop learning, shown in Figure 6.1. Single loop learning is learning to detect and correct error in relation to a given set of operating norms. Step 1 is the process of sensing, scanning, and monitoring the environment. Step 2 involves comparing the results of this information against operating norms—whether, for instance, quality standards are being met. Step 3 is the process of initiating appropriate action to correct any deviation from the operating norms. In double loop learning, however, there is an extra step—2a—the process of questioning whether the operating norms are appropriate that involves learning to learn. Effectively, this involves standing back and asking "Are we doing the right things?" rather than simply doing the job right. The argument is that in today's turbulent business environment, double loop learning is essential for organizational success because the operating norms may quickly become out of date and inappropriate. For double loop learning to occur, though, there must be a climate of openness and trust, where norms and values are open to change, where there is a free exchange of information, and where there are shared "ownership" and commitment to organizational goals.

Also central to this approach are holographic principles. A hologram involves information being stored in such a way that the whole is recorded in each of the parts such that, given one part, the whole can be reconstructed. Pribram (1971, 1976) suggested that the brain functions in accordance with holographic principles. In the brain, each neuron is connected with hundreds of thousands of others, and different kinds of information can be processed simultaneously. Information about the whole is stored in many of the parts, and since much of this connective network is redundant, the system can learn, self-organize, and function effectively when one part malfunctions. Applying these ideas to organizations one can think of a factory where work is performed by autonomous work groups. Each team is a part which replicates the functions of the whole and is self-organizing and able to learn. Within each team, moreover, there are multi-skilled individuals who can perform any of the team's activities and so, again, the whole is replicated in the parts. Furthermore, the malfunctioning of one team does not impact upon the effectiveness of the others. Similarly, networked information systems give everyone access to vital business data, whereas before access to and processing of this may have been confined to particular people or departments.

Applying these ideas to organizations

Senge (1990) applied these ideas to the learning organization, where knowledge sharing and innovation was said to lead to competitive advantage. The following four principles underly the learning organization.

Systems thinking and systematic problem solving

This involves thinking in terms of wholes—not piecemeal changes but fundamental reform—and where the full ramifications of such a change are thought out. The organization is managed in terms of a system and underlying causes and effects are treated, not just the symptoms. Thus, the learning organization would not make the mistake of Heyes's (1998) agrochemical company where training and change was introduced without regard to other systems such as pay and reward and social relations on the shop floor. It failed to achieve its objectives (see later).

Shared vision and personal mastery

This involves everyone having a shared long-term view of where the organization is going and also a willingness and openness to change. Everyone also has a vision of where he or she wants to go and wants to feel a sense of mastery—that this is achievable. In a learning organization, all experiences, and not just formal training courses, are seen as opportunities for learning, and there is a commitment to continual personal development.

*Mental models/focus on experimentation/learning from
past experience*

This involves a willingness to keep examining fundamental assumptions (mental models) so that these can be changed if necessary. There is an interplay between shared and individual mental models and individuals' ideas are not ridiculed under the guise of "this is how we have to do it". Given this, there is an emphasis on experimentation and "learning by doing". In these circumstances, there must not be a fear of failure, and mistakes and failures have to be tolerated and seen as valuable learning experiences. A distinction is made between "unproductive success" and "productive failure". IBM is often cited as an example of a company so successful that it saw no need to change and was consequently overtaken by the microprocessor revolution and nearly went under. Its recent "turnaround" is an example of learning from failure.

Teamwork/learning from others/transferring knowledge

A learning organization is characterized by genuine teams feeding each other ideas that lead to creativity and innovation. Since collections of competitive individuals tend to withhold knowledge and ideas from each other, trust, openness, and a lack of hierarchy have to be encouraged. An organization can also learn from competitors and from strategic alliances. Fundamental assumptions may be implicit and hence not available for scrutiny and change. Knowledge and ideas gained from other organizations can provide the "fresh eye" that detects blindspots.

From this it can be seen that the learning organization has quite a few revolutionary features, among them, openness and the free exchange of information for which an absence of hierarchy and status is seen as essential; every person's ideas need to be heard and valued. The emphasis on constant challenging of assumptions and ways of doing things is the opposite of strict adherence to rules and procedures and an "if it ain't broke don't fix it" mentality. The positive acknowledgement of mistakes and failures, provided that the person and the organization learn from them, is the antithesis of what usually happens in organizations, where failure is punished, and often quite severely. Finally, the learning organization is committed to continuous, fundamental, proactive change and not to evolutionary, reactive change forced by external circumstances. (Note that Kirton's innovators—see Chapter 2—would have a much easier time in a learning organization.)

So much for the hype—what about the problems?

The greatest obstacle to implementing the principles of a learning organization concerns the transmission and management of knowledge. Much organizational knowledge is tacit or implicit. It is based on unvoiced assumptions, is often rooted in action, and is often learned unconsciously through the process of socialisation into the organization and through imitation. It is very hard to communicate and transfer to others. As anyone who has been involved in developing an expert system knows, getting human experts to make all their knowledge explicit can be difficult because much of their knowledge does not lend itself to being represented verbally. Part of the reason for this is the way we acquire skills. As several theorists, notably Anderson (1982) and Fitts and Posner (1967) have suggested, skill learning proceeds in essentially two stages. The first stage involves the conscious, effortful acquisition of declarative knowledge, i.e., knowledge that is explicit. The second stage is the process of using that knowledge so that it gradually becomes implicit and automatic, i.e., procedural knowledge. Thus, when learning a foreign language we may first struggle to put together a simple sentence. As we become more fluent we can "speak without thinking" just as we do when speaking our native language. The same is true of driving a car. At first we are completely overwhelmed by the complexity of all the information we have to process and all the actions we must perform simultaneously. In a skilled driver so much of this has come under automatic control that he or she can engage in other complex tasks such as arguing politics with a passenger. So it is with many tasks—the expert is often not consciously aware of all the information and reasoning which guides his or her decisions and actions. Moreover, trying to make the factors that guide behaviour explicit often disrupts performance to the extent that the person cannot then perform properly. If this is true of the expert knowledge needed to perform the job, it is even more true of implicit norms, values, and assumptions that may never have gone through the declarative knowledge phase but have been picked up unconsciously.

Thus, a major problem for the learning organization, even when workers are willing to share knowledge, is how to make this sufficiently explicit for it to be transmitted to others. Questioning implicit assumptions is even more difficult when this goes against fundamental characteristics of human cognitive functioning. It needs frequent intervention from an outside analyst who has not been socialized into the organization but who may therefore lack vitally important "insider" information.

Another very important factor concerns who owns the means to production. In the industrial age, the owners of business also owned the means of production—the machines and tools that allowed the worker to conduct his or her trade. In the information age, the means of production is knowledge inside people's heads or the personal computers they own or take with them. Thus, knowledge workers own the means to production and can take this to competitors or set up as competitors themselves. Organizations have been slow to realize the implications of this for the balance of power between employers and employees. Its main effects have become glaringly apparent only in economic upturns when there may be shortages of skilled labour. Downsizing organizations may escort people to their desks and out of the building, but they cannot remove the knowledge and skills from their heads. Neither is it always easy to hire their replacement when this becomes necessary. The loosening of organizational ties and the casualization of employment also mean that key personnel can leave at a moment's notice to work for competitors who offer more pay. Another belatedly realized disadvantage of "letting go" older workers is that valuable corporate history is thereby lost and cannot be replaced. All these problems can be magnified in a learning organization because of its heavy reliance on knowledge, which may be freely communicated but not necessarily in a permanent form. However, all organizations are having to turn their attention to the problems of knowledge management to preserve knowledge and expertise (Kessels, 1999).

Promoting a learning organization can also be very costly because relevant training and development is costly. Motorola, in their Dublin plant, for instance, used to give every worker 5–7 days training per year and manufacturing is shut down for an hour per week so that everyone can participate in quality improvement meetings and activities. Though Motorola claims to have saved $6.6 billion in manufacturing costs between 1989 and 1994, it is not clear whether less prosperous companies could embark on this sort of enterprise. A small group of talented, committed, and tightly knit entrepreneurs may naturally create a learning organization for themselves in the early days. Sustaining this as the organization expands may be more difficult. Transforming a large bureaucratic organization into a learning organization may be impossible.

Leadership

Also central to the idea of the learning organization is the notion of leadership. In particular, transformational leadership seems particularly appropriate. Traditional management (usually referred to as transactional leadership in the literature) involves imposing order via systems and procedures and "single loop learning". Management such as this is, of course, essential for the success of organizations but to promote innovation and productivity in today's turbulent business climate, more is needed. According to Bass and Avolio (1990; Bass et al., 1996), transformational leaders are characterized by:

- Charisma—they have a strong vision of where the company is going and communicate this to others.
- Idealized influence—they inspire people with a belief in the attainability of the vision and confidence in their own contribution to achieving the vision.
- Intellectual stimulation—they constantly question set ways of doing things and conduct frequent "reality checks" with colleagues to ensure that their vision does not descend into dogma or "off the wall" ideas; in the process followers also question assumptions and contribute to innovation.
- Personal consideration—they value everyone in the organization regardless of status, and empower and mentor people so that they grow in confidence and achieve personal goals through organizational goals.

All these characteristics would be vital to the development of a learning organization but transformational leaders would seem to be rather rare people, especially in traditional bureaucratic organizations. Very often multi-rater (360 degree) feedback is used in development programmes which attempt to develop transformational leadership qualities in managers. Instruments such as Synchrony (Development Dimensions International) and Benchmarks (Oxford Psychologists Press) are used for this purpose. The manager rates himself or herself on various skills, characteristics, and competencies, which may be related to transformational leadership, and subordinates, peers, and boss also rate the manager. The idea is that this "all round" evaluation will produce a more accurate and balanced picture of the manager's performance. Any discrepancies between the manager's self-ratings and those of others will reveal both strengths and development needs for which a personal development plan can then be devised. (Multi-rater feedback is discussed in more detail in Chapter 8.)

Alimo-Metcalfe (1998b; Alimo-Metcalfe & Alban-Metcalfe, 2000; Alban-Metcalfe & Alimo-Metcalfe, 2000) has recently challenged most leadership assessment in selection and promotion decisions. She argues that since men favour a transactional (traditional management) style (Alimo-Metcalfe, 1995; Bass et al., 1996; Rosener, 1990; Sparrow & Rigg, 1993) and senior managers tend to be male, it is possible that the competencies being assessed are likely to emphasize these types of behaviours at the expense of more transformational styles. They also note that most leadership instruments (and research) have been developed in the US by men, using samples of predominantly male participants in commercial organizations. Thus, transactional leadership is likely to predominate. Finally, they note that transformational leadership research is mostly based on observations of top managers or "distant" leaders, whereas what is wanted is understanding of the characteristics of "close" or "nearby" leaders—those who are in close and regular contact with the staff they manage.

Alimo-Metcalfe's research attempted to circumvent these possible sources of bias. She and Alban-Metcalfe conducted Repertory Grid interviews with more than 150 male and female managers and professionals at all levels in UK local government and the NHS to elicit their constructs of what constitutes an effective nearby leader. In this way, they tried to avoid the bias towards the measurement of transactional and "distant" leadership. Some 2000 constructs were elicited and they then used these to develop a new instrument—The Transformational Leadership Questionnaire (TLQ). This was trialled on more than 3500 managers. Analysis of the data revealed the existence of nine "highly robust scales with high internal reliabilities (alpha = .85), construct validity and convergent validity (range r= .46 to .85)" (Alimo-Metcalfe & Alban-Metcalfe, 2000, p. 16; see also Alban-Metcalfe & Alimo-Metcalfe, 2000). Brief descriptions of the scales are given in Box 6.1.

Alimo-Metcalfe and Alban-Metcalfe believe that their methodology has led to a rather different, more complex, and richer range of leadership dimensions than that produced by Bass and his colleagues in the US. In particular, the TLQ scales almost all relate to notions of transformational leadership, whereas Bass and Avolio's (1990, 1996) research yielded transactional and transformational leadership dimensions. The Metcalfes argue that although the US model emphasizes the leader as role model, their research of male and female "nearby" leaders has thrown up the notion of leader as servant. "Nearby" transformational leaders focus on what they can do for their followers to increase their self-confidence, self-efficacy, motivation, and personal and professional development.

The robustness of the scales has allowed them to develop the Transformational Leadership 360 degree Feedback Questionnaire © in order to meet the need to develop leaders at all levels. This can be used to analyse individual and team/group strengths and development needs. They are now seeking to develop a modified TLQ for the private sector.

BOX 6.1
The Transformational Leadership Questionnaire scales

Scale 1   Genuine concern for others' well-being and development.
Scale 2   Political/stakeholder sensitivity and skills.
Scale 3   Insirational networker and visionary promoter.
Scale 4   Empowers, delegates, develops leadership potential.
Scale 5   Integrity, consistency, honesty, and openness.
Scale 6   Accessibility, approachability, sensitivity.
Scale 7   Decisive, determined, self-confident, resilient.
Scale 8   Clarifies boundaries, involves others in decision making.
Scale 9   Encourages critical and strategic thinking.

Source: B. Alimo-Metcalfe and R. J. Alban-Metcalfe (2000). A new approach to assessing transformational leadership. *Selection and Development Review*, 16(5), 15–17.

Alimo-Metcalfe and Alban-Metcalfe's research indicates that transformational leadership, far from being the key to a learning organization, may itself be in considerable need of rethinking and revision. The question that intrigues me is whether even a gifted transformational leader could operate successfully in very adverse business conditions. Alimo-Metcalfe has said (personal communication) that even in the worst circumstances one can still treat people with consideration and respect. This is undoubtedly true as Herriot and Pemberton's (1995) analysis of the factors that can ameliorate the pain and damage of downsizing shows. They found that things like clear advance communication of bad news, a fair system for selecting those to be made redundant, an appeals procedure, the ability to suggest alternatives, and "outplacement" counselling all improved outcomes. However, I had no answer to one woman who was attending a leadership course when she asked how she could implement her new skills when a "redundancy situation" meant that the trades union had instructed her staff not to speak to her. Can a learning organization develop when there is an overloaded workforce with little time, facilities, and support for learning? One wonders whether the learning organization can become an enduring reality only in the best of circumstances and only then in a workforce without strong vested interests in "the way it was". This conclusion is still positive but it does cast doubt on the notion that the learning organization is a panacea for organizational ills.

Case studies

There is very little evidence for the success of learning organizations and what little there is comes from case studies of organizations that are still in considerable flux. Nevertheless, two interesting case studies, presented at a conference in Dublin in 1997, illustrate several of the points made so far, although at a rather abstract level (see Case studies 6.1 and 6.2).

Case study 6.1:   Motorola (McConnell, 1997)

This involved a "greenfield" site near Dublin with a young and dynamic workforce, most of whom had been recruited straight from school or university. The company is very people oriented. For instance, they have world-wide customer satisfaction teams, which are given time off from other duties to deal with particular projects.

The model of culture design and systems to support learning are as shown in Figure 6.2. Leadership is at the centre and informs all the systems. The vision drives the structure of the organization, its performance management, and other organizational systems, which in turn drive and support teamwork. There are no visible signs of hierarchy and status so there is a single appraisal system and standard benefits for all. There are regular meetings to communicate information and a strong culture of participation so that everyone "owns" and solves problems. There is total commitment to training and development, as already mentioned, which involves a learning centre with computer-based training, job rotation, activity-based learning, and team learning.

Even given this very favourable environment, there were some signs of strain. Careful selection of the "right" people was essential, and it was difficult to recruit high calibre people in sufficient numbers. Since the aim was strategic capability at all levels, recruits had to be willing to improve performance and change to increase their flexibility through knowledge. In 1997, the old system of automatic 5–7 days' formal training per year was replaced with a system of "just in time" learning linked more clearly to performance appraisal and the identification of skills needed *now*. "Total customer satisfaction, participative problem solving teams" were also introduced. Everyone has to be a member of such a team, and manufacturing is shut down to allow time for everyone to contribute. "Recognition systems" for team achievements have also been added.

It is typical of a learning organization that old systems are continuously changed and this was manifestly a successful company. However, since this was a greenfield site and everything was originally designed to promote a learning organization, the fact that some systems were not a success and had to be reformed indicates that the process of achieving a learning organization is not straightforward even when great resources are available.

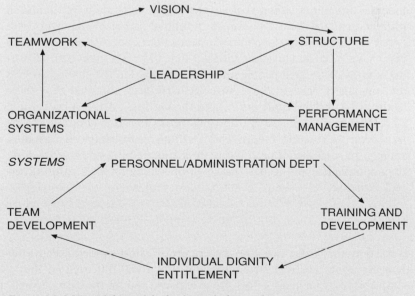

Figure 6.2 Motorola's model of culture design and systems to support learning.

Case study 6.2:   Shell International (Steel, 1997)

Shell is a very different organization to Motorola. This is a huge company suffering from the "tyranny of success", where the need for change could easily be overlooked. However, in 1997, the company was about to make huge investments in evolving markets in Russia and China. There was a felt need for new communication patterns from top to bottom to promote the transitions to new cultures and new learning. Moreover, there was a large existing workforce brought up in the old school who had been sent on technical training courses and promoted for their technical expertise. Now the company wished to promote "people management" and communication skills, and the old culture had to be replaced.

The strategies adopted included sweeping away the symbols of status and initiating a leadership programme, which involved vertical groupings so that managers were trained alongside their staff. (The thinking behind this was that people at different stages of their careers would have different perspectives, but it must have been a threatening environment for those raised in the old hierarchies.) The company vision of everyone owning and contributing to the organizational change was communicated via the slogans "Leaders leading leaders" and "Transformation starts with me". There was an attempt to promote a culture of valuing relationships instead of just intellect and performance.

Gary Steel, who presented this case study, was upbeat and optimistic—the company was on target to transforming itself. But he didn't hide the difficulties either. Among the points he made were that Shell itself had created the old system so shouldn't "rubbish" managers who "grew up" in it, since the company needs their expertise and company history knowledge. He acknowledged that there is a great deal of hurt and confusion so such people must be supported in the change process and managers need to "give succour". He also admitted that there is also a lot of fear. Staff are asking themselves, "Am I good enough to behave in this new way?", and this needs sensitive handling. There is a need to support failure and facilitate learning from mistakes. Finally, he identified a need to create a climate of commitment rather than compliance and to get people to be willing to share information and expertise.

It is a pity that these two case studies are so short on detail and long on statements about abstract structures and processes. But even so they give the impression of immense effort, huge expense and, in the case of Shell, no little hint of desperation. Even in the Motorola "greenfield" site there was an expressed need for "patience". If the learning organization *is* the solution to the "crisis in organizations", it is not one that is easy to implement.

Pearn (1995) provides case studies of more limited interventions that give more details and give grounds for hope. For instance, a group of tanker drivers who had been highly unionized and militant, but who had been downsized from 1100 to 400, now delivered more fuel than before as a result of changes in demarcations and the introduction of flexible working. Following all these changes, the drivers felt insecure and misunderstood by management. If further improvements in productivity were to be delivered management had to understand the drivers' concerns. The consultants suggested that the drivers themselves should conduct this information-gathering exercise and report back to management. Management agreed to this with some reluctance. A project team of drivers then underwent a 3-day workshop to formulate the objectives of the exercise, decide how to communicate them to their fellows, and to design the consultation process. Having decided that structured, facilitated discussions (focus groups) were the best way to collect information, the drivers were trained to conduct such discussions. Over the next 6 weeks the project team conducted 75 focus groups involving all 400 drivers and ancillary staff. The consultants then facilitated the analysis and collation of results before the drivers made recommendations to the management team. Entrusting such a process to "shop-floor" workers is still highly unusual but the outcome of the consultation and the changes agreed by management were enthusiastically received by all parties. "The whole consultation was seen by both drivers and by management as a watershed in their relations. One thing that they realised was that despite years of dissension and distrust they were essentially on the same side" (1995, p. 6). In this manner communication and relations between drivers and management were considerably improved, thus paving the way for increases in productivity.

Conditions for promoting creativity and innovation at work

West (2000b) has recently published an article in *The Psychologist* in which he reviews evidence about the conditions needed to turn creative thinking into innovative practice at work. Although not specifically concerned with learning organizations, much of this research provides evidence for the soundness of the principles underlying them. He first makes a distinction between creativity, which is largely a matter of individuals generating new ideas, and innovation implementation, which is the application of those ideas by teams, organizations, and societies. Paradoxically, workplaces may be too pressured and hectic to encourage individual creativity since high levels of stress encourage a reliance on habitual actions and solutions and rigid thinking (e.g., Kruglansky & Freund, 1983). At the same time, such environments may be those that encourage and demand innovation and in fact several studies have shown that adverse circumstances (e.g., external threat or heavy workloads) were associated with greater innovation. For instance, in a study of 10,000 health service personnel, work demands predicted both stress levels *and* innovation (Bunce & West, 1995). One nurse developed a set of leaflets both to help patients prepare for their visits and to save her time in repeated briefings. Health teams working in areas where there was relative health deprivation were more innovative than teams working in less challenging locations. Companies with low market share (e.g., a uPVC window manufacturer) were more likely to develop new products than those with high market share (West, Patterson, Pillinger, & Nickell, 2000). Although people need some "space" to come up with creative suggestions, implementing innovation is often driven by urgent demands or threats.

However, there are important caveats to these generalizations. First, creativity and innovation are most likely to occur when the organizational climate is safe and supportive. If new ideas are ridiculed or ignored, or failure is punished, people are less likely to innovate. West (2000b) cites as case studies a pharmaceutical company where a leader aggressively challenged his team, with the result that innovative suggestions were rare. In contrast, a US company that makes cables benefited greatly from an innovative solution to a problem made by a part-time shop-floor worker. In the latter case, "the company repeatedly demonstrated that they supported innovative ideas from wherever in the company they emerged" (p. 461). West (2000a) found that a key indicator of innovation was the extent to which team members collectively reflected on objectives, strategies, and processes as well as wider organizational issues. Thus, there is some support for the principle of mental models/focus on experimentation/learning from past experience and maybe some indirect evidence for the principle of shared vision and personal mastery.

Evidence for the principles of systems thinking/systematic problem solving and learning from others/transferring knowledge comes from work that explores innovation in groups. Here the keys to creativity seem to be that teams should be composed of diverse individuals with different skills and knowledge *and* that the team climate and functioning should be good. This implies that knowledge sharing and transfer leads to innovation when the entire system supports it. This is reinforced by research showing that innovation is most likely when team members trust other members' intentions (Edmondson, 1996, 1999). Open discussion of medication errors (administering the wrong drug or the right drug in the wrong amount) led to the replacement of equipment that encouraged such errors, but health-care teams who kept errors to themselves did not learn or improve their performance. (See Chapter 5 for more discussion of the role of trust and reporting of errors in creating a safety culture.)

The meaningfulness of work and the amount of control people have may also be important. Oldham and Cummings (1996) recently reported evidence that the five job characteristics (skill variety and challenge, task identity and task significance, autonomy, and feedback), predicted levels of individual innovation. "Where climates are characterised by distrust, lack of communication, personal antipathies, *limited individual autonomy* and unclear goals, the implementation of these ideas is inhibited (Amabile, Conti, Coon, Lazenby, & Heron, 1996)" (West 2000b, p. 463, my emphasis). If employees are completely constrained by rules and procedures they cannot innovate.

However, West (2000b, p. 463) also points out that innovation also creates conflict and resistance to change or may itself be caused by conflict—dissension generates the energy for innovation: "The notion that creativity and innovation are easy, positive, opportunistic processes is inappropriate." And innovations can sometimes be discovered to be mistakes. Creating a learning organization is not easy!

Thus, there are indications that the principles underlying the learning organization can be successfully implemented but, as for transforming an entire organization on these lines, the jury is most definitely still out!

So much for the ideal—what else is known about the barriers to achieving it?

Training and development paradoxes

Reading the training and development literature, I am struck again and again by how many central issues are paradoxical—at least in terms of what is happening "on the ground". It may be that this discussion is too much dominated by UK experiences and practices and I acknowledge that other countries appear to have a much better record (e.g., France, Germany, and Japan—see, e.g., Steedman, 1990; Steedman & Wagner, 1989). However, these issues may be far more pertinent worldwide than is generally suspected.

Paradox 1: Having a skilled workforce is vital but nurturing the skills of workers is not at all important

This paradox was brought home to me by reading an illuminating chapter on the analysis of organizational training needs by Roscoe (1995). In this work he frequently suggests ways to increase the "credibility" of training activities and training personnel. His first piece of advice is that the training team should have "a high powered and well-recognised source of authority leading it" and in many cases it is desirable that this person is *not* a member of the training team so that "the results can be presented as having status independent from the training specialist" (p. 53). (How about the training specialist giving added credibility to the team of the Finance Director?!) He then goes to great lengths to recommend giving presentations of the results of training needs analysis to senior management in order to achieve a face-to-face encounter with those at the top and to avoid the possibility of a lengthy and carefully prepared written report going unread by those with the power to implement it. Further, he urges training specialists to seek diligently for nontraining solutions to problems they have identified in organizational training needs analysis so that "the credibility of training can be built up by acting responsibly as part of the management team" (p. 65). He adds a list of reasons why training solutions may not be accepted by senior management:

- It will take too long.
- It will cost too much.
- Training resources are not available.
- It will stop/clash with other training.
- There is a lack of learning skills in those needing to learn.
- There is a lack of potential in those needing to learn.
- Training is rejected in this context by management, learners, or the culture of the organization.

He ends with the comment, "Building training into the business makes it an essential service rather than a nice add-on which can be dropped when the going gets tough" (p. 71). Quite so! But one asks, in today's climate, how could any organization possibly *not* build training into the business? Though he never says so directly, Roscoe is obviously a man who has fought many an uphill battle to get training onto the agenda at all.

That Roscoe's experience is not an isolated example of the lowly status of the training and development function is evidenced by many commentators who remark that the training budget, never very generous, is often the first thing to go in hard times. Hamlin (1995), for instance, says that over the decades only major companies have trained skilled workers in significant numbers and these have cut back drastically in economic downturns. As for the rest, "most other organizations have not trained at all but instead have obtained their skilled labour by poaching" (p. 265). Thayer (1997) paints an equally gloomy picture in the US, where only 35% of the workforce are receiving any training at all and most of these are college graduates (Marshall, 1995). While large companies are preoccupied with restructuring and outsourcing, small companies are hiring "downsized", skilled, older workers and see no need to train younger people. "The long term effects of this neglect may be enormous" (Thayer, 1997, p. 27).

Given all that has been said about the learning organization and the importance of training, development, and lifelong learning for the success of organizations and the well-being of individuals, why are they accorded so little status and importance in so many organizations? Why is training so often perceived as an unnecessary current cost instead of as a vital investment in the future? After all, if organizations are really concerned about wasting money on training for people who may not stay long, they can always insist on formal contracts in which employees agree to remain with the company for a specified period afterwards in return for training funds.

One reason is that organizations are often poor at integrating training and development programmes into their strategic business objectives. I once did an analysis of a staff attitudes survey conducted by a large government organization in the UK (Doyle, 1992). One of the most important predictors of positive attitudes to the organization (ranging from job satisfaction, organizational commitment, perceived quality of organizational communication, quality of change management, and so on) was the person's relationship with his or her line manager. This relationship was in turn most strongly predicted by the extent to which the individual's manager took his or her staff development seriously. This particular organization was in the midst of a major organizational development programme, which had many of the hallmarks of a transition to a learning organization, and it was obviously spending a great deal on training and other forms of learning. Despite this, only 29% of managers discussed the objectives of attendance at training courses beforehand and only 30% discussed follow-up action afterwards. Even fewer managers—18%—regularly reviewed how training may have improved the person's job performance.

Even when there is a clear strategy to link training to business objectives, the social processes surrounding skill acquisition and deployment may be ignored, with the result that training does not result in better performance. Heyes (1998) reports an interesting case study of workers in an agrochemical plant. Management wanted to introduce more flexible working patterns by breaking down the old demarcations. Thus, (higher grade) maintenance workers were trained in production tasks and production workers were trained in maintenance tasks. The two sets of workers were then expected to work flexibly as a team. Unfortunately, management conceded to the maintenance workers' insistence on retaining their higher gradings, which meant that once bonuses and overtime payments were added to their higher basic wage, they were paid considerably more than the production workers for doing what was essentially the same job. The production workers reacted to this inequity in two ways. They passed on their skills to the maintenance workers because they needed their cooperation to control the pace of work so they could take rest breaks at times that suited them. However, they refused to undertake any maintenance tasks even though they had frequently *chosen* to do so under the old system—again to control the pace of work. Thus, in the case of production workers, the training had been counterproductive. Meanwhile the maintenance men suffered from low morale because as skilled men they felt demeaned by having to perform lower status production tasks. In fact, though management had intended the training to promote worker empowerment, the most common reaction was demoralization.

Heyes points out that, within HRM, training is not so much a case of providing workers with skills as that these skills should be at management's *disposal* to be used in the pursuit of management's goals. The fact that workers might "use their skills as a tactical resource to pursue non-managerial goals" (p. 99) is often overlooked.

My own experience of attending many IT training courses highlights another problem. Usually, despite an obvious pressing need for the skills thus gained (e.g., spreadsheets and WebCT for student record keeping; use of the internet for research searches, development of distance learning materials, etc.), the typical outcome is that when I get back I am plunged into a huge backlog of work. The result is that I have no time to consolidate and practise my new skills so that a month or so later I have forgotten so much that I may as well not have bothered with the training. So often, time to develop new skills is not factored into the training equation and so the potential benefits appear negligible.

Many people will be familiar with this sort of experience and, in fact, reviews of research into long-term retention of skills show a steady loss over time when they are not used (Annett, 1979; Hagman & Rose, 1983). This is a particular issue when the exercise of skills is very infrequently demanded but, when the need does arise, it is absolutely crucial for the person to be competent. Examples include fault diagnosis in power and chemical plants and in-flight emergencies. Particular faults or emergencies may occur rarely, if ever, in an operator's or pilot's career but if they do, reactions to deal with them must be very rapid if disaster is to be avoided. This is why plant operators and pilots may spend many hours in simulators dealing with potential disasters that might never happen in reality. It is reassuring that relearning can be very rapid and that regular rehearsal in simulators reduces the deterioration of little-used but very important skills (Stammers, 1996).

It is more problematic when employers may not be prepared to provide constant "refresher" training. This may be a particular problem for people who are "intermittent" users of software. After several weeks or months without using the program, people may have to relearn what to do. Until they have achieved this, they are unlikely to be very productive. Similarly, government training schemes to help the long-term unemployed back to work are rendered less effective because there is often a long gap between the training and getting a job that allows the person to actually use the skills they have learned.

In short, if people cannot immediately transfer their new skills and knowledge into their ongoing work, then the benefits of training may be meagre. Training can even be counterproductive. It is very demotivating to arrive back "fired up" with new ideas only to find every attempt to implement them blocked with obstacles and hostility.

Given all this, it is hardly surprising that senior management is often sceptical about the benefits of training and that sending someone on a training course is often given as a reward or because he or she "needs a break". It also explains why learning organizations like Motorola have abandoned traditional training activities in favour of "just-in-time-learning" whereby individuals are taught the skills they need as and when they need them.

If training and development is to become central to business strategy a systems approach is needed (Thayer, 1997; Winter, 1995). From this perspective training and development is seen as a subsystem central to the organization. Thus, the overall business goals and strategies and financial resources influence the design, delivery, and effectiveness of a training programme. Training also influences other subsystems such as pay, career progression, succession planning, and selection. Suppose, for instance, that one wants to introduce new technology. A systems approach would not only involve trials to evaluate its effects on the workforce, but would also elicit the input of the people who would be directly affected into the design of the system. A systems approach would also address the selection of new recruits with the right aptitudes and skills and the training needed for existing employees to use the new technology effectively. Evaluation of the training programmme could well lead to new models of job competencies and measures of job performance, which might then influence appraisal and reward systems. Such an approach may start with an organizational training needs analysis (Roscoe, 1995), which, when done thoroughly, may reveal the causes of organizational ills and suggest both training and nontraining solutions. The full cycle is suggested by Winter (1995) and is shown in Figure 6.3.

But such a process is costly in terms of the resources needed for the analysis, the delivery of training, and its evaluation. If training is low on the strategic agenda and has little organizational "credibility" then the resources will not be found. Interestingly, technology is developing so fast that even an organization committed to its staff's development may not be able to cope. I have been the lucky recipient of a new high-tech phone and a new "all singing and dancing" workstation as a result of efforts to become "millennium compliant". Overall it cost my organization a great deal of money, which it can ill-afford, and I am grateful because both items are

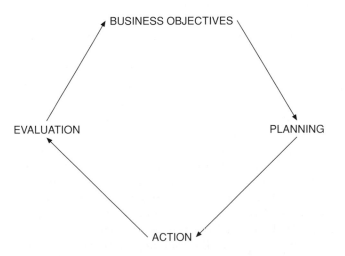

Figure 6.3 Integrating business objectives within a training cycle. From Winter (1995). Reprinted with the permission of Blackwell Publishing Ltd.

essential for my job. Neither have my employers wholly neglected training. I have been given a good 3 hours of training in the use of the new workstation and a manual to help me exploit the full capabilities of the new phone. The result is that, not since I learnt to use a public telephone when I was in the Brownies, age 7, have I felt so helpless and incompetent in the face of a telephone. The wretched thing seems to be erratically switched to voicemail (or not) so that it doesn't ring when I'm sitting at my desk, so I have to unscramble garbled messages and phone back people who think I'm uncontactable and that academics are never at work. Conversely, I am assailed by people who are irate because they haven't been able to leave messages. There are endless nannying electronic messages as to what buttons to press to do what, but I have yet to learn how to get to hear a second message without deleting the first, which I may want to keep, or how to go straight to a saved message without having to re-listen to all the other ones I've saved. Bring back my old phone! I won't bore you with the details of the new workstation's threatened impact on my effectiveness and productivity given the general incompatibility of the software with everything I then used. Suffice it to say that the workstation stayed under my desk for 2 months because I had so much work to do I simply did not dare to install it, despite its manifold short- and long-term benefits. It is not only productivity that can be affected. From feeling totally competent and in control, I was in danger of being rendered a complete ignoramus overnight.

Why are organizations so willing to invest in new technology and so unwilling to invest in adequate training or to consider the likely effects this may have on the productivity of the workforce? Worse, why do senior management place such faith in the new technology that they shed skilled workers before the systems are properly in place and have proved that they can make "efficiency gains"? Chaos in numerous government departments —notably the Passport Office in 1999—is evidence of the folly of sacking people before testing that the automation is working properly. But they do, again and again, possibly because some clever salesperson has told them what they want to hear—that technology will cut wage costs and increase effectiveness and efficiency at the same time. Well it obviously can, but . . .

Paradox 2: Training is too expensive, but it is also too expensive to investigate whether it was worth the cost

This paradox is even starker when one considers that many commentators believe that much costly training is driven by management fads. Campbell was complaining about this in 1971, so this is a long-term problem. More recently, Thayer (1997) singled out the current US vogue for "diversity training", which may genuinely be needed given the changing composition of the workforce. However, he writes, "Programs appear to be instituted without adequate needs assessment, without even a person analysis to determine existing attitudes . . . there is a real need to evaluate such training not only to determine whether such interventions achieve objectives but also to determine what kinds of interventions are effective. Failure to do so may result in their being abandoned as capriciously as they have been adopted" (p. 21).

In the UK much the same could be said about the relatively recent fashion for "team building" courses. Organizations have spent a great deal of money sending their managers on gruelling "outward bound" courses in the hope that in the face of common privation, the group will "bond" together and become mutually reliant. Unfortunately, there is little evidence to indicate that this interesting form of corporate torture is at all effective (see, e.g., Ibbetson & Newell, 1995, 1996). In fact, even a brief examination of what is known about social psychology would lead one to predict that more often than not, such exercises would prove counterproductive. First, people are taken out of their normal environment for a weekend or a few days where they have none of their usual "life-support systems" and where none of the usual social rules apply. Second, people who are maybe more used to Armani suits and chic restaurants are unlikely to relish being plastered in mud and living off "iron rations", so tempers could easily become frayed, especially when less fit and able members slow things down or fail to read the map properly. The most probable result is likely to be friction, discord, and recriminations rather than closer, more cooperative relationships.

Moreover, and this is the important point, there is generally not enough time to establish a new set of social relationships and norms. In contrast, the Armed Forces, who do use mutual privation as a technique to forge close-knit fighting groups, typically spend several weeks or months over the process, and the conditions under which they train are likely to be those that they will encounter in combat. Indiscriminately applied to managers, the same techniques used over a short timescale may actually damage previously existing relationships. Back in the office it may be difficult to forget that you had a furious row with a colleague because of a misread map. Even when the outcomes are considerably less dire than this, a few day's experience that were totally outside the person's normal personal and work life may be difficult to translate into anything relating to the work context.

Failure to clearly establish training needs and instil an appreciation of these needs in participants before the intervention can also be counterproductive. I was once forced to overhear a diatribe against a conventional classroom-based "team building" course on the London Tube. The main objection seemed to be that this had been completely unnecessary since the team had been functioning perfectly well and that the course had therefore been a waste of time and money. Worse, it had totally halted the team's vital work, which now had to be crammed into a considerably reduced working week. Anecdotal though this evidence is, I suspect it is a common part of people's experience. Note that the quality of the course was not an issue; its perceived relevance for participants most certainly was.

TRAINING BENEFITS ANALYSIS

If companies are sometimes prepared to waste money on training, a more common problem is getting them to spend anything on it. Craig (1995) advocates the use of a training benefits analysis, which establishes the training costs in all their various guises relative to the savings to the organization as a result of the training. Since finance directors are more used to dealing with "bottom-line" figures than vague statements about worker well-being and effectiveness, this is a good strategy to use when advocating a training programme. There are five steps in this process:

1   State clearly the problem area, e.g., the introduction of new technology will require retraining of the workforce.
2   Collect and evaluate assumptions made about the problem area, e.g., "this new technology is so complex we may need completely different kinds of people to operate it"—but is this true?
3   Gather information about costs and benefits—who, when, where, why, how, what cost, for how long, how do we measure?
4   Contrast and compare the difference between costs of training inputs and likely benefits from outputs, e.g., a safety training programme might cost £25,000 but if it saved £100,000 in reduced accident payments, its return on investment (ROI) would be £100,000/£25,000 = 4 times.
5   Present the results to top management.

Of course it is not as simple as this brief outline suggests. For a start, many of the benefits may be intangible and subjective, e.g., increased confidence, greater willingness to share ideas, etc. These intangible benefits can be stated in behavioural terms, e.g., "Increased confidence will be demonstrated by . . .", but what if the benefits are negative or "break-even" in monetary terms but are highly positive in terms of the subjective responses of the workers (e.g., Strong agreement with the statement that "This company really looks after its people")? Also, it is difficult to see how any valid cost–benefit analysis can be done *prior* to the training intervention. You can only evaluate the benefits of a safety training programme by comparing accident levels and payouts before and afterwards. Educated guesses can be made by referring to similar studies already done in similar organizations, but if these do not exist, then it is either "finger in the wind stuff" or you must do a pilot study that demands resources. In fact *any* cost–benefit analysis demands resources. If the aim is to get resources, then you have a "Catch-22" situation.

The purveyors of hardware have an advantage in that they can quantify costs much more easily. If the introduction of an industrial robot costs £120,000 and it can work two shifts and replace four people, the return on investment can soon be calculated. Working out the benefits of training the remaining operators to conduct preventative maintenance to reduce "downtime" is less easy. This may explain why new technology tends to be introduced with grossly underestimated training budgets and then fails to deliver its promise of greater productivity (Majchrzak, 1988; Wall, 1996).

TRAINING EVALUATIONS: RESEARCH PROBLEMS

Having said all this, it is not surprising that managers often become impatient with the demands of occupational psychologists for evaluation of training interventions. Trying to show that the training, and the training alone, was responsible for positive organizational effects is well nigh impossible. One is reminded of the old joke about someone who asks the way and is told, "Well, I wouldn't start from here." People grappling with pressing organizational problems have to start from wherever they happen to be and do the best they can. They are not helped by social scientists seeking to emulate the rigour and certainty of the natural sciences, telling them that a host of impossible conditions must be met before they can conclude that the training programme was actually effective and even then they cannot guarantee that it would work again in the same organization with different workers, much less in a different organization altogether.

Here are just some of the things that can influence the apparent outcome of a training programme. For more on this read Fletcher's (1988) seminal article.

* History. Did anything happen during the training programme that might have produced the outcome? For instance, if one manager got the sack, the other managers on the course may have worked flat-out to improve their performance. Thus, it could be the sacking and not the training which improved performance.
* Maturation. People on the training programme might have improved their performance merely because of greater experience in the job gained in amongst the training.
* Selection effects. It is rarely possible to randomly allocate people to training and nontraining groups. At best one might be able to randomly allocate entire departments to one condition or the other, but this can cause demoralization or rivalry effects. In the first case people are so resentful about "being left out" that they deliberately reduce their performance and so the effects of training are exaggerated. In the second case, they strive to outdo the training group so the apparent effects of training are reduced. In any case, nontraining groups may get "second-hand" training from colleagues on the course or managers may try to compensate "excluded" workers by giving them special treatment of some kind, which increases their effort and performance. Both can make the training benefits look negligible.

  Then there is the tendency for managers to send their best or worst workers on training courses—for obvious reasons. The good workers may have greater ability, motivation, and enthusiasm for the training, which results in more positive outcomes than will be the case when more "run-of-the-mill" workers are trained in the future. Many of the "worst" workers may leave or be dismissed before the end of the programme, thus inflating the average post-training scores of those who remain to complete the course.

Early pilot training courses may be delivered by particularly gifted and enthusiastic trainers who foster the expectation that participants will succeed. After delivering the umpteenth training course even the most gifted trainer may be somewhat jaded and give out less powerful signals. Or the later courses may be delivered by minions who are less gifted or who have made little personal investment, so the benefits appear less.

- Pretest. "Before" measures of performance (pretest) are essential as a baseline for evaluating the effectiveness of training afterwards (post-test) but pretests can sensitize participants to what is to be learned and thus inflate their post-test scores. Participants on later courses may not receive a pretest and so their scores may be lower.

- And lastly (in this book at least . . .). If the training does not meet the needs of or is inimical to the climate of a particular organization, it will be ineffective even if it has been a roaring success everywhere else (cf. Bennis, 1977).

The list of pitfalls goes on and on . . . And that's not all. There is still the question of what you measure to evaluate the effectiveness of a training programme. At the most superficial level you may hand out short questionnaires to assess people's impressions of the course. These are scathingly known as "happy sheets" in the trade because they only tap attitudes that may be affected by a host of factors such as how many good jokes the trainer cracked and may have nothing to do with how much was learned or how valuable that learning was. Testing participants for how much they have learned is of little value too if there has been no pretest. You need to find out how much people knew before the training to assess how much they learned from it. The vast majority of training courses do not involve a pretest and if they did, most participants would be resistant to taking a test in something they know nothing about and, indeed, have come to learn about. These two forms of ineffective evaluation are the curse of higher education. At best, all "happy sheets" do is to involve learners more closely in their own education by giving them a voice. Exam performance is, of course, mainly attributed to the student's own ability and effort. Neither method is good for assessing the effectiveness of lecturers' performance. Nor are they much good for assessing the effectiveness of work-based training courses.

At a much deeper level we want to know whether the training made any difference to people's work performance or indeed made a difference to their outlook on life. Take someone who has undergone a leadership course, for instance. Did it improve the person's behaviour so that he or she treated people with more respect and did more to instil confidence and empowerment afterwards? More importantly, did this would-be leader undergo a revolution in his or her thinking and behaviour, which led to the conviction

BOX 6.2
Solomon 4 group design

Experimental Group........... Pretest............. Training .... Post-test
Control Group 1 .... Pretest...................................... Post-test
Control Group 2 .... Training .... Post-test
Control Group 3 .... Post-test

that everyone, however lowly the status in the hierarchy, really does have something vital to contribute to organizational goals? Does this person now believe that the staff who clean the toilets and the offices are as important to company image and success as the Board of Directors? (If this seems far-fetched, consider how you would react to a dirty lavatory whether you were a humble employee or an entrepreneur with a multi-million order in your gift.) Increasingly, employers require this level of attitude change, but how often is such change investigated? And even if the resources were available, how would you go about investigating it?

Purists in the experimental tradition advocate the design given in Box 6.2 for the evaluation of training courses as a fail-safe method of discovering their effectiveness. If possible everyone should be allocated randomly to each group and on no account must they be allowed to speak to each other lest they perhaps deliver second-hand training or create rivalry or resentment effects. No wonder that many managers believe that academics inhabit another planet and reject evaluation and all its works! And there lies another paradox—what can occupational psychologists offer that related professionals (management consultants, HR specialists, etc.) cannot, if it is not the rigour that comes from their scientific training? Yet it is exactly this rigour that is being rejected as unrealistic in its demands.

Dipboye (1997a) raises a number of other issues to explain why the full "rational" model of training design and evaluation is so little used. One suggestion is that the personalities of people attracted to the training profession are unsuited to implementing the scientific model. Leach (1991) found that the best trainers were not analytical and scientific but team oriented, warm, outgoing, and humanistic in their orientation. This is likely to lead to negative attitudes to rigorous evaluation of training on the part of the trainers themselves (Argyris, 1990). Dipoye also defends the use of "happy sheets" because these provide trainees with a voice and involvement in their own training, which promotes a sense of procedural justice. Both procedural and distributive justice can be violated when strictly scientific evaluations are conducted since who gets to be trained can seem to be unfair and the researcher/trainer can be perceived as having too much power and control over the process.

As we have seen in Roscoe's (1995) article, organizational power and politics can also provoke much straying from the pure scientific model.

It has to be said that managers do not usually welcome the news that costly interventions have been ineffective. (Neither do governments—see Robinson, 1998 for a cogent and withering critique of the failure to tackle social exclusion in the UK during the past 30 years despite much knowledge and associated success gleaned from early education interventions in the 1960s and 1970s.) There is thus an inbuilt resistance to effective evaluation, which is odd, considering that "accountability" and "value for money" are high on agendas in the private and public sectors alike. I will resist the temptation to indulge in a critique of "individualistic capitalism" but it does sometimes seem that different rules apply for those with power.

So what is one to do? The answer is the best you can! If it is not possible to use the full scientific model in the field then you resort to whatever is possible. You try to do an analysis of training needs before the intervention, which may instil positive attitudes to the training before you start. You try to ensure random allocation to training and nontraining conditions of departments if not of individuals; you try to include "nonequivalent control groups"— people who are not exactly the same in all their characteristics and conditions of work as the training group but who will act as some sort of baseline indicator. You employ time series designs with multiple pretests and multiple post-tests. If the first and last post-test gives evidence of rises in performance over the last pretest you can be pretty sure that your training (and not history, maturation, etc.) has created the benefits and, what's more, that they are relatively permanent. Ghodsian, Bjork, and Benjamin (1997) advocate methods to evaluate training during the programme itself. Rugg-Gunn (2002) looked at the types of errors made by submarine commanders in "return to periscope depth" training in a simulator, either following a computer-based pretraining programme or without benefit of this experience. He advocates more use of electronic data collection to evaluate computer-based training. Pearn (1995) evaluated the effects of his learning organization intervention on the oil tanker drivers in a 3-day facilitated discussion, which involved an examination of the feelings and attitudes of the drivers towards the company. Much of the evidence involved audio tapes of discussions with management, which would have been unthinkable before the intervention. Certainly, from a strict scientific viewpoint the evidence is weak because there were no pre-intervention audio tapes of discussions with management. Quite so—there *were* no discussions with management to record because they were unthinkable!

The point is that *any* systematic and careful analysis and evaluation surrounding training is vastly better than none at all. If training is worth paying for, it is also worth finding out if it was worth the money.

Paradox 3: Skilled people are vital to our operations but someone else must train them

This is a specific variant of paradox 1 and its logical end point is that no-one gets trained at all; indeed, as we've seen, a lot of organizations are taking this line without heed for the future. The position is exacerbated by organizations generally wishing to hire young people who have yet to establish a secure work identity so they can be moulded to company values and behaviour and are also cheap to employ. Companies tend also to be very specific in what skills and experience they require for certain jobs. But where are these young people going to get their training and experience? One IT specialist recently told me with some bitterness, "What employers want is a 20-year-old with 15 years' experience in the IT industry!" The most casual trawl through job adverts rather confirms this impression.

Even in occupational psychology, commercial and other experience are given as essential prerequisites for most jobs but trainee posts that would allow the person to gain this experience are much less common.

However, before we start berating employers for their lack of foresight and realism, it is well to consider things from their point of view. For a start, much of the 20th century has shown that profitability tends to flow from de-skilling jobs and replacing people with machines. Expensive training, which may then benefit a competitor if the person moves on, does not have such a strong link with profits. Second, if there are already skilled people to be hired then it would be a poor finance director who didn't take advantage of this. Even an inflated salary can be cheaper than years of training for people who may not stay long. (Although formal contracts, as mentioned earlier, could be the answer to these objections.) However, as the section at the beginning of this chapter shows, the experience of training "home-grown" workers has not been a happy one for many UK employers for much of the 20th century. Finally, employers pay their taxes and expect that the education system should produce suitable workers, be they school leavers with BTECs and NVQs or graduates with a range of technical and transferable skills. Certainly Harvey, Moon, and Geall's (1997) survey of what employers want from graduate recruits shows that they want people who can "hit the ground running" and add value from the start. This brings me to the final paradox I want to consider here.

Paradox 4: Education and training are completely separate and distinct but they are also effectively inseparable

There is a fair amount of controversy about the distinctions between education, training, and development. Truelove (1995) gives the following working definitions:

- Education is a process whose prime purposes are to impart knowledge and develop the way mental faculties are used. Education is not primarily concerned with job performance.
- Training endeavours to impart knowledge, skills, and attitudes necessary to perform job-related tasks. It aims to improve job performance in a direct way.

- Development is a process whereby individuals learn through experience to be more effective. It aims to help people utilize the skills and knowledge that education and training have given them—not only in their current jobs, but also in future posts. It embodies concepts such as psychological growth, greater maturity, and increased confidence.

Truelove admits that many education courses have an element of training and vice versa, and that in reality education, training, and development are all inter-related. However, for a long time these distinctions made a great deal of sense, and trainers and educators tended to occupy different professions.

Education was much more general in its aspirations than training, aiming not only to impart knowledge but to "develop the whole child". Higher education was mainly concerned with socializing young people into an academic discipline and "training minds" to become critical, analytical, and capable of juggling and synthesizing ideas. There was a long-standing debate about whether the "trained minds" could apply themselves to any kind of work after graduation. This stemmed from the centuries-old belief that an education in the philosophy, law, history, literature, etc. of Ancient Greece and Rome (preferably in the original written languages) equipped people as general problem solvers, suitable to administer an empire. Irrespective of the merits of such arguments, many employers in many different kinds of business were prepared to hire graduates from any discipline. In any case, in the UK at least, until the 1964 Robbins report and the later expansion at the end of the 1980s, only a small proportion of young people benefited from a university education and until quite recently relatively few managers were graduates.

Training tended to have a lower status than education and was frequently quite narrow in its focus, with an emphasis on imparting physical skills. Though the resulting skill level could be very high it tended to be specific to one particular occupation. Once trained as an electrician or hairdresser, for instance, the person was equipped for and possibly committed to these occupations only. Development, when it occurred at all, came through experience of doing the job. For some people, the training phase was skipped altogether. People left school, learned almost entirely on the job, and progressed by steady promotion to positions of greater responsibility. Proving your capabilities by doing the job was often more important than formal qualifications.

These brief sketches of the traditional distinction between education and training are probably in danger of being caricatures—the truth was certainly always more complex than this. However, if this distinction ever did make any sense, it makes little today. Education provides the training for today's knowledge workers and higher education is frequently more concerned with developing "transferable skills" than socializing into a discipline. If employers want graduates who are good teamworkers, are computer literate, are effective communicators, etc., this is what universities are attempting to deliver. Lecturers are adopting training techniques such as experiential learning exercises, small group discussions, and "hands-on" practicals, and clear learning objectives are mandatory for every class. Not every academic is a gifted educator, much less trainer, but the stereotype of an erudite researcher mumbling incoherently through an hour's lecture while his or her audience yawns, is largely obsolete. (If employers are still dissatisfied with the "products" of education, Arnold, 1997a suggests that this may be partly because the demands of the labour market are rising faster than educational standards.)

If educators are becoming more like trainers, so are trainers becoming more like educators. "Smart" machines increase the complexity of jobs and rather than simply learning and following a set of rules and procedures, workers are required to make inferences, judgements, and diagnoses (Thayer, 1997). Similarly, increasing diversity of the workforce and an emphasis on teamwork creates a need for interpersonal skills training. Flavell (1985) once pointed out that other people are the most complex "objects" that we have to deal with in the world and that for most of us, our highest levels of mental functioning involve our dealings with other people, and indeed, with ourselves. This is emphasized in Hopson and Scally's (1981) basic life skills scheme, which includes such things as managing conflicts, expressing feelings constructively, coping with and gaining from life transitions, managing one's sexuality, making effective decisions, and managing negative emotions. Hopson and Scally believe that many such skills can be taught at school and college and have produced materials to facilitate this. However, none of these skills appear particularly "basic" to me, although they are undoubtedly essential for a satisfying life. Social skills training must thus have a very strong component of cognitive development—something once considered the preserve of educators. As Downs (1995) writes, changing technology and markets mean "people moving away from rote learning and using physical skills to a position where developing concepts is of increasing importance" (p. 79). Trainers have to teach people to "learn how to learn". This, says Thayer (1997, p. 23), is likely to become increasingly important as jobs "dissolve into more flexible clusters of activities" and "just-in-time" training for specific activities rather than general skill development becomes the norm.

Development can take many forms too and does not necessarily involve learning wholly from job experience. Open and distance learning courses, part-time degrees, and even professional doctorates can all be included under this heading. What is becoming clear is that a sound education is one of the most important prerequisites for lifelong learning. It is a tragedy, therefore, that education appears to have failed so many people in the UK and the USA. Drucker (1994) and Howard (1995) have argued that the US educational system is failing, and that too many people do not have the basic skills in reading, writing, and maths to make them suitable for training in complex jobs. Similar arguments have been put forward in the UK, where there has been concerted effort to raise educational standards. A recent government drive to reduce poverty and social exclusion is almost certainly right when it implicates poverty of expectations as much as unemployment and other economic factors in cycles of deprivation running through generations.

The fact is, that even when people succeed relatively well at school, many emerge with very unhappy learning experiences. Downs (1995) has conducted a decade of research into means to help adults to become better learners. Part of this research has involved identifying blockages to learning by asking large numbers of people what had prevented them learning in the past. She then categorized their replies under the following four headings and incorporated this information into a learning blockage questionnaire.

- Poor learning skills—"When I don't understand something I try to memorize it"; "When I'm trying to learn something I can't recover if I get confused early on".
- Problems with concentration—"I find myself thinking about my problems when I ought to be learning"; "I find myself staring out of the window rather than listening to a supervisor/trainer".
- Worries and fears about learning—"I feel embarrassed when I'm asked a question in a group"; "I feel shown up when I make mistakes in front of others"; "People might think I hadn't been listening if I ask questions".
- Learning from others—"People get impatient with me when I don't understand"; "People who teach and train think they're better than us"; "Teachers and trainers don't give me time to think about what they've said before going on to the next thing".

This research gives a fascinating insight into the things that concern and handicap so many people when they confront lifelong learning. The last category, especially, indicates a woeful catalogue of bad experiences of education and training. It seems that if lifelong learning is to become a reality for the majority, a large number of blocks and obstacles have to be overcome first. Perhaps the most serious are people's lack of confidence in their own ability to learn and the number of damaging misconceptions they hold about effective ways to learn.

Luckily, people such as Downs (1995) are gathering a great deal of information about the specialist needs of different trainee groups, which will allow trainers to identify and overcome learning difficulties. More research may be needed and lifespan development theory (Sugarman, 2001) tells us that our perspectives must be constantly updated because changes in society make our theories and research findings obsolete. For instance, the current fear of learning by some older people may disappear as a far larger proportion of the population achieve more and better education and engage in lifelong learning. In the meantime, the problem is there and trainers will need to be aware of the wider psychological literature already existing, which can provide valuable insights into the learning process.

Lessons from developmental psychology

I began my academic life as a developmental psychologist and the one thing that never ceased to astound me and fill me with . . . well awe, really, is the huge feat of learning achieved by almost every child by the time he or she is about 5 years old—learning to speak one, two, and even three native languages. Language learning not only involves vocabulary and grammatical rules but all the concepts that words represent plus a large number of social rules about what to say when, to whom, and how. Tiny babies embark on this endeavour within weeks of birth and in the process learn much of what it is to be human. They appear to do this effortlessly, without formal instruction, and without conscious awareness of all the rules, concepts, customs, and culture they have learned so brilliantly. Moreover, few of us can even express all this vast fund of knowledge. Can you write down a single rule of English grammar? Faced with this question most of my students came up with "i before e except after c", which is a spelling rule that they have been explicitly taught and has nothing to do with how we, for instance, tell someone about something that was going to happen in the future but now won't and why, e.g., "We were going to see my Gran tomorrow but she's poorly so now we can't"—something which your average 5-year-old does with consummate ease. Neither, except with a great deal of effort, can we define words or say how we tackle the problem of what to say after we've said "Hello" (especially to strangers) or how we conclude a telephone conversation.

This learning process is so miraculous that for a long time psycholinguists like Noam Chomsky (1965) felt obliged to conclude that human brains are specially pre-wired to learn language and the process is as natural as learning to walk. Later it came to be realized that, yes, human brains may well have some unique capacity but this has more to do with making sense of the world, understanding human motives and feelings, and in the process learning to categorize—to learn rules and concepts and symbolize them in words and other symbol systems such as numbers. Language, since it is a vitally important part of our world—essential for communication and the construction of shared meanings—is learned as any other aspect of the world is learned.

Jerome Bruner (1979) was a pioneer of this new approach and looked carefully at the role played by parents and care-givers in this mysterious process. He was the first to publicize the term "scaffolding"—the process whereby adults create the conditions for and support the child's learning. He, together with many others, inspired a new wave of research, which has given us great insights into how to become a gifted natural teacher. The main findings regarding what care-givers typically do are summarized in Box 6.3.

BOX 6.3
Parents as gifted natural teachers

Parents typically:

- Behave *as if* the baby can communicate.
- Accept any behaviour as an attempt to communicate (a burp, a smile).
- Treat this behaviour as the baby's "turn" in the conversation.

   (Later on accept any attempt at language use, however inadequate, but often expand the child's utterance e.g., "Car"—"Yes, that's Mum's/Dad's car".)

- Behave consistently in response to the baby's attempts to communicate.
- Provide demonstrations of "how to do it".
- Embed language learning in everyday meaningful human contexts (bathtime, mealtimes, etc.).
- Repeat familiar phrases, using simplified language, in daily "rituals".
- Subtly change their behaviour to match the child's growing mastery e.g., using words with strong nonverbal signals (gestures, etc.) at first and then coming to rely more and more on words alone.
- Encourage young children to explore their world through every-day conversations, question and answer sessions, and word games.
- Do all this through (mainly!) warm and rewarding human contact.
- Do this every day for several years.

In these ways (and more) they set up the conditions that will allow the child to learn his or her native language. However, despite all this support, in the end, it is the child who has to make the connections to learn for himself or herself. Luckily, all but the most seriously damaged or deprived children are equipped and motivated to do this.

   Before reading on you may like to think about the implications of all this for workplace training and learning. How could these principles and behaviours be translated into effective training programmes?

What has all this to do with training adults and young people in work-related skills?

Well, first of all it demonstrates that virtually all human beings begin as highly motivated learners. A 5- or 6-year-old child has not only learned a great deal about how to use language to communicate, but a large number of concepts that words represent and also a good deal about how the world works. This thought should give all educators and trainers pause; if nearly everyone begins with this capacity, what on earth happens to so many of us?

Second, if so many ordinary Mums and Dads are such expert and successful resources for learning, perhaps we should look more closely at their methods and try to emulate them in our training courses. If many people find it difficult to learn concepts in later life (and especially those related to social behaviour, e.g., teamwork, leadership, etc.), then maybe it is because we are not harnessing their natural learning skills. Notice how scaffolding embeds opportunities to learn in the contexts in which the learning is both needed and can be practised. Many training courses are relatively detached from the workplace. Notice the role of demonstrations in scaffolding and the incremental step-by-step character of the learning, which are also characteristics of many good training courses. Scaffolding also involves a positive learning environment; mistakes are tolerated and feedback is unobtrusive, gentle, and continuous. Perhaps learning is inhibited in too many adults because they are too self-conscious and afraid of failure to learn in childlike ways.

Third, the sheer timescale and repetition needed for language learning, to say nothing of long periods when performance is very imperfect, may also provide us with lessons. It's not simply that many training courses are too short but that there is often not a forgiving and supportive work environment to consolidate and develop skills afterwards.

Finally, all this points to the fact that informal, "on the job" learning can be very effective but only if the conditions are right. For the most successful outcomes, workmates, mentors, and role models need to use the skills of parental scaffolding which, among other things, requires time, patience, and a supportive atmosphere. How often do such conditions occur in the workplace?

Interestingly, Downs (1995) asked trainers, works managers, and senior supervisors to think of a supervisor they had had who was good at helping trainees to learn for themselves. They were asked to describe the behaviours which had led to these outcomes. The most cited behaviours involved allowing learners to ask questions, encouraging trainees to identify and correct their own mistakes, and leaving them to work things out by themselves. They did not favour long and detailed expositions, or methods which never allowed the learner to make mistakes. Some of this behaviour is very reminiscent of parental "scaffolding". At the end of this chapter is an exercise which uses Downs', "learning to learn" framework. In the course of this exercise you might like to consider what features of Downs' method resemble "parental scaffolding" and how it might be improved by incorporating more such features.

Designing training programmes

There is not space here to go into great detail about what is a complex and skilled process, but see the work of Patrick (1992, 2000) for good reviews of what is involved. Here I am indebted to Patrick (2000) and will use his case study of a training programme in the steel industry (Patrick, James, & Friend, 1996) to illustrate three stages in the process.

Stage 1: Identify what needs to be learned

The need for training often becomes apparent when some problem arises in the workplace. In the case of the steel plant, sophisticated computer systems controlled much of the process, but the operators were having difficulty diagnosing and correcting faults when things went wrong. From this starting point a two-step analysis was made of what was wrong with the way diagnoses were being made and which diagnostic procedures needed to be incorporated into a training programme. For this, two studies were undertaken. The first of these involved carefully observing and analysing the strategies used and errors made by operators when trying to correct faults. Since faults were rather rare occurences, observation of people on shifts was not enough, so retrospective analyses of reported faults and "talking people through" hypothetical fault scenarios were also used. This gave a clearer picture of what the operators were actually doing and it emerged that their fault-diagnosis strategies were not very systematic or efficient.

The next step was to identify what the operators should be doing and this was achieved using a technique known as hierarchical task analysis (HTA; see Annett, Duncan, Stammers, & Gray, 1971; Patrick, 1992; Shepherd, 1985 for detailed accounts, or Patrick, 2000; Stammers, 1996 for short descriptions). This technique involved interviewing experts to break down the task of fault finding into a series of goals and subgoals and then specifying the sequence of behaviours necessary to achieve each subgoal and goal in pursuit of the overall objective of finding the fault. HTA is a complex process and relies heavily upon the skill of the analyst at the best of times but, in the case of the steel mill, this was complicated by the fact that no-one was a "complete expert" in what should be done and a lot of the knowledge that did exist was implicit and difficult to verbalize. So the goals and subgoals and associated behaviours had to be pieced together from many "experts". Once the goals and subgoals had been specified it was then necessary to specify all the knowledge and skills necessary to achieve them. That done, the content of the training programme had been specified.

Stage 2: Decide how the content of the training programme should be taught

The first step at this stage is to specify the learning objectives for each part of the programme. What has to be learned will determine not only the nature of the objectives but how they are best taught. Researchers have been concerned with identifying different varieties of learning (e.g., Gagne, 1985) and a scheme derived from such work is presented in Box 6.4. Merrill (1983)

BOX 6.4
Defining learning

Maybe we should pause to try to define what learning is, because it is not a unitary concept. Learning comes in several varieties. Gagne (1985) provides an influential starting point.

1   Signal learning
This is classical conditioning as in Pavlov's dogs, who salivated to a light signal which had been paired with food. It happens without conscious awareness or effort and often involves a physical response. Thus as the clock hand approaches 5 pm on a Friday, our spirits may start to rise. However, this type of learning is at its most potent when it is negative. The sight of a bullying boss can provoke feelings of panic in a victim.

2   Stimulus–response learning
This concerns what Skinner (1938) called operant conditioning. If a response to a particular stimulus is reinforced positively then that response becomes more likely in the future. Negative reinforcement comes from the relief we feel when the punishment stops and this can inhibit the response which led to the punishment. However, negative reinforcement is never as effective as positive reinforcement, which can over-ride its effects. Thus praise from the boss may induce us to work harder but censure won't stop us enjoying a good friendly chat with colleagues when his or her back is turned. Task-oriented managers, who give little praise for good work but a lot of criticism for mistakes and failures, are promoting learning to avoid failure, not to increase the quality of work.

These lowly forms of learning are too often ignored in the workplace, as Chapter 3 showed in the discussion of motivation. However, they are always in the background of higher levels of learning and can be very potent. Much of the implicit learning which occurs in the initial informal "socialization" into an organization probably takes these forms as we absorb "how things are done around here" and what leads to reward or punishment.

3   Chaining
What is learned is a chain of two or more stimulus response connections. It is the basis of much skilled action and is largely under automatic control. (See Rasmussen's ladder model in Chapter 5.) The problem is that once they have been overlearned such "chains" of actions are very difficult to change especially if "mistakes" have been overlearned or the situation changes so that familiar routines are no

longer appropriate. Chaining often depends on rote memorization and lots of practice. Downs argues that memorization and rote learning should be kept to a minimum. "In the past a great deal of education and training relied on memorisation and practising. If tasks were done by rote and no decisions were called for, then memorising and practising were sufficient. Today's needs demand a greater understanding and use of initiative on the part of everyone, and so merely memorising would be an inappropriate, if not dangerous learning method." (p. 95)

4   Verbal association

Verbal association is the learning of chains that are verbal. Thus we may learn about rules, regulations, and procedures—if this then do that. These verbal chains can be translated into action if they are regularly used to guide behaviour. However, in unfamiliar situations, learning at the purely verbal level is frequently ineffective. Can you recite the evacuation proceedings from your workplace in the event of a fire? Would you be able to follow them in a real fire and if you did would this save you? The ill-fated Piper Alpha workers followed the verbal associations they had been taught all too well . . . (See Chapter 5.)

5   Multiple discrimination

The person learns to make many different responses to many different stimuli which may or may not resemble each other physically. Thus as a postgraduate student I took part in a study to identify fault displays in a chemical plant and to "parrot" corrective action. I hadn't a clue what I was doing but I would have been a reasonably competent fault operator—providing that I was confronted by only the faults that had been included in the training programme! My learning also included a lot of verbal association since the displays were accompanied by a verbal label and a list of necessary actions and I was able to put the two together very quickly. Such learning need not be so "mindless" when people use their higher level knowledge to interpret stimuli, but a lot of management decision making can appear to involve "knee-jerk" reactions of this sort. Financial difficulties? Cut the workforce! Competition from abroad? Impose the latest "guru-fad"!

6   Concept learning

The learner acquires a capability of making a common response to a class of stimuli that may differ widely in physical appearance. My young son showed that this capacity appears early. One of his first words was "tick-tock", which he applied to a clock, the dial on the bathroom scales, and the overflow outlet in the bath. This too can manifest itself in management decision making. Older worker?

Must be inflexible and out of date—don't employ or get rid! However, concept learning is usually classed as a "higher form" of learning which involves the conscious mind and human intelligence. If I had understood the concept of "Number 1 feed pump blockage", then my control of the chemical plant would have been driven by knowledge and Rasmussen's rule-based level of functioning. However, concept learning can still involve unconscious processes.

7   Principle learning

In simplest terms, a principle is a chain of two or more concepts and guides behaviour via "If A do B" or "If A then B" rules where A and B represent knowledge and understanding rather than verbal associations. Workers as diverse as chefs, decorators, and computer operators can act on instructions such as "combine roux sauce with other ingredients", "prepare wood surface", and "log on to internet" because they have learned the underlying concepts. Similarly a GP can diagnose your ailments from a list of symptoms.

8   Problem solving

This type of learning is said to involve thinking (at last!) whereby two or more previously acquired principles are somehow combined to produce a new capability or new way of doing things. Thus, as a keen amateur cook I can create tasty dishes from whatever ingredients I happen to have because I have learned the principles underlying cooking. Chemical plant operators can diagnose faults because they have learned the principles that underly the system and can thus operate at Rasmussen's knowledge-based level of functioning.

Other varieties of learning

Other writers have added other categories of learning—learning how to learn, mastering general heuristics for attacking problems, how to use symbolic systems such as mathematics to solve problems, and how to invent useful symbolic systems for problem solving.

Identifying types of learning in this way is no bad thing since it provokes a consideration of the best ways to present material for learning and it is wise to heed the fact that much of our learning is largely under automatic control. However, I find such systems rather arid —they don't give enough emphasis to the fact that much learning comes as a result of our capacity to think about thinking—to challenge assumptions and create new ideas and ways of doing things. How do we encourage this sort of activity? The social aspects of learning, especially in its higher forms, are also given little treatment. How useful would you find this scheme for informing the design of a training programme?

linked different kinds of learning to different kinds of objectives using three performance verbs—remember, use, and find. So, for instance, if the objective is for people to *remember* a concept, this is very different from the objective to *use* the concept appropriately when doing the job. To give a concrete example, a safety training programme might have the objective that people can remember safety rules and procedures and the methods to impart this declarative knowledge might involve classroom instruction, computerized interactive tutorials, rote learning, and so on. The objective for people to actually use the rules and procedures appropriately would involve very different forms of instruction to promote procedural knowledge such as fire drills, practising in simulators, and so on. (See, e.g., Gagne, Briggs, & Wager, 1992 for more on different categories of learning that require different training designs.)

One must also consider the characteristics of the trainees—their prior knowledge, aptitudes, age, learning strategies, attitudes, and motivation. In the steel mill example, HTA had done much to specify the objectives of each aspect of the programme because all the subgoals and goals of the overall task had been specified. However, the programme had to be suitable for both experienced operators and apprentices. It was decided to deliver the programme via computerized tutorials based on the knowledge and skills needed to achieve each subgoal. Trainees could select which tutorials to study (thus accounting for differences in prior knowledge), but the programme would not allow them to proceed until the first main goal—"determining the initial symptoms of the fault" had been satisfactorily performed. The programme also included simulated fault scenarios for practice, advice about what tutorial/subtask should be tackled next, and feedback on performance. The knowledge and skills necessary for each subgoal of fault finding were taught separately before the trainee was allowed to tackle the whole task. Writing such a programme also entailed a great deal of effort, and preliminary evaluation was also carried out by trialling the system before formal training began, to eliminate deficiencies in the instructions and simulated fault scenarios.

Stage 3: Evaluation

In the steel mill example, an evaluation of the impact of training on actual job performance was not feasible because major faults occurred so rarely, but pre- and post-training tests on fault finding, using simulated scenarios, were carried out. The results showed that trainees were more systematic in their fault finding after training. They also had positive attitudes to the training programme, particularly in the case of apprentices.

Some conclusions

In comparison with the time, effort, and expense expended in stages 1 and 2, the evaluation phase (stage 3) is perhaps the easiest and cheapest to conduct.

The general lack of evaluation of training programmes must therefore stem more from lack of political will than from economic considerations. But it also demonstrates why training programmes may be ineffective. How many organizations are prepared to fund the activities at stages 1 and 2 adequately? How many can afford to do so? Moreover, how many could afford the time to conduct such painstaking research, especially in the context of "just-in-time learning"? For this reason, many training courses are not "bespoke" programmes to meet specific needs but are "off-the-shelf" modules, hastily adapted to fit today's tender exercise.

Second, educators could learn much from this model and its associated processes, but who can undertake this level of research and analysis in amongst a full-time job delivering many hours of teaching on a variety of topics and at different "trainee" levels every day in every week? It is worth remembering that successive UK governments have spent 10 years developing a National Curriculum for schools using a variety of policy groups and task forces and a forest of publications. Some would argue that they still haven't got it right. An attempt to impose an "undergraduate curriculum" appears to be currently underway. I have no objections to the principles underlying good training design, indeed I think they are essential. However, the resources needed for such projects have to be there. In the steel mill example and in many other safety critical industries, the costs of failure are so high that the resources are made available. In much human resource management, an analysis of the costs and benefits of effective training is frequently lacking and so necessary resources are not made available.

At least in the sphere of education, we can join people like Robinson (1998) in lambasting the idea that teachers can be "trained" in a few weeks of classroom practice. If the design of job training is so complex and skilled, the nurturing of a whole new generation to meet the needs of the economy and promote productive and satisfying lives is not best served by the maxim that "any fool can teach".

Delivering training

There is *so* much more that could be said on the subject of training. Here there is no space except to comment briefly on technological innovations in delivery. There is a feeling that great savings in the delivery and effectiveness of training can be made by harnessing the power of computers with their abilities to combine graphics, video, text, interaction, and active participation on the part of the learner (see also Chapter 10). Once written, such a multi-media package can be used again and again with geographically dispersed learners without the need for the presence of a human trainer or to travel to a fixed site. Similar claims are made for other distance and open learning materials such as the combination of books, workbooks, and videos currently used by the Open University. Stewart and Winter (1995) cite an example of Courtauld's Coventry training centre where, despite high set-up costs, the use of multi-media course delivery is likely to average out at £12 per trainee per course as opposed to £150 for a conventionally delivered course with a tutor. This sort of evidence makes doing away with trainers and educators an attractive proposition for organizations and government. In an article in the *Financial Times*, Ferguson (2000) argued that some of the ills of UK higher education could be solved by more use of the internet for on-line lectures and tutorials. The Department of Trade and Industry in a recent Foresight Report (Mackney, 1999) goes further. In one future scenario, a businesswoman is described as bypassing a terrestrial university except for a few self-development courses, and studies part-time to take a "portfolio of courses from some of the most prestigious universities in the world". But the top class "researchers" who provide this internet ideal are painted as having very light teaching duties: 4 weeks, twice a year, which nevertheless are described in Mackney's article as a "chore and distraction from research". Is this a realistic scenario? Haven't we heard something like this before in the euphoria surrounding computer-assisted learning in the 1970s?

However, it is not as simple as this. There is no doubt that distance learning materials such as WebCT and multi-media CD-ROM materials are a valuable supplement to more traditional forms of delivery but they are not low-cost substitutes. The cost of developing such distance learning materials and the hardware to run them can be very high and the cost of updating the materials increases the expense. It can only be justified when there are large numbers of trainees who are geographically dispersed. Stewart and Winter (1995) also point out that learners still need a great deal of support—technical support with the hardware, software, and course content; counselling and motivational support to provide reassurance and help through difficult periods; help in applying what they have learned to their jobs and time and facilities such as rooms and equipment—only the most motivated will provide all these things themselves. People may also need the additional reward of a recognized qualification and rise in job grade to keep up their motivation to learn.

In short, the idea that providing people with hardware and software, and then expecting them to get on with it, generally invites failure, especially when large-scale programmes are imposed by management. When all these hidden costs are taken into account multi-media training packages do not necessarily prove cheaper or more effective than traditional classroom train-ing. Indeed for some skills they are a good deal more expensive because they incur all these costs but are less effective. Teaching someone social skills, for instance, is much better done via role-playing exercises with other people, not by sitting at a computer! Similar points about "unmanaged" career development programmes are made by Arnold (1997a) and MacCauley and Harding (1996). For these sorts of reasons, the American Psychological Association recently published an article (Murray, 1999) questioning the use of multi-media techniques in higher education. Mackney (1999) also questions the wisdom of this "brave new world" of education via internet surfing. Developing web sites is a very time-consuming, complex, and multi-skilled activity. A good lecturer can provide all the features of a good multimedia package and more. His or her time may be better spent doing what they are paid for—teaching! This is not special pleading. All too often, the potential of new technology fails to be realized because management seizes on the hardware without taking a systems approach to its implementation. Instructional hardware and software, with its promise of cheap delivery, is no exception to this general tendency.

An exercise in concept learning

The reader who wants to know more about the specifics of training design and delivery rather than the general issues considered in this chapter is directed to the further reading at the end. Meanwhile you may like to complete Exercise 6.1, which invites you to consider whether a university is a learning organization. It is based on Downs' (1995) technique to promote learning to learn, which consists of the following keys to understanding:

1 Purposes: Thinking of the purposes of what one wishes to understand. To do so, be prepared to define and describe what needs to be understood, e.g., what purposes do universities serve?
2 Comparisons: Comparing and contrasting with other experiences to identify similarities and differences, e.g., what are the similarities with and differences between university learning and job-based training?
3 Viewpoints: Imagining things from other directions or from others' perspectives, e.g., how does students' learning appear to lecturers?
4 Problems: Thinking of all the problems associated with what you want to understand. What could go wrong? E.g., why might a university not be a learning organization?

The questions based on these four keys are designed to develop concepts through reflection on what the learner already knows. This exercise is best done with a friend who can contribute his or her experience. When you have finished you can compare your answers with those suggested on the following pages, but the exercise will have no value if you skip the thinking process and go straight to the answers!

Before you begin, it is worth pointing out the objectives of this exercise—and there are several.

1 This book is a distance learning device. The exercise invites you to reflect on how effective this is, compared to one conducted in the presence of an educator/trainer/facilitator and a class of people who could all contribute their ideas and experience. This exercise could just as well be delivered via the internet rather than via a book, and indeed this book may well be offered via this medium. Your job is to consider the

relative merits of different delivery systems and to evaluate whether you would have been able to gain more from it if it had been presented via a different medium. Thus, you can begin to make up your own mind whether "distance learning", in all its guises, is an adequate substitute for traditional learning contexts.

2   It is designed to consolidate your understanding of the concept of a "learning organization" and to allow you to apply this concept to something with which you are all familiar—higher education. Given both the nature of learning organizations and the methodology advocated for concept learning by Downs, the challenging of fundamental assumptions is built into the exercise. Questioning whether universities are, in fact, learning organizations, may be somewhat startling. Challenging fundamental assumptions is also incorporated in the form of asking you to consider student learning from the point of view of tutors. You need to be really empathic here, considering what it would be like if *you* were up in front of classes every day. If this book had been designed for lecturers I'd have asked them to consider things from the point of view of students and a lot of complacency would thereby have been severely deflated in the face of student opinions! Even so, the replies from tutors on this topic are likely to make you very angry. Please try to understand the *purpose* of this exercise, and don't let your emotions get in the way of learning. Indeed, consider the role of emotions in learning—this is too often neglected.

3   This is also designed to illustrate Downs' methodology. How useful is it for you; how can it be adapted to other contexts? Take note of the steps in the process and then apply it to the suggested exercise given at the end of the chapter, which invites you to design a training programme to examine your organization's mission statement, barriers to its understanding and implementation, and what is needed to ensure that the mission is really translated into practice.

Keep these objectives in mind and good luck!

EXERCISE 6.1
Is a university a learning organization?

A   Give your views on the following questions:

1   Why do we have universities? What purposes do they serve?
2   Compare and contrast school and university learning. How are they similar and how different? Do the same thing comparing university learning versus job-based learning/training.
3   How does students' learning at university appear to lecturers?

4 Why might a university *not* be a learning organization? What problems may prevent it becoming so?

B Now compare your answers with those following. These answers are not right or wrong, neither are they exhaustive, but they are based on student and staff responses to these questions. You may like to review your answers to the questions in the light of these.

C Consider what you have now learned about a learning organization. Are your ideas clearer than they were before? Would doing this exercise with a tutor as facilitator as opposed to doing this by distance methods have helped?

If so, in what ways?

Suggested answers

1 Why do we have universities?

- So that people can get a qualification which helps them to get a good job.
- So that you can learn more and more about less and less.
- So that people can jump through the hurdles of exams and hang a certificate on the wall.
- To increase knowledge through research and scholarship and communicate this to the next generation.
- To reduce social inequalities by providing educational opportunities for previously disadvantaged groups.
- To increase the economic competitiveness of a country by producing graduates who have good transferable skills and can add value to a company from day 1.
- To produce people who have learned how to learn, are receptive to new ideas, can think for themselves, and are motivated to acquire new skills quickly.
- To develop people's powers of critical analysis and synthesis so that they can quickly absorb and evaluate new information and reach innovative conclusions and solutions.
- To increase the tolerance of a society—if one is used to seeing things from many angles, people are less likely to jump to hasty conclusions or be swayed by intolerant demagogues.
- To act as a fund of expertise and ideas that can be used as a resource for local communities, national and international business, which itself is an income generator.
- To provide a major source of employment and focus of consumers for the local community and businesses.

How many of these purposes coincide with your understanding of the purposes of higher education and your experiences of doing a degree?

2   Contrast and compare school and university learning

Similarities:

- Both involve learning a huge number of facts that have little bearing on the "real world" and are mostly quickly forgotten.
- Both involve exams where you cram information, perform a "brain dump", and forget it as soon as possible.
- Both involve unfair assessments—some people learn easily and pass exams without effort, whereas others work hard and can't demonstrate all they know within exam time limits; some are severely handicapped by exam anxiety, which reduces their performance.
- Both involve having people talk at you while you make notes.
- Both involve a lot of homework, which can seem unreasonably heavy in its demands.
- Both try to promote learning to learn and an appetite for lifelong learning but they do not always succeed.
- Both involve teachers whose job it is to promote and ensure learning.
- Both foster competition in learning rather than cooperation.
- Both advocate learning for learning's sake in the belief that it will make you a better person and lead to a more fulfilled life.

Differences:

- At university you are expected to do far more work on your own and this involves not just practice but reflecting on what you have been taught and learning new material.
- At university you do not only learn "accepted wisdom" but are expected to criticize your elders and betters and come up with your own ideas.
- Schools tend to foster the belief that there are "right answers"; university attempts to demonstrate that there are no right answers and this can provoke a crisis of confidence in learners.
- Universities place much more responsiblity on the learner for his or her own learning; the lecturer faciliates but does not guarantee learning.
- University learning is much less well supported by the state so learners have to take paid employment to support themselves and have less time for study when at the same time they must study more.
- Some university courses are far more geared towards the skills needed in jobs than most school-based learning, especially at A level.
- Universities demand depth of understanding and independent thought to a much greater extent than schools.

- You need above-average ability to succeed at university.
- The pace of learning is very fast at university.
- At university you are expected to contribute to knowledge through your own research and the generation of new ideas.
- Contrast and compare University and job-based learning

Similarities:

- Both can involve learning concepts.
- Both can involve learning transferable skills such as using information technology, giving presentations, and report writing.
- Both can invite reflection on past experience and its relation to current learning.
- Both can involve small group discussion.
- Both may rely on a tutor/trainer being physically present.
- Both may involve "hands-on" skill training and practical work.
- Both involve learning by doing, e.g., one learns research skills by conducting research projects and other assignments
- Both may involve learning from others, e.g., in small group discussion and other group projects.

Differences

- Work-based learning/training is much more clearly job related/job specific.
- University learning relies much more heavily on reading books and other printed materials, whereas training is more likely to involve harnessing the existing skills and knowledge of the group via exercises to create new insights.
- University course delivery is more likely via lectures; in training, theory presentation is punctuated by practical exercises and practice sessions.
- University courses are much more heavily weighted to theory; training is much more weighted to practice.
- University courses are much more long term—even full-time courses usually take at least a year; most training courses are much shorter—measured in days or weeks.
- Attendance at training courses may be infrequent; university courses demand daily or weekly attendance—continual learning and improvement is therefore more likely.
- The content of university courses is much broader, usually involving different aspects of one or more disciplines; training courses are usually very specific to a particular skill set and related body of knowledge.
- University courses are much more about knowledge for its own sake; training is usually linked to some definite job-related purpose.

- Job-based learning involves actually doing the job; at best, most university courses involve preparation for doing the job.

In comparing your lists with these, you may wish to consider to what extent some of the similarities and differences have surprised you. Universities are very different places from those of only a few decades ago when students spent most of their time listening passively to lecturers droning on at the front, or reading in musty libraries. Many courses include periods of work-based learning and a great deal of practical skills training. The general public, many older graduates, and even many students think that universities are entirely concerned with the transmission of interesting but fairly useless knowledge. A lot of students are completely unaware of how many job-related skills they are learning along with knowledge of their chosen discipline. For instance, learning to use a spreadsheet program is obviously a useful job skill but just as useful but somewhat less obvious are the skills of handling, analysing, manipulating, presenting, and interpreting data, which are integral to many disciplines, especially psychology.

Universities have been examining their fundamental assumptions of late, questioning their ways of doing things and undergoing revolutionary and continuing change. These are major characteristics of a learning organization.

3   How do lecturers view student learning?

The best are a joy—they ask stimulating questions, they think of ideas you wish you'd thought of, they write essays and reports you wish you had written. They are interested in the subject, they read widely, and relate what they have learned to their personal experience. They take the time to think and discuss ideas, they cooperate well in groups. They prepare properly so that your carefully prepared learning exercises are successful, and they consolidate their learning afterwards.

The worst students tend to exhibit the following characteristics:

- They think higher education is nothing more than cramming facts and passing exams.
- They will do no more work than is necessary for formal assessment —if it isn't assessed it's a "waste of time".
- They think that turning up for classes should be enough to get them a degree because the tutor should "tell them what they need to know".
- They turn up unprepared for classes that need preparation and disrupt the work of their fellows.
- They do not do the work they have promised to do and group projects are disrupted or collapse.

- They think that all learning should be effortless and if they do not learn it is the fault of their tutors.
- They expect entertainment—anything that is difficult is "boring" and thus the tutor's fault.
- They expect tutors to be constantly available to sort out their shortcomings.
- They make little attempt to solve their own problems—a failed love affair that results in weeks of depression and inactivity must be "compensated" for by special treatment at exam time.
- They believe that higher education is so divorced from the world of work that they do not take advantage of the many opportunities available and emerge totally unprepared for the realities outside.

I have written this book mainly for postgraduate students—hence this "alternative view" exercise is designed for them. I have absolutely no doubt that a similarly disparaging list could be devised for a student's view of lecturers. But consider this extract from a letter written to the *Independent's* Education section (1999) by a recent graduate. Not only does it demonstrate most of the characteristics described here (and more!) but there is an underlying theme that the system is somehow to blame for this person's thoroughly unrewarding and unproductive experience of university.

> Supposedly studying economics and social history, I spent four drink and drug fuelled years at University, and I can hardly remember a thing. It wasn't until I graduated and, apparently "qualified" that I realised how little I had learnt and how ill-prepared I was for life beyond the hedonism to which I had become accustomed. The student's best kept secret is that university life has much more to do with clubs, alcohol, drugs, casinos and getting up late than with scholarly learning.
>
> We had to produce three essays a term, each between 1,000 and 3,000 words and of a standard certainly no more demanding than A Level. They were seen as irritants—interrupters of social life and sleep, something to be rushed through in a couple of days.
>
> And so to the exams. With a 40% pass mark, three hours of waffling generally ensures a scrape through. Even with some freak occurrence (such as falling asleep or missing the exam entirely), there are always resits in September, made "easier to pass" by tutors.
>
> Abbie Kornstein

Who/what *is* to blame? The current system with "so few incentives, so little structure"? Government league tables that impact on funding when every such student is unceremoniously (and justifiably) thrown out to exploit the taxpayer somewhere else? A general lack of understanding of what the higher education enterprise is all about? Schools that send such people to university? The "consumerism" embodied by fees that leads students to think they can buy a degree like a box of chocolates? Tutors who cannot do their jobs and don't care?

Maybe it is a combination of all these factors. Certainly, it is understandable when employers complain about the calibre of many graduates. It is also understandable that many lecturers regard their jobs as a trainer's nightmare. Certainly, if there are many such students (and there are!), universities find it very difficult to be learning organizations. (Incidentally, Ms Kornstein went on to study a postgraduate course in journalism. One wonders whether her letter was part of her degree assessment: a "devil's advocate" exercise to get a publication. If not, doubtless in the future she will direct her manifest intelligence but profound ignorance to "educating" the great British Public via the tabloid press.)

4   What are the obstacles to universities becoming learning organizations?

- Students who don't know why they are there and what they are supposed to be doing (as above).
- Students who are so busy earning enough to live they have little time and energy left for study.
- Tutors who are so overworked and overloaded firefighting they have little time and energy to study and reflect themselves.
- Researchers who are so busy building reputations and careers (to say nothing of bringing funds into cash-starved departments) that they stay well away from any contact with teaching and so their expertise is not passed to the next generation.
- One third of the most "socialized", skilled, and capable "workers" depart every year so a stable "learning culture" cannot be established.
- Mutual incomprehension and distrust between students and tutors; barriers and hierarchies.

What is your verdict?

Mine is that it is extremely difficult for a university to become a learning organization except for a very few of its members. This is a very sad reflection on what has happened to UK higher education in recent years. For a country that hopes to enhance national prosperity through its education system, this is bad news. Occupational psychologists could have a field day dealing with the ills of universities but they are scarcely thought of as "real world" organizations worthy of their attention. And, of course, universities cannot pay "realistic" commercial rates for their services.

Summary

In this chapter I have discussed successive UK Governments' failures to improve the training base of the workforce to meet the economic needs of the country. Some of the reasons for this could be argued to be "self-imposed" by misguided policies, inappropriate use of trades union power and short-termism in industry. However, the needs of the global knowledge economy demand more. As a result, the concept of a learning organization has been embraced by many large organizations, but there is little evidence that such a strategy can be successful, and what there is indicates that it is difficult to achieve, especially when resources are scarce. Business seems to have a paradoxical attitude to training and career development, according it a high priority in the rhetoric of "our people", but little or no priority in reality. If effective leadership and the promotion of creativity and innovation at work are a key to business success, neglect of these is a big mistake. This chapter has acknowledged the problems that business has in integrating training and development into its strategic objectives, but at the same time it is argued that this is essential in the "knowledge economy". I criticize unrealistic demands for "scientific" proof of the effectiveness of training but nevertheless conclude that systematic and valid evaluation is essential if training programmes are to achieve their aims. I end with a case study illustrating the kind of time and labour involved in a properly conducted training intervention, and how these factors may deter top management from engaging in such activities. But they have to decide: Is training and development crucial to the success of business? Many commentators think so. Exercise 6.2 both demonstrates a technique for concept learning and challenges implicit beliefs about the "ultimate" learning organization—a university.

EXERCISE 6.2
Applying Downs' technique to the design of a training exercise

Using the example of Downs' concept learning technique outlined earlier, devise a training programme for any organization with which you are familiar. Focus on the mission statement—which most organizations now feel is indispensible. First consider how employees can be encouraged to understand it and then explore the barriers to its implementation. You may like to end with a training exercise to consider how the mission statement can really be made to drive everyone's endeavours and make a difference to the organization's success.

Suggested further reading

Patrick, J. (1992). *Training: Research and practice.* London: Academic Press.

Patrick, J. (2000). Training. In N. Chmiel (Ed.), *Introduction to work and organizational psychology: A European perspective.* Oxford, UK: Blackwell.

Quinones, M. A., & Erhenstein, A. (Eds.). (1997). *Training for a rapidly changing workplace: Applications of psychological research.* Washington, DC: American Psychological Association.

Senge, P. M. (1990). *The fifth discipline: The art and practice of the learning organization.* London: Century Business.

Truelove, S. (Ed.). (1995). *The handbook of training and development.* Oxford, UK: Blackwell.

7 Getting the right people (and keeping them): Selection and assessment

If you can't stand the heat, get out of the kitchen.

Harry S. Truman, 1884–1972

Both naming and numbering—setting identity and scope—are an essential part of what makes us human.

Kirsten Lippincott, *The story of time*—book/catalogue to accompany the exhibition held at the Queen's House, National Maritime Museum, Greenwich, London, 1 December 1999–24 September 2000; Merill Holbertson Publishers Ltd in association with the National Maritime Museum

Kirsten Lippincott was talking about people's attempts to understand and measure time in the context of a fascinating exhibition devoted to this endeavour. Perhaps we should not be surprised to discover, given the complexities of Einstein's space–time continuum, that time is not quite the simple matter of a linear progression from birth to death, from generation to generation, and so on, that it might at first appear to be. Moreover, people's conceptions of time have varied across the ages and according to their culture. However, one of the things which caught my interest in both *The Story of Time* exhibition and book, was the role of naming and measurement in mythology, theology, philosophy, and the history of ideas. For what else are we doing when we attempt to assess human characteristics, but trying to identify and name what these characteristics are and then to measure the extent to which any one person possesses them?

The idea of measurement seems to come from deep in our psyche. According to Lippincott, in the great religions which grew up around the Mediterranean, "God the Creator" was an engineer—an architect who creates something tangible from nothing but his own ideas. The Prophet Isaiah (40: 12), asks, "Who was it that measured the water of the sea in the hollow of his hand and calculated the dimensions of the heavens, gauged the whole of the earth to the bushel, weighed the mountains in scales, and the hills in a balance?" This rational vision of creation maybe dates back to Pythogoras and beyond, and for some, all this was anathema. Plato created the belief at all questions could be answered by the sufficiently rigorous application of thought alone, and thereby did great damage to the progress of science and technology (which might please some). However, he also banned any artistic endeavour from his vision of an "utopia" because it does not comply with the mathematical coherence of the universe (which will displease many of those he pleased on the first count). William Blake, in the early 19th century, raged against both strands of this tradition because it "strove to impose limiting mathematical blinkers on the 'eye of the imagination' (Lippincott, 1999, p. 020)." For Blake, such representations of the "rational" tradition were the enemy who were:

> Fixing their Systems permanent: by the mathematic power
> Giving a body to falsehood . . .
> *Jerusalem*, chap. 1, plates 12, 11, 12–13; Lippincott, op. cit.

The human capacity for categorization by naming—imposing order upon chaos—has similarly had a contentious career in the history of ideas. In opposition to Plato, Kant in particular concluded that the order we create must be a function of the structure of our own minds. What we conclude is thus as much a result of our biology as of reality. Descartes started all this "scepticism" off in the West. Similar conclusions had been reached by Persian philosophers in the 10th century. They concluded that the only reason they positively knew that they existed was that they experienced their own thought processes—the only phenomena to which we have direct access, in that we do not have to rely on the mediation of our sense organs. The great puzzle of the study of human perception up to the 21st century, is how to explain both the apparent accuracy of the way we walk about in the physical world and the subjectivity of our judgements of what is actually going on in it. Everyone has a different opinion about what is happening in the world of work, and indeed, in every other aspect of life. That is exactly why this book (and most others) is so difficult to write. Even if we agree that reality is largely a social construction, there has to be some consensus about what that construction is, before we can have much chance of agreeing on its causes and consequences.

Anyway, I can at least console myself that the current "love it or loathe it" polarization of attitudes to psychological testing appears to have a pedigree as long as human thought itself. There are many who think that our "naming" of human abilities is inadequate; there are even more who think that our attempts at measurement are not only technically flawed but fundamentally dehumanizing. And yet, what are we doing when we say things like this?

He seems a very genuine person
She's really sociable
She's a real high flyer
He's nice but not very bright
He's irritable today, what's got into him?

People say these sorts of things about each other whenever they get into conversation and when they're not expressing such judgements they are often making them. It's so much a part of everyday social life we take it for granted, but it's actually quite a complex process. All five statements involve naming—this person appears to have qualities such as honesty and integrity, that person has qualities such as intelligence and ambition. They also imply some sort of measurement—if she's *really* sociable, this means she's more sociable than many other people, if she's a *real* high flyer, she's got more ability or is going to be more successful than many others, if he's *not very* bright, it means that he has less ability than most. More and less are numerical terms; they imply that we are measuring people up to some standard of what we consider to be normal or average. Further, all the naming in these judgements are abstractions. We go from observing and describing someone's behaviour to the inference that they must possess some inner quality of personality or ability. That's why we are puzzled when people behave "out of character". Something must have happened to upset this person today because irritability is not part of his or her character. Once we have observed someone and come to a judgement, we expect him or her to behave in ways consistent with that judgement. In other words, we expect past behaviour (and the inner qualities which that behaviour suggests) to predict future behaviour.

Whatever method we use, when we select among people for a job, all we are doing is trying to make our everyday judgements about people more systematic, more explicit, more accurate, and hopefully, more predictive of what they will do in the future. Psychometric instruments (e.g., ability tests, personality questionnaires, etc.) are designed to assist in this process. In selection, the great question is, do the methods we use *work*? For instance, if we use a psychometric test in selecting workers, does this give us workers who are better at doing the job than if we did not use the test? And more importantly, does this give us better workers than if we'd simply relied on our innate ability to judge people just by interacting with them: the conviction that, "I can spot a top salesperson when they walk through the door". Moreover, will this technology give us people who can cope with, and thrive on, the demands of contemporary employment? Can we really select people who can stand the heat of the kitchen? A lot of employers think so, which is one reason why more occupational psychologists are working in the area of selection and assessment than in any other branch of the profession.

BOX 7.1
The ideal selection process

Questions to ask	*Action needed*
What does the job entail?	Job analysis
What sort of people could do it?	Person specification
Where can I find such people?	Attract candidates (recruitment planning, advertising, etc.)
How would I recognize someone who could do the job/be best at it?	Choose selection criteria and assessment methods
How can I avoid bias?	Attend to fairness in selection
How will I know that I've got the best person/got the selection process right?	Conduct a validation study— does performance in selection predict later performance in the job?
What's it worth to get it right?	Perform utility analysis

The selection process: The ideal vs. reality

The basic aim of selection is to choose the best possible person for the job on offer and to do this without any unfair discrimination against certain groups of applicants. The full process is illustrated in Box 7.1. From this it can be seen that a good selection procedure is a complex and lengthy process and is therefore expensive. However, before we delve any further into the "Rolls-Royce" model, we would do well to remind ourselves of what actually happens in most small and medium-sized companies. Although individually such firms will be recruiting small numbers of people, the sector as a whole is important since in the UK, it accounts for most of job vacancies and job turnover. Of UK businesses, 88% employ fewer than 25 people and 73% employ 10 or fewer (Bartram et al., 1992). In fact relatively little research has been conducted into the selection practices in this sector; small firms are unlikely to have specialized personnel officers and the selection task is likely to be taken on as an addition to someone's normal work duties. This in itself might imply that selection will be a rather casual affair. Bartram et al. (1993) found that although responses to adverts in the local press and referrals from the Careers Service, Job Centres, etc. were the best sources for the recruitment of applicants, many vacancies were not advertised at all. Small businesses often take on people when they "turn up at the gate" or on the recommendation of current employees. Interviews were used by most firms, but these usually took the form of a fairly unstructured chat with a single interviewer. Although 15% of small firms reported using numeracy and literacy tests and 20% used work samples (tasks which resemble the work, e.g., a typing test), these were considered far less valuable than interviews as sources of information about applicants. A common assessment method was a probationary work period ranging from a week to several months, and, if performance was satisfactory, then the person would be hired.

White and Doyle (1997) did a survey of small professional firms and practices—GPs, architects, management consultants, solicitors, etc.—to find out how they selected new members and what criteria they used. Although there were some differences between the professions, and they all claimed to advertise posts, there was much evidence of informal "word of mouth"/ personal contact methods being used to recruit applicants. For instance, 89% of the firms of solicitors had used personal contact recommendations, and 44% had used recommendations from current employees. Virtually all the firms employed a formal interview in selection, but very few used ability tests or personality questionnaires. Probationary work periods were popular in GP practices. Apart from professional qualifications, the criteria used in selection emphasized motivation, drive to succeed, job-related experience, and potential to develop professionally.

This emphasis on personal networks and proving that you can do the job in a probationary period may be no bad thing. Schwab (1982), for instance, found that the people most likely to stay in a job tended to have been recommended personally. Similarly, "realistic job previews" (which is effectively what a probationary period is) can be effective in reducing employee turnover (e.g., Makin & Robertson, 1983). This makes sense if you consider that personal recommendation and probation will give the applicant more "insider information" of what it is like to work for the firm than just reading a job description and attending an interview. Probation also means that people who are incompetent or who don't "fit in" can be speedily shown the door.

However, the emphasis on an informal network of contacts has its dangers. It may be reducing the pool of good applicants and may make the firms vulnerable to equal opportunties litigation. Though the professional firms were quite clear in what they wanted from prospective employees, they seemed less clear about how to assess these qualities in selection. The average interview is open to all manner of biases and distortions and may not reveal much about the person except how good he or she is at interviews. Finally, although these methods may work pretty well for the firms themselves in that most people selected are probably good at their jobs, the partners don't really know how effective their procedures are and on the odd occasion, when things go wrong, their methods could lead to disaster. When there are only a few people, personality clashes or incompetence in one member impose a heavy burden. In addition, the consequences of rejecting a potentially excellent employee can be worse than hiring a poor one. The first manuscript of J. K. Rowling (of *Harry Potter* fame) was rejected by several publishers before it was accepted by Bloomsbury, which thereby became a "beyond its dreams" commercial success. Similarly, Beatrix Potter had to publish *Peter Rabbit* privately at her own expense before she could find a publisher willing to back her, but Frederick Warne and Co made millions as a result of its decision to do so. Although neither of these people could be properly described as "employees" in a conventional sense, they nevertheless illustrate the principle that giving anyone a job entails risk and getting it wrong is costly. It follows that the more that this risk can be assessed and taken into account in selection decisions, the greater the prospects for a happy outcome.

Job analysis

It stands to reason that you can't select the best candidate for a job if you don't know what the job entails and thus what knowledge, skills, and attributes are needed to perform it well. Yet Cook (1998) believes that many employers have a very hazy idea of what they want in a new employee. He says that job descriptions and person specifications—what the person is expected to do and the kind of person needed to do it respectively—are often subjective, intuitive, and vague.

Job analysis is much more systematic, detailed, and time consuming than the usual process of drawing up a job description and person specification. It is based on painstaking research involving interviews, observation, and structured questionnaires conducted with people already doing the job. The results are analysed using sophisticated statistical techniques and it sometimes involves comparison with a large database which provides profiles of the job and person, suggested assessment methods and even estimates of pay based on jobs with similar requirements. There are very many different methods of doing job analysis, so many in fact, that Spector (2000) suggests that future effort should be expended on evaluating their effectiveness rather than devising yet another. Space precludes me from describing more than two techniques, selected mainly because they are particularly interesting and readers can try them out for themselves without the need for specialist resources. (See, e.g., Lees & Cordery, 2000; Saal & Knight, 1988; Spector, 2000 for more detailed reviews of other techniques.)

The critical incidents technique

This technique was originally devised by Flanagan (1954) to analyse mistakes and failures in flying during World War II. He interviewed hundreds of flight crews to get them to describe "critical incidents" and what exactly pilots did which led to good and bad outcomes. In this way he was able to analyse what made for good and bad pilots. Translated into a job analysis technique, the sequence is represented in Box 7.2.

The problem with this technique is that when you ask people to describe critical incidents with poor performance, they tend to attribute this to the shortcomings of others and things beyond their control. This tendency to attribute good performance to our own abilities and efforts and poor

BOX 7.2
Job analysis using the critical incidents technique

Job experts provide anecdotes/examples of things done/not done or
witnessed that were critical for quality of work

Job analyst (a) collects large number of incidents
          (b) eliminates redundancies
          (c) organizes remaining incidents into
               categories/job dimensions

Categories or dimensions and associated critical incidents (good and bad)
reflect composite of essential elements of job being analysed

A concrete example might make this clearer. Suppose you were trying to analyse the "job" of being a student and what leads to high performance. As a job analyst you might ask a lot of students questions like:

Tell me about a time when you got very high marks for a piece of work—what did you do?

Answers might include:

• I started planning and reading early and spent a lot of time researching the topic in the library and surfing the internet for information and ideas.

The analyst would then probe further, to pin down the actual behaviours that occurred. The next question might then be:

What did you actually do in the library?

A selection of possible answers follows:

• I analysed the title of the piece, devised a list of questions I wanted to answer—located information and made notes using the questions as headings.
• I decided to play devil's advocate and argue against the proposition in the title—looked for information to support my arguments.
• I realized that material in another course gave me a whole new angle on the topic, so I did more reading in that area.

Having analysed all these replies you might conclude that the characteristics needed for high performance as a student include:

- Good study and information-finding skills.
- Forward planning and organization.
- Deep processing of information.
- Ability to make connections between arguments and ideas.

Neat, isn't it? Before going on, you might like to try this technique yourself with any job with which you are familiar. Think of an incident where your performance or someone else's was particularly good. Try to be as specific as possible about the *behaviours* that resulted in this good performance. Then try to infer the knowledge, skills, and attributes that would lead to these behaviours. Do exactly the same thing with an incident where job performance was poor.

---

performance to external causes is called cardinal attribution error. When asked to describe an occasion when someone got poor marks for a piece of work the answers tended to involve things like poor tuition, inadequate library stocks, and personal traumas that disrupted preparation. The same sorts of questions asked of a part-time student who was a nurse evoked exactly the same pattern of replies. Good performance was attributed to personal skill, knowledge, and ability. A bad incident involved things like acute staff shortages combined with a sudden influx of emergency patients. Did your answers to this exercise display this pattern of replies?

This flaw in the technique means that the information tends to be rather one sided—you tend to learn a lot about desirable qualities but little about the sort of people you would definitely not want to employ. Notice too, that it places great emphasis on the skill of the job analyst to sort and categorize responses and infer the qualities needed to do the job.

Using the repertory grid technique for job analysis

This is a fascinating, recently adapted technique (Smith, 1986; Smith, Gregg, & Andrews, 1989) based on Kelly's personal construct theory and the method he used to investigate the way people construe their worlds—repertory grid. The basic idea is that we all have a set of constructs about how the world is, and these act as "frameworks" which we use to interpret what we experience and to explain and understand it. The repertory grid technique is a method to lay bare what these constructs are and since constructs are akin to our basic assumptions, which are usually implicit and barely capable of articulation, this has to be an indirect approach. Funnily enough, I have never been able to fully communicate this technique to students in writing.

Whatever the detailed instructions I've provided for exercises, I've always had to go round and demonstrate the questioning technique in person for them to really grasp what they were supposed to be doing. Maybe this is due to my lack of written communication skills or, perhaps, it is a feature of qualitative techniques that they can only be learned at the "master's knee". Whatever . . . if you are unfamiliar with rep grid, it is likely that you will have to pay particularly close attention to the text that follows.

When applied to job analysis, you need to think of six or seven major tasks that you have to perform in the course of your job. Smith and his colleagues analysed the job of senior civil servants in the UK government administration and came up with tasks such as "Understanding policy, Appearing before Select Committees, Working on Cabinet papers, Giving presentations to ministers" and so on, as the major tasks of such a job. These tasks are the "elements" in the rep grid and are entered as column headings in the grid. However, for reasons that will become apparent, I cannot continue to explain the rep grid technique using these tasks because I have next to no idea about what they entail and therefore have no constructs associated with them. Instead, I will choose a job likely to be familiar to my readers and certainly familiar to me—the "job" of being a student. (Yes, I know you don't get paid, but it's still work, isn't it?) OK, what tasks do you have to perform as a student? You might come up with a list such as this: attend classes, prepare coursework, design and conduct research projects, sit exams, etc. Now comes the crucial bit. You take three of these tasks at random, and ask yourself "In what way are the skills needed for two of these tasks similar to each other and different from those needed for the third task?" To give an example: Suppose you had chosen preparing coursework, attending lectures, and sitting exams. You might say that preparing coursework and sitting exams were alike in that they both involve communicating your knowledge and understanding to others, whereas attending classes mostly involves comprehending someone else's knowledge and understanding. The first row on your grid might thus have the label "Ability to communicate knowledge and understanding" and this is a skill needed for the job of being a student. At the opposite pole at the right hand of the grid, you might put "Comprehending complex information". You could go on: Preparing coursework and sitting exams depend on you collecting, thinking about, analysing, organizing, and criticizing information for yourself; in class this has largely been done for you by someone else. Thus, your second skill in the grid might be "Ability to assemble information" and your third might be "Ability to analyse critically, and integrate, information into coherent arguments". When you are tired of this comparison you could go on to other comparisons. Comparing sitting exams and attending classes, for instance, you might say that both involve attending promptly at a particular time on a certain date, which is fairly straightforward to enter into your schedule, whereas preparing coursework involves wider time management skills over a longer time period and has to be slotted into the rest of your life, thus

(a) Partial grid

	Tasks					Etc.
	Understanding Policy	Measuring Performance	Lecturing	Appearing before Select Committees	Working on Cabinet Papers	
Ability to express viewpoint	2	1	5	7	3	(18)
Ability to assemble facts	5	5	3	6	4	(23)
Ability to talk convincingly	1	1	6	6	2	(16)
Producing action plans	6	1	3	1	2	(13)
Ability to motivate staff	1	5	4	1	2	(14)
Etc.	(15)	(13)	(21)	(22)	(14)	
Etc.						

Factor analysis of data in grid revealed 8 significant trends in skills needed:

1.	Analytical ability	23%
2.	Oral	16%
3.	Management skills	9%
4.	Detailed specialist knowlege	6%
5.	Drafting skills	5%
6.	Decision-making skills	4%
7.	Breadth of mind	4%
8.	Foresight	3%
	Miscellaneous skills	30%

Figure 7.1 The repertory grid technique in job analysis: (a) a partial grid for senior civil servants (from Smith et al., 1989). From Smith et al. (1989), *Selection Assessment: A New Appraisal*. London: Pitman. Reprinted by permission of Pearson Education Ltd.

requiring more self-discipline. Planning for punctuality may therefore be your fourth skill and the opposite pole might be general self-management. You go on like this, comparing different "triads" and asking the same questions until you can't think of any other similarities and differences and all the skills you think are needed to do your job have been made explicit.

You see the idea? Answering the "triad" questions is intellectually taxing and forces you to make explicit the skills you think you need to do this job. You now have a grid which gives the tasks/elements across the top and the skills needed down the sides. This in itself provides valuable information, but you can then go further by taking each skill and rating how important it is for the successful performance of each task (e.g., 7 = high level of this skill is essential to 1 = task does not involve this skill). You then end up with something resembling the partial grid in Figure 7.1a, which comes from Smith et al.'s civil servants.

(b)

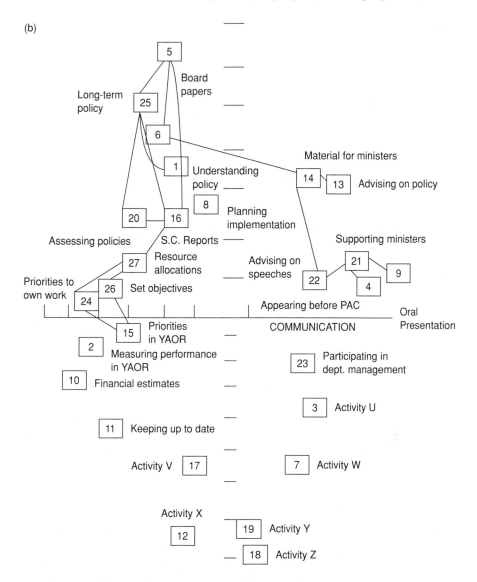

Figure 7.1 (continued) (b) the final results of the job analysis.

Totalling the ratings for the columns tell you at a glance which tasks are most difficult because they require high levels of a lot of different skills. The row totals tell you which skills are most important for the job as a whole since they are needed for many different tasks. In the case of the civil servants, oral presentations and briefings to ministers were the most difficult tasks and the ability to assemble information was the most important skill. You can go further yet and conduct factor analyses and cluster analyses of the grid ratings to explore why some tasks are more difficult than others and what the main clusters of tasks are for any given job. These are sophisticated statistical procedures beyond the scope of this book to explain (but see Tabachnick & Fidell, 1996). In Smith et al.'s analysis, these procedures showed that briefings to ministers were difficult because they had high loadings on analysis, presentation skills, and specialist knowledge. The job of being a top civil servant was revealed to consist of at least two large groups of related tasks—dealing with ministers and dealing with policy—plus a number of more disparate tasks. Software is being developed so that the grids generated by many different people can be combined in these analyses.

A lot of people are rather sceptical about the value of the rep grid technique. Once all the information has been extracted it all seems rather obvious. This is not surprising because what you have revealed is people's fundamental assumptions—if they were to be surprised by the results you would be worried! However, having spent an hour running through a very successful rep grid exercise designed to elicit people's constructs of "world leadership", I sensed a feeling of "So what?" So I asked, "Well, if you knew all that, tell me what makes your friends and acquaintances leaders in your social groups?" A lively and intelligent class suddenly fell silent. They knew the answers at some level, but it was implicit knowledge, and they couldn't put it into words. The rep grid process may be slow but it is necessary. Convincing corporate clients that it *is* necessary may be the biggest obstacle to being able to use this very effective technique. However, it does produce an integrated job description and person specification, and a great deal of information about which skills are most important for assessment in the selection process. It has many other uses, not least in personal development programmes—in making people aware of skills and attitudes they never consciously realized they had.

Job analysis: An evaluation

Good job analysis lies at the heart of much best practice in personnel processes

Once you have done a thorough job analysis, it can be used for many different purposes because it provides the foundations on which so many other things depend (see Exercise 7.1):

- Writing good job descriptions to attract the right candidates.
- Devising structured interviews and application forms.
- Designing fair selection procedures including the use of psychometric instruments.
- Defending the selection procedure against claims of discrimination and unfairness.

- Transferring the use of selection methods (including the use of psychometric instruments) to different jobs that share the same characteristics and skills.
- Devising training programmes so that people have the skills to do the job.
- Careers guidance and career management—advising people about the aptitudes they have and the skills they will need.
- Succession planning—how to "groom" the next generation.
- Designing fair pay and promotion systems.
- Developing good measures of work performance both to evaluate the effectiveness of the selection procedures and to enhance accurate and fair performance management.

EXERCISE 7.1
The uses of job analysis

If you have found this list rather cryptic and cannot easily see how job analysis might help in these matters, it would be a useful exercise to reread what has already been said about it and try to work out how it could contribute to these processes. If you are still uncertain, do some more reading and thinking. You might like to come back to this exercise when you have read the rest of this chapter and this book and add to your answers.

Fair selection

It is worth expanding a little on the fact that fair selection begins with job analysis. With equal opportunity legislation now extended to cover people with disabilities, employers are even more concerned to avoid costly litigation and bad publicity. A simple example will illustrate the value of good job analysis in protecting employers as well as employees. If, for instance, the job analysis *proves* that a person must be able-bodied and over 6 feet tall in order to be able to do the job then employers can legally exclude people who do not fit these criteria from the selection process. The fact that this will exclude many women and people of Asian origin—who tend to be less than 6 feet tall—and people with disabilities cannot legally be challenged, if people who do not fulfil these criteria cannot do the job. Neither can the use in selection of methods such as physical fitness tests be challenged.

However, and here is where protection of potential employees comes in: The proof of the link must be very strong. One Police Authority would not consider women for motorcycle rider training on the assumption that women would not be strong enough to pick up a motorcycle lying on its side. It therefore specified "men only" in its internal adverts. Men who could not do this were also excluded from any further consideration because this *skill* was deemed to be essential to the job of police motorcycle rider. Unfortunately, the Police Authority had mistaken exclusion from selection on the basis of an essential skill (which is legitimate) with exclusion on the basis of membership of a social category (which is not). The ability to lift a heavy motorcycle upright may be rare in women but the policewoman who challenged her nonconsideration *was* able to do this. Thus, the policy of automatically excluding women applicants was shown to be discriminatory. Employers need to be very careful, especially in the case of people with disabilities. Just as technology has removed the need for physical strength in many jobs, so technology may remove the need to be able-bodied. For instance, there are many aids to allow someone whose sight is quite seriously impaired to work as a secretary (Baron, 1998).

Careless job analysis and choice of selection methods got British Rail into trouble because it rejected all the Asian applicants for train driver training because they did badly on a verbal reasoning test (Kellett, Fletcher, Callen, & Geary, 1994). First, it is difficult to see why verbal reasoning is essential for effective performance in driving a train. Second, most of the Asian candidates had English as a second language and, although they were generally fluent in speaking, the test material printed in English may have slowed them down. Third, there may have been cultural differences in that the Asian candidates may have been reluctant to guess or risk making mistakes so a slower, more methodical, but accurate style would have reduced their scores. British Rail was forced to settle out of court and change its selection practices.

Without adequate job analyses we have no idea of what we are requiring of workers

Not often mentioned in the literature is that job analysis can be used in risk assessments for both physical and psychosocial hazards. Observation may show that the physical conditions encourage unsafe behaviours or that the equipment, including software, is leading to suboptimal performance. However, especially when combined with cognitive task analysis and various methods of measuring mental workload (Hart & Staveland, 1988; Hutton & Militello, 1997; Reid & Nygren, 1988; Tattersall, 2000), it is most useful in revealing such aspects as role overload, role conflict, and excessive task complexity. Xie and Johns (1995) investigated the effects of the scope of jobs in over 400 full-time employees who together represented 143 different occupations. They found a curvilinear U-shaped relationship between all their measures of the range of job activities required and emotional exhaustion, which is one of the major facets of burnout (see Chapter 4). Too little or excessive job scope can lead to adverse psychological and physical ill-health. Traditional job analysis and recent work on mental workload in ergonomics need to be integrated for effective analysis of knowledge work. Good job design depends on job analysis.

But sadly . . .

Some commentators believe that the days of traditional job analysis may be numbered. When more and more jobs become short-term constellations of roles that exist only for the duration of a particular project, job analysis is too cumbersome to be useful or feasible. Moreover, with technology changing jobs so fast, employers are finding it increasingly difficult to predict the sort of people they will need in the future. All employers seem to know is that they need people who are flexible, emotionally stable, willing, and able to learn, with good interpersonal skills and who are able to "hit-the-ground-running" and make a difference to the "bottom line" from day 1. Harvey, Moon, and Geall (1997) conducted a study of what employers wanted from their graduate employees and it reads like a "wish-list" for superhumans. Even the authors warn that many undergraduates may become daunted and demoralized when they read what is expected of them. The point is, however, that meticulous analyses of particular jobs may no longer be appropriate or even necessary. As long ago as 1978, Schmidt and Hunter were arguing that assuming necessary job-related knowledge and skills are present, cognitive ability is the best general predictor of success in almost any occupation. Thus, the only needs are for jobs to be classified into more and less complex and a suitable "off-the-shelf" ability test to be used in selection.

Many commentators seem rather resigned to the demise of job analysis although they frequently express the hope that the need to base personnel decisions on good information will never go away (Lees & Cordery, 2000; Schneider & Konz, 1989). However, they also argue that job analysis must be adapted to focus more on business imperatives. Landis, Fogli, and Goldberg (1998), for instance, describe a technique combining traditional job analysis with newer methods to provide future-oriented job analysis. Sanchez (2000) suggests that basing job analysis on information gained solely from people already doing the job is "practically and theoretically unjustified" (p. 207). He also advocates the use of electronic records of work information rather than relying on traditional interviews and paper-and-pencil surveys. Sparrow (1997) suggests that competency-based frameworks can also provide solutions, although more methodological rigour is needed in their formulation and evaluation than is generally the case now. Given the central role that job analysis plays in so much best practice in organizing work, such developments are to be applauded and encouraged.

Choosing assessment methods in selection

There is a bewildering array of methods to assess people for the knowledge, skills, and attributes needed to do a job. Some are more useful than others. Some are better at ensuring fairness in selection than others. Even assuming that the person specification has been carefully constructed, getting from this to the final selection procedure is not always easy, especially if you lack the knowledge to evaluate the various methods. Some general guidelines for choosing methods are given next.

Scope

What range of attributes does the method cover and how general or specific is it? For instance, a general cognitive ability test or a simulated in-tray exercise might be good general predictors of future managerial performance. A test of typing speed and accuracy is much more specific. The method you choose will depend on the nature of the job and your purposes in making the assessment.

Reliability

Any method needs to be evaluated for its reliability. Reliability has a more specialized meaning in psychometrics than it does in everyday language. In general it refers to three main attributes of assessment methods:

1   The accuracy with which the method assesses the characteristic in question.
2   The extent to which the method yields consistent responses.
3   The extent to which people's performance remains stable over fairly short periods of time.

All measurement involves some degree of error. This is true even when directly observable physical characteristics are involved. To emphasize this point to students I used to set a silly exercise whereby they measured the length of each other's forearms 10 times. Most of them did this with good humour and then I would ask, "How many people got exactly the same measurement on all 10 occasions?" In several years of doing this exercise and several hundreds of students not one person ever managed to do this.

When we are measuring psychological characteristics and processes the possibility of error is greater. There are several sources of error. People taking an ability test may underperform because they do not feel very well, or they are worried about some personal problem, or they are distracted by a pneumatic drill outside, or they are paralyzed by test anxiety, or they simply suffer a lapse of attention, which leads them to mark the wrong answer, and so on and so on. If people are being assessed for their performance in a role-play exercise, error can occur if the assessors are insufficiently trained, or have to rate too many aspects of performance, or have too many people to observe. All these sources of error reduce the accuracy of our assessments. There are methods to assess the amount of error in our measurements. For instance, in the role-play example we can assess the reliability of assessors' judgements by correlating the ratings of two different observers. If there is good agreement between their ratings of the same person in the same exercise then we can have more confidence in the accuracy of their ratings. (However, they could both be equally wrong!)

Knowing how accurate our measurements are likely to be is very important in selection. For instance, suppose we decide to select only the people who score above average on a cognitive ability test. How certain can we be that people who score just below average, really have below-average ability? Maybe the inaccuracy in our assessment makes them *look* below average. To assess this we need to look at a statistic called the standard error of measurement (*SEm*), which will be given in the test manual or can be calculated from other information. Put very simply, this statistic tells us the margin of error surrounding someone's score. Supposing that someone scored 100 on a test with an SEm of 5. This means that we can be 68% confident the person's real (or true) score could be as low as 95 (100 − 5) or as high as 105 (100 + 5). Thus we could not safely reject everyone who scored less than 100. We would have to set the cut-off score to take account of this margin of error. Similarly when we have to select just one person from among several candidates, we would want to know the probability that differences in their scores on a test were real differences and were not just caused by error. For these sorts of reasons, best practice suggests that selection decisions should never be based solely on test scores.

The second aspect of reliability concerns the consistency of responses. If a questionnaire designed to measure attitudes produced wildly conflicting responses to questions meant to be exploring views on the same topic, we would be distrustful. Say, for instance, someone strongly agreed with the statement, "This company looks after its people" and also strongly agreed that "This company couldn't care less about its people", we'd be right to resist drawing any conclusions about the person's true attitudes to the company. The internal consistency of responses on a test or questionnaire is measured by statistics known as Cronbach's alpha and the split-half reliability coefficient.

Psychometric techniques are technically quite complex, which is why the British Psychological Society has introduced the Certificate of Competence in Occupational Testing. The Level A Certificate qualifies the person to purchase and use ability tests and occupational interest inventories. The Level B (Intermediate) Certificate qualifies the person to purchase and use one specific personality instrument. Most test publishers run courses leading to these certificates and the BPS has also published an open learning course for Level A (Bartram & Lindley, 1994). So a full understanding of this area requires a considerable investment of time and money. Here, the most important issue to understand is that using an unreliable method is like trying to measure someone's height with a piece of elastic!

The final aspect of reliability is stability, which refers to the expectation that if we are measuring relatively enduring characteristics of the person (skills, abilities, etc.) then their performance on a task/test should not vary much over shortish periods of time. If someone taking an ability test gets a low or average score on one occasion but a few weeks later gets a very high score on the same test, we have to wonder what happened on the first occasion—perhaps the person was ill or did not understand the instructions. If the performance of many people varies greatly from one testing session to the next, then the reliability of the test is suspect.

Validity

Validity concerns the truth of measurement and an investigation of whether the method we're using actually measures what we think it's measuring. A test of creativity or innovative potential may just be a poor measure of intelligence; since highly creative people tend to be highly intelligent too, the test may be picking this up and not measuring creativity at all. The problem is not confined to tests. Do interviews assess qualities important for doing the job or just the ability to interview well? Are group exercises such as a simulated business meeting really assessing interpersonal skills, the ability to influence and persuade, etc., or do they merely show that how one performs in such circumstances depends on the "luck of the draw"—the nature of the other people present? I once took part in such an exercise as part of the selection for a trainee manager post. One person in the group was extremely aggressive and determined to over-ride everyone else's contribution. After some determined attempts to overcome this, it soon became clear that I had the choice of spending the "meeting" in one-to-one combat (thus preventing the group from achieving its goals and excluding other people's contributions as badly as my protagonist sought to do), or to withdraw gracefully and let him "win". What would you have done in these circumstances? Whatever . . . no two group exercises are ever exactly equivalent even if the basic task is the same, because the particular group dynamics have such an influence on performance and outcomes.

What we really want to know is whether performance on selection tasks, whatever they may be, is related to later performance in the job. Do people who do well in selection also do well in the job and vice versa? If so, we can be confident that we're getting selection right. In order to demonstrate this we generally do one of two types of research projects. We can get existing job holders to perform the selection tasks and correlate their performance with measures of how well they do their jobs. If there is a high correlation then we might use the tasks in selecting new employees. This is called "concurrent validity" because the two measures of selection task performance and job performance are collected at the same time, or concurrently. These studies are relatively easy to do but suffer from a number of methodological and statistical shortcomings (see, e.g., Bartram, 1990) A better method is to assess people using some method (e.g., an ability test) and then lock the results away and select on some other criterion (e.g., interview performance). Once successful candidates are settled in the job you then measure their job performance and see how well the test scores predict later job performance. This is called predictive validity (for obvious reasons) and is generally a superior procedure for establishing the validity of selection than concurrent validity studies. However, predictive validity studies are much more difficult and expensive to conduct and, by the time you have collected enough data, the job might have changed so much that the selection procedures will also have changed, so that the investigation of their usefulness is no longer relevant.

Very few researchers can conduct the perfect validity study but one fortunate person was Flanagan (1946) who, uniquely, had access to a large sample of applicants who were *all* selected. During World War II, the US airforce put 1143 men through pilot training, regardless of their scores on an ability test: 77% of the men failed their pilot training but the test scores had a high correlation with later performance in training—*r* = .63. Trust me—those familiar with the average "raw" correlations (i.e., uncorrected for sources of error) found in most validity studies recognize this value as very high indeed—more later on this.

Relevance

An assessment method could be valid in that it is measuring what we want it to measure, but if this attribute is irrelevant to doing the job its use is inappropriate and could result in illegal discrimination. Thus, we must be certain that the method is really assessing some attribute which is relevant to doing the job well. British Rail's choice of a verbal reasoning test for the selection of train driver trainees failed on this criterion.

Suitability

Is the method chosen "fit for purpose"? If you want to assess how likely it is that you'll be able to work comfortably with someone, then a face-to-face interview may be most suitable. If you're a big employer with thousands of applicants who look quite evenly matched on paper, then a well-regarded ability test may be the best way of sifting the most promising people out for further assessment.

If you do decide on a test of some sort, then it must be designed for the pool of applicants you have in mind, and there should be some information on whether it is likely to have a discriminatory bias (adverse impact) on groups such as women and ethnic minorities. Giving a test designed for school-leavers to 5-year-olds would not be fair or sensible. Though the issues are usually much more subtle than this, the same principle applies in selection. Two new challenges are also emerging.

Testing people with disabilities

Equal opportunity laws to protect people with disabilities have recently been enacted in the UK. The use of ability tests with people who lack the physical capacity to take them in the manner intended is clearly a problem and is exercising the minds of most test publishers (see, e.g., Baron & Butterworth, 1997; Clark & Baron, 1992). It is not simply a matter of providing special equipment or giving extra time; varying the conditions under which tests are administered and taken changes the reliability and validity of the resulting scores. We might also question how fair it is for the performance of some-one with a severe sensory disability, for instance, to be compared with able-bodied people. To give one example, a well-known test of numerical ability asks people to analyse data presented in the form of graphs and tables. Extracting information from tables is quite difficult for those who can see them but for someone using braille, it is a nightmare. One slip of the finger or a forgotten column or row label and you are reading the wrong value. Neither is it easy for a blind person to do rough work or calculations on paper.

So there is the danger that the tests will be measuring something quite different in the case of people with disabilities. Research concerning the assessment of people with visual impairments suggests that this could well be the case (Reid, 1994, 1995). In a review of the literature Reid (1997, p. 552) concludes "there are few comprehensive tests available for assessing the intellectual functioning of visually impaired adults and little consensus regarding the utility of those available. The majority of tests reviewed here have never been widely used, and many are no longer available."

Neither are these problems confined to tests of ability. Reid (1998) con-siders the conceptual and measurement issues connected with assessing literacy skills in people with visual impairments. She points out that in most job contexts it is not the basic skills of reading and writing (e.g., in braille) that are important for employers but the person's "functional literacy", i.e., the extent to which he or she can independently access printed and computer information and communicate via printed material with an intended (usually sighted) audience. However, some functional literacy tests have content that is totally unsuited to the everyday experience of people with visual impair-ments. For instance, the Senior High Assessment of Reading Proficiency test, designed to measure reading comprehension, contains reading tasks con-nected with driving a car (Efron & Gibson, 1981). Personality inventories also tend to contain material which is unsuitable for people with visual im-pairments (Reid, 2000). Indeed some material would be quite controversial as to its relevance for many other groups. For instance, one well-respected instrument uses items that address people's readiness to jump out of aircraft and climb mountains as part of its measure of "openness to experience". Fail-ure to relish such thrills is taken as evidence that one has a closed mind!

Assembling a large database of the scores for people with disabilities for the purposes of developing new norms would not be a solution to these problems since there is such a huge range of different disabilities which will affect performance in different ways. Even within the group of people with visual impairments there is a huge range of degrees and types of disability. Some people are almost "sighted" in that they can function effectively with "strong" spectacles and large print whilst others have no vision at all. People who have suffered brain damage may have far more complex disabilities. The great Russian psychologist Luria published a very moving account of the fate of a young man, formerly a university student, who was shot in the head during World War II (Luria, 1973). Though the young man recovered physically and retained his intelligence, self-awareness, and humanity, his sight in one eye was experienced as a "swarm of bees" and in the other he could only see half the visual field, which was in a constant state of flux. One of the worst shocks he encountered on his recovery was that everything he read appeared to be in a foreign language—he had totally lost his capacity to interpret printed material. Despite these and numerous other terrible disabilities, he fought for the rest of his life to overcome them and write an account of his experiences and struggles. Though someone so afflicted would be unlikely to be able to enter the labour market, the case still leads me to question whether the use of psychometric tests in the selection of people with disabilities can ever be justified. A probationary work period would seem to be a much fairer and safer method of selection, although that also raises a host of problems, not least that people with disabilities often need extra skills to compensate that able-bodied people don't need, thus they may need more time than usual to adjust to a new job. Even learning the layout of the building is a greater challenge for people with visual impairments than it is for people like me with no spatial ability! (But see Chapter 10 for some exciting developments in assessment using virtual environments.)

Globalization and testing

A second issue concerns the globalization of business and the fact that tests may be used to select people with very different backgrounds in terms of culture and values from those it was originally designed for. Tests do not always translate easily into other languages. Feltham, Lewis, Anderson, and Hughes (1998) give a good example of this. If you had applied for a job and were asked if you were a hard worker, what would you say? Feltham and his colleagues were involved in a project to translate a test which asked this question into French and used the word "dur". He was surprised that most French managers denied that they worked "dur". It transpired that "dur" has connotations of hard *physical* labour and so it is unsurprising that French managers were reluctant to ascribe this characteristic to themselves. However, even when we get the vocabulary right, there are still considerable cultural differences to contend with (Rousseau & Tinsley, 1997; Shackleton & Newell, 1997).

Acceptability

I once read an anecdote in the computing press of someone who had been grilled mercilessly for 5 days in a selection process that included numerous tests, exercises, simulations, and interviews. At the end of this, he was offered the job, but was so disgusted by his experiences that he told the company that in no circumstances could he be induced to accept it. This is a factor that can be overlooked by employers. The selection process is a social process too, and the candidates are as much concerned with finding the right job and organization for them as companies are with finding the right employees. As long ago as 1989, Herriot argued that selection should be a process of social negotiation and transaction where each party finds out about the other and can terminate the relationship at any stage. Recession soon overtook this optimistic image of more equality between employer and employee within selection, but this alternative approach, which Anderson and Cunningham-Snell (2000) call the constructionist perspective, has recently been gaining ground as organizations come to realize that they must compete for the best people. Anderson (2001) has suggested that the selection process is not just a matter of neutral predicting of who will do the job best. It also serves the function of a pre-entry socialization process whether or not organizations intend this to happen. For instance, says Anderson, even a brief job advert can say a great deal about a company. A long and complex selection process is likely to have a considerable impact on people's attitudes, expectations, and subsequent on-the-job behaviour.

Anderson (2001) writes, "candidate impression formation has been considerably less extensively researched than recruiter impression formation ... leaving gaps in our understanding of these processes" (p. 90). However, the selection process is usually the first contact people have with the organization in which they hope to be investing a great deal of their time, effort, and energy for sizeable chunks of their lives so the impressions formed are likely to be important. If they feel that they have been treated badly or unfairly, they may not stay long, if they accept the job at all. I once attended a highly structured interview where the questions were nearly all designed for new graduates, whereas I had over 20 years of relevant work experience by then. Thus, I had to endure questions relating to my feelings and experiences some 20 years before and very little concerning all my professional experience since then. To be fair, I was obviously an unusual candidate and the structured interview had been designed to ensure equality of treatment of all candidates by asking them the same questions so that everyone had the same opportunity to shine (or not). The answers could then be compared against set criteria. It was based on best practice too—research shows that structured interviews are excellent predictors of later performance (see later). However, this didn't make my experience any the less frustrating, and I retain very negative attitudes towards that organization to this day.

Taken to its logical conclusion a constructivist perspective would dictate a very different approach to selection, but even a "traditional" approach demands that whatever methods are used, they should be perceived by the candidates to be relevant to the job and fair. If tests are used they should *look* as if they are measuring job-related abilities—this is called face validity.

Cost and utility

Unless you are hiring people "at the gate", selection is never cheap. Even if you are using only the most popular process of application form, interview, and references, there are adverts, letters, and candidate's expenses to be paid for as well as the time of everyone involved. Attendance at an assessment centre, a technique involving one or more days of tests, exercises, and interviews, can cost several thousand pounds (euros, dollars, etc.) per candidate. Psychometric instruments (ability tests, personality inventories, etc.) are like the tip of an iceberg. What you see when you take the test gives no inkling of the great amount of research that has gone into developing it and the constant ongoing research to investigate and establish its validity. They are therefore costly to produce. They are sophisticated instruments and people need to be trained to administer them and need even more training to interpret the results. So, especially if there are a lot of candidates, the inclusion of even one test in selection can be expensive.

To justify this expense you need to conduct a utility analysis. There are many sophisticated ways of doing this (Cascio, 1982; Eaton, Wing, & Mitchell, 1985; Schmidt, Hunter, McKenzie, & Muldrow, 1979), but the basic aim is to show how much the organization would gain in greater productivity, etc., if *only* the best workers were to be selected. Schmidt and Hunter give as a rule of thumb that the difference in value to an organization of the work of the worst versus the best worker is between 80% and 140% of the worker's annual wage. Later estimates have reduced this to a more moderate 40% to 70%, but consider a large number of workers over several years of service and the savings soon add up to astronomical sums. Cook (1988) calculated that the US Federal Government was losing $16 billion a year by not using tests.

Cronbach (1990) was very sceptical about these "fairytale" sums because there simply are not enough "best" people out there for every organization to recruit only the most talented and motivated. Be that as it may, even small improvements to the selection procedure can have significant effects. For instance, Cook (1998) gives an example, inspired by Bartram and Dale's (1982) work, of including Eysenck's personality inventory (EPI) to select military pilots. Even though the EPI scores correlate only .15 with later pilot training success, using it to improve the selection procedure can be calculated to save £950 per pilot selected per year and that is without taking training costs into account. In 1995 Bartram introduced his MICROPAT test battery to improve the selection of RAF fighter pilots (see Chapter 10). Since the cost of training pilots is so high, the new test battery's ability to improve the prediction of who would succeed was estimated to save £2 million for each trained fighter pilot!

Commonly used selection methods

The basic aim of good selection is to assess candidates fairly and accurately for the knowledge, skills, and attributes needed to do the job. But before you can decide what assessment methods to use, you need to know what methods are available and how useful they are. Thus, this section summarizes the most commonly used methods and begins with the options for those who do not like psychometric tests.

The "big three": Application forms, interviews, and references

Application forms

The commonly used standard application form is only one of three main types but it is popular because it standardizes the information provided by the candidate so that it can be easily found and compared with that of other candidates or, better still, facilitates comparison with predetermined selection criteria. Cook (1998) reports that there is so much variation in application forms that the only communalities are that they all ask for the name, age, address, and previous employers of the candidate. Keenan (1997) asked graduates whether they ever "made things up . . . to please the recruiters". Although most would not lie about important things such as degree results, a surprising number felt that they did not have to be honest about why they were applying to that company or about their interests and hobbies. Keenan also reports that sifting of application forms tends to be a very unreliable process, and most organizations do not supply any criteria or guidelines for rejecting candidates or inviting to interview. Herriot and Wingrove (1984) found that one in five of the comments of personnel managers, "thinking aloud" while sifting, related to presentation. What the form looked like tended to be more important than any information in it.

Looking at selectors' evaluations of CVs, Finney (2000) comes to similar conclusions, that they use only a small part of the information available to them. Bright and Hutton (2000) also investigated the factors influencing selectors when evaluating CVs. They found that the inclusion in CVs and covering letters of vague "competency statements", such as, "I have excellent skills of organization and can manage my time effectively", increased the likelihood of candidates being shortlisted. Moreover, this happened whether or not the selectors had any information about the specific competences needed for the job. Thus, it seems that selectors were responding to perceived evidence of generic competences rather than assessing the applicant's specific "fit" for the job.

The person's name can also lead to bias. A *Daily Mail* newspaper report, (Vasagar, 1999), cited the case of Mr Tahir Hussein, who was awarded £16,500 following a successful complaint of race and sex discrimination against a recruitment agency. Mr Hussein had used tactics such as posing as a woman and using false names on application forms to demonstrate that he was being discriminated against. By this means he had brought 10 cases to tribunals in 5 years. Of these, he had lost two, won six, and two were still pending. Although not a scientific study, this is quite compelling evidence that bias and discrimination can operate even at the earliest stages of selection. Especially when there are thousands of applicants, bias and unreliability at the sifting of application forms and CVs stage could be a serious threat to good selection.

Another type of application form is the self-assessment of competencies questionnaire. This is essentially a structured written interview. Essential competencies are derived from job analysis and applicants are asked to give examples of a time when they were required to demonstrate each competence, their contribution to the outcome, and the name and telephone number of someone who could verify their accounts. An example question might be like the one in Box 7.3, taken from the UK's former Department of Employment's Management Trainee scheme.

If you tried answering the question in Box 7.3, you will doubtless have discovered that it's not easy! However, consider how you would have responded if you had been asked a similar question at interview. At least in written form you have plenty of time to think about your response. Self-assessment questionnaires are being used increasingly by careful employers and for other purposes too, such as entry to professional organizations, so it

---

BOX 7.3
An example item from a self-assessment of competences questionnaire

Flexibility and Resilience:

Management Trainees need to:

• be flexible to cope with changing situations and manage several tasks at the same time
• deal with ambiguity and uncertainty
• work in situations where they may be isolated and lack support
• withstand criticism
• react quickly and cope with short timescales.

Candidates are asked to provide an example from any aspect of their lives (ie not just work tasks) and to give information about the nature of the task, what they actually did and when, the resulting outcome, and the proportion of this achievement for which they claim credit.

Source: Taken from the Department of Employment's (1992) Trainee Manager Selection Process.

Before reading further, you may like to try to answer that question yourself by writing a paragraph to describe how you have demonstrated these competences.

---

is useful to acquire the knack of writing such entries. The advantages of these types of forms include the care used both in their construction and in the development of criteria for evaluating responses. Many unsuitable candidates de-select themselves when faced with such a task, so they save organizations mountains of application forms from unsuitable candidates. They are considered good practice and are sometimes used by firms of occupational psychologists, but evidence for the validity of self-assessment is inconsistent (see Anderson & Cunningham-Snell, 2000).

The final type of application form is really a heavily disguised test that asks innocent-sounding questions about such matters as age, marital status, and education, which are really criteria for selection because they have been shown to predict later job performance. These "weighted application blanks" (WABS) date back to the 1920s when Goldsmith (1922) used one to predict who would be good insurance salespeople. He found that age, marital status, education, current occupation, previous experience of selling life insurance, and membership of clubs all predicted who would make the best salespeople. These responses were then weighted according to their importance in predicting the most successful workers, and people then end up with a score indicating their suitability. A similar principle applies in calculating car insurance premiums. Certain characteristics make some people a worse risk than others, e.g., being young, male, living in London, etc., are all characteristics that, statistically, make a car insurance claim more likely. So positive answers to these "indicator" questions are weighted, and the higher the score the higher the insurance premium.

Early studies found that WABs were quite good at predicting who would make the best workers. For instance Dunnette and Maetzold (1955) found that whether temporary pea-pickers/canners at Green Giant Company would stay for the full season was best predicted by this unlikely set of characteristics:

- Lived locally.
- Had a telephone.
- Married but no children.
- Not ex-Armed Forces.
- Either young (under 25) or older (over 55).
- Weighed over 150 lbs but under 175 lbs.
- Had more than 10 years education.
- Had worked for the company before.
- Available for work over the summer.
- Preferred field to inside work.

Some of this makes sense. For instance pea-canning would be likely to attract young and semiretired people with few commitments who want a temporary summer job. But why is having a telephone or not being an ex-serviceman important? WABs (and later biodata questionnaires—see next) have always been accused of "blind empiricism". They appear to work but why they work can be a mystery. Why, for instance, should an interest in breeding canaries correlate strongly with dishonesty at work? Another problem is that some questions would be considered offensive or illegal now.

Since the 1960s WABs have tended to be replaced by biodata questionnaires, which are similar in basic technique, but the questions are more transparent and "open" with multiple-choice response alternatives. They are therefore easier to fake. For instance, what sensible person would admit to watching an average of 8–10 hours of TV every day given that employers are not looking for couch potatoes? Some questions are factual and can be verified (e.g., positive vetting for criminal convictions). Other questions resemble the types of items you find in personality inventories, e.g., "I'm usually a happy person". However, biodata tends to predict later job performance better than personality questionnaires. Cook (1998) gives average predictive validity of about .35 for biodata, which is as good as work sample tests that actually get people to perform a job task. Personality inventories rarely exceed the .3 barrier, but the predictive validity of biodata can be as high as .5 or .6. Biodata has also been used to predict success in a wide range of occupations, e.g., salespeople, researchers, engineers, scientists, bus drivers, and police officers (Reilly & Chao, 1982; Schmitt, Gooding, Noe, & Kirsch, 1984).

The disadvantage of biodata is that it is very job specific, and a questionnaire that works well for one job cannot be used for another even if the jobs are similar. For instance the WAB used to select temporary seasonal pea-canners did not work for permanent canning jobs. Thus every job needs its own specific biodata questionnaire and, since this has to be based on extensive research, it can be costly and time consuming, especially if only a few employees can be selected.

"Blind empiricism" remains a problem and can affect the face validity of the process. Some experts recommend the "*Washington Post* test" to judge what items should go in a biodata questionnaire. Imagine, says Cook (1998), what the headlines would say if your activities were discovered by a daily newspaper. "Psychologists reject Police officer recruits because of dislike of colour blue" might bring the profession into disrepute. "Psychologists reject police officer recruits because of fear of heights" seems considerably less bizarre.

Even so, blind empiricism has its uses. Mitchell and Klimoski (1982) went to great lengths to construct a "rational" biodata questionnaire using correlation and factor analysis to discover psychologically meaningful personal history factors that predicted job performance. They compared this rational measure with an empirically derived inventory (i.e., anything, however odd, was included provided it correlated with job success). The empirical measure was a better predictor of the job performance of people already doing the job and the rational measure "travelled better" in that its predictive power didn't "shrink" at all when applied to a group of new applicants. However . . . the empirical measure was still a better predictor of new recruits' later performance even after shrinkage!

Biodata can also have good incremental validity. For instance, Dalessio and Silverheart (1994) used biodata and an interview to select insurance salespeople. If the biodata score was high, then a structured interview didn't add anything to the accuracy of selection decisions. If the biodata score was low, then good performance at interview did have some predictive power, e.g., whether the person would "survive" the first year. Biodata can predict failure very accurately even if a high score doesn't guarantee success, so it is almost certainly a fairer screening technique than the usual biased and unreliable sifting of application forms.

For an interesting and accessible account of the use of biodata techniques in practice see Harvey-Cook (2000).

Selection interviews

Interviewing candidates for a job remains the most popular method of selection, with numerous surveys showing that almost all UK organizations use it. Yet up to the mid-1980s most experts would have said that interviews are a very poor method of selection because interview performance does not predict later job performance. Interviewers were shown to be biased in a number of ways. They may place too much weight on negative information; be influenced by a variety of irrelevant factors such as the age, race, gender, or attractiveness of the candidate; and they tend to make up their minds too fast (in the first 4 minutes according to Springbett, 1958). After the interview they are very poor at remembering and integrating information when making final decisions. All this and more, it was said, made interviews little better than a lottery at best. At worst, they could be vehicles for serious (and illegal) discrimination—a claim made by Wood as recently as 1997.

In fact, the label "selection interview" is used to refer to a range of techniques, each of which can be conducted more or less proficiently. An interview involving an untrained interviewer asking a few haphazard and unplanned questions in a noisy environment amidst constant interruptions is indeed a waste of time. Unstructured interviews in the hands of well-meaning but untrained people who don't know what they're looking for give rise to all those problems of bias and irrelevance. This type of interview was (and still is) all too common and was the focus of the earlier research—hence the bad press.

However, research has now established that "structured interviews, conducted by trained interviewers using systematic assessment procedures to target key skills and attributes identified by job analysis, are . . . comparable to the best selection methods" (Boyle, 1997, p. 15). (See Anderson, 1997; McDaniel, Whetzel, Schmidt, & Maurer, 1994 for reviews.)

Highly structured interviews can be artificial, inflexible, and can hinder the establishment of rapport, as my own experience demonstrates (see p. 278). Dipboye (1997b) gives six main reasons why organizations may prefer to use unstructured interviews, including that it is easier to "sell" the job to good candidates, a wider range of questions can be asked, etc. However, unstructured but carefully planned and sensitively handled interviews can be good predictors of future job performance—for instance, somewhat better than personality inventories.

Interviews can be of three main types, all of which have their advantages and limitations. The *biographical interview* is a semistructured exploration of the candidate's past experiences. This is probably what most candidates expect but it can be difficult to relate the information to job-relevant criteria, which means that the interviewer's personal biases are more likely to influence decisions.

In a *situational interview* questions are based on hypothetical job-related situations and supervisors of people actually doing the job agree on the sort of answers one would expect from "good", "average", and "poor" workers. Cook (1998) gives the following example:

> Your partner and two teenage children are sick in bed with colds. There are no friends or relatives available to look in on them. Your shift starts in 3 hours. What would you do in this situation?

Though situational interviews predict future work performance quite well, some authors claim that they are more like verbal reasoning tests than exchanges of information and could be particularly susceptible to social desirability effects. For instance, in the example above a "good" answer might involve reasoning, "Well, they aren't young children, there will be an adult in the house and they're not really ill—only a cold—so I'd make them as comfortable as I could before I left, leave them with plenty of cold drinks, and go to work as usual." Notice how the person has to attend to, evaluate, and integrate all the information in the question to arrive at such an answer. Da Silva (1979) has shown that this requires a high degree of cognitive development. Presented in such an abstract form, rather than in the context of someone's everyday life, sixth-formers could not always manage this sort of attention to detail and integration of information. Emotional and social factors may also intervene. Someone else, fearing to be seen as unfeeling and uncaring, might give a different answer. Neither reply need necessarily reflect what the person would actually do. Finally, this particular example of a "situational interview question" could be seen as offensive—or even illegal if it was asked only of women candidates, or in interviews for jobs dominated by female workers. The basic principles underlying the construction of situational interviews still apply to better questions, but this example highlights the additional dangers of asking questions that may violate equal opportunities legislation.

Competency-based interviews involve questions relating to important job behaviours, e.g.,

> Describe a time in any job you've held when you were faced with problems and pressures that tested your ability to cope. What did you do?

Such questions make it easy for the interviewer to relate information from the candidate's answers to the skills needed for the job but again the interview has become more of an oral test of intelligence. (In fact, Huffcutt, Roth, & McDaniel, 1996 in a meta-analysis study—see p. 292—found a mean corrected correlation of .4 between interview ratings and cognitive test scores, indicating that cognitive ability plays quite a big role in interview performance—16% of the variance.)

However, it is generally agreed that the main function of the interview is not really to assess ability (although interviewers can accurately assess a number of characteristics such as initiative, analysis, decisiveness, and judgement). Instead, interviews serve an essentially social function. Organizations regard a face-to-face meeting with potential employees as important because they want to assess the candidate's degree of fit with the organization and its culture, or within a team. Despite the common criticism that interviewers favour people who are similar to themselves ("like me" syndrome), selecting a person "one can work with" may be as vital as technical ability to do the job.

There is evidence that interviewers can accurately assess characteristics such as social and communication skills and work motivation even though they sometimes base their judgements on the wrong cues. Herriot (1989) argued that the entire selection procedure is a series of social exchanges and mutual negotiation between employer and applicant, each of which involves the implicit or explicit communication of expectations. At any stage in this process either party can terminate the relationship. If selection is a social process, then the interview as a face-to-face social interaction is vitally important.

Recent research has focused on what happens in interviews and how the characteristics of the parties involved can affect the process. For instance, Graves and Powell (1996) looked at the effects of same- or opposite-sex pairs of interviewer/interviewee. They found that male interviewers did not show any systematic gender bias when rating the performance of men and women. However, female interviewers rated women candidates higher than the men. It could be that women's communication styles, emphasizing empathy and self-disclosure, are more suited to the interview than the task-oriented style favoured by men, and that this tendency is magnified in female pairs. However, it could equally be that the male interviewers had been sensitized to equal opportunity issues and the female interviewers were more careless!

Whether there is racial bias in interviews is a moot question. Anderson (1997) argues against trying to eliminate racist bias in interviews, *not*, I hasten to add, that he condones racism in any context. Rather, he says that if the interview is racially biased, it is likely that this merely reflects racist values in the organization. If so, there is a need for a major intervention to eliminate it "root and branch", and cleaning up selection is merely "window dressing". Better, he says, for applicants to be rejected or reject the organization themselves than to end up working for a racist organization. Be that as it may, one of my undergraduate students, Stephen Awosunle, did a fascinating if modest study to investigate racial bias (Awosunle & Doyle, 2001). Since so many things can influence interviewers to give rise to bias—the candidate's appearance, attractiveness, weight, nonverbal behaviour, etc. —it is very difficult to demonstrate that racial bias, and that alone, influenced outcomes. However, it is possible that if someone has a strong Afro-Caribbean accent most people will assume that the owner of the voice is black. Further, if someone has a "cockney"/East London accent, it may be that most people will assume that the speaker is white. Using this line of reasoning, Awosunle signalled race via accent, and cut out most other nonverbal cues by using audio tapes of interviews rather than videotapes. He got three different people to record a short interview on audio tape. The interview transcript was identical for all three so everyone said exactly the same things in answer to the same questions. Great care was taken to make sure that nonverbal cues such as intonation, and voice qualities such as energy and enthusiasm, were as similar as possible by training the interviewees and getting them to listen to each other's tapes to imitate each other's styles. To avoid gender effects the interviewees were all male. So as far as was possible, the only difference between the three interview tapes concerned the speaker's accents. One interviewee was white and had an East London accent, another was black and had an Afro-Caribbean accent. To check that accent was signalling race as intended a control interviewee was black but had an East London accent. (Ideally, there should have been another control person who was white with an Afro-Caribbean accent, but there are limits to an undergraduate's resources.) One of these three audio tapes was played to groups of white and black people who were asked to rate the person being interviewed for their knowledge and suitability for the job. Ideally, it would have been better if participants had acted as their own controls by listening to all three interviewees, but that might have been very tedious for people. It would also have made the purpose of the study so transparent that participants might have given what they thought was wanted or would seek to sabotage the study. The results are shown in Figure 7.2. This shows that the mean rating scores for each group of participants demonstrated a clear same-race interaction effect. In other words, in the black participants, those who heard the person with an Afro-Caribbean accent rated that person as more suitable than the groups who heard the interviewees with East London accents. In the white participants, the groups who heard the interviewees with East London accents rated those people as being more suitable for the job than the group who heard the person with the Afro-Caribbean accent.

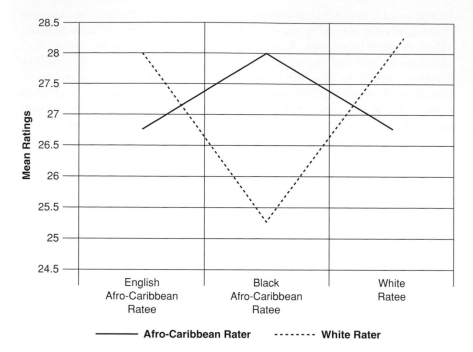

Figure 7.2 Interaction of mean rating between rater and ratee (Awosunle & Doyle, 2001).

Thus, we appear to have here not so much racist bias as "same-race preference", which may be another instance of the "like-me syndrome", which may explain the findings in the Graves and Powell (1996) study of gender biases in interviews. Similar racial preference effects have been reported (see, e.g., Kraiger & Ford, 1985 for a meta-analysis of 74 studies). The problem is, of course, that when the majority of interviewers are white and male, the "like-me" bias can add up to serious discrimination, unless concerted effort is made to avoid it by, e.g., training, structured interviews, and standard decision-making procedures.

Silvester (1997) used attribution theory to analyse what people actually say in interviews and related this to interviewers' ratings of the candidates. She hypothesized that the way successful candidates explain their past successes or failures will be different from less successful candidates. Attributions can be:

Stable: The cause is relatively permanent, e.g., "I've always been interested in business law, that's why I took those options".

Personal: The cause is unique to the speaker, e.g., "You have to be committed and I have that; I mean, I've always worked hard, that's the way I got where I am".

Global:　The cause has many potentially important outcomes rather than a few specific ones, e.g., "My Mum and Dad are quite elderly, so basically I look after the family".

As an example, consider the situation that afflicts many new graduates—taking some time to secure their first "real" job. A period of temporary work or unemployment after graduation is likely to come up at interview. How would you answer questions designed to probe why you didn't go straight from university to a junior post in your chosen career? Consider these two types of answer:

I decided to concentrate on my academic work in my final year to get the best degree I could and so I left making applications too late. But that's me, I always get totally bound up in what I'm doing. In the end though, it's been a good thing because it's given me time to think about my career so I know I'm making the right choice.

Versus:

Our tutors totally overloaded us with work in the final year so I didn't have any time to make any applications. Then when I did have time most of the jobs had gone. Anyway, there just aren't enough jobs around for new graduates and they all want previous experience.

On the face of it, the factors that led to the slow career start are the same in both cases, but the way they are explained differs markedly. In the first case the person takes responsibility for not applying for jobs sooner (personal attribution) and ascribes this to an enduring characteristic (stable attribution) but then goes on to say that commitment has been enhanced (global attribution plus the person has learned from the experience). In the second example, the person ascribes everything to uncontrollable external causes and is basically saying "It's not my fault". This may be true, but what are interviewers to make of this? In the first case they may think, "Here is a person who makes considered decisions, is conscientious and committed, and is likely to stay with the firm and justify our investment with good work and success". In the second case they may think, "Here is someone who can't prioritize and think ahead even in vitally important things. If someone can't cope with the workload on a degree course, what chance in the real world of the job? These kinds of people blame anyone and everything but themselves for their own shortcomings". Unfair though these evaluations may seem, who is likely to get the job?

Silvester (1997) found that more successful candidates were less defensive and more willing to ascribe negative outcomes to stable, personal, and global causes. Interviewers were less impressed by candidates who consistently externalized responsibility when things go wrong. Looked at in this light, selection interviews are quite a minefield for the unwary.

References

Almost all employers think that good references from previous employers or the person's teachers and tutors are essential but there is very little research to indicate whether references are reliable and valid. General requests to write a letter about the candidate yield enormous variations in what is said and how it is said and may reveal more about the writer than the applicant. Baxter, Brock, Hill, and Rozelle (1981) found that referees had their own idiosyncratic ways of describing people so that what one said about a particular person didn't resemble what another referee said about the same person. However, what the same referee said about different people had a lot more in common. Some employers use a form with a standard set of questions, sometimes accompanied by rating scales, and these can be quite effective. For instance, Jones and Harrison (1982) found that head teachers' references for candidates applying for naval officer training, which used a standard form, did predict training success quite well.

One of the major problems with references is that candidates are becoming more litigious and a bad (but maybe honest) reference can be legally challenged. Thus, there is a huge favourability bias in references. At most, referees are likely to "damn with faint praise". In over 20 years of reading thousands of references, I have only encountered two that were unequivocally negative and, in both cases, the writers invited me to contact them for further discussion. This is reflected in Mosel and Goheen's (1958) research in which 97.5% of referees said that they would re-employ the person concerned. This research is rather dated, however, and reflects the paucity of good evidence available.

Some commentators advocate telephone references, which gives referees less time to think and choose their words carefully. Cowan and Cowan (1989) suggest that the most important questions to ask are:

- How long did this person work for you?
- Why did this person leave?
- Would you re-employ this person?

But these are frequently not asked and successful legal cases make referees unwilling to give oral reports.

Another important practical problem is that candidates may be most unwilling to let their current employers know that they are applying for other jobs. If they are unsuccessful, the impact on future prospects in the current job could be severe. This problem may not be solved by contacting employers only after the person has been offered the job. Especially if the candidate occupies a key position, the employer has a vested interest in not being entirely fulsome with praise.

At a more conceptual level, the point of references is the expectation that past behaviour will predict future behaviour but, although this may be true generally, it may not be true in every individual case. Many factors influence whether someone is successful or unsuccessful in a job. The organizational climate may not suit someone's personal style. For instance, someone who is unconventional, innovative, and creative may not thrive in a very formal and hierarchical context but may perform brilliantly in a more "laid back" organization that values such qualities. Or the person may have had troubles with his or her boss or co-workers. The literature on workplace bullying should give us pause when considering the value of references in such cases. So should the evidence of person–environment fit (see, e.g., Burke, 2000b, of which more is said in Chapter 8).

When there may be far more reliable and valid means of predicting people's future behaviour, the continued reliance on references is surprising.

Summary

Traditional methods of selection can be effective but this means more care being exercised than is usually the case in everyday selection. They are also open to considerable (illegal) bias and discrimination if this care is not exercised. All have their advantages and disadvantages and the selection interview, in particular, may not be replaceable simply because it serves an important social function. What can psychometric instruments offer in terms of useful, more objective information?

Ability and aptitude tests

In the 1960s and 1970s the use of mental ability tests in selection fell into disrepute, and they were actually banned in some US states. Their unpopularity stemmed from several sources. First, in 1969, Jensen published a paper in the *Harvard Education Review* in which he suggested that there were ethnic differences in intelligence which were largely racially inherited. The resulting furore was such that psychometric tests came to be associated with "scientific racism". Second, a controversy erupted in the UK over the work of Cyril Burt, who had published work on twin studies which lent a great deal of credence to the view that genetics played a large part in determining someone's intelligence. All sorts of irregularities in the research and its reporting were claimed, some of which have since been disputed. However, the upshot was that research supporting the heritability of intelligence, and by association, the credibility of IQ tests was discredited in the public mind. Worst of all, though, researchers such as Ghiselli (1966, 1973), using the new statistical technique of meta-analysis, which involves pooling the data from many different studies and vastly increasing sample sizes in the process, seemed to show that mental ability tests were not good at predicting later job performance. Moreover, there was great variation in the validity of tests from study to study, even when the same test and the same job was involved. Researchers were forced to conclude that unspecified differences in local conditions affected how well a test would predict job performance and the only way out of this was to conduct "local validity" studies to find out empirically which test would be effective in selecting for a particular job in a particular organization. Since this was an expensive and time-consuming process, employers were already concerned about the use of tests violating equal opportunity legislation, and tests were unpopular with candidates and the public, it is hardly surprising that few employers were prepared to use tests in selection.

All this changed with Schmidt and Hunter's (1977) seminal paper on validity generalization analysis (VGA). Their arguments are quite complex, but their essential point is that there is so much error in the measurement of both ability and job performance, that the size of validity coefficients can be expected to vary widely from study to study. To take just one example, sampling error, caused by the typically small samples in most validity studies, can be expected to produce a range of validity values. (This relates to the well-known statistical fact that the larger the size of the sample, the more the mean is likely to reflect the mean of the underlying population.) Schmidt, Ocasio, Hillery, and Hunter (1985) provided a neat illustration of this effect. They reanalysed the results of a validity study which had used a test to predict the job performance of 1455 postal workers. The correlation of test scores with work performance in the whole sample was .22. Schmidt and colleagues divided this large sample into 63 mini- or pseudo-samples of 68 people, which compared to the average validity study, is still quite a reasonable number. They then correlated test scores and job performance measures for each pseudo-sample. The resulting validity coefficients ranged from −.05 to +.45 just because of chance variation in the composition of each pseudo-sample! Schmidt and Hunter (1977) identified seven such sources of error which could distort the apparent accuracy of test results for predicting later job performance. Four of these sources are deemed to be particulary important and can be either measured directly or estimated statistically, to give a truer picture of the validity of the test.

Technically, VGA "estimates how much variance in validity the four sources of error could account for (estimated variance), then compares this estimate with the actual variance (observed variance) to see if there is any variance (residual variance) left to explain" (Cook, 1998, p. 113). In other words, can all the differences in the size of validity coefficients from study to study be explained by error? The implications of this are also simple. VGA seemed to show that local conditions were not important at all. The differences found in tests' ability to predict job performance from study to study could all be accounted for by error—"noise in the system". Practically, it meant that validity coefficients could be corrected for these sources of error and then ability tests could be shown to be good predictors of job performance. In fact, when corrections for all these sources of error are made, the mean true validity of ability tests seems to be roughly twice as high as the "raw" validity values suggest. For instance, Schmidt, Gast-Rosenberg, and Hunter (1980) claimed that the estimated true validity of the programmer aptitude test is .73 for job proficiency and .91 for training grades.

The main implication of VGA was that ability tests are among the best predictors of job performance—the average true validity is about .5, which means that test scores can account for about a quarter of all the variation in people's later work performance. Test scores were therefore extremely useful additional information. The other implication was that since specific local conditions were not important for the effectiveness of tests in predicting performance, there was no need for local validity studies and tests could be used "off the shelf". Indeed, as has already been mentioned, Schmidt and Hunter (1978) argued that job analysis was no longer necessary either—jobs simply had to be classified into simple and complex to determine how much mental ability was needed so that a suitable test could be selected.

Needless to say, nothing in psychology goes unchallenged and the claims of VGA are no exception. Seymour (1988) produced a scathing argument to the effect that VGA is merely a case of, "If your validity coefficient isn't large enough, inflate it to the desired size by making 'corrections' (Cook, 1998, p. 119)." It is true that different assumptions underlying corrections can produce quite different results (see, e.g., Hartigan & Wigdor, 1989). However, after a careful weighing of all the arguments and evidence, Cook (1998) concludes that ability tests are good predictors of job performance, and certainly provide more accurate information than many other selection methods. Ability tests are, therefore, now used by many organizations.

Personality inventories

It seems plausible to assume that personality must also be implicated in doing a job well. Consider lorry drivers. They have to spend long hours alone in a cab and need to be careful and conscientious if they are not to pose an extreme hazard to other road users. So someone who craves company and likes thrills and risks might not be temperamentally best suited to this job. From good, common-sense insights such as this, we now enter a thicket of controversy.

There is no universally agreed definition of personality, but most definitions emphasize consistent and durable characteristics of the person or features of his or her behaviour, and adaptation to the social and physical environment. There is little consensus in personality assessment because different instruments are linked to particular theoretical traditions. The most famous tradition is derived from Freud's work and the psychoanalytic approach.

The essence of Freudian theory was once described to me as, "Two apes fighting in a dark cellar with a referee trying to put the light on and a very prim maiden aunt berating all concerned". (No, I am not going to ruin a good joke by explaining it!) The psychoanalytic tradition emphasizes the unconscious—a storehouse of impulses, passions, repressed memories, and so on, which are inaccessible to the conscious mind. Thus, personality is so private that the person him or herself is largely unaware of the forces that drive behaviour and these must be revealed by a therapist who interprets free associations, dreams, etc. for the person. Inasmuch as there is any formal assessment in this tradition, it is via projective techniques such as the Rorschach test, in which people are asked to say what they can see in ink blots. Since there is no inherent meaning in ink blots, any meaning must be projected onto them from within the person and thus reflect hidden personality.

Selection and assessment is mainly concerned with trait and factor models of personality. Cook (1998, p. 137) offers the following definitions: "Traits are mechanisms within the individual that shape how he/she reacts to classes of event and occasion, A trait summarises past behaviour and predicts future behaviour. Factors have much in common with traits, but are derived by statistical analysis". Trait and factor models are derived from people's responses to self-report questionnaires and inventories such as Cattell's 16PF and Eysenck's EPI. Though different instruments produce different traits/ factors (with different names), recent research shows that there is a lot of similarity in what they are measuring. Since the early 1990s, factor analysis and meta-analysis studies have shown that most instruments seem to be best construed as measuring five major dimensions of personality. According to Costa and McCrae (1992; Costa, 1996; McCrae & Costa, 1997), these are most sensibly labelled as:

- Neuroticism—extent of emotional stability.
- Extraversion.
- Openness to experience—intellect/intuition/imagination.
- Agreeableness—pleasantness/warmth/tact, etc.
- Conscientiousness—organization/self-discipline/dependableness, etc.

This general consensus about the major dimensions of personality is a great step forward but different theorists believe that each of the five can be sub-divided into particular facets or more specific factors. For instance, Hough (1992) divides extraversion into affiliation (sociability) and potency (degree of impact, influence, and energy). Hogan and Hogan (1997) divides extraversion into ambition (hard working and achievement oriented) and sociability (outgoing, gregarious, attention seeking, and impulsive). Hough also adds two further dimensions: locus of control (the extent to which the person feels control over events) and rugged individualism (decisive, independent, unsentimental). So in effect, there is still disagreement about how many factors are needed for a full description of personality. The implications of this for selection is that there is some uncertainty about what aspects to assess. Hough (1988), for instance, found that some traits which are not part of the "Big Five" were better predictors of job performance. There is also disagreement about which facet "belongs" to which major dimension. For instance, Hough believes that achievement, which is similar to Hogan's ambition, is a facet of conscientiousness, not of extraversion.

However, the biggest controversy concerns whether measures of personality are at all useful in selection. There are at least two strands to the argument. The first concerns "faking" and whether self-reports of personality can ever be a true reflection of what people are "really like". Even if the person does not deliberately set out to mislead by "faking good", there may be an element of self-delusion. The second strand concerns the ability of personality measures to predict future job performance, i.e., their predictive validity. Blinkhorn and Johnson (1990, 1991) have led the "opposition", as the following two quotes demonstrate.

> It is perhaps time that we made up our minds: are personality tests serious measures of personal qualities which predict behaviour, or are they bits of stage managed flummery intended to lend an air of scientific rigour to personnel practice?
>
> (Blinkhorn & Johnson, 1991, p. 39)

> We are not suggesting that personality tests have no uses, or that there are no underlying aspects of temperament which are important in determining behaviour . . . but we see precious little evidence that even the best personality tests predict job performance, and a great deal of evidence of poorly understood statistical methods being pressed into service to buttress shaky claims.
>
> (Blinkhorn & Johnson, 1990, p. 672)

So is there any justification for using personality assessment in selection?

"Faking"

Since inventories usually involve self-report, most questions are fairly transparent, and as when people have applied for a job they usually want to create a good impression, the opportunities and motivation for giving less than honest answers are obvious. Take this (fictitious) example of a statement with which you might be asked whether you agree or disagree: "I find that I can usually get on well with people". If you badly wanted the job would you admit that you usually *didn't?*

There is some evidence that social desirability effects (faking good) may not be that serious (Hough, Eaton, Dunnette, Kamp, & McCloy, 1990; Mount & Barrick, 1995; Ones, Viswesvaran, & Schmidt, 1993). However, a good defence against the faking charge is provided by Hogan, Hogan, and Trickey (1999). They say that there are two aspects of personality. The first is from the point of view of the observer—"how a person is perceived and evaluated by others . . . [in ordinary language—reputation]. The second is personality from the perspective of the actor—the factors inside a person which create his/her reputation . . . [in ordinary language—identity]. Well-constructed personality tests do not measure dimensions which exist inside people. When people respond to items on personality tests they are essentially responding to questions from an anonymous interviewer. Personality tests elicit self-presentations that are characteristic features of a person's interpersonal style" (pp. 7–8). The Hogans go on to argue that since people respond as they would like to be seen—the public aspects of personality that the person projects to the world—the responses are likely to reflect how that person is perceived by others. An important part of the validity evidence for the Hogan personality inventory is therefore the degree of agreement between the person's own scores and the ratings of people who know him or her well. For the most part these correlations are in the range of .3 to .5, indicating reasonable agreement. Thus personality tests have validity *because* they reflect self-presentation and how people tend to "come across" to others. Even allowing for the fact that some people are more self-aware than others and that this can lead to greater or lesser self-criticism or complacency, this argument tends to make the fakeability of personality measures something of a nonissue.

Do personality measures predict later job performance?

Personality inventories suffer from the same problems in establishing validity as ability tests in that they are subject to the same major sources of error—small sample sizes and restricted range in many studies and unreliable tests and measures of work performance. Correcting for these sources of error increases the size of correlations between scores and work performance measures but not to the same extent as with ability tests. However, there are additional problems with measures of personality. Employers often want to know what the "perfect" personality for a particular occupation is. However, the Hogans offer the analogy of the major personality dimensions as being like the three primary colours from which an almost infinite number of tones and hues can be derived. It is the infinite combinations of the five factors and their different facets which create the diversity of human personality. So although we can make some broad generalizations about the types of occupations to which people would be best suited temperamentally, precisely accurate predictions are rarely possible. We can say, for instance, that an unconventional, spontaneous, and intensely creative person may not make the best bank manager or that an energetic, ambitious, outgoing, and agreeable person may be good at sales, but predicting that *this* particular person is best suited to this particular job is more problematic. Just as there are many hues and tones of personality, so are there many ways of being a good manager or salesperson. A cautionary tale comes to mind of laboratory equipment salespeople who were selected on the basis of their extraversion and weren't at all successful in selling products. The reason? These outgoing, energetic, rather "loud" people were trying to sell products to research scientists who were often very introverted and took an immediate dislike to them. In this particular case, being more introverted would have been an advantage.

Another difficulty concerns the question of the extent to which our personalities develop as a result of experience or, indeed, whether the way we react is situation specific. Both social learning theory and humanistic approaches to personality stress the development of the person's self-concept, which is influenced by experience. As I write, the actor Sir Alec Guinness has just died. In his obituaries, everyone who knew him commented on how shy and self-effacing he was, which makes constant public performance an unusual choice of career. Presumably the other qualities that made him a great actor, and thus the success he enjoyed, led him to develop strategies to overcome his shyness in the specific situations of stage and film set. I, for one, am rather thankful that some organizational psychologist or personnel officer didn't reject him for his first acting job because he was temperamentally unsuited to the profession!

Another issue concerns the fact that when it comes to personality, more is not necessarily better. Each facet of personality carries its own strengths and weaknesses. A very agreeable person may be ineffective when difficult issues have to be confronted; a very emotionally stable person may be so "laid back" as to be supine or so complacent as to be totally oblivious to the adverse effects he or she is having on other people; an obsessively conscientious person may be the nightmare, "bean counting" bureaucrat. Technically, this affects the size of correlation coefficients and the results of multivariate analyses since the statistical models assume a linear relationship between variables, e.g., that the higher the person's score on conscientiousness, the higher the work performance. However, at the upper extremes at least, we are talking about nonlinear relationships—something akin to Warr's vitamin model (see Chapter 3), when you can have too much of a good thing.

Given all this, it is hardly surprising that the validity data for personality measures is not all that impressive. A series of meta-analysis studies (Barrick & Mount, 1991; Hough, 1988, 1992; Ones et al., 1993; Salgado, 1997; Tett, Jackson, & Rothstein, 1991) suggest that the use of personality inventories can improve selection although they do not seem to predict general job performance. Cook (1998) summarizes the main findings: Conscientiousness is most strongly associated with work performance, although people with the highest scores are likely to be rigid and inflexible. Barrick and Mount found that extraversion generally predicts success in salespeople and managers, and Salgardo found that emotional stability predicts well for professional jobs. Hough found that personality inventories predicted "nondelinquency" well (correlations up to .52), and the Californian personality inventory (CPI) is best in this respect ($r = .64$). Delinquency is defined as the extent to which people are likely to engage in anti-organizational and out-of-role behaviours so personality measures can help to select honest employees. The Hogan personality inventory (HPI) manual (Hogan & Hogan, 1997) also reports an impressive quantity of research demonstrating the relationship between scores on the HPI and job performance in many different occupations.

Nevertheless the problem with most studies is that they look at the predictive power of single traits in isolation, yet as already mentioned, traits interact with each other. Robertson (1998, 2000) calls for more research into how traits interact and how this relates to job performance. For instance, a very agreeable person will want to minimize conflict at work, but the strategies used to achieve this will likely be very different if the person is also highly extraverted or introverted. An extravert might choose to tackle conflicts "head-on" with amiable chats with colleagues to bring problems out into the open and resolve them. An introvert may choose to ignore them or use more indirect means of resolving them.

I would say that personality measures should be used with great caution in selection. They can provide useful additional information, but it requires very careful interpretation of individual scores, and sensitive feedback to establish the context and how the results fit in with the person's long experience of living with him- or herself, along with any issues which should be explored further at interview. The conclusions drawn from the results of personality inventories must always be regarded as tentative. It is probably true to say that if someone's personality is fundamentally unsuited to a particular occupation, he or she is always going to have to struggle more for success than people who are "naturals". But this doesn't mean that success can't be achieved, only that life may be harder than perhaps it need have been. The real value of personality inventories may thus be more in career guidance/management and personal development than in selection (see Chapter 8). They can also be very useful in teambuilding, as demonstrated in Exercise 1.3. We must *always* remember that tests (of ability and personality) are good for predicting group performance, but that individuals often defy accurate prediction.

A note on emotional intelligence

There is little doubt that some people are less successful in their chosen occupations despite high cognitive ability, whereas some with lesser ability do much better than expected. Given that personality measures have not proved to be very good predictors of eventual performance, employers have latched on to the notion of emotional intelligence as the "missing link" that distinguishes between the average and outstanding performers (Goleman, 1998). The concept of emotional intelligence seems to be a muddled cross between what we in developmental psychology used to call "theory of mind" (i.e., the ability to understand that other people have thoughts, feelings, etc., and to infer what these are via interpretations of behaviour); social skills (well that *would* follow, wouldn't it?); personality factors such as amiability, sociability, and impulse control (all of which would make a person more able to deal with difficult colleagues and situations); and good old "thought police—wishful thinking". The emotionally intelligent person can ignore the most upsetting behaviour and circumstances and return quickly to a positive frame of mind and get on with the work. I was always concerned about this "new orthodoxy" since it seems to be inviting us to repress all our negative emotions at work, whatever the circumstances, if we wish to succeed. I felt that this was somewhat dangerous, given what we know or suspect about the consequences of emotional repression. Indeed, Eisenberg, Fabes, Guthrie, and Reiser (2000) show that emotional regulation is not necessarily a good thing, and the danger is that it can deteriorate into over-control. They also point out that there is a very important distinction to be made between controlling emotion and controlling the behaviours those emotions create. My work colleague may make me feel like punching him or her, but provided that I can control that impulse, do I also need to control the negative emotions that led to that impulse? Maybe a quiet "fume" or "sounding off" to a friend are important "safety valves".

I also felt that the whole concept was ill-informed in management/ occupational psychology compared with the sophistication of theory and research in child development, where there has been a concerted attempt to understand what has to develop for a mature and skilful "theory of mind" and how it develops (see, e.g., Flavell, 1985). Emotional intelligence has also been an important concept in occupational psychology, albeit in different guises, for many years. However, nothing stops a cleverly packaged, intuitively attractive, management "tool". And emotional intelligence tests are already on the market.

I was rather pleased, therefore, when Woodruffe (2000) issued a broadside entitled "Emotional Intelligence: Time for a time-out" where he writes, "Emotional intelligence is a wonderful brand for a set of competencies" (p. 8), but goes on to say that these competencies are neither as new, well-defined nor as simple as their proponents would have us believe. He also says that there is an inherent paradox in self-report measures of emotional intelligence, in that it needs the self-awareness of the emotionally intelligent person to respond with any degree of insight. Thus, the more emotionally intelligent person may actually perceive more deficiencies in their social interactions and thus score lower on a questionnaire than someone with less emotional intelligence! Woodruffe also suggests that it is not "particularly emotionally intelligent to test for emotional intelligence", since it is not empathic to subject someone to such a formal and potentially anxiety-provoking situation. If emotional intelligence is to be assessed, he says that it would be better to do this via assessment centre exercises (see next) or by multi-rater feedback (see Chapter 8). Woodruffe admits that the accessibility of the notion of emotional intelligence recommends itself to managers and the general public, who thereby are encouraged to focus on important aspects of work performance in both selection and personal development. However, he warns that unless occupational psychologists pause for thought, "EI risks seeming like so much hot air" (p. 8). I eagerly await further developments and invite you to make up your own minds by reading more than just Goleman's (1998) book.

Assessment centre methodology

An assessment centre is not a place. According to Seegers (1997, p. 3) it is "an evaluation process which can be used to identify the future potential of employees and job candidates. It consists of the observation of candidates carrying out a variety of assignments, individually or in a group, over a period of several days. The method is systematic, effective and reliable". Central to the process is that each skill or competence needed for the job is assessed by at least two qualitatively different methods. For instance, the ability to influence others may be assessed by means of a group exercise such as a simulated meeting and by a personality inventory. Ability to handle numbers could be assessed by a written exercise using a financial case study and by a test of numerical reasoning. So it is effectively a multi-trait, multi-method means of assessment. Once skills, abilities, etc., have been established via job analysis, suitable assessment methods are chosen which result in an Exercise × Dimension matrix like the one in Figure 7.3.

Simulation exercises often form an important part of assessment centres. They aim to simulate part of the job so that performance can be assessed using trained assessors. They are rigorously developed involving piloting and redesign, re-piloting, and overall evaluation of their eventual effectiveness in selecting good employees. These exercises can involve individuals, e.g., in role play, where a trained actor will take the part of a dissatisfied customer or difficult colleague with whom the candidate must cope, or a written exercise such as dealing with the contents of a typical in-tray, which is used to assess ability to plan, prioritize, delegate, and make decisions. Other exercises may involve groups, e.g., a simulated business meeting where people have to compete for the allocation of resources. Simulation exercises are often popular with candidates because they are clearly job related and people feel that they can demonstrate their skills. However, assessment centres are also likely to include psychometric tests and interviews.

Assessment centres developed almost simultaneously in the UK and the USA around the time of World War II. In the UK they were used for officer selection and in the USA for the selection of spies to work behind enemy lines. (Incidentally, the best predictor of the length of time a spy managed to stay alive was measured intelligence! It makes sense . . .) However, they really took off as a selection method after a series of studies conducted by AT&T in the 1950s (Bray & Grant, 1966): (Although dimensions, and which

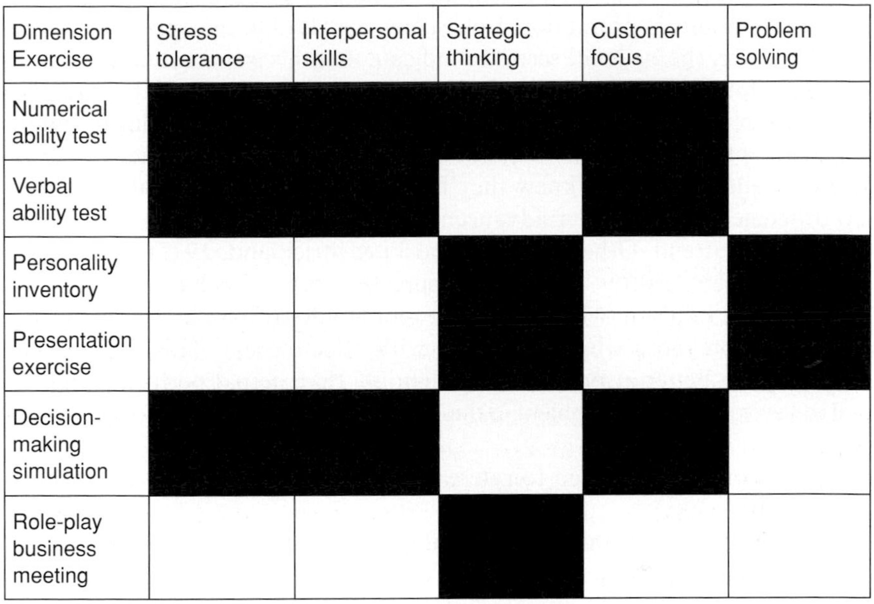

Dimension Exercise	Stress tolerance	Interpersonal skills	Strategic thinking	Customer focus	Problem solving
Numerical ability test	■	■	■	■	
Verbal ability test	■	■		■	
Personality inventory			■		■
Presentation exercise			■		■
Decision- making simulation	■	■		■	
Role-play business meeting			■		

Figure 7.3 An assessment centre exercise × dimension matrix.

aspects each exercise is designed to measure, is much more tightly specified than this might indicate.) 400 candidates who underwent a rigorous assessment process, including a business game, a leaderless group discussion, an in-tray exercise, tests, and interviews, were followed up 5–8 years later. The assessment centre predicted 82% of a college-educated group and 75% of a nongraduate group who reached middle management positions 8 years later. It also predicted 88% of graduates and 95% of nongraduates who failed to make that grade. The validity coefficients were .44 for the college-educated group and .71 for the nongraduates. This was impressive indeed, and results were similar in the UK, where the Civil Service Selection Board pioneered the technique to select government administrators (Vernon, 1950). In the UK the uptake of the use of assessment centres was slow but, by 1993, 75% of top UK employers used them (Goodge, 1997).

Cook (1998) gives a summary of four different studies of assessment centre validity. Assessment centres predicted job performance quite well, but were most useful for identifying "potential". In the studies quoted, validity coefficients for "potential" were .53 and .63. Despite this, Cook comments that, although this very expensive technique appears to work, we don't really know why and there have been criticisms of this method.

There have been accusations that assessment centres simply promote self-fulfilling prophesies, since there have been very few studies where the results of assessment centres were kept secret. Thus, in the case of high scorers, managers may think, "This person has potential so we'll give him/her more challenging tasks." This then promotes the development of skills, confidence, etc., which results in promotion. Low scores may lead to the opposite happening. However, the evidence seems to indicate that this is not actually a serious problem. Jones and Whitmore (1995), for instance, followed up the careers of people who had been selected for a development centre (a similar technique —see Chapter 8), but who weren't able to attend because there were no places available. No-one knew they had been selected at all but there were no differences in the career advancement of this group and the people who actually did attend. Others (e.g., Klimoski & Strickland, 1977) have argued that assessment centres actually measure the sorts of behaviours that top management value but which may have more to do with making a favourable impression on those who count than with effectiveness. This may explain why they are better at predicting "potential" than actual performance.

However, the worst problem is the "exercise effect". The reasoning is this:

- Assessors are supposed to rate each person on dimensions (skills, competencies, etc.).
- If they are doing this, there should be correlations between ratings of the same dimension in different exercises.
- And there should be no correlation between ratings of different dimensions within the same exercise.

To put this in concrete terms, suppose we are assessing decision making. There should be a correlation between the ratings of decision making in a simulation exercise and decision making as assessed by, say, a test such as the Watson Glaser critical reasoning appraisal. There should not be a correlation between ratings of decision making and some totally different competence, such as influencing others, within the same exercise. In fact, the exact opposite happens. For instance, Sackett and Dreher (1982) found that ratings of different competences within the same exercise correlated highly, whereas there was no correlation between ratings of the same competence in different exercises, and this effect has been consistently replicated. In effect assessors appear to be rating people's overall performance on each exercise rather than specific competences across exercises. There are various reasons for this, not least that if the assessor is overloaded with too many people to observe or too many competences to rate, the tendency is to make a global judgement about overall performance in the exercise. However, as Cook (1998) points out, if assessments of decisiveness on task A don't correlate with decisiveness on task B, how can we be sure that these assessments will correlate with decisiveness on the job? In a similar vein, Feltham (1988) analysed data from an assessment centre designed to select senior police officers for promotion. Assessors were supposed to use 13 components/competency ratings to arrive at an overall rating of the candidates' suitability but, in fact, analyses showed that only 4 of these were needed to predict later job performance. In other words, assessors did not seem to be using all the information available to them when making their overall judgements of performance.

Gatewood, Thornton, and Hennessey (1990) also found that global ratings of performance were more reliable than ratings of specific aspects.

Although better training, fewer people to observe or competences to rate, and so forth can improve assessors' ability to rate dimensions rather than overall performance (see Hennessy, Mabey, & Warr, 1998; Lievens, 1998 for reviews), these findings make me question whether assessment centres are doing much more than allowing assessors to have, in assessment terms, long periods of exposure to candidates in a variety of settings and in job-related tasks. Untrained people tend to be good at making global assessments of how well their workmates are performing after a period of time (see Chapter 8), so why shouldn't highly trained people with the benefit of structured situations and clear observation criteria, be equally as good in a shorter timescale? In terms of personality assessment, ordinary people also tend to make global judgements and only notice the more "extreme" aspects of specific characteristics (Psychological Consultancy Ltd, 1997). People are human, and making precise judgements of specific skills is maybe not their main strength. Even individuals themselves seem to be better at judging their own overall performance than their particular strengths and weaknesses (Baldry & Fletcher, 2000a). Maybe this is why assessment centres work—they use the ability of humans to make global assessments, but in a more carefully structured way, which increases their reliability and predictive power. Looked at in this way, the exercise effect may not be a serious problem, and the current vogue for assessing specific competencies may be challenged even more than it has been (Cook, 1998; Robertson, 2000; Sparrow, 1997). If we are generally incapable of making specific judgements (even after extensive training) and global judgements work just as well, maybe the effort to be specific is misguided.

We come back to where we started, in that a lot of people gain employment simply by performing their jobs well in a probationary period. This method is usually a great deal cheaper than an assessment centre and has the advantage that people can "grow" into their jobs or leave quickly for something more suitable.

The future of psychometrics in selection and assessment

Although the basic aims of occupational psychology to improve the fairness and quality of the selection process are both laudable and successful, there have been signs of a possible backlash of late. I have already mentioned the constructionist approach to selection, which implies a much more informal approach to selection and assessment, and so places more emphasis on social relationships. I also considered Anderson's (2001) view that selection acts as pre-entry socialization into the organization. Iles and Robertson (1997) explore evidence for the impact of selection and assessment processes on candidates and make the point that these can have negative effects on people's self-perceptions and behaviour. Herriot and Anderson (1997, p. 1) began the volume they had edited with the words "Traditional personnel and selection psychology is in danger of terminal decline". Fletcher (1997b) also believes that the use of psychometric instruments in organizations is facing perhaps its greatest challenge. All these authors cite the changing nature of work, candidate resistance, and legal challenges to the use of tests, as being among the reasons for a possible future decline in the use of psychometric instruments. Fletcher sets out a number of steps that should be taken to ensure that tests remain acceptable and effective, such as reassuring candidates about the relevance of the tests to job requirements and offering sensitive feedback. However, he adds, "In my experience, it is rare for all these elements to be in place—quite often none are" (p. 11). If he is right, test publishers have cause for concern.

In careers guidance also, the use of formal psychometric tests with some groups is being challenged. Maddocks (2000) cites the example of demotivated and disengaged clients who have not benefited much from their education. Such people should not be subjected to formal and intimidating test sessions which only arouse all their previously learned anxieties, self-doubts, and frustrations. Maddocks argues that the main aim with this client group is to motivate them to open up to their strengths and actively engage in their own personal development. For this we need a "softer" approach, which is more "therapeutic" than "actuarial"; "advisors require instruments that are practical, flexible and ideally fun, where clients can participate in self-discovery" (pp. 6–7). He argues that what is lost in standards of validity, is gained in clients who take control of their own futures and are motivated to develop. Meehan, Birkin, and Snodgrass (1998) also question the appropriateness of tests when unemployed people with disabilities are being assessed to help them decide on realistic job goals.

However, there are some encouraging developments in the test market. In an earlier article, Maddocks (1998) recommended the use of the ABLE series of psychometric exercises (Blinkhorn & Johnson, 1996). The ABLE series (Aptitude for Business Learning Exercises) are unique in the test market. They involve exercises that create job-like situations. While people are doing these exercises they are being assessed on how well they can learn and apply their learning to new situations. In a very real sense they embody Vygotsky's principle of the person's "zone of proximal development". In other words, what is important is not what the person can do now unaided, but what they can learn to do with some assistance and coaching. Thus, we assess aptitude for development. Such techniques reduce the emphasis on traditional normative comparisons and on internal and test–retest reliabilities so they challenge some fundamental assumptions of occupational testing. However, they are well established in the practice of educational psychology. Since employers have a great need to assess adaptability and capacity to learn, it is good to see that occupational psychology is catching up.

On a more political theme, in the 1930s Cattell (1937) was warning of the creation of an underclass of people who would not be able to gain employment if better selection methods excluded all but the most able. Landy (2000) argued that it is unrealistic to try to select only the most able people—there are not enough to go round and it would make more sense to concentrate on fair selection of those with more modest abilities. We should also remember Frese's (1997, 2000, p. 431) concerns about less intelligent people in the industrialized world, which echo Cattell's points; "a continuously unemployed lower class, with a welfare mentality, high crime rates, social unrest and widespread dissatisfaction. We do not yet have a solution but work and organizational psychologists need to develop one". He suggests that we may need to search for job characteristics that do not require high levels of cognitive ability and those of us who are more fortunate may need to subsidize such employment and specialized training schemes.

I would add that the increasing use of speeded cognitive ability tests encourages ageism in the workplace because older people tend to score lower, since they tend to have reduced cognitive processing speeds (Myerson, Hale, Wagstaff, Poon, & Smith, 1990; Welford, 1985) and less efficient working memories (Craik & Jennings, 1990; Salthouse, 1991). However, it is not at all clear whether older workers' work performance is affected by these decrements. Warr's reviews (1996b, 2000) suggest that only on very specific cognitive tasks—those that require fast processing of complex information without environmental aids—is performance likely to deteriorate between 40 and 60 years. In fact, if we exclude jobs that require physical labour, there is little evidence of any decrements in work performance with age, except in very specific occupations. This may be because older people compensate for cognitive slowing with their greater experience and expertise. It is true that older people sometimes find it more difficult to learn new skills, but this may happen for a number of reasons. The current cohort of older workers tend to be less well-educated than their younger counterparts, and so lifelong learning may not have been part of their lifestyle. Thus, as Chapter 6 showed, lack of confidence and motivation may pose problems, but these can be overcome with sensitive training courses. We must also remember that individual differences can be as great in people aged 50 and above as exist among those in their 20s. In the UK it is not yet illegal to discriminate on the grounds of age, but employers who reject applicants on the basis of their date of birth or their ability test scores may be depriving themselves of valuable workers with a fund of expertise. Moreover, no test is completely accurate or fair for every individual, even though at group level it may improve the effectiveness of selection. This is why psychometric instruments should only ever be used as additional sources of information and selection decisions should not be based solely on them.

Most tellingly, Cook, who was a major UK protagonist for the use of tests and other improved methods in selection, ends the third (1998, pp. 302–303) edition of his very successful book on a different note. Productivity isn't everything, he says. The best workers may be workaholics with no time to enjoy life. If the best workers are more productive, fewer workers are needed to supply demand. This means that those in employment work longer and harder whilst others are forced into idleness and unemployment. If fewer and fewer people produce more and more, who will buy it all? He ends with the thought that work serves other puposes besides producing goods and services; "work prevents urban riots", and I agree.

Summary

In this chapter I have argued that job analysis lies at the heart of much of best personnel practice, but that techniques more attuned to commercial imperatives must be developed if this aspect of occupational psychology is to retain its relevance and usefulness. Its loss would be a dangerous and retrograde step for both individuals and organizations. I have outlined the major selection techniques available and highlighted their strengths and weaknesses and some of the main principles for the choice of selection methods. The use of psychometric instruments is only one possible option, and these need to be used responsibly and ethically by those who are well versed in the technicalities of test score interpretation. However, alternative methods are not necessarily any more fair or accurate; in many cases they can be considerably less so. Nevertheless, scores from psychometric instruments should ideally be used only as an additional source of information when making selection decisions and should not be used as the only criteria for job offers or rejection. The value of well-planned and careful selection interviews has been reaffirmed, but we need to know more about what actually goes on in such interviews and the factors which influence decisions. I have discussed assessment centres, and their value in selection as well as their disadvantages. I have looked to the future: the constructionist approach to selection, "soft" methods of assessment, and innovative methods of assessing the potential to learn. I have ended on a note of caution: the potential political and social consequences of too much emphasis on selecting "the best" at the expense of "the rest".

Material related to the content of this chapter may be found in Chapters 8 and 10.

I did not really answer my initial question about whether good selection can help to alleviate or eliminate workplace stress reactions. However, it must be at least a partial solution if the "right people" are selected for the "right jobs" in the "right organizations".

EXERCISE 7.2
Job spec to assessment method

Introduction
Whenever we are designing a selection procedure, the central problem is always how to specify what knowledge, skills, and attributes are needed to do the job and then to decide how to assess candidates to

select the person who has the best fit with what is needed. This exercise takes you through a method for doing this that has a long pedigree and still has much to recommend it in terms of its relative simplicity. At the same time it is more systematic and rigorous than much of what currently passes for "the design" of selection procedures. In this exercise you are the job expert, but you can adapt this technique when dealing with clients, by interviewing job holders or managers to establish the person specification. It may be a good technique to use when advising small/medium enterprises when a full job analysis is not feasible but it has value in almost any organization. To get the most from this exercise, it would help if you looked through test publishers' catalogues/manuals, "off-the-shelf" assessment centre exercises, etc., to find out what is commercially available.

The steps in the process are:

1 Create a person specification using Rodger's "7-point plan".
2 Specify the relevant standards needed for doing the job.
3 Decide on what information to gather/assessment methods.
4 Decide which source of data is most likely to give you good information.
5 Complete the person specification/assessment method grid.

Steps 1 and 2: Creating a person specification
Rodger (1968) suggested the following framework for assessing people in careers guidance. However, it can also be used to create a person specification following his "7-point plan". This involves looking at job requirements and deciding on what is needed under the following seven headings:

1 Physical make-up: e.g., health, physique, appearance, bearing, speech, etc.
2 Attainments: e.g., education, training, experience, qualifications, etc.
3 General intelligence.
4 Special aptitudes: e.g., mechanical ability, dexterity, numeracy, linguistic skills, etc.
5 Interests: e.g. intellectual, practical, occupational, social, etc.
6 Disposition: e.g. dependability, influence, steadiness, self-reliance, etc.
7 Circumstances: e.g., geographical mobility, availability to work particular hours, etc.

Think of a job with which you are very familiar and use the "7-point plan" to create a person specification for that job. Then specify the standards of competence needed for doing that job. For instance, does it need standards of literacy consistent with having attained GCSE

English? Does it need word-processing skills? Does it need average or above-average cognitive ability? Does it need the person to be willing to work unsocial hours or travel away from home a lot? Take care that you do not set the standards too high, because this could result in unfair discrimination, and consider what might compensate for lack of "conventional evidence", e.g., no formal qualifications vs. a lot of prior experience of doing the job; little experience vs. the possibility of training.

Step 3: Gathering information/methods to use in selection
There are three main types of data that you could gather in the selection process.

- Life data (L data): observation, evidence of real life events; e.g., education and work background, membership of groups and societies, evidence from application forms, interview performance/role play exercises, etc.
- Test data (T data): tests of ability, attainment, aptitude, work samples, etc.
- Questionnaire data (Q data): self-report (or by others), results of interest or personality inventories, competency questionnaires, etc.

To illustrate how this can be applied to the person specification derived from the "7-point plan", consider physical make-up. Gathering L data might include noting current sporting activities detailed on the application form or in the CV; an interview allows observation of physical appearance. Gathering T data might involve setting a manual dexterity or motor skill test. Q data might include personality or interest inventories, which might provide information about a person's perceptions of fitness and interest in physically demanding work.

Using the criteria of scope, reliability, validity, fairness, acceptability, and practicality discussed in this chapter, and the framework of the "7-point plan", go through the person specification and decide what information each type of data could give you about each set of attributes (as in the physical make-up example).

Steps 4 and 5: Deciding on the best sources of information and completing the person specification/assessment method grid
Look through what you have written for step 3 and decide which source of data is most likely to give you good information for each of the 7 points. Rate each source for its usefulness according to the following scale: 2 = very good information; 1 = useful supplementary information; 0 = weak or indirect information.

Then fill in the following grid, specifying exactly how you would assess each aspect of the person specification in selection. Note that any data rated 2 should be included. Anything rated 1 is optional.

Since selection is expensive, anything rated 0 should normally be excluded unless there is a very good reason, e.g., compensation for formal qualifications. However, when resources are in short supply you may not be able to include everything even if it is rated 2. In that case, you need to prioritize again: What is *most* important (likely to yield the best information)—rated 3?

Person specification/assessment method grid

	L data	T data	Q data
Physical make-up			
Attainments			
General intelligence			
Special aptitudes			
Interests			
Disposition			
Circumstances			

Now try this technique with a job that is familiar to you by interviewing job-holders and managers. Share your selection procedure design with managers to assess their reactions.

Suggested further reading

Anderson, N., & Cunningham-Snell, N. (2000). Personnel selection. In N. Chmiel (Ed.), *Introduction to work and organizational psychology: A European perspective.* Oxford, UK: Blackwell.

Cook, M. (1998). *Personnel selection: Adding value through people* (3rd ed.). Chichester, UK: Wiley.

Herriot, P., & Anderson, N. (1997). *The international handbook of selection and assessment.* Chichester, UK: Wiley.

Landis, R.S., Fogli, L., & Goldberg, E. (1998). Future oriented job analysis: A description of the process and its organizational implications. *International Journal of Selection and Assesment, 6*(3), 192–197.

Lees, C. D., & Cordery, J. L. (2000). Job analysis and design. In N. Chmiel (Ed.), *Introduction to work and organizational psychology: A European perspective.* Oxford, UK: Blackwell.

Salgado, J.F. (Ed.) (2000). Personnel selection at the beginning of a new millennium: A global and international perspective (Part 1). *International Journal of Selection and Assessment, 8*(4).*

Salgado, J.F. (Ed.) (2001). Personnel selection at the beginning of the new millennium: A global and international perspective (Part 2). *International Journal of Selection and Assessment, 9*(1/2).*

* Note: These excellent collections of articles appeared just as this book was being completed. They are strongly recommended reading.

8   Getting the best from the best: Appraisal and career development

<table>
<tr><td>Good:</td><td>Can jump over tall buildings
in a single leap . . .
Can hit a target 100 miles away . . .</td><td>Poor:</td><td>Trips over own feet

Shoots self in foot
Spoof appraisal scheme</td></tr>
</table>

The idea of career is central . . . for the very reason that it is the only idea which *can* cope with the changes that assail us at the end of the twentieth century.

Herriot (1992)

Most medium to large organizations used to go through an annual appraisal ritual, which was rarely popular with anyone. A pile of appraisal forms would land on the desks of managers and supervisors, who then had to rate the work performance of their staff. Most managers disliked doing this. Although it is easy to rate the best and the poorest workers, distinguishing between the majority who are neither outstanding nor incompetent is both difficult and open to all manner of bias and inaccuracy. Often managers would have only limited knowledge of the workers and the tasks they performed. If they returned a poor report, they then had to live with the consequences of resentful staff; a good report might mean competition for the manager's own job or key people being promoted out of the department.

From the point of view of the person on the receiving end of appraisals, the process could be seen as unfair or traumatic or both. Fletcher (1997a) showed that 80% of the UK organizations in his study were unhappy with the appraisal system currently in use. Employees often regard them as the single most potent violation of procedural justice, especially when pay and promotion decisions might turn on the outcome. Not surprisingly, perhaps, Saal and Knight (1988) paint a picture of people "going through the motions" with everyone getting a reasonably favourable rating amid sighs of relief that it is all over for another year.

This was not a happy state of affairs. Organizations were right to be concerned about the satisfactoriness of staff, but with the advent of globalization and fierce competition this became an obsession with employees' contribution to the "bottom line". In the public sector too, concern with value for taxpayers' money led to a focus on evaluating performance. But just measuring performance was insufficient. Organizations wanted people to improve their performance, to update their skills, to become more interpersonally skilled, better leaders or teamworkers, and to adapt flexibly to often temporary roles. From the employee's point of view, satisfaction was the aim. People who are not rewarded for excellent work are apt to become demoralized or leave. People who feel unfairly treated may become resentful and act out of role. At the same time, increases in downsizing, delayering, casual and contract labour, and so on raised feelings of job insecurity, loosened people's ties of commitment to organizations, and made the concept of self-development and "employability" uppermost in their minds. People wanted marketable skills for their next job. Thus, performance appraisal and personal/career development became inextricably linked together. Years of research effort to make the rating process in traditional forms of appraisal more valid and reliable (see, e.g., Saal & Knight, 1988 for a review) by, for instance, training raters or improving rating questionnaires, didn't address development. New approaches were needed.

Instead of the traditional annual appraisal ritual the notion of performance management developed. The latter is best thought of as a philosophy like that of a learning organization, rather than a particular set of policies and practices. According to some commentators, performance management involves creating a shared vision of organizational goals and helping every individual to understand his or her contribution to them. In this way the performance of both individuals and the organization is managed (Fletcher & Williams, 1992; Williams, 1998). Unlike some other appraisal systems, performance management is driven by line managers rather than by the personnel function and there is an emphasis on developing shared purposes and values. However, this approach does not come as a ready-made "package" but has to be developed by the organization. The "building blocks" include the development of a mission statement and business plan, which is clearly communicated throughout the organization with opportunities for everyone to contribute to its formulation. The role of each person in contributing to the aims and objectives is then clarified and the means to define, measure, and reward individual performance is put in place. However, there is a strong developmental strand so that people can improve their performance further and plan for career progression. By these means organizational goals are translated into individual objectives. The ProMES technique discussed later in this chapter could be described as a form of performance management.

There is some evidence that done well, the performance management approach can lead to enhanced organizational commitment and job satisfaction (Fletcher & Williams, 1996). However, one risk of creating a performance culture is that it may encourage individual achievement and competition at the expense of team effort and the free communication of knowledge. It is interesting to consider whether a performance culture is compatible with a learning culture. In theory they should be virtually synonymous but much will depend on how performance is assessed and whether it is perceived as fair and accurate. So the problems of measuring work performance haven't gone away, they have emerged in a different guise.

EXERCISE 8.1
Harnessing your experience of appraisal systems

Before reading on it may be useful for you to review your experience and knowledge of appraisal systems. Think of any jobs where your performance was assessed and try to answer these questions:

- Were you fully informed about the system, e.g., did you know the criteria on which you would be assessed?
- Did you consider the system to be fair and accurate? What happened if you disagreed with your appraiser's view?
- If the system was less than ideal, what were its worst defects and how did the whole thing make you feel and behave?
- If you have ever found an appraisal system to be helpful and rewarding, e.g., by giving you recognition for good work or helping you to develop, what features made the system successful?

Having done this you may find that you know a lot more about appraisal and career development than you thought you did.

The purposes of appraisal

Fletcher (2000) gives six purposes of performance appraisal, not all of which are compatible.

1 Improving performance. If we are to learn to improve our performance we must have accurate feedback about our strengths and weaknesses. An appraisal can provide this.
2 Making reward decisions. If the best workers are to be rewarded, e.g., by pay rises or promotion, there must be some element of assessment in appraisal. However, this can be difficult and deficiencies can lead to feelings of procedural and distributive injustice.
3 Motivating staff. In Chapter 3 we saw that when good performance is clearly and fairly linked to material rewards then people's job satisfaction is likely to be higher and this may encourage greater effort. More importantly, perhaps, goal-setting theory tells us that setting targets to improve performance, e.g., by identifying and addressing development needs, could be a potent motivational device.

4 Developing staff. Following on from this, formulating a personal development plan and monitoring progress could be a key aim of appraisal.
5 Identifying potential. By identifying the best workers appraisal could contribute to succession planning. Those with most potential could be "groomed" for more demanding future roles via more challenging projects, on-the-job training, and so on.
6 Formal recording of unsatisfactory performance. Appraisals can also be the first step in disciplinary or dismissal proceedings.

Fletcher notes that each of these purposes, on its own, seems "very reasonable and entirely justifiable" but together they form a "formidable agenda" (p. 128). He doubts whether all this can be achieved in one annual process which may only consist of a single interview and report form, and there are many who agree. Randell and his co-workers (Randell, 1989, 1991; Wright & Taylor, 1984) have long argued for three separate appraisal processes:

•   The reward review—based on past performance, assessing for pay, promotion, and firing decisions.
•   The performance review—concerned with the present, identifying strengths and weaknesses to devise a personal development plan and set goals.
•   The potential review—future oriented, identifying the scope for succession planning.

It is possible that the performance and potential reviews could be combined, but the reward review should be kept quite separate and probably ought to be conducted by different people. The reason for this, says Randell, is that people cannot be expected to be honest about their strengths and development needs if they know that this may damage their career prospects or pay levels. Furthermore, line managers cannot play a facilitating, counselling type role to promote development and at the same time adopt a critical, assessing, or disciplinary stance. Thus, assessment for reward and assessment for development and increased motivation usually conflict. (See also Chapter 9.)

And this is by no means the only conflict. There is a great deal of tension between the organization's needs and goals and the individual's needs and goals. (See, e.g., Arthur & Kram, 1989 and Graversen & Johansson, 1998.) Good developmental forms of appraisal and performance management systems have the potential to resolve or lessen this conflict but there are still obstacles, as the table in Box 8.1 shows. Clearly the best outcomes result when these conflicting needs can be reconciled so that each party achieves at least something of what it wants from the other. But appraisal systems differ in their aims and the extent to which they can fulfil needs. Much depends on what aspects of performance are measured and how they are measured—procedural vs. distributive justice again. So the problems of measuring work emerge again in a different guise.

BOX 8.1
Organizational–employee conflicts in the appraisal process

What the organization wants	*What the individual wants*
Maximum employee productivity	Removal of obstacles to performance and perhaps reduction of workload
Employee development to suit specific business goals	Development to maintain and promote employability
Employee accountability: proof that they are serving the bottom line or giving value for money	Recognition and reward for hard work and good performance
Discipline for poor performance	A chance to refute "unjust" criticism
Pay at the lowest acceptable/ market level to ensure continuance and commitment	Pay at the highest possible level to compensate for long hours and reduced personal life

---

Culture clashes: The particular problems of appraising professional staff

Fletcher (1997a) devotes considerable space to this topic, noting that perhaps the most noticable recent trend in appraisal is how its use has been extended to cover professional and technical staff, particularly in the UK public services. Though the issues of the appraisal of professional staff and of appraisals within public services are separable, they are linked because services such as health care and education are dominated by professional employees with specialist skills and high level qualifications—maybe more so than in many commercial organizations. Fletcher argues that appraisal of professionals is particularly problematical because there is an "ethos gap" between the values of professionals and conventional organizations and because, in the UK public services, appraisal systems have often been imposed by Government—not a promising backdrop. Professionals tend to be very work involved and much concerned with ethical codes and standards of excellence. They also tend to be very autonomous and independent, prizing their "clinical judgement" or "academic freedom". Such people are likely to see appraisal to assess their performance, increase their motivation, and raise standards as unnecessary—insulting even. Neither do they take kindly to being "managed" by people who may have wholly different priorities, i.e., to provide a reasonable product or service at the lowest possible cost regardless of professional excellence or codes of ethics. Managing such people has been likened to "herding cats".

Whilst there is almost certainly an element of arrogance in the resistance to appraisal within the ranks of professional staff, there is also a very real clash of culture and values. Fletcher (1997a) argues that if appraisal is to have any chance of success in such workers, there needs to be a great deal of training, preparation, and consultation before any system is put in place. Also essential is a "developmental" rather than an "assessment" focus. Very often even the term "appraisal" is banished and the process becomes a "developmental review". But what do we mean by assessment vs. developmental forms of appraisal? Perhaps it is time to become more specific and contrast two common approaches to appraisal.

Performance-related pay

In the form of piecework, where people are paid according to the number of widgets made, etc., performance-related pay (PRP) has been around for a very long time. It has also existed in sales jobs where all or part of people's pay would be composed of commission. In the late 1980s, however, it came to be applied to a much wider range of jobs, including managerial and professional work. PRP is based on what seems to be an eminently sensible notion: In order to inspire people to greater productivity and achievement, the best and most productive workers should be paid more than less good and less productive workers. Thus, at the heart of PRP systems are appraisal systems that assess worker performance and make comparisons between workers. However, compared to piecework, PRP systems tend to be considerably more complex. They may be combined with a management by objectives approach and some proportion of pay may be put at risk if targets are not met. Other systems may involve assessment of the individual's skills, competencies, and outputs with merit pay or bonuses being added to the person's basic salary. Quite apart from the difficulty of measuring work performance in occupations where outputs are less tangible than a pile of widgets, other factors need to be taken into account. For instance, Kleingeld (1994) cites the example of photocopier service engineers. If PRP was based solely on measures of effectiveness such as the number of repairs correctly performed, highly motivated but less experienced and thus less skilled and slower engineers would not be able to gain high or even medium-sized bonuses and this could prove to be demoralizing. So a proportion of PRP might be based on increases in productivity over the previous year's assessments. However, this might demoralize the more experienced engineers who are already highly effective and can't be expected to increase their productivity by any appreciable amount. Van Tuijl et al. (1997) provide an enlightening discussion (with case studies) of the difficulties and complexities of PRP systems.

Despite the manifest sense of the basic idea, most of the evidence relating to the effectiveness of PRP in motivating workers and increasing productivity tends to be negative. (See, e.g., Alimo-Metcalfe, 1994b; Furnham & Argyle, 1998; Herriot & Pemberton, 1995; Kohn, 1996; Pearce, 1996; Williams, 1998). It is not too difficult to see why this should be. For PRP to be effective it is most important that performance should be accurately and fairly measured and that the relationship between pay and performance should be clear and equitable. This is difficult in relatively simple jobs but it is even harder to do well in more complex jobs, where much of the work is covert and the outputs are more difficult to define, let alone measure.

The UK Government is in the process of introducing PRP for schoolteachers, and this occupation is a good illustration of the problems. In a recent campaign to reverse the "teacher-bashing" culture encouraged by the previous Government and to recruit more teachers, the current administration instituted a TV campaign with the slogan, "Everyone remembers a good teacher". The slogan could be ambiguous—maybe some people can't recall any good teachers. Most of my secondary school teachers just dictated notes and managed to turn the most fascinating subjects into a dreary catalogue of "facts" to be rote memorized. However, going beyond the obvious aspects of poor performance, things get more tricky.

Can you say what it was about any particular teacher that inspired you? In my early life I had difficulty dealing with numbers because my lack of attention to detail led me to make many mistakes in calculations—this was before the days of calculators and computers! I remember one teacher who patiently went through all the examples she had set as homework in class so that I could see where I had gone wrong. Both my confidence and exam marks soared. My biology teacher was simply such a delightful, charming woman that I forgave her the boredom of dictated notes and still retain much of the knowledge she gave me. Her lessons on the human brain, nervous system, and sensory systems were a significant influence on my decision to study psychology at university. Until I came across a particular English teacher, my ambition had been to become a novelist. Her rigorous and disciplined training in the technicalities of writing just about killed my nascent creativity and enthusiasm and I pretty much hated her. But she taught me to spell and punctuate correctly, and most of the fundamentals of English grammar. If I can write well today, it's because of her, and she also injected a healthy dose of reality into my dreams of literary fame. Were they good teachers? Who knows? In any case, they do not appear to have a single characteristic or competence in common apart from the abilty to communicate their knowledge in their very different ways. This brings us back to a point made in the previous chapter when we were discussing personality—there are often many different ways of achieving effective performance at work. While we try to define and measure the skills and competences that are needed for particular jobs, we also run the risk of producing "clones" and stifling innovation. This is also a danger with PRP systems, where the emphasis on measuring performance may lead to rigid criteria about acceptable or "best" forms of behaviour. They can also encourage an emphasis on those aspects of performance that are easiest to measure rather than on what really contributes to positive outcomes. (Remember the folly of rewarding A while hoping for B?)

Another issue concerns the extent to which the person has control over the factors which contribute to performance indicators. A factory worker's output may be compromised by machine downtime, shortages of components, or inadequate quality control in earlier processes. Sales reps may be hampered by the relative affluence of their "patches". A surgeon's ability to conduct serious operations may be limited by the availability of intensive care beds. A teacher in an inner-city school may seem to perform less well than a counterpart in the same locality because of things like a less effective head teacher, a different attitude amongst parents, lower funding, or even a particulary disruptive group of pupils from dysfunctional families. For PRP to be effective, opportunities to improve performance must exist and be within the person's capacity to control. If these are absent, then PRP can be seen as unjust.

The rewards themselves must be valued too. Increased pay is all very well but will it compensate for unrelenting effort, problems with family and personal life, and so on? In *Management Today*'s most recent survey of nearly 2000 UK managers, Rice (2000) reported that a quarter of all the men and half of all the women sampled would trade money for more time for their personal lives. Even if the extra money *is* valued, there are employees' perceptions of hidden agendas intended to keep pay levels low for the majority while rewarding the few. The "sweetener" in the UK of an extra £2000 per year for the best teachers is viewed with cynicism by many in the profession, even though the generally low pay has led most eligible people to apply for it. Similarly, the prospect of earning £40,000 per year as a "super-nurse" is little comfort for the majority, who earn less than a bus driver and considerably less than some car production workers.

Feldman (2000) gives an interesting case study of the problems in implementing PRP systems in that even when the assessment of work performance is seen as fair, the probability of getting merit pay is often very low and the difference in pay for outstanding rather than average performance is often negligible. Consider someone who earns £20,000 for average performance and the PRP system awards 2% more for outstanding performance. This means that outstanding performance attracts only £400 per year more. Add in that only 10% of workers can be awarded the "outstanding" rate of pay and what you have is a 90% chance of *not* getting about £1 extra (after taxes) per day. Why should someone work extra hard all year and strive for excellent performance for such a meagre reward and against those odds? Combine this with any perceived procedural injustice over the assessment of work performance and it really isn't so surprising that PRP can often be a disaster.

Another general problem with PRP is that it can have very negative effects on teamwork since it is usually designed to reward individual effort and success. It can create jealousies between those who get it and those who do not, thus undermining morale and reducing the effectiveness of teams. Finally, it may devalue the motivating potential of intrinsic rewards. If I get paid for the number of school pupils I get through national achievement tests or exams, my teaching may degenerate into test "drilling" rather than "whole child development". Of course, what is wanted is everything—exam success and knowledgeable, skilled, confident, and well-adjusted young adults—but remember the folly of rewarding A while hoping for B?

For all that, done well and fairly, formal appraisals for PRP can achieve the aims of improving performance, giving due reward, identifying potential, and giving notice of unsatisfactory work. It is not so good at motivating *all* staff and has limited potential for developing people. Done badly, it can be a disaster.

Developmental forms of appraisal

Randell (1989, 1991) believes that all these ills can be reduced or eliminated if the appraisal has a purely developmental focus. After all, he says, what is the real purpose of appraisal but to increase the satisfactoriness of staff and their satisfaction, so that productivity and effectiveness can be raised? In that case, what better means to achieve these ends than to identify and remove blocks to progress and develop plans to meet employee needs in order to improve performance?

Arnold (1998) notes that some senior managers have abandoned the idea of organizational involvement in an individual's career management on the basis that the business environment is so turbulent and chaotic that it is a poor use of resources. Sometimes the message has been an aggressive, "You're on your own". However, Hirsh and Jackson (1996) and Parsons and Stickland (1996) report that organizations are beginning to change their views because when people are responsible for their own development they do not always align their self-development with the employing organization's business goals. Why should they? Randell would argue, what better vehicle to align an organization's business goals with individual aspirations than a sensitively conducted appraisal interview where the employee has the "space" to discuss issues and set personal goals in a nonthreatening context? What is more, such a forum can provide an excellent means for upward, downward, and lateral communication. Staff can discuss the barriers to their effectiveness and managers can relay this higher up the organization in their attempts to remove blocks. At the same time, managers can convey their "helicopter view" of the bigger picture to those who may have difficulty in seeing things beyond their immediate roles. Lateral and upward networking by the manager to "smooth the path" of their staff to greater productivity and effectiveness may assist in the dissemination of best practice and shared goals.

Done well, linked to personal development plans and realistic goals that are aligned to business objectives, a developmental appraisal interview can offer a great deal. I have found that developmental reviews can raise difficult issues in a constructive context, can "clear the air" of misunderstandings, resentments, and frustrations, can raise the performance of weaker staff and encourage the best, improve supervisor–staff relationships, motivate the demoralized, and help everyone to work towards common goals. Part of their success for me may have been that they have effectively involved the explicit renegotiation of psychological contracts and while I have had to be careful in what I promise, keeping those promises has led to greater trust and a feeling that we are basically both on the same side.

But there are still dangers. One of the most difficult issues concerns the role of the appraisal interviewer who must be very socially skilled—counselling training is a distinct advantage. Most managers find it very difficult to handle giving negative feedback and most employees will react with defensiveness, anxiety, and depression when it is done badly. My tactic has always been to raise an issue in such a way that, with luck, the person will admit to short-comings themselves. Or they will raise real blocks to performance that can maybe be addressed by action at a higher level or by a development plan. Developmental reviews can also give people the chance to discuss what they really want to do in the future to further their goals and aspirations. But . . . if you cannot deliver what they want despite all your ingenuity and lateral thinking, or somehow reconcile their desires with business imperatives, all is in vain.

A creative, problem-solving, realistic but positive approach is vital but this needs to be sustained beyond the confines of the review—it is no good being a caring and supportive manager once a year! The good news is that some-times small things can make all the difference. Lubitsh (2002; Lubitsh & Doyle, 2001) is evaluating an intervention to increase productivity by dealing with "bottlenecks" or constraints in work systems. The theory of constraints (TOC; Goldratt, 1989) generates a systematic approach to im-proving productivity without increasing resources or workloads. Goldratt argued that in every system there is a chain of dependency of events and the overall efficiency of a system is determined by its weakest link or constraint. Therefore by improving the efficiency of the constraint, e.g., by offloading it or making sure it is working all the time, the efficiency of the whole system can be improved. The work context Lubitsh is concerned with is an NHS hospital (see Knight, 2000–2001), and there, one of the main "bottlenecks" is the time of consultant surgeons. They are involved with patient care from diagnosis to discharge but each one has only a finite time to do all this; their time is precious and dictates the speed of treating patients throughout the system. However, since they were moving about between different hospitals they were spending half an hour or more simply finding a parking space between each venue. Allocating dedicated parking spaces at hospitals to these consultants would therefore release them to see between three and six more outpatients or conduct one more routine operation per venue switch. If support staff were helped to have every patient ready for consultation or surgery (with all the necessary documentation, preparatory drug treatment, support staff, etc.) the second that the consultant was free to attend to them, then more patients could be seen and waiting lists of seriously ill people would be reduced. A guaranteed parking space doesn't necessarily maximize the surgeon's productive time. It is also necessary to support this "constraint" by ensuring that the whole system is geared to making sure that when a consultant is ready, so is everything else needed. This was facilitated by installing a telephone link between wards and theatre so ward staff could be more easily alerted to start getting the next patient ready. However, if the consultant surgeon is hunting for a place to park the car, all the other (and considerable) efforts of staff to get the patients ready for consultation and surgery don't improve efficiency or reduce waiting lists.

If the reader finds the relevance of this "diversion" somewhat opaque, consider this. A major goal of developmental forms of appraisal is to devise/learn better ways of doing things. TOC is an intervention designed to do just this by challenging people to identify and cope with "constraints" to increase the effectiveness and efficiency of the entire system. The changes introduced in the NHS Trust following the TOC intervention were not "trivial adjustments", but serious performance management initiatives. Other advantages and disadvantages of developmental forms of appraisal are summarized in Box 8.2.

From all this it can be appreciated that developmental forms of appraisal are not "soft" options in comparison with more "objective" and formal methods such as PRP. To be successful they require a lot of training and skill on the part of the appraiser and the investment of considerable resources. Done badly, they can be a counterproductive waste. There is, however, one technique that seems to integrate the best aspects of development reviews and formal assessment, discussed next.

PRODUCTIVITY MEASUREMENT AND ENHANCEMENT SYSTEM

Productivity measurement and enhancement system (ProMES) is a system developed by Pritchard (1990, 1995) and widely used in Europe (see, e.g., Algera & Kleinbeck, 1997b). ProMES is a method for developing tailor-made performance management systems and aims to address three fundamental questions:

- In what way can people contribute to the effectiveness of the organization?
- What kinds of motives do people have to contribute to organizational effectiveness?
- How can people actually improve performance?

ProMES is developed in four phases (Algera, Monhemius, & Wijnen, 1997).

1   Identify the key outcomes or "products" that the work team is responsible for by asking questions such as "What are we responsible for?"

BOX 8.2
Further advantages and disadvantages of developmental forms of appraisal

Advantages

Can be used to align business goals with personal goals and aspirations

Can promote a "helicopter view" and the harmonization/alignment of business goals throughout the organization

Can improve communication throughout the organization and a sense of common purpose

Can promote a sense of procedural justice—gives appraisees "a voice" and enables their participation in the process (Fletcher, 2000)

Can include objective criteria for judging performance and can be used to resolve problems of unsatisfactory performance

Can be very effective vehicles for improving performance

Potential disadvantages

Goal-setting training is needed—collusion in setting too easy goals or an unskilled interviewer setting goals too high are dangers

Both appraiser and appraisee need a clear understanding of business goals and their own roles in achieving them. Deficient understanding can result in fragmented and disparate action plans in different departments

Appraiser and appraisee can have different agendas which can affect the outcomes. Organizational politics can affect managers' assessments of staff, e.g., good reports to enhance the status of their departments; lukewarm reports to prevent the promotion of staff out of their departments (Bernadin & Beatty, 1984; Dulewicz & Fletcher, 1989), Appraisees' motives range from enhancing self-esteem to refuting "unfair" criticism. Different/conflicting agendas hinder communication

Can be as open to bias as other forms of appraisal, e.g., female managers in NHS received less useful feedback in appraisal interviews than male managers (Alimo-Metcalfe, 1994a)

Tend to be more effective when "soft" criteria are used. Use for disciplinary or pay and promotion purposes is incompatible with developmental purposes. Not well-suited for comparisons between workers

Follow-up action after the interview is essential—best seen as a continuous process rather than a once-a-year exercise. Can therefore be expensive in time, energy, and resources and can result in employee demoralization if hopes are raised but nothing much happens

2   Identify quantifiable measures of performance (indicators) for each key
     outcome or "product" by asking questions such as "How can we meas-
     ure how well we succeed in realizing our responsibilities?"
3   Define contingencies: The indicators are ordered in terms of their im-
     portance and given a "nonlinear weighting" (contingency) so that they
     can be converted into an organizational effectiveness score—the extent
     to which the work group contributes to the overall effectiveness of the
     organization.
4   Design a feedback system: Information on performance outcomes is fed
     back to the workgroup and management.

There are several interesting features of this system. First, it is designed for
workgroups rather than individuals (although it can be adapted for use with
individuals). Second, the process of developing the system is largely under
the control of the workgroup. The first two phases involve discussions
between the workers with a supervisor to act as facilitator and a manager to
give an organizational perspective. Crucially, the workgroup itself identifies
the indicators for which they will take responsibility. Even though management can intervene if they think that an important aspect of performance
has been omitted, the workers still decide how it will be measured. In this
way, the indicators are likely to be within the workers' control and of course
the whole process ensures a sense of procedural justice. Third, in defining
the contingencies, management is challenged to ask, "If the group concentrated on this set of indicators, and set priorities according to this set of contingencies, what would be the short- and long-term risks for the company?"
Moreover, the contingencies need to be regularly reviewed in the light of
changing circumstances. In this way, managers gain an overview of the
organization's effectiveness.

Van Tuijl et al. (1997) give numerous case studies to demonstrate this
process in action. One case study involved photocopier repair and maintenance technicians. At some times during the year a backlog of service calls
would build up and customers would become annoyed because they would
have to wait a long time for repairs. Response time was outside the control
of the technicians because they were told by the "despatcher" department
which customers to go to and in what order. However, they could contribute
indirectly to response times by the efficiency with which they worked, so this
was chosen as an indicator. However, when there was a backlog (termed a
red alert), it was agreed that the technicians would concentrate on making
as many calls a day as possible by making repairs to a minimal standard and
not doing any maintenance. During "red alert" periods, the average calls
per day indicator got a very steep contingency (or wrighting). However,
management was concerned that, if calls per day was the only indicator then
the technicians would not be motivated to do any maintenance and this
would mean customer dissatisfaction as photocopiers became unreliable. So
a maintenance indicator was added and this got a steeper contingency in

times of normal workload. Finally, the company felt that greater customer satisfaction would increase market share so the technicians devised indicators for correct behaviour towards clients. In turn, the company added 10 minutes to the expected labour time indicator to give the technicians more time for client-centred behaviour. A similar process was operating in other workgroups within the company, e.g., the dispatchers, so that the organization was able to pursue several hierarchically organized objectives.

The assessment part of the process can be successfully linked to PRP but Van Tuijl and his co-workers (1997) comment that ProMES works better when this is not done. In general the feedback alone is valued and even indicators that are not perfectly controllable will be accepted if they provide helpful information about core aspects of job performance.

However, ProMES also has a developmental component in that the feedback given to the workgroup stimulates thinking about ways to do things differently in order to improve performance. Since the indicators have been carefully chosen to be largely within the control of the workers, they are likely to be able to effect improvements. For example, a group of factory workers took responsibility for a machine uptime indicator and thereafter began to think of factors that contributed to downtime. This led them to ask questions about machine set-up procedures, which they realized were very haphazard. They then devised a standard procedure for machine set-ups, and uptime improved considerably. Similarly, an intensive care team took responsibility for an indicator "moving patients to a medium care ward too early". Complaints from staff on the medium care ward that they were having to deal with too many very seriously ill patients led the intensive care team to define precise criteria and rules for moving patients. The medium care nurses' job satisfaction improved as a result.

Although ProMES appears to be a promising technique for performance management, Schmidt and Kleinbeck (1997) warn that the organizational context can hinder its success. For instance, in one case study, the pay system was incompatible with the indicators so that if workers improved their performance they would actually lose money. In another, conflict arose when a supervisor insisted on focusing on quantity indicators to the exclusion of quality indicators. These problems could be resolved but the main implication is that several contextual conditions have to be changed at the same time that ProMES is introduced if it is to be successful in increasing productivity. Another important issue is that the network of performance indicators across departments should be compatible. In the photocopier technicians example, for instance, if the despatchers did not comply with the "red alert" procedures, then the calls per day indicator would not result in greater productivity and customer satisfaction.

ProMES also depends on accurate and quantifiable measures of job performance and this has always been the "Achilles heel" of performance appraisal. Though the involvement of workers in the selection of indicators removes one source of dissatisfaction, in that these are more likely to be within the workers' control, the difficulties of good measurement still apply. Perhaps more so, since the complexities of contingencies may make accurate record keeping for feedback more difficult. It would still be difficult to apply ProMES to very complex jobs where there are less tangible outputs. Most of the performance indicators that I can think of for my job are only partly under my control—student results for instance—but when I'm next standing over a photocopier or supplying yet more documentation for yet another quality review I will yearn for the built-in, formal prioritization of objectives given by ProMES!

The contribution of appraisal to career development

In today's work climate, employees are far less likely to be able to progress steadily up the career ladder. Flatter organizational structures mean that there are fewer rungs on the ladder and when promotion does come, it is likely to lead to a much greater "jump" in terms of roles and responsibilities than hitherto. People are also far more likely to change jobs frequently and even change occupations in the course of their careers. Arthur (1994) has coined the term "boundaryless career" to refer to the fact that either through choice or necessity, people must cross many boundaries during the course of their working lives, within and between organizations and occupations.

For some people the "death" of the traditional career has engendered a good deal of cynicism and the feeling that the whole notion of a career is obsolete. Arnold (1998, p. 2) says that this is because the term career is being defined in a very narrow way. He defines career as "the sequence of employment related positions, roles, activities and experiences encountered by a person". This, he says, has several important implications. "Careers are owned by an individual, they have subjective as well as objective components, they explicitly involve the future and the past as well as the present, they are not confined to high status occupations, they include phenomena such as unemployment or vocational education." However, he warns about overestimating the scale of changes in the workplace. For many people the career landscape is still pretty much as it was. However he, like many others (e.g., Herriot, 1992; Herriot & Stickland, 1996), believes that because careers have become more complex and difficult to navigate, the need for lifelong learning and career management is greater than ever. An illustration of this need comes from Feldman (2000), who speaks of a flight from organizations. In the US, many young people are seeking not to work their way up an organization but to work their way out. A large organization can give them experience, mentoring, accumulated financial resources, and credibility, the better to launch out on their own in entrepreneurial activities. At the other end of the employment lifespan, Feldman claims that many older workers are seeking to take early retirement and to use compensation packages to set up their own businesses.

Arnold points out that there is relatively little evidence for the effectiveness of career management interventions but there is evidence that people are very concerned about opportunities for training and development. For instance, Doyle (1992) found that satisfaction with these aspects of work were the strongest predictors of satisfaction with many other facets of organizational life. Orpen (1994) found that the extent to which supervisors, middle managers, and their organizations engaged in career management was related to measures of career success such as salary growth and promotion as well as career satisfaction. In place of organizational commitment (Meyer & Allen, 1984) there seems to be an increase in commitment to one's own career or, as touched on in Chapter 3 and neatly encapsulated by my doctoral student Ceri Diffley, "commitment to doing a good job". Thus, the feedback that comes from appraisal is valued if it contributes to people's ability to manage their careers.

An excursion into adult development (and an advert and an apology . . .)

Increasingly, appraisal has a developmental focus and two techniques— development centres and 360 degree or multi-rater feedback—are increasingly being used by organizations both to assess potential and increase core competences. Traditionally, careers guidance was only for the young, but the "new" careers demand such assistance throughout people's working lives. This blurring of the distinction between appraisal and career development makes it difficult to know what to include where in this chapter. However, most writers on this topic begin with a consideration of theories of adult development so it is perhaps worth pausing to consider these before looking at specific techniques. However, before we begin I feel the need for an apology, in that a short chapter can only scratch the surface of this area and risks gross over-simplification. By the time this book is published, Léonie Sugarman's (2001) new text, *Lifespan Development: Theories, Concepts and Interventions* (revised edition) will be on the market. In my view her book should be required reading for every management consultant, manager, or human resource specialist who believes that the workforce can be treated as an amorphous mass without regard to their individuality, and coerced into conformity with whatever is current policy.

Early in her book, Sugarman describes the tenets of lifespan developmental psychology "as an inclusive philosophy of 'both/and' rather than 'either/or'. No one perspective, theory or discipline is sufficient but together they can provide what Baltes (1987) [p. 612] claims is a 'coherent metatheoretical view on the nature of development'." A little later in her book she tells us that one hallmark of mature thinking is the person's ability to deal with contradiction and ambiguity. Both aspects are admirably demonstrated in her book. Sugarman ranges effortlessly across theories and perspectives taken from traditions as diverse as sociology, the psychoanalytic tradition, literature, and journalism. Then, just when the reader might be feeling rather overwhelmed, she knits everything together in a discussion of the major recurring themes of trust and dependency, authority and autonomy, and cooperation and competition, which we use when constructing our own narratives of our life courses—the stories we tell about ourselves which create a sense of continuity and meaning.

Contradiction is a recurring theme in the book. It is inherent in life itself, as when the young adult strives for both independence and intimacy or when a retired person both relinquishes the world of employment but looks for new achievement outlets. It is found in the fact that development is not simply a linear process but also circular, as we repeatedly undergo transitions and revisit old conflicts. Most of all, it is reflected in the important insight that lifespan development is not just about change, but about continuities and stabilities and each person's struggle to maintain a coherent sense of self.

She challenges many commonly held assumptions such as the notion that the life course can be described as a series of stages involving growth, maintenance, and decline. The general turbulence of life in Western countries with changes in the workplace, society, and ways of living, to say nothing of increasing health and longevity, make this model look too static and outdated. The notion of a "mid-life crisis" is questioned—there is limited evidence that this is a "normative event" and many people in mid-life strive to maintain a sense of stability and continuity. Neither are the post-retirement years simply a matter of disengagement and decline. Increasing infirmity comes to many of us and death comes to us all, but there are still many developmental tasks to accomplish—coming to terms with our own mortality, successfully adjusting to the death of a partner, and spiritual growth among them. Other thought-provoking ideas are that social support may not always be a good thing and that there are possible flaws in all the models of helper/professional–client relationships, which can lead to negative outcomes in interventions.

She is inclusive in her discussion of variations in the life course. Rather than focusing on white heterosexual males, she makes frequent reference to the lives of women, lesbians and gays, and people from different cultures and races. Even though her book is quite short, it demonstrates that my efforts to chart the significant events of the life course in a few pages must be inadequate. All I can say is, read her book too!

Theories of adult development and career stages

In a world that was more stable, if not necessarily simpler, it made sense to look at life as a series of fairly predictable stages, which people passed through as they matured and grew old. Thus, the stages were closely linked to chronological age and, in addition, the paths that people took tended to be different according to their gender. Most of the occupationally related theories tend to reflect traditional male life courses: a period of preparation for work in education; a period of establishing occupational identity and one's working "niche"; a plateau or period of stability for many; for some, a period of increasing status and power; and at last, a gradual process of decline and disengagement from work. For women, the stages were mainly defined by their biology, with very little said about the time after mid-life except for the "empty nest syndrome". Even before the changes in the nature of work and gender roles in Western countries, there were very many people who did not fit these stereotypical life courses. Their relevance is even more dubious now.

However, one of my favourite theories of adult development is that of Erickson (1968). This is because his views are not unduly gendered, they fit my personal experience very well, and they are basically optimistic—most of adult life can be a period for growth and creative striving. For Erickson, adolescence and early adulthood is a time for establishing a sense of identity—who one is and where one is going. The next developmental task is to develop intimacy and commitment to another person or some important cause, whereas from the age of about 35 people want to accomplish something of lasting value. This may involve bringing up a family or contributing to the community or society. In any case, there is concern for the next generation. In maturity (age 65+) the task is to feel satisfied with one's choices and one's life. At each of these stages there can be positive and negative outcomes depending on how well the major developmental task has been handled. For instance, at the identity stage one can either emerge with a strong self-concept or feel a lack of direction and a confused sense of "who one is"; in mid-life a failure to establish intimacy or concern oneself with the next generation can lead to people treating themselves as their own children with a selfish and superficial lifestyle; at the maturity stage one can feel satisfaction with one's life or full of regrets about past mistakes, now too late to rectify.

In his early work Super (1957) proposed four similar age-linked stages, more clearly related to employment:

- Exploration (15–24): Involves increasing self-awareness and investigation of the world of work to find occupations that fit.
- Establishment (25–44): The person eventually finds a occupational niche and strives for success.
- Maintenance (45–65): The person strives to maintain his or her position in the face of technological change and competition from younger people.
- Disengagement (65+): People gradually distance themselves from the world of work and become observers rather than participants.

Arnold et al. (1998) observe that though there are similarities between these two theories, Super is rather more pessimistic: Middle age is a time for "hanging on" to what you've got rather than for growth. In his later writings Super (1980, 1990) developed a more flexible framework by identifying six roles that people perform in Western societies: homemaker, worker, citizen, leisurite, student, and child. At any point in one's life each of these roles can assume a different level of importance or priority and people can be at different stages within them. Take, for instance, a woman who decides to change the course of her life once all her children are in full-time education. As a homemaker she may be in the maintenance stage. As a mature student she may be in the establishment stage, while as a citizen and worker she may be at the exploratory stage, maybe becoming interested in social issues and considering career options. With a busy schedule she may be relatively disengaged as a leisurite.

Even so, flexibility in role priorities does not adequately describe or explain how people cope flexibly with their work role alone throughout life, which is increasingly being expected. In addition, can these theories account adequately for individual differences? A successful career woman without children has a number of choices she can make as she approaches mid-life. She can shift her priorities completely and "downsize" her career to concentrate on homemaking and childcare; she can decide to become a parent but accord equal priority to her work role; or she could decide not to have children and maintain work as her priority. Erickson's (1968) framework could explain why many women feel the urge to have children later in life (quite apart from biological imperatives) and why men often devote far more time to second families after divorce than they ever did to their first. Both are expressions of "generativity"—the need to become involved with the next generation. A very strong work identity developed earlier may incline some to continue to make work a priority with or without parenthood. If they choose not to have children, then the work itself may satisfy generativity, as for instance in teaching, politics, or other occupations that have a strong impact on the future. Or people may find that they become involved with mentoring or succession planning at work or with voluntary community work. Failure to work at the task of generativity would lead to a regretful old age in Erickson's scheme, so an egocentric lifestyle can also be explained, provided that such people *do* feel regretful in old age.

Other theories have emphasized the role that transitions play in our lives. Perhaps Levinson and his co-workers (1978) have provided the most influential model, although it is based on interviews with a tiny sample of American men between the ages of 35 and 45. Levinson et al. proposed that there are major transitions at about age 30, 40, 50, and 60. The "mid-life" crisis at around age 40, for instance, results from the realization that one is no longer young and that time is beginning to run out. This may prompt a major reappraisal of one's life and the choices that have shaped it. By this stage people have a realistic idea of how much further they are likely to progress and whether their career and other ambitions will be achieved. This may trigger fundamental changes in one's occupation and other important aspects of one's life. Or the person may reaffirm their previously made commitments, and Sugarman (2001) reviews evidence that this may be the more common reaction. Whatever the choice, the rest of adult life is a process of implementing and living with mid-life decisions.

Gilligan (1982) criticized the male bias in these theories and proposed a theory based on interviews with women. She argued that the different socialization of boys and girls led them to have very different concerns. For boys the aim is to achieve separation and independence; for girls the aim is to achieve interconnectedness and reciprocity. The challenge for women is therefore to move from an exclusive concern for "caring for others" to a more balanced concern with "caring for oneself". Both Levinson et al.'s (1978) and Gilligan's theories can explain why both men and women sometimes undergo major transitions in middle adulthood. In Gilligan's case, after years of homemaking and caring for others, women may suddenly launch into caring for themselves, e.g., in a university course and a whole new career. Further, as women's careers start to resemble men's, Levinson's mid-life transition can explain both a female Gauguin abandoning everything for a Pacific island and women abandoning employment to become full-time mothers and homemakers.

I feel as if I'm swimming through treacle here: The frameworks are so general they appear to be able to explain any eventuality. But this may be the point. Why should we expect something as complex as human lifespan development to fit into simple frameworks? Remember that an understanding of lifespan development has to be informed by a variety of different perspectives and each on its own is inadequate. There is a need for mature thinking here—we need to be able to tolerate contradiction and ambiguity. Top managers may be very good at this when considering risky business ventures. They can often seem less willing to take this stance when dealing with their workforces, when they seem to want simple frameworks that prescribe "levers" which will affect everyone in the same way.

Nevertheless I am gripped with a feeling of deep dissatisfaction with all these frameworks. They all seem too static, too outdated, too stereotypical and, in their proposed later stages, too pessimistic. There is a feeling that they do not really explain anything about the factors determining people's choices and actions at different points in their lives. On the contrary, Sugarman (2001) makes clear that lifespan developmental psychology "challenges the frequently implicit assumption of a growth–maintenance–decline model of development". To give some anecdotal examples of the inadequacy of the "maintenance and decline" view: A friend of mine, as he was approaching 70, enrolled on and graduated from a fine arts degree after a working life as a mining engineer. Another, lucky enough to retire at 55, took to round-the-world sailing. Another in her 50s was selected for the England Senior Ladies Golf team and regularly jets off to represent her country in international tournaments. Even I, at the age of 50 and after 26 years with the same organization, have begun weekly commuting from the North to the South of England to take up a new and deeply satisfying job just at the time when I thought my concerns were turning to retirement planning and disengagement. My circle of acquaintances may be somewhat narrow in terms of things like social class and opportunity but it doesn't include huge numbers of people. To find these examples in such a restricted sample may indicate not that these instances are exceptional, but that people's expectations about what growing older means, may have changed in some significant way. Certainly, the choices and actions of my friends don't look like the backward-looking disengagement proposed by the later stages of theories. What does unite us is the simple fact that circumstances meant that we *could* do these things. My friends were fit and healthy enough and had the leisure. I was lucky to escape the ageism so prevalent in today's workplace and was offered a great new job, which has rejuvenated my career.

I think the stages are more like cycles, which people can repeatedly engage in at any age, provided they are well and circumstances permit. I believe that the stage theories were more applicable in a world where most people's lives were more circumscribed, their horizons were narrow, and when people grew old quickly. Of course, all too many people still suffer these conditions and get trapped into the life course their earliest decisions have dictated, so the theories can still have some currency and usefulness.

Cognitive age

However, some researchers are arguing that instead of using chronological age when investigating priorities, values, and attitudes throughout the lifespan, we should use other measures of age. The concept of "cognitive age" has been developed, which has at its heart the old adage, "you're as young as you feel". Barak and Schiffman (1981) argue that the individual's identity and behaviour may depend not just on chronological age but on the perceived or subjective age—the cognitive age. They found that as the person's chronological age increased, the greater the discrepancy between the age they thought and felt themselves to be and their age in terms of years became. Summarizing a number of studies that support these findings, Hubley and Hultsch (1994) found that the majority of older adults (50–80%) feel between 12 and 15 years younger than they actually are. These perceptions may not simply reflect self-delusion. The reality is that in developed nations, improvements in general health and life expectancy mean that people who are now in their 50s can have very different outlooks on life and levels of fitness from their counterparts of 40 years ago. Clarke, Long, and Schiffman (1999) have added two more dimensions to Barak and Schiffman's original instrument to measure cognitive age. These are "health age" and "think age", which refer respectively to how the person feels in terms of perceived physical condition and in terms of thinking processes. They found a consistent tendency for people to classify themselves as younger on all the dimensions of cognitive age but the "think age" dimension contributed most to the overall cognitive age score. The lower the "think age" score, the younger the overall cognitive age score.

Chronological age is a rather crude measure of time since birth, which can hide a multitude of individual differences in vigour, energy, enthusiasm, fitness, and so on. Cognitive age could be a facet of personality related to openness to experience. People who retain their curiosity, flexibility, and zest for new experiences later in life are likely to have a cognitive age considerably lower than their chronological age and the former may be a much better guide to attitudes and behaviour and therefore as a basis for lifespan development frameworks. In fact, consumer psychology provides evidence that cognitive age is a much better guide to people's buying habits, leisure pursuits, and so on, than chronological age (Schiffman & Sherman, 1991; Stephens, 1991). Employers might consider this when they are encouraging ageism in the workplace and thereby discarding a wealth of experienced, productive workers who may be the repositories of company history and culture. Me? I shall be happy to ruminate on my life when I am finally physically incapacitated, but not before.

The one thing I find most positive about the "new careers" is that they oblige people to get out of their ruts or prevent them ever getting into one; they afford lifelong learning so that people don't become fearful about their ability to learn and do new things; they oblige flexibility so people don't lose their capacity to adapt. And a good thing too, since Western societies will realize that they need their older workers when the numbers of young people entering the workforce begin to diminish in the next few decades. From this perspective the future looks quite bright.

Job transitions

Given the new realities, understanding how people manage job transitions and the turbulence in their working lives is probably more useful from a practical point of view than grand theories of adult development. Nicholson and West (1988) found that the frequency with which managers changed jobs was increasing and some of these moves could be quite dramatic, involving changes of both status and function. Over a decade later, Rice (2000) reports on a survey of UK managers which indicates that this trend has accelerated. Nearly 43% of this sample said that that their loyalty is now to themselves and not to their organizations in that they did not expect to be with their present employers 2 years from now; "For a large minority, ruthless self-interest has become the number one survival strategy" (p. 48).

Nicholson (1990) proposed a four-stage process of job transition— preparation, encounter, adjustment, and stabilization. Successful negotiation of one stage influences the outcomes of the next. Preparation occurs before the person starts the job and involves a process of information exchange and negotiation similar to Herriot's (1989) social model of selection (see Chapter 7). Both sides have a vested interest in presenting themselves in the best possible light but this may lead to unrealistic expectations. This has stimulated work on the effectiveness of realistic job previews (e.g., Premack & Wanous, 1985; Wanous, 1989; Wanous, Poland, Premack, & Davis, 1992), which have been found to reduce turnover in new employees and increase the job satisfaction of those who stay.

The encounter stage is essentially a matter of gathering information about the organization and the job and "how things get done around here".

Sometimes this information is gathered explicitly by asking questions or consulting written sources but simply observing and listening to what is going on seems to be an effective strategy. Some people are better at gathering and assimilating information than others and some organizations appoint established staff to act as mentors to help the newcomer (Kram, 1985).

Adjustment occurs when people understand the new work environment and now consider how they are going to perform their jobs in the medium to long term. Schein (1971) defined three basic approaches the person could adopt:

- Custodianship: The person accepts the role as given.
- Content innovation: The person accepts the role/goals but finds his or her own way of implementing them.
- Role innovation: Both the role and the methods to enact them are redefined.

Van Maanen and Schein (1979) believe that how the person is socialized into the organization can influence the approach they will adopt. For instance, Ashford and Saks (1996) found that organizations that sent their new people on structured induction and training courses tended to produce workers with a custodian approach, since everyone is exposed to the same rather narrow set of experiences. In contrast, Gortex (Rhodes, 1982) used to hire promising people and then ask them to find their own role and develop it by "wandering about" through departments until they discovered their own niches. Many organizations operate somewhere between these two extremes, but Arnold et al. (1998) comment that organizations probably reward "custodians" most because they conform to the existing culture. Nevertheless, organizations are likely to *claim* that they value content innovators more.

The stability phase is when the person is firmly established in the job. Paradoxically, many people spend least time in this stage before moving on. Their careers are therefore a constant sequence of transitions. Parker and Lewis (1981) discuss the dangers of leaving a job too soon. People may start off with a false sense of competence but quickly realize that a steep learning/relearning curve is needed. This may lead to a happy or unhappy outcome depending on the person's capacity to deal with this kind of difficult transition effectively. The danger of this kind of "dangerous transition" increases as people move employers more often in search of career advancement and the old tried and tested, measured career advancement routes disappear. Organizations are therefore more at risk of appointing unsuitable people to senior positions. The old "law" of people being promoted to their level of incompetence becomes an even greater risk than before.

Others find themselves "plateaued" in a job—unable to move on even if they want to. Some people may decide that this suits them well since they do not want more challenge and responsibility (Howard & Bray, 1988), but for others this is a source of frustration and dissatisfaction (Goffee & Scase, 1992).

Many solutions to a "plateaued" career involve development of one sort or another, for instance training if there is a lack of skill, secondment to another department if there is a lack of experience, coaching if there is a specific problem. So we return to the role of assessment and appraisal, or rather, we see that a person's performance in the "new careers" depends on a continuous cycle of adjustment, which depends on continuous development. A possible integration is given in Box 8.3, which also includes some practical suggestions for people's needs at different stages in the cycle. Though there is little that is new in this integration, the simple fact that the stages could involve iterative cycles or an entire working life depending on circumstance gives it much greater flexibility in describing people's working lives. With a little adjustment, it could be applied to other life roles. The main point is that disengagement—and the various forms this can take—does not have to be the final life stage but can be the start of a new cycle up to

---

BOX 8.3
A possible integration of lifespan development and job transitions theory

Stages/transitions	*Associated needs/actions*

Exploration (Super)
Preparation (Nicholson)
Selection as a social process/
   constructivist perspective
   (Herriot, Anderson, &
   Cunningham-Snell)
     ↓
	Self-assessment
	Careers guidance
	Further education/
	   training courses
	Realistic job previews
	
	     ↓

Establishment (Super)
Encounter/adjustment
   (Nicholson)
 	
     ↓
	Feedback/appraisal
	Self-development/career
	   management
	Mentoring
	     ↓

Maintenance (Super)
Stability (Nicholson)
Generativity (Erickson)
 	
     ↓
	Feedback/appraisal
	Career management and
	   development
	Assessment for potential
	     ↓

Disengagement
Career plateau (retiring
   on the job)
Unemployment
Retirement
	"Plateau" solutions,
	   e.g., coaching,
	   careers guidance
	Succession planning
	Retirement planning
	Return to exploration stage

↓	↓
Extreme old age or incapacity	Long-term care

extreme old age provided that the person has the health, energy, motivation, and means to make it so.

Career management

Traditionally, careers guidance was for the young, but the new careers mean that there is an increasing need for adults to get this sort of help especially when dealing with "career derailment", which might occur when a senior person is suddenly made redundant. The phenomenon of a "plateaued career" or the processes that lead people to reassess their lives may prompt fundamental changes of direction. People who reach their mid- to late thirties without finding an employment niche, perhaps because of childcare respon- sibilities or a succession of different jobs, are increasingly looking to start a substantial new career. Arnold (1998) believes that even those in stable and established careers need to engage in career management and to prepare for the worst. Once things have started to look dodgy at work, he says, it's probably already too late to avoid "derailment", redundancy, or unemploy- ment. For these sorts of reasons, many occupational psychologists make a good living assessing people and advising on suitable occupations. One approach to helping people to find the right occupation and organization involves trying to match the person's interests, abilities, personality, and skills to jobs and organizations, and a number of useful theoretical frame- works can assist in this process.

In a sense an organization's selection process is the end of a very long pro- cess of self and career development whereby people prepare themselves to be the most suitable job applicant. This is true whether this occurs at the beginning or later in the person's working life. But people differ in their approach to making career decisions and managing their careers. Phillips, Friedlander, Pazienza, and Kost (1985) identified three decision-making styles in career management:

- Rational: Where the person exhaustively investigates self-characteristics and career options—perhaps with the help of a careers advisor or an occupational psychologist who will carry out a full psychological assessment.
- Intuitive: Where decisions are made more on a "gut feeling"—what feels right. Such people may try out any experience or career opportunity that presents itself without having any definite plan of where it might take them.
- Dependent: The person waits for other people or circumstances to dictate what to do. In Erickson's framework, such people may not have developed a strong sense of identity so they "follow in their parent's footsteps", accept jobs simply because they are available, follow other people's advice whether or not it's right for them, and begin to think of their future only after redundancy.

Most people employ a mix of styles and Case study 8.1 illustrates this. See if you can identify the three decision-making styles at each point.

Case study 8.1:   Career decision-making styles

Sue had a good education. She was bright and academic success came easily. However, in early adolescence she was stunned by the sudden death of her father and her interest in school work disappeared. Though the family was not poor she felt that she ought to contribute financially so she left school at 16 with minimal qualifications and took a secretarial course because it was the quickest and easiest route to a reasonably well-paid job. She got a job as an office junior in a law firm and though she stayed for 3 years, she found much of the work routine and boring.

When she was 19 her mother remarried and this prompted Sue to think about her own future. A television series inspired her to go to university, with the aim of becoming a forensic psychologist. After a term or two she discovered that this was a great mistake—psychology seemed to be all scientific rigour and statistics, not at all what she had expected. So she changed to a history course, which was a subject she had always enjoyed. She did well and emerged with first-class honours. She was encouraged by her tutors to embark on a PhD. In the meantime, she had fallen in love with a medical student who still had 2 years of study before graduation. A PhD seemed an attractive prospect which would further her current interests and keep her close to the person she valued, so she accepted the offer and successfully completed her PhD. Later, she accepted a post as a junior university lecturer because this seemed a natural extension of her career so far.

When she was 30 Sue's circumstances changed. For various reasons, her childless marriage failed and she had become very dissatisfied with university work. But what else could she do with a PhD in history? The University Careers Service told her that many employers would regard her as both over- and under-qualified for virtually any job. It was clear that she would have to gain yet more qualifications if she was to change her career. Sue thought long and hard about her future. She could not face the thought of another 3 years of doing a degree followed by more training and that ruled out most professional jobs. She read widely in the Careers Service library and discovered that she could take a shorter graduates' conversion course in law. She thought back to her early days in the law firm. Typing other people's work and routine legal documents, and acting as a filing clerk had been rather boring but much of the lawyers' work had seemed very interesting. She had bought a house when she had been married and when it was sold, the loan paid off, and her ex-husband had taken his share, there was just enough profit left to pay for the course and *very* modest living expenses.

Going back to study and living on a student's income was hard but, as usual, her ability ensured success and she found the law fascinating. Armed with her new qualification she took out a bank loan, had a smart haircut, bought herself a sharp suit, and sent out applications to begin a new career as a lawyer. She was lucky. She was bright enough and still young enough to get a job quickly.

Think back on your own career—to what extent did different moves and transitions depend on luck or judgement or some combination of the two? What prompted you to delve into occupational psychology and what do you need to do to further your career aspirations? You might want to devise and write down a personal development plan that will enable you to achieve your career goals. To what extent would this demand self-generated development and what could you do to get help from your employer? If you haven't thought much about these things before, start now!

Sue's case study demonstrates a number of points. She may seem privileged in her ability and opportunities but notice the role of ill-luck/luck in her career decisions. One traumatic experience initially deflected her from university and a professional career. Better luck made her early experience in the law firm one that guided her to her eventual "niche". Notice too how easily she was deflected from her goal of becoming a forensic psychologist, which itself had a very flimsy basis. Third, note how her choice of degree course exerted a great influence not only on her subsequent career but also on her attempts to change its direction. Again luck played a part. If her marriage had not failed when it did and she had stayed at her university job a few more years maybe she would not have been able to change at all. Glib statements that in the future people will flexibly pursue a range of different careers should therefore be treated with caution. The sad fact is, that our earliest, often least-considered decisions can determine the rest of our lives, and each generation has to learn this anew. When we are young, anything and everything may seem possible and there appears to be ample time to do all this. This perception is largely false, but "old-timers" rarely convince the young.

The obstacles against using wholly rational decision-making styles when making career decisions are admirably discussed by Arnold (1997b) in a paper that considers theories of adult cognitive development and their implications for effective career management. For instance, "post-formal" theories of thinking (in the sense that they go beyond Piaget's stage of formal operations, see, e.g., Flavell, 1963; Boden, 1994) stress the relativistic nature of knowledge, an acceptance of contradiction, and a striving to reconcile contradiction. The implications of this are that the person:

- Rejects the ideas that (a) there is only one possible "perfect career" and (b) that all possible careers would be equally suitable.
- Is open to personal change through the process and challenge of dealing with career problems.
- Recognizes apparently contradictionary tendencies in values and attitudes (e.g., valuing autonomy *and* working in a team).
- Engages in internal dialogues in the quest to resolve contradictions; internal "arguments" may involve many different "voices".

Notions of what is meant by "wisdom" add some texture to this scheme. For instance Arlin (1990) emphasizes "problem finding"—instead of just accepting "what is" or "what one is told", the wise person questions, and imagines alternatives. The Berlin-based research team of Smith, Baltes, Staudinger, and colleagues (e.g., Baltes & Smith, 1990) emphasize good judgement and the ability to give advice about important but uncertain matters of life. Cowan (1995) questions whether we have placed too much value on "experts". Being too expert in a rapidly changing world may be a disadvantage if one is unable to adapt. The "wisest expert" may be the "novice who is always willing to learn".

There are a few important implications of this:

1 How many people are capable of this level of thinking and wisdom?
2 Even if there were large numbers, wouldn't this sometimes lead to over-complex decision making? (Yes, career management is complex but sometimes there are simple matters of fact to be navigated, e.g., one needs an MSc in Occupational Psychology to become a chartered occupational psychologist!)
3 It takes a long time to become an "expert" (maybe 10 years?). If everything is changing so fast will anyone ever make it to "expert" (including occupational psychologists and careers guidance counsellors!).
4 What about the "not-so-smart" people and those without opportunity?

It is well to remind ourselves again, that for very many people, there are *not* limitless opportunities. In fact, Roberts (1968, 1977) was arguing 30 years ago that opportunity and not choice governs the way in which young people enter employment. He was citing factors such as social disadvantage, discrimination, and poverty of expectations as major barriers and limiters of choice, but he also implicated personal factors such as values held and levels of encouragement received. Later theories have elaborated on the role that the development of the person's self-concept has on choice of occupation. For instance, Miller-Tiedeman and Tiedeman (1990) regard career development as an ongoing process of differentiating ego identity. The person has to learn to distinguish between "common reality"—what everyone says is right for you (e.g., that teaching is a good occupation for a woman); and "personal reality"—what is right for me (e.g., woman or not, I'd be a good merchant banker). Gottfredson (1981, 1996) puts forward a theory which explains why it may be very difficult for people to make this distinction. The development of the self-concept proceeds in two main phases. Circumscription involves successive delineations and refinements of the self, which start at a fundamental level, e.g., I am a boy, but become increasingly abstract, e.g., I am a talented/talentless person; I belong to the middle class; I am a good Muslim; and so on. Gottfredson argues that each such delineation results in a narrowing of the range of options the person will consider. So, for instance, girls as young as 6 years old may decide that maths and computers are "boy things" and thus very many prestigious occupations are rendered "gender inappropriate". The next phase is compromise, which involves a process of vetting the preferred occupational alternatives on the basis of "external reality" or accessibility. Your social class, race, family contacts, geographical location, and so on all then become opportunities or barriers according to how favourable or advantageous they are. So in this scheme, self-concept (gender, social class, perceived ability, interests and values, etc.) and occupational "images" (gender appropriateness, perceived status, and field of work) determine people's occupational preferences. Then there is a compromise between what the person would like and what the person deems possible. This framework can be applied to the career choices of women who often "select themselves in" to low-status or low-paid occupations but it can be applied to almost any disadvantaged group. The sad thing is, even if people "throw off" these self-limiting conceptions of themselves later in life, very many find themselves effectively trapped in their circumstances.

To summarize:

1   For many younger and older people there may be little real choice of career. Limited ability, skills, experience, local job opportunities, and limiting self-concepts may circumscribe those crucial early decisions. Later, financial and domestic responsibilities and ageism amongst employers can reduce the options even though there are far more opportunities for further education and training for people in mid-life than there were 20 years ago.

2   Various forms of prejudice conspire to thwart the aspirations of many and in addition to this, there are real seniority/juniority barriers even for the most enlightened of employers. Progressing in one career and getting to the top of even a modestly paid grade may render someone "too expensive" for a junior position in a new occupation. Employers may fear that the drop in income may be too much and the person will soon be forced to leave. On the other hand, paying more than the going rate for the job may create feelings of inequity in fellow workers. So even with goodwill on all sides, major mid-life career changes are usually a challenge. Real discrimination in the workplace stops many before they can start.

For these sorts of reasons, when people come for advice and assessment, there needs to be care in raising unrealistic expectations while avoiding negative self-fulfilling prophecies. Dave Williams, who taught me on my MSc, once quoted the story of a man he had counselled who had unfortunately lost a leg but was desperate to become a roofer. Despite all advice, he demonstrated his ability to cope with ladders and roofs and got a job. The line between over-optimistic encouragement and discriminatory discouragement is very fine. In the end it has to be the person's own drive and determination to succeed that must steer the career choice and development process.

Individual versus organization models of career development

The previously mentioned case of the roofer is also a good reminder that people are not always imprisoned in their circumstances but can and do make autonomous career choices. Two models help to explain people's initial and later career-related decisions and are useful frameworks for guidance advice.

Schein's career anchors

Schein (1993) proposed the notion of "career anchors", which involve fundamental aspects of the person—a mixture of values, needs, motives, and abilities. They are so important that people are unwilling to give them up even in the most difficult circumstances. Schein's ideas are summarized in Box 8.4. Arnold et al. (1998) point out that one of the most difficult choices is that between the career anchors themselves since most people would want to say that several are important to them. However, if you had to choose just one what would it be? That is your real career anchor.

According to this view, people are likely to be most satisfied when they choose occupations and organizations compatible with their dominant career anchor. Those with a security anchor may be satisfied with a mundane job provided there is little fear of redundancy and it gives them a steady wage. People with a service anchor may be best suited to occupations such as teaching, nursing, and social work. A pure challenge anchor would be an advantage in occupations such as professional football and high finance. People with a strong autonomy anchor may thrive best when they are self-employed.

Arnold et al. (1998) point out that this framework also has implications for how people are managed in organizations. The distress of many nurses who feel that financial considerations are coming before patient care can be explained if most of them have a service anchor. Forcing a research and development team to work to standard hours and procedures is likely to cause trouble if they have strong autonomy anchors. It will be difficult for people with a security anchor to cope with major organizational change and "portfolio" careers, and the long working hours culture prevalent in the UK will be a challenge for people with a lifestyle integration anchor. The situation of engineers who have a technical anchor can be particularly difficult.

BOX 8.4
Schein's career anchors

1   *Managerial competence*: These people want to manage others and prefer to be generalists rather than technical experts. They are interested in advancement, responsibility, and leadership and tend to be motivated by pay.

2   *Technical/functional competence*: People with this career anchor value their technical expertise and actually doing the job well is important to them. They are particularly concerned with developing and maintaining their expertise.

3   *Security*: These people are most concerned about having a safe, predictable, and familiar work environment. Job security is obviously important but so are things like familiar routines and staying in one location.

4   *Autonomy and independence*: These people want to be free to do their work in their own way and chafe at restrictions, rules, and procedures.

5   *Entrepreneurial creativity*: People with this anchor want to produce goods and services and build up their own businesses and organizations.

6   *Pure challenge*: These people are highly competitive and want to win against all the odds.

7   *Service/dedication*: These people want work that reflects their social, political, or religious beliefs, and values within an organization that endorses and enacts those values.

8   *Lifestyle integration*: These people are most concerned to achieve a balance between their work and personal lives so that no one aspect dominates to the detriment of any other.

It is worth pausing to consider the engineers' case in some detail because it provides a good illustration of the usefulness of the career anchor framework (see Case study 8.2).

It has always been a mystery to me why professionals who have excellent technical skills have to become managers in order to progress their careers. What seems particularly illogical to me is that it is usually those who are technically most excellent who get promoted out of the job they are so good at. One finds it in so many occupations—among them teaching and nursing. In my study of senior academic women (Doyle, 1998), researchers with international reputations were spending much of their time struggling with financial management, for which they had had little or no training. It always amazed me that a high-tech company, which relied on the development of leading-edge technology, did not have *practising* hardware and software engineers

Case study 8.2: Engineers and scientists

Dalton and Thompson (1986) studied the careers of hundreds of engineers and scientists and came to the conclusion that some professionals in organizations passed through four distinct career stages. Interestingly, these were *not* age related. The average age of the professionals in each of the four stages varied by only 3 years—38 to 41. Neither did formal positions in the organizational hierarchy account for progress through the stages. More than half at stage III had no formal supervisory or managerial position and even a significant number at stage IV had only informal influence. However, those who had reached stage IV were far more valued by their organizations than those at stages I and II.

Stage I. People in this stage usually worked under the supervision of another professional and did most of the detailed and routine work in larger projects.
Stage II. People at this stage tended to specialize in one area and were responsible for their own projects or a clearly definable part of larger projects. They worked independently and developed an internal and sometimes an external reputation.
Stage III. People in this stage had a greater breadth of technical skill and could apply those skills in broader areas. They become involved in the development of others through providing ideas and information or acting as mentors or leaders of small groups. They also acted for the group by mediating with outside groups, e.g., getting research funding or liaising with higher management.
Stage IV. People in this stage provided direction for a significant part of the organization and exercised a good deal of formal or informal power. They represented the organization to internal or external individuals and groups and they sponsored promising individuals for crucial future roles.

Since these individuals were all of a similar age and were all technical experts in their field, what could explain the different rates of progress and the career stage attained? Maybe differences in levels of technical expertise could explain some of the variation but Dalton (1989) links progress through these stages to Schein's career anchors. Those still at stage I may have had an autonomy or independence anchor, which meant that they moved constantly between organizations, unable to find a satisfactory niche. An alternative for such people is to operate on the periphery of organizations as independent consultants, hired for their technical skills only. Such people may constitute many of those at stage II. People at stage IV demonstrated the leadership function consistent with Schein's managerial anchor. It is interesting to note that few of these engineers and scientists were able to progress their careers unless they took on a wider managerial role, corroborating Bailyn (1980) who came to similar conclusions. Technical skills were not enough and indeed Dalton (1989) argues that processes within organizations can actually hamper the development of technical competence in such people by, for instance, keeping them too long on projects using obsolete technology or failing to provide adequate training and development. Certainly, it was my husband's experience in a computing firm, that "career development" in the R & D team tended to consist of taking excellent programmers and promoting them to become untrained and inadequate managers who soon lost their technical edge.

on its Board of Directors, but a separate career structure for technical staff seems to be quite rare. The only reasons for this puzzle seem to lie in politico-sociological arguments about the value we currently place on managerial as opposed to any other kind of expertise. In any case, the folly of suppressing the development of professionals who have a technical anchor should be apparent. At best an organization is likely to lose key technical experts; at worst, it may be left with resentful, demoralized staff with outdated skills.

Holland's theory of occupational choice

Holland (1985) believed that there are six pure types of vocational personality and that occupational environments can be classified in the same terms. Individuals seek to achieve congruence between their personality and their work environment. The six types are briefly described in Box 8.5.

Few of us can be described as "pure" types. Most people have stronger preferences for or similarities to some types than others. The relationships of

---

BOX 8.5
Holland's types of vocational personality

Realistic: This sort of person is practical, down to earth, and hard-headed. They may have mechanical ability but may lack social skills. They like realistic jobs such as mechanic, surveyor, farmer, plumber, and electrician.

Investigative: This type is analytical, curious, independent, and introspective. They may have good scientific and mathematical ability but may lack leadership skills. They are best suited to investigative jobs such as biologist, chemist, physicist, and engineer.

Artistic: This type of person tends to be original, creative, unconventional, emotionally expressive, and impulsive. They are often artistically skilled in writing, music, painting, and design but tend to lack attention to detail and clerical skills. Most suitable jobs include composer, musician, stage or film director, writer, actor, interior designer, and advert designer.

Social: This type of person is friendly and empathic, warm, and tactful. They have highly developed social skills but may lack mechanical and scientific ability. They are best suited to jobs which involve close interaction with other people such as teacher, religious worker, counsellor, and clinical psychologist.

Conventional: This type of person is careful, conscientious, and conforming but can be inflexible and unimaginative. They may have clerical and arithmetic abilities but often lack artistic abilities. They are best suited to jobs such as bookkeeper, financial analyst, banker, tax expert, and accountant.

Enterprising: This type of person is adventurous, ambitious, energetic, self-confident, and sociable. They have good leadership and speaking skills but may lack scientific ability. Most suitable jobs include salesperson, manager, business executive, television producer, and buyer.

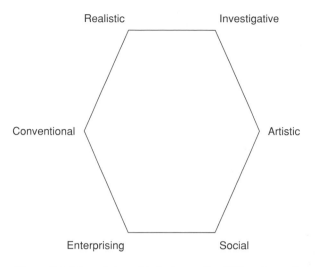

Figure 8.1 The relationship between the different vocational personality types within the individual.

each type to the other are usually represented in a hexagram as in Figure 8.1. The hexagon format tends to emphasize that types on opposite corners are generally speaking opposites in their vocational interests and personality. Adjacent types are more similar to each other. Holland (1985) suggests that people can be usefully described in terms of the three types they most closely resemble and that since people influence the climate and culture to which they belong, some people will be more "fitted" to some organizations than others. Thus someone who has the strongest similarity to the artistic type with some elements of the social and enterprising types may fit best in an organization valuing creativity and originality, such as a television advertising agency. Such a person may not thrive in a high street bank or a rigidly bureaucratic culture. Someone whose preferences are mainly investigative but with elements of the artistic and social would make a good research scientist and may be the sort of person who reaches stage IV in Dalton and Thompson's (1986) scheme.

The interest of employers in achieving these kinds of person–organization fit are reflected in the increasing use of personality instruments in selection and development processes. Burke (2000b) has produced some fascinating evidence to show that congruence between the values and needs of individuals and organizations not only led to higher job satisfaction but also had a positive impact on the bottom line. Using a large database he measured individuals' needs and values using the Motivation Questionnaire (Baron, Henley, McGibbon, & McCarthy, 1998), which included factors such as need for achievement and need for affiliation. Measurement of organizational culture via the Corporate Culture Questionnaire (Davies, Phelp, & Warr, 1997) gave rise to two main factors. The first of these he called rational

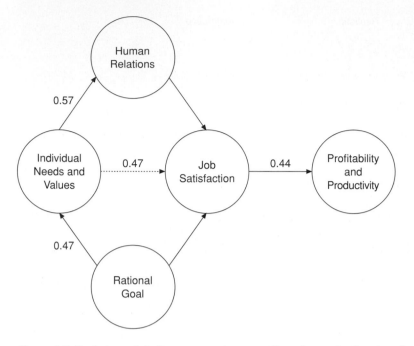

Figure 8.2 Burke's model of person–environment fit and organizational performance. Reprinted with permission of the author.

goals—the extent to which the organization had an orientation to customer care, favoured a longer-term view, and had clear organizational goals. The second involved human relations—the extent to which the organization showed concern for career development, sought to empower its workers, and valued creativity. He then analysed the data using a statistical technique called structural equation modelling. What this does is to allow you to construct models of the relationships between variables and then to test which of the hypothesized models actually fits the data best. As a result, Burke (2000b) developed the model in Figure 8.2 of the relationships between individual needs and values, organizational culture, individual job satisfaction, and organizational profitability and productivity. If Burke is correct, nearly 20% of the variability in organizational performance can be explained by the fit between individual needs and values and organizational climate and culture. He concludes, "knowledge of the links between individual needs and values can provide powerful information in managing organizational culture through selection either by hiring those people who will maintain the culture wanted . . . or through development by increasing employees' awareness of the match or otherwise between their individual needs and values and the cultural factors important to organizational success" (p. 141).

Burke would probably regard these initial findings as rather tentative, but they are promising and point to the value of frameworks such as Schein's

EXERCISE 8.2
How far do Schein's and Holland's frameworks work for you?

Decide which is your career anchor and which of Holland's types you most resemble. Then choose which types are closest to you in second and third place. Then do two things:

1 Examine the consistency of the two frameworks: Is what they tell you about yourself compatible? Does one add insights which the other doesn't?
2 Consider to what extent your needs, values, and personality fit the culture of your current organization. What incongruences do you see and how does this influence your feelings and behaviour? What sort of organization would fit you best and how might this influence your future career choices?

It is very important to emphasize that this exercise can only be very tentative and indicative. Even a full assessment of your interests and personality by a qualified professional could give you no more than some helpful leads and possible insights. So don't take the results of this too seriously!

career anchors and Holland's theory of occupational choice in career guidance and career management and development.

I feel that it is time for another exercise, so please turn to Exercise 8.2.

A summary of conclusions so far

It seems to me that we have covered a lot, and maybe the reader needs to pause for breath and consider what all this means. What follows are the conclusions I have come to in the course of researching and writing this chapter.

*   Though the various lifespan and career stage models can provide some insights into people's decisions and behaviour, most are too static, narrow in focus, and stereotypical to be particularly useful to explain today's "boundaryless careers".
*   More useful is the work on transitions, and this prompts the suggestion that far from being age-related inexorable phases in the life path, career stages may be constantly repeated cycles, as people change jobs and even occupations several times in the course of their working lives.
*   The question of the flexibility and adaptability of older workers is raised. Demographic changes mean that, in the developed world, there will be fewer young people entering the workforce and employers will be forced

to rely more on older workers. (Commentators are also predicting that the difficulties of providing adequate resources for retirement will force many people to continue working into old age.) Ageist attitudes are not helpful in this endeavour and some lifespan theories (e.g., Super's maintenance stage) encourage negative age stereotypes. Cognitive age may be a better indicator of what older workers may have to offer than chronological age, maybe because it reflects fundamental values and aspects of personality. The young at heart may be "younger" than the young in body.

- The issue of what organizations can do to help individuals make transitions and improve their performance is also raised. In perhaps simpler days, a formal induction programme and informal organizational socialization, especially in professional and managerial occupations, was maybe enough. Now, it is clear that for many people, this process must be repeated several times in their working lives and, if people are to become maximally effective in the shortest possible time, they need help to cope with transitions. This may be provided by a constructivist approach to selection with realistic job previews, and a mentoring scheme in the encounter phase. Personal development plans together with careful sequencing of projects and challenges in the adjustment/ stability stages can contribute to increased effectiveness. These may also prevent "plateauing" and "retiring on the job", and keep key people productive and on board.

- Frameworks that promote the identification of the basic orientations of individuals and organizations and the fit between them are valuable in the processes of career guidance, selection, and career management and development. Increasingly, the fit between an individual's personality, needs, and values, and organizational culture and values is seen as important not just for well-being and job satisfaction but for productivity and profitability. Here we may glimpse one of the missing links between job satisfaction, motivation, reward systems, and performance. It is a moot point whether basic facets of personality can be "developed" or changed, but increasing a person's self-awareness of the congruence, or not, between individual and organizational value systems at least allows the option of sensible career management. An organization that is clear about its own value system can be more clear-sighted in the types of people it wants to select and mould.

- Potentially, development activities represent a "win–win" situation for individuals and organizations. Individual aspirations and talents can be aligned with business objectives. Attention to "fit" by selection, development, or both, can contribute significantly to business success. Individuals can build on their strengths and work on their weaknesses and their commitment to the organization may thereby be enhanced even in the context of short-term contracts and the "Me plc" approach. People looking to enhance their skills, CVs and employability for the next job aren't in the business of being incompetent in their present posts. Even if they don't always stay as long as employers might like, anything that enhances their performance in the meantime must be a good thing.

- A hundred factors can operate to thwart this rosy picture. Financial necessity and lack of alternatives may prompt people to accept and continue in unsuitable occupations and inimical organizations. Organizations may be financially constrained to regard developing people who may not stay long as an expendable business cost rather than a crucial investment in their future and profitability. Even so, looked at in the light of these ideas and findings, an aggressive "You're on your own"/self-development approach to human resources seems extraordinarily short-sighted from an organizational point of view. In such circumstances, what else are people to do but to serve the bottom line of their own self-interest and to use their organizations insofar and as long as it suits them? Fortunately, not every organization is so blinkered (see, e.g., Parsons & Stickland, 1996), and some are coming to realize that even "self-development" needs to be supported if it is to result in enhanced performance (Stickland, 1996). Arnold (1998) comments that organizations are again entering into partnership with employees to promote career management and development.
- Since both business success and the formulation of effective personal development plans seem to rely on accurate assessment of people's strengths and weaknesses, we are back with the notion of appraisal of work performance. Can appraisal and development be more effectively integrated to serve individual and organizational needs? Perhaps they can.

Approaches to career development

Arnold et al. (1998) list 15 different career development interventions that can be implemented in organizations, ranging from mentoring and coaching, to career planning workshops and outplacement counselling. Here I have space to consider just two, chosen because they combine assessment and development—development centres and multi-rater feedback.

Development centres

Goodge (1997) charts the progress of assessment centres (ACs) in the UK since the 1970s. The first generation of ACs were purely assessment oriented and could often be very stressful. Over several days, participants might have no respite from being observed and judged from the moment they appeared at breakfast until they retired to bed. Googe says that ACs became "tests of nerve and stamina" and could be quite inhumane. If they were used to assess potential or to select for promotion from within existing staff, they often had a demoralizing and demotivating effect. The "second generation" of ACs, which emerged in the 1980s, were designed to be more employee friendly. Participants were more involved in the process, were given briefing sessions, and were allowed to ask questions. Detailed feedback was given to candidates after the AC, and sometimes this would be linked to personal development planning. They became much more relaxed affairs; assessors would strive to be friendly and approachable and candidates would be told exactly when they were being assessed and when they could relax their guard. Goodge notes that although they were often called development centres, especially when existing staff were involved, they were still linked to appointment decisions and people knew that important career decisions would hinge on their performance. As tools for development—if, for instance, they were used to assess potential—post-centre inaction could still limit their usefulness.

Goodge (1997) believes that true development centres (DCs) did not start to be widely used until the mid-1990s. Although there was still an element of assessment, the real purpose was for the DC to be a learning and development exercise in itself. Candidates were renamed as participants and assessors were called coaches or advisors. The role of assessors became that of facilitators, who gave detailed feedback after, and sometimes during, the exercises. The aim was that the exercises should become open and honest discussion about performance and development needs and the DC itself was intended as just the first stage of a much larger performance-enhancing process. In the course of this metamorphosis, tests and "off-the-shelf" exercises were replaced with real-life business problems, with senior managers sometimes giving presentations to explain the issues facing the company and participants having access to all the available information. If done well, these "true" DCs could not only identify individuals with potential but could serve a valuable career development function.

Lee (2000) argues that the transformation from ACs to DCs was never as clear-cut as Goodge (1997) suggests, and in his paper he gives an interesting discussion of some of the practical issues surrounding the implementation of DCs. He describes the use of a "fourth generation" design defined as a "peer centre". A peer centre involves "peer feedback and coaching after each exercise, integration of off-the-shelf tests and exercises, real life problems and activities to identify personal values, personal and group planning on the centre, greater emphasis on follow-up e.g. through mentoring" (p. 11). Multi-rater feedback is often incorporated into the centre and there is the intention to continue peer coaching and support after the centre. Lee issues some warnings; there is still a need to train participants to observe and give sensitive feedback, there is a need for a period of reflection to assimilate all the feedback and translate it back to the workplace before true development can begin, and there must be mechanisms to turn the centre's outcomes into practice before their impact fades. Gaining top level support for the DC, whether line managers should be involved, and sustaining the development process afterwards all seem to be rather thorny issues, although various solutions and case studies are offered.

Though DCs can be valuable, they are expensive in terms of their design and development, the training of assessors to observe, record, and give feedback, the time of all the participants during the DC, and all the follow-up needed afterwards. Furthermore, the timescales of DCs are not suitable for assessing development needs in some competences, e.g., those that concern balancing short- and long-term goals and pressures. Multi-rater feedback is much cheaper and may be equally effective.

Multi-rater feedback

Multi-rater feedback is a more intensive, sustained, and systematic form of developmental appraisal, which also includes formal assessment. The process begins with the person completing a questionnaire that asks for self-ratings of performance on the competences required to do the job. Some of these instruments have been developed by test publishers, e.g., *Synchrony* (Development Dimensions International), *Benchmarks* (Oxford Psychologists Press), and the *Perspectives on Management Competencies* (Saville & Holdsworth) but many more are constructed in-house. These questionnaires are designed to measure performance dimensions, competences, leadership qualities, and so on. In addition to self-ratings, the person's performance is also rated by his or her boss and by a number of the person's peers and direct reports. The idea is that the number of raters, all with different perspectives and knowledge of the person, will together produce a more accurate and rounded picture of the person's strengths and weaknesses. Once completed, all the questionnaires are returned to a central point and the results are turned into a confidential written report, which often uses graphics to highlight discrepancies between the person's self-ratings and others' ratings. A trained facilitator discusses the results with the focal person and helps him or her to to plan development activity. Sometimes this process may also include discussion with the colleagues who completed the questionnaire, but they need training to handle this sensitively—giving specific examples of behaviour is most helpful.

Geake, Oliver, and Farrell (1998) report that in a survey of medium to large UK companies about half of those sampled currently use multi-rater feedback and 74% expected to expand its use. It is mainly used to develop senior managers (81% of users), but it is also used for junior managers (43%), supervisors (18%), and other grades (17%). Almost all said it was a success and among the reported uses were individual coaching, changing managerial style, career reviews, performance management, identification of training needs, and teambuilding. Almost all respondents claimed to use it for developmental purposes but half also used it for performance appraisal and a small proportion (7%) linked it to PRP.

So it is becoming a widely used technique, but does it work? McEvoy and Beatty (1989) found that staff ratings were better short- to medium-term predictors of managerial performance than assessment centres. Baldry and

Fletcher (2000b) found that the congruence between self and others' ratings of a sample of managers increased over time because the others' ratings became more favourable—the implication being that the multi-rater feedback and associated development process had improved the managers' competence. Burr (1998) conducted a study of financial services salespeople over 9 months and found that the impact of multi-rater feedback was greatest upon the performance of the least competent people. Alimo-Metcalfe (1998a) also reviews a good deal of evidence for the effectiveness of the technique.

Despite all this positive evidence, some issues, till need to be addressed. It is hardly surprising that 75% of user companies said that their employees felt threatened by multi-rater feedback. If the process is handled badly it could have a very destructive effect. For instance, Hind (2000) suggested that multi-rater feedback may be inappropriate for young inexperienced managers because it tends to produce an imbalance of very negative feedback that may be demotivating. It is easy to see how people could become overwhelmed by their perceived deficiencies and merely become anxious or depressed. Alternatively, to protect their identities, they might reject the feedback entirely.

Alimo-Metcalfe (1998a) and Clifford and Bennett (1997) have formulated guidelines for best practice. All commentators agree that multi-rater feedback should only be used for developmental purposes so linking it to PRP is very dubious practice. It is important that the rating questionnaire should be appropriate for the person's job and is valid and reliable. Fletcher et al. (1998) conducted a pilot study with a multi-rater instrument used by an oil company and revised it in the light of their findings. The improved psychometric properties of the final instrument produced "dramatic" improvements in the accuracy and quality of the feedback. This issue is worrying because many questionnaires are produced in-house and are not investigated for their accuracy and validity. Other safeguards include the need for very careful introduction of multi-rater feedback systems. Employees should be fully informed about its purposes, advantages, and limitations. It is all very well telling someone that criticism merely involves subjective judgements, but in personal relationships it is subjective impressions that count as reality (e.g., if everyone says that you have little social sensitivity, then you may be inclined to think that this must be true). Employees must have the opportunity to ask questions and deal with their fears. Other principles of good practice are:

1   The process should be voluntary.
2   The data should be owned by the individuals, not the organization.
3   Confidentiality should be assured.
4   Individuals should choose their others.
5   Others' ratings should be presented as averages to preserve anonymity.
6   The process must be supported by a sensitive feedback session.
7   Follow-up support and development opportunities are essential.

Another issue concerns the extent to which ratings are open to bias. Goodge and Burr (1999) note that it is often difficult to get people to make negative ratings, but if real weaknesses are not identified there is no motivation to develop. Warr and Bourne (1999, 2000), among many others, found that self-ratings tend to be higher than others' ratings, although their later paper suggested that this applied more to self-ratings of interpersonal skills than to perceptions of technical effectiveness. Nilsen and Campbell (1993) argue that people rate their competences higher than they actually are, citing evidence from a meta-analysis by Harris and Schaubroeck (1988), which shows that on ratings of job performance, peers and supervisors agree to a much greater extent than self-raters and supervisors or self-raters and peers. However, Warr and Bourne (1999) found more agreement between people's self-ratings and the ratings of peers and followers. Bosses' ratings were most negative and appeared to be influenced by stereotypes. For instance, older managers were negatively rated on flexibility, creativity, and innovation. Such discrepancies in ratings might be expected since what bosses value may not be the same as what followers value, and each group will see a different side of the manager's behaviour. Indeed, Bourne, Oliver, and Warr (1998) argue that the discrepancies between different groups of raters gives multi-rater feedback its richness and value. This may be true but, if the "messages" given to the focal person are very inconsistent, on what basis should a development plan be made?

An interesting literature is developing concerning the influence of personality on the multi-rater feedback process. Warr and Bourne (1999) found that the people who over-rated themselves also scored higher on the socially confident, innovating, controlling, achieving, and competitive scales of the Occupational Personality Questionnaire. People who under-rated themselves scored high on the worrying, traditional, and modest scales. Alimo-Metcalfe (1998a) quotes evidence that women are more likely to under-rate themselves or have few discrepancies with their others' ratings than men— traditional modesty perhaps? However, Alimo-Metcalfe believes it could be that women have a more transformational leadership style and so ask for more feedback in the normal course of events. Thus, they are more aware of the impact they are having on others. Gray and Farrell (1999) are developing a model of how personality influences the way people react to the multi-rater feedback process. Furnham and Varian (1990), studying reactions to personality questionnaires, found that extroverts were more likely to accept positive feedback and reject negative feedback than introverts, and the higher people scored on the neuroticism (emotional instability/ stability) scale on the EPI, the more likely they were to accept negative feedback. Gray and Farrell believe that similar effects are likely to occur with multi-rater feedback. This work must raise some concerns about the possible negative effects of multi-rater feedback on vulnerable people's self-concepts and self-esteem, especially if best practice guidelines are ignored.

There is some controversy about why multi-rater feedback is effective. Goodge and Burr (1999) suggest that when ratings come from a trustworthy source, critical evaluations make the person feel uncomfortable and motivated to change. Others stress the role of self-awareness—it is only when we can see our weaknesses that we can do something about them. However, Baldry and Fletcher (2000a) found that managers were much more aware of their overall performance than of specific strengths and weaknesses. Perhaps, however, it is not so much the multi-rater feedback process itself which matters, as what happens afterwards. Edwards (2000), writing from a practitioner perspective, stresses the importance of the self-managed development activities that follow. In that case, all the multi-rater feedback does is to give good information about what is needed. The real development occurs when the manager plans to do something about it, actually learns what is needed, and then transfers it to the job. This is only possible if there is a supportive organizational framework. Unsurprisingly, but perhaps significantly, Bass, Avolio and Atwater (1996) found that managers who attended a leadership training programme after multi-rater feedback only showed improvements on the dimensions they had chosen to work on. Feedback is of no value if you don't act on it, or more importantly, if there is no opportunity to act on it. It could be argued that, in the end, what really improves performance is an environment that provides good training and development support.

Suggested further reading

Algera, J. A., & Kleinbeck, U. (Eds.). (1997). Performance improvement programmes in Europe. *European Journal of Work and Organizational Psychology*, 6(Whole No. 3).

Arnold, J. (1997). *Managing careers into the 21st century*. London: Paul Chapman Publishing.

Fletcher, C. (2000). Performance appraisal: Assessing and developing performance and potential. In N. Chmiel (Ed.), *Introduction to work and organizational psychology: A European perspective*. Oxford, UK: Blackwell.

Fletcher, C., & Baldry, C. (2001). Multi-source feedback systems: A research perspective. In I. Robertson & C. L. Cooper (Eds.), *Personnel psychology and HRM: A reader for students and practitioners*. Chichester, UK: Wiley.

Herriot, P., & Stickland, R. (Eds.) (1996). The management of careers. *European Journal of Work and Organizational Psychology*, 5(Whole No. 4).

Payne, T. (Ed.). (1998). 360 degree assessment and feedback. *International Journal of Selection and Development*, 6(Whole No. 1).

9 How to stop worrying and learn to love work: Counselling and individual development

In durance vile here must I wake and weep,
And all my frowzy couch in sorrow steep

O wad some Pow'r the giftie gie us
To see oursels as others see us!
It wad frae mony a blunder free us,
And foolish notion

Robert Burns, 1759–1796

Like all great poets and thinkers, Scotland's favourite son, Robbie Burns, can get to the heart of human experience in a few words. Looking for an appropriate epithet to summarize the spirit of this chapter I found this marvellous conjunction of what it means to endure despair about our lives and what counselling is all about. Traditional wisdom has it that Burns was being rather scathing about our tendency to think well of ourselves and thus "pride goes before a fall". But his verse could just as easily be turned on its head. The point is that too many of us do *not* think well of ourselves and imagine all sorts of failings and inadequacies, which can sometimes rob us of the ability to act to solve the problems that inevitably confront us in life. I will never forget the comment made by Beverley Alimo-Metcalfe in a personal development programme; "Think about how you talk to yourself —if your friends said that to you, would you ever speak to them again?" Maybe this is why our friends don't tell us what we need to know about ourselves! However, the point is that we are often our own worst critics and one basic aim of counselling is to prompt us to consider more positive and assertive ways of viewing things. The hope is that this may open up solutions to an apparently hopeless situation. Alternatively, we may be behaving in inappropriate ways—unable to see things from the point of view of others for instance—that may be making life more difficult than it needs to be.

Whatever the background theory or particular technique, counselling has at its heart the desire to give "unconditional positive regard"—the sort of thing your perfect mother would have given you if she could have put herself permanently in your shoes to see the world from your point of view, and hadn't been so needful, tired, and distracted herself. Unconditional positive regard is designed to give you the safety and space to see and acknowledge what is wrong, challenge your misconceptions, and thereby solve your own problems in your own way. This is potentially the "Pow'r" that does indeed give us the gift "to see oursels as others see us".

What has all this to do with the workplace? Well, a quick trawl through some recent textbooks (Arnold et al., 1998; Chmiel, 2000; McKenna, 2000) reveals that they all devote considerable space to the topic of job-related stress and they all quote research claiming that stress-related ill-health has risen sharply in the last decade. Significantly, it has been estimated that the costs per year of sickness absences for stress and mental disorders amount to 10% of the gross national product in the UK and 9.6% in Europe as a whole (Cartwright & Cooper, 1996). There also appears to have been a change in the nature of stressors at work. In the past, physically unpleasant or dangerous work conditions were the focus of attention. Although these are still important, the decline in heavy manufacturing industry and more rigorously enforced health and safety legislation means that relatively fewer people are exposed to serious physical hazards in the workplace. Now the most frequently cited sources of stress are likely to be work overload, time pressures, problems with social relationships at work, and inability to balance work and personal lives. In other words, psychosocial hazards are coming to prominence. Moreover, several landmark cases, most notably *Walker v. Northumberland County Council* (1995), where a social worker was awarded damages because his excessive caseload had led to two "nervous breakdowns", has led to legislation in the UK that emphasizes employers' responsibility to provide a psychologically healthy environment as well as a physically safe one.

The rising costs of stress-related ill-health and fear of litigation are prompting many organizations to set up Employee Assistance Programmes (EAPs). These can take many different forms, e.g., the provision of a fitness centre, health education programmes, and stress management training, but most often they involve, or also involve, a counselling service. In fact, Carroll (1996) comments that there may now be more people being counselled in schemes set up by organizations than there are in traditional private counselling settings. Counselling is therefore becoming an increasingly important part of organizational life.

What might counselling be able to offer troubled employees? First, stress reactions appear to depend on the person's perception that some aspect of the environment poses a threat to well-being. So, if this appraisal process could be changed so that the stressor was no longer perceived as so threatening, then the person may be able to cope better and feel less strain. For instance, a seemingly impossible workload may have arisen from a multitude of causes not necessarily connected with the job itself. The person may be reluctant to delegate, inefficient at prioritizing, too much of a perfectionist, or lacking in some skill that would make the job easier and faster. Once the person has identified and accepted that the problem may lie in his or her approach to the job, then an action plan can be formulated to combat the root cause. The person can then take control and experience a sense of self-efficacy and mastery instead of feeling overwhelmed and unable to cope.

Second, counselling can help when people are suffering severe reactions to "objective" stressors. Someone who has just been told that he or she is about to be made redundant will experience a range of negative emotions—shock, anger, betrayal, fear for the future, grief, loss, and so on. The counsellor can acknowledge the legitimacy of these feelings, allow their expression, and so help the person to work through them and come to a more constructive approach to planning the future. In the process people may discover that this job, or even this particular occupation, went against the grain of their essential selves—was not what they really wanted or needed—and so a new identity and a more satisfying life may be constructed.

However, the provision of a counselling service is only one way to help employees to combat stress at work. What are the other alternatives?

Murphy (1988) suggested that there are three levels of intervention to reduce stress-related ill-health:

- Primary level: Reduce the sources of stress, e.g., ergonomically designed systems and workspaces, job redesign (e.g., more worker participation and control), better management systems and practices, etc.
- Secondary level: Change the person, e.g., training, stress management, personnel selection (person–environment fit), mentoring and coaching, health and fitness programmes.
- Tertiary level: Treat the after-effects, e.g., employee assistance pro-grammes (EAPs), counselling, psychiatric treatment.

There are problems associated with all these interventions. It may well be thought that changes at the primary level would be most effective, e.g., reducing people's workloads by hiring more staff. However, increasing global competition and the need for economic survival makes organizations reluctant to take this route. Instead, primary interventions are more likely to involve increasing worker autonomy and control but this strategy is not a panacea and has had mixed success (see Jones & Fletcher, 1996 for a recent review). Also, job redesign has the potential to create as much pressure as it relieves since any change can be stressful in itself.

Secondary-level interventions focus on individual differences in reactions to stressors, sometimes to the extent that personal inadequacies are blamed for stress-related ill-health. As Semmer (1996, p. 52) notes, "there is a ten-dency to emphasise individual differences to the point where stress is being reduced to nothing but a problem of idiosyncratic appraisals and coping styles". Several commentators have criticized the effectiveness of stress-management interventions (e.g., Briner, 1999c), and Frese (1989) argues that they may even be counterproductive. Stress-management training may encourage the use of relatively unfamiliar and under-learned coping strategies, which itself could create more anxiety and stress and makes "relapse" likely. Indeed, Hockey (1997) makes it clear that long-term, active coping has costs for the individual, which may result in ill-health.

So we are left with the growth of interventions at the tertiary level, which some might say are a case of "closing the stable door after the horse has bolted". Kompier and Cooper (1999a, 1999b) take this line, arguing that it is better to prevent stress in the first place by improving the workplace than it is to treat already-damaged individuals. They present a series of case studies of best practice in stress prevention in a range of European organizations. But is this judgement of the value of workplace counselling too harsh? What are the advantages and disadvantages of EAPs? Are they effective, and if so what are the benefits? If they are not always effective what can be done to make them more so?

Counselling versus counselling skills

It is worth starting this discussion with some consideration of the role of counselling in occupational psychology. In general, occupational psychologists are not trained and qualified counsellors but they need to use counselling skills. One of the most important arenas for the use of counselling skills is in consultancy. There are various models of the consultant's role (Blake & Mouton, 1972; Heron, 1990), only one of which is based on the traditional medical model where the consultant acts as an expert, comes in and diagnoses organizational ills, and prescribes the "medicine" the client is expected to take, with not much say in the matter. Another model, which many occupational psychologists find more conducive to their philosophies, resembles a counselling relationship. The consultant starts by building a relationship of trust and negotiating a psychological contract. At this stage it is also important to establish how the client organization perceives the problem. Further information is then gathered and the consultant may be able to use a "fresh eye" to uncover the causes of the symptoms, which present as the immediate problem. This information, which may well challenge deeply held assumptions, is then fed back to the client organization. The organization is then encouraged to work with the consultant to devise an action plan to tackle the root causes. In this way the people most affected are empowered to own the problems and their solutions and are more likely to be committed to the action needed. Care also needs to be exercised when terminating the relationship. Hopefully, the organization has avoided excessive dependency and will be more proactive in dealing with its problems in the future. However, the consultant may also offer further support and services if these are needed.

Coming back to the counselling process, this has echoes of Egan's "skilled helper" model of counselling (e.g., Egan, 1994, 1998; Egan & Cowan, 1979). Sugarman (2001) notes that the model can be used reactively in helping

---

BOX 9.1
Egan's skilled helper model of counselling: A simplified description

1	Establishing the client's perspective (understanding the current scenario)	Involves "skilled listening"—giving the client *full* attention; "empathic listening"—"putting yourself in the client's shoes"
2	Facilitating new perspectives (defining the preferred scenario)	Involves reading between the lines and achieving a "helicopter view", asking probing questions, getting the client to work through the problem space; may involve "challenging"—more forceful questioning of assumptions that may be preventing the client from moving forwards—almost a "shock tactic" to jolt the person into a new way of thinking
3	Developing a clear plan of action	Involves the development of strategies to prompt the client to think how to get from the current to the desired scenario
4	Action implementation and evaluating progress	Involves facilitating the generation of solutions and helping the client to implement the plans and monitor their progress/success

---

people to cope with "problem situations" and proactively in the development of opportunities. Egan prefers to speak of "problem management" rather than "problem solving" because most difficulties of living have to be adapted to rather than solved or removed. His model of counselling proceeds in four main phases characterized by the main activities at each stage of the process (although after the first phase, any one session may range backwards and forwards and skilled listening and questioning are important throughout). This is summarized in Box 9.1.

This model of counselling occupies the middle ground between those where the therapist is more prescriptive and "instructional" and those that involve the counsellor as simply a "sounding board" who reflects back (repeats) what the clients have to say and then leaves them to come up with their own answers (see Feltham, 1999; Nelson-Jones, 1995 for discussion of various controversies and theoretical frameworks). Each stage in Egan's model in-volves a data-collection phase and, based on the data, a decision-making phase. So, for instance in the first phase, establishing the client's perspective is followed by agreement on what aspects should be focused on. In the fourth phase, the first step involves trying out plans and the second involves evaluating the reasons for their success or failure. Each phase is cumulative in the sense that each is dependent both on the success with which the issues of the preceding phase have been addressed and in the development of skills needed for the next phase. Some phases may take far more time, effort, and resources than others. The process is not a smooth, linear sequence.

Any effective counselling is a complex and intellectually challenging process and is often emotionally draining too. However, Egan's "skilled helper" model is a good one for the nonspecialist to use. Thirty or so hours of intensive training can allow most people to understand the basic tenets of the approach and develop the skills of listening and questioning that will suffice in many different situations. As well as in consultancy, it can be used in developmental appraisal interviews, negotiating goals and action plans, dealing with difficult colleagues, resolving relatively minor conflicts at work, giving feedback in assessment and development centres, delivering bad news, some aspects of careers guidance, and helping people to cope with many less serious personal and work problems. The trick is knowing the limits of your own competence. In particular, people who have suffered major trauma or who have serious mental health problems need to be referred for specialist help.

Many occupational psychologists go no further than this level of skill. Many managers are also expected to demonstrate at least this level of competence. In a climate of employee empowerment and transformational leadership, it may seem a natural part of the manager's job. However, Carroll (1996) argues that there are dangers associated with expecting line managers and HR specialists to act in a formal counselling role, the main one being role conflict. Especially in traditional "command and control" organizations, the line manager has a disciplinary function and is often involved in formal appraisals for pay and promotion decisions. In these circumstances, expecting staff to confide personal and other problems that may be adversely affecting their work performance is probably unrealistic. There is also the issue of confidentiality. If the line manager knows that the person's problems are damaging work performance and organizational survival, is it reasonable for him or her to keep quiet about it and exercise a nonjudgemental stance? HR specialists probably suffer similar problems. However, just as with occupational psychologists, the good interpersonal skills that counselling training helps to promote are vitally important competencies for managers. We must, however, distinguish very carefully between what a highly skilled and qualified counsellor can offer as compared to the nonspecialist with heightened interpersonal skills.

For this reason, some occupational psychologists choose to become fully qualified counselling psychologists too and specialize in this area. At the very least, an occupational psychologist may be called upon to advise an organization on whether more training, organizational change and job redesign, setting up an employee assistance programme (EAP), or all three simultaneously, would provide solutions for organizational problems. For this, one needs to understand the issues involved and so the rest of this chapter will be concerned with the pros, cons, challenges, and potential of providing a fully professional counselling service for employees.

A brief history of the development of counselling at work in the UK

The Industrial Revolution created great changes and stresses in society. The movement of the population from the land to the factories and cities disrupted family and kinship networks and created great changes of lifestyle. Factory work was dangerous and challenging in many ways. However, an upsurge in religious fervour prompted many philanthropic factory owners to try to improve the living conditions of their workers. Examples include the Cadbury and Fry families and Titus Salt in Yorkshire. However, for most factory workers the conditions in which they lived and worked were appalling. From as early as 1802, various Factory Acts were passed to try to reduce the rates of injury and death at work and gradually employers began to realize that it was in their own best interests to have a healthy and well-fed workforce. Thus, from the early 19th century, employers began to provide works' doctors, nurses, and social assistants, but nationally and locally this provision was usually uncoordinated and unsystematic.

During World War I and the advent of large numbers of women into the munitions factories, welfare provision became a legal requirement. Between the wars, companies' welfare provision became well established. Welfare workers were responsible for social conditions in the workplace such as canteens, facilities for drying coats, rest rooms, and so on. They also gave advice to workers on domestic and other personal matters and provided services such as visiting sick workers. Two factors contributed to these trends. First, the rise of Trade Unionism led to improvements in working conditions and second, with universal franchise, the growth of a liberal democracy encouraged corporate responsibility. So prominent employers provided occupational health officers, advice and welfare officers, retirement provisions, and facilities such as sports clubs.

After World War II the Welfare State was introduced, with free health care and the provision of pensions and many other benefits. Corporate taxation led many employers to ask why they should pay twice for the welfare of their workers so services were run down to minimum health and safety legislation levels. Throughout the 1970s and 1980s welfare provision remained minimal and things became worse during the recession of the early 1990s, when there was great pressure to cut costs by large-scale redundancies. Welfare in these circumstances might be limited to "outplacement" counselling for those who had lost their jobs—and these were the lucky ones!

Against this background, the growth of EAPs in recent years may seem somewhat surprising. EAPs have a long history in the USA—the first goes back to the 1920s at the Western Electric company of Hawthorne studies fame. Early schemes were set up mainly to deal with alcohol and substance abuse but they came to be concerned with the general social and psychological adjustment of employees. The aim was not entirely philanthropic, however; they were oriented to the achievement of an integration of corporate goals and employee behaviour, i.e., conformity and productivity. They were integrated by design into the organization, its management, and its culture.

In the UK, the growth of EAPs was later and much slower. We have already seen that a major impetus in the 1990s was company and governmental concern about the rising costs of stress-related ill-health, and health and safety legislation being increasingly interpreted to cover psychosocial hazards. However, many downsized companies also recognized that they had a problem with the morale and productivity of the traumatized survivors. The first EAPs were "in-house" and developed from the old welfare function, but as personnel increasingly became an "arm" of mainstream management there was a reluctance to take over the EAP function. The need for a separate, confidential counselling function came to be appreciated. Moreover, with the trend to "outsource" all but core business functions, EAPs were also set up as external businesses to which employees could have recourse.

Diversity of provision

This rich history of employee welfare provision means that there is now great diversity of provision both in its scope, quality, and above all, purpose (Carroll, 1996)—an issue to which we will return. Reddy (1993) conducted a survey and, from 400 replies from UK companies, found that 85% believed they were providing some form of counselling service to employees. Encouraging though this is, the diversity of provision can be gauged by the fact that, at that time, EAPs had been adopted by only 4% of the companies surveyed, and, in 60%, stress counselling was provided by personnel departments or line managers or both. The role conflict inherent in the latter option makes it less than ideal. A later survey commissioned by the Health and Safety Executive (Highley & Cooper, 1995) showed that 22% of workplace counsellors had no formal qualification or held only a basic certificate, and 45% rated the amount of further training they had received from providers as "nonexistent". Although this picture may now be changing it is instructive to compare this with the outline of a "complete" EAP provider suggested by Reddy (1997), which is shown in Figure 9.1. This provides a wide range of services from a stress helpline and stress management counselling, to careers counselling, development, and outplacement, to performance management, to providing training, to informing and shaping management policy. When evaluating the value of workplace counselling, this diversity clearly has to be borne in mind.

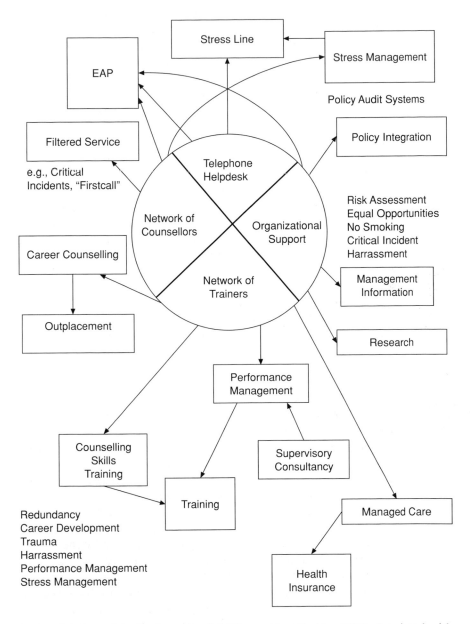

Figure 9.1 A model of a "complete" EAP provider (Reddy, 1997). Reprinted with the permission of the author.

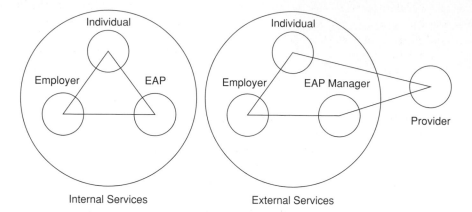

Figure 9.2 The tripartite relationship in workplace counselling (Reddy, 1997). Reprinted with the permission of the author.

The context of workplace counselling

Counselling within the workplace is fundamentally different from that in more traditional counselling contexts. The main one is that it involves not just a personal relationship between a counsellor and client but a tripartite relationship, which includes the employer who directly or indirectly pays the counsellor's wages. This is true whether the service is provided in-house or externally. The external provider may be one step removed from the organization, linked perhaps by an internal EAP manager, but the employer is still part of the relationship. This is shown in Figure 9.2.

This provokes the obvious question: Who is the client? And this raises immediate issues of conflicts regarding the confidentiality of the counsellor client/worker relationship, which is essential for trust and may determine whether the service will be used at all. Does the counsellor have a duty to disclose information to his or her employer that indicates a threat to other workers or the business? Reddy (1997, pp. 87–88) says that it goes further than this. "The essence of the debate is not about confidentiality at all, but about the legitimate rights, interests and expectations of employee and employer along a much broader continuum. That spectrum includes policy and practice in grievance and disciplinary procedures . . . and, with the ever shifting boundary between the commercially, politically or ideologically inspired "realities" of the right to employment, of diversity and equal opportunity in employment as opposed to the right to manage and to satisfy institutional shareholders." In other words, there is likely to be a clash of values between the counsellor's concern for the client and the employer's concern for business objectives. This is summed up in two other quotations: "There is no doubt that the aim of counselling is to promote growth and autonomy, to encourage clients to care for themselves, to be assertive and to develop their

Client not bound by confidentiality. —
∴ info to empl. (may be diff
How to stop worrying and learn to love work 363

potential" (Carroll, 1997, p. 14) versus . . . "The main criteria for therapy in the business context is that the method must fix the performance problem and must fix it fast" (Yeager, 1983, p. 137).

And that's not all, says Carroll (1996). Clients are not bound by confidentiality as are counsellors, and they are not averse to using the counselling for their own purposes. They may, for instance, tell their managers that the counsellor has recommended that they take time off from work or that the counsellor believes that poor management style is to blame for all their problems. This can make the counsellor's life very difficult.

The suggestion that values and agendas may not be aligned is a valuable insight, but against this, it could be said that counsellors and clients are not always in harmony in other contexts. Shea and Bond (1997), for instance, suggest that there is not enough diversity within the counselling profession and maybe too much of a preponderance of white, middle class, "educated" values. My former colleague Sarah Lewis pointed out that workplace and traditional counselling contexts have at least three features in common. Both are concerned with survival, growth, and performance or functioning of the person. In the business context, if the employer's concern is more about the person's role in the survival, growth, and performance of the company, does this make that much difference at a practical level? Provided the person is empowered towards growth, coping, and more effective functioning, do the different perspectives really conflict? As I said at the start of this book, pragmatism and "enlightened self-interest" have to inform the practice of occupational psychology. Moreover, Carroll (1994) describes the role of counsellors within organizations as one of "building bridges" or "sophisticated mediation", because counsellors stand at the crossroads of two worlds—counselling and business. In an ideal world, counsellors could play a major role in humanizing the workplace by their influence on management policy and practice—of which more later.

The purpose of workplace counselling

Perhaps this lies at the heart of the debate about the value of workplace counselling and whether it is a "sticking plaster" (or worse, a cynical ploy to avoid litigation for damages and unfair dismissal), or something that transforms organizational life and genuinely contributes to enhanced health, safety, and job satisfaction. Berridge (1999) believes that there is a continuum of employers' motives for setting up counselling provision, ranging from the angelic to the diabolical, as summarized:

1   A disinterested concern for employee well-being.
2   A recognition of the increasingly stressful nature of work.
3   A willingness to accept responsibility (equivalent to the "polluter pays").
4   A desire to create an image as a "caring employer" to increase morale and attract recruits.

5   A need to reduce the costs of workplace stress, e.g., absenteeism, turnover, retraining, etc.
6   A wish to improve quality of product or service via more committed,
less stressed staff.
7   A plan to avoid legal costs and awards for damages.
8   A plan to maintain or increase productivity in times of change, e.g.,
restructuring, downsizing, etc.
9   A tactic to supplement disciplinary procedures: An employee who does
not cooperate with counselling and its outcomes can be lawfully
dismissed.

Most employers probably fall somewhere in the middle of this range and
will have a mix of motives, but at least a quasi-disciplinary aspect can rear
its head even when intentions are good. Andrew Bull (1997) quotes an
anecdote of when he was interviewed by Trades Union representatives for a
counselling job. He was given the scenario of a woman coming for counselling with an unspecified problem but whose body odour was causing
problems on the shop floor. What would he do about it? He said he would
do nothing about the body odour unless this emerged as an issue they both
agreed to work on. A long intense discussion then ensued where it became
clear that the Trades Union saw counselling as a "diagnosis–instruction–
action" process—they wanted *their* problem fixed! This medical model of
counselling conflicts with most counsellors' view of their role but may be
very common amongst lay people, who may have a very hazy idea of what
counselling entails. If this is the case, it is hardly surprising that most managers think that the main purpose of counselling is to fix the problem and
get people back to work as soon as possible.

More seriously, Leymann (1996) quotes cases where people bullied to the
point of post-traumatic stress disorder have been ordered to undergo psychiatric examinations, which then resulted in diagnoses of paranoia or severe
personality disorder. This then allowed their employers to dismiss them and
severely reduced their chances of ever finding work again. Though these are
extreme examples, there is a real danger that workplace counselling could be
used to blame the individual for organizationally induced stress-related ill-
health. In the worst scenario, the very act of consulting a counsellor could
be interpreted to mean that the person was "not up to the job".

Clearly the dominant motives for counselling provision will have a
great impact on the nature of the service provided and, indeed, whether any
counsellor with an eye to professional ethics would choose to work for the
organization.

The impact of organizational culture on counselling

There have been many attempts to categorize organizations according to
different types of culture. In reality organizations do not embody pure types

but combine a mix of tendencies, some of which may be more dominant than others. Carroll (1996) uses Harrison's (1972) framework of four major types of organizational culture to assess the likely impact on counselling in each. *Culture Depts*

- In a *role culture* people and tasks are defined by their roles and responsibilities. Role cultures are bureaucratic and hierarchical, and are characterized by rules and procedures. The main dangers for employees in such cultures is that individuals may be sacrificed to organizational goals; roles may become artificial rather than "real" or personal ("not my job's worth"); and there is resistance to innovation and change. Such organizations are resistant to setting up counselling schemes but if they do, there is likely to be a "fix-it" emphasis. There may be a punitive element for troublesome employees, and counsellors will have very little opportunity to influence organizational policy.
- An *achievement culture* emphasizes tasks rather than roles, with individuals driven by enthusiasm and a desire to get the task done. The atmosphere will be innovative and collaborative and there will be constant change. The dangers of this type of organization are that individuals will sacrifice their own well-being for the sake of the team; creativity and innovation may be cherished for their own sake rather than their contribution to organizational goals; and there is the possibility that the lack of structure will result in chaos. Such an organization will find it difficult to accept counselling since the need for it will be seen as weakness. If counselling figures at all it will be outsourced to an external provider and there will be an emphasis on accountability—"fix-it-quick" again. It could be dropped as unpredictably as it was set up.
- A *power culture* emphasizes strength, dominance, control, and rationality. People's feelings will be largely ignored and what is valued is loyalty and hard work with clear (monetary) reward systems. The dangers of this type of organization include (again) that individuals will be sacrificed to organizational goals; individuals who do not or cannot live up to expectations will be punished; and there will be a generally negative view of human nature. In such organizations, if counselling services are provided at all, they are likely to be externalized and medicalized. The need for counselling will be seen as personal weakness and so will be marginalized. Counsellors will thus have no impact on organizational change.
- A *supportive culture* is one where relationships, mutuality, and communication are the dominant values. There will be an atmosphere of collectivity, autonomy, trust, continuous personal development, support, and intrinsic reward. The danger of this type of organization is that it emphasizes personal growth at the expense of the task; it could descend into "navel-gazing"; anyone who does not share the dominant values

only create dysfunctional conflict but will be roundly rejected.
is, the most promising context for a successful counselling func-
not fertile ground either. Since counselling will be seen as a
integrated aspect of the culture and part of everyone's job, for-
nselling services will be difficult to establish!

From this it might be concluded that establishing an effective EAP is a hopeless enterprise. Such a view is maybe too pessimistic but this analysis certainly illustrates the obstacles that must be overcome.

Case study 9.1: In the Navy

One of my professional doctorate students, Georgina Slaven, has been conducting a study of stress in the Royal Navy (Slaven & Doyle, 2001). Her remit specifically excluded acute battle stress so she was concerned only with naval personnel doing a job of work like anyone else. Her initial audit of job stressors, which involved nearly 2000 people (and an 80% response rate!), revealed the familiar litany of work overload, time stressors, lack of resources to do the job, and lack of autonomy and control in the lower ranks. But people in the Navy suffer additional (and often unavoidable) stressors in that they must spend long months at sea separated from their families, and sometimes they cannot plan their personal lives because shortages of personnel provoke unpredictable recalls to duty. On board ship, their living conditions can be very poor.

The Royal Navy is an interesting organization in that it seems to embody Harrison's four organizational culture tendencies in almost equal measure. It is obviously a very hierarchical role culture but also most definitely a power culture. At the same time it can be a supportive culture in that a career in the Navy is a way of life rather than a job, and, in preparation for battle conditions, groups need to be close-knit and mutually supportive. The least well-developed tendency is the achievement culture, but funding cuts, the "civilianization" of many roles, and staff shortages, which require improvization to get the job done, and so on, tend to blur the bureaucratic roles. Moreover, initiative and innovation are required in battle and are therefore valued—at least in the higher ranks.

The organization takes its support structures seriously and overall there is an emphasis on creating a close-knit and mutually supportive climate. The provision of employee assistance and counselling services are many and varied and reflect the diversity of organizational culture. For instance, the power culture aspect is reflected in a "medical" psychiatric service, which is responsible for identifying and treating people with serious psychiatric disturbances. Sick-bay personnel could also provide help with work and personal problems but most people were reluctant to use this service for anything but physical/medical complaints. The supportive culture finds expression in the service provided by chaplains but many will not avail themselves of this service because they are "not religious". There is also a kind of internal social services department. It is possible that the power and achievement culture elements may discourage people from seeking help from any source and there was some evidence to suggest that this was the case. Even so, many people simply prefer to talk to their friends when they are troubled.

As a role culture, one of the main sources of support is the Divisional Officers. Every naval rating has a Divisional Officer who is that person's line manager and has a number of responsibilities with regard to the rating's professional and moral well-being. It is sometimes difficult for an outsider to understand fully the nature of roles and relationships and their function within the hierarchy of the Royal Navy. Despite being line managers, Divisional Officers do not have an explicitly disciplinary function, except in so far that all naval personnel have a duty to maintain order in their vicinity. (It is the Commanding Officer who has responsibility for discipline on board his ship, but "discipline" has a very specific meaning in the Royal Navy. Flogging, etc., are outlawed but military transgressions can still be punished with imprisonment.) Divisional Officers have a counselling function, can offer guidance and advice, and also act as the accused's friend in any disciplinary procedures. They are also expected to refer people for specialist help when they are giving cause for concern. Thus, it seems that the Divisional Officers have an explicit welfare function in addition to their role as people's line managers. This role might parallel the position of "considerate" managers (transformational leaders?) in civilian life. Such people are task focused but also treat their staff with consideration and respect. The most effective leaders are said to inspire and empower their followers to achieve high quality work. However, it can be difficult for line managers to achieve this delicate balance between supportive leadership and the authoritative direction needed to "get the job done". It would hardly be surprising if some Divisional Officers were more skilled in achieving this balance than others. Maybe for this reason, some of Slaven's respondents were unwilling to make use of this resource when they needed help.

Thus, we have an extensive support infrastructure that is not functioning as effectively as it might be. And yet great care and expense has gone into creating and maintaining the support structure and yet more concern is evidenced in the Navy's commissioning of Slaven's research—the main purpose of which is to assess the effectiveness of what is already in place and to determine what more is needed. Moreover, there is little cause to doubt that all support personnel are dedicated to doing the best job they can.

This could be seen as a cautionary tale which many organizations might take to heart. The provision of counselling and support services may not prevent or manage adverse stress reactions. The Royal Navy may have more justification than many other organizations for saying that some stressors are either impossible or very difficult to eliminate. One could hardly have an effective Navy that did not deploy at sea! (With all the disruption to family and personal life that must then ensue.) Furthermore, warships are never going to be luxury cruise liners, and even though the design of new ships may pay more attention to the comfort and privacy of naval personnel, the timescales of shipbuilding and deployment must make this a very slow process.

In addition, funding for any service provided by the state depends on the decisions of the government of the day. In recent decades in the UK, Defence, in common with Health, Education, and many other public services, has tended to be seen as a drain on the taxpayer. A drive to reduce government spending led to successive cuts in the funding available to provide many services. In many instances, evidence that a service could still "deliver" despite serious cuts in funding led to the expectation that there must be a great deal more "fat" that could be usefully eliminated by further cuts. So working harder and longer, and enduring more strain to maintain an excellent service in adverse circumstances, was not rewarded. In such circumstances, a loss of morale becomes likely and it may become more difficult to recruit and retain staff, which then exacerbates the problems of work overload for those who remain. Private companies can also make the mistake of governments. Since cutting the workforce did improve profitability in the 1990s, company directors and shareholders may think that further cuts will do likewise. In fact, further cuts may remove the "muscle and bone" of a company which then reduces its ability to function. But when do you know when things have gone too far? When you can't fulfil your function? When you can't recruit or retain the people you need to supply the demand for your product or service? When you go bankrupt? Maybe we need more proactive measures to prevent these disasters.

Inability or failure to tackle the root causes of stress may not be compensated for by the provision of counselling and support services. Further, it is well to remember that an adverse economic climate, work overload, severe disruption of family life, and an organizational culture that tends to equate stress reactions with personal weakness, are features of people's worklife in a wide range of occupations.

Politics again ... tackling objective work stressors vs. economic survival

There is little point in arguing that objectively existing stressors cannot be tackled because economic survival is at stake. It cannot be an either/or argument. As Schabracq, Winnubst, and Cooper (1996) point out, if doing the job becomes unbearable, then people will not do it if they have any other options available. If this happens, organizations will not have the staffing resources to survive and people will lose all the benefits of meaningful work—a lose–lose situation. This already appears to be happening in some occupations, especially in capital cities. Poor pay and conditions plus very expensive housing costs means that vital support workers such as teachers, nurses, bus drivers, and so on cannot be recruited in sufficient numbers in London, and the Government is offering a number of inducements such as wages while training and low cost mortgage schemes to attract more recruits. They are also encouraging the immigration of workers from abroad. These trends can only get worse. Europe as a whole has one of the lowest birth rates in the world—there will be a great shortage of "homegrown" labour in the future. "Band aid" remedies will not suffice and transferring production overseas may, in the long term, encourage economic growth in those countries at the expense of economic and social collapse at home.

Multi-national corporations may not care but democratic governments, and their electorates, do. The first stirrings of (largely domestic) unease and unrest were seen in the (as yet fairly incoherent) anti-capitalist riots in London, Seattle, and Prague. That tide may turn to include a much wider cross-section of the population. We have already seen in Europe a general public backlash against genetically modified foods, which owes as much to distrust of the technology as to the perception that powerful corporations are exercising that power without people being informed, consulted, or given a chance to consent. The appalling spectacle in the UK of the transfer of BSE to new-form human CJD, via the food chain, has shaken people's confidence in the competence and willingness of governments to protect the populace from the disasters that can stem from too much unregulated commercial influence. Serious errors on the part of government, the civil administration, and agro-commerce almost destroyed the UK beef industry (Phillips report, 2000). Nike has been humbled by young consumers who, discovering that their trainers were made by exploited Third World child labour for a fraction of what they paid for them, stared at the cameras and said, "We made you and we can break you." Nike was forced to clean up its act (Rawsthorne, 2000). Similarly, the proliferation of internet "suck sites" where large numbers of disaffected consumers, and current and ex-employees, vent their bile can inflict serious damage on a company's reputation and brand image (Crush, 2000). Two recent books by respected authors (Klein, 2000; Monbiot, 2000) are "straws in the wind" regarding the extent to which corporations can continue to operate without regard for public opinion in Western democracies.

As Arnold et al. wrote mildly in 1998, "Organizations must begin to manage people at work differently, treating them with respect and valuing their contribution, if we are to enhance the psychological well-being and health of workers in the future" (p. 439). The consequences of not doing so, may be much worse than the suffering of dispensible workers—however great their numbers. A few years ago Charles Handy published an entertaining series of articles in *Management Today* where he exhorted readers to look to unlikely sources for inspiration, in particular, past literary masterpieces. Perhaps Gibbons' *Decline and Fall of the Roman Empire* should be required reading for MBA students and managers alike, for its case study of how unbridled greed, exploitation, and consequent decadence destroyed an empire. Just because it hasn't happened to us yet doesn't mean that it won't. The Roman Empire relied on slave labour and thought itself invincible in its riches and the stability of the "Pax Romana". Look what happened to them!

(As I am making the final revisions to this book, it is with some horror that I realize that I wrote virtually all of the last few pages, and certainly the last paragraph, a year or more before the terrorist attacks on New York and Washington on 11 September 2001. Many people are saying that the world has changed, I do hope it is for the better . . .)

Now let us turn to what might happen in a better world if the full potential of counselling psychology is harnessed. If organizations are going to spend scarce resources on EAPs, they may as well do it in a manner that is likely to bring real business benefits.

Integrating the counselling function into central business strategies

Egan and Cowan (1979) distinguish between "upstream" and "downstream" tactics. What is the point, they argue, of rescuing and resuscitating "drowning" individuals "downstream" to send them back "upstream" in the organization to become victims of the system again? The answer may be for counsellors to have an input into the formulation of policy and for management to make much greater use of the skills they can offer, especially in the management of organizational change. Carroll (1996) lists the skills counsellors have for facilitating organizational change and ameliorating its worst effects, as shown in Box 9.2.

In addition to this, counsellors can promote awareness that problems can reside in the individual or the organization but most probably in both. Looked at from this point of view, counselling, far from being a "band aid/ sticking plaster", has the potential to be used to intervene at the primary, secondary, and tertiary levels.

But before we get carried away, there are some cautions. One concerns the difficulty of persuading top management that counselling has this potential,

BOX 9.2
Carroll's list of counsellors' skills for facilitating organizational change

1 *Providing a forum*: Counsellors are in a unique position to gather and provide information (made suitably anonymous) about the real thoughts and feelings of the workforce; if top management heeds and takes these into account in their planning, this could result in greater humanization of the workplace; workers may feel that they have a voice and that their views are respected.

2 *Training*: Counsellors are well placed to provide interpersonal skills training that might help to eliminate poor management practice; simultaneously, they can provide "succour" for managers who feel threatened by their changing roles.

3 *Consulting with managers*: Again, their privileged position outside the management structure means that they can give advice to create more effective and efficient systems.

4. *Managing change and transitions*: Facilitating growth and change is the counsellor's stock in trade, i.e., helping people to cope with loss, confusion, uncertainty, and move on to "letting go" and creating a new identity; acknowledgement of these feelings and helping people to work through them may make the change process less traumatic.

5 *Helping deliver the bad news*: The relationship of trust between counsellors and clients allows them to deliver clear messages—we tell the truth and we help you to deal with it.

6 *Outplacement counselling*: Counsellors understand the impact of redundancy on individuals, and can help them to work through their feelings of shock and anxiety to move on; downsizing exercises are conducted with humanity and respect and this is likely to have a positive impact on survivors too.

7 *Modelling professional relationships*: The counsellor–client relationship can act as an exemplar of ethical and professional relationships throughout the company; it can act as a "call to conscience", to behave with respect, compassion, and concern.

8 *Empowering individuals and groups*: The main focus of counselling can become the model for organizations; managers can be trained to use counselling skills in their dealings with staff.

9 *Creating awareness of individual differences*: The workforce is not a uniform "mass" but comprises diverse individuals with different concerns, perspectives, and aspirations.

10 *The value of considering contexts in growth and change*: Counsellors can take a systemic approach, understanding that change in one part affects other parts; e.g., how top managers treat lower level managers cascades down the organization to the way

> customers are treated (Hampden-Turner, 1994); so one way to im-
> prove the quality of customer service is to change top management!
> 11   *Understanding individual, group, and organizational dynamics*: Coun-
> sellors know that there are constant shifts within and between
> people and in the organization as a whole and are sensitive to the
> "shadow side" of organizations (Egan, 1994)—the unconscious or
> unacknowledged ways of working, etc., which can have a profound
> impact on how people think, feel, and behave.

much less getting them to actually use it. Another is that some organizations
are totally unsuited to counselling solutions.

The "stressed" organization

Berridge (1999) proposed the concept of a "stressed organization", which is
exhausted and dysfunctional. A stressed organization is characterized by
an inappropriate mission, philosophy, or goals; unsuitable or outmoded
structures, communications, or control processes; lack of attention to job
design and demands; and ineffectual or ill-adapted managerial criteria and
supervisory styles. All this may be accompanied by external events such as
competitors' aggressive tactics, government over-regulation, corporate relocation, mergers, takeovers, and business closures. In these circumstances,
employee clients may be the most visible sign of an organization in deep
trouble. The counsellor's role in such an organization then becomes problematic. How should a counsellor deal with problems relating to real conflicts and dysfunctions within the organization? Should counsellors promote
optimism and positive coping when the situation is effectively incapable of
remedy? Counsellors may themselves become dysfunctional by trying to
promote values that conflict with those of the stressed organization.
In short, organizations must be assessed for the appropriateness of
counselling provision and, if the decision is taken to provide a counselling
service, its nature must be matched to the culture. Flowers do not generally
bloom in a desert; neither can counselling flourish in the wrong context.

Changes to the counsellor's role

Carroll's (1996) list of counsellors' skills implies quite a radical departure
from the way most organizations currently use the counselling function (if
they have one at all). In particular, the counsellor would assume a multi-
plicity of roles. He suggests that these might include:

- Setting up and ensuring suitable counselling provision.
- Advising line managers about approaching troubled employees.

- Counselling employees.
- Training and health education.
- Welfare.
- Casework supervision.
- Critical incident debriefing.
- Research.
- Advising on equal opportunities.
- Publicising the service.
- Educating staff about the role of counselling.
- Developing counselling provision.
- Monitoring effectiveness.
- Administration of the service.
- Making referrals.
- Mediating between client and organization.
- Managerial responsibilities.
- Facilitating organizational change.

In addition, the counsellor must attend to his or her own continuing professional development.

Clearly, if one person were to attempt all these different functions there would be severe role overload and overwork. But supposing there was a well-resourced team of counsellors, there may still be problems of role conflict. The most serious danger may be that counsellors come to be seen as another arm of management. Their privileged position of trust and independence would then be seriously compromised. Even if this danger was avoided, does counsellor training really equip people to fulfil all these roles, especially communication with top management and helping to formulate business policy? Many counsellors may be temperamentally unsuited to such tasks. Some indication of what may be needed is contained in the CV of the former Director of the Post Office's (now the Royal Mail Group) EAP (Highley & Cooper, 1995). He had several years' experience of operational management within a commercial organization and was a chartered occupational psychologist and a chartered counselling psychologist. People with that range of qualifications and experience are quite rare!

Other challenges faced by workplace counsellors include becoming the organization's "conscience", being used to do the organization's "dirty work", having to justify the cost of the service and avoid the threats to reputation by "failure" cases, being overwhelmed by the case load, succumbing to pressure to follow the organization's agenda (e.g., terminating therapy too soon), maintaining confidentiality, and dealing with isolation/marginalization (Carroll, 1997). From this, it is clear that the workplace counsellor's lot is not always a happy one.

What may be needed is for a team of occupational psychologists and personnel professionals to mediate between the counselling function and top management and help with some of the roles such as training, so that counsellors can concentrate on doing what they're best at—working with clients. Another alternative may be for organizations to use an external provider. A small in-house service with one or a few staff could not match the range of skill specialisms that may be available in a large external EAP firm.

Should counselling be "in-house" or "outsourced"?

Carroll and Walton (1997b) provide an extensive discussion of the relative strengths and weaknesses of internal versus external providers. As well as being able to offer a wider range of services, the main advantage of external providers is their greater independence, which means that they can distance themselves from the politics of the organization, challenge what is taken for granted internally, and offer clearer confidentiality. The main disadvantage is also their greater independence, which means that they may not understand the culture and politics of the organization and cannot educate the system in what counselling means or influence policy. Individual counsellors attached to external EAPs may not have experience of workplace counselling and the provider firm has to make a profit, both of which can limit flexiblity. Berridge (1999) is concerned about the maintenance of professional standards in some external EAPs. In the early days, EAP firms were run mainly by entrepreneurial professional psychologists, but a recent trend has been for counselling firms to be taken over by "large players in the personal and financial service sectors". In these circumstances, he is concerned that "being overly concerned with volumetric growth, increase in market share, reduction in unit costs, enhanced return on capital employed and satisfying client firms' needs" may threaten professional standards (p. 261). In effect, external EAPs are beginning to look very similar to the organizations whose workforces they are seeking to serve, with all the same pressures and dehumanizing tendencies. Who, one may ask, is going to counsel these counsellors?

Like external providers, the advantages and disadvantages of in-house counselling functions tend to stem from the same source, but this time it concerns the fact that they are a part of the organization. This gives them intimate knowledge of the culture, politics, formal and informal structures, processes, and practices within the organization. This helps them to adapt flexibly to client and organizational needs and to provide mediation. At the same time this makes counsellors more vulnerable to organizational politics, which may threaten their professional independence and make maintaining confidentiality more difficult. Other advantages and disadvantages of an internal service have been discussed. In the best of circumstances a well-resourced team of counsellors could do much to facilitate organizational change and humanize the workplace. In the worst of circumstances, one or two overloaded counsellors can be marginalized and exploited by an organization that wants merely to "cover its back".

Does workplace counselling work?

There is in fact, very little evidence about the effectiveness of workplace counselling in the UK. Most research has been conducted in the USA, which has a very different history of workplace counselling. Claims have been made that more than four dollars were saved in increased production, decreased sickness absence, etc., for every dollar spent on counselling.

In the UK there has been little research evaluating EAPs. This may be because of their relatively recent introduction. Certainly few, if any, companies appear to have integrated counselling into business objectives as advocated by Carroll. However, Highley and Cooper (1995) published an evaluation of the effectiveness of the Post Office's (now the Royal Mail Group) EAP. They found that absenteeism was considerably reduced, workers' awareness of stress and stressors was greater, and, in the view of the counsellors, coping behaviours were improved. However, job satisfaction and relationships with the employer were not improved. It is interesting to consider the context of this study. The Royal Mail Staff Attitudes Survey (Summers, 1993), revealed that 70% of employees were unhappy at work—"Uncertainty over privatisation, reorganisation of the service, new technology and worries over job security, all contributed to rock bottom morale" (p. 8). The EAP had been set up around the time of this survey and the fact that, in these circumstances, the EAP had any positive impact at all, says much for the potential power of workplace counselling.

Acute stress counselling and post-traumatic stress disorder

Before leaving this topic, it is worth considering another aspect of workplace counselling; that which is now routinely offered to those closely involved in major traumas and disasters, especially rescue workers. The UK courts have long been awarding damages to people who, while not physically injured themselves, develop post-traumatic stress disorder as a result of their experiences. Such cases include *Alcock v. Chief Constable of South Yorkshire Police* (1992) following the Hillsborough football stadium disaster where over 90 people were crushed to death, and *Hale v. London Underground* (1994) following the horrific Kings Cross underground station fire. Even without the incentive to avoid litigation, many employers, especially in the emergency services, now recognize the psychological trauma suffered by people who have to deal with death and destruction or acute physical threat. Some of these people go on to develop post-traumatic stress disorder, which can mean that they have to leave their occupation—as happened to the fireman in the Kings Cross case—or indeed, are unable to work again. For this reason, employers offer counselling after any serious incident, in an attempt to prevent post-traumatic stress disorder developing. But does such counselling help? Rick and Briner (2000) conducted a study to investigate this and found that sometimes the counselling did more harm than good because the quality of the counselling varied so much, and because counselling can make people vividly re-live the experience and thus compound the original trauma. However, most people appreciated management's provision of a counselling service and, as a result, felt that their employers were more caring.

Conclusions

This gives us two clues about the effectiveness of workplace counselling. First, the counselling must be of high quality—an untrained person, however sympathetic, is unlikely to have much positive impact. Second, the provision of workplace counselling may serve more of a managerial than a therapeutic function. Even the partial implementation of Carroll's (1996) model, if done sensitively by a management that genuinely has the well-being of its workforce at heart, may be effective because it makes people feel that they are being treated with humanity and respect. This is more than "shutting the stable door after the horse has bolted".

Summary

In this chapter I have argued that having counselling skills are important competencies for practitioners, managers, and human resource professionals in today's workplaces, and I have outlined Egan's "skilled helper" model as one that is useful for nonspecialists. However, I have also stressed that a fully qualified counsellor can offer a great deal more than this, and the relative independence of the counsellor's role avoids some of the problems associated with line managers trying to fulfil both disciplinary and counselling functions. I have also put forward the view that employee assistance programmes (EAPs) are often set up by organizations, not out of a disinterested concern for employee well-being, but to avoid litigation. There is a tension within any organizationally sponsored counselling service because the employer is always a part of the therapeutic relationship. This raises a number of difficult issues of professional ethics for the counsellor. In the worst scenarios, counsellors can be exploited to serve cynical organizational ends. I have explored Carroll's arguments for an expanded role for counsellors in the formulation of business policy and "humanization" of the workplace. Despite applauding the general idea, I have pointed out the dangers of this, not only because counsellor training alone rarely equips a person for such a role (or rather roles), but also because the counselling function could come to be seen as another arm of management. I have also discussed the general dangers of commercial pressures and dehumanizing tendencies making EAPs very like the organizations whose damaged workforces they are meant to serve. I have reviewed the meagre evidence of the effectiveness of workplace counselling (at least in the UK) and have concluded that at least two factors contribute to the success of counselling interventions: the quality of the counselling and the perceptions of the workforce that employers care about their well-being.

EXERCISE 9.1
Counselling dilemmas

Alone or in small groups consider one or more of the following case studies. In each case:

- What are the relevant counselling issues?
- What are the relevant organizational issues?
- What ethical issues are raised?
- What, within the three-way relationship, may have contributed to this dilemma arising?
- What earlier action might have prevented this dilemma from arising?
- If you were the counsellor what might you do?

Case A
In the course of counselling it emerges that a male client is drinking on the job and endangering the health and welfare of others. What does the counsellor do? Where are her responsibilities to the organization?

Case B
A client admits in a counselling session that she falsified information at an industrial tribunal that resulted in the dismissal of a senior manager. What does the counsellor do?

Case C
A manager phones the counselling service to tell the counsellor that a member of his department is about to be made redundant. Since she (the manager) knows that this member of her department is coming to the counsellor for personal counselling, she wonders if the counsellor will break the bad news to the client.

Case D
The workplace counsellor sees three individuals, all from the same department, and all complaining about the management style of the head of section. However, none of them is prepared to "go public" with this information. What does the counsellor do?

Case E
A client who has just had a very poor appraisal that affects both his pay and his career prospects tells his counsellor that his manager (who did the appraisal) has "had it in for him" for some time and has told him that even though he is doing very good work his appraisal will be poor because the manager does not want him in his department. What does the counsellor do?

Case F

A middle manager comes for counselling because his marriage is breaking up and his wife intends leaving the city and moving away. It will mean little contact with his children. He is distraught and the counsellor picks up that he has suicidal and violent thoughts. It is possible that the employee could be a danger to others, especially in stressful situations. What does the employee counsellor do? Has she responsibility to the organization as well as to the individual client?

Source: Reprinted with permission from M. Carroll (1996). *Workplace counselling*. London: Sage.

Suggested further reading

Carroll, M. (1996). *Workplace counselling*. London: Sage.
Carroll, M., & Walton, M. (1997). *Handbook of counselling in organizations*. London: Sage.
Feltham, C. (Ed.) (1999). *Controversies in psychotherapy and counselling*. London: Sage.

10 Where do we go now? (Well, I wouldn't start from here . . .)

There's work to be done and wars to be fought

William Shakespeare: Captain Fluellen *Henry V*

Shakespeare made the pugnacious and misguidedly enthusiastic Fluellen a figure of fun in *Henry V*. I always thought this was a bit hard on the poor Welshman. After all, he might be an ideal employee for many organizations nowadays. He is tireless in the pursuit of his duties, enjoys his work, encourages others to effort, has a sense of honour and integrity, and is intensely loyal to his master's cause (except for that small matter of the leek and a certain insensitivity to diversity . . .). So, what if you haven't read or seen *Henry V* and don't know what I'm talking about? Well, a pity, but you can take comfort in that most top management probably haven't either; if they had they would not be trying to turn us all into Fluellen clones. The point is, that for all his excellent qualities, he is pretty much a fool.

Still, not so much a fool, since he has given me (via Shakespeare of course), one of my favourite sayings whenever energy and exertion are required. "There's work to be done and wars to be fought", is my favourite rallying cry to both myself and my long-suffering companions. However, there is also a darker side to this. For many people work is a continual daily battle in the war to earn a living—always has been, always will be. Many others experience work as prisoners of war, forced into work which they do not really enjoy and subject to constant scrutiny by the "thought and performance police". Maybe your experience is different. Lucky you! But I must return to the themes of Chapter 2. Has work changed so much in recent years that for many it is becoming unbearable, or have we just changed our expectations? The "life isn't a rehearsal" mentality may have made people less accepting of the hardships that were taken as inevitable in the past. There is an interesting discussion of these issues in Rice (2000). You will probably recall that she reported on a survey of nearly 2000 UK managers and wrote that "half of Britain's managers feel too mentally and physically exhausted to do anything but work and sleep . . . nearly 30% say that their lives and work are out of control" (p. 48). In fact, what can be concluded is that 50% and 30% of the *sample* of people included in the research reported these reactions. Extrapolation to all UK managers is more tricky. Nevertheless, these results are interesting, not least because *Management Today*, which has sponsored this research amongst its readership every year for the past few years, has been reporting ever more pessimistic results, albeit based on smaller numbers of respondents with each successive survey. Rice speculates on some of the trends. Employment allowing a work–life balance was once seen as a "woman's issue", but Rice speculates that changing attitudes to parenthood and the increased participation of women in the workforce means that men are also becoming concerned with this balance, bringing it into the "mainstream". However, on the matter of working mothers, even women who don't happen to have children are resentful of the extra demands which are made on them as a result of those who do. "Captains of Industry", some of them women, say reasonably that if working mothers can't compete in hours and commitment, they can't expect special treatment. But if the dissatisfaction with work–life balance is general and work-related ill-health is increasing, can this problem continue to be ignored?

Should work consume almost all of a person's life? Didn't we try to abolish this in the 19th century? It is a fierce debate, and there are many strong economic (and historical and biblical) arguments to support the necessity of unrelenting labour. Are we in the West just getting soft?

All is not well in the occupational psychology camp either. Adams (2000c) suggests that the profession is currently undergoing something of an identity crisis and says this about the reasons: "Public confusion as to what occupational psychologists actually do, increasing competition from members of other professional bodies, and a rapidly changing workplace are all leading to a good deal of soul searching" (p. 15). To this I would add what I see as a totally unnecessary and unjustified split between the academic and practitioner arms of the profession (Doyle, 1999, 2000). At the 2000 UK BPS Occupational Psychology Conference, participants took part in an intervention known as a search conference (Emery & Purser, 1996; Holman & Devane, 1999). Three eminent practitioners acted as facilitators to guide up to 100 delegates through a structured series of exercises, workshops, and plenary sessions culminating with a set of agreed outcomes and actions for which participants took shared responsibility. Accounts of the process and the outcomes can be found in papers by Adams (2000a, 2000b), Azizollah (2000), Beech (2000), Buckland (2000), Crawshaw (2000a, 2000b), Frith (2000), Loughran (2000), Roseveare (2000), and Ryan (2000). However, three things struck me most. One is the richness of our shared history in occupational psychology/work and organizational psychology, but perhaps a change of name might clear up some of the confusion about what we do in the public mind. The second is the way the influence of our profession has waxed and waned throughout the 20th century. It has not been a steady increase in perceived importance but rather a series of spurts followed by decline—in fact, "booms and busts" in the fortunes of the profession. Many delegates found this reflection on our shared history to be the most moving and important aspect of the search conference, especially as some could give their experience of working with the pioneers and "giants" of the profession. The third point, which I want to make, is how much common ground we delegates from all sorts of backgounds still share and how much our basic priorities are coherent and unified. This last is easy to overlook when a group of intelligent, opionated, and vociferous professionals get together in a meeting or in print!

Most introductory textbooks in occupational psychology end with an account of the challenges facing the profession (see, e.g., Frese's excellent chapter in Chmiel, 2000), but in a sense I have tried to cover such issues throughout this book and so I want to do something different. Most of all, I want to continue the positive atmosphere of the search conference and end on an upbeat note. To this end, this chapter is composed of a personal selection of what I think are the most interesting and exciting areas for research and practice for occupational psychology in the early part of the 21st century.

Perhaps, given the "network world" (see Chapter 2, pp. 51–53) and its capacity to transform our lives, it is not surprising that my selection mostly involves applications of technology. In the area of the design of environments and of work, I shall consider new ways of working—telework and virtual teams. Rice (2000) suggests that this may be the answer to excessive work stress and may allow a better balance between work and personal life. Maybe . . . but I would argue that occupational psychology has a lot to offer to help such initiatives succeed in their intended purpose. In the area of selection and assessment I shall look at the revolution that is offered in the guise of computer-based assessment. This is not simply a matter of transferring traditional paper and pencil tests to computer mode. The dynamic capabilities of the VDU screen allow much better forms of assessment in job selection for people as diverse as fighter pilots, chief firefighters, and keyhole surgeons. There are important implications for training too. However, there are also challenges in this area, most notably the increasing use of the internet in selection, and here again, occupational psychology can lead the way in establishing best practice. In the area of human–computer interaction, I shall look at the way well-designed technology can make a real difference to the quality of life for people with disabilities. In particular, virtual reality systems seem to have a great future in rehabilitation and training for people with learning difficulties or brain injury. I shall end with some general thoughts about the future of the profession: our need to expand our activities into the large sector of small and medium enterprises, and the need for evidence-based practice and techniques that meet business imperatives as well as maintaining professional ethics and good practice.

In the end, I hope you will agree with me that work and organizational psychology is a vibrant and *useful* discipline, which can not only meet its own challenges, but which can offer much to solving the problems that confront organizations and the individuals who work for them. The future is bright if we make it so.

New ways of working: Telework and virtual teams

Some people would dispute whether doing some or all of your work from home is anything new; rather we have reinvented the practice that was almost universal before industrialization. Moreover, homeworking has historically been linked with sweatshops and exploitation, and with low-skilled, and low-paid work. As recently as 1999, Felstead and Jewson conducted interviews with 338 sewing machinists, packers, assemblers, etc., and found many examples of people who worked for less than £1 per hour (the current legal minimum wage in the UK is just over £4 for most adults) and suffered ill-health and injury without recourse to employment protection law. They also assert "the assumption that working from home makes for a happy combination of employment and childcare has been comprehensively disproved" (p. 34).

However, Standen (2000) remarks that "In many ways modern society has evolved to keep work and home life separate" (p. 85). Going to your *separate* place of work each day, being *seen* to work, and adhering to a company and management culture designed to keep you focused on your tasks was, and probably still is, the norm for most of us. On the other hand, home is often seen as a refuge from the workplace, and people can resent any intrusion of employment into it. However, this separation is something of a myth even in conventional work. People bring their personal worries and domestic concerns to work with them. Many people do "unofficial" overtime at home in the evenings and at weekends. In the latter sense, I, in common with most academics and many other professionals, have always done quite a considerable part of my paid work from home and sometimes wonder what all the fuss is about.

So what *is* new about telework or, as it is sometimes called, telecommuting? As we shall see, telework can take many different forms, but a list of common features include:

1   It commonly involves knowledge workers—often highly skilled and highly paid professionals and managers. (Although it can be extended to occupations such as data entry, word processing, and "call centre"/ telephone booking work.)
2   It involves full-time or part-time work remote from head office or a centralized workplace.
3   It relies heavily on communication/information technology, e.g., PC and modem, e-mail, internet, telephone, fax, etc.

4 In contrast to the self-employed, e.g., freelance journalists, accountants working from a spare bedroom, etc., true teleworkers are not "self-contained" but remain employees and rely on central organizational resources.

The real innovation in all this is that people who would normally work under the watchful eyes of their managers and supervisors in some central workplace, can now do so at some distant location, often at times to suit themselves. And all this is made possible by advances in communications technology. (Virtual teams are something else again and I'll come back to that topic later.)

According to some authorities (e.g., Kurland & Bailey, 1999), there are four main types of "true" telework:

1 Home-based telecommuting—the person's home is either the sole or part-time workplace.
2 Satellite office work—the person works at a more local "branch" office.
3 Telecentre or telecottage—the person works at a well-equipped local office, which is rented by several different companies: Telecottages are in rural areas.
4 Mobile teleworking—the person travels to customers/clients and uses the car, airport, or hotel room as a mobile office. "Base" may be any of the previously listed places, or central headquarters.

The research literature on the spread and extent of telework and its benefits and disadvantages for individuals and organizations is marred by a general failure to distinguish between different kinds of telework. Smith (1995) complains that all manner of very different types of workers are "lumped" together under the heading of teleworkers. Types of worker include anyone who is self-employed (from journalists, accountants, interior designers, etc.), full-time and part-time sales reps, and the traditional (exploited) "homeworkers" doing manufacturing/assembly-type tasks. For this reason, there are great variations in estimates of the prevalence of telework. For instance, Felstead and Jewson (1999) reckon that the numbers employed in industrial homeworking and telework in the UK rose from 345,920 in 1981 to 680,612 in 1998. They estimate that about 25% of the UK workforce is currently employed at home some or all of the time and predict that this will rise to 50% by the end of the first decade of the 21st century. In contrast to this, Huws (1999), reports that over 2 million people in the UK are teleworkers and that this represents 7.6% of the workforce! Smith believes that the term telework should be reserved solely for organizations that choose to have a part of their permanent workforce working away from the office on a regular and *formal* basis. On this definition, the "upsurge" in telework throughout the world may largely be a myth and all the data needs to be examined in relation to the definitions used.

Dooley (1996), reporting on an EU research programme that looked at telework in rural areas, gives us some insight into the diversity of telework. Within her relatively small sample of 192 rural teleworkers throughout Europe, there were people who were self-employed, freelance, worked for one or several organizations, had fixed working hours, were hourly paid, or were on piece rate. The types of work included stock control, bookkeeping, computer programming, management, filing business records, evaluation and documentation, data input/amendment, and word processing; 86% had had no training for telework and 65% had had no health and safety information. More men (56%) than women comprised the sample and two thirds spent 50% or more of their time working in their companies' central offices. This picture is echoed by Slepicka (1999), who reported on a survey in the USA, which found that, especially in sparsely populated Western states such as Utah and Arizona, a third to a half of companies claimed to operate a telework programme, and most said they would be expanding it. But . . . most companies had no formalized telework programmes, didn't provide special training for either teleworkers or their managers, didn't evaluate programmes for their effectiveness, and didn't provide ongoing technical support for teleworkers. The impression one gains is that a lot of telework is often an informal and somewhat haphazard affair that involves very different types of workers, but nevertheless encompasses an increasing proportion of the workforce in many countries.

This should not be surprising. Doubtless the first moves from the land to the factories was a piecemeal and haphazard affair—indeed, in my Pennine, Yorkshire homeland you are surrounded by the remnants of the first industrialized mills in rural river valleys; the concentration of populations in towns did not happen overnight. What excites me about telework is that we may be witnessing a reverse revolution in the making and one that *could* be far less traumatic. However, given the manifest advantages of avoiding the stress, wasted time, and environmental pollution of a daily commute, to say nothing of the benefits to organizations of cutting down on the costs of "downtown" offices, relocation expenses of staff, keeping key workers who cannot relocate or commute, and the ability to draw on a geographically dispersed pool of talent, the wonder is that telework is not far more widespread than it currently is. If this is the future of work in a world that is capable of such rapid transformation, why is it coming so slowly?

History and technological limitations

Oborne (1996) and Pliskin (1998) give fascinating insights into the technological changes that have made "true" telework possible and the challenges still remaining. They tell us that telework was not really feasible before the advent of the personal computer (PC), because mainframe computers and terminals were too expensive for home use. Nevertheless, multi-user software and telephone links from user terminals to the "host" computer gave people geographically dispersed about the company site access to centrally stored information. Thus, the term information technology was born, and a few workers such as programmers and data entry clerks were allowed to work from home.

The "PC revolution" in the 1980s introduced user-friendly software, which made using computers easier for nonspecialists, and there was a corresponding rise in the home ownership of computers. Word processing became an occupation ripe for telework. Meanwhile, laptops enabled mobile computer use, and e-mail was beginning to emerge. Nevertheless, PCs functioned in single user mode, so disconnecting computing from corporate information. Solutions to this problem included software that imitated the old terminal/host system and Local Area Networks (LANs), which enabled database sharing, e-mail file transfer, and so on. However, LANs only operated at one location.

Remote access from home or on the road was only available towards the end of the 1980s, and this suffered from a large technological impediment. With remote access to central information, "bandwidth" is all. Early systems relied on telephone lines, which are designed for minutes-long conversations *not* hours-long computer connections and data downloads. The narrow bandwidth of telephone lines makes access very slow, especially when the data involves video and voice, and is therefore expensive. Meanwhile, at the centralized workplace, broader bandwidth data communication lines with client/server computing proliferated, making the gap between office and home/road access to information even wider in the 1990s. So despite great technological advances, the ability to work effectively from home actually decreased during the 1990s.

Further technological advance helped somewhat. Digital technology in the form of integrated services digital networks (ISDN lines) allowed the transmission of more information in the same "time packet", but a well-known "in-joke" is that ISDN stands for "It's Still Doing Nothing"! Solutions were sought in highly developed cable and satellite broadband networks plus software techniques such as picture compression and digital signal compression. Even with all this, the amount of data that must be transmitted within a short space of time, e.g., in video conferencing, makes the use of this technology prohibitively expensive.

Some countries had built-in advantages. For instance, the USA had cable and satellite broadband networks already widely available and free local phone calls. In the UK, cable TV was much less widespread and even local phone calls can be very expensive when they extend for several hours. Thus, in the UK, home internet users have the common experience of spending hours trying to find useful information and suffering large phone bills. More advanced ADSL technology is gradually becoming available in the

UK but not in many rural areas where telecommuting might be particularly advantageous to workers. In the workplace, fast broadband data connection lines are usually provided and the organization pays the phone bills. Hence, those working from home remain economically disadvantaged. (See Daniels, Lamond, & Standen, 2000 for a fascinating discussion of other economic, political, and social influences on the spread of telework in various countries.)

Issues concerning the well-being and management of teleworkers

Even if these technological limitations can be overcome (and undoubtedly they will!), there are still some challenges that are univeral, and these concern the well-being and management of teleworkers. Box 10.1 summarizes some of the major issues according to the type of telework involved. What is clear, even from this brief outline, is that our "organizationally oriented" society is a major barrier to reaping the full potential of telework. This is seen in many different ways. Managers are distinctly uneasy about the work performance of people they cannot directly supervise and are not sure about how to manage in these circumstances. There is a fear that organizational culture cannot be adequately inculcated in or expressed by these "remote" workers, and that teleworkers are somehow not as serious about or committed to their work as conventional employees. The problems of measuring work performance are magnified in the minds of those who expect to be able to oversee work performance minutely. There can be a temptation to monitor and regulate work output even more rigorously than is the case with conventional workers. There have even been reports of teleworkers being required to go out of their front doors and enter their workspaces by another door at conventional office hours. Teleworkers may be monitored electronically, downgraded from permanent, full-time work to short-term contract work, or they may be paid solely by output (piecework) rather than by hours worked. Such practices can make the only advantage of telework the absence of a long commute to work, which may not compensate for the disadvantages.

Both workers in headquarters and in the general community may feel that working from home is not "real work". There may be jealousy and misunderstanding from "traditional" colleagues and the feeling that one can be interrupted and called upon for errands and services by family and friends. It is not surprising that women often find it more difficult to establish the "space" and routines necessary for successful telework than men.

From the teleworker's point of view, the boundaries between work and home can become blurred—work is always present and there is a danger that, far from easing work–family conflict, it just makes things worse. Another concern of teleworkers is that "out of sight" in the central office may mean "out of mind" when it comes to training and promotion opportunities, even

BOX 10.1
Problems associated with different types of telework and suggested solutions

Type	Advantages	Disadvantages	Solutions
Working FT or PT from home	Reduces central office costs: space, heat, light, etc. Worker autonomy and flexibility: work when and how they prefer; greater productivity and job satisfaction; lower absenteeism. Less time wasted on commuting: less stress, traffic congestion, and pollution. Distraction-free environment (?). Widens talent pool available to organization and helps retain valuable workers; no need to relocate. Work/family balance: benefits workers with child care responsibilities (?) and those with disabilities. People can live where they choose.	1 Technical problems and exploitation (?). Who pays for equipment, home phone bills, etc. 2 Problems instilling corporate culture. 3 Management concerns about monitoring and measuring performance; loss of management control concern. 4 Loss of opportunity for mentoring, coaching, and informal learning. Social and professional isolation.	1 Companies should provide equipment, ISDN lines, etc. 2 FT office work *before* teleworking. Require regular attendance at office (PT homeworking best). Select *good* office workers for homeworking. 3 Train teleworkers and their managers. Performance management by *results* not time spent at a desk (a problem if work has few tangible outputs). Some work can be monitored electronically. 4 Institute social, etc., programmes for homeworkers.

	5 Degraded communication with office staff. Jealousy, hostility of office staff. Problems organizing/coordinating work if flexible hours means teleworker can't be contacted.	5 Educate nonteleworking force: teleworking culture; formal guidelines/policy. Agree contact hours; choose type of work, e.g., requiring long periods without interruptions.
	6 "Out of sight, out of mind"—less training/promotion, etc.	6 Advantages of homeworking may outweigh lack of promotion.
	7 Blurring of work/personal life: work is *always* there vs. friends, family not respecting work times/space.	7 Yes! Encourages workaholics: individual has to set boundaries. Teleworking does *not* provide a substitute for childcare! Men more successful in achieving work respect than women!
	8 Enforcing rights and protection: Trades Union involvement and health & safety issues.	8 "EU plans directive to protect 'outworkers'", *People Management* (1997) 3(3), 9. Controversy.
Satellite office	Reduces cost of city centre offices. Less commuting so greater ability to balance work/personal life. Better technology.	Still major concerns about performance monitoring and measurement; loss of managerial control.
		Satellite offices often seen as best compromise between traditional office work and homeworking.

	Advantages	Disadvantages	Solutions
	Corporate culture may be replicated—more informal interactions possible so more mentoring and informal learning so reducing professional isolation. Social isolations less of a problem. Clearer boundaries between home and work.		Good preparation for telework and solutions as for homeworking.
Telecentre/ telecottage	As above (except for corporate culture). Telecottages help in regeneration of rural economies.	Professional isolation still a problem —not enough employees from same firm for firm-specific environment. Shares many of the disadvantages of homeworking especially management concerns.	
Mobile working	Reduction of office costs as above. Greater productivity —can work in cars, trains, airports, hotel rooms, etc. Customer proximity— worker goes to customers instead of vice versa.	Has same technical problems as homeworkers. Annoyance to other passengers: use of mobile phones in cars can be dangerous. Social professional isolation. Problems with work/family balance— always away from home so possible low morale. More travelling time, less time with customers. Quality of work in highly distracting environments?	No obvious solutions.

After Kurland and Bailey (1999) *Organizational Dynamics*, 28(2), 53–68.

though telework frequently results in greater effectiveness and productivity. Teleworkers also run the danger of social and professional isolation—they miss the opportunities for networking, mentoring, and vicarious learning over coffee and the water fountain, to say nothing of all the other socializing that goes on in organizations.

In addition there is some evidence (Hodson, 1992) that not all forms of work are suitable for telework. Cognitively demanding work that involves discussion, negotiation, and decision making may best be done in face-to-face meetings. On the other hand, work that requires a lot of concentration without interruption may best be done away from the office.

None of these problems is insurmountable. My own experience of home telework has been a huge success, and I certainly couldn't be doing the job I'm doing now without it. I tend to spend 3 days a week at the university, teaching, meeting with students and colleagues, and attending to all the administration. On the other 2–4 days a week I work at home doing all my reading, thinking, and writing, including most of my preparation. I often think that I am most productive when I work from home but this could be the result of years of practice doing unofficial overtime!

Standen (2000) recommends that the home teleworker has to devise his or her own strategies to ensure effective working and employers can do much to ensure a smooth transition by training teleworkers, their colleagues, and managers. Careful selection of home teleworkers is also desirable, since without the structure of the office, work requires good self-management skills. People who derive a lot of satisfaction from social contacts at work may not be suitable. Home telework is most successful when there is a pre-existing climate of trust between management and workers. Hodson (1992) reports findings that, once established, the climate of trust is not affected by worker location. However, there must be good channels of communication and teleworkers' job satisfaction was higher when their managers were able to fight for their interests and ideas. Working in the central office for at least part of the week is often seen as a good compromise, since a lot of the benefits of full-time home telework are gained while the potential disadvantages are reduced. Dooley (1996) found that job satisfaction tended to increase with the number of years spent teleworking, indicating that feelings of social isolation were not necessarily a long-term problem. Hodson also suggests that home telemanagement works best when goals are clear and set participatively. This reduces the teleworker's uncertainty and allows outputs to be measured more effectively.

However, it is important to distinguish between different types of telework because each presents different potential problems and suggested solutions. For instance, a satellite office may be indistinguishable from conventional work. Mobile working is quite another matter. Apart from the fact that technology plays a large part in allowing this type of work, it shares very few of the characteristics of other forms of telework. On the contrary, such people spend long periods travelling and away from home and may also suffer all the effects of isolation from the central office.

In fact, although telework can seem good for both individuals and organizations, it implies some fundamental changes in attitude and several important practical issues remain to be resolved. Guthrie (1997) looked at the emerging ethics of home telework. He asked 30 business people to judge scenarios involving home teleworkers, their managers, and employing organizations in terms of the ethics of the behaviour described. For instance, is it right for someone who finishes work ahead of schedule to attend to personal work but remain available by phone until close of business? There tended to be a lack of consensus about what was appropriate. For instance, in answer to a scenario involving a company that allowed home telework provided that employees supplied all their own equipment, 30% thought it was ethical, 30% said it was ethically questionable, and 30% felt it was unethical. Guthrie concludes that home telework poses a major challenge to traditional work/home boundaries and relationships between managers and staff. For instance, should managers monitor people's personal space by checking that the car is in the drive or by monitoring phone calls?—23% thought that such behaviour was justified, even though this would be considered a gross violation of privacy in the case of conventional workers.

When the home is also the workplace, there are a number of thorny health and safety issues. If the teleworker is injured, should the employer be liable? Should employers have the right to inspect the person's home workspace to ensure that it complies with Health and Safety regulations? In fact, health and safety legislation in the UK is designed to protect workers whether or not they work in the office or at home. For teleworkers the Health and Safety (Display Screen Equipment) Regulations 1992 are especially relevant. These stipulate that the employer should provide homeworkers with necessary equipment, maintenance checks, and training as well as carrying out workstation assessments in the home (Little, 2000). However, the guidelines for teleworkers are somewhat ambiguous. A "pragmatic approach" means that HSE inspectors will only visit domestic premises following a complaint from employees or after incidents have already been reported. They are also mindful of how reasonable it is to expect the employer to have control over the employee's workspace if, for instance, the employee only works from home on ocasions rather than permanently. Further, if teleworkers are very dispersed geographically, it can be expensive and impractical for employers to carry out the necessary checks. Quite apart from the invasion of privacy, many teleworkers may be unwilling to challenge their employers over health and safety issues at home for fear of losing their jobs, so these may be neglected. The European Union (EU) is aware of this problem and has it on its list of health and safety priorities for 2002/03 (Health and Safety at Work, 2002) but for now it remains a "grey area". So teleworkers themselves need to take responsibility for negotiating fair contracts with their employers.

In conclusion, although telework may have much to offer in making people's working lives easier, it is not something individuals and organizations should enter into lightly. It is not a panacea for stress and overwork, and it is not just a good way to cut down costs on office space.

Virtual teams

Like telework, a virtual team is not just a single way of working. Pape (1997) defines a virtual team as "any task-focused group that meets without all members necessarily being in the same room or even working at the same time" (p. 29). What makes this possible is advances in communications technology that allow conference telephone calls, videoconferences, e-mail, and communication tools such as groupware or computer-supported cooperative work. Pape gives a case study (see Case study 10.1) that illustrates the potential power of virtual teams and gives an immediate flavour of what is involved.

Whether the incident in Case study 10.1 describes Verifone's normal level of operations or the ideal they aspire to, the principles are clear. It is also

---

Case study 10.1:   The workings of a virtual team

At 4.30 pm a Greek sales rep for Verifone products is challenged by a bank customer who wants a new payment service technology but doubts the company's ability to deliver. This technology is not much used in Greece. The rep knows that Verifone is the major supplier in the US but doesn't know the details. Once out of the meeting, the rep hooks up his laptop to the nearest phone and sends an e-mail SOS to all Verifone sales, marketing, and technical support staff worldwide. This e-mail creates a virtual team, which gathers customer testimonials and other data to make a sales case while the Greek rep sleeps. In San Fransisco a member of the international marketing staff gets the SOS at 6.30 am (his time) and he organizes a conference call with two other marketing staff in Atlanta and Hong Kong (9.30 am and 10.30 pm respectively). They decide how to handle the worldwide data coming in. The US team speak on the phone later and use the company's wide area network to fine-tune a sales presentation prepared by the San Fransisco team. The presentation is also sent to Hong Kong for the addition of Asian information. The Greek rep gets up and retrieves the finished presentation from the network, gets to the bank at 8 am and the bank manager is so impressed he signs the contract.

clear what a boon well-functioning virtual teams must be for globalized business. They are often used to create 24-hour project work. When the Europeans stop work, the US team takes over, and when they stop, the Japanese team begins. If they are all working on the same project, with good knowledge management and coordination, the project gets finished much faster. This way of working is often used by international law firms when drawing up major contracts. The NCR Corporation created a virtual team of more than 1000 people in 17 different locations to develop a next-generation computer system and completed the project on budget and ahead of schedule. (But notice the hours worked in the case study—the US team were already at work at 6.30 am, the Hong Kong team were still at work at 10.30 pm. Hopefully, the same people were not expected to work from 6.30 am to 10.30 pm.)

The major difference between virtual teams and most telework is that team members are usually office based and thus have the full benefit of the most advanced technology—high speed, full bandwidth, audio/visual/data links. Apart from that, virtual teams can take many forms. They can be very simple, as in an e-mail discussion forum where people collaborate to pool knowledge, discuss ideas, and solve problems. Or they can involve "virtual organizations" (Sheehy & Gallagher, 1996) where there may be few or no physical premises. They may be transitory as in the case study example or permanent as in the virtual organization. They may also differ according to function: a short-term problem-solving task team or long-term operational teams responsible for some aspect of day-to-day functioning. They can exist within an organization or transcend organizational boundaries, perhaps including nonemployee experts or even customers. Lipnack and Stamps (1997) quote the case study of three rival publications in the men's magazine market who were challenged by an advertiser to work together on a campaign, otherwise the contract would go to a much larger market leader with the biggest circulation. The three smaller companies created a virtual team and won the contract.

Lipnack and Stamps (1997) give a number of such case studies to illustrate the effective workings of virtual teams, but in general there seems to be much "hype", but little hard evidence. Based on years of experience, using and working in virtual teams, Pape (1997) sets out a list of prerequisites for effective virtual teamwork. First, he stresses the necessity of adequate training—everyone must be able to use the technology—but written procedures and agreed frameworks are also essential. He then goes on to describe four crucial steps to creating a successful virtual team.

1   The team's purpose must be clearly defined and put in writing. This is because the purpose determines the team's membership, what information needs to be collected, how quickly a conclusion must be reached, what the team will/will not try to accomplish, which technologies will be used, and what defines success.

2   Recruit members. Three to seven members with the right skill and personality mix is recommended, but some major project teams are enormous, thus posing major coordination challenges.

3   Determine duration. Transitory, short or long term.

4   Select technology that is fit for purpose. For instance:

- Keeping in contact remotely—bleepers, mobile phones, voicemail.
- Disseminating information—fax, e-mail, application sharing over the network.
- Decision making—e-mail, conference calls, videoconferencing.

At Verifone they find that technology problem-solving teams often use videoconferencing so that all members can see the equipment. Marketing teams often use groupware so that all members can share presentation slides and make suggestions. Problem-solving teams can share results by e-mail and follow this up with conference calls to challenge the information and decide amendments and next actions. E-mail is good for sharing information but poor for resolving conflicts and arguments. Resolving misunderstandings is best done in a phone conversation or face to face. Negotiation is best done face to face, especially in sitations where trust is both required and low. Most commentators recommend that the team meets physically at least once and preferably more often during its lifetime. The early phase when team members are getting to know each other and are defining their purposes and goals is an important time for face-to-face meetings. But towards the end of the project, when deadlines are looming and major decisions have to be made, can also be a crucial time.

All this seems eminently sensible advice, and the potential of virtual teams does seem very exciting and not just for business. International research teams are already operating in this way. More modestly, I have set up an electronic discussion group for my doctoral students to share their knowledge and expertise and offer mutual support between our monthly meetings. This sort of thing is now common practice in higher education. The benefits are also apparent for anyone who has to live and work in a geographically remote location. However, given the problems that conventional teams can experience in functioning effectively, it would be good to know what processes in virtual teams lead to success. Haywood (1998) questioned over 500 managers in hi-tech organizations and found that many of them had great reservations about virtual teams and felt that their management skills didn't translate easily into the virtual workplace. Lamond (2000) also discusses the problems of managing a dispersed workforce, and Sparrow (2000a, 2000b) warns that virtual organizations are unlikely to compensate for the deterioration in psychological contracts over the past few years. Merrick (1996, p. 41) quotes Alison Hardingham, director of the firm of business psychologists Interactive Skills, as saying, "People might be seduced into thinking they can communicate entirely through IT, and that nasty little problems and group dynamics won't impinge, but what they find is that they impinge in spades."

There is very little research evidence about the workings of virtual teams and what there is tends to involve student groups (e.g., Rockett, Valor, Miller, & Naude, 1998). However, Jarvenpaa, Knoll, and Leidner (1998) conducted an interesting study of 75 teams of between four and six masters students, each of whom lived in a different country—from the US to Australia. After a number of electronic teambuilding exercises, their task was to collaborate to produce a web page via e-mail over a period of 8 weeks. A prize was offered for the best page. Ostensibly, the study aimed to look at the determinants of trust between team members as the project progressed. Early on, the perceived ability of other team members had most effect on trust, but as virtual relationships developed, perceived benevolence—the extent to which others were seen to exhibit interpersonal care and willingness to contribute—became most important in predicting trust. One of the most interesting findings was that the most effective teams exhibited "swift trust". That is, since there was no time to gradually develop trust, members behaved as if it existed from the start. (Perhaps this is one reason why initial face-to-face teambuilding is so important.) However, for me, the most fascinating findings concerned the qualitative analyses of the e-mails of the three "highest trust" and three "lowest trust" teams. The characteristics of the behaviour of these two sets of teams are summarized in Box 10.2.

This study has limitations. Students are not paid employees and their motivations may be different. In particular, some of them were more concerned with getting credits towards their degrees than with doing a good job or winning the prize. They had very restricted technology compared with commercial virtual teams and they were also self-managed, whereas work teams will almost certainly have a manager. However, I think this study is important because it is the only one I have been able to discover to date that looks so closely at the processes that contribute to the success or failure of virtual teams. (Doubtless there will be many other studies by the time this book appears in the shops, so please don't write to complain!) My view is that trust seems to develop as a result of successful teamwork, rather than causing it. The "swift trust" in the least successful teams soon evaporated as a result of inaction and lack of cooperation. What this study also shows is that good teams are very socially skilled even when interacting via e-mail. However, they did not "suffer fools gladly"; having been given a chance, uncooperative members were dismissed. The study also showed the importance of clear goals. Whereas the good teams asked for clarification from the researchers, the poor teams asked each other what they were supposed to be doing. The need for frequent communication is also evident. The good teams wanted feedback fast and members warned each other when this might not be possible. Importantly, the good teams limited their interdependence while

BOX 10.2
The behaviour and interactions of effective and ineffective virtual teams

"High trust"/effective teams

Proactive
Exhibited initiative, volunteered for roles, expelled "loafers", informed one another when they would be away but still tried to log on—extra effort.

Task orientation
Very little socializing chat —all task focused but still empathic and supportive. Very little time discussing procedures—produced high quality work and shared it with the rest for improvement.

Positive tone
Expressed excitement, encouragement, and compliments; disagreements handled very gently.

Rotating leadership
All members exhibited leadership qualities and took the lead as required. Leadership based on skill needed at that time.

Task goal clarity
Discussed goals of assignment more and contacted project coordinator with questions. Also linked project goals to own personal goals.

"Low trust"/ineffective teams

Nonproactive
Asked questions but didn't volunteer or deliver work; ignored "loafers"; didn't notify others of imminent absences.

Little task orientation
Little communication social or otherwise; but also little empathy; emotion expressed uncertainty about anyone reading messages or frustration about lack of others' contributions. More time spent trying to evade responsibility and get others to do the work.

Negative tone
Focused on what they might lose if performance poor rather than gain if performance good; focused on differences in course credits received for completing project—not fair if some got more!

Ineffective leadership
No leadership or leader without followers.

Lack of task goal clarity
Little discussion of task goals but lots of "don't know what we're supposed to be doing" messages—not acted on. Personal goals—"spend as little time as necessary".

Role division and specificity
  Roles emerged after person took initiative but these were not pursued independently—several iterations of feedback and rework.

Role division
  Divided work so they could work completely independently of others.

Time management
  Explicitly discussed schedules, milestones, deadlines, etc.; monitored and reminded each other and kept to them; also managed global clocks to maximize time spent by *someone* on project.

Time management
  None!

Feedback
  High quality comments and suggestions on others' work.

Feedback
  Very little at all; "OK", "looks good to me"—little value added.

Frequency and pattern of interaction
  Much more frequent; intense bursts of activity—members needed rapid feedback so told each other when they would be absent.

Frequency and pattern of interaction
  Very little; frequent messages, "is anyone out there?" Lengthy unexplained lapses of communication followed by sudden unexpected emergencies.

still collaborating, by sending work for comment after having prepared it as individuals. Thus, they adjusted to the limitations of the technology at their disposal and used it to best effect. The least successful teams worked as individuals, if they worked at all.

Some of Pape's (1997) recommendations are vindicated in this study, e.g., the need for clear procedures, frameworks, and goals, and the need to use the technology appropriately, for particular purposes. Despite the limitations of this study, it is possible that the transactional approach adopted by the least successful teams could be replicated in work teams. Some of the students were aggrieved that others were getting more credits for the work than they were and this appears to have made them reluctant to contribute. There was a tendency to ask for volunteers rather than to volunteer, and, having agreed to do a job, some would do nothing more than that particular job, even though there was a clear need for other work. In work teams this might be translated into effort according to pay levels, a "that's your job" mentality, and general "social loafing". What the study does show is that technology alone does not make for an effective virtual team—a point that employers and managers would do well to consider.

So to conclude this section, I believe these new ways of working hold much promise both for individuals and for business, but there are many challenges. In particular, the command and control model of management may no longer be appropriate. If these forms of working, especially virtual teams, increase, the demands on managers will be for knowledge management and coordination and the facilitation of knowledge pooling, transfer, and recording (Baker, Barker, Thorne, & Dutnell, 1997; Kessels, 1999). Especially on large, complex projects, the amount of information from a large number of different sources, which must be assimilated and coordinated in a short timescale to complete each stage and decide what to do next, must pose considerable challenges for human cognition and be difficult to do well. Do we know enough about how to make this kind of knowledge management effective? Or do we already know quite a lot about why it is often ineffective? To me, it sounds like handling the amount of information needed to run a nuclear power plant without any computerized aids to understanding and decision making! If this analogy is anywhere near the truth, then we might expect knowledge management and coordination to be rather a "seat-of-the-pants" affair.

Both telework and virtual teams imply great organizational change and a need for much learning and training. Face-to-face communication remains as important as ever in this brave new world but the effects on communication via these new media add new complications and are only beginning to be understood. There is plenty of work for occupational psychologists.

Computer-based assessment

In 1994, Bartram commented that "stand-alone" computer-based assessment (CBA) systems had had a significant impact only in the previous decade, and most of them had had the "mundane use" of converting traditional pencil and paper tests and questionnaires to computer delivery. The reasons for this were, as ever, cost cutting. Computer delivery of tests was seen to cut down on the need for test administrators, who became more like invigilators. The programme could provide accurate scoring, create instant local norms, and even generate feedback for the candidate. "Adaptive" tests could generate a short set of questions tailor-made for the candidate's level of ability, thus saving the time wasted on a long test, where most of the items would either be too easy or too difficult. The full capabilities of a full CBA system are described by Burke (1997, 1998) and an outline is presented in Figure 10.1.

At the assessment generation stage an expert system is embedded in the software, which then generates tests that can be adapted to the individual

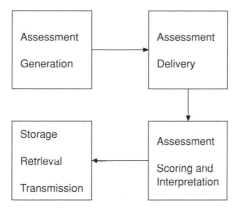

Figure 10.1 The elements of a full CBA system (Burke, 1997, 1998). Reprinted with the permisstion of the author.

candidate and that can produce several versions of the same test for use in investigating reliability or giving as practice. This reduces the effects of "test wiseness". Delivery can be modified so that, for instance, a speed test can manipulate the amount of time an item is exposed on the screen, thus reducing the distorting effects of some candidates' strategies for care and accuracy. At the scoring stage, the computer is faster and more accurate than any human, and the program can also undertake test diagnostics. For instance, if a candidate scores lower than if he or she had just guessed the answers, then we must question the result—were the instructions misunderstood; was the candidate ill? The program can reveal something of the process by which candidates achieved their scores. This is very difficult to do "by eye" in a paper and pencil version. Expert systems can also generate narrative reports to give feedback to candidates after they have completed a personality inventory, although a human expert can amend and add to the computer's interpretation. Finally, the computer can maintain a convenient database, which can be transmitted to geographically dispersed clients.

Despite all these advantages, there are criticisms of these "conventional" uses of CBA. Booth (1998) says that, far from being a cheap alternative to paper and pencil versions, CBA is hugely expensive to develop since it needs a large interdiciplinary team of experts and constant upgrades of hardware and software. There are also validity issues to be considered. A test presented on a computer can result in much lower scores because test takers are unfamilar with, or fearful of, the system. On the other hand, much higher scores can result because reading a single item then pressing one of five keys is much faster than finding and reading one item on a page of items, finding the right set of answer alternatives on a sheet of answer sets, and then carefully marking your chosen answer so the automatic scanner can "read" it. All this requires the collection of new norms and more investigations of the validity of the computerized test, all of which add to the expense of development. People are sometimes very resistant to taking computerized tests, and may be especially hostile to computers interpreting their personalities. There is very little research on the effects of CBA on test fairness. All these factors may make their use more open to legal challenge and yet more expense.

Booth (1998) argues that user interface (UI) design is central to effective human computer interaction and it can involve "a considerably complex myriad of perceptual and cognitive dynamics" (p. 62). Yet, according to him, this aspect is rarely considered in the CBA literature. Furthermore, EU directives on common standards for UI could create conflicts between the legal requirements and the demands for good psychometrics.

All this does not preclude the possibility of good computerized testing, but it is not the "quick fix" to reduce selection costs that organizations sometimes think it is. In my view, if there are paper and pencil tests of proven worth, and the savings of putting them on computer are largely illusory, and they may be rendered less reliable, valid, and fair in the process, why do it? However, Bartram (2001), expresses the view that computer-managed and computer-delivered assessment will become the "default" and paper and pencil testing will be the exception. Among the reasons Bartram gives for this shift is the far greater control test publishers would have over their products if they are delivered via a computer or over the internet. If a test user buys a paper and pencil test the publishers have to rely on training and codes of ethics for the continued integrity of their instrument. In theory, there is nothing to stop the user from telling friends and relatives the answers, making illegal copies of test booklets and answer sheets, and committing all manner of other abuses from sloppy test administration to carelessly leaving materials on a train. With computer-based tests, whether delivered via a local test centre or the internet, control remains with the test provider since there are no tangible question and scoring sheets and the provider controls the software that delivers the test, and thus its administration.

Even so, what I find far more exciting is the use of computers to assess abilities that cannot be accessed by paper and pencil tests; abilities and aptitudes that may be much better predictors of future performance because they are more central to doing the job.

Bartram (1995) was one of the pioneers in using the full capabilities of the dynamic computer screen when he developed his MICROPAT test battery for selecting trainee fighter pilots. In one of the subtests the screen "grows" several lines heading down towards "score" boxes at the bottom. Lines move at different speeds and can disappear at random before reaching the score box. The candidate has to bet on the best line and switch between them, e.g., a good strategy might be to switch to a line just before it reaches its score box. The test can be made more difficult by increasing the speed of the lines, which means that the person has to attend to and act on multiple sources of unpredictable and rapidly changing information. MICROPAT has greater predictive validity than previous pilot training selection tests, and has been adopted by several civil airlines.

More recently, Burke, Kitching, and Valsler (1999) have produced the PILAPT (Pilot Aptitude Tester) battery. This uses an "in-built" expert system and item generator. Among the subtests is one called TRAX, which is a pursuit tracking task that uses a 3D display that moves about the screen and simulates dealing with 3D dynamics as in real flight. Validity data are so far rather sparse, but in a study of 165 RAF university air squadron cadets, TRAX scores correlated .51 with training grades.

Also in 1999, Bartram, Crawshaw, Geake, and Sherman presented the preliminary results of a CBA system designed to predict training success in "keyhole" knee surgery. Success in this delicate technique depends on good spatial orientation and hand–eye coordination, as the surgeon relates the image on a TV monitor to his/her actions in manipulating the surgical instruments within the person's body. Bartram and colleagues tried to develop a computerized test that improved on the traditional paper and pencil spatial reasoning tests in predicting training success. Bartram's selection test involved a dynamic but very simple spatial task—keeping a cross within a small green square that moved round a triangle. Only 14 people took part in this study but none of them had any previous experience of medicine, anatomy, or surgery so no-one had any relevant prior experience. Further, all of them were included in the study irrespective of how good or bad their scores on the computerized test were. Thus, this was the equivalent of selecting people for a training course at random. Using a plastic knee joint these people were trained over a number of weeks to conduct knee operations. The dynamic spatial task score was a good predictor of training success overall and differentiated more between trainees as training proceeded.

CBA has also been applied to select senior personnel in the emergency services. Danielsson and Ohlsson (1997) investigated the demands made on fire chiefs when managing major fires. The main problems facing those who direct the emergency operations were found to be:

- Lack of information in the initial stages of the emergency.
- Situations that were nonroutine and therefore unfamiliar.
- Communication deficiencies—no one person had all the necessary information.
- Feelings of isolation.
- Delays in information that would aid decisions to scale up the operation.

In addition, the emergency directors had to prioritize life-saving, decide on evacuation, and the fire-fighting strategy. Clearly getting the right person to do such a job is quite important. Burke (2000a) reported on how he used "command interviews" to select and train senior people in the London Fire Brigade. These were paper and pencil fire scenarios based on "critical incidents" from real fires. Candidates talk aloud about how a situation should be managed and their responses are evaluated in terms of the decisions made by experts who had actually attended the fires. This technique has been extended to a CBA system to select air traffic controllers. The VDU screen is used to produce a dynamic graphic display of a busy airport with several planes in the process of taking off and landing. At one point in the exercise, an emergency arises and a plane is coming in with an engine on fire and has to be given priority over all other traffic, some of which are about to take off or land. Candidates are taken to various "decision points" and have to state their priorities, the actions they propose to take and their reasons for selecting them. An example of a "decision point" might be, "What are you going to instruct the pilot waiting to take off on runway A to do and the pilot coming into land on runway B to do?" when both these manoeuvres would clearly obstruct the speedy landing of the stricken plane. These responses are then compared with the decisions of experts. (Unfortunately, these simulations are quite difficult to explain in words; an on-screen demonstration is far more effective. I hope readers have gained a flavour of what is involved, but those who are particularly interested in these techniques should perhaps contact the researchers/authors directly. Incidentally, this is a good illustration of the limitations of traditional distance learning media. If this book were to be delivered by the internet, this would be an ideal point to include on-screen demonstrations of MICROPAT, PILAPT, and Burke's air traffic control task.)

Burke's (2000a) tool can also be used in training and development, as can many other forms of computer simulation. In many hazardous industries, emergencies are so rare that the normal course of job experience cannot prepare people to cope with them so many hours must be spent in simulators. Computer simulation is also used in basic training since practice in the "real thing" would be far too expensive in terms of lives and equipment in the event of accidents. Flight simulators are very well established but such comprehensive systems are very expensive both in terms of hardware and the presence of highly trained assessors/trainers. Simpler, PC-based simulations of, for instance, power plant scenarios, have been around for a long time but these are gaining in sophistication and fidelity to the situations they represent. Moreover, they are being used to supplement, not replace, more traditional training techniques. For instance, my doctoral student Mike Rugg-Gunn (2002) is evaluating the effectiveness of a CBA system to shorten the amount of time trainee submarine commanders have to spend in the full-scale simulator in order to become proficient at safely returning the submarine to periscope depth.

There is also increasing use of computer-based testing and training scenarios to assess complex problem solving. Funke (1998) lists the advantages of such systems as allowing the construction of complex scenarios, which change over time and so pose new requirements; there is process-oriented data storage and at least partial computer interpretation of the results.

These sorts of exercises are also popular with candidates who can see their direct relevance to doing the job. However, there are disadvantages. Sometimes the scenarios are so complex that even the developer doesn't know the optimal solution, and this means that candidates can only be compared with each other and not some ideal level of performance. The dynamic and interactive nature of these exercises means that a small mistake early on can change the nature and complexity of the exercise. (I am reminded of my own bitter experience of arithmetic tests in primary school when a single early miscalculation could render a simple sum a horror of long multiplication and division complete with fractions, and I'd *still* get zero for my answer despite demonstrating considerably more arithmetical competence overall than those who got it right!) In short, the same scenario can be measuring different abilities and competences in everyone who attempts it. Finally, PC simulations do not always include everything that would be relevant to actually doing the job. For instance, a simulation designed to assess decision making to increase the size of a van delivery fleet might omit information about the actions of competitors, which would be vital in real life. Funke and Schuler (1998) concluded that the fidelity (and usefulness) of simulations to real life lies not so much in the way that information is presented as in the relevance of the responses required. For instance, an audio or videotape of a difficult customer may be an excellent simulation of what can happen to a hapless shop assistant or call centre operator, but typing "a" to a multiple choice answer set may not be much help in responding to the real situation later.

There is one major problem with computer simulations and that is that they do not reproduce the same emotional responses as the "real thing". Sixsmith (personal communication) reported cases of people who successfully completed air traffic controller training for military aircraft but, when confronted with a real mission, suffered so much anxiety that their voice quality posed a serious communication problem, and thus, safety hazard, to pilots. Maybe training should make more of the differences between simulated scenarios and the "real thing". Telling trainees that some (unspecified) scenarios in the next series of missions may be simulated or real, while (unbeknown to trainees) keeping control of the real situations with experts, may help trainees to make the adjustment from "protected" enviroments to situations where the newly qualified have to take full responsibility. But it is a difficult matter, involving professional ethics. It is a poor analogy, but I remember the terror I felt as a newly qualified driver, when I first took to the roads alone without the dual controls of my instructor. How much worse must this feeling be, when you are suddenly expected, alone and unaided, to guide the landing of passenger jets with hundreds of people on board. Training has to reproduce the emotional responses that must be coped with in these sorts of circumstances. Technical competence may not be enough.

To conclude, my view is that work and organizational psychology/occupational psychology has much to offer in this promising area of CBA and computer-assisted training, if only because there are so many traps for the unwary. Booth (1998) says that "The days where one could plan, implement and deliver a complete CBT [CBA] system single-handedly are a technological shadow of the past" (p. 58). The danger is that in the multi-disciplinary teams now required, experts in psychometrics, ergonomics, and psychological processes may lose control of both process and outputs. Without rigorous evaluation of the reliability, validity, and fairness of CBA systems, their use could have very negative effects on both individuals and organizations.

Psychological assessment and the internet

The use of several computers in one room to assess candidates either with tests or problem-solving/decision-making tasks is long established, as is the use of systems such as JIGCAL and GRADSCOPE for careers guidance. The next logical step is to have remote centres where people can go to some convenient place and have the results of their assessments sent via a central agency to potential employers, etc. The temptation is for "do-it-yourself" assessment, rather like filling your car with petrol, since the technology takes care of everything and all the test taker has to do is repond to instructions. Bartram (1997, 1999, 2000) thinks this raises a number of issues that must be confronted. Without a test administrator, or at least a test invigilator on hand, how do we know the real identity of the test taker; what if several people are involved in deciding on the answers; what if people use books and other aids to help them answer correctly? There is nothing wrong with local psychological assessment centres and distance testing; all that is needed is for there to be a qualified person on hand to prevent such abuses.

However, tests taken on the internet have the potential to suffer from all these problems and more. Bartram (1997) envisaged a day when the complete selection process could be conducted on-line. Careers guidance software might be available for downloading so that people can explore their interests and likely careers. Browsing for company information and job adverts is already with us, and job preview exercises and work samples may soon be published along with the "further details" of jobs. On-line application forms are already available, and candidates can send their CVs by e-mail. Companies could then access candidates' ability scores and personality profiles from databases sent from local test centres. Even interviews might be held via videoconferencing. Much of this scenario is already in place so this is not the remote future and the globalization of business makes this not only likely but necessary. However, Bartram (1999) offers the scenario in Box 10.3 to illustrate the potential problems.

BOX 10.3
The potential problems of testing via the internet

Job applicant: Italian
Test Centre: in France
Test language: English
Test Publisher: in Australia but . . .
    running from an Internet provider in Germany
Company is Dutch-based subsiduary of . . .
    US multi-national
Job applied for: manager of Tokyo office
Test results held on multi-national's internet server in US
Sent to applicant's potential line manager in Japan
Having first been interpreted by the company's outsourced HR
    consultancy in Belgium.

To which scenario, my reaction is . . . !!!!! But of course, this is exactly the sort of complexity to which globalization leads in any aspect of business. However, to occupational psychologists steeped in their professional conduct of assessments and their interpretation, and the ethics of fair testing, this is something for which we are ill-prepared. Bartram (1999) goes on to list some of the questions and issues that arise from this situation:

- Which country's test standards and code of practice apply?
- Who is the test user?
- How does the test supplier decide on test user qualification issues?
- In which country does the test user need to have their qualifications?
- Where does the responsibility lie for ensuring that the test is suitably adapted to the culture and language of the applicant?
- Who is responsible for ensuring that the report generated is appropriate for the client?
- Who chooses the language of assessment?
- What norms are used for interpreting the results?
- Who is responsible for secure and accurate storage of result data and what recourse does the applicant have for checking them?
- What redress is available for the test taker who feels unfairly treated—who, in what country?

Bartram (1999) says that some of these problems are simply matters of standards and good professional practice, but other issues must be addressed via internationally agreed legislation. The British Psychological Society (BPS, 2000) has issued a code of best practice for CBA, but testing via the internet requires, according to Bartram, a need to rethink relationships between all the stakeholders in cyberspace rather than geographical locations: test developers, test publishers, test users, test takers, consumers of test results, professional bodies, and law makers.

In fact, technology moves so swiftly in this field that almost anything I write today will almost certainly be out of date by the time this book is published. According to Bartram (2001), many of the issues that were problematical in 1997 and 1999 have already been addressed. For instance, the International Test Commission has agreed guidelines for testing over the internet, which are available at its web site (www.InTestCom.org). The internet has changed the focus of employers from an almost exclusive concern with selection (cf. Chapter 7) to an equal emphasis on sourcing, screening, and sifting applicants. Many employers advertise jobs only on the internet and will only accept applications via the internet. Applicants can complete assessment inventories and biodata questionnaires on-line. They may also be asked to undertake a preliminary ability test—to which there is open access. This is easy to do because once an item pool has been validated a subset can be used to generate hundreds of different tests so that no applicant gets the same test. People who are selected for further assessment can then be given another full version of the test under controlled conditions, e.g., at a test centre. Feedback can be sent back to candidates via their own personal "filing cabinet".

The advantages for recruiters are that they can access much wider applicant pools, the sifting process can be made much more reliable and objective, and the whole recruitment and selection process can be speeded up. For applicants, the advantages are access to a great deal of employment-related information and a much faster application process. Rejection and feedback or a job offer can come within a week in contrast to the weeks, months, or complete silence that is associated with traditional selection. This can be a boon for people (e.g., new graduates) who may have made many applications and who can now track the progress of each one instead of agonizing over whether to accept this job offer or risk waiting for another more desirable job offer, which may not materialize.

All this relates to activities that are carefully regulated by national professional bodies and codes of professional ethics, but the internet currently appears to be beyond the control of any institution, government or otherwise. Given the availability of easy-to-use authoring software, anyone can set up a "service" offering any old rubbish as a so-called psychological assessment instrument and make a lot of money in the process. There were (and probably still are) plenty of dubious paper and pencil tests on the market, but professional bodies like the BPS took strong measures to tighten up standards and inform the public. No such constraints can control the internet "cowboys". Organizations need to be made aware of the dangers of getting psychometrics for selection "on the cheap". As Bartram (1999) says, "In testing, the medium is not the message, as the quality of the test is always hidden in the technical data" (p. 11), so it is impossible to distinguish a good from a bad instrument merely by looking at it. Engineers wouldn't choose steel for bridge building simply by eye. They would seek out reputable and reliable suppliers and insist on rigorous quality checks. The same principles apply to the use of tests in selection. In fact, the International Test Commission is in the process of reviewing the quality of tests offered over the internet and this will result in a "kitemark" symbol of quality, which will reassure test users and takers that this is a reputable psychometric instrument. Bartram believes that the emphasis placed on technical and ethical standards and good practice by major test publishers will become increasingly important.

Once the person has been hired, the internet (or in-house network) is being increasingly used in personnel processes. For instance, the viability and ease of use of multi-rater feedback has been greatly increased by all the distributed "others" being able to fill in the form on-line and send it to a central location at the click of a mouse. Personal development planning and tracking, performance management, job analysis, culture, climate, and employee attitude surveys, and distributed teamwork are all facilitated by use of the internet or the in-house network (Bartram, 2001).

People with disabilities: The contribution of ergonomics and virtual reality

There are, within the profession of occupational therapy/physiotherapy, a proportion of people who are very circumspect about the use of technological aids to help people to cope with disabilities (see, e.g., Jeffreson, 1997). It is argued that such aids frequently encourage dependence and a failure to develop residual capacities and adapt to a life that may be changed but which still has personal meaning. Further, such aids can increase the person's feeling of "otherness" by drawing attention to the disability and tend to a loss of dignity and feelings of humiliation. To illustrate some of the evils, Campbell (1994), cites the case of a person who had held down a professional job, but had to give it up because her personal helper had been replaced with technological "aids". She could now "manage by herself" but it took her 3 hours to get dressed and another 3 hours to get ready for bed, leaving her drained for any activity in what little time remained. There are also reports of people being offered "aids" and little else, so obliging them to use technology which they found unpleasant and demeaning. Far better, say the proponents of this view, to offer people intensive therapy to achieve a meaningful life by their own efforts and their own choices.

I have a lot of sympathy with this ethos. Crass technology, developed without regard to the psychology of the intended users, is worse than useless. A good example was the loud auditory devices designed to warn people with severe visual impairments of obstacles in their path. These were never successful or popular, partly because they were far less efficient than the skilled use of a white stick and partly because few people want to be accompanied by uproar wherever they go. Hearing aids are also unpopular because they magnify all sounds, rather than just speech, thus creating an uncomfortable, incoherent babble of background noise. It is also important to consider people's sensitivities. When a revolutionary new ear operation was introduced a few years ago, many profoundly deaf parents of children with equally bad hearing impairments were very ambivalent about it and unwilling to let their offspring undergo the operation. They felt that the restoration of hearing would damage the children's identity, and cut them off from their families and the deaf community in which they had grown up. The decision to turn their children into hearing people seemed like a betrayal of their identity and culture.

However, having said that, I don't see this as an either/or argument. There is a need for both intensive therapy and ergonomically designed technological aids. To use aids to replace therapy or a personal helper is just cost-cutting stupidity and can be regarded as a latent error in the system. To dispense with, or condemn, all technological aids is equally absurd. Some degree of disability comes to most of us through illness, accidents, or simply by growing old, and most of us would welcome any aid that helped us to maintain independence or quality of life. I'm sure the "therapy camp" would agree with me on this.

It seems to be the high-tech "gizmos"—ill-conceived, badly designed, promising the earth, and *imposed*—that attracts their ire and rightly so. But it doesn't have to be like that. Consider Stephen Hawkings' voice synthesizer, which allows him to transcend the ravages of motor neurone disease. There are also a raft of electronic aids that would allow, e.g., someone with quite severe visual impairment to work as a secretary (Baron & Butterworth, 1998). With recent laws in the UK to ban employment discrimination on the basis of disability, employers would do well to inform themselves about what techological aids are available. However, what I want to do here is to discuss the development of one aid that combines good ergonomics with considerable technological innovation.

The MoBIC travel aid, funded by the EU, has been developed to help blind people plan journeys and navigate through the more distant environment (Johnson & Petrie, 1998; Petrie & Johnon, 1996; Strothotte et al., 1996). The aim of the project was to make independent travel for blind people "safe, comfortable, graceful, efficient and stress free" (Johnson & Petrie, 1998, p. 27). To this end, the researchers began by conducting extensive interviews and discussion groups with blind and partially sighted people to establish their needs and what they would want from the proposed aid. Two of the chief anxieties about independent travel for people with visual impairments concern getting lost or finding themselves in unsafe areas. The kinds of information they wanted "is knowing which street they are on and which direction they are heading in, orienting themselves in relation to landmarks and knowing how to reach their destination" (p. 27) —things which sighted people take for granted. They were also concerned about their personal safety: knowing the state of the pavements, whether they were approaching a kerb or a temporary obstacle like roadworks and scaffolding, whether they were at the right intersection or crossing, knowing whether they had reached their destination. Some of these problems could be helped by a guide dog but others, such as knowing that they actually were in the location they thought they were, remained. (Guide dogs do not know the right London Tube stop—the person counts the stations or relies on the public address system.) They were also concerned about using public transport: finding the right bus stop, boarding the right bus. Most of all they wanted to feel in control and prepared for any eventuality. People were also asked what would be their main requirements of the proposed aid. These were that it should be light to carry and unobtrusive. The mode of delivery of information was also discussed and as a result an auditory stream of information via a light headset similar to a personal stereo was selected.

Armed with this information, the researchers set out to design a system that would meet all these needs and take the anxiety out of independent travel. The resulting MoBIC system is in two parts. The first is a journey planner, which involves an ordinary PC, or one that is suitably adapted to the needs of the user. This provides access via computer-based geographical information systems (GIS) to a large number of databases, which include minute details of the route to be traversed such as landmarks, intersections, shops, and so on, and also information such as bus and train timetables. In this way people could put together a detailed itinerary that would guide them on every step of their journey and tell them exactly where they were at any time and what was immediately ahead of them. This was then loaded onto the second part of the system—a mobile computer, linked to the satellite Global Positioning Sytem (GPS), which would pinpoint their exact location on any part of the journey. Stored information about this location would be transmitted via the headset. This system was designed to supplement usual aids such as guide dog and long stick to allow the person to avoid immediate obstacles.

Extensive trials were carried out with blind people using "mock-ups" of the eventual system and by dint of many iterations in the design process and great technological innovation the final system met all user requirements. Though not yet commonly available, it has been a great success with users, allowing people who were formerly too afraid to travel independently to make journeys alone with confidence, safety, and dignity. What is important in this example is the role of the ergonomists in carefully establishing user requirements. This is not always easy to do because when faced with a new system people do not always know what they want and defects only become apparent when it is actually being used. The researchers tried to circumvent these problems by getting people to think generally about their worries and problems when travelling independently and then to test prototypes to iron out remaining problems. I think it is a splendid example of how ergonomics and advanced technology *together* really can improve the quality of people's lives.

The potential of virtual reality

Virtual reality (VR) (or virtual environments; VEs), has long outgrown its computer games applications. Liz Attree (2000, p. 3) defines virtual reality as "an artificial environment, created with computer hardware and software, that can be presented to the user in such a way that it appears and feels like a real environment". However, VE can vary according to the level of "immersion" experienced by the user. At the simplest level, the person can simply view and "move about in" a 3D environment presented on a VDU screen. At the next level the person can manipulate objects in that environment using a keyboard or mouse. Full immersion requires the person to wear sensory input devices such as a headset and datagloves so that real-world external stimuli are substituted by computer-generated stimuli.

VEs have been developed as training aids where training in real-life situations would be too dangerous and/or expensive: for pilots, divers, parachutists, and firefighters (see Rose et al., 2000 for details). However, it is also being used in assessment, therapy, rehabilitation, and training for people with disabilities and those recovering from brain injury. Cognitive deficits are characteristic of many medical conditions involving neurological damage or degeneration. VEs can provide a safe, everyday environment for assessment without sacrificing the need for analytic control. For instance, the precise assessment of memory impairments may be difficult in a mulifaceted real environment but the VE can be carefully controlled to pinpoint particular deficits (Attree, 2000). VEs may be particularly useful in therapy and rehabilitation for people with learning difficulties, physical disabilities, and brain damage (see Sharkey, Rose, & Lindstrom, 1998 for an interesting set of studies and Rose & Foreman, 1999). For instance, at the University of East London, David Rose, Liz Attree, and other colleagues are investigating the use of VE in training people with learning disabilities. This project is in association with MENCAP and forms part of a European-wide project funded in part by the Italian Government. They have used 3D images presented via VDU screens together with keyboard manipulation to train people in kitchen safety, supermarket shopping, and simple industrial assembly tasks. Rose et al. (2000) have investigated the extent to which training in VEs transfers to real environments, using a sensorimotor task. They found no differences between the later performance of healthy volunteers in the virtual or real training conditions so both seemed to be equally effective. However, they conclude that more research is needed to ascertain the precise conditions needed to ensure transfer of training. Perhaps Funke and Schuler's (1998) findings discussed earlier in this chapter may have some bearing here—the fidelity of the VE response to what is needed in the real environment may be a significant factor.

This is an exciting emerging research area that is very relevant to the concerns of occupational psychology, although the researchers are by no means all occupational psychologists. I am excited by the multi-disciplinary nature of this endeavour, the way that it unites academic and applied psychology, and its promise of many new and useful applications within both therapy and rehabilitation and mainstream occupational psychology. Perhaps the assessment tools in selection in the future will involve VEs (Aguinis, Henle, & Beaty, 2001), especially as all major test publishers are currently very exercised by the challenge of complying with the new disability discrimination laws.

Small to medium enterprises

Scattered throughout this book there have been occasional references to small businesses, but occupational psychology has been almost exclusively concerned with large organizations, or at least, most of what gets published concerns this latter sector. There are signs that this is changing. The growth of independent practitioners in the UK, who work alone or in collaboration with one or two colleagues, means that many more occupational psychologists are coming into contact with small and medium-sized enterprizes (SMEs), and doubtless a lot of interesting and important work is going on. Unfortunately, little of this finds its way into print, and our knowledge of what goes on in this sector is limited. I was therefore delighted to see a seminar on SMEs organized by the BPS Occupational Psychology Section and later published as a special edition of *The Occupational Psychologist* (1999). Margaret Chapman, who organized the seminar and wrote the foreword to the special edition, points out the importance of this sector in the UK economy: "99.4% of businesses employ less than 500 people; only 4000 employees are in organizations with more than 500 staff; and only 18,000 businesses are not small" (p. 3). (Presumably the public sector is excluded from these figures.)

Chell (1999) opened the proceedings by looking at the notion of the "entrpreneurial personality". This is an important topic because most big business begins with someone with vision and enterprise, working from the garage or kitchen table. Chell says that psychology's traditional concerns with traits, etc., perhaps assumes a homogeneity of personal characteristics that do not exist, and is inadequate. She uges us to look at what entrepreneurs actually do and points to at least one important distinction between the people who run SMEs. There are "true" entrepreneurs who create and pursue opportunities for wealth creation, and "lifestyle" owner-managers who are more concerned to live a balanced life as their own bosses while still making a decent living. Moran (1999) pursues this theme of diversity within the sector, investigating the "growth orientation" of the small business owner-manager in an attempt to understand why some businesses grow and some do not. High growth oriented owner-managers seem more likely to rely on intuition and "gut feelings" and are unlikely to be particularly interested in the systematic and formal systems offered by work and organizational/ occupational psychology, since these might be seen as slowing them down or entangling them in red tape. "A support system for such owner managers would need to reflect their approach to business and encompass attributes of disorganisation, chaos, change, innovation and learning-by-doing so as to provide a stimulating environment for dealing with critical business development issues and accelerating stategic management capability" (p. 20). Moran argues that there is no substitute for occupational psychologists building a relationship with SMEs over a long period of time and "getting their hands dirty" to appreciate the culture of the firm and its complexity and diversity.

Given the tubulence of the current business climate with its pressing imperatives and ever shorter timescales, this is advice that colleagues working in large organizations would be wise to heed. As a profession, we need to know much more about the work of practitioners working with SMEs: the techniques and interventions they employ, the innovations and creative problem solving they are undoubtedly forced to use, their successes and failures, and the reasons for them. It is within the unforgiving environments of SMEs that we are likely to find the "fast response", business-oriented solutions needed in big business.

Work and organizational/occupational psychologists as evidence-based practitioners

I began this book with a consideration of what occupational psychology is for, and I feel compelled to return briefly to this theme at the end. Briner (1998) called for occupational psychologists to ground their practice in systematic evidence and evaluation if they are to avoid the "quick fix" trap. "Quick fixes" involve the rapid implementation of a policy or technique with the aim of resolving a presenting problem, which is often driven by the need to be "seen to be doing something" rather than on careful analysis of the underlying causes, and can be strongly influenced by fads and fashions. They can be championed by an "issue-seller", who has much to gain but little to lose from the adoption of his or her recommendations, and there is a focus on style of presentation rather than substance. Interventions are rarely evaluated and when they do not work, may be followed by another "quick fix", and so the process continues with failures rapidly subject to organizational amnesia.

There are many advantages associated with "quick fixes", which makes their use a rational strategy for top management. By definition, they are quick; they can be politically expedient; they are "do-able" in a difficult situation; and the implementers can "move on" before the full effects become apparent. They are also very ethically dubious, often ineffective, and wasteful of resources. The delayering and downsizing of organizations in the last recession is a classic case of a "quick fix". Even one of its main proponents, Charles Handy, was taken aback by the scale of the reaction and has toned down his pronouncements of late. The immediate costs were mass unemployment and great burdens on the State, traumatized and demoralized survivors, and a crisis in human resource management. The medium-term costs include workers committed to their own ends rather than their organizations' goals, and a severe skill shortage in some industries. The long-term consequences have yet to be fully worked through but the rising costs of work-related ill-health are beginning to be realized. The fact that all this has been accompanied by an economic upturn in many Western countries has obscured the true costs. In a report of a recent CIPD survey (*The Psychologist*, 2000), only 10% of UK companies see personnel issues as having a top priority over marketing and finance, despite much evidence that how staff are managed has an important link with business performance. The research is interpreted to show "how little value is placed on employees by many companies" (p. 540).

Such a denial of the value of evidenced-based practice would not be tolerated in fields such as medicine, and "seat-of-the-pants" decision making will not suffice in occupational psychology either. I couldn't agree more with Briner's (1998) arguments. What else have occupational psychologists to offer that many related professionals do not, if it is not this careful approach to the accumulation of good evidence and the evaluation of the success of our interventions? This does not have to mean slavish adherence to the traditional experimental, positivistic, scientific paradigm. This would make us rigid, inflexible, and unable to meet the pressing needs of our clients—and has perhaps contributed to negative perceptions of the profession's expertise in the past. There is no room for experimental purity in applied research, but we do need to know what we would do in an ideal world so that we are alive to the limitations of what we do in this one. Thus, we can draw appropriate and cautious conclusions and avoid the "guru syndrome" of miracle cures for all ills. The challenges that confront individuals and organizations in the changing workplace of the 21st century are too serious for a superficial approach.

Anderson, Herriot, and Hodgkinson (2001) published a thought-provoking article just as this book was going to press. In it they lament the fact that there has been a drift away from what they call "pragmatic science", which is high in both rigour and professional relevance. This has happened because researchers/academics and practitioners now rarely collaborate. The scramble for research funding has led the latter into "pedantic science", which may be very rigorous but has little or no relevance to anything in the real world of work. "The continued proliferation of studies investigating outmoded research questions and refinements of measurement procedures in relation to peripheral methodological concerns exemplifies this trend" (p. 399). On the other hand, practitioners have been driven by commercial pressures to move into "popularist science", which "draws upon concepts and methods that constitute currently fashionable solutions to issues. These often have little theoretical underpinning . . . Arguably, much of the recent research in the areas of emotional intelligence and managerial competencies exemplifies this trend" (p. 399). Pedantic and popularist science together lead to "irrelevant theory and in untheorized and invalid practice" or "puerile science". The authors advocate that perhaps the only way to reverse these trends is to "engage in political activity" (p. 407) to try to influence major stakeholders such as Trades Unions, Government, and private sector companies. Since my aims in writing this book were to champion "pragmatic science", to avoid academic pedantry in the presentation, and to engage in some modest "political activity", I am encouraged that such eminent people appear to share my views.

Another way forward would be to incorporate more professional doctorates into our continuing professional development. Here at the University of East London we have a programme specifically designed for busy practitioners to incorporate their ongoing work into a period of part-time study and development, which has research skills to enhance their own practice and advance the profession at its heart. We are specifically looking for new ways to conduct applied research that are responsive to business needs and maintain and develop good practice (Doyle, Slaven, & Day, 2001). This may also be a means to greater unity between the the researcher and practitioner arms of the profession. Someone once said there was nothing so practical as a good theory. Occupational psychology has plenty of these. What we need is more good evidence, collected in the real world of work to support them, and so enhance their usefulness.

Suggested further reading

Patterson, F. (Ed.) (2001). Emerging issues and future trends in work psychology: A centennial celebration. *Journal of Occupational and Organizational Psychology*, *74*(Whole No. 4).

This volume contains the article by Anderson et al. mentioned in the text, plus several other articles equally interesting and useful. All are written by leading work and organizational psychologists.

BOX 10.4
The finale ... which maybe encapsulates the essential message of this book in a joke

I can't resist finishing this book with a joke. It's for you to judge how funny or relevant it is but I hope you enjoy it.

"A shepherd was tending his sheep when a new Range Rover screeched to a halt next to him. The driver, a young man dressed in an Armani suit, Cerutti shoes, Ray-Ban sunglasses and a Ferragamo tie, said to the shepherd; "If I can tell you how many sheep you have, will you give me one?" "All right," said the shepherd. The young man connected his laptop into his cellphone; entered a NASA website; scanned the ground using his GPS; opened a database with 60 Excel table algorithms; then printed a 150 page report on a high-tech mini-printer. Finally he turned to the shepherd and said; "You have exactly 1586 sheep". "That's correct," answered the shepherd. "I suppose you can have your sheep."

The young man started putting it into the Range Rover, when the shepherd looked at him and asked; "If I guess your profession, will you return my sheep to me?" The young man smiled and said; "Why not?". "You're an investment banker," said the shepherd. Quite surprised, the young man replied; "Yes, how did you know?". "Very simple," said the shepherd. "First, you come here without being asked. Second, you make me pay for something I already know. And third, you haven't a clue about what I do—you've just picked up my dog."

The Times Magazine, 2 September 2000. Reprinted with permission.

References

Abrahams, M. (2001). *Higher education lecturer burnout: Structural equation modelling of relationships between job characteristics, job satisfaction and burnout.* Unpublished MSc Dissertation, University of East London.

Adams Atomic Energy Inc. (1996, April). *Chernobyl health effects.* Retrieved 24 April 2002 from http://www.ans.neep.wisc.edu/~ans/point_source/AEI/apr96/effects.html

Adams, J. S. (1965). Inequity in social exchange. In L. Berkowitz (Ed.), *Advances in experimental social psychology, Vol. 2.* New York: Academic Press.

Adams, J. S., & Jacobsen, P. R. (1964). Effects of wage inequities on work quality. *Journal of Applied Psychology, 69,* 19–25.

Adams, M. (2000a). Join the internet debate on the future of occupational psychology. *Occupational Psychologist, 39,* 16.

Adams, M. (2000b). Results from the virtual debate on the future of occupational psychology. *Occupational Psychologist, 40,* 26–27.

Adams, M. (2000c). Shaping the future of occupational psychology. *Selection and Development Review, 16*(2), 15–16.

Adams-Guppy, J., & Guppy, A. (2000). The management of fatigue in an international sample of truck drivers. In *The British Psychological Society occupational psychology conference book of proceedings* (pp. 47–51). Leicester, UK: British Psychological Society.

Adler, P. S. (1993). Time-and-motion regained. *Harvard Business Review,* January–February, 97–107.

Adler, P. S., & Cole, R. (1995). Designed for learning: A tale of two autoplants. In A. Sandberg (Ed.), *Enriching production.* Aldershot, UK: Avebury.

Aguinis, H., Henle, C. A., & Beaty, J. C., Jr (2001). Virtual reality technology: A new tool for personnel selection. *International Journal of Selection and Assessment, 9*(1/2), 70–83.

Aitkenhead, A. M., & Slack, J. M. (1985). *Issues in cognitive modeling.* Hove, UK: Lawrence Erlbaum Associates Ltd.

Akerstedt, T. (1985). Adjustment of physiological circadian rhythms and the sleep–wake cycle to shiftwork. In S. Folkhard & T. H. Monk (Eds.), *Hours of work: Temporal factors in work scheduling.* Chichester, UK: Wiley.

Akerstedt, T. (1988). Sleepiness as a consequence of shift work. *Sleep (Association of Professional Sleep Societies), 11*(1), 17–34.

Alban-Metcalfe, B. M., & West, M. A. (1991). Women managers. In J. Firth-Cozens & M. A. West (Eds.), *Women at work: Psychological and organizational perspectives.* Milton Keynes, UK: Open University Press.

Alban-Metcalfe, R. J., & Alimo-Metcalfe, B. (2000). An analysis of the convergent and discriminant validity of the Tranformational Leadership Questionnaire. *International Journal of Selection and Assessment*, *8*(3), 158–175.

Alderfer, C. P. (1972). *Existance, relatedness and growth: Human needs in organizational settings*. New York: Free Press.

Algera, J.A., & Kleinbeck, U. (1997a). Foreword. *European Journal of Work and Organizational Psychology*, *6*(3), 257–260.

Algera, J. A., & Kleinbeck, U. (Eds.) (1997b). Performance improvement programmes in Europe. *European Journal of Work and Organizational Psychology*, *6*(Whole No. 3).

Algera, J. A., Monhemius, L., & Wijnen, C. J. D. (1997). Quality improvement: Combining ProMES and SPC to work smarter. *European Journal of Work and Organizational Psychology*, *6*(3), 261–278.

Alimo-Metcalfe, B. (1994a). Gender and appraisal: Findings from a national survey of managers in the British National Health Service. In L. Heslop (Ed.), *The ties that bind: The Global Research conference on women and management, Ottawa, Canada, October, 1992*. Canadian Consortium of Management Schools.

Alimo-Metcalfe, B. (1994b, October 20). The poverty of PRP. *Health Service Journal*.

Alimo-Metcalfe, B. (1995). An investigation of female and male constructs of leadership and empowerment. *Women in Management Review*; *10*(2), 3–8.

Alimo-Metcalfe, B. (1998a). 360 degree feedback and leadership development. *International Journal of Selection and Assessment*, *6*(1), 35–44.

Alimo-Metcalfe, B. (1998b, July). *A new transformational leadership questionnaire (LQ) (Free of gender bias)*. Paper presented at the International Work Psychology conference, Institute of Work Psychology, University of Sheffield, UK.

Alimo-Metcalfe, B., & Alban-Metcalfe, R. J. (2000). A new approach to assessing transformational leadership. *Selection and Development Review*, *16*(5), 15–17.

Amabile, T. M., Conti, R., Coon, H., Lazenby, J., & Heron, M. (1996). Assessing the work environment for creativity. *Academy of Management Journal*, *39*, 1154–1184.

Anderson, J. R. (1982). Acquisition of cognitive skill. *Psychological Review*, *4*, 369–406.

Anderson, N. (1997). The validity and adverse impact of selection interviews. *Selection and Development Review*, *13*(5), 13–17.

Anderson, N. (2001). Towards a theory of socialization impact: Selection as pre-entry socialization. *International Journal of Selection and Assessment*, *9*(1/2), 84–91.

Anderson, N., & Cunningham-Snell, N. (2000). Personnel selection. In N. Chmiel (Ed.), *Introduction to work and organizational psychology: A European perspective*. Oxford, UK: Blackwells.

Anderson, N., Herriot, P., & Hodgkinson, G. P. (2001). The practitioner–researcher divide in industrial, work and organizational (IWO) psychology: Where are we now and where do we go from here? *Journal of Occupational and Organizational Psychology*, *74*(4), 391–412.

Anderson, N., & West, M. (1995). *Team climate inventory*. Windsor, UK: NFER-Nelson.

Annett, J. (1979). Memory for skill. In M. M. Gruneberg & P. E. Morris (Eds.), *Applied problems in memory*. London: Academic Press.

Annett, J., Duncan, K. D., Stammers, R. B., & Gray, M. J. (1971). *Task analysis* (Training Information No. 6). London: HMSO.

Apter, M. J. (1982). *The experience of motivation: The theory of psychological reversals.* London: Academic Press.

Apter, M. J. (1989). *Reversal theory: Motivation, emotion and personality.* London: Routledge.

Apter, M. J. (Ed.). (2001). *Motivational styles in everyday life: A guide to reversal theory.* Washington, DC: American Psychological Association.

Apter, M. J., & Batler, R. (1997). Gratuitous risk: A study of parachuting. In S. Svebak & M. J. Apter (Eds.), *Stress and health: A reversal theory perspective.* Washington, DC: Taylor & Francis.

Argyle, M. (1989). *The social psychology of work.* Harmondsworth, UK: Penguin.

Argyris, C. (1960). *Understanding organizational behaviour.* Homewood, IL: Dorsey Press.

Argyris, C. (1990). Inappropriate defenses against the monitoring of organizational development practice. *Journal of Applied Behavioural Science, 26,* 299–312.

Argyris, C., & Schon, D. A. (1978). *Organizational learning: A theory of action perspective.* Reading, MA: Addison-Wesley.

Arlin, P. K. (1990). Wisdom: The art of problem finding. In R. J. Sternberg (Ed.), *Wisdom: Its nature, origins, and development.* Cambridge, UK: Cambridge University Press.

Arnold, J. (1997a). *Managing careers into the 21st century.* London: Paul Chapman.

Arnold, J. (1997b). Nineteen propositions concerning the nature of effective thinking for career management in a turbulent world. *British Journal of Guidance and Counselling, 25*(4), 447–463.

Arnold, J. (1998, January). *The psychology of career management.* Paper presented at the British Psychological Society Occupational Psychology conference, Eastbourne.

Arnold, J., Cooper, C. L., & Robertson, I. T. (1998). *Work psychology* (3rd ed.). Harlow, UK: Financial Times/Prentice Hall.

Arnold, J., Robertson, I., & Cooper, C. L. (1991). *Work psychology.* London: Pitman.

Arthur, M. B. (1994). The boundaryless career: A new perspective for organizational enquiry. *Journal of Organizational Behaviour, 15,* 295–306.

Arthur, M. B., & Kram, K. E. (1989). Reciprocity at work: The separate yet inseparable possibilities for individual and organizational development. In M. B. Arthur, D. T. Hall, & B. S. Lawrence (Eds.), *Handbook of career theory.* Cambridge, UK: Cambridge University Press.

Arvey, R. D., Bouchard, T. J., Segal, N. L., & Abraham, L. M. (1989). Job satisfaction: Environmental and genetic components. *Journal of Applied Psychology, 74,* 187–192.

Arvey, R. D., McCall, B. P., Bouchard, T. J., Taubman, P., & Cavanaugh, M. A. (1994). Genetic influences on job satisfaction and work values. *Personality and Individual Differences, 17,* 21–33.

Ashford, B. E., & Saks, A. M. (1996). Socialization tactics: Longitudinal effects on newcomer adjustment. *Academy of Management Journal, 39,* 149–178.

Attree, E. (2000, March). *Introduction to human–computer interaction and the potential of virtual reality.* Paper presented at the University of East London.

Awosunle, S., & Doyle, C. (2001). Same-race bias in the selection interview. *Selection and Development Review, 17*(3), 3–6.

Azizollah, H. (2000). The search conference: A personal account. *Occupational Psychologist, 39,* 14–15.

Baddeley, A. (2000). The episodic buffer: A new component of working memory? *Trends in Cognitive Sciences, 4*(11), 417–423.

Baddeley, A. D., & Hitch, G. J. (1974). Working memory. In G. H. Bower (Ed.), *The psychology of learning and motivation: Advances in research and theory, Vol. 8.* New York: Academic Press.

Bailyn, L. (1980). *Living with technology: Issues at mid-career.* Cambridge, MA: MIT Press.

Bainbridge, L. (1987). Ironies of automation. In J. Rasmussen, K. Duncan, & J. Leplat (Eds.), *New technology and human error.* Chichester, UK: Wiley.

Baker, M., Barker, M., Thorne, J., & Dutnell, M. (1997). Leveraging human capital. *Journal of Knowledge Management, 1*(1), 6–7.

Baldry, C., & Fletcher, C. (2000a). The distribution and measurement of managerial self-awareness in the context of multi-source feedback: Findings from a field study. In *The British Psychological Society Occupational Psychology conference book of proceedings* (pp. 176–181). Leicester, UK: British Psychological Society.

Baldry, C., & Fletcher, C. (2000b). The impact of multiple source feedback on management development: Findings from a longitudinal study. In *The British Psychological Society Occupational Psychology conference book of proceedings* (pp. 104–108). Leicester, UK: British Psychological Society.

Baltes, P. B. (1987). Theoretical propositions of life-span developmental psychology. *Developmental Psychology, 23*(5), 611–626.

Baltes, P. B., & Smith, J. (1990). Towards a psychology of wisdom and its ontogenesis. In R.J. Sternberg (Ed.), *Wisdom: Its nature, origins, and development.* Cambridge, UK: Cambridge University Press.

Bandura, A. (1986). *Social foundations of thought and action.* Englewood Cliffs, NJ: Prentice Hall.

Bandura, A. (1989). Perceived self-efficacy in the exercise of personal agency. *The Psychologist: Bulletin of the British Psychological Society, 10,* 411–424.

Bandura, A. (1997). *Self-efficacy: The exercise of control.* New York: W.H. Freeman.

Barak, B., & Schiffman, L. G. (1981). Cognitive age: A non-chronological age variable. *Advances in Consumer Research, 8,* 602–606.

Barber, B. R. (2001, October 20). Ballots versus bullets. *Financial Times*, Weekend, p. I.

Barker, J. R. (1993). Tightening the iron cage: Concertive control in self managing teams. *Administrative Science Quarterly, 38,* 408–437.

Baron, H. (1998). The Disability Discrimination Act: Implications for test users. In *The British Psychological Society Third Test User conference book of proceedings* (pp. 7–9). Leicester, UK: British Psychological Society.

Baron, H., & Butterworth, A. (1997). Good practice for fair selection. In *The British Psychological Society Division of Occupational Psychology Second Test User conference book of proceedings* (pp. 25–28). Leicester, UK: British Psychological Society.

Baron, H., Henley, S., McGibbon, A., & McCarthy, T. (1998). *Motivation questionnaire manual and user's guide.* Thames Ditton, UK: Saville & Holdsworth.

Baron, J. N., Davis-Blake, A., & Bielby, W. T. (1986). The structure of opportunity: How promotion ladders vary within and among organizations. *Administrative Science Quarterly, 31,* 248–273.

Barrett, B., & Howells, R. (1997). *Occupational health and safety law* (3rd ed.). London: Financial Times/Pitman Publishing.

Barrick, M. R., & Mount, M. K. (1991). The big five personality dimensions and job performance: A meta-analysis. *Personnel Psychology, 44*, 1–26.

Bartlett, F. C. (1932). *Remembering*. Cambridge, UK: Cambridge University Press.

Bartlett, F. C. (1943). Fatigue following highly skilled work. *Proceedings of the Royal Society, B131*, 247–257.

Bartram, D. (1990). Reliability and validity. In J. R. Beech & L. Harding (Eds.), *Testing people: A practical guide to psychometrics*. Windsor, UK: NFER-Nelson.

Bartram, D. (1994). Computer-based assessment. In C. L. Cooper & I. T. Robertson (Eds.), *International review of industrial and organizational psychology, Vol. 9* (pp. 31–69). Chichester, UK: Wiley.

Bartram, D. (1995). Validation of the Micropat battery. *International Journal of Selection and Assessment, 3*, 84–95.

Bartram, D. (1997). Distance assessment: Psychological assessment through the internet. *Selection and Development Review, 13*, 10–14.

Bartram, D. (1999). Testing and the internet: Current realities, issues and future possibilities. *Selection and Development Review, 15*, 3–12.

Bartram, D. (2000). Internet recruitment and selection: Kissing frogs to find princes. *International Journal of Selection and Assessment, 8*(4), 261–274.

Bartram, D. (2001, December). *Testing on the internet: Opportunities, issues and challenges*. Paper presented at the University of East London.

Bartram, D., Crawshaw, M., Geake, A., & Sherman, K. (1999). Predicting performance in arthroscopic surgery with a computer-based tracking task. In *British Psychological Society Occupational Psychology conference book of proceedings* (pp. 138–142). Leicester, UK: British Psychological Society.

Bartram, D., & Dale, H. C. A. (1982). The Eysenck personality inventory as a selection test for military pilots. *Journal of Occupational Psychology, 55*, 287–296.

Bartram, D., & Lindley, P. A. (1994). *Psychological testing: The BPS "level A" open learning programme*. Leicester, UK: BPS Books.

Bartram, D., Lindley, P. A., & Foster, J. (1992). *The selection of young people by medium sized and large organizations* (NPAL Rep.). London: Department of Employment Careers Service Branch.

Bartram, D., Lindley, P. A., Marshall, L., & Foster, J. (1993). *The recruitment and selection of young people by small businesses*. London: Department of Employment Careers Service Branch.

Baruch, G. K., Biener, L., & Barnett, R. C. (1987). Women and gender in research on work and family stress. *American Psychologist, 42*, 130–136.

Baruch, Y., & Hind, P. (1999). Perpetual motion in organizations: Effective management and the impact of the new psychological contracts on "Survivor Syndrome". *European Journal of Work and Organizational Psychology, 8*(2), 295–306.

Bass, B. M. (1999). Two decades of research and development in transformational leadership. *European Journal of Work and Organizational Psychology, 6*(1), 9–25.

Bass, B. M., & Avolio, B. J. (1990). *Transformational leadership development: Manual for the multifactor leadership questionnaire*. Palo Alto, CA: Consulting Psychologist Press.

Bass, B. M., Avolio, B. J., & Atwater, L. (1996). The transformational and transactional leadership of men and women. *Applied Psychology: An International Review, 45*(1), 5–34.

Battram, A. (1998). *Navigating complexity: The essential guide to complexity theory in business and management*. London: The Industrial Society.

Baxter, J. C., Brock, B., Hill, P. C., & Rozelle, R. M. (1981). Letters of recommendation: A question of value. *Journal of Applied Psychology, 66*, 296–301.

BBC News Europe (2002). *Deadly toll of Chernobyl.* Retrieved 24 April 2002 from http://news.bbc.co.uk/hi/.../world/europe/newsid_722000/722533.stm

Beech, D. (2000). The search conference (continued): Adding value at a strategic level. *The Occupational Psychologist, 40*, 21–25.

Beer, M., Spector, B., Lawrence, P. R., Quinn-Mills, D., & Walton, R. E. (1984). *Managing human assets: The ground breaking Harvard Business School program.* New York: Macmillan.

Belbin, R. M. (1981). *Management teams: Why they succeed or fail.* London: Heinemann.

Bellows, R. M. (1954). *Psychology of personnel in business and industry* (2nd ed.). New York: Prentice Hall.

Benchmarks (Multi-rater feedback instrument). Oxford, UK: Oxford Psychologists Press.

Bennis, W. G. (1977). Bureaucracy and social change: An anatomy of a training failure. In P. H. Mirvis & D. N. Berg (Eds.), *Failures in organizational development and change.* New York: Wiley.

Berg, D. N. (1998). Resurrecting the muse: Followership in organizations. In E. B. Klein, F. Gabelnick, & P. Herr (Eds.), *The psychodynamics of leadership.* Madison, CT: Psychosocial Press.

Bernadin, H. J., & Beatty, R. W. (1984). *Performance appraisal: Assessing human behaviour at work.* Boston: Kent.

Berridge, J. (1999). Employee assistance programmes and stress counselling: At a crossroads? In C. Feltham (Ed.), *Controversies in psychotherapy and counselling.* London: Sage.

Blake, R., & Mouton, J. (1972). *The diagnosis and development matrix.* Houston, TX: Scientific Methods.

Blinkhorn, S., & Johnson, C. (1990). The insignificance of personality testing. *Nature, 348*, 671–672.

Blinkhorn, S., & Johnson, C. (1991). Personality tests: The great debate—the case. *Personnel Management*, September, 38–39.

Blinkhorn, S., & Johnson, C. (1996). *The ABLE series manual and user's guide.* Oxford, UK: Oxford Psychologists Press.

Boden, M. A. (1981). *Minds and mechanisms: Philosophical psychology and computational models.* Brighton, UK: Harvester Press.

Boden, M. A. (1994). *Piaget* (Modern Masters, 2nd ed.). London: Fontana.

Bohle, P., & Tilley, A. J. (1989). The impact of night work on psychological well-being. *Ergonomics, 32*, 1089–1099.

Booth, J. F. (1998). The user interface in computer-based assessment: Applied and theoretical problematics of an evolving technology. *International Journal of Selection and Assessment, 6*(2), 61–81.

Booth, P. (1989). *An introduction to human–computer interaction.* Hove, UK: Lawrence Erlbaum Associates Ltd.

Bourne, A., Oliver, K., & Warr, P. (1998). Agreement and disagreement in 360 degree feedback. *The British Psychological Society Third Test User conference book of proceedings* (pp. 21–26). Leicester, UK: British Psychological Society.

Boyle, S. (1997). Researching the selection interview. *Selection and Development Review, 13*(4), 15–17.

Bray, D. W., & Grant, D. L. (1966). The assessment center in the measurement of potential for business management. *Psychological Monographs, 80*(17, Whole No. 625).

Breslow, L., & Buell, P. (1960). Mortality from coronary heart disease and physical activity of work in California. *Journal of Chronic Diseases, 11*, 615–625.

Bright, J. E. H., & Hutton, S. (2000). Impression management in the resume. *International Journal of Selection and Assessment, 8*(2), 41–53.

Briner, R. B. (1996). Making occupational stress management interventions work: The role of assessment. In *Proceedings of the British Psychological Society Occupational Psychology conference* (pp. 49–54). Leicester, UK: British Psychological Society.

Briner, R. B. (1997). Beyond stress and satisfaction: Alternative approaches to understanding psychological well-being at work. In *Proceedings of the British Psychological Society Occupational Psychology conference* (pp. 95–100). Leicester, UK: British Psychological Society.

Briner, R. B. (1998). What is an evidence-based approach to practice and why do we need one in occupational psychology? In *The British Psychological Society Occupational Psychology conference book of proceedings* (pp. 39–44). Leicester, UK: British Psychological Society.

Briner, R. B. (Ed.) (1999a). Emotional at work. *European Journal of Work and Organizational Psychology, 8*(Whole No. 3).

Briner, R. B. (1999b, January). Feeling and smiling. *The Psychologist,* pp. 16–19.

Briner, R. B. (1999c, October 26). *Organizational stress as a trivial concept and modern myth: Alternative approaches to understanding work and well-being.* Paper presented at the University of Surrey, UK.

Briner, R. B., & Daniels, K. (1999). Work and well-being: Current understanding and developing new approaches. *Occupational Psychologist, 37*, 28–29.

Briner, R. B., & Hockey, G. R. J. (1988). Operator stress and computer-based work. In C. L. Cooper & R. Payne (Eds.), *Causes, coping and consequences of stress at work.* Chichester, UK: Wiley.

British Psychological Society. (2000). *Guidelines for the development and use of computer-based assessments.* Leicester, UK: Professional Affairs Board Steering Committee on Test Standards, British Psychological Society.

Broadbent, D. E. (1958). *Perception and communication.* Oxford, UK: Pergamon Press.

Brockner, J., Grover, S. L., & Blonder, M. (1988). Predictors of survivors' job involvement following lay-offs: A field study. *Journal of Applied Psychology, 73*, 436–442.

Brockner, J., Tyler, T. R., & Cooper-Schneider, R. (1992). The influence of prior commitment to an institution on reactions to perceived unfairness: The higher they are, the harder they fall. *Administrative Science Quarterly, 37*, 241–261.

Brodsky, C. M. (1976). *The harrassed worker.* Toronto, Canada: Lexington Books/D.C. Heath & Co.

Brotherton, C. (1999). *Social psychology and management: Issues for a changing society.* Buckingham, UK: Open University Press.

Brown, M. (1997, August). The perks that work. *Management Today,* pp. 61–64.

Brown, R. (1988). *Group processes.* Oxford, UK: Blackwell.

Brown, W. (1979). Social determinants of pay. In G. M. Stephenson & C. J. Brotherton (Eds.), *Industrial relations: A social psychological approach.* Chichester, UK/New York: Wiley.

Bruner, J. (1979). From communication to language: A psychological perspective. In V. Lee (Ed.), *Language development*. London: Croom Helm.

The BSE Inquiry: The Report (2000). House of Commons papers 1999-00 887. House of Commons: Lord Phillips of Worth Maltravers, J. Bridgeman, & M. Ferguson-Smith. London: Stationery Office.

Buckland, S. (2000). The search conference (continued): The demands of the market-place. *Occupational Psychologist, 40*, 16–17.

Bull, A. (1997). Models of counselling in organizations. In M. Carroll & M. Walton (Eds.), *Handbook of counselling in organizations*. London: Sage.

Bunce, D., & West, M. A. (1995). Changing work environments: Innovative coping responses to occupational stress. *Work and Stress, 8*, 319–331.

Bunn, G. (2001). C.S. Myers Lecture: Charlie and the chocolate factory. *The Psychologist, 14*(11), 576–579.

Burke, E. (1997). Technology and testing: Advances and issues. In *The British Psychological Society Second Test User conference book of proceedings* (pp. 7–13). Leicester, UK: British Psychological Society.

Burke, E. (1998). Computer-based assessment: Technological advances and professional issues. In *The British Psychological Society Third Test User conference book of proceedings* (pp. 35–45). Leicester, UK: British Psychological Society.

Burke, E. (2000a). Assessing and selecting decision-makers for risk critical roles. In *The British Psychological Society Occupational Psychology conference book of proceedings* (pp. 68–73). Leicester, UK: British Psychological Society.

Burke, E. (2000b). The economic impact of the fit between the values of individuals and organizational culture. In *The British Psychological Society Occupational Psychology conference book of proceedings* (pp. 136–141). Leicester, UK: British Psychological Society.

Burke, E., Kitching, A., & Valsler, C. (1999). Computer-based assessment for pilots: The *Pilot Ap*titude Tester (*PILAPT*). In *The British Psychological Society Occupational Psychology conference book of proceedings* (pp. 95–99). Leicester, UK: British Psychological Society.

Burr, J. (1998). *An evaluation of a 360 degree feedback development programme.* Unpublished MSc dissertation, London Guildhall University.

Caldwell, L. S., & Lyddan, J. M. (1971). Serial isometric fatigue functions with variable intertrial intervals. *Journal of Motor Behaviour, 3*, 17–30.

Campbell, J. (1994). Equiped for independence or self-determination? *British Journal of Occupational Therapy, 57*(3), 89–90.

Campbell, J.P. (1971). Personnel training and development. *Annual Review of Psychology*. Palo Alto, CA: Annual Reviews.

Carnall, C. (1995). *Managing change in organizations* (2nd ed.). London: Prentice Hall International.

Carpenter, S. (2001). Research confirms the virtues of "sleeping on it". *Monitor on Psychology, 32*(9), 49–50.

Carroll, D., Ring, C., Shrimpton, J., Evans, P., Willemsen, G. H. M., & Hucklebridge, F. (1996). Secretory immunoglobulin A and cardiovascular responses to acute psychological challenge. *International Journal of Behavioural Medicine, 3*, 266–279.

Carroll, M. (1994). *Building bridges: A study of employee counsellors in the private sector.* Unpublished MSc dissertation, City University, London.

Carroll, M. (1996). *Workplace counselling*. London: Sage.

Carroll, M. (1997). Counselling in organizations: An overview. In M. Carroll & M. Walton (Eds.), *Handbook of counselling in organizations*. London: Sage.

Carroll, M., & Walton, M. (Eds.) (1997a). *Handbook of counselling in organizations*. London: Sage.

Carroll, M., & Walton, M. (1997b). Introduction. In M. Carroll & M. Walton (Eds.), *Handbook of counselling in organizations*. London: Sage.

Cartwright, S., & Cooper, C. L. (1996). Public policy and occupational health psychology in Europe. *Journal of Occupational Health Psychology, 1*, 349–361.

Cascio, W. F. (1982). *Costing human resources: The financial impact of behaviour in organizations*. Boston: Kent.

Castells, M. (1997a). *The information age: Economy, society and culture: Vol. 1. The rise of the network society*. Oxford, UK: Blackwell.

Castells, M. (1997b). *The information age: Economy, society and culture: Vol. 2. The power of identity*. Oxford, UK: Blackwell.

Castells, M. (1998). *The information age: Economy, society and culture: Vol. 3. End of the millennium*. Oxford, UK: Blackwell.

Cattell, R. B. (1937). *The fight for our national intelligence*. London: P.S. King.

Chapanis, A. (1965). On the allocation of function between men and machines. *Occupational Psychology, 39*, 1–11.

Chapman, M. (1999). Foreword. *Occupational Psychologist, 38*, 3–4.

Chell, E. (1999). The entrepreneurial personality—past, present and future. *Occupational Psychologist, 38*, 5–12.

Chernobyl No More (n.d.) *Chernobyl 'costs'*. Retrieved 24 April 2002 from http://www.ecn.cz/private/c10/costs.html

Cherrington, D. (1989). *Organizational behaviour: The management of individual and organizational performance*. Boston: Allyn & Bacon.

Chesbrough, H. W., & Teece, D. J. (1996, January–February). When is virtual virtuous? *Harvard Business Review*, 65–73.

Chiles, W. D. (1955). *Experimental studies of prolonged wakefulness* (WADC Tech. Rep. No. 55-395). Dayton, OH: Wright-Patterson Airforce Base.

Chmiel, N. (1998). *Jobs, technology and people*. London: Routledge.

Chmiel, N. (Ed.) (2000). *Introduction to work and organizational psychology: A European perspective*. Oxford, UK: Blackwell.

Chomsky, N. (1965). *Aspects of the theory of syntax*. Cambridge, MA: MIT Press.

Clark, R., & Baron, H. (1997). *Guidelines for testing people with disabilities*. Thames Ditton, UK: Saville & Holdsworth.

Clarke, S. D., Long, M. M., & Schiffman, L. G. (1999). The mind–body connection: The relationship among physical activity level, life satisfaction, and cognitive age among mature females. *Journal of Social Behaviour and Personality, 14*, 221–241.

Clifford, L., & Bennett, H. (1997). Best practice in 360 degree feedback. *Selection and Development Review, 13*(2), 6–9.

Collier, J. G., & Davies, L. M. (1986). *Chernobyl: The accident at Chernobyl Unit 4 in the Ukraine, April 1986*. Barnwood, UK: Central Electricity Generating Board.

Colligan, M. J., & Rosa, R. R. (1990). Shiftwork effects on social and family life. *Occupational Medicine: State of the Art Reviews, 5*, 315–322.

The Committee on Higher Education (Cmnd 2154) (the Robbins Committee) (1963). *Higher Education: Report of the Committee on Higher Education* (1963). London: HMSO.

The Committee on Safety and Health at Work 1970–72 (Cmnd 5034) (the Robens Committee) (1972). *Safety and Health at Work* (1972). London: HMSO.

Computing (2000, May 25). Labour delivers its plan to end IT disasters.

Connor, E., & Lake, L. (1994). *Managing organizational change* (2nd ed.). Westport, CT: Praeger.

Connor, S. (2000, November 22). Deep sleep and good memory may be the happiest bedfellows. *The Independent*, p. 5.

Cook, M. (1988). *Personnel selection and productivity* (2nd ed.). Chichester, UK: Wiley.

Cook, M. (1998). *Personnel selection: Adding value through people* (3rd ed.). Chichester, UK: Wiley.

Cooper, C. L. (1997, July). *The changing nature of work: Future stressors and their implications*. Paper presented at the fifth European Congress of Psychology, Dublin, Ireland.

Cooper, C. L., Cooper, R. D., & Eaker, L. H. (1988). *Living with stress*. Harmondsworth, UK: Penguin.

Cooper, M. D. (1998). *Improving safety culture: A practical guide*. Chichester, UK: Wiley.

Cooper, M. D., Phillips, R. A., Robertson, I. T., & Duff, A. R. (1993). Improving safety on construction sites by the utilisation of psychologically based techniques: Alternative approaches to the measurement of safety behaviour. *European Review of Applied Psychology, 43*, 33–41.

Costa, A. C., Roe, R. A., & Taillieu, T. (2001). Trust within teams: The relation with performance effectiveness. *European Journal of Work and Organizational Psychology, 10*(3), 225–244.

Costa, P. T. (1996). Work and personality: Use of the NEO-PI-R in industrial/organizational psychology. *Applied Psychology: An International Review, 45*, 225–241.

Costa, P. T., & McCrae, R. R. (1992). *The NEO PI-R professional manual*. Odessa, FL: Psychological Assessment Resources.

Cowan, D. A. (1995). *Practical wisdom for long-term organizational survival: Aquiring multi-dimensional awareness*. Paper presented at the National Academy of Management meetings, Vancouver, Canada.

Cowan, N., & Cowan, R. (1989, December). Are references worth the paper they're written on? *Personnel Management*, p. 38.

Craig, M. (1995). Techniques for analysis. In S. Truelove (Ed.), *The handbook of training and development* (2nd ed.). Oxford, UK: Blackwells.

Craik, F. I. M., & Jennings, J. M. (1992). Human memory. In F. I. M. Craik & T. A. Salthouse (Eds.), *The handbook of aging and cognition*. Hillsdale, NJ: Lawrence Erlbaum Associates Inc.

Craik, K. J. W. (1940). *Fatigue apparatus* (FPRC Rep. No. 119). London: Air Ministry.

"Cranfield Man". (1969). Industrial use of ergonomics. *Applied Ergonomics, 1*, 26–32.

Crawshaw, C. M. (2000a). The search conference: Overview. *Occupational Psychologist, 39*, 3.

Crawshaw, C. M. (2000b). The search conference (continued): Overview. *Occupational Psychologist, 40*, 12.

Cronbach, L. J. (1990). *Essentials of psychological testing* (5th ed.). New York: Harper & Row.

Cropanzano, R., & Folger, R. (1992). Procedural justice and worker motivation. In R. M. Steers & L. W. Porter (Eds.), *Motivation and work behaviour* (5th ed.). New York: McGraw-Hill.

Cropanzano, R., James, K., & Konovsky, M. A. (1993). Dispositional affectivity as a predictor of work attitudes and performance. *Journal of Organizational Behaviour*, *14*, 595–606.

Crush, P. (2000, November). Out to get you. *Management Today*, pp. 94–97.

Cummings, T., & Blumberg, M. (1987). Advanced manufacturing technology and work design. In T. D. Wall, C. W. Clegg, & N. J. Kemp (Eds.), *The human side of advanced manufacturing technology*. Chichester, UK: Wiley.

Curral, L. A., Forrestier, R. H., Dawson, J. F., & West, M. A. (2001). It's what you do and the way that you do it: Team task, team size, and innovation-related group processes. *European Journal of Work and Organizational Psychology*, *10*(2), 187–204.

Curtis, B., Krasner, H., & Iscoe, N. (1988). A field study of the software design process for large systems. *Communications of the ACM*, *31*, 1268–1287.

Cyert, R. M., & March, J. G. (1963). *A behavioural theory of the firm*. Englewood Cliffs, NJ: Prentice Hall.

Dalessio, A. T., & Silverheart, T. A. (1994). Combining biodata and interview information: Predicting decisions and performance criteria. *Personnel Psychology*, *47*, 303–315.

Dalton, G. (1989). Developmental views of careers in organizations. In M. B. Arthur, D. T. Hall, & B. S. Lawrence (Eds.), *Handbook of career theory*. Cambridge, UK: Cambridge University Press.

Dalton, G., & Thompson, P. (1986). *Novations: Strategies for career development*. Glenview, IL: Scott Foresman.

Danford, A. (1998). Work organization inside Japanese firms in South Wales: A break from Taylorism? In P. Thompson & C. Warhurst (Eds.), *Workplaces of the future*. Basingstoke, UK: Macmillan Business.

Daniels, K., Lamond, D. A., & Standen, P. (Eds.) (2000). *Managing telework: Perspectives from human resource management and work psychology*. London: Business Press/Thomson Learning.

Danielsson, M., & Ohlsson, K. (1997). Models of decision making in emergency management. In D. Harris (Ed.), *Engineering psychology and cognitive ergonomics: Vol. 2*. Aldershot, UK: Ashgate.

Da Silva, W. A. (1979). The formation of historical concepts through contextual cues. In A. Floyd (Ed.), *Cognitive development in the school years*. London: Croom Helm.

Davidson, M. J. (1997). *The black and ethnic minority woman manager: Cracking the concrete ceiling*. London: Paul Chapman.

Davidson, M. J., & Cooper, C. L. (1992). *Shattering the glass ceiling: The woman manager*. London: Paul Chapman.

Davies, B., Phelp, A., & Warr, P. (1997). *Corporate culture ouestionnaire manual and user's guide*. Thames Ditton, UK: Saville & Holdsworth.

Davies, D. R., Shackleton, V. J., & Parasuraman, R. (1983). Monotony and boredom. In G. R. J. Hockey (Ed.), *Stress and fatigue in human performance*. Chichester, UK: Wiley.

Davis, L. E. (1972). Job satisfaction research: The post-industrial view. In L. E. Davis & J. C. Taylor (Eds.), *Design of jobs*. Harmondsworth, UK: Penguin.

Davis-Blake, A., & Pfeffer, J. (1989). Just a mirage: The search for dispositional effects in organizational research. *Academy of Management Review*, *15*, 385–400.

Day, A. (2001). *An investigation into the impact of the introduction of multi-skilled, semi-autonomous work groups on groups and individuals in two "brownfield" manufacturing sites: The impact of multi-skilled, semi-autonomous work groups in a manufacturing environment—a longitudinal field study*. Unpublished D. Occ. Psych. thesis, University of East London.

Decker, P. J., & Borgen, F. H. (1993). Dimensions of work appraisal: Stress, strain, coping, job satisfaction, and negative affectivity. *Journal of Counselling Psychology, 40*(4), 470–478.

De Jong, R. D., Bouhuys, S. A., & Barnhoorn, J. C. (1999). Personality, self-efficacy and functioning in management teams: A contribution to validation. *International Journal of Selection and Assessment, 7*(1), 46–49.

Department of Organizational Psychology Birkbeck College (1998–1999). *Annual report: 1998–1999*. Unpublished report, University of London.

De Vries, R. E., Roe, R. A., & Taillieu, T. C. B. (1999). On charisma and need for leadership. *European Journal of Work and Organizational Psychology, 8*(1), 109–127.

Dinges, D. F., Orne, M. T., & Orne, E. C. (1984). Sleepiness during sleep deprivation: The effects of performance demands and circadian phase. In M. H. Chase, W. B. Webb, & R. Wilder-Jones (Eds.), *Sleep research: Vol. 13*. Los Angeles: University of California.

Dipboye, R. L. (1997a). Organizational barriers to implementing a rational model of training. In M. A. Quinones & A. Ehrenstein (Eds.), *Training for a rapidly changing workplace: Applications of psychological research*. Washington, DC: American Psychological Association.

Dipboye, R. L. (1997b). Structured employment interviews: Why do they work? Why are they under-utilised? In N. Anderson & P. Herriot (Eds.), *International handbook of selection and assessment*. Chichester, UK: Wiley.

Dix, A., Finley, J., Abourd, G., & Beale, R. (1998). *Human–computer interaction* (2nd ed.). London: Prentice Hall Europe.

Dixon, N. F. (1981). *Preconscious processing*. London: Wiley.

Donaldson, M. (1978). *Children's minds*. Glasgow, UK: Fontana.

Dooley, B. (1996). At work away from work. *The Psychologist, 9*(4), 155–158.

Downs, S. (1995). Learning to learn. In S. Truelove (Ed.), *The handbook of training and development* (2nd ed.). Oxford, UK: Blackwells.

Doyle, C. E. (1992). *Analysis of a staff attitudes survey and towards the development of a shorter survey questionnaire*. Unpublished MSc dissertation, University of Hull, UK.

Doyle, C. E. (1998). The work experience of senior academic women: Stress, coping and career progression. In *International Work Psychology conference book of proceedings*. Sheffield, UK: Institute of Work Psychology.

Doyle, C. E. (1999). The professional doctorate in occupational psychology at the University of East London. *European Journal of Work and Organizational Psychology, 8*(3), 487–490.

Doyle, C. E. (2000). The British Psychological Society: The 2000 Occupational Psychology conference, Brighton, UK, 5–7 January, 2000. Some personal highlights. *European Journal of Work and Organizational Psychology, 9*(2), 293–297.

Doyle, C. E. & Hind, P. A. (1997, 2 February). Women in psychology: A survey of female psychology lecturers. In *Proceedings of the British Psychological Society, 5*(1).

Doyle, C., & Hind, P. A. (1998). Occupational stress, burnout and job status in female academics. *Gender, Work and Organization, 5*(2), 67–82.

Doyle, C., Slaven, G., & Day, A. (2001). Continuing professional development and evidence-based practice: The role of the professional doctorate at the University of East London. *Occupational Psychologist, 43*, 17–20.

Dreary, I. J., & Tait, R. (1987). Effects of sleep disruption on cognitive performance and mood in medical house officers. *British Medical Journal, 295*, 1513–1516.

Drucker, P. F. (1994). The age of social transformation. *Atlantic Monthly, 247*(5), 53–80.

Drummond, S. P. A., Brown, G. A., Gillin, J. C., Stricker, J. L., Wong, E. C., & Buxton, R. B. (2000). Altered brain response to verbal learning following sleep deprivation. *Nature, 403*, 655–657.

Dulewicz, S. V., & Fletcher, C. (1989). The context and dynamics of performance appraisal. In P. Herriot (Ed.), *Assessment and selection in organizations*. London: Wiley.

Duncan, D. C. (2001). Response to "The identity of occupational psychology" (TOP, August 2000). *Occupational Psychologist, 42*, 14–17.

Dunnette, M. D., & Maetzold, J. (1955). Use of a weighted application blank in hiring seasonal employees. *Journal of Applied Psychology, 39*, 308–310.

Dutton, J. E., & Dukerich, J. M. (1991). Keeping an eye on the mirror: Image identity in organizational adaptation. *Academy of Management Journal, 34*, 517–554.

Eaton, N. K., Wing, H., & Mitchell, K. J. (1985). Alternative methods of estimating the dollar value of performance. *Personnel Psychology, 38*, 27–40.

Edmondson, A. C. (1996). Learning from mistakes is easier said than done: Group and organizational influences on the detection and correction of human error. *Journal of Applied Behavioural Science, 32*, 5–28.

Edmondson, A. C. (1999). Psychological safety and learning behaviour in work teams. *Administrative Science Quarterly, 44*, 350–383.

Edwards, D. (2000). 360 degree feedback as a longitudinal development intervention: A consultancy perspective. *Selection and Development Review, 16*(3), 9–14.

Efron, J. R., & Gibson, J. (1981). Modification and development of proficiency tests for visually handicapped senior high school students. *Journal of Visual Impairment and Blindness, 75*, 286–291.

Egan, G. E. (1994). *The skilled helper: A systematic approach to effective helping* (5th ed.). Monterey, CA: Brooks/Cole.

Egan, G. E. (1998). *The skilled helper: A problem-management approach to helping* (6th ed.). Pacific Grove, CA: Brooks/Cole.

Egan, G. E., & Cowan, M. A. (1979). *People in systems: A model for development in the human-service professions and education*. Monterey, CA: Brooks/Cole.

Eisenberg, N., Fabes, R. A., Guthrie, I. K., & Reiser, M. (2000). Dispositional emotionality and regulation: Their role in predicting quality of social functioning. *Journal of Personality and Social Psychology, 78*(1), 136–157.

Emery, M., & Purser, R. E. (1996). *The search conference*. San Francisco: Jossey-Bass.

Empson, J. (1989). *Sleep and dreaming*. London: Faber & Faber.

Erickson, E. (1968). *Identity, youth and crisis*. New York: Norton.

Evans, P., Bristow, M., Hucklebridge, F., Clow, A., & Pang, E. Y. (1994). Stress, arousal, cortisol and secretory immunoglobulin A in students undergoing assessment. *British Journal of Clinical Psychology, 33*, 575–576.

Evans, P., Bristow, M., Hucklebridge, F., Clow, A., & Walters, N. (1993). The relationship between secretory immunity, mood and life events. *British Journal of Clinical Psychology, 32*, 227–236.

Evans, P., Clow, A., & Hucklebridge, F. (1997, July). Stress and the immune system. *The Psychologist*, pp. 303–307.

Evening Standard (2000, June 7). Safety at work shake-up will hit bosses in pocket.

Evening Standard (1999, October 6). Report on the Paddington rail crash.

Farquarson, A. (1999, April 17). I'll make your life a misery. *Guardian*, p. 32.

Feldman, D. C. (2000). The Dilbert syndrome. *American Behavioural Scientist, 43*(8), 1286–1301.

Felstead, A., & Jewson, N. (1999). Domestic product. *People Management, 5*(24), 34–37.

Feltham, C. (Ed.) (1999). *Controversies in psychotherapy and counselling*. London: Sage.

Feltham, R. (1988). Assessment centre decision making: Judgmental vs. mechanical. *Journal of Occupational Psychology, 61*, 237–241.

Feltham, R., Lewis, C., Anderson, P., & Hughes, D. (1998). Psychometrics: Cultural impediments to global recruitment and people development. *Selection and Development Review, 14*(4), 16–21.

Ferguson, N. (2000, November 4). Dreaming spires and speeding modems. *Financial Times*, Weekend.

Festinger, L. (1957). *A theory of cognitive dissonance*. Evanston, IL: Row & Peterson.

Festinger, L. A., Schachter, S., & Back, K. (1950). *Social pressures in informal groups*. New York: Harper & Row.

Finney, M. (2000). CV biodata: Its use for CV screening and applicant impression formation. *Occupational Psychologist, 40*, 3–6.

Fisher, S. G., Hunter, T. A., & Masrossen, W. D. K. (2001). A validation study of Belbin's team roles. *European Journal of Work and Organizational Psychology, 10*(2), 121–144.

Fitts, P. M. (1951). Engineering psychology and equipment design. In S. S. Stevens (Ed.), *Handbook of experimental psychology*. New York: Wiley.

Fitts, P. M. (1962). Functions of man in complex systems. *Aerospace Engineering, 21*, 34–39.

Fitts, P. M., & Jones, R. E. (1961). Psychological aspects of instrument display 1: Analysis of 270 "pilot error" experiences in reading and interpreting aircraft instruments (Aeromedical Laboratory Rep. AMRL/TSEAA-694-12A, July). In W. Sinaiko (Ed.), *Selected papers in the design and use of control systems*. New York: Dover. (Original work published 1947)

Fitts, P. M., & Posner, M. I. (1967). *Human performance*. Belmont, CA: Brooks/Cole.

Flanagan, J. C. (1946). The experimental validation of a selection procedure. *Educational and Psychological Measurement, 6*, 445–466.

Flanagan, J. C. (1954). The critical incident technique. *Psychological Bulletin, 51*, 327–358.

Flavell, J. H. (1963). *The developmental psychology of Jean Piaget*. New York/London: Van Nostrand.

Flavell, J. H. (1985). *Cognitive development* (2nd ed.). London: Prentice Hall.

Fletcher, B., C., & Payne, R. L. (1980). Stress and work: A review and theoretical framework I. *Personnel Review*, *9*(1), 19–28.

Fletcher, C. (1982). Assessment centres. In D. Mackenzie-Davey & M. Harris (Eds.), *Judging people*. London: McGraw-Hill.

Fletcher, C. (1988). Occupational psychology: Some difficulties of doing experimental research. *Bulletin of the British Psychological Society*, *33*, 11–14.

Fletcher, C. (1997a). *Appraisal: Routes to improved performance* (2nd ed.). London: Institute of Personnel and Development.

Fletcher, C. (1997b). The impact of psychometric assessment: Fostering positive candidate attitude and reactions. *Selection and Development Review*, *13*(4), 8–11.

Fletcher, C. (2000). Performance appraisal: Assessing and developing performance and potential. In N. Chmiel (Ed.), *Introduction to work and organizational psychology: A European perspective*. Oxford, UK: Blackwell.

Fletcher, C., Baldry, C., & Cunningham-Snell, N. (1998). The psychometric properties of 360 degree feedback: An empirical study and a cautionary tale. *International Journal of Selection and Assessment*, *6*(1), 19–34.

Fletcher, C., & Williams, R. (1992). *Performance appraisal and career development* (2nd ed.). London: Stanley Thornes.

Fletcher, C., & Williams, R. (1996). Performance management, job satisfaction and organizational commitment. *British Journal of Management*, *7*, 169–179.

Flin, R. H., Mearns, K. J., Fleming, M., & Gordon, R. (1996). *Risk perception in UK off-shore workers*. Report OTH 94454 to OSD, HSE. Suffolk: HSE Books.

Flynn, J. (1998). *The future of work*. Unpublished undergraduate paper, Trinity and All Saints College of the University of Leeds, UK.

Folkard, S. (1996). Body rhythms and shiftwork. In P. Warr (Ed.), *Psychology at work* (4th ed.). Harmondsworth, UK: Penguin.

Folkard, S., & Monk, T. H. (1979). Shiftwork and performance. *Human Factors*, *21*, 483–492.

Forgacs, I. (1995, April 8). Differences in perception of the health service. *Guardian*, Letters to the Editor.

Frankenhaeuser, M. (1986). A psychobiological framework for research on human stress and coping. In M. A. Appley & R. Trumbell (Eds.), *Dynamics of stress: Physiological, psychological and social perspectives*. New York: Plenum Press.

Frayne, C. A., & Gerlinger, M. (1990). *Self-management practices and performance of international joint venture general managers*. Paper presented at the annual meeting of the Academy of Management, San Francisco.

Fredriksson, K., Koster, M., Bildt Thorbjornsson, C., Toomingas, A., Torgen, M., Kilbom, A., & Alfredsson, L. (1999). Risk factors for neck and upper limb disorders: Results from 24 years of follow-up. *Occupational and Environmental Medicine*, *56*(1), 59–66.

French, W. L., & Bell, C. H., Jr (1999). *Organizational development: Behavioural science interventions for organizational improvement* (6th ed.). Upper Saddle River, NJ: Prentice Hall.

Frese, M. (1989). Theoretical models of control and health. In S. L. Sauter, J. J. Hurrell, Jr, & C. L. Cooper (Eds.), *Job control and worker health*. Chichester, UK: Wiley.

Frese, M. (1997, July 6–11). *New problems and prospects for work and organizational psychology in the 21st century*. Paper given at the 5th European Congress of Psychology, Dublin, Ireland.

Frese, M. (2000). The changing nature of work. In N. Chmiel (Ed.), *Introduction to work and organizational psychology: A European perspective*. Oxford, UK: Blackwell.

Frese, M., & Zapf, D. (1994). Action as the core of work psychology: A German approach. In H. C. Triandis, M. D. Dunnette, & J. M. Hough (Eds.), *Handbook of industrial and organizational psychology, Vol. 4* (2nd ed.). Palo Alto, CA: Consulting Psychologists Press.

Frey, K. P. (1997). About reversal theory. In S. Svebak & M. J. Apter (Eds.), *Stress and health: A reversal theory perspective*. Washington, DC: Taylor & Francis.

Frith, L. (2000). The search conference: A personal account. *Occupational Psychologist, 39*, 11–13.

Funke, J. (1998). Computer-based testing and training with scenarios from complex problem-solving research: Advantages and disadvantages. *International Journal of Selection and Assessment, 6*(2), 90–96.

Funke, J., & Schuler, H. (1998). Validity of stimulus and response components in a video test of social competence. *International Journal of Selection and Assessment, 6*(2), 115–123.

Furnham, A. (1990). *The protestant work ethic*. London: Routledge.

Furnham, A. (1992). *Personality at work*. London: Routledge.

Furnham, A. (1997). *The psychology of behaviour at work: The individual in the organization*. Hove, UK: Psychology Press.

Furnham, A., & Argyle, M. (1998). *The psychology of money*. London: Routledge.

Furnham, A., & Varian, C. (1990). Predicting and accepting personality test scores. *Personality and Individual Differences, 9*, 735–748.

Gagne, R. M. (1985). *The conditions of learning and theory of instruction*. New York: CBS College Publishing.

Gagne, R. M., Briggs, L. J., & Wager, W. W. (1992). *Principles of instruction design* (4th ed.). New York: Harcourt Brace Jovanich.

Galer, A. R. (Ed.) (1987). *Applied ergonomics handbook* (2nd ed.). London: Butterworths.

Ganster, D. C. (1989). Worker control and well-being: A review of research in the workplace. In S. L. Sauter, J. J. Hurrell, Jr, & C. L. Cooper (Eds.), *Job control and worker health*. Chichester, UK: Wiley.

Gatewood, R., Thornton, G. C., & Hennessey, H. W. (1990). Reliability of exercise ratings in the leaderless group discussion. *Journal of Occupational Psychology, 63*, 331–342.

Geake, A., Oliver, K., & Farrell, C. (1998). *The application of 360 degree feedback: A survey*. Thames Ditton, UK: Saville & Holdsworth.

Ghiselli, E. E. (1966). *The validity of occupational aptitude tests*. New York: Wiley.

Ghiselli, E. E. (1973). The validity of aptitude tests in personnel selection. *Personnel Psychology, 26*, 461–477.

Ghodsian, D., Bjork, R. A., & Benjamin, A. S. (1997). Evaluating training during training: Obstacles and opportunities. In M. A. Quinones & A. Ehrenstein (Eds.), *Training for a rapidly changing workplace: Applications of psychological research*. Washington, DC: American Psychological Association.

Giddens, A. (1999). *Runaway world* (BBC Reith Lecture). London: Profile Books. (Also available at www.polity.co.uk/giddens/reith.htm)

Gilligan, C. (1982). *In a different voice: Psychological theory and women's development*. Cambridge, MA: Harvard University Press.

Gmelch, W. H., Wilke, P. J., & Lovrich, N. P. (1986). Dimensions of stress among university faculty: Factor-analytic results from a national study. *Research in Higher Education, 24*, 266–286.

Goffee, R., & Scase, R. (1992). Organizational change and the corporate career. *Human Relations, 44*(4), 363–385.

Goleman, D. (1998). *Working with emotional intelligence.* London: Bloomsbury.

Goldratt, E. (1989). *The goal: A process of ongoing improvement.* London: Gower UK.

Goldratt, E. M., & Cox, J. (1986). *The goal.* Great Barrington, MA: North River Press.

Goldsmith, D. B. (1922). The use of the personal history blank as a salesmanship test. *Journal of Applied Psychology, 6*, 149–155.

Goodge, P. (1997). Assessment and development centres: Practical design principles. *Selection and Development Review, 13*(3), 11–14.

Goodge, P., & Burr, J. (1999). 360 degree feedback—for once the research is useful. *Selection and Development Review, 15*(2), 3–7.

Gottfredson, L. S. (1981). Circumscription and compromise: A developmental theory of occupational aspirations. *Journal of Counselling Psychology, 28*, 545–579.

Gottfredson, L. S. (1996). Gottfredson's theory of circumscription and compromise. In D. Brown & L. Brooks (Eds.), *Career choice and development* (3rd ed.). San Francisco: Jossey-Bass.

Graversen, G., & Johansson, J. A. (Eds.) (1998). The individual and the organization. *European Journal of Work and Organizational Psychology, 7*(3), 257–264.

Graves, L. M., & Powell, G. N. (1996). Sex similarity, quality of the employment interview and recruiters' evaluation of actual applicants. *Journal of Occupational and Organizational Psychology, 69*, 243–261.

Gray, A., & Farrell, C. (1999). *The impact of personality on 360 degree feedback.* Paper presented at the British Psychological Society Occupational Psychology conference, Blackpool.

Green, B. L., Grace, M. C., Lindey, J. D., Gleser, G. C., Leonard, A. C., Korol, M., & Winger, C. (1990a). Buffalo Creek survivors in the second decade: Stability of stress symptoms. *American Journal of Orthopsychiatry, 60*, 43–54.

Green, B. L., Lindy, J. D., Grace, M. C., Gleser, G. C., & Leonard, A. C. (1990b). Buffalo Creek survivors in the second decade: Comparison with unexposed and nonlitigant groups. *Journal of Applied Social Psychology, 20*, 1033–1050.

Greenberg, J. (1988). Equity and workplace status: A field experiment. *Journal of Applied Psychology, 73*, 606–613.

Gregg, P., & Wadsworth, J. (1995). A short history of labour turnover, job tenure, and job security, 1975–93. *Oxford Review of Economic Policy, 11*, 73–90.

Griffiths, A., & Cox, T. (1993, September). *The management of musculo-skeletal disorders in VDU users.* Paper presented at the European Network of Organizational Psychologists third workshop on Personnel Psychology in Healthcare Institutions, Krakow, Poland.

Guest, D., & Conway, N. (1997). *Fairness at work and the psychological contract: Issues in people management.* London: IPD.

Guest, D., & Conway, N. (1998). *Motivation and the psychological contract: Issues in people management.* London: IPD.

Guest, D., & Conway, N. (1999, July 1). *How miserable and insecure are British workers?* Summer seminar, Birkbeck College, Department of Psychology, London.

Guest, D., Conway, N., Briner, R., & Dickman, M. (1996). *The state of the psychological contract in employment*. London: IPD.

Guest, D., Williams, R., & Dewe, P. (1980). Workers' perceptions of changes affecting the quality of working life. In K. D. Duncan, M. Gruneberg, & D. Wallis (Eds.), *Changes in working life*. Chichester, UK: Wiley.

Guthrie, G. (1997). The ethics of telework. *Information Systems Management, 14*(4), 29–33.

Hacker, W., Skell, W., & Straub, W. (1968). *Arbeitpsychologie und wissenschafilich-technisch Revolution*. Berlin, Germany: Deutscher Verlag der Wissenschaften.

Hackman, J. R. (1994). Trip wires in designing and leading workgroups. *Occupational Psychologist, 23*, 3–7.

Hackman, J. R., & Oldham, G. R. (1980). *Work redesign*. Reading, MA: Addison-Wesley.

Hagman, J. D., & Rose, A. M. (1983). Retention of military tasks: A review. *Human Factors, 25*, 199–213.

Hakim, C. (1999). *Social change and innovation in the labour market*. Oxford, UK: Oxford University Press.

Hall, R. N. (1999). *Continuity and change in British work attitudes*. Unpublished MSc thesis, University of East London.

Hamlin, B. (1995). National training policies in Britain. In S. Truelove (Ed.), *The handbook of training and development* (2nd ed.). Oxford, UK: Blackwell.

Hampden-Turner, C. (1994). *Corporate culture*. London: Piatkus.

Hancock, P. A., & Scallen, F. F. (1996). Allocating functions in human–machine systems. In R. Hoffman (Ed.), *Psychology beyond the threshold: A festscrift for William N. Dember*. Hillsdale, NJ: Lawrence Erlbaum Associates Inc.

Handy, C. (1984). *The future of work*. Oxford, UK: Basil Blackwell.

Handy, C. (1995). *The age of unreason*. London: Arrow Books.

Handy, L. (1996). *360 degree feedback: Unguided missile of powerful weapon*. Berkhamsted, UK: Ashridge Management College.

Harma, M. I., Ilmarinen, J., Knauth, P., Rutenfranz, J., & Hanninen, O. (1988). Physical training intervention in female shift workers: II. The effects of intervention on the circadian rhythms of alertness, short-term memory and body temperature. *Ergonomics, 31*, 51–63.

Harrington, J. M. (1978). *Shiftwork and health: A critical review of the literature*. London: HMSO.

Harris, M. M., & Schaubroeck, J. (1988). A meta-analysis of self–boss, self–peer, and peer–subordinate ratings. *Personnel Psychology, 41*, 43–62.

Harrison, J. E., Mandryk, J. A., & Fromer, M. S. (1993). Work-related road fatalities in Australia, 1982–1984. *Accident Analysis and Prevention, 25*, 443–451.

Harrison, R. (1972). Understanding your organization's character. *Harvard Business Review, 50*(23), 119–128.

Harrison, Y., & Horne, J. A. (2000). The impact of sleep loss on decision making: A review. *Journal of Experimental Psychology: Applied, 6*, 236–249.

Hart, S. G., & Staveland, L. E. (1988). Development of a NASA TLX (task load index): Results of empirical and theoretical research. In P. Hancock & N. Meshkati (Eds.), *Human mental workload*. Amsterdam: Elsevier.

Hartigan, J. A., & Wigdor, A. K. (1989). *Fairness in employment testing*. Washington, DC: National Academy Press.

Hartley, J. (1996). Organizational change. In P. Warr (Ed.), *Psychology at work* (4th ed.). Harmondsworth, UK: Penguin.

Hartley, J. (1997, July 6–11). *Organizational psychology in the changing context of market, state and civil society.* Paper presented at the 5th European Congress of Psychology, Dublin, Ireland.

Harvey, L., Moon, S., & Geall, V. (1997). *Graduates' work: Organizational change and student attributes.* Birmingham, UK: Centre for Research into Quality.

Harvey, R. J., Billings, R. S., & Nilan, K. J. (1985). Confirmatory factor analysis of the Job Diagnostic Survey: Good news and bad news. *Journal of Applied Psychology, 70*, 461–468.

Harvey-Cook, J. (2000). Demystifying biodata: A description of a practical application. *Selection and Development Review, 16*(3), 15–19.

Hayes, N. (1999). The psychological contract: All things to all people? In *The British Psychological Society Occupational Psychology conference book of proceedings.* Leicester, UK: British Psychological Society.

Haynes, A. C. (1992). United 232: Coping with the loss of all flight controls. *Flight Deck, 3*, 5–21.

Haywood, M. (1998). *Managing virtual teams.* Norwood, MA: Artech.

Health and Safety at Work (2002). *EU shifts towards a global approach to well-being at work.* London: Health and Safety at Work.

Heckhausen, H., Schmalt, H. D., & Schneider, K. (1985). *Achievement motivation in perspective.* New York: Academic Press.

Hellgren, J., & Isaksson, K. (1997, July 6–11). *Effects of organizational downsizing on survivors' job attitudes.* Paper presented at the 5th European congress of Psychology, Dublin, Ireland.

Hellgren, J., Sverke, M., & Isaksson, K. (1999). A two dimensional approach to job insecurity: Consequences for employee attitudes and well-being. *European Journal of Work and Organizational Psychology, 8*(2), 179–196.

Hennessy, J., Mabey, B., & Warr, P. (1998). Assessment centre observation procedures: An experimental comparison of traditional, checklist and coding methods. *International Journal of Selection and Assessment, 6*(4), 222–231.

Heron, J. (1990). *Helping the client.* London: Sage.

Herriot, P. (1989). Selection as a social process. In M. Smith & I. T. Robertson (Eds.), *Advances in staff selection.* Chichester, UK: Wiley.

Herriot, P. (1992). *The career management challenge.* London: Sage.

Herriot, P., & Anderson, N. (1997). Selecting for change: How will personnel and selection psychology survive? In N. Anderson & P. Herriot (Eds.), *International handbook of selection and assessment.* Chichester, UK: Wiley.

Herriot, P., & Pemberton, C. (1995). *New deals.* Chichester, UK: Wiley.

Herriot, P., & Stickland, R. (Eds.) (1996). The management of careers. *European Journal of Work and Organizational Psychology, 5*(Whole No. 4).

Herriot, P., & Wingrove, J. (1984). Decision processes in graduate pre-selection. *Journal of Occupational Psychology, 57*, 269–275.

Hershenson, D. (1981). Work adjustment, disability and the three Rs of vocational rehabilitation: A conceptual model. *Rehabilitation Counselling Bulletin, 2*, 91–97.

Hershenson, D. (1996). A systems reformulation of a developmental model of work adjustment. *Rehabilitation Counselling Bulletin, 49*, 2–10.

Herzberg, F. (1966). *Work and the nature of man.* Cleveland, OH: World Publishing.

Herzberg, F. (1968). One more time: How do you motivate employees? *Harvard Business Review, 46,* 53–62.

Heyes, J. (1998). Training and development in an agrochemical plant. In C. Mabey, D. Skinner, & T. Clark (Eds.), *Experiencing human resource management.* London: Sage.

Highley, J. C., & Cooper, C. L. (1995). *An assessment of UK EAPs and workplace counselling programmes.* London: Health & Safety Executive.

Hildebrandt, G., Rohmert, W., & Rutenfranz, J. (1974). Twelve and 24 hour rhythms in error frequency of locomotive drivers and the influence of tiredness. *International Journal of Chronobiology, 2,* 175–180.

Hind, P. (2000). D*evelopmental damage: The dark side of 360 degree feedback.* Paper presented at the British Psychological Society Occupational Psychology conference, Brighton, UK.

Hind, P., & Doyle, C. (1996). A cross cultural comparison of perceived occupational stress in academics in higher education. *International Journal of Psychology, 31*(3&4), 354.112.

Hind, P., Rowley, S., & Frost, M. (1997, July). The resilient organization: Success in the face of adversity. In *Fifth European Congress of Psychology book of abstracts* (Abstract No. 325). Dublin, Ireland: Psychological Society of Ireland.

Hirsh, W., & Jackson, C. (1996). *Strategies for career development: Promise, practice and pretence.* Brighton, UK: Institute for Employment Studies.

Hochschild, A. R. (1989). *The second shift: Working parents and the revolution at home.* New York: Viking.

Hochschild, A. R. (1997). *The time bind: When work becomes home and home becomes work.* New York: Metropolitan Books.

Hochwarter, W. A., Perrewe, P. L., Zellars, K. L., & Harrison, A. W. (1999). The interactive role of negative affectivity and job characteristics: Are high-NA employees destined to be unhappy at work? *Journal of Applied Social Psychology, 29,* 2203–2218.

Hockey, G. R. J. (1970). The effect of loud noise on attentional selectivity. *Quarterly Journal of Experimental Psychology, 22,* 28–36.

Hockey, G. R. J. (1986). Changes in operator efficiency as a function of environmental stress, fatigue and circadian rhythms. In K. R. Boff, L. Kaufman, & J. P. Thomas (Eds.), *Handbook of perception and human performance, Vol. 2.* New York: Wiley.

Hockey, G. R. J. (1993). Cognitive energetical control mechanisms in the management of work demands and psychological health. In A. D. Baddeley & L. Weiskrantz (Eds.), *Attention, selection, awareness and control: A tribute to Donald Broadbent.* Oxford, UK: Oxford University Press.

Hockey, G. R. J. (1997). Compensatory control in the regulation of human performance under stress and high workload: A cognitive-energetical framework. *Biological Psychology, 45,* 73–93.

Hockey, G. R. J. (2000). Work environments and performance. In N. Chmiel (Ed.), *Introduction to work and organizational psychology: A European perspective.* Oxford, UK: Blackwell.

Hockey, G. R. J., Payne, R. L., & Rick, J. T. (1995). Intra-individual patterns of hormonal and affective adaptation to work demands: An n = 2 study of junior doctors. *Biological Psychology, 42,* 393–411.

Hodgeson, J. T., Jones, J. R., Elliott, R. C., & Osman, J. (1993). *Self-reported work related illness: Results from a trailer questionnaire on the 1990 Labour Force Survey in England and Wales.* Sudbury, UK: HSE Books.

Hodgson, G. (1995). *People's century: From the dawn of the century to the start of the Cold War*. London: BBC Books.

Hodson, N. (1992). *The economics of teleworking*. Ipswich, UK: BT Laboratories.

Hogan, R., & Hogan, J. (1997). *Hogan personality inventory: UK edition*. Tunbridge Wells, UK: Hogan Assessment Systems with Psychological Consultancy.

Hogan, R., Hogan, J., & Trickey, G. (1999). Goodbye mumbo-jumbo: The transcendental beauty of a validity coefficient. *Selection and Development Review, 15*(4), 3–9.

Holding, D. (1983). Fatigue. In G. R. J. Hockey & P. Hamilton (Eds.), *Stress and fatigue in human performance*. Chichester, UK: Wiley.

Holland, J. L. (1985). *Making vocational choices* (2nd ed.). Englewood Cliffs, NJ: Prentice Hall.

Holman, P., & Devane, T. (Eds.) (1999). *The change handbook: Group methods for shaping the future*. San Francisco: Berrett-Koehler.

Homans, G. (1950). *The human group*. New York: Harcourt Brace.

Homans, G. C. (1961). *Social behaviour: Its elementary forms*. New York: Harcourt, Brace & World.

Hopson, B., & Scally, M. (1981). *Lifeskills teaching programme, No. 2*. London: McGraw-Hill.

Horne, J. A. (1988). *Why we sleep: The functions of sleep in humans and other mammals*. Oxford, UK: Oxford University Press.

Horne, J. A. (1992, January 4). Stay awake, stay alive. *New Scientist*, pp. 20–24.

Horne, J. A. (2001). State of the art: Sleep. *The Psychologist, 14*, 302–306.

Horne, J. A., & Pettitt, A. N. (1985). High incentive effects on vigilance performance during 72 hours of total sleep deprivation. *Acta Psychologia, 58*, 123–139.

Horne, J. A., & Rayner, L. A. (1999). Vehical accidents related to sleep: A review. *Occupational and Environmental Medicine, 56*, 289–294.

Horne, J. A., & Wilkinson, R. T. (1985). Chronic sleep reduction: Daytime vigilance performance and EEG measures of sleepiness, with particular reference to "practice" effects. *Psychophysiology, 22*, 69–77.

Hough, L. M. (1992). The "big five" personality variables—construct confusion: Description versus prediction. *Human Performance, 5*, 139–155.

Hough, L. M. (1988, April 21). *Personality assessment for selection and placement decisions*. Paper presented at the third annual conference of the Society for Industrial and Organizational Psychology, Dallas, TX.

Hough, L. M., Eaton, N. K., Dunnette, M. D., Kamp, J. D., & McCloy, R. A. (1990). Criterion-related validities of personality constructs and the effect of response distortion on those validities. *Journal of Applied Psychology, 23*, 537–546.

Howard, A. (1995). Rethinking the psychology of work. In A. Howard (Ed.), *The changing nature of work*. San Fransisco: Jossey-Bass.

Howard, A., & Bray, D. W. (1988). *Managerial lives in transition*. New York: Guilford Press.

Howes, M. J. A. (1991). *Fragments of genius: The strange feats of idiots savants*. London: Routledge.

Hubley, A. M., & Hultsch, D. F. (1994). The relationship of personality trait variables to subjective age identity in older adults. *Research on Ageing, 16*(4), 415–440.

Hudson, P., Reason, J., Wagenaar, W., Bentley, P., Primrose, M., & Viser, J. (1994). Tripod-Delta: Proactive approach to enhanced safety. *Journal of Petroleum Technology, 40*, 58–62.

Huffcutt, A. I., Roth, P. L., & McDaniel, M. A. (1996). A meta-analytic investigation of cognitive ability in employment interview evaluations: Moderating characteristics and implications for incremental validity. *Journal of Applied Psychology*, *81*, 459–473.

Hughes, D. (1995, January 30). Incidents reveal mode confusion: Automated cockpits special report, part 1. *Aviation Week and Space Technology*, p. 5.

Hunt, J. W. (2001, November 14). Women who choose. *Financial Times*.

Hunter, H. (1995, November 16). Unison survey highlights nurse gloom "time-bomb". *Health Services Journal*.

Hurley, M., & Schaumann, F. (1997). KPMG survey: The IT outsourcing decision. *Information Management and Computer Security*, *5*(4), 126–132.

Hutton, R. J. B., & Militello, L. G. (1997). Applied cognitive task analysis (ACTA): A practitioner's window into skilled decision making. In D. Harris (Ed.), *Engineering psychology and cognitive ergonomics: Vol. 2*. Aldershot, UK: Ashgate.

Huws, U. (1999). Wired in the country. *People Management*, *5*(23), 46–48.

Iaffaldano, M. T., & Muchinsky, P. M. (1985). Job satisfaction and job performance: A meta-analysis. *Psychological Bulletin*, *97*, 251–273.

Ibbetson, A., & Newell, S. (1995). Winner takes all: An evaluation of adventure-based experiential training. In *The British Psychological Society Occupational Psychology book of proceedings* (pp. 33–38). Leicester, UK: British Psychological Society.

Ibbetson, A., & Newell, S. (1996). A comparison of a competitive and cooperative outdoor management development programme: An evaluation methodology. In *The British Psychological Society Occupational Psychology book of proceedings* (pp. 207–212). Leicester, UK: British Psychological Society.

Iles, P. A., & Robertson, I. T. (1997). The impact of personnel selection procedures on candidates. In N. Anderson & P. Herriot (Eds.), *International handbook of selection and assessment*. Chichester, UK: Wiley.

Isaksson, K. (1995). *Factors related to well-being in older employees after organizational downsizing*. Paper presented at the seventh congress of the European Association of Work and Organizational Psychology, Gyor, Hungary.

Ishmael, A. (1999). *Harassment: Bullying and violence at work*. London: The Industrial Society.

Jahoda, M., Lazarsfeld, P. F., & Zeisel, H. (1971). *Marienthal: The sociography of an unemployed community*. New York: Aldine-Atherton.

James, L. R., & Tetrick, L. E. (1986). Confirmatory analytic tests of three causal models relating job perceptions to job satisfaction. *Journal of Applied Psychology*, *71*, 77–82.

Janis, I. L. (1982). *Groupthink*. Boston: Houghton Mifflin.

Jarvenpaa, S. L., Knoll, K., & Leidner, D. E. (1998). Is anyone out there? Antecedents of trust in global virtual teams. *Journal of Management Information Systems*, *14*(4), 29–65.

Jeffreson, P. (1997). Arthritis: Using assistive devices to promote independence. *British Journal of Therapy and Rehabilitation*, *4*(10), 528–534.

Jensen, A. R. (1969). How much can we boost IQ and scholastic achievement?, *Harvard Educational Review*, *39*, 1–123.

Jex, S. M., & Bliese, P. D. (1999). Efficacy beliefs as a moderator of the impact of work-related stressors: A multi-level study. *Journal of Applied Psychology*, *84*(3), 349–361.

Johnson, J. V., & Hall, E. M. (1988). Job strain, workplace social support, and cardiovascular disease: A cross-sectional study of a random sample of the Swedish working population. *American Journal of Public Health, 78*(10), 1336–1342.

Johnson, L. C., & Naitoh, P. (1974). *The operational consequences of sleep deprivation and sleep deficit* (NATO/SGARDograph No. 193). London: Technical Editing and Reproduction.

Johnson, V., & Petrie, H. (1998). Travelling safely: The problems and concerns of blind pedestrians. *British Journal of Visual Impairment, 16*(1), 27–31.

Johnson, W. (1991). Global work force 2000: The new world labour market. *Harvard Business Review, 69*, 114–127.

Jones, A., & Harrison, E. (1982). Prediction of performance in initial officer training using reference reports. *Journal of Occupational Psychology, 55*, 35–42.

Jones, F., Bright, J. E., Searle, B., & Cooper, L. (1998). Modelling occupational stress and health: The impact of the demand–control model on academic research and on workplace practice. *Stress Medicine, 14*, 231–236.

Jones, F., & Fletcher, C. (1996). Job control and health. In M. J. Schabracq, J. A. M. Winnubst, & C. L. Cooper (Eds.), *Handbook of work and health psychology*. Chichester, UK: Wiley.

Jones, H. (1992). Biography in management and organizational development. *Management Education and Development, 23*(4), 199–206.

Jones, J. R., Hodgeson, J. T., Clegg, T. A., & Elliott, R. C. (1998). *Self-reported work-related illness in 1995—results from a household survey*. Sudbury, UK: HSE Books.

Jones, R. G., & Whitmore, M. D. (1995). Evaluating developmental assessment centres as interventions. *Personnel Psychology, 48*, 377–388.

Jonssen, B., & Lank, A. G. (1985). Volvo: A report on production technology and the quality of working life. *Human Resource Management*, Winter, 455–465.

Judge, T. A., Bono, J. E., & Locke, E. A. (2000). Personality and job satisfaction: The mediating role of job characteristics. *Journal of Applied Psychology, 85*(2), 237–249.

Kahn, R. L., Wolfe, D. M., Quinn, R. P., Snoek, J. D., & Rosenthal, R. A. (1964). *Organizational stress: Studies in role conflict and ambiguity*. New York: Wiley.

Kamali, J., Moodie, C. L., & Salvendy, G. (1982). A framework for integrated assembly systems: Humans, information and robots. *International Journal of Production Research, 20*, 431–448.

Karasek, R. A. (1979). Job demands, job decision lattitude and mental strain: Implications for job design. *Administrative Science Quarterly, 24*, 285–308.

Karasek, R. A. (1990). Lower health risk with increased job control among white collar workers. *Journal of Organizational Behaviour, 11*, 171–185.

Karasek, R. A., & Theorell, T. (1990). *Healthy work: Stress, productivity and the reconstruction of working life*. New York: Basic Books.

Katz, D., & Kahn, R. L. (1966). *The social psychology of organizations*. New York: Wiley.

Katz, D., & Kahn, R. L. (1978). *The social psychology of organizations* (2nd ed.). Chichester, UK: Wiley.

Katzell, R. A., & Thompson, D. E. (1990). Work motivation: Theory and practice. *American Psychologist, 45*, 144–154.

Kawachi, I., Colditz, G. A., Stampfer, M. J., Willett, W. C., Manson, J. E., Peizer, F. E., & Hennekens, C. H. (1995). Prospective study of shiftwork and risk of coronary heart disease in women. *Circulation, 92*, 3178–3182.

Keenan, T. (1997). Selection for potential: The case of graduate recruitment. In N. Anderson & P. Herriot (Eds.), *International handbook of selection and assessment.* Chichester, UK: Wiley.

Keep, E. (1989). Corporate training strategies: The vital component? In J. Storey (Ed.), *New perspectives in human resource management.* London: Routledge.

Kellett, D., Fletcher, S., Callen, A., & Geary, B. (1994, January). Fair testing: The case of British Rail. *The Psychologist,* pp. 26–29.

Kerr, S. (1996). On the folly of rewarding A, while hoping for B. In R. M. Steers, L. W. Porter, & G. A. Bigley (Eds.), *Motivation and leadership at work* (6th ed.). New York: McGraw-Hill. (Original work published 1975)

Kessels, J. W. M. (1999, June). *Knowledge management: A corporate curriculum for the knowledge economy.* Institute of Personnel and Development lecture, London.

Kiecolt-Glaser, J. K , Dura, J. R., Speicher, C. E., Trask, O. J., & Glaser, R. (1991). Spousal caregivers of dementia victims: Longitudinal changes in immunity and health. *Psychosomatic Medicine, 53,* 345–362.

Kiecolt-Glaser, J. K., Malarkey, W. B., Chee, M., Newton, T., Cacciopo, J. T., Mao, H. Y., & Glaser, R. (1993). Negative behaviour during marital conflict is associated with immunological down-regulation. *Psychosomatic Medicine, 55,* 395–409.

Kinnunen, U., Mauno, S., Natti, J., & Happonen, M. (1999). Perceived job insecurity: A longitudinal study among Finnish employees. *European Journal of Work and Organizational Psychology, 8*(2), 243–260.

Kirton, M. J. (1961). *Management initiative.* London: Acton Society Trust.

Kirton, M. J. (in press). *Adaption–innovation: Problem solving style in change and diversity.* Hove, UK: Psychology Press.

Kjellberg, A. (1977). Sleep deprivation and some aspects of performance: I. Problems of arousal changes; II. Lapses and other attention effects; III. Motivation, comment and conclusions. *Waking and Sleeping, 1,* 139–143, 145–148, 149–153.

Klandermans, B., & van Vuuren, T. (1999). Job insecurity: Introduction. *European Journal of Work and Organizational Psychology, 8*(2), 145–153.

Klein, N. (2000). *No logo: Taking aim at the brand bullies.* London: Flamingo.

Kleingeld, P. A. M. (1994). *Performance management in a field service department: Design and transportation of a productivity measurement and enhancement system (ProMES).* Unpublished doctoral dissertation, Eindhoven University of Technology, The Netherlands.

Klimoski, R. J., & Strickland, W. J. (1977). Assessment centers—valid or merely prescient? *Personnel Psychology, 30,* 353–361.

Knight, A. (2000–2001). Healing the National Health Service. *Directions: The Ashridge Journal,* Winter, 8–15.

Kogi, K. (1985). Introduction to the problems of shiftwork. In S. Folkard & T. H. Monk (Eds.), *Hours of work: Temporal factors in work scheduling.* Chichester, UK: Wiley.

Kohn, A. (1996). Why incentive plans cannot work. In R. M. Steers, L. W. Porter, & G. A. Bigley (Eds.), *Motivation and leadership at work* (6th ed.). New York: McGraw-Hill.

Komaki, J. L., Coombs, T., & Schepman, S. (1996). Motivational implications of reinforcement theory. In R. M. Steers, L. W. Porter, & G. A. Bigley (Eds.), *Motivation and leadership at work* (6th ed.). New York: McGraw-Hill.

Kompier, M., & Cooper, C. L. (1999a). Introduction: Improving work, health and productivity through stress prevention. In M. Kompier & C. L. Cooper (Eds.),

Preventing stress, improving productivity: European case studies in the workplace. London: Routledge.

Kompier, M., & Cooper, C. L. (1999b). *Preventing stress, improving productivity: European case studies in the workplace.* London: Routledge.

Korabik, K., & Rosin, H. (1997). Factors contributing to why professionals stay with their organizations. *Abstracts of the fifth European congress of Psychology, Dublin, Ireland* (Abstract No. 329).

Kornstein, A. (1999). Letter to the Editor. *Independent Newspaper Education Section*, 30 September.

Kotter, J. P. (1973). The psychological contract. *California Management Review, 15,* 91–99.

Kraiger, K., & Ford, J. K. (1985). A meta-analysis of ratee race effects in performance ratings. *Journal of Applied Psychology, 70,* 56–65.

Kram, K. E. (1985). *Mentoring at work.* Glenview, IL: Scott Foresman.

Kruglansky, A. W., & Freund, T. (1983). The freezing and unfreezing of lay influences: Effects on impressional primacy, ethnic stereotyping and numerical anchoring. *Journal of Experimental Social Psychology, 19,* 448–468.

Kurland, N. B., & Bailey, D. E. (1999). Telework: The advantages and challenges of working here, there, anywhere and anytime. *Organizational Dynamics, 28*(2), 53–68.

Kyotani, E. (1996). The bright and dark sides of the Japanese Labour process. Unpublished paper cited in Thompson, P. & Warhurst, C. (1998). Hands, hearts and minds: Changing work and workers at the end of the century. In P. Thompson & C. Warhurst (Eds.), *Workplaces of the future.* Houndmills: Macmillan Business.

La Croix, A. Z., & Haynes, S. G. (1987). Gender differences in the health effects of workplace roles. In R. C. Barnett, L. Biener, & G. K. Baruch (Eds.), *Gender and stress.* New York: Free Press.

Lamond, D. A. (2000). Managerial style and telework. In K. Daniels, D. A. Lamond, & P. Standen (Eds.), *Managing telework: Perspectives from human resource management and work psychology.* London: Business Press/Thomson Learning.

Landis, R. S., Fogli, L., & Goldberg, E. (1998). Future oriented job analysis: A description of the process and its organizational implications. *International Journal of Selection and Assessment, 6*(3), 192–197.

Landy, F. (2000). *Public policy and assessment: Which is the cart and which the horse?* Keynote address at The British Psychological Society Occupational Psychology conference, Brighton, UK.

Landy, F., & Becker, W. S. (1987). Motivation theory reconsidered. *Research in Organizational Behaviour, 9,* 1–31.

LaPorte, T. R., & Consolini, P. M. (1991). Working in practice but not in theory: Theoretical challenges of "high reliability" organizations. *Journal of Public Administration Research and Theory, 1,* 21–34.

Lazarus, R., & Folkman, S. (1984). *Stress, appraisal and coping.* New York: Springer Publications.

Leach, J. A. (1991). Characteristics of excellent trainers: A psychological interpersonal profile. *Performance Improvement Quarterly, 4,* 42–62.

Le Blanc, P., de Jonge, J., & Schaufeli, W. (2000). Job stress and health. In N. Chmiel (Ed.), *Introduction to work and organizational psychology: A European perspective.* Oxford, UK: Blackwell.

Lee, G. (2000). The state of the art in development centres. *Selection and Development Review, 16*(1), 10–14.

Lees, C. D., & Cordery, J. L. (2000). Job analysis and design. In N. Chmiel (Ed.), *Introduction to work and organizational psychology: A European perspective.* Oxford, UK: Blackwell.

Legge, K. (1989). Human resource management: A critical analysis. In J. Storey (Ed.), *New perspectives on human resource management.* London: Routledge.

Levinson, D. J., with Darrow, C. N., Klein, E. B., Levinson, M. H., & McKee, B. (1978). *Seasons of a man's life.* New York: Knopf.

Lewin, K. (1951). *Field theory in social science.* New York: Harper & Row.

Leymann, H. (1996). The content and development of mobbing at work. *European Journal of Work and Organizational Psychology, 5*(2), 165–184.

Lievens, F. (1998). Factors which improve the construct validity of assessment centres: A review. *International Journal of Selection and Assessment, 6*(3), 141–152.

Lipnack, J., & Stamps, J. (1997). *Virtual teams: Reaching across space, time and organizations with technology.* Chichester, UK: Wiley.

Little, A. D. (2000). Display screen regulations: Risk assessments and how to carry them out. *Course notes.* London: Quadrilect.

Locke, E. A., & Henne, D. (1986). Work motivation theories. In C. L. Cooper & I. T. Robertson (Eds.), *International review of industrial and organizational psychology.* Chichester, UK: Wiley.

Locke, E. A., & Latham, G. P. (1990). *A theory of goal-setting and task performance.* Englewood Cliffs, NJ: Prentice Hall.

Locke, E. A., Shaw, K. M., Saari, L. M., & Latham, G. P. (1981). Goal setting and task performance: 1969–1980. *Psychological Bulletin, 90,* 125–152.

Loewenthal, K. M., Eysenck, M., Harris, D., Lubitsh, G., Gorton, T., & Bicknell, H. (2000). Stress, distress and air traffic incidents: Job dysfunction and distress in airline pilots in relation to contextually-assessed stress. *Stress Medicine, 16,* 179–183.

Loher, B. T., Noe, R. A., Moeller, N. L., & Fitzgerald, M. P. (1985). A meta-analysis of the relation of job characteristics to job satisfaction. *Journal of Applied Psychology, 70,* 280–289.

Loughlin, C., & Barling, J. (2001). Young workers' values, attitudes and behaviours. *Journal of Occupational and Organizational Psychology, 74*(4), 543–558.

Loughran, J. (2000). The search conference (continued): Integrating the scientist and practitioner sides of the profession. *Occupational Psychologist, 40,* 18.

Lubitsh, G. (2002). *A longitudinal study of the impact of theory of constraints (TOC) on three departments in an HHS Trust.* Unpublished D. Occ. Psych. thesis, University of East London.

Lubitsh, G., & Doyle, C. (2001). A longitudinal study of the impact of theory of constraints (TOC) on productivity and morale in the NHS. In *VIIth European congress book of abstracts* (Abstract No. 169). London: European Federation of Professional Psychologists Associations.

Luria, A. R. (1973). *The man with a shattered world: The history of a brain wound.* London: Cape.

Lyons, G. (1997). Learning the hard way: Using competency-led assessment centres with head teachers. *Selection and Development Review, 13*(4), 12–14.

Mabey, C., Skinner, D., & Clark, T. (Eds.) (1998). *Experiencing human resource management.* London: Sage.

MacCauley, S., & Harding, N. (1996, April 4). Drawing up a new careers contract. *People Management,* pp. 34–35.

Mackney, P. (1999, December). Virtual globaloney. *The Lecturer,* p. 15.

Maddocks, J. (1998). Thinking ahead: The future of psychometrics and other approaches to assessment. *Assessment Matters: The National Journal of Vocational Assessment, 7*(Spring), 3–4.

Maddocks, J. (2000). Assessing the demotivated: Compromise objectivity. *Selection and Development Review, 16*(5), 6–8.

Maier, N. R. F. (1952). *Principles of human relations: Applications to management.* New York: Wiley.

Maier, N. R. F., & Solem, A. R. (1952). The contribution of a discussion leader to the quality of group thinking: The effective use of minority opinion. *Human Relations, 5,* 277–288.

Maitland, A. (2001, November 14). What women really want. *Financial Times.*

Majchrzak, A. (1998). *The human side of factory automation.* San Francisco: Jossey-Bass.

Makin, P. J., & Robertson, I. T. (1983). Self-assessment, realistic job previews and occupational decisions. *Personnel Review, 12,* 21–25.

Mallon, M. (1998). From public sector employees to portfolio workers: Pioneers of new careers? In C. Mabey, D. Skinner, & T. Clark (Eds.), *Experiencing human resource management.* London: Sage.

Malnick, T. (2001). On the side of the psyche—some next steps for organizational psychology. *Occupational Psychologist, 42,* 23–27.

Mann, S. (1998). Don't tell me to "have a nice day"! In *The British Psychological Society occupational psychology conference book of proceedings* (pp. 102–105). Leicester, UK: British Psychological Society.

Marshall, K. (1995, March 28). Labor chief checks out high-tech changes in textile industry. *Observer,* pp. D1–2.

Martin, G., Beaumont, P., & Staines, H. (1998). Changing corporate culture: Paradoxes and tensions in a local authority. In C. Mabey, D. Skinner, & T. Clark (Eds.), *Experiencing human resource management.* London: Sage.

Martin, R., & Wall, T. D. (1987). Attentional demand and cost responsibility as stressors in shopfloor jobs. *Academy of Management Journal, 32,* 69–84.

Maslach, C., & Jackson, S. E. (1986). *MBI: Maslach Burnout Inventory: Manual research edition.* Palo Alto, CA: Consulting Psychologists Press.

Maslow, A. H. (1954). *Motivation and personality.* New York: Harper & Row.

Maslow, A. H. (1968). *Toward a theory of being.* New York: Van Nostrand Reinhold.

McClelland, D. C. (1961). *The achieving society.* Princeton, NJ: Van Nostrand.

McClelland, D. C. (1962). Business drive and national achievement. *Harvard Business Review, 40,* 99–112.

McClelland, D. C. (1965a). Achievement motivation can be developed. *Harvard Business Review, 43,* 6–24.

McClelland, D. C. (1965b). Toward a theory of motive acquisition. *American Psychologist, 20,* 321–333.

McClelland, D. C. (1971). *Assessing human motivation.* New York: General Learning Press.

McConnell, I. (1997). Company case B: Motorola Inc. In *Fifth European congress of Psychology, Dublin, Ireland* (Abstract No. 333). Dublin: Psychological Society of Ireland.

McCrae, R. R., & Costa, P. T. (1988). Reinterpreting the Myers–Briggs type indicator from the perspective of the five-factor model of personality. *Journal of Personality, 57,* 17–40.

McCrae, R. R., & Costa, P. T. (1997). Personality trait structure as a human universal. *American Psychologist*, *52*, 509–516.

McDaniel, M. A., Whetzel, D. L., Schmidt, F. L., & Maurer, S. D. (1994). The validity of employment interviews: A comparative review and meta-analysis. *Journal of Applied Psychology*, *81*, 599–616.

McEvoy, G. M., & Beatty, R. W. (1989). Assessment centres and subordinate appraisals of managers: A seven year examination of predictive validity. *Personnel Psychology*, *42*(1), 37–52.

McGregor, D. (1960). *The human side of enterprise*. New York: McGraw-Hill.

McHugh, P. (1968). *Defining the situation: The organization of meaning in social interaction*. Indianapolis, IN: Bobbs-Merrill.

McKenna, E. (2000). *Business psychology and organizational behaviour. A student's handbook* (3rd ed.). Hove, UK: Psychology Press.

McKinley, A., & Taylor, P. (1997). Foucault and the politics of production. In A. McKinley & K. Starkey (Eds.), *Foucalt, management and organization*. London: Sage.

Meehan, M., Birkin, R., & Snodgrass, R. (1998). Employment assessment (EA): Issues surrounding the use of psychological assessment material with disabled people. *Selection and Development Review*, *14*(3), 3–9.

Merrick, N. (1996). Remote control. *People Management*, *2*(19), 40–42.

Merridenand, T., & Bird, J. (1999, May). Exploding IT myths. *Management Today*, Management Today/Microsoft Suppl.

Merrill, M. D. (1983). Component display theory. In C. M. Reigeluth (Ed.), *Instructional design theories and models: An overview of their current status*. Hillsdale, NJ: Lawrence Erlbaum Associates Inc.

Metro London. (1999, May 10). Big Brother may watch over staff.

Metro London. (2000, September 4).

Meyer, J. P., & Allen, N. J. (1984). Testing the side-bet theory of organizational commitment: Some methodological considerations. *Journal of Organizational Behaviour*, *69*, 372–378.

Midgley, S. (2000, December). Doors must open to all. *The Lecturer*, p. 3.

Milhill, C. (1996, January 18). NHS managers up 400% on 1989. *Guardian*, p. 6.

Miller, E. (1995). Comment on an ethical issue. *Clinical Psychology Forum*, *80*, 7–8.

Miller, G. A. (1956). The magical number seven, plus or minus two: Some limits on our capacity for processing information. *Psychological Review*, *63*, 81–97.

Miller, S. J., Hickson, D. J., & Wilson, D. C. (1999). Decision making in organizations. In S. R. Clegg, C. Hardy, & W. R. Nord (Eds.), *Managing organizations: Current issues*. London: Sage.

Miller-Tiedeman, A. L., & Tiedeman, D. V. (1990). Career decision making: An individualistic perspective. In D. Brown & L. Brooks (Eds.), *Career choice and development: Applying contemporary theories to practice* (2nd ed.). San Francisco: Jossey-Bass.

Mitchell, T. W., & Klimoski, R. J. (1982). Is it rational to be empirical? A test of methods for scoring biographical data. *Journal of Applied Psychology*, *67*, 411–418.

Mitler, M. M., Caskadon, M. A., Czeisler, C. A., Dement, W. C., Dignes, D. F., & Graeber, R. C. (1988). Catastrophies, sleep and public policy: Consensus report. *Sleep*, *11*, 100–109.

Mohrmap et al. (1998). Quality of work life and employee involvement. In C. L. Moldaschl & W. G. Weber (Eds.), The "three waves" of industrial group work:

Historical reflections on current research on group work. *Human Relations, 51*(3), 347–384. (Original work published 1986)

Monbiot, G. (2000). *Captive state: The corporate takeover of Britain.* Basingstoke, UK: Macmillan.

Moran, P. (1999). The growth-orientation of the small business owner-manager. *Occupational Psychologist, 38,* 13–21.

Morgan, G. (1986). *Images of organization.* London: Sage.

Morgan, G. (1997). *Images of organization* (2nd ed.). London: Sage.

Mosel, J. N., & Goheen, H. W. (1958). The validity of the employment recommendation questionnaire in personnel selection: I. Skilled traders. *Personnel Psychology, 11,* 481–490.

Mount, M. K., & Barrick, M. R. (1995). The big five personality dimensions: Implications for research and practice in human resources management. *Research in Personnel and Human Resources Management, 13,* 153–200.

Mulder, G. (1986). The concept and measurement of mental effort. In A. W. K. Gaillard & M. G. Coles (Eds.), *Energetics and human information processing.* Amsterdam: Nijhoff.

Murphy, L. (1988). Workplace interventions for stress reduction and prevention. In C. L. Cooper & R. Payne (Eds.), *Causes, coping and consequences of stress at work.* New York: Wiley.

Murray, B. (1999). Technology invigorates teaching, but is the pizzazz worth the price? *American Psychological Association Monitor, 30*(4), 1, 36.

Myers–Briggs Type Indicator. Instrument Materials and Manual available from Oxford Psychologists Press, Oxford, UK.

Myerson, J., Hale, S., Wagstaff, D., Poon, L. W., & Smith, G. A. (1990). The information loss model: A mathematical theory of age-related slowing. *Psychological Review, 97,* 475–486.

Naylor, K. (1994). Part-time working in Britain—an historical analysis. *Employment Gazette, 102,* 473–484.

Nelson-Jones, R. (1995). *The theory and practice of counselling* (2nd ed.). London: Cassell.

Nemeth, C., & Owens, P. (1996). Making workgroups more effective: The value of minority dissent. In M. A. West (Ed.), *Handbook of work group psychology.* Chichester, UK: Wiley.

Nicholson, N. (1990). The transition cycle: Causes, outcomes, processes and forms. In S. Fisher & C. L. Cooper (Eds.), *On the move: The psychology of change and transition.* Chichester, UK: Wiley.

Nicholson, N., & West, M. A. (1988). *Managerial job change: Men and women in transition.* Cambridge, UK: Cambridge University Press.

Nilsen, D., & Campbell, D. P. (1993). Self-observer rating discrepancies: Once an over-rater, always an over-rater? *Human Resource Management, 32,* 265–281.

Nixon, S. (2000, September). Quitting the City. *Management Today,* pp. 82–87.

Nof, S. Y., Knight, J. L., Jr, & Salvendy, G. (1980). Effective utilization of industrial robots: A job and skills analysis approach. *AIIE Transactions, 12,* 216–225.

Norman, D. A. (1981). Categorization of action slip. *Psychological Review, 88*(1), 1–15.

Nuclear Regulatory Commission. (1994). *An analysis of operational experience during low power and shut down and a plan for addressing human reliability assessment issues* (Report No. NUREG/CR-6093). Washington, DC: US Regulatory Commission.

Oborne, D. J. (1995). *Ergonomics at work* (3rd ed.). Chichester, UK: Wiley.

Oborne, D. J. (1996). Technological issues for flexible working. *The Psychologist*, 9(4), 167–170.

Oborne, D. J., Branton, R., Leal, F., Shipley, P., & Stewart, T. (1993). *Person-centred ergonomics: A Brantonian view of human factors*. London: Taylor & Francis.

Observer Business/Gallup Poll. (1994). The workplace revolution. *Observer*, 25 September.

The Occupational Psychologist. (1999). Special edition: Small to medium enterprises, 38.

Oldham, G. R., & Cummings, A. (1996). Employee creativity: Personal and contextual factors at work. *Academy of Management Journal*, 39, 607–634.

O'Leary, M., & Chappell, S. L. (1996). Confidential incident reporting systems create vital awareness of safety problems. *ICAO Journal*, 51, 11–13.

O'Leary, M., & Fisher, S. (1993). *British Airways confidential human factors reporting programme: First year report, April 1992–March 1993*. Hounslow, UK: British Airways Safety Services.

O'Leary, M., & Pidgeon, N. (1995). Too bad we have to have confidential reporting programmes. *Flight Deck*, Summer, 11–16.

Ones, D. S., Viswesvaran, C., & Schmidt, F. L. (1993). Comprehensive meta-analysis of integrity test validities: Findings and implications for personnel selection and theories of job performance. *Journal of Applied Psychology*, 78, 679–703.

Orpen, C. (1994). The effects of organizational and individual career management on career success. *International Journal of Manpower*, 15, 27–37.

Osborn, A. (2000, October 12). Workplace blues leave employers in the red: A dramatic increase in stress levels has led to spiraling anxiety, burnout and depression across the globe, the UN's labour arm warns. *Guardian*.

Ostberg, O. (1980). Risk perception and work behaviour in forestry: Implications for accident prevention policy. *Accident Analysis and Prevention*, 12, 189–200.

Pape, W. R. (1997). Group insurance. *Inc.*, 19(9), 29–31.

Parker, C., & Lewis, R. (1981). Beyond the Peter Principle—Managing successful transitions. *Journal of European Industrial Training*, 5(6), 17–21.

Parker, S. K., & Wall, T. D. (1996). Job design and modern manufacturing. In P. Warr (Ed.), *Psychology at work* (4th ed.). Harmondsworth, UK: Penguin.

Parker, S. K., & Wall, T. D. (1998). *Job and work design: Organizing work to promote well-being and effectiveness*. London: Sage.

Parsons, G., & Stickland, R. (1996). How Vauxhall Motors is getting its employees on the road to lifelong learning. *European Journal of Work and Organizational Psychology*, 5(4), 597–608.

Pasnau, R. O., Naitoh, R., Stier, S., & Kollar, E. J. (1968). The psychological effects of 205 hours of sleep deprivation. *Archives of General Psychiatry*, 18, 469–483.

Patrick, G. T. W., & Gilbert, J. A. (1896). On the the effects of loss of sleep. *Psychological Review*, 3, 469–483.

Patrick, J. (1992). *Training: Research and practice*. London: Academic Press.

Patrick, J. (2000). Training. In N. Chmiel (Ed.), *Introduction to work and organizational psychology: A European perspective*. Oxford, UK: Blackwell.

Patrick, J., James, N., & Friend, C. (1996). A field study of training fault-finding. *Le Travail Humain*, 59, 23–44.

Patton, W., & McMahon, M. (1999). *Career development and systems theory: A new relationship*. London: Brooks/Cole.

Payne, T. (1998). Editorial—360 degree assessment and feedback. *International Journal of Selection and Assessment*, 70(1), 16–18.

Pearce, J. L. (1996). Why merit pay doesn't work: Implications from organizational theory. In R. M. Steers, L. W. Porter, & G. A. Bigley (Eds.), *Motivation and leadership at work* (6th ed.). New York: McGraw-Hill.

Pearn, M. (1995, December 14–15). *Breaking with convention: Case studies in organizational learning.* Paper presented at City University Business School New Deal in Employment conference.

Pearn, M., Roderick, C., & Mulrooney, C. (1995). *Learning organizations in practice.* Maidenhead, UK: McGraw-Hill.

Pease, R. A. (2000, April 3). What's all this apples and oranges stuff, anyhow? *Electronic Design*, Suppl., 131–134. (Original work published 1994)

Perrow, C. (1984). *Normal accidents: Living with high-risk technologies.* New York: Basic Books.

Perspectives on Management Competencies (PMC) (Multi-rater feedback instrument). Available from Saville & Holdsworth Ltd, Thames Ditton, Surrey.

Petrie, H. L., & Johnson, V. (1996). *Defining user requirements for a new navigational aid for blind travellers* (Tech. Rep. No. 3). Hatfield, UK: Sensory Disabilities Research Unit, University of Hertfordshire.

Phillips, S. D., Friedlander, M. L., Pazienza, N. L., & Kost, P. P. (1985). A factor analytic investigation of career decision making styles. *Journal of Vocational Behaviour, 26*, 706–719.

Pisano, G. P. (1996 March–April). Letter to the Editor. *Harvard Business Review*, p. 162.

Pliskin, N. (1998). Explaining the paradox of telecommuting. *Business Horizons, 41*(2), 73–79.

Pollitt, C. (1993). *Managerialism and the public services* (2nd ed.). Oxford, UK: Blackwell.

Porras, J., & Robertson, P. (1992). Organizational development: Theory practice and research. In M. Dunnette & L. Hough (Eds.), *Handbook of industrial and organizational psychology* (2nd ed.). Palo Alto, CA: Consulting Psychologists Press.

Porteous, M. (1997). *Occupational psychology.* London: Prentice Hall.

Preece, J., Rogers, Y., Sharp, H., Benyon, D., Holland, S., & Carey, T. (1994). *Human–computer interaction.* Harlow, UK: Addison-Wesley.

Premack, S. L., & Wanous, J. P. (1985). A meta-analysis of realistic job preview experiments. *Journal of Applied Psychology, 70*, 706–719.

Pribram, K. (1971). *Languages of the brain.* Englewood Cliffs, NJ: Prentice Hall.

Pribram, K. (1976). Problems concerning the structure of consciousness. In G. Globus et al. (Eds.), *Consciousness and the brain.* New York: Plenum Press.

Price, H. E. (1985). The allocation of functions in systems. *Human Factors, 27*, 33–45.

Pritchard, R. D. (1990). *Measuring and improving organizational productivity: A practical guide.* New York: Praeger.

Pritchard, R. D. (1995). Lessons learned about ProMES. In R. D. Pritchard (Ed.), *Productivity measurement and improvement: Organizational case studies.* Westport, CT: Praeger.

Prowse, M. (2001, October 20). Why a peace-loving nation is seen as a threat. *Financial Times*, Weekend p. XXIV.

Psychological Consultancy Ltd. (1999). *BPS level B (intermediate) pre-course review.* Tunbridge Wells, UK: Author.

The Psychologist. (2000, November). Report on CIPD survey.

Randall, P. (1997). *Adult bullying: Perpetrators and victims*. London: Routledge.

Randell, G. (1989). Performance appraisal. In C. Molander (Ed.), *Human resource management*. Bromley, UK: Chartwell-Bratt.

Randell, G. (1991, January 9–11). *Managing people: A skills approach*. Paper presented at the Manchester Business School: The Management of Higher Education conference.

Rasmussen, J. (1981). Models of mental strategies in process plant diagnosis. In J. Rasmussen & W. B. Rouse (Eds.), *Human detection and diagnosis of system failures*. New York: Plenum Press.

Rasmussen, J. (1986). *Human information processing and human machine interaction*. Amsterdam: North-Holland.

Rasmussen, J. (1993). Learning from experience? Some research issues in industrial risk management. In B. Wilpert & T. Qvalve (Eds.), *Reliability and safety in hazardous work systems*. Hove, UK: Lawrence Erlbaum Associates Ltd.

Rawsthorn, A. (2000, October 20). Message on a bottle. *Financial Times*, Weekend p. VII.

Reason, J. (1987). The Chernobyl errors. *Bulletin of the British Psychological Society*, *40*, 201–206.

Reason, J. (1990). *Human error*. Cambridge, UK: Cambridge University Press.

Reason, J. (1997). *Managing the risks of organizational accidents*. Aldershot, UK: Ashgate.

Rechtschaffen, A. (1998). Current perspectives on the functions of sleep. *Perspectives in Biology and Medicine*, *41*, 359–390.

Reddy, M. (1993). *EAPs and counselling provision in UK organizations: An ICAS report and policy guide*. Milton Keynes, UK: ICAS.

Reddy, M. (1997). External counselling provision for organizations. In M. Carroll & M. Walton (Eds.), *Handbook of counselling in organizations*. London: Sage.

Reid, G. B., & Nygren, T. E. (1988). The subjective workload assessment technique: A scaling procedure for measuring mental workload. In P. Hancock & N. Meshkati (Eds.), *Human mental workload*. Amsterdam: Elsevier.

Reid, J. M. V. (1994). Assessing the numeracy and literacy skills of visually impaired adults. *British Journal of Visual Impairment*, *12*, 60–62.

Reid, J. M. V. (1995). Assessing the verbal and nonverbal ability of visually impaired adults. *British Journal of Visual Impairment*, *13*, 12–14.

Reid, J. M. V. (1997). Standardized ability testing for vocational rehabilitation in visually impaired adults: A literature review. *Journal of Visual Impairment and Blindness*, *91*, 546–554.

Reid, J. M. V. (1998). Assessing the literacy of adults who are visually impaired: Conceptual and measurement issues. *Journal of Visual Impairment and Blindness*, *92*, 447–453.

Reid, J. M. V. (2000). Personality testing with visually impaired adults in applied occupational settings: A review of the literature. *Journal of Visual Impairment and Blindness*, *94*, 771–780.

Reilly, R. R., & Chao, G. T. (1982). Validity and fairness of some alternative employee selection procedures. *Personnel Psychology*, *35*, 1–62.

Reinberg, A., Andlauer, P., De Prins, J., Malbec, W., Vieux, N., & Bourdeleau, P. (1984). Desynchronisation of the oral temperature circadian rhythm and intolerance to shiftwork. *Nature*, *308*, 272–274.

Rhodes, L. (1982, August). The un-manager: No ranks, no titles, nothing but profits. W. L. Gore & Associates has an unusual approach to management structure— none at all. *Inc.*

Rice, A. K. (1963). *The enterprise and its environment.* London: Tavistock Publications.

Rice, B. (1982). The Hawthorne defect: Persistence of a flawed theory. *Psychology Today, 16,* 70–74.

Rice, M. (2000, August). Age of the flex exec. *Management Today,* pp. 47–52.

Rick, J., & Briner, R. B. (2000). Trauma management vs. stress debriefing: What should responsible organizations do? In *The British Psychological Society Occupational Psychology conference book of proceedings* (pp. 126–130). Leicester, UK: British Psychological Society.

Ridgeway, C. C. (2000). Eight years on: "What's so special about chartered occupational psychologists?" *Occupational Psychologist, 41,* 13–15.

Rijsman, J. B. (1999). Role-playing and attitude change: How helping your boss can change the meaning of work. *European Journal of Work and Organizational Psychology, 8*(1), 73–85.

Roberts, K. (1968). The entry into employment: An approach towards a general theory. *Sociological Review, 16,* 165–184.

Roberts, K. (1977). The social conditions, consequences and limitations of careers guidance. *British Journal of Guidance and Counselling, 5,* 1–9.

Robertson, I. (1998). Personality and organizational behaviour. *Selection and Development Review, 14*(4), 11–15.

Robertson, I. (2000). *Research in personality and work performance: Past, present and future.* Keynote address at the British Psychological Society Occupational Psychology conference, Brighton, UK.

Robertson, J. (1985). *Future work, jobs, self-employment and leisure after the industrial age.* London: Gower Publishing.

Robinson, W. P. (1998). Early childhood education: Notes from the past for the future. *International Journal of Educational Research, 29,* 7–24.

Rockett, L., Valor, J., Miller, P., & Naude, P. (1998). Technology and virtual teams: Using globally distributed groups in MBA learning. *Campus-Wide Information Systems, 15*(5), 174–182.

Rodger, A. (1968). The seven-point plan. In B. Hobson & J. Hayes (Eds.), *The theory and practice of vocational guidance.* Oxford: Pergamon.

Roethlisberger, F. J., & Dickson, W. J. (1939). *Management and the worker.* Cambridge, MA: Harvard University Press.

Rolfe, J. (1996). Craik and the Cambridge Cockpit. *The Psychologist, 9*(2), 69–71.

Roos, P. A., & Treiman, D. J. (1980). DOT scales for the 1970 census classification. In A. R. Miller, D. J. Treiman, P. S. Cain, & P. A. Roos (Eds.), *Work, jobs and occupations: A critical review of the dictionary of occupational titles.* Washington, DC: National Academy Press.

Roscoe, J. (1995). Analysis of organizational training needs. In S. Truelove (Ed.), *The handbook of training and development* (2nd ed.). Oxford, UK: Blackwell.

Rose, F. D., Attree, E. A., Brooks, B. M., Parslow, D. M., Penn, P. R., & Ambihaipahan, N. (2000). Training in virtual environments: Transfer to real world tasks and equivalence to real task training. *Ergonomics, 43*(4), 494–511.

Rose, F. D., & Foreman, N. (1999). Virtual reality. *The Psychologist, 12*(11), 550–554.

Rose, M. J. (2000). *Future tense—are growing occupations more stressed-out and de-pressive?* (Working Paper No. 3). Work Centrality, Careers and Household project, ESRC Future of Work.

Rosener, J. (1990, November–December). Ways women lead. *Harvard Business Review*, pp. 119–125.

Roseveare, J. (2000). The search conference (continued): Graduate socialisation. *Occupational Psychologist*, *40*, 19–20.

Rousseau, D. M. (1995). *Psychological contracts in organizations: Understanding written and unwritten agreements*. London: Sage.

Rousseau, D., & Tinsley, C. (1997). Human resources are local: Society and social contracts in a global economy. In N. Anderson & P. Herriot (Eds.), *International handbook of selection and assessment*. Chichester, UK: Wiley.

Rubery, J., Smith, M., & Fagan, C. (1995, April). *Changing patterns of work and working time in the European Union and the impact on gender divisions*. Brussels: European Commission.

Rugg-Gunn, M. (2002). *The evaluation of computer-based training: Exploring a new approach*. Unpublished D.Occ.Psych. thesis, University of East London.

Rundmo, T. (1992). Risk perception and safety on off-shore petroleum platforms: Part I. Perception of risk; Part II. Perceived risk, job stress and accidents. *Safety Science*, *15*, 39–68.

Rutenfranz, J., Haider, M., & Koller, M. (1985). Occupational health measures for nightworkers and shiftworkers. In S. Folkhard & T. H. Monk (Eds.), *Hours of work: Temporal factors in work scheduling*. Chichester, UK: Wiley.

Ryan, F. (2000). The search conference as a method of participative strategic planning. *Occupational Psychologist*, *39*, 4–10.

Rystedt, L. W., Johansson, G., & Evans, G. W. (1998). A longitudinal study of workload, health and well-being among male and female bus drivers. *Journal of Occupational and Organizational Psychology*, *71*, 35–45.

Saal, F. E., & Knight, P. A. (1988). *Industrial/organizational psychology: Science and practice*. Pacific Grove, CA: Brooks/Cole.

Sachs, R., Chrisler, J. C., & Sloane-Devlin, A. (1992). Biographic and personal: Characteristics of women in management. *Journal of Vocational Behaviour*, *41*, 89–100.

Sackett, P. R., & Dreher, G. F. (1982). Constructs and assessment center dimensions: Some troubling empirical findings. *Journal of Applied Psychology*, *67*, 401–410.

"Safety at work shake-up will hit bosses in pocket". (2000, June 7). *Evening Standard*.

St Ather, T. (1999). Where do we go from here . . . again? *Occupational Psychologist*, *38*, 59–61.

Salgado, J. F. (1997). The five factor model of personality and job performance in the European Community. *Journal of Applied Psychology*, *82*, 30–43.

Salthouse, T. A. (1991). *Theoretical perspectives on cognitive aging*. Hillsdale, NJ: Lawrence Erlbaum Associates Inc.

Sanchez, J. I. (2000). Adapting work analysis to a fast-paced and electronic business world. *International Journal of Selection and Assessment*, *8*(4), 207–215.

Savva, C. (2000, October). Follow-up report on bullying in further and higher education. *The Lecturer*, p. 3.

Schabraq, M. J., Winnubst, J. A. M., & Cooper, C. L. (Eds.) (1996). *Handbook of work and health psychology*. Chichester, UK: Wiley.

Schaubroeck, J., & Merritt, D. E. (1997). Divergent effects of job control on coping with work stressors: The key role of self-efficacy. *Academy of Management Journal, 40*(3), 738–754.

Schaufeli, W. B., & Buunk, B. P. (1996). Professional burnout. In M. J. Schabraq, J. A. M. Winnubst, & C.L. Cooper (Eds.), *Handbook of work and health psychology.* Chichester, UK: Wiley.

Schein, E. H. (1971). Occupational socialization in the professions: The case of the role innovator. *Journal of Psychiatric Research, 8,* 521–530.

Schein, E. H. (1980). *Organizational psychology* (3rd ed.). Englewood Cliffs, NJ: Prentice Hall.

Schein, E. H. (1988). *Organizational psychology* (3rd ed.). (International student edition). Englewood Cliffs, NJ: Prentice Hall International.

Schein, E. H. (1993). *Career anchors: Discovering your real values* (Rev. ed.). London: Pfeiffer & Co.

Schiffman, L. G., & Sherman, E. (1991). Value orientations of a new-age elderly: The coming of an ageless market. *Journal of Business Research, 22,* 187–194.

Schmidt, F. L., Gast-Rosenberg, I., & Hunter, J. E. (1980). Validity generalisation results for computer programmers. *Journal of Applied Psychology, 65,* 643–661.

Schmidt, F. L., & Hunter, J. E. (1977). Development of a general solution to the problem of validity generalisation. *Journal of Applied Psychology, 62,* 529–540.

Schmidt, F. L., & Hunter, J. E. (1978). Moderator research and the law of small numbers. *Personnel Psychology, 31,* 215–232.

Schmidt, F. L., & Hunter, J. E. (1984). A within setting empirical test of the situational specificity hypothesis in personnel selection. *Personnel Psychology, 37,* 317–326.

Schmidt, F. L., Hunter, J. E., McKenzie, R. C., & Muldrow, T. W. (1979). Impact of valid selection procedures on work-force productivity. *Journal of Applied Psychology, 64,* 609–626.

Schmidt, F. L., Ocasio, B. P., Hillery, J. M., & Hunter, J. E. (1985). Further within-setting empirical tests of the situational specificity hypothesis in personnel selection. *Personnel Psychology, 38,* 509–524.

Schmidt, K. S., & Kleinbeck, U. (1997). Relationships between group-based performance measures, feedback, and organizational context factors. *European Journal of Work and Organizational Psychology, 6*(3), 303–320.

Schmitt, N., Gooding, R. Z., Noe, R. A., & Kirsch, M. (1984). Meta-analyses of validity studies published between 1964 and 1982 and the investigation of study characteristics. *Personnel Psychology, 37,* 407–422.

Schneider, B., & Konz, A. M. (1989). Strategic job analysis. *Human Resource Management, 28,* 51–63.

Schruijer, S. G. L. (1992). Work design at the production department of a camera plant. In S. Vickerstaff (Ed.), *Human resource management in Europe: Text and cases.* London: Chapman & Hall.

Schruijer, S. G. L., & Vansina, L. S. (1999a). Epilogue. *European Journal of Work and Organizational Psychology, 8*(1), 135–138.

Schruijer, S. G. L., & Vansina, L. S. (1999b). Leadership and organizational change: An introduction. *European Journal of Work and Organizational Psychology, 8*(1), 1–8.

Schwab, D. P. (1982). Recruiting and organizational participation. In K. Rowland & G. Ferris (Eds.), *Personnel management.* Boston: Allyn & Bacon.

Schwab, R. S. (1953). Motivation in measurements of fatigue. In W. F. Floyd & A. T. Welford (Eds.), *Symposium on fatigue.* London: H. K. Lewis.

Schwartz, B. (1992, May 14). *Statement*. Mission Control Houston.

Scott, W. (1987). *Organizations: Rational, natural and open systems*. Englewood Cliffs, NJ: Prentice Hall.

Seegers, J. (1997). What is an Assessment Centre? In P. Jansen & F. de Jongh (Eds.), *Assessment centres: A practical handbook*. Chichester, UK: Wiley.

Semmer, N. (1996). Individual differences, work stress and health. In M. J. Schabracq, J. A. M. Winnubst, & C. L. Cooper (Eds.), *Handbook of work and health psychology*. Chichester, UK: Wiley.

Senge, P. (1990). *The fifth discipline: The art and practice of the learning organization*. London: Centuary Business.

Senior, B., & Swailes, S. (1998). A comparison of the Belbin Self-Perception Inventory and Observer's Assessment Sheet as measures of an individual's team roles. *International Journal of Selection and Assessment*, *6*(1), 1–8.

Seymour, R. T. (1988). Why plaintiffs' counsel challenge tests, and how they can successfully challenge the theory of "validity generalisation". *Journal of Vocational Behaviour*, *33*, 331–364.

Shackleton, V., & Newell, S. (1997). International assessment and selection. In N. Anderson & P. Herriot (Eds.), *International handbook of selection and assessment*. Chichester, UK: Wiley.

Shamir, B. (1996). Meaning, self and motivation in organizations. In R. Steers, L. W. Porter, & G. A. Bigley (Eds.), *Motivation and leadership at work* (6th ed.). New York: McGraw Hill International. (Original work published 1991)

Sharkey, P., Rose, F. D., & Lindstrom, J. (Eds.) (1998). *Proceedings of the 2nd European conference on Disability, Virtual Reality and Associated Technologies*, Skovde, Sweden, 10–11 September.

Shaw, T. F. (1992, April). What's so special about chartered occupational psychologists? *Occupational Psychologist*, pp. 10–12.

Shea, C., & Bond, T. (1997). Ethical issues for counselling in organizations. In M. Carroll & M. Walton (Eds.), *Handbook of counselling in organizations*. London: Sage.

Sheehy, N., & Gallagher, A. (1996). Can virtual organizations be made real? *The Psychologist*, *9*(4), 159–162.

Shepherd, A. (1985). Hierarchical task analysis and training decisions. *Programmed Learning and Educational Technology*, *22*(3), 162–176.

Shimmin, S., & Wallace, D. (1994). *Fifty years of occupational psychology*. Leicester, UK: British Psychological Society.

Silvester, J. (1997). Spoken attributions and candidate success in graduate recruitment interviews. *Journal of Occupational and Organizational Psychology*, *70*, 61–73.

Singleton, W. T. (1969). Display design: Principles and procedures. *Ergonomics*, *12*, 519–531.

Skinner, B. F. (1938). *The behaviour of organisms*. Englewood Cliffs, NJ: Prentice-Hall.

Skriver, J., & Flin, R. (1997). Emergency decision making on offshore installations. In D. Harris (Ed.), *Engineering psychology and cognitive ergonomics, Vol. 2*. Aldershot, UK: Ashgate.

Slater, J. A., & West, M. (1995). Satisfaction or source of pressure: The paradox of teamwork. *Occupational Psychologist*, 30–34.

Slaven, G., & Doyle, C. (2001). *A longitudinal study of stress, neuroticism and coping style*. VIIth European Congress Book of Abstracts (Abstract No. 218). London: European Federation of Professional Psychologists Associations.

Slepicka, M. (1999). Remote workforces gaining in strength. *America's Network,* *103*(18), 16.

Smith, A. (1995). Is teleworking really taking off? *Management, 42*(9), 118–119.

Smith, A., Johal, S., Wadsworth, E., Davey Smith, G., Harvey, I., & Peters, T. (1998a, May/June). The scale of occupational stress. *Occupational Health Review,* pp. 19–22.

Smith, A., Johal, S., Wadsworth, E., Davey Smith, G., Harvey, I., & Peters, T. (1998b, September /October). Stress at work II: Results from a pilot study. *Occupational Health Review,* pp. 11–13.

Smith, D. (1997, May). Paranoia in the workplace. *Management Today.*

Smith, L., Folkard, S., & Poole, C. J. M. (1994). Increased injuries on night shift. *Lancet, 344,* 1137–1139.

Smith, J. M. (1986). A repertory grid analysis of supervisory jobs. *International Review of Applied Psychology, 35*(4), 501–512.

Smith, J. M., Gregg, M., & Andrews, D. (1989). *Selection and assessment: A new appraisal.* London: Pitman.

Smith, P. B., & Peterson, M. F. (1988). *Leadership, organizations and culture: An event management model.* London: Sage.

Sonnentag, S., & Schmidt-Braße, U. (Eds.) (1998). Expertise at work: Research perspectives and practical interventions for ensuring excellent performance at the workplace. *European Journal of Work and Organizational Psychology, 7*(4), 449– 454.

Sparks, K., Faragher, B., & Cooper, C. L. (2001). Well being and occupational health in the 21st century workplace. *Journal of Occupational and Organizational Psychology, 74,* 489–509.

Sparrow, J., & Rigg, C. (1993). Job analysis: Selecting for the masculine approach to management. *Selection and Development Review, 9*(2), 5–8.

Sparrow, P. (1994). The psychology of strategic management: Emerging themes of diversity and cognition. *International Review of Industrial and Organizational Psychology, 9,* 147–182.

Sparrow, P. R. (1997). Organizational competencies: Creating a strategic behavioural framework for selection and assessment. In N. Anderson & P. Herriot (Eds.), *International handbook of selection and assessment.* Chichester, UK: Wiley.

Sparrow, P. R. (2000a). New employee behaviours, work designs and forms of work organization: What is in store for the future? *Journal of Managerial Psychology, 15*(3), 202–218.

Sparrow, P. R. (2000b). Teleworking and the psychological contract: A new division of labour? In K. Daniels, D. A. Lamond, & P. Standen (Eds.), *Managing telework: Perspectives from human resource management and work psychology.* London: Business Press/Thomson Learning.

Spector, P. E. (2000). *Industrial and organizational psychology* (2nd ed.). New York: Wiley.

Sperandio, A. (1978). The regulation of working methods as a function of workload among air traffic controllers. *Ergonomics, 21,* 367–390.

Springbett, B. M. (1958). Factors affecting the final decision in the employment interview. *Canadian Journal of Psychology, 12,* 13–22.

Stammers, R. (1996). Training and the acquisition of knowledge and skill. In P. Warr (Ed.), *Psychology at work* (4th ed.). Harmondsworth, UK: Penguin.

Standen, P. (2000). Organizational culture and telework. In K. Daniels, D. A. Lamond, & P. Standen (Eds.), *Managing telework: Perspectives from human resource management and work psychology.* London: Business Press/Thomson Learning.

Stanton, N. A., Young, M., & McCaulder, B. (1998). Drive-by-wire: The case of driver workload and reclaiming control with adaptive cruise control. *Occupational Health and Industrial Medicine, 38*(3), 121.

Staw, B. M., & Ross, J. (1985). Stability in the midst of change: A dispositional approach to job attitudes. *Journal of Applied Psychology, 70,* 469–480.

Steedman, H. (1990, August). Improvement in workforce qualification: Britain and France 1979–88. *National Institute Economic Review.*

Steedman, J., & Wagner, K. (1989, May). Productivity, machinery and skills: Clothing manufacture in Britain and Germany. *National Institute Economic Review.*

Steel, G. (1997). Company case C: Shell International. In *Fifth European Congress of Psychology, (Abstract No. 343).* Dublin, Ireland: Psychological Society of Ireland.

Steers, R. M., & Porter, L. W. (Eds.) (1991). *Motivation and work behaviour* (5th ed.). New York: McGraw-Hill International.

Steers, R. M., Porter, L. W., & Bigley, G. A. (Eds.) (1996). *Motivation and leadership at work* (6th ed.). New York: McGraw-Hill.

Stephens, N. (1991). Cognitive age: A useful concept for advertising? *Journal of Advertising, 20*(4), 37–48.

Stevens, G., Faragher, B., & Sparks, K. (2000). The relationship between working hours and health in an international sample of managers. In *The British Psychological Society Occupational Psychology conference book of proceedings* (pp. 7–11). Leicester, UK: British Psychological Society.

Stewart, D. A., & Townsend, A. S. (2001). There is more to "Health and Safety is good business" than avoiding unplanned costs: A study into the link between safety performance and business performance. Available at http://www.behavioural-safety.com/articles...re_than_just_reducing_unplanned_costs/

Stewart, J., & Winter, R. (1995). Open and distance learning. In S. Truelove (Ed.), *The handbook of training and development* (2nd ed.). Oxford, UK: Blackwell.

Stickland, R. (1996). Career self-management: Can we live without it? *European Journal of Work and Organizational Psychology, 5*(4), 583–596.

Stromberg, A. H., & Harkness, S. (1978). *Women working.* Palo Alto, CA: Mayfield.

Strothotte, T., Fritz, S., Michel, R., Raab, A., Petrie, H., Johnson, V., Reichert, L., & Schalt, A. (1996). *Development of dialogue systems for a mobility aid for blind people: Initial design and usability testing.* Paper presented at ASSETS '96, Vancouver, Canada.

Stryker, S. (1980). *Symbolic interactionism: A social structural version.* Menio Parl, CA: Benjamin/Cummings.

Sugarman, L. (2001). *Life-span development: Theories, concepts and interventions* (2nd ed.). Hove, UK: Psychology Press.

Summers, D. (1993, June 14). Management—the right attitude—staff surveys are popular, but can be fraught with pitfalls. *Financial Times,* p. 8.

Sundstrom, E., Town, J. P., Rice, R. W., Osborne, D. P., & Brill, M. (1994). Office noise, satisfaction and performance. *Environment and Behaviour, 26,* 195–222.

Sunman, K. (2000). *A study of equal opportunities between different groups of individuals at work through the assessment of their attitudes towards satisfaction with training and development, respect and equal opportunities, career opportunities and performance appraisal.* Unpublished dissertation, University of East London.

Super, D. E. (1957). *The psychology of careers*. New York: Harper & Row.

Super, D. E. (1980). A life-span, life-space approach to career development. *Journal of Vocational Behaviour, 13*, 282–298.

Super, D. E. (1990). A life-span, life-space approach to career development. In D. Brown & L. Brooks (Eds.), *Career choice and development* (2nd ed.). San Francisco: Jossey-Bass.

Svebak, S., & Apter, M. J. (Eds.) (1997). *Stress and health: A reversal theory perspective*. Washington, DC: Taylor & Francis.

Synchrony (Multi-rater feedback instrument). Available from Development Dimensions International, Pittsburgh, 1225 Washington Pike, Bridgeville, PA 15017-2838.

Tabachnick, B., & Fidell, L. S. (1996). *Using multivariate statistics* (3rd ed.). New York: Harper Collins.

Tattersall, A. J. (2000). Workload and task allocation. In N. Chmiel (Ed.), *Introduction to work and organizational psychology: A European perspective*. Oxford, UK: Blackwell.

Taylor, F. (1911). *Principles of scientific management*. New York: Harper & Brothers.

Taylor, S. (1998). Emotional labour and the new workplace. In P. Thompson & C. Warhurst (Eds.), *Workplaces of the future*. Basingstoke, UK: Macmillan Business.

Tepas, D. I., Armstrong, D. R., Carlson, M. L., Duchon, J. C., Gersten, A., & Lezotte, D. V. (1985). Changing industry to continuous operation: Different strokes for different plants. *Behaviour Research Methods, Instruments and Computers, 17*, 670–676.

Terry, D. J., & Jimmieson, N. L. (1999). Work control and employee well-being: A decade review. In C. L. Cooper & I. T. Robertson (Eds.), *International review of industrial and organizational psychology, Vol. 14*. Chichester, UK: Wiley.

Tester, N. (1998, July). Mr Chips learns to manage. *Management Today*, pp. 50–53.

Tett, R. P., Jackson, D. N., & Rothstein, M. (1991). Personality measures as predictors of job performance: A meta-analytical review. *Personnel Psychology, 44*, 703–742.

Thayer, P. W. (1997). A rapidly changing world: Some implications for training systems in the year 2001 and beyond. In M. A. Quinones & A. Ehrenstein (Eds.), *Training for a rapidly changing workplace: Applications of psychological research*. Washington, DC: American Psychological Association.

Thomas, M., Sing, H., Belenky, G., Holcomb, H., Mayberg, H., Dannals, R., Wagner, Jr, H., Thorne, D., Popp, K., Rowland, L., Welsh, A., Balwin Ki, S., & Redmsnd, D. (2000). Neural basis of alertness and cognitive performance impairments during sleepiness. One: Effects of 24h of sleep deprivation on waking human regional brain activity. *Journal of Sleep Research, 9*, 335–3.

Thompson, P., & Warhurst, C. (1998). Hands, hearts and minds: Changing work and workers at the end of the century. In P. Thompson & C. Warhurst (Eds.), *Workplaces of the future*. Basingstoke, UK: Macmillan Business.

Tilley, A. J., & Wilkinson, R. T. (1982). Sleep and performance of shiftworkers. *Human Factors, 24*, 629–641.

Tomkins, P. (1999, March 20). Old father time becomes a terror. *Financial Times*, Weekend, p. I.

Torsvall, L., & Akerstedt, T. (1988). Disturbed sleep while being on call: An EEG study of ships' engineers. *Sleep, 11*(1), 35–38.

Traynor, M. (1994). The views and values of community nurses and their managers: Research in progress—one person's pain, another person's vision. *Journal of Advanced Nursing, 20,* 101–109.

Treiman, D. J. (1977). *Occupational prestige in comparative perspective.* New York: Academic Press.

Trist, E. L. (1982). The evolution of Sociotechnical Systems as a conceptual framework and as an action research program. In A. Van de Ven & W. F. Joyce (Eds.), *Perspectives on organizational design and behaviour.* New York: Wiley.

Trist, E. L., & Bamford, K. W. (1951). Some social and psychological consequences of the longwall method of coal getting. *Human Relations, 4*(3), 3–38.

Truelove, S. (1995). Developing employees. In S. Truelove (Ed.), *The handbook of training and development* (2nd ed.). Oxford, UK: Blackwell.

Tuckman, B. W. (1965, November). Developmental sequence in small groups. *Psychological Bulletin,* pp. 384–399.

Tyler, C. (2000, June 3). Memo to the future. *Financial Times.*

Uttal, B. (1983, 17 October). The corporate culture vultures. *Fortune.*

Van Maanen, J., & Schein, E. H. (1979). Toward a theory of organizational socialization. In B. M. Staw (Ed.), *Research in organizational behaviour, Vol. I.* Greenwich, CT: JAI Press.

Van Mierlo, H., Rutte, C. G., Seinen, B., & Kompier, M. (2001). Autonomous teamwork and psychological well-being. *European Journal of Work and Organizational Psychology, 10*(3), 291–302.

Van Offenbeek, M. (2001). Processes and outcomes of team learning. *European Journal of Work and Organizational Psychology, 10*(3), 303–318.

Vansina, L. S. (1998). The individual in organizations: Rediscovered or lost forever? *European Journal of Work and Organizational Psychology, 7*(3), 265–282.

Van Tuijl, H., Kleingeld, A., Schmidt, K., Kleinbeck, U., Pritchard, R. D., & Algera, J. A. (1997). Measuring and enhancing organizational productivity by means of ProMES: Three practical implications. *European Journal of Work and Organizational Psychology, 6*(3), 297–302.

Van Vianen, A. E. M., & De Dreu, C. K. W. (2001). Personality in teams: Its relationship to social cohesion, task cohesion, and team performance. *European Journal of Work and Organizational Psychology, 10*(2), 97–120.

Van Vuuren, T. (1990). *Met ontslag bedreigd: Werknemers in onzekerheid over hun arbeidsplaats bij veranderingen in de organisatie.* Amsterdam: VU-uitgeverij.

Van Vuuren, T., Klandermans, B., Jacobson, D., & Hartley, J. (1991). Employees' reactions to job insecurity. In J. Hartley, D. Jacobson, B. Klandermans, & T. van Vuuren (Eds.), *Job insecurity: Coping with jobs at risk.* London: Sage.

Vasagar, J. (1999, July 17). The £16,500 job snub. *Daily Mail.*

Vernon, P. E. (1950). The validation of Civil Service Selection Board procedures. *Occupational Psychology, 24,* 75–95.

Vince, M. (1996). Recollections of Kenneth Craik. *The Psychologist, 9*(2), 67–68.

Von Bertelanffy, L. (1950). The theory of open systems in physics and biology. *Science, 3,* 23–29.

Vroom, V. (1964). *Work and motivation.* New York: Wiley.

Vrugt, A. (1996). Perceived self-efficacy, work motivation and well-being. In M. J. Schabraq, J. A. M. Winnubst, & C. L. Cooper (Eds.), *Handbook of work and health psychology.* Chichester, UK: Wiley.

Vygotsky, L. S. (1962). *Thought and language.* Boston: MIT Press.

Wagenaar, W. A. (1986). *The causes of impossible accidents* (The Sixth Duijker Lecture). Amsterdam: University of Amsterdam.

Wagenaar, W. A., & Groeneweg, J. (1987). Accidents at sea: Multiple causes and impossible consequences. *International Journal of Man–Machine Studies, 27,* 587–598.

Wahba, M. A., & Bridwell, L. G. (1976). Maslow reconsidered: A review of research on the need hierarchy theory. *Organizational Behaviour and Human Performance, 15,* 212–240.

Wall, T. D. (1996). Working with robots. *The Psychologist, 9*(4), 163–166.

Wall, T. D., & Martin, R. (1994). Job and work design. In C. L. Cooper & I. T. Robertson (Eds.), *Key reviews in managerial psychology: Concepts and research for practice.* Chichester, UK: Wiley.

Wanous, J. P. (1989). Installing a realistic job preview: Ten tough choices. *Personnel Psychology, 42,* 117–133.

Wanous, J. P., Poland, T. D., Premack, S. L., & Davis, K. S. (1992). The effects of met expectations on newcomer attitudes and behaviours: A review and meta-analysis. *Journal of Applied Psychology, 77,* 288–297.

Warhurst, C., & Thompson, P. (1998). Hands, hearts and minds: Changing work and workers at the end of the century. In P. Thompson & C. Warhurst (Eds.), *Workplaces of the future.* Basingstoke, UK: Macmillan.

Warr, P. (1987). *Work, unemployment and mental health.* Oxford, UK: Oxford University Press.

Warr, P. (1996a). Employee well-being. In P. Warr (Ed.), *Psychology at work* (4th ed.). Harmondsworth, UK: Penguin.

Warr, P. (1996b). Younger and older workers. In P. Warr (Ed.), *Psychology at work* (4th ed.). Harmondsworth, UK: Penguin.

Warr, P. (1998). Well-being and the workplace. In D. Kahneman, E. Diener, & N. Schwartz (Eds.), *Foundations of hedonic psychology: Scientific perspectives on enjoyment and suffering.* New York: Russell Sage.

Warr, P. (2000). Work performance and the ageing workforce. In N. Chmiel (Ed.), *Introduction to work and organizational psychology: A European perspective.* Oxford, UK: Blackwell.

Warr, P., & Ainsworth, E. (1999). 360 degree feedback—some recent research. *Selection and Development Review, 15*(3), 3–6.

Warr, P., & Bourne, A. (1999). Factors influencing two types of congruence in multi-rater judgements. *Human Performance, 12*(3/4), 183–210.

Warr, P., & Bourne, A. (2000). Associations between rating content and self-other agreement in multi-source feedback. *European Journal of Work and Organizational Psychology, 9*(3), 321–334.

Wason, P. C., & Johnson-Laird, P. N. (1972). *Psychology of reasoning: Structure and content.* London: Batsford.

Waterhouse, J. M., Folkard, S., & Minors, D. S. (1992). *Shiftwork, health and safety: An overview of the scientific literature 1978–1990.* London: HMSO.

Weber, M. (1958). *The protestant work ethic and the spirit of capitalism* (T. Parsons, trans.). New York: Scribner.

Weick, K. E. (1987). Organizational culture as a source of high reliability. *Californian Management Review, 24,* 112–127.

Weiner, E. L. (1989). *Human factors of advanced technology ("glass cockpit") transport aircraft* (Tech. Rep. No. 117528). Washington, DC: NASA.

Welch, J. (1997). EU plans directive to protect "outworkers". *People Management*, *3*(3), 9.

Welford, A. T. (1985). Changes of performance with age: An overview. In N. Charness (Ed.), *Aging and human performance*. Chichester, UK: Wiley.

Wells, R. (1999, June). *Making it in the creative industries*. University of East London seminar, London.

West, M. (1994). *Effective teamwork*. Leicester, UK: BPS Books.

West, M. A. (2000a). Reflexivity, revolution and innovation in work teams. In M. Beyerlein (Ed.), *Product development teams: Advances in interdisciplinary studies of work teams*. Stamford, CA: JAI Press.

West, M. A. (2000b). State of the art: Creativity and innovation at work. *The Psychologist*, *13*(9), 460–464.

West, M. A., Lawthom, R., & Patterson, M. (1995). Productivity, innovation and well-being: Psychological perspectives on company performance. In A. Oswald & A. Layard (Eds.), *Economic performance*.

West, M. A., Patterson, M., Pillinger, T., & Nickell, S. (2000). *Innovation and change in manufacturing*. Birmingham, UK: Aston University Business School.

West, M., & Slater, J. A. (1995). Teamwork: Myths, realities and research. *Occupational Psychologist*, *24*, 24–29.

Westman, M., & Eden, D. (1996). The inverted-U relationship between stress and performance: A field study. *Work and Stress*, *10*(2), 163–173.

Whatmore, L., Cartwright, S., & Cooper, C. L. (1999). United Kingdom: Evaluation of a stress management programme in the public sector. In M. Kompier & C. L. Cooper (Eds.), *Preventing stress, improving productivity: European case studies in the workplace*. London: Routledge.

White, L., & Doyle, C. (1997). Recruitment and selection in small professional firms and practices. *Selection and Development Review*, *13*(6), 3–8.

Whyte, W. F. (1955). *Money and motivation: An analysis of incentives in industry*. New York: Harper & Row.

Wilkinson, R., Allison, S., Feeney, M., & Kaminska, Z. (1989). Alertness of night nurses: Two shift systems compared. *Ergonomics*, *32*(3), 281–292.

Williams, H. L., Lubin, A., & Goodnow, J. J. (1959). Impaired performance with acute sleep loss. *Psychological Monographs*, *73*(14, Whole No. 484).

Williams, R. (1998). *Performance management*. London: Thomson Business Press.

Wilpert, B. (1997). One hundred years of work and organizational psychology: Progress, deficiencies and promise. In R. Fuller, P. Noonan-Walsh, & P. McGinley (Eds.), *A century of psychology*. London: Routledge.

Winefield, A. (1997, July). *Occupational strain in university staff* (Abstract No. 347) Paper presented at the fifth European congress of Psychology, Dublin, Ireland.

Winter, R. (1995). An integrated approach to training and development. In S. Truelove (Ed.), *The handbook of training and development* (2nd ed.). Oxford, UK: Blackwell.

Wood, R. (1997). The interview: Just when you thought it was safe. . . . *Selection and Development Review*, *13*(2), 15–17.

Woodruffe, C. (2000). Emotional intelligence: Time for a time-out. *Selection and Development Review*, *16*(4), 3–9.

Woods, D. D. (1984). Some results on operator performance in emergency events. *Institute of Chemical Engineers Symposium Series*, *90*, 21–31.

Woods, D. D. (1986). Paradigms for intelligent decision support. In E. Hollnagel, G. Mancini, & D. D. Woods (Eds.), *Intelligent decision support in process environments*. New York: Springer-Verlag.

Woods, D. D. (1987). Technology alone is not enough. In R. Anthony (Ed.), *Human reliability in nuclear power*. London: IBC Technical Services.

Woods, D. D. (1999). *Human factors, politics, and stakeholders*. Available at http://www.hfes.org/News/0999news/item2.html

Woods, D. D., O'Brien, J. F., & Hanes, L. F. (1987). Human factors in process control: The case of nuclear power plants. In G. Salvendy (Ed.), *Handbook of human factors*. New York: Wiley.

Wright, C., & Lund, J. (1996). Best-practice Taylorism: "Yankee speed-up" in Australian grocery distribution. *Journal of Industrial Relations, 38*(2), 196–212.

Wright, P. L., & Taylor, D. S. (1984). *Improving leadership performance: A practical new approach to leadership*. London: Prentice-Hall International.

Xie, J. L., & Johns, G. (1995). Job scope and job stress: Can job scope be too high? *Academy of Management Journal, 38*(5), 1288–1309.

Yankelovich, D. (1979, August). On today's workers. *Industry Week*.

Yeager, J. (1983). A model for executive performance coaching. In J. Manuso (Ed.), *Occupational clinical psychology*. New York: Praeger.

Yorks, L., & Whitsett, D. A. (1985). Hawthorne, Topeka and the issue of science versus advocacy in organizational behaviour. *Academy of Management Review, 10*, 21–30.

Zapf, D., & Leymann, H. (Eds.) (1996). Mobbing and victimization at work. *European Journal of Work and Organizational Psychology, 5*(Whole No. 2).

Zisook, S., Schuchter, S. R., Irwin, M., Darko, D. F., Sledge, P., & Resovsky, K. (1994). Bereavement, depression, and immune function. *Psychiatry Research, 52*, 1–10.

Author Index

Subject Index